CW01590128

DATA PROTECTION STRATEGY

IMPLEMENTING DATA PROTECTION COMPLIANCE

DATA PROTECTION STRATEGY

IMPLEMENTING DATA PROTECTION COMPLIANCE

3rd edition

by

Richard Morgan, FBCS, CITP

IT Consultant

and

Ruth Boardman

Partner, Bird & Bird

SWEET & MAXWELL

THOMSON REUTERS

1st edition 2003
2nd edition 2012

Published in 2019 by Thomson Reuters, trading as Sweet & Maxwell.
Thomson Reuters is registered in England & Wales, Company No.1679046.
Registered Office and address for service: 5 Canada Square, Canary Wharf, London, E14 5AQ. For further information on our products and services, visit http://www.sweetandmaxwell.co.uk

Typesetting by Servis Filmsetting Ltd, Stockport, Cheshire.
Printed and bound in the UK by CPI Group (UK) Ltd, Croydon, CR0 4YY

No natural forests were destroyed to make this product: only farmed timber was used and replanted.

A CIP catalogue record for this book is available from the British Library.

ISBN 978 0 414 060203

Crown copyright material is reproduced with the permission of the Controller of HMSO and the Queen's Printer for Scotland.
EU material in this publication is acknowledged as © European Union, 1998–2019. Only EU legislation published in the electronic version of the Official Journal of the European Union is deemed authentic.

All rights reserved. No part of this publication may be reproduced, or transmitted in any form, or by any means, or stored in any retrieval system of any nature, without prior written permission, except for permitted fair dealing under the Copyright, Designs and Patents Act 1988, or in accordance with the terms of a licence issued by the Copyright Licensing Agency in respect of photocopying and/or reprographic reproduction. Application for permission for other use of copyright material, including permission to reproduce extracts in other published works, should be made to the publishers. Full acknowledgement of the author, publisher and source must be given.
Material is contained in this publication for which publishing permission has been sought and for which copyright is acknowledged. Permission to reproduce such material cannot be granted by the publishers and application must be made to the copyright-holder.

Precedents in this publication may be used as a guide for the drafting of legal documents specifically for particular clients, though no liability is accepted by the publishers or authors in relation to their use, but not for republication. Such documents may be provided to clients for their own use in print or electronic form but distribution to third parties is otherwise prohibited. Precedents are provided "as is" without warranty of any kind, express or implied, including, but not limited to, fitness for a particular purpose. The publishers and the author cannot accept any responsibility for any loss of whatsoever kind, including loss of revenue business, anticipated savings or profits and loss of goodwill or data, or for any direct or consequential loss whatsoever to any person using the precedents or acting or refraining from actions as a result of the material in this publication.

Thomson Reuters, the Thomson Reuters Logo and Sweet & Maxwell ® are trademarks of Thomson Reuters.

© Richard Morgan and Ruth Boardman

Acknowledgements

We gratefully acknowledge permission to reproduce UK statutory material, UK court judgements, and guidance from the Information Commissioner under the Government's permission (*http://www.nationalarchives.gov.uk/doc/open-government-licence/version/3* [Accessed 15 May 2019]).

We must also thank the European Commission and the Court of Justice of the European Union, for permission to reproduce their material including Article 29 Working Party and European Data Protection Board papers. We must also thank the Council of Europe and the European Court of Human Rights for permission to quote from their material. Further thanks are due to the British and Irish Legal Information Institute (BAILII) for enabling us to quote from their invaluable service. None of these various organisations can be responsible for or provide any guarantees in respect of the materials they have allowed us to use.

Finally we must thank London data protection team at Bird & Bird, as well as Ed Young of Bird & Bird and Edmund Morgan, for assistance in preparing this book.

Richard Morgan
Ruth Boardman
12 May 2019

Contents

Part III Data Protection Compliance

Part IV Appendices

Precedents

Table of Cases

England and Wales

European Court of Justice

European Court of Human Rights

Table of Statutes

Table of Statutory Instruments

Table of European Legislation

Decisions

Table of Information Commissioner's Office Guidance

Table of Article 29 Working Party Guidance

Table of European Data Protection Board Guidance

Introduction and How to Use This Book

0.1 This book is intended for those tasked with responsibility for compliance with data protection legislation within their organisation. It assumes that the reader has no prior knowledge of the legislation and, to assist this reader, explains concepts from first principles, with extensive cross referencing when topics are discussed in more detail elsewhere in the book. Although the reader we had in mind when writing this book may be new to data protection, we hope that the book will also be useful to those who already work in the field.

0.2 **Part I** of the book covers the essentials of the legislation, the General Data Protection Regulation (the "GDPR") as amended and amplified by the Data Protection Act 2018 (the "DPA 2018"). The GDPR is over 100 pages long, and the DPA 2018 is 340 pages. In many parts the legislation is not easy for the layman to understand and it is buttressed by substantial guidance from the Information Commissioner. We start with a discussion of key concepts and players, in **Chapter 1**, to assist the reader with finding his or her way around the terminology and concepts which recur throughout other chapters.

0.3 **Part II** is concerned with conducting a data audit, on the principle that an organisation cannot comply with the legislation unless it knows what personal data it processes and why.

0.4 **Part III** is concerned with setting up procedures for compliance with all the provisions of the legislation and maintaining that compliance in the future. We included commentary on compliance in the first two editions of this book. The GDPR introduces a new "accountability" principle, giving even greater prominence to this topic.

0.5 The DPA 2018 also deals with the more recondite areas of law enforcement and the intelligence services. For completeness we devote a chapter to these provisions, but have placed it in **Part IV**, so as not to inconvenience readers who do not need it.

0.6 We anticipate that lawyers as well as non-lawyers will find the approach useful. For the benefit of lawyers we have included the usual Tables of Statutes, Cases, and European Legislation, and we have also retained the titles of judges—e.g. "J" after a name for "Mr Justice", "LJ" for "Lord Justice", "MR" for "Master of the Rolls", and "VC" for Vice-Chancellor", etc.

0.7 Much of the guidance as to how the legislation is to be observed comes from the Information Commissioner (whose job we explain at **1.3.8**), and we have also included a Table of Commissioner's Guidance so that readers can lay their hands easily on the authority for a particular recommendation. The Commissioner's website is further discussed at **1.3.8.11**.

0.8 Text in *italics* is a direct quotation—from the legislation, or a reported case, or the Commissioner's guidance, etc., as the case may be. The Commissioner's guidance used to be available both in html and pdf format and the latter included page numbers. Regrettably, during the winter of 2018–19, the Information Commissioner removed the page-numbered pdf versions of her guidance on the GDPR from her website. As a result, we have only been able to include page numbers for quotations in older guidance from the Commissioner.

0.9 The book is extensively cross-referenced in **bold** so that if a reader forgets some vital piece of information he can at once turn it up. A reference beginning with a number is a reference to the main text of the book. Other cross-references are to the General Data Protection Regulation (and other EU legislation) in the form of art. for article, and rec. for recitals. For the Data Protection Act 2018 (and other Acts) we use s. (for section, plural ss.) followed by the relevant number of the section of the Act, or Schedule, for a reference to the Schedules of the Act.

0.10 We should also point out that the GDPR uses the word "data" as a plural, meaning either "information" or "items of information". In the real world "data" is universally used as a singular noun meaning simply "information" and nothing else. We have followed ordinary usage and treated "data" as a singular, except when we are quoting directly from European legislation or similar sources.

0.11 In the second edition published in 2012 we remarked on the accretion of new legislative material, the emergence of data breach as a substantial issue, and technological/social changes since the first edition some nine years earlier. Although only seven years have elapsed since the last edition, the matter has been transformed not only by the GDPR, but also by the matter of Brexit. We return to Brexit at the end of these introductory comments.

0.12 After the main text there are a series of **Appendices**. **Appendix 1** describes the background to the legislation and its relationship to the newer field of privacy legislation. This is a huge topic outside the general scope of this book and although it is not essential reading before going straight to **Ch. 1**, we think many readers will find this outline useful, either before starting to consider the detail of the legislation, or saved for consideration at a later stage in their reading.

0.13 The remaining **Appendices** provide in tabular form some of the detail for special cases, so as to keep the main text as uncluttered as possible. Where we refer to an Appendix in the main text, we have prefaced it with an "A" followed by the number of the Appendix.

0.14 Set out at the very end of the book to allow for easy access, we have a series of **Precedents**, which we hope will prove useful. These should like all precedents be used with discretion and only when the conditions are appropriate. The reader is recommended to study the corresponding main text before using any Precedent. Optional wording is enclosed in square brackets. Where we provide alternative wording it is in the form of two square-bracketed phrases: [this][or that]. Precedents are referenced in the main text with a "P", followed by the number of the relevant precedent.

0.15 Brexit

0.15.1 We have written this book in the latter part of 2018 and early 2019, when the UK is still a member of the European Union, but neither the short-term, nor longer-term, implications of Brexit are clear. As of April 2019, three main options were being discussed:

(1) the Draft Agreement on the withdrawal of the United Kingdom of Great Britain and Northern Ireland from the European Union and the European Atomic Energy Community, as agreed at negotiators' level on 14 November 2018 (the "Withdrawal Agreement") and the Political Declaration on the Future Relationship between the EU and the UK (the "Political Declaration"), rejected by the UK Parliament three times, but still the only negotiated exit to which the EU has agreed (*https://www.gov.uk/government/publications/progress-on-the-uks-exit-from-and-future-relationship-with-the-european-union*);

(2) a no-deal Brexit (*https://www.gov.uk/government/publications/data-protection-if-theres-no-brexit-deal*); or

(3) a form of Brexit involving a customs union with the EU.

0.15.2 There is no certainty as to whether one, or indeed, any, of these options will be agreed or not. The implications of the Withdrawal Agreement, or a no-deal Brexit, for data protection are broadly clear. Nothing has been published by the UK Government or the EU about the impact of a customs union on data protection. However, the objective of this approach, seems to be to secure the approval of the UK Parliament for the Withdrawal Agreement, on the basis of a commitment to a customs union after the transitional period ends. At least for the transitional period, therefore, we can look to the Withdrawal Agreement to see the impact on data protection.

0.15.3 In the event of a no-deal Brexit, section 3(1) of the European Union (Withdrawal) Act 2018 ("EUWA") will provide that the GDPR will continue to apply in the UK post-Brexit. However, in the event of a no-deal Brexit, the GDPR cannot be applied in the UK without amendment. For example, in multiple places, the GDPR refers to EU institutions which will have no further direct relevance to the UK. To address these deficiencies, the Government has introduced secondary legislation, the Data Protection, Privacy and Electronic Communications (Amendments etc) (EU Exit) Regulations 2019 (the "Data Protection (EU Exit) Regulations"). These introduce a concept of the "UK GDPR", being the GDPR "*as it forms part of the law of England and Wales, Scotland and Northern Ireland by virtue of section 3 of the European Union (Withdrawal) Act 2018*" and make consequential changes to the UK GDPR and the DPA 2018. By way of example of these changes, references in the GDPR to "*Member State law*" become references to "*domestic law*" and references to the EU Commission are replaced with references to the Secretary of State. The UK Government has published Keeling schedules which show the effect of these changes, by way of marked-up copies of the GDPR and the DPA 2018 (*https://www.gov.uk/government/publications/data-protection-law-eu-exit*).

0.15.4 The Withdrawal Agreement provides for a transitional period, which will run until the end of 2020 (unless extended). During this transitional period, art.127 provides that EU law will apply to the UK and will produce the same effect in, and in respect of the UK, as it does in the rest of the EU. However, the UK will not (ordinarily) participate in EU institutions, bodies or agencies during this period (art.7(1)). The future relationship between the Information Commissioner and her EU peers is addressed in the Political Declaration which promises "*appropriate co-operation between regulators*". If the Withdrawal Agreement is approved, therefore, there will be fewer changes to data protection law – at least during the transitional period. The changes to UK data protection law after that date are unclear – although one assumes that the changes similar to those described at **0.15** above would have to be implemented at that point.

0.15.5 Whether the Withdrawal Agreement becomes effective, or whether there is a no-deal Brexit, organisations will still have to address compliance with the GDPR. The substance of the obligations which apply to them and the rights granted to individuals will not change. Brexit will have most effect on:

(1) the role of the Information Commissioner and the operation of the co-operation and consistency mechanisms in the GDPR (Ch.1);

(2) the material and territorial scope of data protection legislation in the UK (Ch.2); and

(3) transfers of personal data (Ch.9)

and we address the impact of Brexit in further detail in these chapters. As it is not clear when, or if, the changes to UK data protection law described at **0.15** will become effective, we have not otherwise generally attempted to anticipate these changes.

0.15.6 Finally, as a drafting point:

(1) Whenever we refer to Member States of the European Union, this should be taken to mean both EU Member States and the UK, up to the point at which the UK ceases to be an EU Member State; and

(2) Whenever we talk about the GDPR, we mean the GDPR up to Brexit, or, post-Brexit, its incorporation into the law of the United Kingdom by the EUWA.

Part I

Introduction to Data Protection

CHAPTER 1

Processing Data

1.1 INTRODUCTION

1.1.1 Before the reader can consider the obligations which data protection legislation places on their organisation, we need to consider first what data protection legislation means by "personal data" (**1.2.2**), what it means by "processing" (**1.2.5**), and then consider the players involved in personal data. The main players are the data subject and the controller, possibly with involvement of a third party known as the processor (**1.3.2–1.3.5**). The Information Commissioner (the regulator of data protection legislation in the UK), is also a key player and this chapter introduces the Commissioner and her enforcement powers together with the system of appeals from these (**1.3.8**). The General Data Protection Regulation (Regulation (EU) 2016/679) (GDPR) required the UK to make sweeping changes to its previous data protection legislation and introduced a new and influential player, the European Data Protection Board (EDPB) and a new set of rules for handling investigations relating to cross-border processing. The EDPB and these rules are discussed at **1.4.2**.

1.2 PROCESSING PERSONAL DATA

1.2.1 Introduction

1.2.1.1 Data protection legislation applies to:

> "*the processing of personal data wholly or partly by automated means and to the processing other than by automated means of personal data which form part of a filing system or are intended to form part of a filing system*" (GDPR art.2(1)).

In order to understand the scope of data protection legislation, it is necessary to consider what "*personal data*" means and when, by contrast, data may be anonymous and so fall outside the scope of the legislation. It is also necessary to understand what is meant by processing by automated means, or in non-automated "*filing systems*". In this section, we also look at certain types of personal data: special category data, information about criminal offences and convictions, and health related data—which are called out for special treatment under data protection legislation. In addition to the Information Commissioner's "*Guide to Data Protection*" (the "*Guide*"), we also refer to a separate guidance note from the Commissioner on the meaning of personal data: *What is personal data,* Vol. 1.0, 24 May 2018. There is also *Opinion No.4/2007 on the concept of personal data* (WP 136) issued by the Article 29 Working Party (a body whose role we describe at **1.4.1.3**).

1.2.2 Personal data

1.2.2.1 The main definitions in the GDPR are to be found in art.4. "Personal data" is defined at art.4(1), as:

> "*any information relating to an identified or identifiable natural person*"

and an "*identifiable natural person*" is defined as:

> "*one who can be identified, directly or indirectly, in particular by reference to an identifier such as a name, an identification number, location data or an online identifier, or one or more factors specific to the physical, physiological, genetic, mental, economic, cultural or social identity of the individual*".

So, an individual can be identified by an identifier—such as a name or number—or by a combination of factors which allow an individual to be "*singled out*" (rec.26).

Online identifiers

1.2.2.2 The definition makes clear individuals can be identified by their online activity and this is further emphasised by rec.30 which notes that:

> "*Natural persons may be associated with online identifiers provided by their devices, applications, tools and protocols, such as internet protocol addresses, cookie identifiers or other identifiers such as radio frequency identification tags*".

There is guidance from the Information Commissioner on all aspects of the legislation. In her detailed guidance on *Determining What is Personal Data* she gives the examples of MAC addresses, advertising IDs, pixel tags, account handles and device fingerprints: these are all examples of different types of reference numbers, or other forms of identification, used to allow publishers, advertisers and others to single out those who are online. Some of these are considered in more detail in **Ch.14**.

1.2.2.3 Very often it is not clear whether some of these types of data refer to an individual or not. For example, IP addresses may or may not refer to a single living individual. Thus, *john.smith1234567@suchandsuchmail.com* probably is a personal identifier, but probably not *theblogginsfamily@suchandsuchmail.com* nor *info@jonesltd751.co.uk*. Such personal identifiers as IP addresses or cookies have been helpfully described as "non-obvious identifiers" by a previous Information Commissioner in his *Personal Information Online Code of Practice* (July 2010) p.9, and his advice was that if you cannot tell if it is personal data or not, you should still treat it as personal data.

Direct and indirect identification

1.2.2.4 An individual will be directly identified where the information itself shows who the individual is—for example, because name and address are included. An individual will be indirectly identifiable where the data, when combined with other information, allows the individual to be identified. This has been considered by the Court of Justice of the European Union (CJEU), in the context of IP addresses.

1.2.2.5 The case of *Scarlet Extended SA v SABAM* (C-70/10) 24 November 2011 [51] confirmed that IP addresses held by internet service providers (ISPs) would be personal data. This is not surprising: the ISP would be able to correlate the IP address with the details of the subscriber to whom the address had been allocated.

1.2.2.6 Organisations publishing websites will also hold IP addresses of those visiting their sites, where these addresses are recorded in the publisher's web-logs. If a website visitor registers to use a site, the publisher will know to whom an IP address relates. However, in other situations, the publisher will not know this. The case of ***Patrick Breyer v Bundesrepublik Deutschland*** (C-582/14) 19 October 2016 [45] confirmed that dynamic IP addresses contained in web-logs held by a website publisher would *also* be personal data if it was reasonably likely that the publisher would be able to access the identification information held by the ISP.

1.2.2.7 Recital 26 states that

> "*account should be taken of all the means reasonably likely to be used ... either by the controller or by another person to identify the natural person directly or indirectly*".

Breyer considered the equivalent provisions in the old data protection Directive 95/46 on the protection of individuals with regard to the processing of personal data and on the free movement of such data (now repealed but in force at the time), confirming that:

> "*The fact that the additional data necessary to identify the user of a website are held not by the online media services provider, but by that user's internet service provider does not ... exclude that dynamic IP addresses ... constitute personal data*" [43].

The CJEU confirmed that we must consider whether this access is *likely*:

> "*it must be determined whether the possibility to combine a dynamic IP address with the additional data held by the internet service provider constitutes a means likely reasonably to be used to identify the data subject.*
> *... that would not be the case if the identification ... was prohibited by law or practically impossible on account of the fact that it requires a disproportionate effort in terms of time, cost and man-power, so that the risk of identification appears in reality to be insignificant*" [45], [46].

Likelihood of identification

1.2.2.8 Recital 26 states that:

> "*To ascertain whether means are reasonably likely to be used to identify the natural person, account should be taken of all objective factors, such as the costs of and the amount of time required for identification, taking into consideration the available technology at the time of the processing and technological developments*".

The recital states that you must consider what is available *at the time of processing*—so this may change over time. As the Commissioner notes in her detailed guidance on *Determining What is Personal Data*, this should be kept under review and conclusions documented. The Commissioner also notes there that organisations should not just consider the methods likely to be used by an ordinary individual—they should also consider what a determined person, with a particular reason to want to identify the individual, may do—this could be an investigative journalist or an estranged partner. If the data relates to someone who has a high profile, then this would also be relevant.

Examples of personal data considered in cases

1.2.2.9 There are now a large number of CJEU cases which have considered whether data is, or is not, personal. Some useful conclusions are listed below:

- personal data is intentionally a wide concept, made clear by the reference to "any information" in the definition; it is not restricted to sensitive or private information; it includes subjective information such as opinions and assessments; it includes information written by a candidate in an exam (although not the exam questions); it also includes the comments of the examiner—which would be personal data about both the candidate and the examiner (***Nowak*** (C-434/16) 20 December 2017 [33], [34], [42], [44]);
- only natural persons can benefit from data protection rights—however, this would include legal persons (such as partnerships) where the official title of the legal person identifies a natural person—i.e. where the partnership has the name of the individual partners; the fact that information relates to an individual's professional life is not relevant—there is no reason to exclude this from protection (***Volker und Markus Schecke GbR*** (C-92/09) and ***Hartmut Eifert v Land Hessen*** (C-93/09) EU:C:2010:662 [53], [59]);
- legal analysis about an individual does not itself amount to personal data—although it may include some personal data (such as facts about the individual) (***YS v Minister voor Immigratie, Integratie en Asiel*** (C-141/12) and ***Minister voor Immigratie en Asiel v M and S*** and (C-372/12) ECLI:EU:C:2013:838 [39]);

- Photos, where individuals can be identified, are personal data; the fact those photographed are public officials and that the data relates to individuals in a professional capacity does not stop the data being personal (***Sergejs Buivids v Datu valsts inspekcija*** (C-345/17) EU:C:2019:122 [31], [44], [46].

When does personal data "relate to" an individual?

1.2.2.10 For data to be personal, it must "*relate to*" an identified or identifiable individual. For a considerable period, the UK approach to the definition of personal data was confused by the case of ***Durant v Financial Services Authority*** [2003] EWCA Civ 1746. Mr Durant had complained about Barclays Bank to the Financial Services Authority (FSA). When the FSA rejected his complaint, Mr Durant made a subject access request (that is, he asked to see a copy of his personal data—a data subject right under the Data Protection Act 1998 ("1998 Act") as well as under the GDPR—see **6.5**) to the FSA. The papers held by the FSA included information about the systems and controls in place at the bank, which had been collected because of Mr Durant's complaint. The Court of Appeal concluded, amongst other things, that the information held by the FSA was not Mr Durant's personal data because it did not relate to him—noting that "*mere mention of the data subject in a document held by a data controller does not necessarily amount to his personal data*" and suggesting two "*notions*" which may assist in determining when data are personal—being whether the:

> "*information is biographical in a significant sense, that is going beyond the recording of the putative data subject's involvement in a matter or an event that has no personal connotations, a life event in respect of which his privacy could not be said to be compromised*"

and

> "*. . . focus. The information should have the putative data subject as its focus rather than some other person with whom he may have been involved or some transaction or event in which he may have figured. . .*" [28].

1.2.2.11 The emphasis in the CJEU cases listed above on the breadth of "*personal data*" makes clear that the comments about biographical significance and focus cannot be read too literally. However, the case predated these CJEU cases and did cause considerable confusion in the UK. A good example of this can be found in another case involving the FSA, ***Edem v Information Commissioner & Financial Services Authority*** [2014] EWCA Civ 92. Here with very similar facts to ***Durant***, a Mr Edem had complained to the FSA and then sought to obtain information from the FSA under the Freedom of Information Act 2000 (FOIA) about the handling of his complaints, including details of the employees at the FSA who had been involved in these. Under s.40 of the FOIA there is an exemption from the provisions of the FOIA for data that is personal data under the data protection legislation. The First-tier Tribunal concluded that this information did not amount to personal data—following ***Durant***—on the basis that it was not of biographical significance and there was no focus on the individual. It is hard to see how individuals' names could not be personal data—and the Court of Appeal had no difficulty distinguishing ***Durant*** and finding this to be the case. A good suggestion for the best way to read the comments in ***Durant*** can be found in the Court of Appeal case of ***Secretary of State for the Home Department and the Home Office v TLU and TLV*** [2018] EWCA Civ 2217 which concludes that:

> "*I am unable to accept that . . . Auld LJ was doing more than state a broad, practical working assumption. On no view was he seeking to reformulate the statutory test, whereby personal data encompasses data and other information from which an individual could be directly or indirectly identified*" [42].

1.2.2.12 *The Guide*, following the Article 29 Working Party Paper WP 136, gives straight-forward guidance that:

> "*When considering whether information 'relates to' an individual, you need to take into account a range of factors, including the content of the information, the purpose or purposes for which you are processing it and the likely impact of that processing on the individual*".

Purpose and impact can be context-specific. The Commissioner's detailed guidance on *Determining What is Personal Data* gives this example:

> "*Emails written by a lawyer to their client about their client's matter all contain references to the lawyer's name and place of work, which will be the lawyer's personal data. However, the content of the emails are not about the individual lawyer, but about the client's instructions. The content of the email is not, therefore, personal data where it concerns legal advice about the client's legal query. If a complaint was then made about the lawyer's performance and the emails were then used to investigate this, the legal advice given in them would become personal data*".

1.2.3 Anonymous data and pseudonymous data

1.2.3.1 Data that is truly anonymous that is, where the individual cannot reasonably be identified falls outside data protection legislation. However, it can be difficult to produce genuinely anonymous information (**5.5.6.2**). The Information Commissioner produced an *Anonymisation Code of Practice* under the 1998 Act, which is currently being updated and so has been removed from the Commissioner's website. Detailed guidance is, however, still available from the Article 29 Working Party, which, in 2014, adopted *Opinion 05/2014 on Anonymisation Techniques* (WP 216). WP 216 summarises a wide range of anonymisation techniques and, for each one, it comments on its strengths and weaknesses. The Opinion suggests that the effectiveness of anonymisation techniques should be assessed against three tests—can the individual be singled out from the data; does the data allow records to be linked; and can information about an identifiable individual be inferred from the data. Readers should note that the Opinion has been criticised as being overly strict (for example, El Emam and Alvarez: *A critical appraisal of the Article 29 Working Party Opinion 05/2014 on data anonymisation techniques*, available on *https://www.researchgate.net*).

1.2.3.2 Anonymous data must be distinguished from "pseudonymous data". The GDPR introduces a new definition of "pseudonymisation"—that is:

> "*the processing of personal data in such a manner that the personal data can no longer be attributed to a specific data subject without the use of additional information, provided that such additional information is kept separately and is subject to technical and organisational measures to ensure that the data are not attributed to an identified or identifiable natural person*" (art.4(5)).

The definition describes data where an individual cannot be identified because the elements of the data which could identify the individual are held separately and securely. Data collected during a clinical trial fits this example well. The sponsor of the trial (that is the legal entity which obtains authorisation to conduct the trial) needs to receive results about the individuals participating in the trial, at an individual level. However, the sponsor does not need to know the identity of each patient. The investigator applies a unique code to each patient record and sends the sponsor the data with the code, but with other identifying information removed. The investigator retains a look-up table linking the unique code with the patient. This table can only be accessed in certain situations. For example, in the event that patients have to be contacted on safety grounds or for clinical audit requirements.

1.2.3.3 As the example of clinical trial data shows, in most situations the sponsor will not be able to identify patients—however, in appropriate situations, the sponsor *will* be able to do this, and the system is designed to ensure that this can happen. As a result, the data still relates to identifiable individuals and is still personal data. Recital 26 of the GDPR makes clear that pseudonymisation does not stop data being personal:

> "*Personal data which have undergone pseudonymisation, which could be attributed to a natural person by the use of additional information should be considered to be information on an identifiable natural person*".

1.2.3.4 Pseudonymisation certainly helps to protect personal data—for example, a personal data breach involving pseudonymous data is likely to pose less threat to individuals than a personal data breach where identifiers are also exposed. However, organisations which have pseudonymised personal data must still ensure that they comply with all aspects of data protection legislation—as rec. 28 notes:

> *"The application of pseudonymisation to personal data can reduce the risks to the data subjects concerned and help controllers and processors to meet their data protection obligations. The explicit introduction of 'pseudonymisation' in this Regulation is not intended to preclude any other measures of protection"*.

Anonymous data, by contrast, falls completely outside the scope of the legislation.

1.2.3.5 The interaction between freedom of information and data protection means that public authorities in particular have had to give considerable attention to when data ceases to be personal, so that it can be released more easily under the FOIA. An interesting example is to be found in the House of Lords case: ***Common Services Agency v Scottish Information Commissioner*** [2008] UKHL 47. This was a Scottish case about the FOIA (Scotland) 2002. Section 38 of this Act, like s.40 of the English FOIA, has an exemption from the duty to divulge if the data is personal data and where releasing the data would breach certain provisions of data protection legislation. The case turned on the extent to which apparently anonymised data might still be personal data. An MSP's researcher asked for information from the Common Services Agency in Scotland as to all incidents of childhood leukaemia for both sexes from 1990–2003 for all of Dumfries and Galloway broken down by postal area within census ward. The purpose of the question was to identify clusters of occurrences of the disease which might be related to specific nuclear and other installations within the area.

1.2.3.6 The problem with the request was that by ward per year the number of occurrences was in many cases tiny—often just one—and as such the data could relate to a single individual. The Agency therefore refused to give the information on the grounds that it was personal data. The MSP's researcher appealed to the Scottish Information Commissioner. (The Scottish Information Commissioner is concerned with the FOIA (Scotland). He does not have authority for data protection in Scotland.) He, as a compromise, suggested that the Agency release the data not broken down by ward, but the researcher refused this. The next suggestion was that the data should be "barnardised". This is a statistical technique for handling very low numbers whereby certain values are modified. The purpose is to ensure that the numbers in the range 1–4 cannot be identified with certainty while still recognising that they are very low numbers. This is done by arbitrarily adding -1, 0 or +1 to each of them. The numbers five and above are unchanged. The Commissioner ordered the Agency to release the data in this form. The Agency appealed. Their Lordships decided that the request should be resubmitted to the Commissioner for him to consider whether the barnardised data was still personal data (and if it was, whether it was also sensitive personal data as being about the health of individuals), or whether it was sufficiently anonymised for it to cease to be personal data and so releasable to the MSP's researcher.

1.2.3.7 A more recent case considering the release of datasets is ***Information Commissioner v Miller*** [2018] UKUT 229 (AAC). In this case, a freedom of information request had been made to the Department of Communities and Local Government (DCLG), for release of homelessness statistics between 2009–2012. The DCLG refused to release the information, arguing that a motivated intruder would be able to identify the individuals concerned, so making the data personal. Neither the First-tier Tribunal nor the Upper Tribunal were convinced that this would be the case. The Upper Tribunal considered that the approach of the First-tier Tribunal (which looked at likelihood of identification) was reasonable. Considerable emphasis was placed on the fact that it seemed very unlikely to the Tribunal that anyone would be motivated to try to identify the individuals. The Tribunal was also influenced by the fact that neither the Commissioner nor the DCLG had provided detailed evidence to support their claims that the data could be identifiable.

1.2.4 Special types of personal data

Special category data

1.2.4.1 Within the broad category of personal data, data protection legislation distinguishes certain kinds of information which it regards as needing special protection. These are referred to as "*special categories*" of personal data (and are sometimes also referred to as "sensitive personal data" which was the definition used in the 1998 Act). Data protection legislation prohibits the processing of this type of data, unless one of the more stringent conditions set out in art.9 of the GDPR or in the DPA 2018 can be met (**6.11.3**).

1.2.4.2 Special category data is listed in art.9(1) of the GDPR and consists of personal data:

> "*revealing racial or ethnic origin, political opinions, religious or philosophical beliefs, or trade union membership, and the processing of genetic data, biometric data for the purpose of uniquely identifying a natural person, data concerning health or data concerning a natural person's sex life or sexual orientation*".

1.2.4.3 There is a strong correlation between special category data and information which could be used to discriminate against someone (with the exception of gender and age). Genetic data, biometric data used for identification and sexual orientation were added by the GDPR to the special categories of data listed in the previous Data Protection Directive 95/46.

Genetic data is defined at art.4(13) as:

> "*personal data relating to the inherited or acquired genetic characteristics of a natural person which gives unique information about the physiology or the health of that natural person and which results, in particular, from an analysis of a biological sample from the natural person in question*".

Recital 34 notes that this may, in particular, be the result of DNA or RNA analysis.

1.2.4.4 Biometric data is also defined in art.4(14) as:

> "*personal data resulting from specific technical processing relating to the physical, physiological or behavioural characteristics of a natural person, which allow or confirm the unique identification of that natural person, such as facial images or dactyloscopic data*" [i.e. fingerprints].

The definition would cover unique behaviours—such as handwriting or gait—as well as physical facts such as fingerprints. However, this information only falls within the definition of biometric data if it could be used to confirm the unique identity of an individual.

1.2.4.5 Many systems which use biometrics to identify someone do not store a copy of the actual biometric (for example, the fingerprint). Instead, for reasons of security, the biometric data is transformed by an algorithm into a unique digital representation of the raw biometric. The fact that the definition covers personal data "resulting from" the processing of the biometric characteristic is important: it means that the definition will cover both the "raw" biometric and also, the transformed digital record of the biometric. For more information on biometric data, readers should refer to the Article 29 Working Party *Working document on biometrics*, adopted on 1 August 2003 (WP 80).

1.2.4.6 Recital 51 notes that photographs should not automatically be regarded as covered by the definition of biometric data: if they are subjected to facial recognition technology, in order to tag all photos of a particular individual, they will be biometric data; if they are not used for this purpose, they will not be. Photographs may also reveal information about religion, racial or ethnic origin, health or sexual orientation, which are also special categories of data. Recital 51 says nothing about whether photographs should, therefore, automatically be treated as a special category of data. This was briefly considered in ***David Murray (by his litigation friends Neil Murray & Joanne Murray) v Express Newspapers and Big Pictures (UK) Ltd*** [2007] EWHC 1908 (Ch). The case concerned pictures taken of JK Rowling's infant son in a pushchair on the street. At first instance arguments were raised as to whether or not the photographs should be treated as sensitive personal data. The first instance decision was overturned on appeal. However, the appeal was on other grounds and the comments of Patten J on photographs being sensitive data were not considered at all. His comments were:

> "*It seems to me that if a photograph and the information it contains constitutes personal data then it is hard to escape from the conclusion that insofar as it indicates the racial or ethnic origin of the data subject it also consists of sensitive personal data. I do not however accept that the present photograph also comprises sensitive personal data under s.2(e)* [of the 1998 Act]. *For that to be the case it would have to be of someone with some clearly identifiable physical condition which was exposed by the photograph. A photograph of an apparently healthy individual in fact tells one nothing about his actual state of health*" [80].

Data concerning health

1.2.4.7 Health data has a wider definition than purely information about a medical condition. Article 4(15) provides that "*data concerning health*" means:

> "*personal data relating to the physical or mental health of a natural person, including the provision of health care services, which reveal information about his or her health status*".

The fact that someone is a patient at a particular facility may, therefore, also be data concerning health. Recital 35 notes that this would include the "*past, current or future*" health status—and would include information collected to register persons for health care services and numbers or symbols assigned to uniquely identify people for health purposes. Recital 35 also notes that data can concern health irrespective of the source of the information, for example, whether the source is a health care professional, a hospital, medical device or diagnostic kit.

1.2.4.8 The DPA 2018 distinguishes between data concerning health (s.205) (any health data, irrespective of source) and "health records" (also s.205) (which are those created by healthcare professionals). Organisations should be alert to processing either type of data: as set out in **10.2.2**, there are special rules for subject access requests involving data concerning health, in order to avoid releasing information to the individual which may cause serious harm. There are also special rules for health records, to prevent individuals being required to use subject access rights to obtain health records and provide the records to third parties—for example, to potential employers or insurers.

Criminal convictions and offences

1.2.4.9 The GDPR art.10 treats information about "*criminal convictions and offences or related security measures*" as a unique type of personal data, providing that it may only be processed "*under the control of official authority*" or when the processing is authorised by EU or Member State law. Further a comprehensive register of criminal convictions can only be kept under the control of official authority.

1.2.4.10 In the UK, s.10(5) of the DPA 2018 provides that the conditions for processing in Sch.1 to the Act, which allow special category data to be processed for certain purposes, also apply to data about criminal convictions. There are also some conditions for processing which apply specifically to criminal conviction data (at Sch.1 Pt 3) (**4.5.2.2**). However, the UK is unusual in the way it approaches this and in many EU Member States, criminal conviction data can only be processed in limited situations/by official bodies.

1.2.4.11 Section 11(2) of the DPA 2018 provides that information about criminal convictions and offences includes personal data relating to:

> "*a) the alleged commission of offences by the data subject; or*

b) *proceedings for an offence committed or alleged to have been committed by the data subject or the disposal of such proceedings, including sentencing*".

The Information Commissioner conducted an investigation into the trade in illegal personal data, resulting in a report to Parliament in May 2006: *What price privacy?* As part of this investigation, the Information Commissioner held information about 305 journalists, who were customers of a private investigator, found to be illegally trading in personal data. The Information Commissioner received freedom of information requests for information about the investigation—including the names of these journalists. In ***Information Commissioner v Colenso-Dunne*** [2015] UKUT 471 (AAC) the Upper Tribunal had to decide if the Information Commissioner was correct to treat this information as information about the alleged commission of offences. The Upper Tribunal concluded that this was not the case: the fact that the journalists had commissioned this investigator need not have been because they knew or connived at his illegal actions and so was not sufficient as to amount to an assertion of criminality in relation to the journalists, nor did the fact that the public may misconstrue the information as amounting to allegations of offences mean that it fell into this category [48].

1.2.5 Processing

1.2.5.1 Article 2(1) of the GDPR provides that:

"*This Regulation applies to the processing of personal data wholly or partly by automated means and to the processing other than by automated means of personal data which form part of a filing system or are intended to form part of a filing system*".

"Processing" is defined at art.4(2) as:

"*any operation or set of operations which is performed on personal data, or on sets of personal data whether or not by automated means, such as collection, recording, organisation, structuring, storage, adaptation or alteration, retrieval, consultation, use, disclosure by transmission, dissemination or otherwise making available, alignment or combination, restriction, erasure or destruction*".

The definition is extremely broad. The CJEU has held that the equivalent definition under the old Directive 95/46 covered references to individuals, with their name and telephone number, on an internet page (***Bodil Lindqvist***, CJEU, C-101/01 [27]) and the crawling and indexing of internet pages carried out by search engines (***Google Spain SL, Google Inc, v Agencia Espanola de Proteccion de Datos, Mario Costeja Gonzalez*** CJEU, C-131/12 [28]).

1.2.5.2 In the UK, in ***Johnson v MDU*** [2007] 1 All E.R. 467, the Court of Appeal was asked to consider whether the analysis and scoring carried out by the

Medical Defence Union's risk assessors amounted to "processing" of personal data under the 1998 Act. Some of the relevant records were held on computer and some largely on paper. The actual process of scoring—which determined if the MDU would continue to provide cover for a health-care professional—was not automated and was carried out by the risk assessor in her head. The Court of Appeal, in a majority decision, concluded that this was not processing by automated means. The GDPR is wider than Directive 95/46, as it applies to processing "*wholly or partly*" by automated means: we think this means that the decision in ***Johnson*** is in this respect of limited further relevance—the information consulted by the risk assessor was held on computer, so her activities were partly involving automated means.

Filing systems

1.2.5.3 As well as applying to wholly or partly automated processing of personal data, data protection legislation also applies to personal data which is not processed automatically if the data forms part of, or is intended to form part of, a "*filing system*". This is defined at art.4(6) as:

> "*any structured set of personal data which are accessible according to specific criteria, whether centralised, decentralised or dispersed on a functional or geographical basis*".

Most manual files will consist of paper records. It is, however, worth remembering that manual files can be broader than this. So, for example, collections of x-rays or tissue samples could amount to a manual record.

1.2.5.4 Non-automated filing systems were considered by the CJEU in the Jehovah's Witnesses Community case (***Tietosuojavalutuutettu, intervening parties Jehovan todistajat-uskonnollinen yhdyskunta***, 10 July 2018, C-25/17). One of the questions the Court was asked was whether the paper records collected by preachers from the community, consisting of names, addresses and other information, amounted to a "*filing system*" for the purposes of Directive 95/46 (which had the same definition as that in the GDPR). The CJEU emphasised that the definition was intended to be broad—shown by the fact that the definition referred to "*any*" structured set of personal data. The CJEU noted that the set must be structured so as to allow "*easy access*" to the personal data and the criteria used to structure the records must relate to individuals—however, the Court thought this part of the definition simply confirmed the requirement that the personal data should be easily retrievable. The Court concluded that there was no requirement for the files to include particular search methods or specific lists:

> "*the specific criterion and the specific form in which the set of personal data collected by each of the members who engage in preaching is actually structured is irrelevant, so long as that set of data makes it possible for the data relating to a specific person who has been contacted to be easily retrieved*".

1.2.5.5 Directive 95/46 (rec.27) allowed Member States to determine the criteria for relevant filing systems. The definition of a "*relevant filing system*" in the UK's 1998 Act was more restrictive than that of a "filing system" in the Directive itself and in the GDPR. In the ***Durant*** case (**1.2.2.10**), the Court of Appeal was concerned about the burden a broad term could impose on controllers dealing with access requests and concluded that this term was limited to files which:

- were clearly structured so as to indicate at the outset of any search whether specific information capable of being personal data was held in the files and, if so, in which file or files; and
- which have a sufficiently detailed and sophisticated means of readily indicating whether and where in an individual file specific information about an individual can be located [50].

Given the broader definition which now applies under the GDPR and given the comments in the ***Jehovah's Witnesses*** case about the breadth of the definition, it seems that this element of *Durant* has been superseded.

1.2.5.6 Finally, for public authorities there is a further type of record to note—this is entirely unstructured manual records, known as "*manual unstructured processing of personal data*". The FOIA provided that all personal data held by public authorities is subject to data protection legislation (albeit with wide exemptions) even if the information is not structured. This concept is carried forward by DPA 2018 s.21(2) and (4), and considered in more detail at **12.3.2**.

1.3 THE PLAYERS

1.3.1 We have considered what "personal data" and "processing" mean in the legislation. We now have to turn our attention to some individuals who are identified or defined in the legislation.

1.3.2 Data subjects

1.3.2.1 The GDPR art.4(1) uses the term data subject to describe

"*an identified or identifiable natural person*"

and goes on to say:

"*an identifiable natural person is one who can be identified, directly or indirectly,*

and refers to the types of identifier we discussed at **1.22** above.

1.3.2.2 The GDPR and DPA 2018 grant data subjects the following rights summarised here as:

- to access personal data that relates to them, to be provided with certain explanatory information and, in some circumstances, to require a copy of their data to be provided to them or another organisation in a portable format;
- to prevent organisations from using their personal data in certain situations (such as processing for purposes of direct marketing) and not to be subject to significant and entirely automated individual decision-making;
- to require inaccurate data to be corrected; and
- to require data to be erased, or to require the processing of data to be restricted—so that the data can be stored but not otherwise used.

These rights are considered at Ch.6. It is important to note that these rights are not restricted to UK residents; the DPA 2018 grants rights to all individuals to whom personal data relates.

1.3.2.3 The GDPR does not apply to personal data of deceased persons—although rec. 27 in saying this, permits Member States to provide for rules in this area if they so wish. The DPA 2018 does not do this. However, if an organisation operates in other EU Member States, it should be alert to the fact that some Member States have adopted rules which relate to this. For example, the French *Loi Informatique et Libertés*, provides for this. In the UK, the Access to Health Records Act 1990 touches on one aspect of this. Although mostly repealed by the 1998 Act, it survives in limited form to allow, under s.3(1)(f), the representatives of a deceased patient rights of access to that patient's records.

1.3.3 Controllers

1.3.3.1 Most of the burden of complying with data protection legislation falls on the controller. This is the:

> "*natural or legal person, public authority, agency or other body which, alone or jointly with others, determines the purposes and means of the processing of personal data*" (art.4(7)).

Any type of organisation can be a controller—public or private sector, or an individual – so long as that person determines purposes and means of processing. Government departments are often legally treated as being one legal entity (on the principle that they are all part of the Crown, which is one entity for legal purposes). However, for data protection purposes, s.209(2) of the DPA 2018 provides that each government department is to be treated as a separate person – so each government department is a separate controller.

1.3.3.2 Every organisation is likely to process personal data relating, at the very least, to its staff, its customers and business contacts. It will determine the reasons why it processes such personal data and the way in which such personal data is processed (for example, who, within the organisation is allowed to access the information and how the information should be obtained, processed, stored and eventually destroyed). The Article 29 Working Party adopted *Opinion 1/2010 on the concepts of 'controller' and 'processor'* (WP 169) and this Opinion (p.12) describes these kinds of cases as examples of "*control stemming from implicit competence*", noting that:

> "*existing traditional roles that normally imply a certain responsibility will help identifying the controller: for example, the employer in relation to data on his employees, the publisher in relation to data on subscribers, the association in relation to data on its members or contributors.*
> *In all these cases, the capacity to determine processing activities can be considered as naturally attached to the functional role of a (private) organisation, ultimately entailing responsibilities also from a data protection point of view*".

1.3.3.3 The GDPR and the DPA 2018 note that, in some cases, a specific law will set out which person is to be the controller. Section 6(2) of the DPA 2018 provides that:

> "*. . . where personal data is processed only–*
> *a) for purposes for which it is required by an enactment to be processed, and*
> *b) by means by which it is required by an enactment to be processed,*
> *the person on whom the obligation to process data is imposed by the enactment . . . is the controller*".

It will be relatively rare that a private organisation will process personal data *only* for purposes which are specified by an enactment – and even rarer that that enactment will also specify the means of processing. However, this could cover situations where organisations are required to provide personal data to government bodies in a prescribed format or using prescribed databases or portals.

1.3.3.4 The Information Commissioner has published detailed guidance on controllers and processors (*https://ico.org.uk/for-organisations/guide-to-data-protection/guide-to-the-general-data-protection-regulation-gdpr/controllers-and-processors* [Accessed 14 May 2019]). This comments on s.6(2) as follows:

> "*Some controllers may be under a statutory obligation to process personal data. Section 6(2) of the Data Protection Act 2018 says that anyone who is under such an obligation and only processes data to comply with it will be a controller*".

The commentary does *not* address the requirement in s.6(2) of the DPA 2018 that the enactment must also specify "means" of processing. The 1998 Act contained a similar provision at s.1(4), addressing occasions where "*personal data are processed only for purposes for which they are required by or under any enact-*

ment to be processed". However, the DPA 2018 is in different terms—and has to be, as it is in line with the definition of "controller" in the GDPR, which also refers to laws determining "*purposes and means*" of processing. It seems that the Information Commissioner's guidance on this point is not correct and still reflects the position under the 1998 Act.

1.3.3.5 The UK courts have considered whether the liquidator of an insolvent company would be a controller—***Re Southern Pacific Personal Loans Ltd, Oakley Smith v Information Commissioner*** [2013] EWHC 2485 (Ch). In this case, the joint liquidators of the insolvent company continued to receive subject access requests, which were costly to process to such an extent that processing the requests would prejudice the distribution of available funds to creditors. The liquidators applied to court for guidance as to whether they would be considered as data controllers, separately from the company, and whether they could dispose of personal data in their control in this capacity. The court concluded that the joint liquidators were acting as agents of the company, rather than as separate controllers, so that they were not personally responsible for compliance. The court also allowed the liquidators to dispose of personal data which was not required either for litigation or to deal with access requests made before the date of disposal of the data.

1.3.4 Joint controllers

1.3.4.1 Organisations can also be controllers "jointly with others" if they act together to determine purposes and means of processing. The Information Commissioner's detailed guidance also notes that organisations "*are not joint controllers if they are processing the same data for different purposes*". Two CJEU cases have considered joint control.

1.3.4.2 In the ***Facebook Ireland*** case (***ULD v Wirtschaftsakademie Schleswig-Holstein GmbH; interveners Facebook Ireland Ltd, Vertreter des Bundesinteresses beim Bundesverwaltungsgericht*** (C-210/16) 5 June 2018), a private company in Schleswig-Holstein, which provided education-related services, was ordered by the ULD (the data protection authority for Schleswig-Holstein) to deactivate its Facebook fan page. The ULD considered that the fan-page did not comply with data protection law, because no information was given to visitors to the fan-page about the processing of personal data or the use of cookies. The ULD claimed that this was the responsibility (either wholly or partly) of the local company [16]. One of the questions referred to the CJEU was whether the administrator of a fan-page would be a controller.

1.3.4.3 The CJEU noted that Facebook collected and processed data from the fan-pages by means of cookies. Some of the data was used by Facebook to improve its advertising. In addition, Facebook provided anonymous statistics to the administrator of the fan-page – for example about the types of visitors to the page [33]–[37]. The administrator never had access to the data processed by Facebook. However, the administrator was able to define the criteria in relation to which Facebook would compile statistics—for example, requesting statistics about age, sex, occupation, lifestyle and purchasing habits and geographical information. The CJEU concluded that this meant that the administrator must be categorised as a joint controller with Facebook Ireland [44]. The fact that the administrator did not have access to the actual personal data, and that it was using a platform provided by Facebook, did not exempt it from being responsible for compliance. The CJEU specifically emphasised that fan-pages could be visited by people who are not Facebook users (so do not have Facebook accounts and would not have seen Facebook's terms or privacy policy): this meant that there was a particular responsibility on the administrator in regard to these people [41]. The CJEU did, however, note that [43]:

> "*joint responsibility does not necessarily imply equal responsibility of the various operators involved in the processing of personal data. On the contrary, those operators may be involved at different stages . . . and to different degrees, so that the level of responsibility of each of them must be assessed with regard to all the relevant circumstances of the particular case*".

1.3.4.4 The second recent case to consider this is the ***Jehovah's Witnesses*** case (***Tietosuojavaltuutettu intervening parties Jehovan todistajat – uskonnollinen ydhyskunta*** (C-25/17) EU:C:2018:551). This case has already been discussed under **1.2.5.4** in respect of the definition of a filing system. It will be recalled that members of the Jehovah's Witnesses Community make notes about persons they visit. These notes include name and address, information about religious belief and family circumstances, as well as details of requests not to visit a household. They can be used by other members of the Community when visiting the same person. No information was given to those visited about this practice and no consent was obtained. The details of what data is collected and how is it used would be a matter for the particular member of the Community. However, the Community knows that such data is collected and encourages members to do so. The Community also co-ordinates and organises the activities of the Community members, who then make use of the notes. Given this background, the CJEU confirmed that the religious Community is a controller, jointly with its members. Again, the fact that the Community itself had no access to the actual data did not stop the Community being a controller, nor did the fact that it had not given written guidelines or instructions to its members.

1.3.4.5 The Article 29 Working Party (see below at **1.4.1.3**), in its Opinion, WP 169 (p.21), notes that the fact that one controller shares personal data with another does not make them joint controllers:

> "*. . . the mere fact that different subjects cooperate in processing personal data, for example, in a chain, does not entail that they are joint controllers in all cases, since an exchange of data between two parties without sharing purposes or means in a common set of operations should be considered only as a transfer of data between separate controllers*".

WP 169 gives the example of a travel agent sharing personal data with airlines and a chain of hotels—all of whom would be separate controllers. By contrast,

WP 169 suggests that if these same controllers set up a common platform to share information and improve co-operation and agree on important matters such as which data will be stored, the means to be used and who will have access to the information, then they will become joint controllers. WP 169 emphasises (p.22) that it is important not to look just at a micro-level (where different processing operations in a chain can seem disconnected and with a different purpose), but also to consider whether "*at macro-level these processing operations should not be considered as a 'set of operations' pursuing a joint purpose or using jointly defined means*".

1.3.4.6 Of course, in each of the ***Facebook Ireland*** case and the ***Jehovah's Witnesses*** matters, the case was initiated because the overall processing activities did not meet data protection requirements. The most important lesson to be drawn from the cases, therefore, is that when controllers collaborate with other organisations they should consider if—overall—the processing meets data protection requirements. The GDPR now formalises this requirement, with art.26 requiring joint controllers to determine their respective compliance obligations in a transparent manner and to make essential elements of this available to data subjects (**13.7.4**). Controllers should, therefore, be alert to occasions where they may be considered to be "jointly" determining purposes or means of processing with others, so as to ensure that this is done. One common example of joint controllers may be that of group companies, where members of the group jointly take decisions about elements of processing.

Implications of being a controller (joint or otherwise)

1.3.4.7 Controllers must comply with:

- the data protection principles set out in art.5 of the GDPR (relating to fair, transparent and lawful processing; purpose limitation; data minimisation and accuracy; storage limitation; security and accountability) (**Ch.5**);
- obligations to have a lawful basis for all processing (**Ch.4**);
- individuals' rights (**Ch.6**);
- more detailed security, accountability and privacy by design obligations (**Chs 8, 13 and 14**); and
- restrictions on transfers of data outside the European Economic Area (**Ch.9**).

1.3.4.8 Data protection legislation does not apply equally to all controllers. There are exemptions from certain parts of the legislation for certain types of data processing. For example, the broadest exemption applies where personal data is processed only for personal or household affairs and is considered at **10.5.8.** Here, to all intents and purposes, the legislation ceases to apply. In addition to this broad exemption, data protection legislation contains more limited exemptions to certain aspects of the GDPR and the DPA 2018, such as the data subject's right of access to the data, and these are set out in detail in **Ch.10**.

1.3.5 Processors

1.3.5.1 Data protection legislation distinguishes between controllers and processors. Under the 1998 Act, almost all obligations only applied to controllers. The GDPR alters this, placing independent obligations on processors in relation to:

- security and personal data breaches (**Ch.8**);
- implementing contracts with controllers and assisting controllers in dealing with individuals rights, security, appointment of data protection officers and data protection impact assessments and data breaches (**Ch.13**);
- maintaining records of processing (**Ch.13**); and
- data transfers (**Ch.9**).

Data processors can also be fined by data protection authorities and sued by individuals (**Ch.3**).

1.3.5.2 Despite this increase in liability, however, processors still have fewer compliance obligations than controllers. A processor should not process personal data except on instructions of the controller (art.29). It is, therefore, important for organisations to know if they act as a controller or a processor—and to know whether those they appoint are controllers or processors. As the Information Commissioner's detailed guidance notes, as a controller you are "*accountable for your own compliance and the compliance of your processors*". It is, therefore, important for controllers to be clear when they are appointing a processor and to check that the processor is suitable. This is also required by art.28 of the GDPR (**13.7.3**).

1.3.5.3 A processor means:

> "*a natural or legal person, public authority, agency or other body which processes personal data on behalf of the controller*" (art.4(8)).

The processor, therefore, processes personal data on behalf of the controller, rather than on its own behalf. The processor is usually a contractor.

1.3.5.4 If a processor in fact determines the "*purposes and means of processing*" then it becomes a controller (art.28(10)). A processor, in other words, may carry out the physical processing of personal data but is not responsible for determining purposes and manner of processing. A good example of a processor would be a company that carries out payroll processing for other companies. A payroll processor handles personal data. However, the payroll processor is not free to use the payroll data for other purposes without its client's approval. Furthermore, the client will specify the manner in which the payroll processor uses the personal data (i.e. to make certain payments on certain dates, to update the data in accordance with agreed procedures and so forth).

1.3.5.5 It can sometimes be difficult to determine whether an organisation is a data controller or a data processor. This is a particular difficulty where a service provider is given a substantial degree of discretion as to how it processes personal data. For example, in many cases where an organisation outsources the processing of personal data, it may give the service provider substantial discretion as to the detailed manner in which the service provider actually processes the personal data. Thus, the service provider may be given complete discretion as to the software applications that it uses to process the data. The Information Commissioner's detailed guidance confirms that:

> "*. . . where allowed for in the contract, a processor may have the freedom to use its technical knowledge to decide how to carry out certain activities on the controller's behalf. However, it cannot take any of the overarching decisions, such as what types of personal data to collect or what the personal data will be used for*".

1.3.5.6 The detailed guidance also notes that it is "*common* [for a controller] *to allow its processor discretion over how the processing takes place using its own expertise*". This means that the fact that an organisation is providing a service to someone else does not necessarily automatically mean it will be a processor: the degree of discretion afforded to the service provider is key. Specialist providers, who have independent professional obligations, are more likely to be controllers. According to the Information Commissioner's detailed guidance:

> "*If specialist service providers are processing data in line with their own professional obligations, they will always be acting as the controller. In this context, they cannot agree to hand over or share controller obligations with the client*".

1.3.5.7 The Information Commissioner suggests that you will be a controller if you decide:

- to collect the personal data in the first place and assess the legal basis for doing this;
- which personal data to collect;
- the purpose(s) for which it can be used;
- which individuals to collect data about;
- whether to disclose the data and to whom;
- what to tell individuals about the processing;
- whether subject access and other rights apply and how exemptions should be handled;

- how long to retain the data and whether to make non-routine changes to the data.

By contrast, a processor could still have authority to take the following decisions:

- what IT systems or other methods to use;
- how to store the data;
- the detail of the security;
- how to transfer data to another organisation;
- how to retrieve data about someone;
- the method for ensuring a retention schedule is followed;
- the means used to delete or dispose of personal data.

1.3.5.8 The Information Commissioner's detailed guidance also contains worked examples looking at a number of commonly recurring scenarios. We have singled out two of these below, but others may also be helpful:

- market research companies will be (joint) controllers if the company appointing them gives the market research company discretion as to how to sample interview methods and presentation of results. A bank will be a joint controller when it commissions the research and determines the purpose for which the data will be used;
- mail delivery services will usually be controllers when they process addressing information to send correspondence; but will not be controllers or processors in relation to the content of the correspondence, to which they have no access.

1.3.5.9 If this analysis sounds confusing then, as a further aid to distinguishing between controller and processor, we suggest applying the following tests. These tests have no statutory or other authority, but we have found them useful in a number of cases.

Does Organisation A have a relationship with the data subject independent of that of Organisation B? This could be prior to the transaction that triggers the question to be considered, or subsequent to it, or both.

Does Organisation A do anything with the data other than in furtherance of the interests of Organisation B?

Does Organisation A get anything out of working with Organisation B other than payment by B?

Organisation B is definitely a controller. Organisation A is an organisation which may be a controller, or a processor on B's behalf. Where the answer to these questions is "no", the relationship is likely to be that of processor and controller. Where it is "yes", it is likely to be that of two controllers or joint controllers.

1.3.6 Recipients

1.3.6.1 As well as "controllers" and "processors" data protection legislation also refers to "recipients". A recipient is defined at art.4(9) as:

> "*a natural or legal person, public authority, agency or another body, to which the personal data are disclosed, whether a third party or not*".

The phrase "*whether a third party or not*" means that a recipient could be another legal person to whom personal data is disclosed (a processor, or another controller) —or it could be another department or team within the same organisation. To give an example, the HR department may disclose information about an employee to the legal department if they need to seek advice on a potential claim by the employee: the legal department would then be a recipient of the data.

1.3.6.2 Controllers must be alert to the "recipients" of personal data, because information on recipients, or categories of recipients, must be:

- included in privacy notices (art.13(1)(6) and art.14(1)(e) and **6.4**);
- included in the information provided in response to a subject access request (art.15(1)(c) (**6.5**)); and
- included in records of processing activity maintained by the controller (art.30) (**13.5**).

In addition, if a controller receives a request to correct personal data, or to erase it, or restrict the processing of personal data, then, under art.19, the controller must notify all recipients of the personal data in its incorrect, un-erased or unrestricted form (**6.9**, **6.10**). This can only be done, if the controller keeps a list of all recipients of each category (or in some cases each item) of personal data.

1.3.6.3 Article 4(9) goes on to provide that:

> "*... public authorities which may receive personal data in the framework of a particular inquiry in accordance with Union or Member State law shall not be regarded as recipients; the processing of those data by those public authorities shall be in compliance with applicable data protection rules according to the purposes of the processing*".

Recital 31 gives the example of tax and customs authorities here. The effect of art.4(9) is that a controller will not be in breach of its obligations of transparency, or record keeping, if it has not anticipated, and included details of, this type of request from an authority.

1.3.7 The data protection officer

1.3.7.1 Controllers and processors have often appointed someone to take responsibility for data protection within the organisation. Sometimes this person has been called the data protection officer, or chief privacy officer. The GDPR, at arts 37–39, creates a specific, formal, role of "data protection officer", often abbreviated to "DPO". The obligation to appoint a DPO and the position and tasks for a DPO are considered more thoroughly at **13.2**. For now, the key points to note are that only certain organisations have to appoint a DPO (public authorities; those whose core activities involve certain higher risk processing):

- the DPO has to have expert knowledge and appropriate support from the organisation appointing him or her—this includes a right to report directly to the highest management;
- the DPO must be free from any conflict of interests; cannot be told how to do his her or her role; and cannot be dismissed or penalised for performing his or her tasks;
- the DPO is to be a point of contact for individuals and the supervisory authority; has an obligation to co-operate with the supervisory authority; has to inform and advise on compliance; to monitor compliance and provide advice—in particular on data protection impact assessments (**13.2**).

Where we refer to the data protection officer, or DPO, in this book, we mean a person appointed in line with the above requirements. Organisations could have other personnel who have responsibility for data protection and, in order to avoid confusion, we have referred to such personnel as "data protection professionals".

1.3.8 The Information Commissioner

1.3.8.1 The Data Protection Act 1984 originally created the office of the Data Protection Registrar. This was continued by the 1998 Act and, now, by the DPA 2018, albeit that the Registrar is now the Information Commissioner. This reflects the shift away from the Registrar's original focus on maintaining a register of data controllers and recognises the Commissioner's additional responsibilities for other information law matters, particularly under the e-Privacy Regulations (**7.4**), FOIA and for environmental information. In addition to these responsibilities, the Information Commissioner also has responsibilities:

- as the supervisory body for the eIDAS Regulations 2016, which set out rules for electronic identification and trust services (including rules for electronic signatures);
- under the INSPIRE Regulations 2009 relating to mapping data produced by public authorities and bodies covered by Environmental Information Regulations 2004;

- for handling complaints under the Re-use of Public Sector Information Regulations 2015; and
- to regulate relevant digital service providers under the Network and Information Systems Regulations 2018.

1.3.8.2 The GDPR refers to the UK Information Commissioner and her opposite numbers in other Member States as a "supervisory authority" (arts 4(21)–(22) and 51 and following). The current Information Commissioner is Ms Elizabeth Denham. DPA 2018 Sch.12 para.2(3) provides that appointment is for a maximum of seven years; an Information Commissioner cannot be re-appointed. Although formal powers and responsibilities are placed on the Commissioner personally as a "corporation sole", the Information Commissioner also has a large staff, referred to as the Information Commissioner's Office, or "ICO".

Tasks and powers

1.3.8.3 The Information Commissioner's tasks are set out at art.57 of the GDPR, where she is mandated to fulfil any tasks related to the protection of personal data. These include:

- monitoring and enforcing the application of the Regulation, including by conducting investigations, handling complaints, keeping records of infringements and monitoring relevant developments (including in technology and commerce);
- raising awareness—amongst the public, controllers and processors;
- giving advice to Parliament, the government and other institutions on data protection;
- fulfilling specific tasks foreseen by the GDPR in relation to certification, codes of conduct and data protection seals and marks (**13.1**);
- issuing lists of activities where data protection impact assessments ("DPIA") should be carried out and advising controllers if a DPIA shows there is an unmitigated high risk (**13.6**);
- adopting standard contract clauses for appointing data processors (**13.7**);
- authorising standard contract clauses for data transfer purposes and approving binding corporate rules (**9.5**); and
- participating in the European Data Protection Board and co-operating with supervisory authorities for data protection in other Member States (see also **1.4.2**).

1.3.8.4 Article 57(3) provides that supervisory authorities cannot charge data subjects or data protection officers ("DPO") for the performance of their tasks.

There is, however, an exception to this at art.57(4) where the requests of a data subject or DPO are manifestly unfounded or excessive, in particular because they are repetitive. Here the Information Commissioner has discretion whether to decline the request or to charge a reasonable fee, based on administrative costs. These provisions are reflected at ss.134–135 of the DPA 2018, which – perhaps with an eye to future funding of the ICO—also provides that the Commissioner may require that people other than data subjects and data protection officers pay a reasonable fee for services provided.

1.3.8.5 The Information Commissioner's powers are set out at art.58. These consist of:

- authorisation and advisory powers, corresponding to the tasks listed at **1.3.8.3** above;
- investigatory powers: to order information to be produced; to audit; to notify organisations of alleged infringements; to obtain access to personal data and other necessary information and to obtain access to premises and data processing equipment (all set out in more detail in Pt 6 of the DPA 2018 (s.131 of which provides that, aside from certain provisions under the Regulation of Investigatory Powers Act and the Investigatory Powers Act, no enactment or rule of law which prohibits or restricts disclosure of information is to preclude a person from providing information to the Commissioner which is necessary for the discharge of her functions) and Sch.15 of the DPA 2018) (these are explored in much greater detail in **3.4.2**); and
- corrective powers: to issue warnings and reprimands; to order compliance, or to prohibit processing including suspending trans-border data flows; to withdraw certification and to impose administrative fines (referred to as penalties in the DPA 2018) (Pt 6 and Sch.16 of the DPA 2018) (these are explored in much greater detail in **3.4.3**).

1.3.8.6 In addition to these specific powers, GDPR rec.120 notes that supervisory authorities should be provided with "*the financial and human resources, premises and infrastructure necessary for the effective performance of their tasks*". This is to include a separate, public, annual budget. As at the date of writing, the Commissioner's budget was £24 million (speech given by Elizabeth Denham to the Centre for Research into Information Surveillance and Privacy, delivered on 14 March and reproduced at *https:// www.ico.org.uk>2018/03>money-law-courage*).

Safeguards

1.3.8.7 The Commissioner must comply with the procedural requirements of the DPA 2018 when exercising her powers of enforcement, and these provide safeguards on the exercise of her powers. In addition, the Commissioner and her staff are subject to a statutory duty of confidentiality, at s.132, in relation to information which is obtained or provided to them in the course of discharging the Commissioner's functions. Breach of this provision is an offence – although the offence is not made out if there is lawful authority for the disclosure—for example, if the disclosure was in the public interest (e.g. **3.4.3.5**).

1.3.8.8 A further safeguard is set out at s.133. This requires the Information Commissioner to draw up and publish guidance as to how she will deal with privileged communications (i.e. material subject to legal professional privilege (as to which see **6.5.3.36**)). As para.335 of the Explanatory Notes explains, the Commissioner must address:

> "*. . . how she will a) limit the use and disclosure of privileged communications she obtains or has access to during the course of carrying out her functions to ensure this goes no further than is necessary; and b) ensure that she does not have access to privileged communications which she is expressly prohibited from accessing under section 143 (restrictions on information notices), section 147 (restrictions on assessment notices), paragraph 11 of Schedule 15 (powers of entry and inspection) or under equivalent provisions in other enactments . . .*"

Codes of practice and guidance

1.3.8.9 The Commissioner produced a number of codes of practice under the 1998 Act. Some of these old codes are still available on the ICO website (*https://www.ico.org.uk*) and are in many cases of value, and we shall refer to some of them from time to time.

1.3.8.10 The DPA 2018 requires the Information Commissioner to produce specific codes of practice, which must take account of the interests of data subjects and others. Codes of practice must be produced in relation to:

- data sharing (s.121);
- direct marketing (s.122 and **Ch.7**);
- age appropriate design for information society services likely to be used by children (s.123 and **14.1.3**); and
- journalism (s.124), where the Commissioner also has to prepare a report as to how the processing of personal data undertaken for journalism complies with good practice and legislation (s.178) (**10.5.6**).

Under s.128, secondary legislation can be promulgated requiring the Commissioner to produce other codes of practice. Codes of practice are to be laid before, and approved by, parliament (s.125). Codes of practice are admissible in legal proceedings, and courts and tribunals, and the Information Commissioner herself must have regard to codes which have been approved by parliament (ss.127(3) and (4)). However, failure to follow a code does not, of itself, make someone liable to proceedings (s.127(1)).

1.3.8.11 In addition to these formal codes of practice, the Information Commissioner has issued a large number of additional guidance papers, both on particular legal topics and for specific industry sectors. These are all available from the Commissioner's website *http://www.ico.gov.uk*. The website is very helpful and anyone with responsibility for data protection should make use of the resources available there. The Table of Commissioner's Guidance on **p.liii** shows how heavily we have drawn on this useful source of information.

1.3.8.12 The Information Commissioner reports directly to the UK Parliament and produces an annual report. This too is a useful source of information on the Commissioner's policies and enforcement activities.

International roles

1.3.8.13 The Information Commissioner has certain international roles—in particular, the Information Commissioner participates in the EDPB and is required by arts 60–62 to participate in the co-operation and consistency mechanisms which aim to ensure consistent application of the GDPR across the EU. The EDPB and these mechanisms are discussed further at **1.4.2**.

1.3.8.14 The Information Commissioner also has an international role in relation to the Law Enforcement Directive and Convention 108, set out at Sch.13 to the DPA 2018. She is also tasked with a wider international role by s.120 (reflecting rec. 116 of the GDPR), which requires her to liaise with third countries and international organisations with a view to facilitating effective enforcement of data protection on an international basis and to exchange information on legislation and practice relating to jurisdictional conflicts with third countries.

Impact of the one-stop shop

1.3.8.15 The "one-stop shop" is the term often used to describe the mechanism, set out at arts 60–62 of the GDPR, which allows one supervisory authority to act as sole lead authority on an investigation or enforcement activity, but consulting and engaging in joint operations with other concerned authorities. The one stop-shop is described in more detail at **1.4.3** below. The one stop-shop is described in more detail at **1.4.3** below. Organisations which have more than one establishment in the EU may therefore find that the supervisory authority of a different EU Member State handles a complaint, investigation or enforcement activity which affects them.

Appeals from the Commissioner's rulings

1.3.8.16 There are rights of appeal from any investigatory or enforcement notices served by the Information Commissioner, including penalty notices (ss.162–164), to a tribunal within the General Regulatory Chamber. There are also rights for individuals to apply to the tribunal:

- if they consider that the Information Commissioner has not taken appropriate steps in response to a complaint made by the individual to the Information Commissioner (s.166); and

- in relation to the exemptions which apply once a national security certificate is issued (ss. 27, 79 and 111).

These appeals are ordinarily handled by the First-tier Tribunal—unless Tribunal Procedure Rules determine that the matter should be heard by the Upper Tribunal (as is the case, for example, for national security matters). Section 203 of the DPA 2018 allows Tribunal Procedure Rules to be promulgated and the Explanatory Notes to the DPA 2018 (para.586) explain that these rules will be made in accordance with the Tribunals Courts and Enforcement Act 2007. The Tribunal can cancel, vary or uphold notices issued by the Information Commissioner. There is a right of appeal from First-tier Tribunal decisions, on points of law, to the Upper Tribunal. Decisions of the Upper Tribunal may also be challenged, on points of law, and appeals are usually heard by the Court of Appeal. The Upper Tribunal may refer questions of interpretation of the GDPR to the CJEU.

1.4 THE EUROPEAN UNION, THE EUROPEAN DATA PROTECTION BOARD AND THE ONE-STOP SHOP

1.4.1 Introduction

1.4.1.1 In **Ch.2** and in **Appendix A1** we explain the links between UK data protection legislation and European conventions and laws, both via the Council of Europe and the EU. UK data protection legislation is not a stand-alone matter.

1.4.1.2 The main impetus behind Directive 95/46 and its successor, the GDPR was a desire to harmonise the laws relating to personal data protection within the EU. Directive 95/46 established a working party, consisting of a representative of the supervisory authority from each Member State, the European Data Protection Supervisor (EDPS) (the individual responsible for supervising data protection compliance by EU institutions and bodies, currently Mr. Giovanni Buttarelli) and from the Commission. As the working party was established by Article 29 of the Directive, it was known as the: Article 29 Working Party (WP 29). One of the objectives in setting up WP 29 was for it to "*contribute to the uniform application*" of data protection measures in each Member State (Directive 95/46 art.30(1)(a)) and it did this by adopting Opinions on a wide-range of topics. Although these Opinions are on Directive 95/46, as the GDPR is based on and extends that Directive, they remain largely relevant and we refer to them throughout this book. The Opinions are available at *https://ec.europa.eu/justice/article-29/documentation/Index_en.htm* [Accessed 14 May 2019].

1.4.1.3 There is a difference between the EU and the European Economic Area (EEA) (the latter comprising the Member States of the EU plus the European Free Trade Agreement states of Norway, Iceland and Liechtenstein). EU data protection rules are also relevant to the EEA and the GDPR has been incorporated into the EEA Agreement (the agreement which governs relations between the EFTA States and the EU), albeit with some amendments (for example, relating to the ways in which supervisory authorities of EFTA States participate in the European Data Protection Board) (see *http://www.efta.int/EEA/news/Incorporation-GDPR-EEA-Agreement-508041* [Accessed 14 May 2019]. When we refer to the EU, or EU Member States, therefore, readers should note that the comment could also apply to Norway, Iceland and Liechtenstein.

1.4.2 The European Data Protection Board

1.4.2.1 WP 29 is replaced by a new EDPB, whose primary task is to "*ensure consistent application*" of the GDPR (art.70(1)). The EDPB's role is strengthened by comparison to that of WP 29. In particular, it is empowered to issue binding decisions in certain situations (**1.4.3.1**) and it is now established as an EU body with its own legal personality (art.68(1)). The composition of the EDPB is the same as that of WP 29. It has a chair (currently Ms. Andrea Jelineck, the head of the Austrian data protection authority) and two vice-chairs. The EDPS provides the secretariat for the EDPB. Decisions of the EDPB are, usually, taken on a simple majority basis (art.72(1)). The Commission does not vote (art.68(5)) and the EDPS's voting rights are restricted when the EDPB takes decisions which will have binding effect. Here, the EDPS only has voting rights on decisions applicable to the EU institutions which the EDPS supervises and where those institutions are subject to rules which correspond in substance to those set out in the GDPR (art.68(6)). Like the WP 29, the EDPB is to act independently when performing its tasks or exercising its powers (art.69).

1.4.2.2 The EDPB must publish its opinions etc. and must, where appropriate, also consult interested parties and give them an opportunity to comment on its decisions (art.70(3) and (4)); it must also publish an annual report (art.71). These are all available at *https://EDPB.europa.eu [Accessed 14 May 2019]).* As the EDPB is able to issue binding decisions, there must be a right for those affected to challenge these decisions. This can be done pursuant to art.263 of the Treaty on the Functioning of the European Union (TFEU). As rec.143 explains, this provides a right for controllers, processors or complainants to challenge decisions where they are of direct and individual concern to them. Supervisory authorities to whom decisions of the EDPB are addressed can also challenge decisions. In each case, there is a two-month time limit to bring a challenge. This runs from the date a decision is notified to a supervisory authority or, for others, is published on the EDPB's website. There were no similar mechanisms for consultation or appeal in relation to the WP 29 and it will be interesting to see how the EDPB adapts to its new status and obligations.

1.4.2.3 The tasks of the EDPB are set out art.70, with, as mentioned above, its primary task being to ensure consistent application of the GDPR. Its tasks are:

- to adjudicate on the actions of supervisory authorities, by issuing opinions (art.64) and by adopting binding decisions in the event of disputes between supervisory authorities (art.65) (arts 70(1)(a) and 70(1)(t)) (**1.4.3.8** below);

- to issue guidelines, recommendations and best practices to encourage consistent application of the GDPR and to review how these are applied. There is both a general task to this effect (art.70(1)(e) and (l)) and a requirement to issue these in relation to certain specific topics, being:
  - automated individual decision-making involving profiling (art.70(1)(f)) (**6.11**);
  - personal data breach (art.70(1)(g)–(h)) (**8.4**);
  - binding corporate rules (art.70(1)(i) (**9.5.5**);
  - derogations allowing transfers of personal data to third countries (art.70(1)(j) (**9.6**);
  - the powers of supervisory authorities and the setting of administrative fines (art.70(1)(k)) (**3.4**).

The WP 29 issued Opinions on all of these topics and the EDPB approved these during its first meeting on 25 May 2018. Recital 124 also notes that the EDPB is able to issue guidelines on certain matters relating to the one-stop shop procedure. The WP 29 has also issued an Opinion on this:

  - erasing personal data once it has been made public by a controller (art.70(1)(d) (**6.9.5**);
  - procedures for natural persons to report to supervisory authorities and arrangements to ensure that confidentiality for such reports (art.70(1)(m);

- to undertake roles in relation to codes of conduct and certification (art.70(1)(n), (p), (x) (**13.1**);
- to issue opinions to the Commissioner—both in general, and specifically in relation to binding corporate rules, certification, icons and whether third countries and international organisations offer adequate protection for personal data (art.70(1)(b), (c), (q), (r), (s)); and
- to exchange information and best practices both between EU supervisory authorities and worldwide and to promote common training programmes and personnel exchanges, again both on an EU and international basis (art.70(1)(u), (v), (w)).

1.4.3 The one-stop shop

1.4.3.1 As mentioned at **1.3.8.15** above, this is the mechanism which allows a supervisory authority in one EU Member State to be the lead authority on a matter which also involves other concerned supervisory authorities. We consider which authority will be the "lead" and which will be "concerned" at **1.4.3.9**. The aim of the one-stop shop is to produce a decision which will be accepted by, and binding on, all relevant supervisory authorities. The one-stop shop consists of:

- co-operation procedures, which aim to produce a one-stop shop by consensus (arts 60–62); and
- a consistency mechanism, which enforce consistency by means of a binding decision issued by the EDPB (arts 63–66).

1.4.3.2 These procedures were described as a one-stop shop when the Commission published its Proposal for a Regulation (*https://eur-lex.europa.eu/legal-content/EN/TXT/PDF/?uri=CELEX:52012PC0011&from=EN* [Accessed 14 May 2019], p.12). The term is commonly used to describe these arrangements, so we adopt it in our book. One-stop shop suggests convenience, simplicity and, indeed, that there will be one stop. Readers should note that the term is an example of Orwellian double-speak: the rules are complex and, for some organisations, there may be a row of check-outs, rather than one-stop, while others will not be allowed to enter the shop at all. The WP 29 revised and adopted guidelines for identifying a controller or processor's lead supervisory authority on 5 April 2017 (WP 244 rev.01).

Cross-border processing

1.4.3.3 The one-stop shop procedures apply where there is "*cross border processing*". This is defined at art.4(23) as meaning either:

> "*a) processing of personal data . . . in the context of the activities of establishments in more than one Member State of a controller or processor in the Union . . .; or*
>
> *b) processing of personal data which takes place in the context of the activities of a single establishment of a controller or processor in the Union but which substantially affects or is likely to substantially affect data subjects in more than one Member State*".

The test under limb a) is more lenient than under limb b). If an organisation has establishments in multiple Member States, and if the processing is in the context of their activities, then it will be cross-border processing, irrespective of the seriousness of the processing. By contrast, if only a single establishment is relevant, then the processing must actually have, or be likely to have, a substantial effect on data subjects in other Member States. As WP 244 notes (p.3):

> "*The intention of the wording was to ensure that not all processing activity, with any effect and that takes place within the context of a single establishment, falls within the definition of 'cross-border processing'*".

WP 244 notes that "*likely to*" means something more than a remote possibility; the effect must be more likely than not (p.3). WP 244 suggests criteria relevant to determine if there is a substantial effect (p.4). These are whether the processing causes, or is likely to cause:

- damage, loss or distress;
- loss of or limitations to rights or opportunity;
- an effect on health, well-being or peace of mind;
- an effect on financial or economic status or circumstances;
- discrimination or unfair treatment;
- individuals to change behaviour in a significant way;
- embarrassment or other negative outcomes, including reputational damage;

or:

- involves analysis of special categories of data, or otherwise intrusive data, or involves children's data; or
- involves processing of a wide range of data.

Procedures for co-operation and consistency

1.4.3.4 As mentioned at **1.4.3.1** above, the co-operation procedures rely on consensus, whereas the consistency mechanism is designed to force the point. There are references throughout all of the provisions to arrangements being agreed for electronic exchange of information between supervisory authorities and with the EDPB and there is also provision, at art.67, for the Commission to adopt implementing acts to specify these arrangements.

Co-operation

1.4.3.5 Article 60 imposes an obligation on the lead authority to co-operate with other concerned supervisory authorities so as to "*endeavour to reach consensus*". There are obligations for the lead authority to communicate and to submit draft decisions to the other authorities (art.60(3)); obligations for authorities to provide mutual assistance (art.61) and deadlines for responses to be provided. Article 60 also sets out rules as to who will communicate with the controller or processor (usually the lead authority) and who will communicate with a complainant (the supervisory authority which has received the complaint) (arts 60(7) – (9)). Any eventual consensus decision, or decisions, will be adopted by the lead supervisory authority.

Joint operations

1.4.3.6 Article 62 applies to joint investigations and enforcement measures involving cross-border processing. It establishes that concerned supervisory authorities have a right to be involved in such investigations and enforcement measures and that the lead authority must notify them of such measures. The article also contains provisions clarifying which Member State's law applies when staff of one authority take part in a joint operation run by another authority and setting out arrangements for liability and compensation in the event that one authority incurs liability as a result of damage caused by another authority's personnel.

Consistency

1.4.3.7 Article 64 provides for the EDPB to give Opinions:

- in specified situations, so as to avoid a proliferation of inconsistent national measures. These situations are when supervisory authorities publish: mandatory criteria for conducting data protection impact assessments DPIAs (art.64(1)(a) and discussed at **13.6**); matters relating to codes of conduct with impact on other Member States (art.64(1)(b)); criteria relating to accreditation of bodies who can monitor compliance with codes of conduct or for certification bodies (art.64(1)(c)); approved standard contract clauses to be used when appointing a data processor or when transferring personal data to a third country (art.64(1)(d) (**9.5.4**)); or when they authorise ad hoc data transfer clauses or authorise binding corporate rules (arts 64(1)(e) and (f) (**9.5.5**)); and
- when requested by any supervisory authority, the Chair or the EDPB or the Commission. These requests may, in particular, be made if a supervisory authority has failed to follow the rules for co-operation or joint operations.

Opinions of the EDPB are to be given within eight weeks, capable of extension by a further six weeks for complex matters and are to be adopted on a simple majority basis (art.64(3)).

Dispute resolution (binding decisions)

1.4.3.8 Article 65 requires the EDPB to adopt a binding decision, to resolve disputes, if:

- the co-operation procedure (i.e. the one-stop shop) has not produced a consensus decision (i.e. if a concerned authority raises a relevant and reasoned objection to a decision of the lead authority or if the lead authority rejects such an objection) (art.65(1)(a));
- there are conflicting views as to which supervisory authority should be the lead authority for the main establishment (art.65(1)(b)); or
- where a supervisory authority does not follow the procedures for EDPB Opinions at art.64.

Binding decisions of the EDPB must be adopted within one month of the referral to the EDPB, or within a maximum of two months for complex subject matters. As this is a binding decision, it has to be taken on a two-thirds majority basis. If the EDPB cannot reach a decision on this basis, then a decision will be taken, within a further two weeks, on a straight majority basis, with the Chair having the casting vote if there is a split decision (art.65(2) and (3)). There are urgency mechanisms at art.66 if a supervisory authority needs to take urgent action such that the mechanisms above cannot be followed.

Lead authority and concerned authorities

1.4.3.9 It will be apparent from the description of the co-operation procedure above that knowing which authority is the "lead authority" is key. As WP 244 notes, aside from enforcement or investigations, this is also important for controllers so that they know whom to consult if they need to consult a supervisory authority after conducting a DPIA (**13.6**), or to provide details of their data protection officer to a supervisory authority (**13.2**) (p.6).

1.4.3.10 Article 56 sets out the rules for this, providing that where there is a single establishment of the controller or processor, that the supervisory authority for that establishment will be the lead. Where there are multiple establishments, then one looks to see which establishment is the "*main establishment*" (see below); the authority competent for the main establishment is the lead.

1.4.3.11 There are two exceptions to this:

(1) in the case of public authorities, who process personal data because it is required by law, or because this is for a task in the public interest, then their national supervisory authority is always the competent authority (art.55(2)); and

(2) if the complaint or investigation relates solely to an establishment in a particular Member State or substantially affects data subjects in that Member State only, then the supervisory authority for the main establishment has to tell the other authority if it wishes to keep the case or not; if it does not, then the other, relevant, local authority handles the matter, using the mutual assistance and joint operations provisions at arts 61 and 62.

It is quite difficult to think of an occasion when the second occasion will apply—matters which only really involve one Member State are unlikely to be cross-border processing in the first place. However, WP 244 has a good example (pp.9–10):

> *"This might be the case where a marketing company with its main establishment in Paris launches a product that only affects data subjects residing in Portugal. In such a case the French and Portuguese supervisory authorities might agree that it is appropriate for the Portuguese supervisory authority to take the lead in dealing with the matter".*

1.4.3.12 If an authority is not the lead authority, it may be a "concerned" authority. Article 4(22) provides that:

> "'*supervisory authority concerned*' *means a supervisory authority which is concerned by the processing of personal data because:*
>
> *a)* *the controller or processor is established on the territory of the Member State of that supervisory authority;*
> *b)* *data subjects residing in the Member State of that supervisory authority are substantially affected or likely to be substantially affect by the processing; or*
> *c)* *a complaint has been lodged with that supervisory authority*".

Main establishment

1.4.3.13 The "main establishment" means (art.4(16)):

> "*a)* *as regards a controller with establishments in more than one Member State, the place of its central administration in the Union, unless the decisions on the purposes and the means of the processing of personal data are taken in another establishment of the controller in the Union and the latter establishment has the power to have such decisions implemented, in which case the establishment having taken such decisions is to be considered to be the main establishment;*
> *b)* *as regards a processor with establishments in more than one Member State, the place of its central administration in the Union, or, if the processor has no central administration in the Union, the establishment of the processor in the Union where the main processing activities . . . take place . . .*".

The definition applies different tests for controllers and processors. For controllers, the emphasis is on where decisions are taken. Recital 36 notes that this means "*the effective and real exercise of management activities determining the main decisions as to the purposes and means of processing through stable arrangements*". This is not the same as where the personal data is actually processed. As WP 244 notes (p.8) there is no scope for forum shopping; this is a question of fact and will not be determined solely based on statements made by the organisation. For processors, the main establishment will either be central administration, or the place where the main processing takes place.

1.4.3.14 As mentioned at **1.4.3.13** above, the main establishment concept is not simple and may not produce any, or any one, lead authority.

- Not all organisations will benefit from a lead authority:
  - The definition always requires an establishment in the EU and if there is no EU establishment there can be no lead authority (WP 244 p.10).

- For groups of undertakings, recs 36 and 37 provide that the undertaking which exerts a dominant influence over the others, whether by ownership, financial participation, governing rules or control specific to personal data processing, is to be regarded as the controlling undertaking and the main establishment of the group. If this decision-making entity is not in the EU, then the organisation will *only* benefit from a lead authority if an entity in the EU has the power to take and implement decisions about personal data processing (WP 244, p.8).

- Some organisations may have multiple lead authorities:
  - This is the case for controllers where different establishments are responsible for different areas of personal data processing (WP 244 (p.6) gives the example of a bank with its HQ in Frankfurt, which takes decisions on banking matters, but with an entity in Vienna which takes decisions on its insurance business and notes that it would have two separate lead authorities, one for personal data processed for banking purposes and one for insurance).
  - Where an investigation or complaint involves a processor and its controller clients, then rec. 36 provides that the supervisory authority (or authorities) competent for the controller clients will be the lead authority.

The GDPR does not set out how the concept will be relevant for joint controllers. Here, WP 244 concludes (pp.7–8) that if they wish to benefit from a lead authority that they should designate one establishment with the power to implement decisions about processing of personal data with respect to all joint controllers. This may be feasible where there are joint controllers within a group of companies (although here one would, in any event, presumably look to the controlling undertaking rule as set out at the first bullet to **1.4.3.14** above), but where arms-length organisations are joint controllers it is hard to see that they would be willing to agree that one of them would have power to implement decisions with respect to all of them.

1.5 BREXIT

1.5.1 The position on Brexit and the options available (insofar as they are known) were analysed at **0.15**. The main impact of Brexit on the matters described in this chapter affects the Commissioner's relationship with the EDPB (**1.4.2**) and the operation of the co-operation and consistency mechanism (**1.4.3**).

1.5.2 Impact of the Withdrawal Agreement

1.5.2.1 During the transitional period (**0.15.4**), the UK would continue to apply the GDPR, including the co-operation and consistency mechanism. However, in accordance with arts.7(1) and 128 of the Withdrawal Agreement, the UK would not participate in European Union institutions or bodies, which would include the EDPB. Article 128(5) of the Withdrawal Agreement provides that, exceptionally and upon invitation, the UK may be invited to take part in meetings if the discussion concerns persons in the UK, or if the presence of the UK is necessary and in the interest of the Union – in particular for the effective implementation of Union law during the transition period. UK participants at such meetings will not have voting rights. The Information Commissioner will, therefore, ordinarily cease to participate in the EDPB. She may be invited to participate, where this is appropriate—for example, if the EDPB is taking a decision affecting a UK controller or processor or individuals in the UK (**1.4.3.8**), but she will not be able to vote on that decision.

1.5.3 Impact of no-deal Brexit

1.5.3.1 In the event of a no-deal Brexit, the co-operation and consistency procedure will cease to apply to organisations in the UK. (Of course, if such organisations also have establishments in the EU, then it may apply to those establishments). The Information Commissioner will cease to participate in the EDPB in any capacity.

CHAPTER 2

Scope of the Legislation

2.1 INTRODUCTION

2.1.1 This chapter deals with two separate topics which need to be understood first if the reader is to progress in compliance with the legislation. In **2.2** we explain the territorial scope of the GDPR and the DPA 2018. This is relevant for those who, while established outside the EU, nevertheless need to be compliant with the legislation (e.g. if they sell goods or services to people in the EU). Yet other readers may have questions as to which parts of their business need to comply with data protection legislation – for example, if they work for an international business which also has operations outside the EU.

2.1.2 In **2.3** we focus on another aspect of the legislation. The DPA 2018 says at s.1(2) "*most processing of personal data is subject to the GDPR*". The implication is that *some* processing of personal data is not subject to the GDPR. There are a number of types of processing of personal data which lie outside the GDPR and so have their own processing regime, separate from the GDPR. Some readers may work for law enforcement authorities or the intelligence services—or they may work for organisations who provide services to them. The GDPR does not apply here—but different parts of the DPA 2018 do apply and this section also explains this aspect of scope of the DPA 2018. **Chapter 15** is for readers who need to know about law enforcement processing or processing by the intelligence services in more detail. **Appendix A2** also contains a table showing when the various Parts and Schedules of the DPA 2018 apply to processing outside the scope of the GDPR.

2.2 TERRITORIAL SCOPE OF THE GDPR

2.2.1 Territorial scope

2.2.1.1 This is set out in art.3, which has three limbs:

(1) dealing with controllers and processors established in the EU, as applicable;

(2) dealing with extra-territorial scope where controllers or processors which are not established in the EU process personal data in connection with the offer of goods or services to EU customers, or with monitoring individuals in the EU; and

(3) dealing with situations where Member State law applies as a matter of public international law.

2.2.1.2 The first and second limbs are usually those of most relevance. The principle is that organisations should comply with data protection legislation if they are based here or if they intend to sell to, or if they monitor, individuals here. The EDPB (**1.4.2**) has issued detailed guidance on the provisions on territorial scope, in its Guideline 3/2018, adopted on 16 November 2018 and issued for public consultation.

Controllers and processors established in the EU

2.2.1.3 Article 3(1) provides that:

"*This Regulation applies to the processing of personal data in the context of the activities of an establishment of a controller or processor in the Union, regardless of whether the processing takes place in the Union or not*".

Establishment

2.2.1.4 The reader must first identify who the controller, or processor, is for the relevant processing (**2.2.1.1**), before then considering if that controller or processor has an establishment in the EU. Recital 22 makes clear that "*establishment*" is given a wide interpretation, implying:

"the effective and real exercise of activity through stable arrangements. The legal form of such arrangements, whether through a branch or a subsidiary with a legal personality, is not the determining factor in that respect".

2.2.1.5 The wide concept of "establishment" is made clear in the ***Weltimmo*** case (***Weltimmo sro v Nemzeti Adatvédelmi és Információszabadság Hatóság***, CJEU, C-230/14). Weltimmo was a Slovakian company, which ran a property website, in Hungarian, listing Hungarian properties. Weltimmo employed an individual in Hungary as a representative, and had a Hungarian bank account and letter box. The CJEU concluded that this could be enough to amount to an establishment in Hungary, such that the Hungarian Commissioner could have authority.

Context of activities

2.2.1.6 As the EDPB notes in Guideline 3/2018 (p.6):

"*. . . it is not necessary that the processing in question is carried out 'by' the relevant EU establishment itself.*"

2.2.1.7 The GDPR will apply to any processing which is carried out "*in the context of the activities of*" that establishment, whether or not the processing takes place in the EU. However this concept:

"*should not be interpreted too broadly to conclude that the existence of any presence of in the EU with even the remotest links to the data processing activities of a non-EU entity will be sufficient to bring this processing within the scope of EU data protection law*".

2.2.1.8 The case which established the so-called "right to be forgotten", the ***Google Spain*** case (***Google Spain SL, Google Inc v AEPD, Mario Costeja González*** C-131/12; see also **6.9.2.8**) looked at what the equivalent phrase meant in Directive 95/46 (i.e. under the old pre-GDPR legislation). Google Inc had a subsidiary in Spain which was responsible for selling advertising space targeting individuals in Spain. This contributed to the revenues of Google Inc and the listing of Spanish search results performed by Google Inc only made economic sense because of the activities of the Spanish entity. The CJEU held that there was an "inextricable link" between the establishment in Spain and the listing of search results carried out by Inc: the processing was, therefore, carried out in the context of the activities of the Spanish establishment.

Nationality and residence are not relevant

2.2.1.9 There is often a (mistaken) assumption that EU data protection law applies when an organisation processes personal data of EU citizens or residents. This is not correct and is addressed explicitly in GDPR rec. 14 which states that:

"this Regulation should apply to natural persons, whatever their nationality or place of residence . . .".

2.2.1.10 The EDPB has a good example of how this could play out at p.8 of Guideline 3/2018:

"Example 4: A French company has developed a car-sharing application exclusively addressed to customers in Morocco, Algeria and Tunisia. The service is only available in those three countries but all personal data processing activities are carried out by the data controller in France.
Whilst the collection of personal data takes place in non-EU countries, the subsequent processing of personal data in this case is carried out in the context of the activities of an establishment of a data controller in the Union. Therefore, even though processing relates to personal data of data subjects who are not in the Union, the provisions of the GDPR will apply . . .".

EU-established processors

2.2.1.11 Article 3(1) applies when there is an establishment of a controller or processor in the Union. Here, the EDPB notes (p.10) that only the provisions of the GDPR which apply to processors will be relevant in this case,

"this does not cause the non-EU controller to become subject to the GDPR controller obligations. That is to say, a 'non-EU' controller. . . will not become subject to the GDPR simply because it chooses to use a processor in the Union".

2.2.1.12 The provisions relevant to processors include entering into a data processing agreement with the controller (**13.7**). Ordinarily, a data processing agreement would require the processor to agree to assist the controller to comply with the controller's obligations under the GDPR: the EDPB accepts that this need not be included in the contract, as a controller would not have any such obligations (p.11).

Offering goods or services to, or monitoring, individuals in the EU

2.2.1.13 Article 3(2) provides that:

"This Regulation applies to the processing of personal data of data subjects who are in the Union by a controller or processor not established in the Union, where the processing activities are related to:

a) the offering of goods or services, irrespective of whether a payment of the data subject is required, to such data subjects in the Union; or
b) the monitoring of their behaviour as far as their behaviour takes place within the Union".

2.2.1.14 The legislation, therefore, deliberately has extra-territorial reach—in order, as rec. 23 puts it, "*to ensure that natural persons are not deprived of the protection to which they are entitled* . . .". As mentioned at **2.2.1.9** above, the provision is *not* linked to nationality or residence—although many individuals in the EU will be EU nationals or residents, this is not the criterion and any individual who is in the EU can benefit from the provisions in the GDPR.

Offering of goods or services

2.2.1.15 There is an important clarification of this provision at rec. 23, which states that:

> "*In order to determine whether such a controller or processor is offering goods or services to data subjects who are in the Union, it should be ascertained whether it is apparent that the controller or processor envisages offering services to data subjects in one or more Member States in the Union. Whereas the mere accessibility of the controller's, processor's or an intermediary's website in the Union, of an email address or of other contact details, or the use of a language generally used in the third country where the controller is established, is insufficient to ascertain such intention, factors such as the use of a language or a currency generally used in one or more Member States with the possibility of ordering goods and services in that other language, or the mentioning of customers or users who are in the Union, may make it apparent that the controller envisages offering goods or services to data subjects in the Union*".

2.2.1.16 An organisation which unintentionally happens to transact with EU customers, therefore, will not have to deal with the GDPR. Instead there must be an element of intent (the controller or processor must "envisage"dealing with such individuals). Further, this is not just a matter of the organisation's private intent—there must be some public evidence of this intent (which must be "apparent"). The factors listed in rec. 23 and quoted in full above are useful indicators of what may be sufficient to show this intent. Guideline 3/2018, at pp.15 and 16, has further examples, which are:

- references to the EU or Member States in connection with the goods or services;
- paying search engines to display listings to consumers in the EU;
- marketing and advertising campaigns targeting the EU;
- dedicated addresses or phone numbers to be reached from an EU country;
- use of top-level domain which is linked to the EU ("*.eu*") or a Member State ("*.de*");
- description of travel instructions from the EU;
- offers to deliver to EU Member States.

2.2.1.17 The EDPB suggests that, taken alone, one of these criteria may not be sufficient to bring an organisation within scope of the GDPR—overall analysis should be undertaken (p.16). There is a helpful example on p.17 of Guideline 3/2018:

> "*Example 14: A Swiss University in Zurich is launching its Master degree selection process, by making available an online platform where candidates can upload their CV and cover letter, together with their contact details. The selection process is open to any student with a sufficient level of German and English and holding a Bachelor degree. The University does not specifically advertise to students in EU Universities, and only takes payment in Swiss currency.*
> *As there is no distinction or specification for students from the Union in the application and selection process for this Master degree, it cannot be established that the Swiss University has the intention to target students from particular EU member states. The sufficient level of German and English is a general requirement that applies to any applicant whether a Swiss resident, a person in the Union or a student from a third country. Without other factors to indicate the specific targeting of students in EU member states, it therefore cannot be established that the processing in question relates to the offer of an education service to data subject* [sic] *in the Union, and such processing will therefore not be subject to the GDPR provisions.*
> *The Swiss University also offers summer courses in international relations and specifically advertise this offer in German and Austrian universities in order to maximise the courses' attendance. In this case, there is a clear intention from the Swiss University to offer such service to data subjects who are in the Union, and the GDPR will apply to the related processing activities*".

Monitoring behaviour within the Union

2.2.1.18 The monitoring criterion is wider: here there is no reference to or requirement for intent on the part of the controller or processor. Recital 24 states that:

> "*In order to determine whether a processing activity can be considered to monitor the behaviour of data subjects, it should be ascertained whether natural persons are tracked on the internet including potential subsequent use of personal data processing techniques which consists of profiling a natural person, particularly in order to take decisions concerning her or him or for analysing or predicting her or his personal preferences, behaviours and attitudes*".

(The term "profiling" has a specific meaning in the GDPR under art.4(4) which is discussed in detail at **6.11.2**, but for the moment the reader can rely on the word's ordinary meaning in considering this passage.)

2.2.1.19 The EDPB's Guideline 3/2018 makes clear that the recital does not mean that the only form of monitoring which is relevant is online monitoring:

rather the intent of the recital is to make clear that online tracking *is* covered, not to suggest that other forms of monitoring are not covered (p.18). The Guideline (again, at p.18), lists types of monitoring which could be included:

- through wearables or smart devices;
- targeted advertising;
- geo-localisation activities, in particular for marketing;
- online tracking through cookies or device fingerprinting (**Ch.7**);
- personalised diet and health analytics services online;
- CCTV;
- market surveys and other behavioural studies based on individual profiles;
- monitoring or regular reporting on an individual's health status.

Public international law

2.2.1.20 The last occasion when the GDPR or the UK GDPR applies is when, as art.3(3) provides "*Member State law applies by virtue of public international law*". Recital 25 notes that this would be the case for diplomatic missions or consular posts of Member States. The EDPB, in Guideline 3/2018, gives the example of ships which are registered to a Member State, where that State's laws apply when the ship is in international waters (p.19).

Representatives

2.2.1.21 Where the GDPR applies on an extra-territorial basis pursuant to art.3(2), the controller or processor outside the EU, must appoint a representative within the EU (art.27). The representative can then be contacted by supervisory authorities or data subjects, instead of, or as well as, the controller or processor itself (art.27(4)).

2.2.1.22 There is an exception, at art.27(2) for processing which is "*occasional*" and which is

> "*unlikely to pose a risk to the rights and freedoms of natural persons, taking into account the nature, context, scope and purpose of the processing*".

However, this exception cannot apply to processing, on a large scale, of special categories of data or data relating to criminal convictions and offences. The requirement that the processing be "*occasional*" means that it is likely to be of very limited use. Public authorities and bodies also do not have to appoint a representative.

2.2.1.23 The representative must be designated in writing (art.27(1)) and must be given a mandate to deal with queries by supervisory authorities and individuals (art.27(4)). To facilitate this, the identity and contact details of the representative must be included in the privacy notice provided to individuals under arts 13 or 14 (**6.4**). The representative must be located in a Member State where data subjects are located, whose personal data are processed by the controller or processor (art.27(3)). The EDPB, in Guideline 3/2018 recommends choosing a Member State where the majority of data subjects are based—but is clear that this is a non-binding recommendation (p.22). The representative must also maintain a record of the processing activities of the controller or processor under art.30 (**13.5**)—although, in practice, as the EDPB notes (p.23) this will likely require support from the controller or processor itself.

2.2.1.24 The GDPR says very little about the role of the representative, so the EDPB's Guideline 03/2018 spells out some additional considerations from the EDPB. In particular, the EDPB confirms that whilst a representative can act for multiple controllers and processors, in the EDPB's view the representative cannot also act as the external data protection officer (because the representative will be instructed how to undertake its role, whereas the data protection officer cannot be instructed how to perform his or her role (**13.2.3**)), neither can a data processor be the representative (because of the potential for conflict of interest. Presumably this might arise if there was a query as to whether the processor or the controller was responsible for a matter which was the subject of an investigation or complaint) (both p.20).

2.2.1.25 Article 27(5) provides that the

> "*designation of a representative by the controller or processor shall be without prejudice to legal actions which could be initiated against the controller or the processor themselves*"

so, this is to be an additional route, not something which precludes action directly against the overseas controller or processor. Recital 80 notes that "*the designated representative should be subject to enforcement proceedings in the event of non-compliance by the controller or processor*" and Guideline 3/2008 notes, at p.23, that

> "*it was the intention to enable enforcers to initiate enforcement action against a representative in the same way as against controllers or processors. This includes the possibility to impose administrative fines and penalties, and to hold representatives liable*".

In the light of this risk, it remains to be seen how many organisations will be willing to act as representatives.

2.3 Territorial scope of the DPA 2018

2.3.1 Section 207(2) of the DPA 2018 provides that the Act applies to processing of personal data "*in the context of the activities of an establishment in the United Kingdom, whether or not the processing takes place in the United*

Kingdom". Section 207(7) provides more detail as to what amounts to an establishment in the United Kingdom, including individuals who are ordinarily resident in the United Kingdom, bodies which are incorporated under the law of the United Kingdom, partnerships or other unincorporated associates which are formed under the law of the United Kingdom and other persons who maintain or carry on activities through stable arrangements in the United Kingdom, which include an office, branch or agency. The DPA 2018 also contains an equivalent provision to the extra-territorial provisions of the GDPR. Section 207(3) provides that, where the GDPR applies in this way, then the DPA 2018 will also so apply provided that the offering of goods or services is to, or the monitoring is of, individuals in the United Kingdom and that the processing is not carried out in the context of the activities of an establishment of a controller or processor in an EU member state. This extra-territorial provision does not apply to processing by law enforcement agencies, the intelligence services, or the applied GDPR.

2.4 AMBIT OF THE UK LEGISLATION

2.4.1 Introduction

2.4.1.1 So far we have been looking at the GDPR which repealed and replaced Directive 95/46, coming fully into force on 25 May 2018. As an EU Regulation, the GDPR applies directly in all EU Member States without the need for implementing legislation. However, the UK still needs domestic data protection legislation:

- to make provision for the Information Commissioner; and
- to address areas which the GDPR says *must* be addressed by each Member State (such as the interaction between processing of personal data and freedom of expression (art.85), or which the GDPR says Member States *may* address if they so wish (such as additional conditions where special categories of personal data may be processed (art.9(2)(g)), or exemptions (art.23)).

The DPA 2018 repeals the vast majority of the previous UK data protection legislation, the Data Protection Act 1998 and addresses these points in Pt 1, Chs 1 and 2 and associated Schedules. The matter is complicated by the fact that the DPA 2018 also addresses areas of data protection legislation beyond the scope of the GDPR.

2.4.2 Processing by law enforcement agencies and the intelligence services

2.4.2.1 The 1998 Act had applied to all processing of personal data in the UK—including these three areas. It follows that the repeal of the 1998 Act, without replacing these provisions, would lower the standard of data protection in the UK. Replacement provisions are also required to implement an EU

Directive relating to protection of personal data by law enforcement authorities and to ensure that the UK continues to meet its obligations under the Council of Europe's Convention for the Protection of Individuals with regard to Automatic Processing of Personal Data (Convention 108). The departure of the UK from the EU does not affect our membership of the Council of Europe of which the UK is a founder member.

Law enforcement

2.4.2.2 At the same time as the GDPR was adopted, the EU also adopted a Law Enforcement Directive (2016/680), to come into force by 6 May 2018. As this is a Directive, rather than a Regulation, it had to be implemented into national laws by Member States, including the UK. Part 3 of the DPA 2018 is the UK's implementation of this Directive.

2.4.2.3 The DPA 2018 still needs to include definitions for terms used in the Law Enforcement Directive, these are set out either in s.3 of the DPA 2018, or in Pt 3 of the DPA 2018. This means that, somewhat confusingly, the initial provisions of the DPA 2018 contain definitions of—for example—personal data, data subject and processing—but these relate *only* to areas of processing outside the scope of the GDPR—notably law enforcement processing and processing by the intelligence services—and so are irrelevant to most of the readers of this book who are not involved in these specialist areas. This is discussed at **15.1.**

Intelligence services

2.4.2.4 There are certain areas in which the EU cannot legislate—the Information Commissioner in pages on her website headed "Data Protection Act 2018" [Accessed 8 October 2018], gives the example of national security. As the DPA 2018 repeals almost all of the 1998 Act, it also needs to make new provision for data protection laws to apply to activities which fall outside EU competence—to avoid the UK having no laws in this area and, as a result, be in breach of its commitments under Convention 108. The UK addresses this by setting out provisions in Pt 4 of the DPA 2018 which apply to processing of personal data by the intelligence services (that is MI5, MI6 and GCHQ). This is discussed at **15.2.**

2.4.3 The applied GDPR

2.4.3.1 The DPA 2018 also introduces a concept of the "applied GDPR". This addresses processing of personal data to which neither the GDPR, nor the law enforcement provisions, nor the provisions for the intelligence services apply. The principal example of such processing would be completely manual unstructured personal data processed by a public authority. Another example, would be processing of personal data in connection with foreign policy. As such processing of personal data was covered by the 1998 Act, again, the Government has needed to ensure that the repeal of the 1998 Act does not lower standards in this area. The approach taken in the DPA 2018 is to create a concept of the "*applied*

GDPR" where the GDPR is legislated to apply "*as if its Articles were part of an Act extending to England and Wales, Scotland and Northern Ireland*" (s.22). The GDPR cannot be applied wholesale to such processing: to take an example, as such processing falls outside EU law, the mechanisms for co-operation and consistency between EU supervisory authorities can have no relevance to it (**1.4.3**). The DPA 2018 therefore also includes a long schedule, Schedule 6, introducing amendments to the GDPR, largely to disapply this type of provision. The applied GDPR is of limited application to most organisations and, as explained at **2.5.4**, it seems likely that, at some stage post-Brexit, the applied GDPR will cease to exist. Given this, we mention the applied GDPR only rarely in this book.

2.5 BREXIT

2.5.1 If the Withdrawal Agreement applies, then, during its transitional period (**0.15.4**), there will be no change to the territorial scope of UK data protection law.

2.5.2 In the event of a no-deal Brexit, territorial scope becomes more complex. For controllers or processors which are established only in the UK, but which offer goods or services to individuals in the EU, or which monitor the behaviour of individuals in the EU, the GDPR will continue to apply, but on an extra territorial basis as described at **2.2** above. Such controllers or processors will need to appoint a representative in the EU (**2.2.1.21**). Such organisations will also have to comply with the DPA 2018 which will continue to apply where there is an establishment of a controller or processor in the UK, and where the processing is in the context of the activities of that establishment. However, the extra-territorial scope of the DPA 2018 will be altered, so that EU-based controllers or processors which deal with data subjects in the UK are subject to UK data protection law on an extra-territorial basis in just the same way as UK-based controllers or processors dealing with EU data subjects. Accordingly, art.3 of the UK GDPR will apply whenever a controller or processor which is not established in the UK, offers goods or services to, or monitors the behaviour of, individuals in the UK. Such controllers or processors will also have to appoint a representative in the UK. As with the current provisions, this extra-territorial scope does not apply to processing by law enforcement agencies, the intelligence services or to the applied GDPR.

2.5.3 If the Withdrawal Agreement applies, then there will be no change to the material scope of UK data protection legislation during the transitional period. The UK government has to continue to apply EU law during this period and, as regards the rules relating to the processing of personal data by the intelligence services, the departure of the UK from the EU does not affect our membership of the Council of Europe of which the UK is a founder member.

2.5.4 In the event of a no-deal Brexit, the Data Protection (EU Exit) Regulations will take the opportunity to simplify matters so far as the applied GDPR is concerned. They will provide that the UK GDPR (arts.2(1), (1A) and (2)) will apply to *all* processing of personal data (other than that carried out by an individual in the course of purely personal or household activities (**1.3.4.8**—see also **10.5.8**), or processing to which the law enforcement provisions or the intelligence services provisions apply (**15**). This is specifically stated to include

> "*processing in the course of an activity which, immediately before exit day, fell outside the scope of EU law, . . . processing in the course of . . . common foreign and security policy activities . . .* [and] *the manual unstructured processing of personal data held by an FOI public authority*" (as to which, see **10.2.5.2**).

The provisions relating to the "applied GDPR" will all be omitted and the transitional arrangement provisions at Sch. 21, Pt 2 of the DPA 2018 will confirm that the applied GDPR is, as from exit day, to be merged with the main legislation, and that all references to data protection legislation after exit day are to include the applied GDPR. Even if the Withdrawal Agreement applies, it would be logical for this same approach to be taken to the applied GDPR on the expiry of the transitional period.

CHAPTER 3

Consequences of Failure

3.1 INTRODUCTION

3.1.1 Readers may wonder why we deal with the consequences of failure to observe the legislation, before they have been told what their full obligations under the legislation are. The reason is simple: although the legislation may appear to a layman as a matter simply of bureaucracy, the consequences of failing to observe it can be extremely serious. First the Information Commissioner has powers to inflict fines ("penalties") on organisations. Under the 1998 Act, the maximum fine which could be imposed by the Commissioner was £500,000. The Commissioner has regularly exercised her power to impose penalties—with a penalty of the maximum amount being imposed on Equifax and Facebook. Although the penalty notices are dated after 25 May 2018 (so after the entry into force of the GDPR and the DPA 2018), both penalties were issued under the 1998 Act. The GDPR and the DPA 2018 provide for penalties of up to €20 million or 4% of annual worldwide turnover – a vast increase. The Commissioner also has the power to institute other enforcement proceedings on your organisation under the DPA 2018—ranging from compulsory audit by means of assessment notices (**3.4.2**) to orders prohibiting processing of personal data (**3.4.3.4**).

3.1.2 Second, some breaches of data protection legislation amount to criminal offences (**3.2**) and in certain cases an individual manager or other officer of an organisation can incur personal criminal liability for breaches of the DPA 2018 (**3.2.1.1**).

3.1.3 In addition, legal action and claims for compensation by individuals or groups on behalf of individuals are possible under the legislation. An individual may also be able to require modifications not just to your data, but also to your procedures and even in an extreme case to your software, which may prove very expensive.

3.1.4 Finally, it must always be borne in mind that the press is also often interested in claims that an organisation has breached privacy requirements. The damaging publicity that follows may prove to be the worst consequence of all for organisations who have infringed the legislation (**3.5.2**).

3.2 CRIMINAL OFFENCES

3.2.1 Offences by the controller, its officers, managers, members or partners

3.2.1.1 In a number of cases, an organisation's failure to comply with the legislation will mean that it commits a criminal offence. In most of these cases the

Commissioner initiates such legal action. In the first nine months of 2018 there were at least 13 prosecutions under similar provisions in the 1998 Act. Where acts are carried out by limited companies or other legal entities, then in most cases, any criminal liability will be incurred by the limited company or other legal entity. However, in some circumstances, members of the management may find themselves personally liable for the commission of an offence. DPA 2018 s.198 is relevant here. This provides that:

> "*(1) Subsection (2) applies where –*
> *(a) an offence under this Act has been committed by a body corporate, and*
> *(b) it is proved to have been committed with the consent or connivance or to be attributable to any neglect on the part of –*
> *(i) a director, manager, secretary, or similar officer of the body corporate, or*
> *(ii) a person who was purporting to act in any such a capacity.*
> *(2) The director, manager, secretary, officer or person, as well as the body corporate, is guilty of the offence and liable to be proceeded against and punished accordingly*".

3.2.1.2 The DPA 2018 has similar penalties for a member of a body corporate which is managed by its members, where a member acts in connection with his management functions in relation to the body as if he were a director of a body corporate (s.198(3)). Partners in Scottish partnerships may be similarly liable (s.198(4)–(5)).

3.2.1.3 The intent behind s.198 is that where an offence has been committed under the Act by a limited company or other named body, but is actually attributable to the instructions of, or negligence of, its management, the relevant manager should be able to be pursued personally. Section 198 specifically mentions company directors and the company secretary who have statutory obligations in relation to a limited company. However, it could also cover other individuals who have management powers. A data protection officer might fall within this section if he or she had a sufficient level of authority and could be shown to be culpable by connivance or neglect.

3.2.1.4 The Information Commissioner has made use of the equivalent provision under the 1998 Act (s.61) when dealing with organisations which disregard her investigatory and enforcement powers. For example, on 1 May 2018, prosecutions were obtained against both a company and a company director for failing to respond to information notices. Another example dates from 7 December 2017, where the ICO website reported a case of a firm of loss adjusters found guilty of disclosing personal data illegally obtained under DPA 1998 s.55 (see **3.2.3**). In addition to the conviction of the firm ("*body corporate*"), a director and a senior loss adjuster employed by the firm were found personally liable under s.61, as well as two contracted private investigators who were evidently self-employed. The fines reported on the ICO website 5 January 2018 were £50,000 plus £20,000 costs against the firm, £75,000 and £20,000 costs against the director, and £20,000 plus £20,000 costs against the senior loss adjuster.

3.2.1.5 This could be extremely useful in persuading board members of the need to take an interest in and responsibility for data protection; management can incur liability under this section if they neglect data protection, as well as if they deliberately flout the legislation.

3.2.1.6 Similar powers in respect of the Privacy and Electronic Communications (EC Directive) Regulations 2003 (SI 2003/2426), whose relevance to data protection legislation is described at **7.4**, are provided by the Privacy and Electronic Communications (Amendment) Regulations 2018 (SI 2018/1189).

3.2.1.7 The DPA 2018 provides for criminal sanctions in relation to the following areas:

(a) offences relating to unauthorised obtaining or disclosure of personal data;

(b) an offence of re-identification of de-identified personal data;

(c) offences relating to abuse of individuals' subject access rights; and

(d) offences of interfering with the exercise of the Commissioner's powers.

These are all considered in further detail below.

3.2.2 Unlawful obtaining or disclosure of personal data

3.2.2.1 Section 170 of the DPA 2018 makes it an offence to obtain or disclose personal data without the consent of the relevant controller. The most obvious application of this section is to enquiry agents who obtain information about particular individuals by deception; for example, by purporting to be the individual concerned. The ICO tends to refer to this offence as "blagging". It is also sometimes referred to as "pretexting".

3.2.2.2 Section 170 provides that:

"*(1) It is an offence for a person knowingly or recklessly–*

(a) to obtain or disclose personal data without the consent of the controller,

(b) to procure the disclosure to another person without the consent of the controller, or

(c) after obtaining personal data, to retain it without consent of the person who was the controller in relation to the personal data when it was obtained".

3.2.2.3 This is not a strict liability offence. An individual only commits this offence if they obtain or disclose personal data knowing that, or being reckless as to whether or not, the controller has consented to this.

3.2.2.4 It is also an offence for someone who has obtained data in breach of s.170 to sell, or to offer to sell data so obtained. Any advertising of the personal data is an offer to sell (s.170(4)–(6)).

3.2.2.5 There are a number of defences to s.170. These cover:

- the prevention or detection of crime;
- disclosures required or authorised by an enactment;
- disclosures in the public interest;
- disclosures for journalistic or similar purposes ("the special purposes"—see **10.5.6**); or
- acts where the individual reasonably believed he had a legal right to obtain, etc. or had, or would have had, the consent of the controller to obtain or disclose the information.

3.2.2.6 The defences are set out at s.170(2)–(3):

"*(2) It is a defence for a person charged with an offence under subsection (1) to prove that the obtaining, disclosing, procuring or retaining –*
(a) was necessary for the purpose of preventing or detecting crime,
(b) was required or authorised by an enactment, by a rule of law or by the order of a court or tribunal, or
(c) that in the particular circumstances, was justified as being in the public interest.
(3) It is also a defence for a person charged with an offence under subsection (1) to prove that –
(a) the person acted in the reasonable belief that the person had a legal right to do the obtaining, disclosing, procuring or retaining,
(b) the person acted in the reasonable belief that he would have had the consent of the controller if the controller had known about the obtaining, disclosing, procuring, procuring or retaining and the circumstances of it, or
(c) the person acted –
(i) for the special purposes,
(ii) with a view to the publication by a person of any journalistic, academic or literary material, and
(iii) in the reasonable belief that in the particular circumstances the obtaining, disclosing, procuring or retaining was justified as being in the public interest".

3.2.2.7 The matter of whether or not the accused had the controller's assent is further illuminated by s.170(7) which deals with cases where a processor who is found to be dictating the purposes and means of processing is thereby deemed to be the controller, or where there is more than one controller of the same data—

presumably where there are joint controllers. A processor who is considered a controller because he decides the purposes and means of processing is not a valid controller in the present context. If there is more than one controller of the personal data, the consent of any one of the controllers is sufficient. It says:

"*(7) In this section –*
(a) references to the consent of a controller do not include the consent of the person who is a controller by virtue of article 28(10)) of the GDPR or section 59(8) or 105(3) of this Act (processor to be treated as controller in certain circumstances);
(b) where there is more than one controller, such references are references to the consent of one or more of them."

3.2.2.8 In addition to these specific defences, there is a general exemption for information which is exempt under some of the provisions in the DPA 2018 at ss.24 and 26. These relate to:

- disclosure, without consent, of completely unstructured personal data held by a public authority (see **10.2.5** DPA 2018 s.24; and
- exemptions required for national security or defence purposes (see **10.4** DPA 2018 s.26).

3.2.2.9 Although the provisions are of most obvious application to enquiry agents, this is not their only application. Section 170 could also, for example, cover disclosures of personal data made by staff in banking or insurance call centres in breach of their employers' policy on disclosures. This is a permanent problem for organisations handling large amounts of personal data. An example of this under the corresponding s.55 of the 1998 DPA appeared as a news item on the ICO website on 6 December 2012. The partner of a man who was divorcing was a bank employee and called up his wife's bank account to provide him with ammunition in contesting the amount of maintenance. The bank employee ended up with a criminal conviction, a £500 fine, victim surcharge of £15 and £1,410.80 prosecution costs. She also lost her job.

3.2.2.10 A further complication is that in practice, individuals with bank accounts, insurance policies, etc. will often expect the service provider to deal with family members. So, for example, a husband or wife will often call up on behalf of the other to check the balance in a particular account. Callers can sometimes be difficult if staff do not release such information. However, in a number of cases the individual calling will not have the authority of the other party. It is very important that organisations operating in this sector have clear policies as to when information will be released to callers and that they make these policies clear, both to their customers and to call centre staff. Call centre staff also should be given training on the policies. Policies should include guidance as to how the identity of callers will be obtained and verified and how the organisation will check if the caller has the authority of the person to whom the account relates to disclose information. As there could be potential criminal sanctions for a member of staff who fails to adhere to these policies, it is essential that such service providers offer appropriate staff training. Failure to adopt these kinds of policies and to offer appropriate staff training could also mean that an organisation is, itself, in breach of its security obligations (described in detail at **Ch.8**), as it may not have taken appropriate organisational measures to protect the security of the data.

3.2.2.11 There were a fair number of prosecutions for the 1998 Act s.55 offence (the offence corresponding to DPA 2018 s.170): out of the 13 prosecutions under the 1998 Act during January–September 2018, eight relate to breach of s.55.

3.2.2.12 One of the most high-profile cases is the prosecution, in the Crown Court, reported by the ICO on 10 June 2011, of two employees of T-Mobile who stole customer data and sold it on. They together pleaded guilty to 20 offences under s.55, and were ordered to pay confiscation costs, one of £45,000 and the other of £28,700. On 25 April 2014 the ICO reported another Crown Court case: a private investigator called Spencer who was convicted under DPA 1998 s.55. Although his fine was relatively modest (£12,000), he was also hit with a confiscation order of over £69,000 under the Proceeds of Crime Act 2002. His discomfiture was completed by prosecution costs of £8,000 (bringing the cash total to just shy of £90,000) and he was disqualified from being a Director for eight years.

3.2.2.13 The case of ***Paul Shepherd v The Information Commissioner*** [2019] EWCA Crim 2 considered the somewhat similarly worded defence under the 1998 Act and contrasted it with that in the DPA 2018. They also discussed the extent to which the defence engaged art.6 of the European Convention on Human Rights. The 1998 Act subsection (2) began with the unusual words "*Subsection (1) does not apply to a person who shows . . .*". The DPA 2018 s.170(2) by contrast uses the more usual wording: "*It is a defence for a person charged with an offence under subsection (1) to prove. . .*". The court agreed with Mr Shepherd's counsel that this wording in the 1998 Act was deliberate. Mr Shepherd did not have a legal burden to prove that one of these subsections was made out. Instead there was a lower requirement, an evidential burden simply to raise one of these provisions, at which point the Information Commissioner must disprove it, to the criminal standard of proof. The Court of Appeal went on to contrast this with the DPA 2018 [54], quoting para.490 of the *Explanatory Notes* which state:

> "*. . . As worded, the section places a legal burden on the defendant to prove the relevant defences on the balance of probabilities.*"

Thus, the 1998 Act had a lower threshold for the defendant than does the DPA 2018. The court concluded:

> "*. . . we agree with the opinion that the new section imposes a legal burden of proof on the defendant. We express no view on whether s.170(2) is compatible with the defendant's art.6 rights.*"

3.2.3 Re-identification of de-identified personal data

3.2.3.1 This offence has no counterpart in the 1998 Act. Under s.171 of the DPA 2018

"It is an offence for a person knowingly or recklessly to re-identify information that is de-identified personal data without the consent of the controller responsible for de-identifying the personal data."

3.2.3.2 As we saw at **1.2.2**, the GDPR distinguishes between:

- Personal data where an individual is identified or identifiable, taking into account all means reasonably likely to be used; and
- anonymous data where the individual is no longer identifiable and which is not within scope of the GDPR (rec.26).

The GDPR (art.4(5)) also introduces the concept of "pseudonymisation", meaning

"the processing of personal data in such a manner that the personal data can no longer be attributed to a specific data subject without the use of additional information, provided that such additional information is kept separately and subject to technical and organisational measures to ensure that the personal data are not attributed to an identified or identifiable natural person".

3.2.3.3 In other words, anonymisation is the removal of all identifiers, whereas pseudonymisation refers to cases where the identifiers are not removed and erased completely but are held elsewhere, rather in the way that a publisher of a pseudonymous novel will keep the author's identity secret and secure.

3.2.3.4 The GDPR points out (recs 28–29) that pseudonymisation can reduce the risks to data subjects and help controllers and processors meet their data protection compliance objectives. By way of example, if there is a personal data breach affecting pseudonymous data, then, so long as the identifying information is not compromised, the risk to individuals is likely to be much reduced or even non-existent. Pseudonymisation is one of a range of mechanisms mentioned in art.25 (Data protection by design and by default) to provide safeguards, and it heads the list of such mechanisms in art.32 on security of processing.

3.2.3.5 It follows that any failure of pseudonymising must be a serious matter and individuals should be subject to sanction if they deliberately seek to circumvent controls which a controller has put in place in relation to identifying material. The DPA 2018 s.171 responds to this policy objective. Section 171(2) states that:

"personal data is 'de-identified' if it has been processed in such a manner that it can no longer be attributed, without more, to a specific data subject; a person 're-identifies' information if the person takes steps which result in the information no longer being de-identified . . .".

3.2.3.6 The Explanatory Notes, at para.494, state that the definition "*reflects the definition of pseudonymisation in Article 4(5) of the GDPR*". In fact, it seems to us that the definition is more subtle than this—and it could cover both data which has been pseudonymised and data which has been anonymised.

3.2.3.7 There are possible defences to a charge of re-identification under s.171(3)–(4) where the re-identification was:

- necessary for the purposes of preventing or detecting crime;
- authorised under an enactment;
- in the circumstances, in the public interest;
- the re-identification is performed by the data subject in question;
- made with a reasonable belief that the person carrying out the re-identification is the data subject or was carried out with the data subject's consent, or would have been carried out with the data subject's consent had the data subject known the details;
- made with, or in the reasonable belief of having, the controller's consent, or carried out in the reasonable belief that the person re-identifying the data is the controller responsible for the de-identification;
- for the special purposes, with a view to publication, and in the reasonable belief that the re-identification was in the public interest (**13.3.2.4.1**).

3.2.3.8 There is an additional defence under "effectiveness testing conditions" described in s.172. Where a person acted:

- with a view to testing the effectiveness of the de-identification;
- without intending to cause or threaten to cause damage or distress to anyone;
- in the reasonable belief that what he was doing was in the public interest; and
- he notified the Commissioner or controller without delay of the re-identification (where feasible in 72 hours or less).

Where there is more than one controller, notification of any one controller is sufficient.

This defence recognises that security measures need to be constantly tested for effectiveness and many controllers bring in consultants expressly to see if they can break their security measures, and sometimes are approached by members of the public who tell them they have been able to break the security.

3.2.3.9 A further related offence in s.171(5) arises where a person knowingly or recklessly processes such re-identified data. Apart from the effectiveness testing conditions of s.172, the same defences as in **3.2.3.7** are available under s.171(6)–

(7) with an additional defence that the defendant had a reasonable belief that the processing was lawful.

3.2.3.10 A processor who is treated as a controller because he determines the purposes and means of processing (GDPR art.28(10)) is not a controller for the purposes of this s.171 and so cannot authorise re-identification.

3.2.4 Subject-access related offences

Enforced subject access

3.2.4.1 An individual can obtain copies of personal data relating to him under GDPR art.15 and this is discussed at **6.5**. This right is called the subject access right. A practice grew up under the original 1984 Act (which had a similar subject access provision), whereby employers would ask prospective employees to use their subject-access rights to obtain a copy of their police record. Provision of this police record would then be a condition of the employer considering the individual's application. The then Data Protection Registrar (predecessor of the Information Commissioner) labelled this practice enforced subject access as the employer was forcing the applicant to use the rights granted to him under the 1984 Act. The Data Protection Registrar considered this practice to be extremely objectionable, largely as the police records obtained revealed details of cautions and spent convictions, as well as "current" convictions, thereby undermining the principle of rehabilitation.

3.2.4.2 The 1998 Act contained provisions to criminalise this practice. Section 56 of that Act applied to specific criminal and related records listed in the Act. This is now covered by s.184 of the DPA 2018, whereby it is an offence for a person to require the supply of relevant records in connection with the recruitment or continued employment of an individual or for the supply of services by that individual. It is also an offence for anyone to require an individual to produce these records before they can receive goods, facilities, or other services that are provided to the public. "Relevant records" are defined in Sch.18; they include police records, but also now include health records and records held for certain statutory functions, including the Disclosure and Barring Service and for sentencing purposes.

3.2.4.3 If an organisation can show that it was legally required to obtain this record or that, in the particular circumstances, requiring the production of the record was justified because it was in the public interest, then there is a defence. However, organisations should note that it is not possible to argue that, as a matter of policy, it is in the public interest to require individuals to produce these records on the grounds that this is for the purpose of the prevention or detection of crime. This is specifically excluded from the defences in the DPA 2018 (s.184(4)).

3.2.4.4 Section 184 recognises that in many circumstances the person or organisation which might be seeking enforced subject access will be able to bring pressure on the data subject to provide this. Thus, the word "require" is further illustrated by s.184(5) which makes it clear it means asking someone to provide this material, while "*(a) knowing that, in the circumstances, it would be reasonable for the other person to feel obliged to comply with the request, or*

(b) being reckless as to whether, in the circumstances, it would be reasonable for the other person to feel obliged to comply with the request."

3.2.4.5 There is clearly a legitimate interest for some organisations to be able to check the complete criminal records of potential employees. Where it is legitimate or required to seek such an assurance (for example when recruiting staff to work with unsupervised access to children), employers and others should turn to the Disclosure and Barring Service, set up by the Protection of Freedoms Act 2012 s.87(1) to combine the old Criminal Records Bureau and the Independent Safeguarding Authority. In Scotland there is a body called Disclosure Scotland. For Northern Ireland there is AccessNI; there is information about, or links to, these bodies at *https://www.gov.uk/criminal-record-checks-apply-role*.

Alteration of data to prevent disclosure to a data subject

3.2.4.6 DPA 2018 s.173 applies to two data subject rights: subject access and data portability. Subject access is the right for an individual to receive a copy of his or her personal data; portability is the right to receive certain data in a structured and machine-readable format (so a more "portable" format). The rights are considered in more detail at **6.5** and **6.7**. Section 173 provides that it is an offence for a controller, or someone employed by or subject to the direction of a controller, to alter, block, erase, destroy or conceal information from the data subject making the request, with the intent of preventing disclosure of information to which the individual is entitled. There is a defence if the person can prove

- that the alteration, etc. would have occurred anyway in the absence of the request. This might arise in the case of a CCTV system whose data is regularly overwritten every month; or
- the person reasonably believed that the data subject was not entitled to the information.

3.2.4.7 Section 197 provides that proceedings for this offence must be brought within six months of the day on which the prosecutor knows of evidence which would be sufficient to bring proceedings. There is also a long-stop date of three years from the date on which the offence was committed.

3.2.5 Offences relating to the Commissioner's powers

3.2.5.1 The role of the Information Commissioner was discussed at **1.3.8**. The Commissioner's powers are dealt with at **3.4.** and in particular the various notices which the Commissioner can serve on persons are discussed at **3.4.5** and **3.4.6** below, but here we are only concerned with a person, who, having received one of these notices, is less than open in providing the information and co-operation that the Commissioner requires. Failure to co-operate with the Information

Commissioner in the exercise of her powers, almost invariably, amounts to the commission of a criminal offence.

3.2.5.2 Where the Information Commissioner has served an information notice (**3.4.2.1**), it is then, by virtue of DPA 2018 s.144, an offence for anyone knowingly or recklessly to make a statement to the Information Commissioner which is false in a material respect.

3.2.5.3 Section 148 applies to information notices (**3.4.2.5**) and assessment notices (**3.4.2.14**). It is an offence when receiving one of these notices

> "*(a) to destroy or otherwise dispose of, conceal, block or (where relevant) falsify all or part of the information, document, equipment, or material, or*
>
> *(b) to cause or permit the destruction, disposal, concealment or blocking or (where relevant) falsification of all or part of the information, document, equipment or material,*
>
> *with the intention of preventing the Commissioner from viewing, or being provided with or directed to, all or part of the information, document, equipment or material.*"

There is a defence if it can be shown that the destruction etc. would have occurred in any event without the notice. Thus (as we mentioned above at **3.2.4.6**), the regular overwriting of CCTV footage on say a monthly basis could still go ahead, despite an assessment notice. However, to be on the safe side, a controller should probably not push this too far.

3.2.5.4 Similar provisions were available under DPA 1998 s.47(1). There seems to have been only one case where this kind of thing was considered. In ***Medway Council v The Information Commissioner*** [2015] EA/2014/0227, the Council reported themselves to the ICO over an incident of mis-sending of sensitive personal data—due to a software bug. The ICO served a notice of intent for a monetary penalty on the grounds that it appeared to be an infringement of DPA 1998 7th Data Protection Principle (security obligations). Medway then advised the ICO that, in fact, this was a case of human error, where the employee who mis-addressed the sensitive personal data had made changes to the database to try to cover their tracks, and Medway invited the ICO to re-open its investigation. The ICO did so but also sent Medway an information notice asking for a full explanation. Medway appealed against the information notice on the grounds that they had already given this information—and then unwisely gave a third explanation. The First-tier Tribunal dismissed Medway's appeal, but in doing so mentioned [30] the possibility that Medway, by their prevarication and failure to provide a single correct explanation of the data breach, might have been guilty under DPA 1998 s.47(2) which says;

> "*A person who, in purported compliance with an information notice...*
>
> *(b) recklessly makes a statement which is false in a material respect is guilty of an offence.*"

3.2.5.5 Finally, under Sch.15, para.15, it is an offence intentionally to obstruct the Commissioner's staff when they are exercising search and seize warrants. It is also an offence to fail without reasonable excuse to give the Commissioner's staff reasonable assistance when they exercise their powers under such a warrant.

3.2.6 Procedures relating to offences

3.2.6.1 The Information Commissioner has hitherto usually been the person who brings proceedings for offences under the Act. In addition, the Director of Public Prosecutions, in England and Wales and, in Northern Ireland, the Director of Public Prosecutions for Northern Ireland may also give consent for proceedings for offences to be brought. In Scotland, the Procurator Fiscal would give consent. This is set out at s.197 of the DPA 2018.

3.2.6.2 In practice, the Commissioner may decide to issue a caution instead of prosecuting an offence. The Act does not contain any formal provisions relating to cautions. However, the Information Commissioner has adopted a practice of issuing a caution where the Office wishes to give a formal warning that, in the event of further breach, the Commissioner reserves the right to bring the previous breach to the attention of the court. The Commissioner may also require an undertaking from the controller to take or refrain from taking some appropriate action (**3.4.3.16**).

3.2.6.3 The offences of obstructing the Commissioner in the exercise of a search and seize warrant or of failing to give reasonable assistance in the execution of a warrant can be tried only in the Magistrates Court. However, all other offences could, in theory, also be tried in the Crown Court. The significance of this is that there is no statutory maximum fine in the Crown Court; in the Magistrates Court, the maximum fine is currently £5,000. It will be noticed that in the T-Mobile and Spencer cases mentioned above (**3.2.2.12**), the proceedings, resulting in much higher fines, were remitted to the Crown Court. Lastly, readers should note that government departments and the Corporate Officers of the Houses of Parliament cannot face criminal liability under the legislation (ss.209(6) and 210(6)).

3.3 LEGAL ACTIONS

3.3.1 Legal actions by individuals

3.3.1.1 The paragraphs which follow describe the remedies available to individuals via the courts—however, organisations should be aware that individuals can also complain to the Information Commissioner, who will then investigate their complaint at no cost to them. This is considered further at **3.4.1.2** below. The DPA 2018 grants individuals two types of remedy:

(1) a right to seek a compliance order—that is, an order requiring an organisation to do certain things, or to stop doing certain things (s.167); or

(2) a right to seek compensation for contravention of the legislation (ss.168–169).

Compliance orders

3.3.1.2 Section 167 applies where a court is satisfied that there has been a breach of a data subject's rights. At the request of an affected individual, a court may order a controller, or a processor acting on behalf of a controller, to take such steps, or to refrain from taking such steps, as are specified in the order, so as to comply with any of an individual's rights. So, for example, the court could order the controller to rectify some personal data, to cease processing some personal data, or to erase some personal data (**6.6**).

3.3.1.3 Organisations should note that the court is not obliged to enforce individuals' rights under s.167: rather, s.167(2) provides that the court "may" make an order to secure compliance. The 1998 Act also gave the courts discretion as to when they would order compliance. In 2003, Mumby J described the court's discretion as "*general and untrammelled*" in ***R. (on the application of Lord) v Secretary of State for the Home Department*** [2003] EWHC 1073, [160], a phrase cited approvingly by the Court of Appeal, in ***Durant v Financial Services Authority*** [2003] EWCA Civ 1746, [74]. For a discussion of this and more recent cases, see **1.2.2.10** above.

Compensation

3.3.1.4 Before we look at provisions under the GDPR and the DPA 2018 relating to claims for compensation, we start by seeing what can be learned from cases under the 1998 Act. We have grouped these into two main categories:

(1) claims where data protection issues were bound up with broader claims for breach of privacy and/or confidentiality—often celebrity privacy cases; and

(2) claims which focus solely on data protection.

A further complication is raised by group litigation and representative actions, and these too are discussed below **(3.3.1.19)**.

Mixed privacy/confidentiality and data protection claims

3.3.1.5 A number of cases where compensation has been awarded for breach of the 1998 Act relate to processing by the press and also involve broader claims of breach of confidence and privacy. This makes them of somewhat limited use as a guide to damages for breach of data protection obligations alone. One example of this is the ***Naomi Campbell*** case (***Campbell v Mirror Group Newspapers Ltd*** [2002] EWCA Civ 1373; [2003] 1 All E.R. 224), where damages were awarded at first instance on a combined basis in relation to breach of confidence and breach of the Act. Naomi Campbell sued Mirror Group over publication of details of her treatment for drug addiction. Most of the case turns on the very detailed provisions in the Act exempting the press (the "special purposes" provisions dealt with at **10.5.6**) and, is therefore, of limited relevance to general considerations of damages recoverable for breaches of the DPA. At first instance, the Judge awarded Ms Campbell £3,500 both for breach of confidence and data protection without ear-marking specific amounts for each element. Of this, £1,000 was for aggravated damages in recognition of the extremely aggressive manner in which Mirror Group had handled Ms Campbell's story after her complaints for breach of confidence and data protection were brought. The Court of Appeal overturned the first instance decision. The House of Lords ([2004] UKHL 22) judgment reinstated the original award for damages for breach of confidence, but shed no more light on the data protection aspects (Hale LJ spoke at [130] the "*claim under the Data Protection Act 1998 which it is agreed adds nothing to the claim for breach of confidence*").

3.3.1.6 A sting in the tail for the defendants was that although the damages at £3,500 were small, the order for costs was not. They amounted to £1,086,295.47. A further appeal to the House of Lords on this matter of costs was dismissed (***Campbell v MGN Ltd** (No.2)* [2005] UKHL 61). Litigation does not come cheaply, and this will not be the last case where the damages are not very significant but the costs most certainly are.

3.3.1.7 Another case was that of Michael Douglas and Catherine Zeta-Jones who had paid £1 million to *OK!* magazine for control of the taking and publishing of exclusive photographs of their wedding, when a rival magazine *Hello!* had destroyed this exclusivity by taking their own unauthorised photographs and releasing them for publication (***(1) Michael Douglas; (2) Catherine Zeta-Jones; (3) Northern & Shell Plc v (1) Hello! Ltd; (2) Hola SA; (3) Eduardo Sanchez Junco; (4) The Marquesa de Varela; (5) Neneta Overseas Ltd; (6) Philip Ramey*** [2003] EWHC 786 (Ch). On these facts Lindsay J awarded damages to the Douglases of £3,750 each for distress caused by the unauthorised photographs, £7,000 each for the cost and inconvenience of having to make a hurried choice of the authorised photographs, and a nominal £50 each for the breach of the DPA. Thus, though awarded £10,800 each, only £50 of this was for the DPA breach. By contrast *OK!* was awarded £1,026,706 for loss of profit and a further £6,450 for wasted costs. There was no mention of the DPA, as it was not engaged by this part of the claim). The matter went to the Court of Appeal (***Douglas v Hello! Ltd** (No.3)* [2005] EWCA Civ 595) which upheld the award to the Douglases, but not the (non-DPA) award to *OK!*. The further appeal to the House of Lords under the title ***OBG Ltd v Allan, Douglas v Hello! Ltd, Mainstream Properties Ltd v Young*** [2007] UKHL 21 was only in respect of *Hello!*'s obligations in tort to *OK!*.

3.3.1.8 Another important privacy/confidentiality case is ***Gulati*** (***Gulati v MGN Ltd.*** [2015] EWHC 1482 Ch). Various people, some celebrities, other people who were friends or associates of celebrities, had their phones hacked consistently (often several times a day) by the staff and agents of Mirror Group Newspapers over a number of years. The publication of the material so obtained was not just deeply upsetting to the victims. It also engendered a climate of suspicion in which the victims, realising that only one or two people knew the facts the press was flaunting, came to believe that their friends, lovers or family had betrayed this material to the press—doubtless for gain. In more than one case the break-up of a marriage was at least in part attributed to the suspicion so caused. The case is significant because the judge, Mann J, included a summary of claims for breach of privacy/confidentiality and also discussed in detail the factors to form the basis of compensation. It is the leading case which gives guidance as to how compensation in such cases should be determined. Mann J notes that:

- compensation is not necessarily to be just for distress [148];
- each article published constitutes a separate cause of action [149]–[159];
- any aggravated damages are compensatory, not punitive, and may be payable in cases where the defendant's behaviour (e.g. high-handed, malicious, insulting or oppressive) justifies them [203]–[215];
- not all the claimants received aggravated damages;
- there can be possible mitigation of damages by the defendant's good behaviour—not much in the instant case [216];
- the court should consider the degree to which the material was circulated. This meant looking at the millions of copies of each paper printed and read (each copy by 2.5 people) [221].

3.3.1.9 The case is discussed almost entirely in privacy terms rather than data protection terms. Nonetheless, the factors listed could also be relevant to data protection cases—for example, looking at the number of people who have had access to the material could be relevant in the case of a personal data breach.

Claims where data protection has been the focus

3.3.1.10 For a long period, cases here were hampered by the fact that the provisions allowing for claims for compensation in the 1998 Act only applied (in most cases) where the claimant suffered damage, or damage and distress, with damage being interpreted as meaning physical harm or financial loss. As the celebrity privacy cases show, infringement of privacy (and breach of data protection) may produce significant distress—but not necessarily any financial loss or physical harm.

3.3.1.11 It was only in 2015, that the Court of Appeal, in ***Google Inc v Judith Vidal-Hall*** [2015] EWCA Civ 311, addressed this and found the 1998 Act to be out of step with the Directive 95/46 in treating "*damage*" as purely financial damage and ignoring distress unless also accompanied by damage. The court found that the UK had mis-implemented Directive 95/46 and that the requirement for damage as a pre-condition for a claim should be "*disapplied*". We are now back in step with the EU Regulation (the GDPR) since DPA 2018 s.168(1) talks of "*material and non-material damage*" and makes clear that non-material damage includes distress.

3.3.1.12 This requirement for "damage" has shaped and restricted earlier case law. We have listed some cases which act as useful reference points below (**3.3.1.13–3.3.1.18**).

3.3.1.13 ***Sean Robert Grinyer v Plymouth Hospital NHS Trust*** unreported 28 October 2011, (but summarised at *http://www.unitystreetchambers.com/blog/*) is an interesting case on a claim for damages. Mr Grinyer had a personality disorder. His then partner, who was a nurse, illegally accessed his records. She worked at the same hospital where Mr Grinyer was being treated, but in a different department. This was not only a breach of the DPA 1998 by the nurse, but also a breach of the DPA by her NHS Trust employer (i.e. a breach of its security obligations under the 7th Principle on security (now the 6th Principle) (**Ch.8**)). Mr Grinyer's condition was exacerbated by this breach and the NHS Trust's handling of his complaint, which also caused him to lose a job opportunity. HHJ Cotter awarded Mr Grinyer £12,500 for exacerbation of a pre-existing condition and £4,800 for loss of earnings.

3.3.1.14 In ***Halliday v Creation Consumer Finance Ltd*** [2013] EWCA Civ 333, the Court of Appeal considered the amount of compensation to be awarded for distress caused by incorrect disclosure of information to a credit reference agency. Mr Halliday purchased a TV and, in the process, entered into a credit agreement with Creation Consumer Finance (CCF). There were proceedings between Mr Halliday and CCF, partly in relation to breaches of data protection legislation, which led to the credit agreement being discharged and to a consent order being approved, whereby CCF agreed to delete Mr Halliday's data and to provide him with a list of third parties to whom his data had been released. CCF also agreed to ensure deletion of Mr Halliday's data by any third party to whom it had released the data. Mr Halliday discovered that CCF had made incorrect entries on its system and had provided these to the credit reference agency Equifax. Equifax, in turn, then showed Mr Halliday as owing amounts to CCF. So CCF, far from doing what it had said it would do in the consent order, had shared inaccurate information with a credit reference agency. Mr Halliday sought fairly substantial amounts in compensation from CCF. He suggested that the Court of Appeal should look to cases awarding compensation for discrimination as a reference point. However, the Court of Appeal rejected this approach, noting that in discrimination cases there was usually an element of loss of equality of opportunity which was not the case here [26]. The court accepted that it should make an award, but felt that it was not the intention of the legislation that awards for distress should be substantial [36]: a notional £1 for damage was awarded and £750 for distress [48].

3.3.1.15 ***Woolley and Woolley v Akbar or Akram*** 2017 S.L.T. (Sh Ct) 175; Sheriffdom of Lothian & Borders at Edinburgh [2017] SC EDIN 7 is also worth noting. The pursuers and defender shared a two-story semi-detached dwelling, the pursuers having the upper storey and the defender the lower storey. There was also a garden divided roughly between them. The defender ran her property as a guest house and did not live there. Relations between the parties broke down in 2013, both installing CCTV equipment. That of the pursuers focused only on the exterior of their own property (car-parking area in front, passage and external access stair to the side, and garden at the back). The defender's system by contrast covered much of the pursuers' property from four cameras, and was further supported by an audio recording system with four boxes. Every word uttered in the pursuers' garden was recorded on this. CCTV and audio tapes were kept for five days before being overwritten. There was no notice either at the scene or to interested parties like the pursuers as to the existence or purpose of the systems.

3.3.1.16 The court found the defender was the data controller of the systems. The pursuers had apparently sought copies of the data under DPA 1998 s.7 (Subject Access Request 6.5), and when the defender did not respond engaged the ICO. The defender made "minimal disclosure" to the ICO and wrongly asserted she lived at the property. About this time the defender "*notified*" with the ICO as data controller (as required by ss.16–26 of the 1998 Act). It is not clear what if any action the ICO took.

3.3.1.17 The court evidently was not asked for an injunction but was asked to award damages. The court described the systems as intrusive, excessive and unjustified and with no legitimate purpose. The response to the pursuers' s.7 requests was inadequate. The systems were unfair. There was no data retention policy. There was no lawful basis for processing. The data were excessive and kept for longer than necessary. So, multiple provisions of the legislation were infringed. The pursuers claimed a nominal £10 a day each for the intrusion. The court noted that there was little guidance on the amount to claim. "*This aspect would benefit from an authoritative decision*" [114]. The court awarded the requested £10 a day for 912 days less the four weeks when the pursuers were absent on holiday—£8,634 for each pursuer (£17,268 in total) with interest from the date of judgment. There is no mention of an injunction, though the systems appear not to be still in use. It may be that the ICO had closed the systems by an enforcement order.

3.3.1.18 In ***TLT v Secretary of State for the Home Department*** [2016] EWHC 2217 (QB), an asylum seeker whose personal data including name was inadvertently posted on the Home Office website brought an action on behalf of himself and also his family who, although not named were identifiable from his name. Mitting J considered that the claimant and his wife should be awarded £12,500 each and their teenage daughter, who had to a degree been protected from the consequences of this personal data breach, should receive £2,500. The case was appealed but the quantum of damages was not queried. It is hard to think of a more worrying and distressing breach of data protection: the case suggests that awards for compensation here will, indeed, be modest.

Group litigation and representative proceedings

3.3.1.19 Recently, there have been cases involving groups of claimants for breach of data protection or privacy laws. ***Gulati*** is an example of this, although for breach of privacy rather than data protection, the claimants being people whose phones had been hacked by Mirror Group Newspapers. ***Wm Morrison Supermarkets Plc v Various Claimants*** [2018] EWCA Civ 2339, is also an example of this. This was a claim on behalf of some 5,518 Morrisons' employees (out of a total workforce of almost 100,000) whose salary information (including bank account details) had been broadcast over the web by a disaffected ex-employee. The member of staff was jailed for eight years for offences including under the Computer Misuse Act as well as s.55 of the DPA 1998. The issue in the group action was the extent to which Morrisons as a company and the erstwhile employer of the member of staff were liable to their own staff. The first instance judge and the Court of Appeal distinguished between direct liability, which could only be found if Morrisons had failed in their observance of data protection law and particularly security under the old 7th Principle of the 1998 Act (still of course highly relevant under arts 32–34 of the GDPR), and indirect or vicarious liability where the issues were the extent to which the tortious action by the member of staff could be related to his work. The courts found no reason to criticise Morrisons' security arrangements except in one minor way which neither caused nor contributed to the tort. But the first instance judge and the Court of Appeal found Morrisons vicariously liable in that the tort was effectively close enough to the member of staff's employment duties. Morrisons has stated that it intends to appeal to the Supreme Court.

3.3.1.20 The circumstances which led to the ***Vidal Hall*** case are also behind an interesting representative action, ***Richard Lloyd v Google LLC*** [2018] EWHC 2599 (QB). Both cases were triggered by the workaround deployed by Google between 2011–2012 which allowed it to override settings in Apple's Safari browser software, so as to collect data about users. In ***Vidal Hall*** the courts determined that compensation had to be available for distress alone, irrespective of whether individuals had suffered damage. In ***Richard Lloyd*** the claimant sought compensation—not just on his own behalf but in a representative capacity on behalf of a class of residents in England and Wales said to be affected by the Safari workaround. (The case was brought as a representative action, rather than as group litigation—the practical difference being that group litigation requires a group litigation order to be made by the court to proceed, whereas a representative action does not, although the courts can control such actions at a later date.) Representative proceedings can be brought in reliance on CPR r.19.6, where the person starting the proceedings has the same interest as others in the claim [42]–[44]). The claimant did not advance any evidence of financial loss or even of distress. In the letter of claim, a figure of £750 per person was advanced—given the size of the potential class, Google estimated the liability to be somewhere between £1 and £3 billion [4]. All parties accepted that Google's actions were in breach of data protection legislation: what was at issue was whether this should automatically give rise to compensation—i.e. whether infringement has to be compensated either per se [23] or whether to deprive Google of the profits it made out of the Safari workaround [24]. The claimant had secured funding for the case through litigation funders in an amount of up to £15.5 million.

3.3.1.21 In order to bring proceedings, the claimant needed the court's permission to serve notice of claim on Google out of the jurisdiction. Warby J rejected the claimant's argument that breach of data protection legislation must—as a matter of principle—be compensated. He took the view that the claimant had to show that the breach of the legislation had actually caused some distress; if the claimant could not show this, then other remedies (such as deletion or correction of data) may be appropriate, but compensation would not be awarded [56]. The judge accepted that loss of control over data *may* give grounds for compensation—but the person alleging this would have to actually advance a case that the breach had caused some form of irritation or interference with their life and the claimant had provided no evidence to this effect [59]. Warby J also held that there was no authority to award damages to censure Google [75] or to deprive it of profits [76]. Warby J also considered that the claimant should not be allowed to proceed with a representative action on the basis that he would not have the same interests as others in the class—the class was expressed to be everyone using Safari during 2011–2012, but not everyone in that class would have suffered any damage (interpreted as including distress) as they would react to the data protection breaches differently [89] and would have made use of Safari in different ways and amounts [91]. Warby J also thought it would not be possible to define the class with certainty [94].

3.3.1.22 Warby J noted that "*the main beneficiaries of any award at the end of this litigation would be the funders and the lawyers, by a considerable margin*" [102]. He denied permission to serve proceedings out of the jurisdiction on the basis that there was no real prospect of success for the claimant—both because no damage was suffered or claimed and because the court would inevitably refuse to allow this type of representative claim to continue.

3.3.1.23 The case is an interesting cautionary tale: although the claim here failed, it does illustrate well the types of large claims which could be brought where large numbers of users are affected (for example, in a personal data breach) and the likely costs of dealing with such litigation. It also shows that litigation funders are alive to these possibilities: this is unlikely to be the last case of this type.

The future under the GDPR

3.3.1.24 Under the GDPR art.82, a data subject who has suffered material or non-material damage as a result of an infringement of the Regulation is entitled to compensation. The provisions of art.82 are supplemented by s.167 in the DPA 2018. Section 168 addresses claims for compensation for data protection legislation other than the GDPR. Article 82 contains many innovations, so is worth reading in full. It provides as follows:

> "1. *Any person who has suffered material or non-material damage as a result of an infringement of this Regulation shall have the right to receive compensation from the controller or processor for the damage suffered.*
>
> 2. *Any controller involved in processing shall be liable for the damage caused by processing which infringes this Regulation. A processor shall be liable for damage caused by processing only where it has not complied with obligations of this Regulation specifically directed to processors or where it has acted outside or contrary to lawful instructions of the controller.*

3. *A controller or processor shall be exempt from liability under paragraph 2 if it proves that it is not in any way responsible for the event giving rise to the damage.*
4. *Where more than one controller or processor, or both a controller and a processor, are involved in the same processing and where they are, under paragraphs 2 and 3, responsible for any damage caused by processing, each controller and processor shall be held liable for the entire damage in order to ensure effective compensation of the data subject.*
5. *Where a controller or processor has, in accordance with paragraph 4, paid full compensation for the damage suffered, that controller or processor shall be entitled to claim back from the other controllers or processors involved in the same processing that part of the compensation corresponding to their part of responsibility for the damage, in accordance with the conditions set out in paragraph 2".*

3.3.1.25 The following key points should be noted.

(1) Under the 1998 Act, claims could only be brought against a controller. The GDPR allows claims to be brought against a processor, but recognises that the scope of responsibility of controllers and processors is different.

(2) The GDPR recognises that where multiple parties are involved in processing an individual's data, it can be difficult for the individual to know who is to blame. Accordingly, the GDPR establishes the principle of compensate first and allocate responsibility afterwards. In effect, a type of joint and several liability is created. This could apply both as between controller and processor and between joint—or indeed, separate—controllers.

(3) To further tip the scales in favour of the individual, the burden of proof is reversed. The controller or processor is to be liable unless they can show that they were not in any way responsible.

(4) However, causation and the need to show that damage or non-material damage flowed from an infringement of the GDPR remains (the point addressed in ***Richard Lloyd***).

3.3.1.26 Article 80 of the GDPR provides that individuals can mandate a not-for-profit body or organisation to represent them—both in the courts and in relation to the Information Commissioner. The Article also allows Member States—if they so wish—to provide that such a body can receive compensation on their behalf.

3.3.1.27 Section 168 makes provision for compensation to be awarded in pursuance of this provision. Section 187(2) and following introduces equivalent provisions in relation to data protection legislation other than the GDPR. Section 188 allows for secondary legislation to be introduced relating to the management of claims by such representative bodies. It seems that the Government has some nervousness as to how such provisions will operate, as s.189 provides that operation of these provisions must be reviewed 30 months after they come into force. This review must, in particular, look at how the provisions address children's rights and whether bodies should be authorised to bring claims on behalf of children even when they are not mandated to this by data subjects, which is a possibility anticipated by art.80(2) of the GDPR.

3.3.1.28 Article 81 of the GDPR visualises the circumstances where two or more EEA Member States are dealing with the same data protection subject matter. In those circumstances, a Member State Court should contact the court in the other jurisdiction(s) to seek confirmation of whether in fact the subject matter is the same in the two cases. If they are, the proceedings may be suspended to take account of this, and a court may even decline jurisdiction if the court in the other member state can establish jurisdiction and its law permits the two cases to be consolidated. How this will work out for the UK post-Brexit remains to be seen.

3.4 ENFORCEMENT BY THE INFORMATION COMMISSIONER

3.4.1 Introduction

3.4.1.1 The first thing to notice is that, whereas under the DPA 1998, only a data controller could face disciplinary action, under the GDPR a processor may also be liable. Article 58 (which we shall consider in detail shortly) lists the actions that may be taken by the Commissioner against a controller *or processor* (e.g. art.58(1)(a) and (2)(a), etc.).

3.4.1.2 The second point to note is that, although we talk above about individuals pursuing claims via the courts, in practice an individual who is affected by a breach of data protection legislation is more likely to complain to the Information Commissioner and to ask the Commissioner to investigate the matter, rather than initiate proceedings themselves. This is cost-free for the individual and also gives the individual the benefit of the Commissioner's (now extensive) investigatory powers. So, by DPA 2018 s.165 (building on GDPR art.57(1)(f) and (2) and art.77), a data subject can complain to the Commissioner about any infringement of the GDPR.

3.4.1.3 The third point to note is that the Commissioner's powers to take enforcement action in relation to the Privacy and Electronic Communications (EC Directive) Regulations 2003 (SI 2003/2426), are dealt with separately from her other powers. These Regulations, often called the PECR, deal with such matters as unsolicited telephone calls, faxes, emails (spam) and text messages. In the case of a breach of the PECR, the powers granted to the Information Commissioner remain those under the previous legislation, the 1998 Act. The PECR and the associated enforcement powers for the Commissioner are considered in more detail at **7.4**.

3.4.1.4 The Commissioner's powers have been greatly extended by the GDPR and DPA 2018. GDPR art.58 which defines the powers of a supervisory authority (i.e. the Commissioner) must be the starting point. They are divided into investigative powers (art.58(1)) and corrective powers (art.58(2)). What the GDPR calls "corrective powers" are called "enforcement" in the DPA 2018 ss.142–179, and include fines which are called "penalties" in the DPA 2018 ss.155–159. "Infringements" are called "failures" in the DPA 2018. The Commissioner can impose a penalty on an organisation which does not comply with a notice exercising her powers (s.155(1)(b)) (see also **3.4.3**).

3.4.1.5 Before we consider these two types of powers in more detail, it is worth pausing to look at the Information Commissioner's *Regulatory Action Policy*. The Commissioner is required, by s.160 of the DPA 2018, to publish guidance as to how she will exercise her powers and the *Regulatory Action Policy* meets this requirement. The Policy has to be laid before Parliament for approval under a negative resolution procedure (that is, it will be approved unless there is a resolution not to approve it) and the Commissioner's Policy was laid before Parliament on 19 July 2018 and it was approved on 11 September 2018.

3.4.1.6 Section 160 specifies some of the content of the Policy—for example, stipulating that it must include guidance as to when the Commissioner will consider it appropriate to issue formal notices, and when urgency provisions would be invoked. So the Policy is important as it shows what we can expect from the Commissioner and her staff. As the Policy notes (p.3), this type of predictability is important. In particular, it is inherently important to know the factors which will be taken into account, and that enforcement will not be arbitrary or random; this matters for particular investigations, as organisations can see how their specific factors line up against the criteria called out by the Commissioner as significant; it can also be essential in training and awareness raising—for example, so organisations can train their staff on what to expect from assessment notices.

3.4.1.7 The Policy includes guidance on each of the investigatory and enforcement powers available to the Commissioner: much of this is repetitive of content in the GDPR, but what we think are the more interesting comments from these sections are considered in the appropriate sections below **(3.4.2–3.4.3).** In addition, the Policy also includes insights into the Commissioner's overall priorities and approach—and we have summarised these here.

Five objectives

3.4.1.8 The Commissioner (p.6) has five overarching objectives which her staff must seek to meet when considering and undertaking action. These are:

(1) to respond swiftly and effectively to breaches of legislation for which the Commissioner has enforcement responsibility—focusing on those involving highly sensitive information; adversely affecting large groups of individuals; or impacting vulnerable individuals;

(2) to be effective, proportionate and dissuasive (this objective comes straight from art.83 of the GDPR), targeting the most serious powers for those suspected of repeated or wilful misconduct or serious failures; or where formal regulatory action will have a deterrent effect;

(3) to promote compliance by promoting good practice and by providing targeted advice;

(4) to be pro-active in identifying and mitigating new or emerging risks—either from technology of social change;

(5) to work constructively with other regulators and interested parties.

3.4.1.9 On being selective, the Commissioner (p.10) largely repeats criteria mentioned in art.83 (imposition of fines or penalties and considered below (**3.4.3.17–3.4.3.53**)). However, in addition to these she also declares that she will have regard to whether or not:

- any critical national infrastructure or service is involved;
- whether the issue is representative of similar issues affecting a particular sector or group which makes it more important to address it; and
- the cost of measures to mitigate risk.

She also mentions the importance of providing an effective deterrent—i.e. that there is an inherent interest in regulatory action being taken.

Types of breaches

3.4.1.10 We have considered the Commissioner's powers—and what the *Regulatory Action Policy* says about them—below (**3.4.2–3.4.3**). The powers available to the Commissioner sometimes depend on the particular provision of data protection legislation which has been breached and, at s.149, the DPA 2018 groups the breaches into four types of provision. Accordingly, before looking at these powers in detail it is as well to consider the particular kinds of failure by a controller or processor identified in DPA 2018 s.149 as follows:

3.4.1.11 The first group (s.149(2)) is:

- a failure to comply with the principles, the rules for special categories of personal data or personal data relating to criminal convictions and offences (GDPR Ch.2 arts 5–11, and DPA 2018 Pt 3 Ch.2, Pt 4 Ch.2);
- transparency, privacy notices and the rights of the data subject (GDPR arts 12–22 and DPA 2018 Pts 2 and 3);
- controller's and processor's responsibilities, including security, records or processing, data protection impact assessments, prior consultation with the Commissioner and appointing a data protection officer (GDPR arts 25–39 and DPA 2018 ss.64–65);
- requirements to communicate details of a personal data breach to the Commissioner (GDPR arts 33–34 and DPA 2018 ss.67–68 and 108); and
- details of transfers to third countries, etc. (GDPR arts 44–49 and DPA 2018 ss.73–78 or 109).

This first group is far and away the most important, and most of the failures we shall discuss refer to this group. For ease of reference, we have referred to this group as "substantive breaches" in the remainder of this chapter.

3.4.1.12 The second type of failure under DPA 2018 s.149(3) is where a body which has a remit to monitor codes of conduct has failed, or is failing, to comply with GDPR art.41 on monitoring approved codes of conduct (**13.1.2**).

3.4.1.13 The third type of failure under DPA 2018 s.149(4) relates to certification providers where:

- the provider does not meet the requirements for accreditation;
- has failed or is failing to comply with an obligation under GDPR arts 42 or 43 on certification of controllers or processors;
- has failed or is failing to comply with any other provision of the GDPR, whether as certification provider or otherwise.

3.4.1.14 The fourth type of failure under DPA 2018 s.149(5) is where a controller has failed to pay the Commissioner's fees under DPA 2018 s.137 (see **3.4.3.35**).

3.4.2 The Commissioner's investigative powers

3.4.2.1 The Information Commissioner has the following investigative powers:

(1) to issue information notices (requiring the provision of information);

(2) to issue assessment notices (requiring access to premises or documents so as to allow the Commissioner to conduct an assessment of compliance); and

(3) to obtain a search warrant allowing her staff to enter premises, to inspect and seize materials.

Each of these powers is considered below (**3.4.2.5–3.4.2.32**).

3.4.2.2 There are largely identical exemptions from each of these powers where the information sought is protected by legal advice privilege or litigation privilege (**10.5.4**) and relates to advice or proceedings connected with data protection legislation, or where complying with the notice would infringe the privileges of either House of Parliament. There are also exemptions protecting the interests of those processing personal data for the special purposes (i.e. for purposes of journalism, literary or artistic purposes)—here the precise details of the exemption do vary slightly and so they are considered below (**3.4.2.9**).

3.4.2.3 There are also parallel offences of knowingly, or recklessly, making statements which are false in a material respect in relation to information notices and when the Commissioner exercises a search warrant (at s.144 in relation to information notices and at Sch.15 para.15(2) in relation to search warrants).

Under DPA 2018 s.148, there is also a ban on destroying or otherwise disposing of or concealing, blocking, falsifying all or part of any information, document, equipment or other material, or causing or permitting such destroying, etc. There is a possible defence to such actions if the destruction etc., would have happened anyway in the absence of the person being given the notice. This might arise where the data was from a CCTV system which was automatically overwritten on a regular one-month cycle.

3.4.2.4 There are also provisions, in relation to each of the powers, setting out that, generally, the Commissioner cannot use the information she has obtained in evidence against someone as part of a prosecution for an offence under the DPA 2018 (for example, this is set out at s.143(8) in relation to information notices). The Commissioner *is* allowed to use this information if the individual tries to adduce as evidence a statement which is inconsistent with what the Commissioner has been told. The provision against self-incrimination also only applies to prosecutions for *offences* under the DPA 2018: there is nothing to stop the Commissioner using the information obtained as evidence when she imposes a penalty, or issues an enforcement notice against the controller or processor.

Information notices

3.4.2.5 The investigative powers of the Commissioner are listed in art.58(1). The first of these is the power to seek information:

> "*(a) to order the controller and the processor, and, where applicable, the controller's or the processor's representative, to provide any information it requires for the performance of its* [the Commissioner's] *tasks*"

3.4.2.6 These simple words are amplified by ss.142–144 of the DPA 2018, which describe the procedures for seeking this information by means of an information notice (corresponding to DPA 1998 s.43). Section 142(1) makes clear there are different types of information the Commissioner is permitted to demand from a controller or processor. The first is:

> "*information that the Commissioner reasonably requires for the purposes of carrying out the Commissioner's functions under the data protection legislation*".

and the second is the Commissioner's power to

> "*require any person to provide the Commissioner with information that the Commissioner reasonably requires for the purposes of—*
>
> *(i) investigating a suspected failure of a type described in section 149(2)* [i.e. substantive breaches of the legislation, see **3.4.1.11** above] *or a suspected offence under this Act, or*

(ii) determining whether the processing of personal data is carried out by an individual in the course of a purely personal or household activity."

This last is of course an exemption as being outside the scope of the GDPR under art.2(2)(c)—see also **11.3.2.7** below)

3.4.2.7 The information notice from the Commissioner to the controller or processor (or to his representative if he is outside the EU (s.142(9)) must state:

- whether it is given under s.142(1)(a), (b)(i) or (b)(ii);
- why the Commissioner requires the information;
- the consequences of failure to provide the information—i.e. that the Commissioner may seek an information order (**3.4.2.2** below), impose a penalty, or even prosecute the possible commission of a criminal offence under s.144 (see **3.2.5.2** above); and
- the controller's or processor's right of appeals etc. under ss.162 and 164 ((ss.142(2) and (4))—see **1.3.8**).

3.4.2.8 It may:

- specify or describe particular information or a category of information;
- specify the form in which the information must be provided;
- specify the time at which, or the period within which, the information must be provided, though this must leave sufficient time for an appeal by the controller or processor (s.142(6));
- the place where the information must be provided (s.142(3)); and
- whether, and if so, why, the Commissioner thinks the information is required urgently (s.142(7)). Ordinarily, a controller or processor need not reply to an information notice until the time allowed for appeal has expired—however if the Commissioner asserts that compliance is urgently required, then this provision is disapplied and a response must be provided within the timescales specified in the notice (provided at least 24 hours' notice is given).

3.4.2.9 In addition to the exemptions mentioned above (**3.4.2.2**), there are exemptions as follows:

- at s.143(1) an information notice in respect of personal data processed for the special purposes (journalism—see **10.5.6**) can only be issued where the Commissioner either suspects, or needs additional information to determine, or already has made a written determination that the data is not being processed only for the special purposes or not being processed with a view to publishing something not previously published, and the Commissioner must provide this written notice of determination to the controller or processor. This determination cannot take effect until the period for an appeal has passed without an appeal (s.174(3)–(6); and

- at s.143(6) and (7), if providing the information would reveal evidence of the commission of an offence, other than an offence under the DPA 2018, s.5 of the Perjury Act 1911, s.44 of the Criminal Law (Consolidation) Act 1995 or art.10 of the Perjury (Northern Ireland) Order 1979 (these last three all refer to false declarations under oath).

In addition, by s.142(8), the Commissioner may cancel an information notice.

3.4.2.10 *The Regulatory Action Policy* suggests (p.15) that the Commissioner may serve an information notice – as opposed to informally asking a controller or processor for information – where her staff think this is justified based on the risk of harm posed to individuals; where it would be useful to require a formal response within a set time period; where they want to test responses—specifically because making a false statement in response to an information notice is an offence; and where there is a public interest in the response. In other words, the Commissioner may start out asking for information in a less formal way—but if an organisation does not respond or the Commissioner thinks the organisation is being less than trustworthy with its responses, she will resort to formal procedures. In a high profile or significant investigation this may also (possibly) be the approach from the start (p.15).

3.4.2.11 As an example of a situation where an urgent response may be required, the Policy gives the example of a personal data breach, where requiring an early report on the breach may allow the Information Commissioner to advise the controller on notification to individuals and mitigation of the breach (p.16).

3.4.2.12 The Commissioner's ability to serve information notices under ss.142 and 143 has been considered in ***Doorstep Dispensaree v Information Commissioner*** [2019] UKFTT 2018/265 (GRC). The Commissioner had received information about the appellant from the Medicines and Healthcare Products Regulatory Authority and commenced an investigation. The appellant refused to provide the requested information so the Commissioner served an information notice under s.142, requiring the information to be provided. The appellant appealed the notice, arguing that the notice was invalid or void because it was written in general terms, so could require the provision of incriminating information. The First-Tier Tribunal General Regulatory Tribunal rejected this, explaining that the effect of s.143(6) was to allow a person to raise with the Commissioner the possibility that information would be incriminating and should not be provided. There was no requirement for the Commissioner to anticipate this and draft the notice in a way that would avoid this: indeed, she would likely not have the necessary information to be able to do this. The Tribunal did, however, note that when the Commissioner served an information notice, she should include information alerting the recipient to the provisions of s.143(6).

Information orders

3.4.2.13 The consequences of failure to comply with an information notice may, if the Commissioner applies to a Court, result in the Court making an order to the controller or processor to provide the information; and any other information which the Court is satisfied the Commissioner requires to enable her to comply with her reasons for seeking information under s.142(2)(b).

3.4.2.14 This information order may specify the form of the information, timescale for and place of compliance (s.145(3)).

Assessment notices

3.4.2.15 The Commissioner's second investigative power under GDPR art.58(1) is as follows:

> "*(b) to carry out investigations in the form of data protection audits*"

and, linked to this;

> "*(e) to obtain, from the controller and the processor, access to all personal data and to all information necessary for the performance of its tasks*".

This is referred to as an assessment notice under DPA 2018 ss.146–147.

3.4.2.16 Section 146(1) allows the Commissioner to serve a designated controller or processor with an assessment notice for the purpose of enabling the Commissioner to carry out an assessment of whether the controller or processor has complied or is complying with data protection legislation. The limitation whereby, under the 1998 Act, assessment applied only to government departments or public authorities has gone. Assessments can apply to any controller or processor.

3.4.2.17 There is nothing in the legislation to suggest what may trigger an assessment notice, though it is reasonable to suppose that it may often arise from a complaint by a data subject, but equally it may have some quite different origin—e.g. a press story. The *Regulatory Action Policy* (p.17) notes that an assessment notice may be issued in *any* investigation—however the Commissioner will have regard to what is appropriate and proportionate, in particular considering:

- where the Commissioner has concluded, through regulatory action, that there is a probability that personal data is not being processed in a compliant manner, together with a likelihood of damage or distress;
- it is necessary to verify compliance with an enforcement notice;
- communications with the controller, or information (e.g. in the press) suggest that they are not complying; and
- they have failed to respond to an information notice within an appropriate time.

3.4.2.18 Putting these factors together, ordinarily, an organisation should not expect to receive an assessment notice "out-of-the blue" from the Information Commissioner (save in the most high-profile and serious matters). Usually, there will already have been some kind of investigation—coupled either with a degree of lack of co-operation, or an indicator that the matter could have a more serious impact on individuals. However, the Commissioner's comment that assessment notices *may* be used on any investigation is designed to keep options open for her staff.

3.4.2.19 The assessment notice requires the controller or processor to:

a) permit the Commissioner to enter specified premises;

b) direct the Commissioner to any documents on the premises that are of a specified description;

c) assist the Commissioner to view any information of a specified description that is capable of being viewed using equipment on the premises;

d) to comply with any request from the Commissioner for a copy (in such form as may be requested)—

 (i) of any of the documents to which the Commissioner is directed;

 (ii) of any of the information which the Commissioner is assisted to view;

e) direct the Commissioner to any equipment or other material on the premises which is of a specified description;

f) permit the Commissioner to inspect or examine any of the documents, information, equipment or material to which the Commissioner is directed or which the Commissioner is assisted to view;

g) provide the Commissioner with an explanation of such documents, information, equipment or material;

h) permit the Commissioner to observe the processing of any personal data that takes place on the premises;

i) make available for interview by the Commissioner a specified number of persons of a specified description who process personal data on behalf of the controller, not exceeding the number who are willing to be interviewed. These words in (i) "*on behalf of the controller*" would seem also to apply to any relevant processor.

3.4.2.20 The assessment notice must include for each requirement imposed by the notice;

- the time at which the requirement is to be complied with; or
- the period during which the requirement is to be complied with;

- the consequences of any failure to comply;
- particulars of the right of appeal under ss.162 and 164. The times specified must allow sufficient time for the controller to appeal.

3.4.2.21 There is a mechanism for an urgent assessment under s.146(8)—this requires the controller or processor to comply within seven days beginning with the date the notice is given. The Commissioner must state in the assessment notice that the requirement to comply is urgent and give the Commissioner's reasons for so deciding.

3.4.2.22 Section 146(9) provides for what we might call a super-urgent assessment if

- the Commissioner states that there are reasonable grounds for believing that a substantive breach has occurred or is occurring, or an offence has been or is being committed—see **3.4.2.7** above;
- the assessment notice specifies the nature of the suspected failure or offence;
- does not apply to the domestic premises;
- states that in the Commissioner's opinion compliance must be in less than seven days; and
- gives the Commissioner's reasons for reaching that conclusion.

In this case, there is no minimum time limit for the assessment notice to apply. The Commissioner could, therefore, use this super-urgent assessment notice provision as a way to obtain immediate access to premises. Whereas the escalation from an information notice is for the Commissioner to obtain an information order from the court, the escalation from an assessment notice is for the Commissioner to obtain a warrant: this allows similar access to premises and documents (see below (**3.4.2.28**)), but also allows such reasonable force as is necessary to gain entry.

3.4.2.23 The *Regulatory Action Policy* notes that, amongst other factors the Commissioner may use this super-urgent procedure when urgent investigation is necessary to prevent or limit the risk of serious harm to individuals or serious intrusion into their privacy, or when urgent investigation is needed to prevent sanitisation or destruction of evidence (p.17).

3.4.2.24 The Commissioner has the power to cancel an assessment notice by a written notice to the controller on whom it was served (s.146(10)). Where an assessment notice is served on a processor, the Commissioner must, "*so far as reasonably practicable*", serve a copy on each controller for whom the processor processes personal data. The Commissioner will usually need to get that information from the processor – if necessary by an information notice.

3.4.2.25 Exemptions and restrictions on compliance with assessment notices are set out in s.147 and, in addition to those discussed at (**3.4.2.2**) above, include:

- the data is processed for the special purposes (journalism, etc.—see **10.5.6** below);
- the controller or processor receiving the assessment notice is a security body, as specified under Freedom of Information Act 2000 s.23(3), or the Office for Standards in Education (Ofsted) Children's Services and Skills in respect of data of its functions under s.5(1)(a) of the Care Standards Act 2000.

3.4.2.26 The *Regulatory Action Policy* has a useful list of documents and information "*which define and explain how obligations have been met under the legislation and the governance controls in place to measure compliance*" and which, therefore, the Commissioner may require access to as part of an assessment notice. This (non-exhaustive) list comprises (p.18):

- strategies;
- policies;
- procedures;
- guidance;
- codes of practice;
- training material;
- protocols;
- frameworks;
- memoranda of understanding;
- contracts;
- privacy statements;
- privacy impact assessments;
- control data;
- job descriptions.

3.4.2.27 To these an organisation should add its record of processing activities (GDPR art.30), legitimate interest assessments (GDPR art.6) and any documentation determining whether or not a data protection officer is needed (GDPR art.37, **1.3.7**). A useful precaution would be for an organisation to ensure that as and when it creates any of the documents above (**3.4.2.26**), that they are added to a data protection compliance resource, so as to allow them to be provided if needed, and with a minimum of disruption. Of course, being able to put one's hands easily and quickly on such documentation will tell its own story about the organisation's approach to compliance, by comparison with having to hunt around to produce materials.

Summary of rights of entry and inspection

3.4.2.28 In addition to the powers of entry conferred by assessment notices (DPA 2018 ss.146–147 and **3.4.2.14**), the Commissioner has powers of entry and inspection on warrant issued by a circuit judge (s.154 and Sch.15).

3.4.2.29 The Commissioner may apply to a circuit judge for a warrant of entry and inspection if:

(1) the Commissioner reasonably believes that a controller or processor has contravened or is contravening one of the substantive provisions of the DPA 2018 (**3.4.2.7**) or an offence under the DPA 2018 has been or is being committed, and that evidence of the contravention or offence will be found on the premises or can be viewed using equipment on the premises; or

(2) the Commissioner certifies on oath that that a controller or processor has failed to comply with a requirement imposed by an assessment notice.

The warrant will authorise the Commissioner to enter the premises, to search them, to inspect, examine, operate and test equipment found there, and to inspect and seize documents and other material.

3.4.2.30 Usually, the Commissioner must give seven days' notice in writing to the occupier of the premises before seeking a warrant. A warrant will then only be issued if access has been unreasonably refused or, the occupier unreasonably refused to comply with the search (Sch.15 para.4).

3.4.2.31 Some readers may recall the photographs of the Commissioner's staff entering the premises of Cambridge Analytica exercising search warrants. They may also recall that there was some delay before the Commissioner's staff were able to do this. This experience led to late amendments to the Data Protection Bill—resulting in a provision that the requirement for seven days' notice does not apply if the judge is satisfied that compliance with the notice requirement would defeat the object of the entry or the Commissioner urgently requires access to the premises. Warrants must be exercised within seven days of the date of issue.

3.4.2.32 Schedule 15 para.5 requires individuals to explain documents or material found on the premises. Paragraph 16 provides that such explanations may not generally be used in evidence against that person—there are exceptions for perjury and related matters and if the individual later seeks to admit evidence which is inconsistent with what was said whilst the warrant was being exercised.

3.4.3 The Commissioner's corrective powers

3.4.3.1 The GDPR art.58(2) lists the Information Commissioner's corrective powers. They are:

(a) to issue warnings to a controller or processor that intended processing is likely to infringe the GDPR;

(b) to reprimand a controller or processor for an infringement;

(c) to order a controller or processor to comply with a data subject's rights;

(d) to order a controller or processor to bring operations into compliance with the GDPR, with ability to specify how and within what period;

(e) to order a controller to communicate a personal data breach to a data subject;

(f) to ban, temporarily or permanently, particular processing;

(g) to order rectification, erasure or restriction under arts 16, 17 and 18, and to order notification of such actions to those to whom the personal data have been disclosed under arts 17(2) and 19;

(h) to withdraw or not issue a certification or to order a certification body to do that;

(i) to impose a fine pursuant to art.83, in addition to or instead of actions in art.58(2); and

(j) to order the suspension of the flow of personal data to a third country or international organisation.

3.4.3.2 Section 115(2) of the DPA 2018 makes general reference to these powers (and to the tasks allocated to the supervisory authority by art.57 of the GDPR). In the above **(3.4.3.1)** list powers (a) and (b) do not call for any special comment and are not specifically addressed in the DPA 2018, beyond the general cross reference to the GDPR in s.115(2). Section 115 provides that the remaining powers are all to be exercised exclusively through the powers granted to the Information Commissioner to issue Enforcement Notices (art.58(2)(c)–(g) and (j)—see **3.4.3.32**), and to issue penalties (art.58(2)(i)—see **3.4.3.17**).

Enforcement notices

3.4.3.3 The DPA 2018 ss.149–153 sets out the rules relating to enforcement notices. As mentioned at **3.4.1.11–3.4.1.14** above, the four main types of infringement are in summary:

- failure to comply with most of the provisions of the GDPR relevant to controllers or processors (arts 5–39, 73–78 and 109) (which we have referred to as substantive breaches);
- failure of a monitoring body to comply with art.41 on codes;
- failure to comply with art.43 on certification; and
- failure to pay fees dues to the ICO under DPA 2018 s.137.

3.4.3.4 The Commissioner may serve an enforcement notice on a controller or processor if the Commissioner is satisfied that the controller or processor has failed or is failing to comply in respect of the matters in the preceding paragraph. This notice may require the controller to take, or refrain from taking, certain steps. (A notice may even require both refraining from one type of action and implementing another.) The notice is, therefore, akin to an injunction. There are also urgency procedures.

3.4.3.5 In deciding whether to serve an enforcement notice, the Commissioner is required to consider whether compliance with the Enforcement Notice would be an appropriate way of remedying the failure. The Secretary of State may by Regulation give the Commissioner enforcement powers in respect of other kinds of failure (s.149(6)–(8)). In the *Regulatory Action Policy* (p.22), the Commissioner explains that they will be issued where specific corrective action (or prevention) is required—and examples are given of repeated failure to meet information rights, obligations or timescales (for example, repeatedly delayed access requests); or where transfer of data to a third country fails to meet legislative requirements.

3.4.3.6 The enforcement notice must identify the failure and give the Commissioner's reasons for reaching the opinion that there is a failure. In the case of the first type of failure (s.149(2) infringement of the GDPR's obligations on controllers and processors), the Commissioner must consider whether the failure has caused, or is likely to cause, any person damage or distress. The Commissioner's powers include banning all processing of personal data by the controller or processor or banning the processing of a particular subset of personal data defined by one or more of its description, purpose or time of processing (s.150(1)–(4)).

3.4.3.7 The enforcement notice must include (s.150(5)–(7)):

- consequences of failure to comply;
- the controller's or processor's rights of appeal under ss.162 and 164; and
- a time for compliance provided it leaves time for any appeal.

3.4.3.8 There is a mechanism for an urgent enforcement notice, which requires the Commissioner to state why she thinks the matter is urgent (s.150(8)). There is also a power for the Commissioner to cancel or vary an enforcement notice (s.153).

3.4.3.9 In s.151, special conditions attach to enforcement notices seeking to compel a controller or processor to rectify or erase, or restrict personal data, or where there is some other complaint about accuracy.

3.4.3.10 Where accuracy is an issue and the controller or processor has correctly recorded the data given but it proves to be inaccurate, the enforcement notice may require the controller:

- to take specified steps to ensure the accuracy of the data. The purposes for which the data was obtained and further processed may be relevant;

- if relevant, to ensure that the data records the data subject's view that the data is inaccurate; and
- to supplement this with a statement of the true facts, approved by the Commissioner (s.151(3)–(4)). These provisions closely track earlier provisions in the 1998 Act.

3.4.3.11 In the case of the rights of rectification or erasure, whether because the controller or processor has failed to rectify or erase, or because there was a failure of other conditions of s.151(1)—i.e. accuracy, the controller may be required "if practicable" to notify third parties to whom the data was disclosed of the rectification or erasure. To determine this practicability, the Commissioner should consider the number of people who would need to be notified.

3.4.3.12 Where an enforcement notice involves the special purposes (journalism, etc.—see **10.5.6**), the Commissioner can only issue an enforcement notice where they have:

(1) first reached a determination under s.174 (i.e. has concluded that the processing is not only for the special purposes, or is not being undertaken with a view to publication of material, see **10.5.6.25**); and

(2) obtained leave of the court. The courts may grant leave only if it involves a matter of substantial public importance; they will also require notice to be given to the affected controller or processor unless the matter is urgent (s.152(2)).

3.4.3.13 A controller or processor need not comply with an enforcement notice to the extent that to do so would infringe the privilege of either House of Parliament (s.152(3)).

3.4.3.14 The classic instance of the use of enforcement powers under the 1998 Act was part of the action against The Consulting Association in 2007. In 2007 the ICO closed down an illegal service called The Consulting Association, which provided profiles of workers to the large building trade companies, enabling the companies to identify trouble-makers. Some of the personal data was sensitive (trade union memberships). The Consulting Association had never notified its processing to the Commissioner (i.e. it hadn't fulfilled the registration requirements under the legislation), and the personal data was collected covertly without the data subjects' knowledge or consent. The ICO successfully prosecuted for the failure to notify, and by an enforcement notice prevented the Association from processing any further personal data of this type, thereby effectively closing it down.

3.4.3.15 Other examples include:

- In January 2016 the Alzheimer's Society were ordered to take action to stop volunteers from using their personal email addresses for patient data and failing to encrypt and otherwise store securely the data. They also needed to be trained and supervised better.

- In April 2016, West Dumbartonshire Council were issued with an enforcement notice for failing to implement staff training. Their failure to do so had contributed to a child's medical reports being stolen. The Council were warned that they faced court action if they failed to implement training.
- In September 2018, the London Borough of Lewisham was required to respond to outstanding subject access requests, following a backlog of dealing with over 100 requests, some of which were more than five years old.
- Enforcement Notices can also be used by the Commissioner under the Privacy Regulations (the Privacy and Electronic Communications (EC Directive) Regulations 2003 (SI 2003/2426) reg.31).
- A large number of enforcement notices sent to organisations engaging in telephone or email marketing in breach of the Privacy Regulations. By way of example, six enforcement notices were issued in respect of this in the first nine months of 2018.

Signed undertakings

3.4.3.16 Historically, the Commissioner has also required organisations to give an undertaking to put right some poor practice or infringement of data protection legislation and the Commissioner regarded this as part of the office's enforcement strategy. These undertakings are often published on the ICO website. The Commissioner offers the undertaking as an alternative to a formal enforcement notice or penalty. The Commissioner typically requires that an undertaking is signed by an organisation's CEO or other senior officer—thus ensuring effective attention to the matter at issue by the organisation henceforth—and where a breach of the legislation leads to criminal sanctions, making it easier for the Commissioner to take action against the company's management personally. The Commissioner's new *Regulatory Action Policy* makes no reference to undertakings and although they are still listed as a form of enforcement action on the Commissioner's website, as of May 2019 no undertakings appear to have been issued since the coming onto force of the GDPR and DPA 2018. It will be interesting to see to what extent they are to be replaced by the Commissioner's new, tougher, enforcement powers.

Penalties generally

Factors to be taken into account when deciding whether to impose a penalty

3.4.3.17 We have already seen that the Commissioner has powers under GDPR art.58(2)(i) to impose fines. The conditions which apply to these fines are set out in art.83. The Article starts by enunciating some general principles:

> "*1.* *Each supervisory authority* [that is, the Information Commissioner] *shall ensure that the imposition of administrative fines pursuant to this Article*

in respect of infringements of this Regulation referred to in paragraphs 4,5 and 6 [the paragraphs that deal with the amount of a fine] *shall in each case be effective, proportionate and dissuasive.*"

3.4.3.18 Article 83 goes on to enumerate the factors to be taken into account (far more numerous than those under the DPA 1998 s.55A):

"2. *Administrative fines shall, depending on the circumstances of each individual case, be imposed in addition to, or instead of, measures referred to in points (a) to (h) and (j) of Article 58(2)* [other enforcement measures]. *When deciding whether to impose an administrative fine and deciding on the amount of the administrative fine in each individual case due regard shall be given to the following:*

(a) the nature, gravity and duration of the infringement taking into account the nature scope or purpose of the processing concerned as well as the number of data subjects affected and the level of damage suffered by them;

(b) the intentional or negligent character of the infringement;

(c) any action taken by the controller or processor to mitigate the damage suffered by data subjects;

(d) the degree of responsibility of the controller or processor taking into account technical and organisational measures implemented by them pursuant to Articles 25 and 32 [art.25 Data protection by design and by default; art.32 Security of processing—see **Ch.8** below];

(e) any relevant previous infringements by the controller or processor;

(f) the degree of cooperation with the supervisory authority, in order to remedy the infringement and mitigate the possible adverse effects of the infringement;

(g) the categories of personal data affected by the infringement;

(h) the manner in which the infringement became known to the supervisory authority, in particular whether, and if so to what extent, the controller or processor notified the infringement;

(i) where measures referred to in Article 58(2) [the other 'corrective' measures available to the Commissioner] *have previously been ordered against the controller or processor concerned with regard to the same subject-matter, compliance with those measures;*

(j) adherence to approved codes of conduct pursuant to Article 40 or approved certification mechanisms pursuant to Article 42 [see **13.1.2**]; *and*

(k) any other aggravating or mitigating factor applicable to the circumstances of the case, such as financial benefits gained, or losses avoided, directly or indirectly, from the infringement."

3.4.3.19 From these factors we can derive guidance which controllers or processors will wish to observe.

(i) before any infringement, to reduce the chances of incurring any fine:

- implement full security measures (d); and
- adhere to approved codes or approved certification (as and when these become available) (j); and

(ii) if and when an infringement has occurred, to mitigate the severity of any impending fine:

- take such action as you can to mitigate the damage to data subjects (c);
- tell the Commissioner, before she finds out from other sources (h); and
- fully co-operate with the Commissioner (f). This is in any event required under art.31 which says:

> "*The controller and the processor and, where applicable, their representatives, shall cooperate, on request, with the supervisory authority* [the Information Commissioner] *in the performance of its tasks.*"

3.4.3.20 The Commissioner may, in appropriate circumstances, decide *not* to issue a penalty. Recital 148 alludes to this, stating that

> "*in case of a minor infringement or if the fine likely to be imposed would constitute a disproportionate burden to a natural person, a reprimand may be issued instead of a fine*".

The Art.29 Working Party, on 3 October 2017, adopted *Guidelines on the application and setting of administrative fines for the purposes of the Regulation 2016/679* (WP 253). The main focus of these Guidelines is to emphasise the need for supervisory authorities to ensure that the sanctions they impose are equivalent with those imposed by their peers in other Member States. There is also, though, an interesting comment on rec.148. WP 253 refers to the recital and notes that:

> "*The assessment of the criteria ... may lead the supervisory authority to believe that in the concrete circumstances of the case, the breach for example, does not pose a significant risk to the rights of the data subjects concerned and does not affect the essence of the obligation in question. In such cases, the fine may (but not always) be replaced by a reprimand*" (p.9).

WP 253 also has an interesting example of what may amount to a deliberate breach of data protection legislation, which would be an aggravating factor justifying a higher amount (p.12):

> "*the trade of personal data for marketing purpose i.e. selling data as 'opted in' without checking/disregarding data subjects' views about how their data should be used*".

This may support continued focus by the Commissioner on direct marketing.

The Commissioner's *Regulatory Action Policy* considers the factors which will be taken into account as to whether a penalty should be imposed and the amount of the penalty together, so we have summarised interesting features from the Commissioner's Policy below (**3.4.3.42–3.4.3.43**), where we look at the amounts of a penalty.

3.4.3.21 Sections 155–159 of the DPA 2018 deal with the ICO's administration of fines (or penalties as the DPA 2018 calls them). Any infringement that falls within the definitions in s.149 (**3.4.1.11–3.4.1.14**) may give rise to a penalty. Because the DPA 2018 addresses not just the GDPR, but the applied GDPR, processing by competent authorities for law enforcement purposes and the intelligence services, s.155 repeats, largely verbatim, the criteria set out in the GDPR at art.83.

Procedure for imposing penalties

3.4.3.22 The details of the ICO's administrative procedures for penalties are set out at Sch.16 (substantially following the procedures under the DPA 1998). DPA 2018 Sch.16 para.2 requires the Commissioner to precede the penalty notice by a notice of intent, effectively giving the organisation opportunity to make representation about the imposition of a penalty. The Commissioner must send any penalty notice within six months of issuing the notice of intent, though the Commissioner and apparently infringing controller or processor may agree to extend that period.

Notice of intent

3.4.3.23 The notice of intent must contain the following (Sch.16 para.3(1)–(5)):

- name and address of the intended recipient;
- reasons for giving a penalty notice, to include:
  - a description of the circumstances of the failure; and
  - where the failure is of the s.149(2) type (**3.4.1.8**) (i.e. a substantive breach), the nature of the personal data involved;
- an indication of the amount the Commissioner proposes to impose, including any aggravating or mitigating factors to be taken into account;
- a statement that the recipient may make written representations about the Commissioner's intention to give a penalty notice; and
- the period within which such representations may be made (not less than 21 days from the notice of intent).

The Commissioner may also use the notice of intent to invite oral representations from the recipient, although the *Regulatory Action Policy* (pp.25–26) suggests that this will be a relatively rare arrangement.

3.4.3.24 The sending of a notice of intent would ordinarily be a private matter between the parties (ICO and allegedly infringing data controller or processor). However, the Commissioner's policy on *Communicating Regulatory Activity* makes clear that the Commissioner may publish a notice of intent where she considers that there is an overriding public interest in so doing. This was done in relation to the notice of intent issued to Facebook, linked to the Cambridge Analytica investigation—see **3.4.3.49** below. This can only increase the pressure on the recipient controller or processor.

3.4.3.25 The Commissioner is obliged to consider any written (or oral, where permitted) representations by the recipient of the notice of intent and in the light of them reconsider the proposed penalty. Following this either the penalty notice is served within six months or the data controller is advised that there will be no penalty notice (Sch.16 para.4).

The penalty notice

3.4.3.26 The penalty notice must contain (Sch.16 para.5):

- the name and address of the recipient;
- details of the notice of intent already given;
- whether the Commissioner has received any written or oral representations from the recipient;
- the reasons for imposing the penalty which will include:
  - a description of the circumstances of the failure; and
  - where the failure is of the s.149(2) type (**3.4.1.11**) (i.e. a substantive breach), the nature of the personal data involved;
- the reasons for the amount of the penalty and any aggravating or mitigating circumstances;
- details of how the penalty is to be paid;
- details of the rights of appeal under s.162; and
- details of the Commissioner's enforcement powers under Sch.16.

3.4.3.27 Payment must be made within the period specified in the penalty notice, not less than 28 days from the date of the notice. The Commissioner may also vary (but not increase) the amount (using a penalty variation notice, which itself may be subject to appeal) or indeed cancel the penalty notice (DPA 2018 Sch.16 paras 6–8).

3.4.3.28 Once the periods for appealing and for paying have elapsed, if any part of the penalty is still outstanding, the Commissioner can invoke the support of the courts (County Court or High Court in England and Wales, and in Northern Ireland, and sheriff court in Scotland (Sch.16 para.9)).

3.4.3.29 A penalty which concerns the special purposes (journalism and the like—see **10.5.6**) has additional procedures to comply with, set out in ss.156(1)–(2) and 174. The Commissioner may not issue a penalty notice in respect of any personal data where the purposes and manner of processing are determined by or on behalf of either House of Parliament. There are also exemptions from penalties for the Crown Estate Commissioners or controllers acting on behalf of the Royal Household, Duchy of Lancaster or Duchy of Cornwall (s.156(3)–(4) and 209(4)).

Maxima for penalties

3.4.3.30 Under the 1998 Act, the Data Protection (Monetary Penalties) Order 2010 (SI 2010/31) provided for a maximum penalty of £500,000. That figure was reviewable after three years but was never in fact reviewed. Now we have a very different regime. GDPR art.83 and DPA 2018 ss.157–159 deal with this. Article 83(3) states:

> "*If a controller or processor intentionally or negligently, for the same or linked processing operations, infringes several provisions of this Regulation, the total amount of the administrative fine shall not exceed the amount specified for the gravest infringement.*"

This is small comfort to an infringing controller or processor, when he sees the maximum allowed.

3.4.3.31 The maxima are in two bands, art.83(4) describing the less serious infringements, and art.83(5) the more serious.

Article 83(4) lists various articles whose infringement attracts less serious penalties:

- art.8 [children's consent—see **14.1**];
- art.11 [processing which does not require identification—see **6.3.3.4**];
- arts 25 to 39 [data protection by design or by default—see **14.1.3**, joint controllers, representatives of non-EU controllers or processors, processors requirements, records of processing activities, co-operation with the supervising authority (i.e. the Commissioner), security and data breach, impact assessment and prior consultation, data protection officer—see **1.3.7, 13.2**];
- arts 42 and 43 [certification, including obligations on a certifying body—see **13.1.2**]; and
- art.41(4) (the obligations on the monitoring body [a body set up to regulate a code of conduct established under art.40—see **13.1.2**].

Infringements of any of these Articles are subject to administrative fines of up to €10 million, or in the case of an "undertaking" (as to the meaning of this, see

3.4.3.37 below), up to 2% of a total worldwide annual turnover of the preceding financial year, whichever is higher.

3.4.3.32 The more serious infringements are those that concern:

- art.5 [the principles—see **Chs 5, 8,** and **13.1.1**];
- art.6 [lawfulness of processing—see **Ch.4**];
- art.7 [consent—see **4.2**];
- art.9 [special categories of personal data—see **1.2.4**];
- arts 12–22 [data subjects' rights—see **Ch.6**];
- arts 44–49 [transfers to a third country—see **Ch.9**];
- arts 85–91 [any obligations under Member State law—see **Ch.10**]; and
- non-compliance with a supervisory authority [the Information Commissioner] in exercising certain of its investigative or corrective functions under arts 58(1) or (2) (**3.2.5**).

Infringements of these Articles can attract fines of up to double those for the less serious infringements—i.e. €20 million or for "undertakings" 4% of annual worldwide turnover.

3.4.3.33 The DPA 2018 s.157 refers to the two bands described as the higher maximum amount (€20 million etc.) and the standard maximum amount (€10 million etc). Section 157(1) confirms that the maxima set out in GDPR art.83 are to be applied. Section 157 of the DPA 2018 adds that if an amount is not specified in art.83, the standard maximum applies. It goes on to say that:

- for infringements in Pt 3 (law enforcement) of
  - ss.35–40 the data protection principles
  - s.44 controller's general duties;
  - ss.45–49 and 52–53 data subject's rights; and
  - ss.73–78 transfers to third countries;
- for infringements in Pt 4 (intelligence services) of
  - ss.86–91 the data protection principles;
  - ss.93–94 data subject's rights of access;
  - s.100 data subject's right of rectification; and
  - s.109 transfers to third countries;
- and for failures to comply with an information notice, assessment notice or an enforcement notice the higher maximum (**3.4.3.32**) applies.

3.4.3.34 The DPA 2018 still gives these values in euros. The penalty must be based on the rate of exchange as set by the Bank of England on the day the penalty notice was given (s.157(7)).

3.4.3.35 The DPA 2018 by s.137 requires the Secretary of State to make regulations to require controllers to pay a charge to the Commissioner. The charges are in three bands: £40, £60 and £2,900 per annum (**13.5.2**). This replaces the process of notification under ss.16–26 of the 1998 Act, but the new Act does not require the controller to provide the Commissioner with details of the processing as they did in the old notification process. The old Register of controllers is no more. The Regulation as to fees payable by controllers to the Commissioner prescribed by s.137 is already in force. The Data Protection (Charges and Information) Regulations 2018 (SI 2018/480) came into force on 25 May 2018. It defines what the fees are and requires that they be paid.

3.4.3.36 Section 155(1) allows the Commissioner to issue a penalty notice to a controller who fails to pay the prescribed amount. This is to be a fixed penalty amount (s.158). It is for the Commissioner after consultation to produce and lay before Parliament a document specifying the amount of the penalty for failure to comply with this, up to a maximum of 150% of the charge in question.

Organisations defined as undertakings

3.4.3.37 This has nothing to do with promises of amended behaviour extracted by the Commissioner from erring controllers (**3.4.3.16** above). In GDPR art.83, the word "undertaking" has a distinct and different meaning. For organisations who are defined as "undertakings", fines are to be assessed based on total worldwide turnover in the preceding financial year, or the set amount, whichever is higher. Understanding what is meant by an "undertaking" in this context is, therefore, key. Recital 150 of the GDPR points the reader to competition law, as set out in arts 101 and 102 of the Treaty on the Functioning of the EU. WP 253 helpfully summarises the law in this area, noting that:

> "*. . . the concept of an undertaking is understood to mean an economic unit, which may be formed by the parent company and all involved subsidiaries. In accordance with EU law and case law, an undertaking must be understood to be the economic unit, which engages in commercial/economic activities, regardless of the legal person involved*".

3.4.3.38 "Undertakings" are highly likely to include all companies within a corporate group—for example, in the competition law case of ***Groupe Gascogne SA v European Commission*** (C-58/12) EU:C:2013:770, it was not necessary for the Commission to show whether the parent company could exercise a decisive influence on all of its subsidiaries – it was sufficient that it exercised decisive control over the infringing company for the fine to apply to the whole group. Indeed, competition law cases have also applied the concept of an "undertaking" beyond group companies, where one entity has decisive influence over another. For example, in the case of joint ventures, where there is evidence that that both top-companies exercise decisive influence over the joint venture, all three entities may be deemed to make up an economic unit—see ***Dow Chemical v European***

Commission (C-179/12); ***El du Pont de Nemours and Company v European Commission*** (C-172/12).

3.4.3.39 In some cases, although relatively rarely, pure financial investors have been fined for breaches of a portfolio companies. The European Commission has taken the view that involvement in strategic, financial or investment issues in the portfolio companies can be evidence of direct control. A good example was an investment by Goldman Sachs amounting to a shareholding of around 90% in a company called Prysmian. The Commission found Goldman Sachs had the right to appoint board members, and had exercised that right, and that was sufficient to amount to a decisive influence.[1]

3.4.3.40 Where a penalty is imposed on someone other than an undertaking (perhaps an individual?), rec.150 states that the supervisory authority should

> "*take account of the general level of income in the Member State as well as the economic situation of the person in considering the appropriate amount of the fine*".

3.4.3.41 Finally, the Secretary of State may introduce secondary legislation to give more specificity to this. The secondary legislation could provide that specified persons are, or are not, to be treated as undertakings, and set out how an undertaking's turnover is to be determined (DPA 2018 s.159).

Quantum

3.4.3.42 Penalties under data protection legislation now have the potential to be a very significant factor. Organisations may take some comfort from the fact that, in the *Regulatory Action Policy*, the Commissioner states (p.24) that:

> "*In the majority of cases we will reserve our powers* [to issue penalty notices] *for the most serious cases, representing the most severe breaches of information rights obligations*".

So, a more minor infraction should not lead to a large fine. As mentioned above, the Commissioner has said that she will use the criteria set out in art.83 (**3.4.3.17** and **3.4.3.18** above) and amplified in the *Regulatory Action Policy* both to determine if a penalty notice should be imposed and to determine the quantum of any penalty. Where a significant penalty (which the Commissioner considers would be those over £1 million) is to be imposed, then the Commissioner may convene a panel of non-executive advisers to consider the findings of the investigation and representations made before recommending the penalty to be applied (p.26).

---

[1] Note that Goldman Sachs has appealed that decision; the appeal is pending.

3.4.3.43 The *Regulatory Action Policy* also outlines a five-step approach to setting penalties (which builds on the approach used under the 1998 Act). This is (p.27):

1) remove any financial gain from the breach;
2) add in any element needed to censure the breach based on scale and severity, looking at the factors listed in data protection legislation;
3) add in an amount for any aggravating factors;
4) add in an amount for deterrent effect for others;
5) reduce the amount (other than the amount arrived at under step 1) to take account of mitigating factors, including ability to pay.

Examples of penalties

3.4.3.44 The legislation on penalties is not retrospective so at the time of writing we have no examples of how the Commissioner will impose penalties for infringements of the GDPR/DPA 2018. But we have many examples to draw on in respect of penalties under the 1998 DPA.

3.4.3.45 For example, a penalty of £325,000 was imposed on Brighton & Sussex University Hospital NHS Trust in June 2012. About 1,000 hard drives on redundant equipment were disposed of by the Trust without removing the data. The data referred by name to tens of thousands of patients, including HIV and Genito-Urinary Medicine (GUM) patients. The drives had been handed over to a contractor, Sussex Health Informatics Services (HIS), for them to destroy. The drives were stolen from a supposedly secure building and sold on, four drives turning up on an internet auction website. The ICO investigated and were assured that only these four drives were affected. It later transpired that at least 252 drives were taken. This is a case involving a processor whose degree of negligence is not clear. The same facts today would no doubt bring out in more detail what the failings were, and it might well be that the penalty for the controller might be quite small and that for the processor rather larger. It is reasonable also to conclude that the Trust did themselves no favours by suggesting the loss was small (four drives) and then discovering that more than 50 times that number were compromised. When reporting a loss, an inadequate statement to the Commissioner is not a good start.

3.4.3.46 TalkTalk, the internet service provider, was fined £400,000 by the ICO in October 2016 in respect of a serious hacking attack. TalkTalk took over Tiscali in 2009. Tiscali had webpages which gave its customers access to its database. TalkTalk left these webpages up. The database software was an obsolete version of MySQ, which had a security bug which was curable by a published fix. TalkTalk neglected to fix this. A cyberattack taking advantage of these weaknesses obtained personal data including bank account data of 15,656 customers. There were some mitigating factors: the breach was reported to the ICO by TalkTalk and they had been co-operative. They had taken remedial action. The customers were all notified and offered compensation. TalkTalk had suffered much adverse publicity. It remains to be seen how much the penalty for a similar infringement might be in the future, but it seems TalkTalk's turnover in the previous year was in the order of £1.8 billion. 2% of that is in the order of £3.6 million.

3.4.3.47 In the dying days of the old 1998 legislation, two organisations have been fined the full maximum of £500,000. Equifax, the credit reference agency, was issued with a £500,000 in September 2018, for a breach which occurred in 2017 (so under the previous legislation). The breach affected up to 15 million UK citizens. The breach was a cyber-attack which affected Equifax Inc in the US—however, the Commissioner concluded that the UK entity, Equifax Ltd was the controller responsible for data relating to UK citizens and that the US entity was processing the data as a data processor on Equifax Ltd's behalf. The Commissioner concluded that there had been a failure to take adequate security measures, in this case by failing to patch fully a vulnerability to which Equifax had been alerted by the US Department of Homeland Security Computer Emergency Readiness Team—and also (as is often the case in enforcement relating to personal data breaches) that the data had been retained for longer than necessary, as it was retained in the US even after the relevant system had been migrated to run in the UK. The Commissioner also considered that Equifax had no lawful basis for some of the processing which it undertook, as Equifax relied on consent to justify its processing which the Commissioner concluded was invalid—so an investigation into a personal data breach led to wider investigations into data retention and lawful basis for processing. The enforcement notice also found failings in that Equifax Ltd did not carry out any audits or checks of Equifax Inc and failed to ensure that its parent had appropriate security measures in place or that appropriate standard contractual clauses were in place to meet data transfer requirements: organisations often overlook the need to implement and enforce data processing agreements intra-group. The Equifax case shows the danger of looking externally only and not applying the same rigour to internal arrangements. The Commissioner was also critical of the delay in communications between Inc and Ltd—noting that it took one month for Inc to notify Ltd of the breach.

3.4.3.48 Again, details provided by Equifax to the Commissioner changed as the investigation progressed and the enforcement notice makes reference to the fact that the Commissioner served an information notice on Equifax in the course of the investigation. It is clearly best to avoid changing details – although this is difficult to do, when communications to a regulator happen in tandem with the live internal investigation. The enforcement notice also shows the importance of actually addressing what may seem like procedural compliance requirements: the failure of Equifax group, for example, to put in place appropriate data transfer agreements provided the Information Commissioner with a finding of fault which could easily have been avoided.

3.4.3.49 In October 2018, the UK Information Commissioner imposed a monetary penalty of £500,000 on Facebook Ireland Ltd and Facebook Inc as part of her Office's investigation into Cambridge Analytica, under the 1998 Act. There are multiple important points to note from the notice—not least the Commissioner's statement that:

> "*but for the statutory limitation on the amount of the monetary penalty, it would have been reasonable and proportionate to impose a higher penalty*".

3.4.3.50 Dr Kogan of Cambridge Analytica wrote an app for use on Facebook to harvest personal data of 1 million UK Facebook users (including data about users' friends and their email addresses) over the period November 2013–May 2015. The data had been illegally shared with others (Cambridge Analytica and Dr Kogan's company, Global Science Research Ltd). The harvesting stopped only when the *Guardian* published an article about it.

3.4.3.51 The Commissioner found that some of the data shared with these companies was likely to have been used for purposes of political campaigning. Facebook advised the Commissioner that the only individuals whose data was used in this way were US residents—however, the Commissioner noted that some of those would have used Facebook while visiting the UK (p.13) and so would have amounted to UK users at that point.

3.4.3.52 The app breached multiple provisions of Facebook's Platform Policy—in particular:

- data about friends of users should only have been used to augment the experience of the user, whereas it was used for the app developer's own purpose;
- the sale of data to third parties breached the Policy;
- the transfer of the data to third parties breached the Policy; and
- the app requested permission from users to obtain personal data that the app itself didn't need.

3.4.3.53 Dr Kogan gave a fraudulent undertaking to Facebook that data was purely for research, but the Commissioner found that Facebook took inadequate steps to monitor or restrain Dr Kogan;

> "*The Facebook Companies permitted the App to operate in such a way that it collected personal data about Facebook friends of users of the App, without those friends being informed that such data was being collected ... The Facebook Companies did not attempt to prevent the App from collecting data in this manner... By permitting the App to operate in this way, the Facebook Companies unfairly processed the personal data of the Facebook friends of uses of the App*".

Facebook are now seeking an appeal.

3.5 OTHER CONSEQUENCES OF FAILURE

3.5.1 Introduction

3.5.1.1 A penalty imposed by the Information Commissioner is of course not the only risk in a breach of the legislation. In addition to the matters discussed in this chapter there are other dangers to guard against in respect of data protection breaches including:

- risks of loss or damage to data resulting in expense in reconstructing/recovering the data;
- risks of confidential information getting into the hands of competitors . . .
- or other unauthorised persons such as violent criminals;
- risks of legal action including risk of defamation actions based on data getting to unauthorised persons;
- risks of intervention and possible fines from other regulators (e.g. Financial Conduct Authority or the Advertising Standards Authority);
- in special circumstances compromising major public responsibilities—e.g. police work, national security etc.

3.5.2 Bad publicity

3.5.2.1 Lastly, but not least, organisations should be aware that breach of data protection legislation can lead to substantial adverse publicity. For many organisations this can be a worse consequence than the possibility of criminal sanctions or legal actions, resulting in a loss of confidence in the organisation by its customers. Publicity indicating that an organisation has failed to comply with privacy requirements can be extremely damaging for any organisation that relies on consumer trust and goodwill.

3.5.2.2 There may also be a personal cost. Those who saw the CEO of TalkTalk on television the day the news of the hacking attack broke (see **3.4.3.46**) will appreciate the personal anguish a senior officer may undergo.

3.5.2.3 The power of publicity is not lost on the Information Commissioner's Office. *The Information Commissioner's Annual Reports* include case studies that provide details of some of the Commissioner's investigations into named companies. Furthermore, the organisations giving undertakings, or subject to penalties, enforcement notices or assessment—even consensual assessment—are often named on the Commissioner's website in prominent news items on the home page. From there the stories are often picked up and widely disseminated by the mainstream press. The consequences to organisations of the adverse publicity may outweigh fines imposed for criminal offences and sometimes even monetary penalties under the DPA 2018.

CHAPTER 4

Lawful Basis for Processing

4.1 THE NEED FOR A LAWFUL BASIS FOR PROCESSING

4.1.1 Article 6 of the GDPR provides that

"*Processing shall be lawful only if and to the extent that at least one of the following* [lawful bases] *applies*".

A controller must be able to point to a lawful basis set out in art.6 for every processing activity it undertakes. Where one activity is for multiple purposes—for example, where a controller processes personal data to fulfil a contract with its customers and also so it can understand what interests them for future marketing—then the controller must find a lawful basis for each purpose.

4.1.2 Where a controller processes special category data, then—in addition—the controller must have a further lawful basis, set out in art.9. Similarly, under art.10, processing of data about criminal convictions and offences also requires an additional lawful basis, above and beyond the ones set out in art.6. There are six lawful bases set out in art.6 and a further 10 in art.9. The DPA 2018 sets out a large number of additional conditions relevant to special category data and criminal offence data. Secondary legislation may also be promulgated, under s.10(6) of the DPA 2018, introducing further conditions.

4.1.3 Consent by the relevant individual is a possible lawful basis in both arts 6 and 9. In addition, many of the additional lawful bases in the DPA 2018 only apply when consent cannot be obtained. For this reason, we have looked at 'consent' before any of the other conditions. Many conditions also only apply where the processing is "necessary" for the specified purpose: accordingly, we must look at the meaning of "necessary".

4.1.4 A controller must include details of the lawful basis—or bases—for its processing in the privacy notice which it gives individuals. The ICO also recommends in the guide, *Consent Guidance*, that controllers document which lawful basis they consider is appropriate as part of their accountability documentation. A controller can only provide the notice and document this correctly if it decides which lawful basis is appropriate at the outset of any processing. The ICO provides an interactive lawful basis assessment tool on its website to help with this.

4.1.5 The choice of lawful basis should be undertaken carefully. The ICO advises in the guide that "*you should not swap to a different lawful basis at a later date without good reason*". This is particularly important where consent is the lawful basis because:

> "*Leading the individual to believe they had a choice is inherently unfair if that choice will be irrelevant* [because an organisation would switch to a different lawful basis if consent were to be withdrawn]".

Controllers should note that meeting a condition in arts 6 and 9 will help to make processing lawful – but is not all that is required. In addition, controllers should be aware of the over-arching first data protection principle, set out at art.5(1)(a), which requires that personal data shall be:

> "*processed lawfully, fairly and in a transparent manner in relation to the data subject...*".

4.1.6 Transparency is addressed in Ch.6. There is commentary on lawful and fair processing in the guide. This notes that:

> "*Lawfulness also means that you don't do anything with the personal data which is unlawful in a more general sense. This includes statute and common law obligations, whether criminal or civil ...*".

The Guide includes examples of breach of confidence and infringement of copyright. The Information Commissioner is, however, unlikely to focus on "*allegations which are primarily about breaches of . . . other laws outside our remit and expertise as a data protection regulator*". However, it is clearly still important for the organisation to comply—both from a wider compliance perspective and because the GDPR gives individuals a right to require their personal data to be erased when it has been processed unlawfully (**6.9.3.1**).

4.1.7 On fairness, the guide states that:

> "*. . . If any aspect of your processing is unfair you will be in breach of this principle – even if you can show that you have a lawful basis for the processing. In general, fairness means that you should only handle personal data in ways that people would reasonably expect and not use it in ways that have unjustified adverse effects on them . . .*
> *. . . if anyone is deceived or misled when the personal data is obtained, then this is unlikely to be fair.*
> *. . . If you have obtained and used the information fairly in relation to most of the people it relates to but unfairly in relation to one individual, there will still be a breach of this principle.*
> *Personal data may sometimes be used in a way that negatively affects an individual without this necessarily being unfair. What matters is whether or not such detriment is justified*".

Many of the lawful bases for processing set out at arts 6 and 9 require quite technical, detailed analysis. However, a controller should not overlook the bigger picture—of fair and lawful processing.

4.2 CONSENT

4.2.1 Legislative provisions and guidance

4.2.1.1 Article 4(11) provides that:

> "'*consent' of the data subject means any freely given, specific, informed and unambiguous indication of the data subject's wishes by which he or she, by a statement or clear affirmative action, signifies agreement to the processing of personal data relating to him or her*".

Article 7 is dedicated solely to consent. It sets out rules relating to the form for consent; the requirement for the controller to be able to prove that an individual has given consent; and the ability to revoke consent. It also contains further requirements for consent to be valid.

4.2.1.2 In addition to these requirements, in some situations consent must be "explicit"—see **4.2.4**. This is the case where a controller wishes to rely on consent to process special category data (but not criminal offence data, where by DPA

2018, Sch.1, Pt 3, para.29, ordinary consent will be sufficient), to undertake significant, and entirely automated, decisions about people or to transfer personal data outside the EEA.

4.2.1.3 Consent is also relevant under the ePrivacy Directive. This requires that organisations obtain consent if, amongst other things, they wish to send unsolicited email marketing to individuals or wish to use cookies or similar technology for purposes which are not strictly necessary to deliver an online service requested by a user. The references to consent in the ePrivacy Directive depend on the definition of consent in the GDPR (**7.3.3.5**).

4.2.1.4 The ICO has issued detailed consent guidance (*Lawful basis for processing: Consent*, May 2018), and the EDPB has also issued Guidelines on Consent (WP 259). The Article 29 Working Party also issued an Opinion on the definition of consent in 2011 (WP 187). Although WP 187 relates to the old Data Protection Directive, it is still relevant to the GDPR, because, as the EDPB itself notes: "*the GDPR codifies existing WP29 guidance and general good practice and most of the key elements of consent remain the same under the GDPR*" (WP 259, p.3).

4.2.2 Role of consent

4.2.2.1 Consent is the first lawful basis for processing personal data in art.6 (for normal data) and art.9 for special category data. However, this does not mean consent is better than other conditions and there is no suggestion that controllers should look to consent before the other conditions. As the ICO notes in the guide, "*No single basis is better or more important than the others*".

4.2.2.2 It is difficult to obtain valid consent under the GDPR and the ICO advises that "*consent won't always be the most appropriate or easiest*".[1] Controllers should use consent where there is a genuine choice for the individual and where the organisation can delete that data if consent is then withdrawn at a later date. If the requirements for valid consent under the GDPR cannot be met, controllers should not purport to ask for consent. For example, if consent cannot be freely given because of some constraint on the individual, any "consent" purported to be elicited by the controller must be invalid.

> "*If you would still process the personal data without consent, asking for consent is misleading and inherently unfair*"
> "*Relying on invalid consent could destroy trust and harm your reputation – and may also leave you open to large fines*" (ICO *Consent Guidance*).

4.2.2.3 Where consent is appropriate, it meets one requirement under the GDPR—providing a lawful basis for processing personal data (or for carrying out automated decision-making or transferring personal data outside the EEA). Obtaining consent does not avoid the need to meet other requirements of the GDPR—as the EDPB notes in WP 259:

---

1 *Consent Guidance*, p.15

"*Even if the processing of personal data is based on consent of the data subject, this would not legitimise collection of data which is not necessary in relation to the specified purpose of processing and* [which is] *fundamentally unfair*".

This is because under art.5(1)(c), personal data should be "*limited to what is necessary in relation to the purposes for which they* [the data] *are processed*".

4.2.3 Rules for valid consent

Freely given

4.2.3.1 The ICO *Consent Guidance* puts this succinctly:

"*Consent means giving people genuine choice and control over how you use their data. If the individual has no real choice, consent is not freely given and it will be invalid*".

This makes it difficult to obtain valid consent where the controller is in a position of power in relation to the individual—for example a public authority, or an employer in relation to an employee.

4.2.3.2 Recital 43 of the GDPR states that:

"*... consent should not provide a valid legal ground for the processing of personal data in a specific case where there is a clear imbalance between the data subject and the controller, in particular where the controller is a public authority and it is therefore unlikely that consent was freely given in all the circumstances of that specific situation*".

Organisations in this position may read rec. 43 and conclude that they should never rely on consent. However, this is not necessarily the case. On some occasions, controllers who are in position of power in relation to the individual *will* be able to offer individuals a real choice—and on these occasions consent will be valid.

4.2.3.3 The ICO *Consent Guidance* notes that

"*public authorities and employers are not banned from using consent as their lawful basis. Even if you are in a position of power, there may be situations when you can still show that the consent is freely given*".

The ICO includes the following example to demonstrate this:

"*A local council runs a number of fitness centres. It wants to find out what people think of the facilities in order to decide where to focus improvements. It decides to email a questionnaire to individuals who have fitness memberships to ask them about the facilities.*

The decision as to whether or not to take part in the survey is entirely optional, and . . . there is no real risk of adverse consequences for failing to respond. The council could consider relying on consent to process the responses".

4.2.3.4 In this example, it will be absolutely clear to individuals that there is no risk in not providing consent to the local authority. This may not always be the case, though, so the ICO advises that "*you may need to take steps to ensure that the individual does not feel any pressure to consent and allay any concerns over the consequences of refusing consent*".

4.2.3.5 In this example the powers of the local authority over the individuals are very limited. It is more difficult if the controller is dealing with employees. If a company wishes to show pictures of its area managers on the website, with their names and contact details, then unless it is has somehow already obtained valid consent beforehand, it must ask each area manager for his consent. An area manager may suspect that if he says "no", he may be penalised—e.g. by being treated as uncooperative or having his promotion prospects reduced. Even though his fears are entirely groundless, if he believes this may be so, his consent cannot be freely given. To obtain valid consent, the company must make it clear to all the area managers that they may legitimately say "no", do not need to give any reason, and will not be penalised in any way. If only one area manager says "no", the project cannot go ahead.

4.2.3.6 Another example of a situation where consent is unlikely to be freely given is where a controller insists that individuals give consent as a condition of providing goods or services. Although the controller may argue that the individual has a free choice whether or not to do business with it, the GDPR sets a presumption that consent obtained in this way will be invalid. Article 7(4) provides:

"*When assessing whether consent is freely given, utmost account shall be taken of whether, inter alia, the performance of a contract, including the provision of a service, is conditional on consent to the processing of personal data that is not necessary for the performance of that contract*".

4.2.3.7 In some situations, the controller may not be able to fulfil a contract without processing the individual's personal data (for example, in order to ship goods). Here, the controller could potentially rely on consent as the lawful basis to process the personal data. Recital 43 clarifies that the mischief being prevented is making "*the performance of a contract . . . dependent on . . . consent despite such consent not being necessary for such performance*".

4.2.3.8 In most situations, if the controller must be able to process personal data in order to fulfil a contract, it will be able to justify its processing of personal data as being "necessary for the performance of a contract" (art.6(1)(b))—so that there will be no need to ask for consent. However, this contractual necessity condition does not apply to processing of special categories of personal data under art.9, so organisations offering services where they must be able to process sensitive data to meet the individual's request will be able to insist on consent and to make clear that they cannot accept an order unless this is given. The ICO *Consent Guidance* includes an example of a pregnancy yoga class to illustrate this:

> "*. . . although the individual cannot sign up to the class without revealing information about their pregnancy, explicit consent is still likely to be the appropriate condition for processing health data. The processing is objectively necessary to provide the requested class, and the individual has a free choice whether or not to sign up to that class*".

4.2.3.9 The Article 29 Working Party Guideline WP 259 (p.9) notes that:

> "*consent cannot be considered as freely given if a controller argues that a choice exists between its service that includes consenting to the use of personal data for additional purposes on the one hand, and an equivalent service offered by a different controller on the other hand*".

Recital 43 also suggests that consent will not be freely given if an individual will suffer "detriment" as a result of not giving, or withdrawing consent:

> "*Consent should not be regarded as freely given if the data subject has no genuine or free choice or is unable to refuse or withdraw consent without detriment.*"

4.2.3.10 If read literally, this is problematic. In the example of the yoga class above (**4.2.3.8**), the participant would suffer detriment if she refuses consent—as she would not be able to attend the class. Loyalty schemes and other offers where a consumer gets a benefit in return for agreeing that a retailer or service provider can process their data would also be affected. The ICO *Consent Guidance* is constructive on this point, noting that:

> "*The ICO's view is that it may still be possible to incentivise consent to some extent. There will usually be some benefit to consenting to processing. For example, if joining the retailer's loyalty scheme comes with access to money-off vouchers, there is clearly some incentive to consent to marketing. The fact that this benefit is unavailable to those who don't sign up does not amount to a detriment for refusal. However, you must be careful not to cross the line and unfairly penalise those who refuse consent*".

This is helpful as far as it goes. However, it may be difficult for businesses to heed the ICO's advice not to "cross the line" when it is not clear where the line is drawn.

4.2.3.11 The last example which the GDPR gives, of practices which will result in consent not being freely given, is where an organisation relies on consent for several different purposes, but requests consent for all of these purposes together. Consent should allow individuals to decide if they wish to allow their data to be processed: in this example, because multiple purposes are conflated into one request, the individual has less control than she or he should do.

4.2.3.12 Recital 43 is relevant for this and provides that "*consent is presumed not to be freely given if it does not allow separate consent to be given to different processing operations despite it being appropriate in the individual case . . .*". The GDPR definition at art.4(1) requires that consent must be "specific". The ICO refers to this as "blanket" consent. Despite sounding cosy, this is to be avoided. Instead, organisations should offer individuals the ability to say yes, or no, to each different processing activity for which consent is needed.

Specific and informed

4.2.3.13 The ICO *Consent Guidance* provides that:

> "*You must clearly explain to people what they are consenting to in a way they can easily understand. The request for consent needs to be prominent, concise, . . . and in plain language.*
> *If the request for consent is vague, sweeping or difficult to understand, then it will be invalid. In particular, language likely to confuse – for example, the use of double negatives or inconsistent language – will invalidate consent*".

Simply "agreeing to a privacy policy" will fail this test: it is sweeping and does not ask for consent to specific processing activities. The CJEU case of *Volker and Markus Schecke v Land Hessen* joined cases C-92/09 and C-93/09 confirmed the latter point [63], noting that an acknowledgment of a privacy policy is not the same as consent to the processing of personal data. The requirement for consent to be "informed" is, therefore, linked to the GDPR's transparency obligations in art.5(1) and art.12 which require any communication relating to processing to be "*in a concise, transparent, intelligible and easily accessible form, using clear and plain language . . .*" (**6.2.2**).

4.2.3.14 For consent to be "specific" it will need to be relatively detailed. Where one purpose includes several processing activities then, according to rec.32 "*consent should cover all processing activities carried out for the same purpose or purposes. When the processing has multiple purposes, consent should be given for all of them*". However, if an organisation asks for consent for several different purposes, then it should consider if it is appropriate to offer separate choices for each purpose, so as to ensure consent is freely given.

4.2.3.15 For consent to be informed, "*the data subject should be aware at least of the identity of the controller and the purposes of the processing for which the personal data are intended*" (rec.42). As the ICO *Consent Guidance* states:

> "*This means you need to identify yourself, and also name any third-party controllers who will be relying on the consent. If you buy in 'consented' data, that consent is only valid for your processing if you were specifically identified.*"

The requirement to identify controllers relying on consent will have a significant impact on organisations seeking to trade lists of consumer email addresses (**7.4.2.7**).

4.2.3.16 Furthermore, a practice has developed for webpages to give minimal information about controllers—often a name and if you are lucky a small box in which the individual can try and cram an emailed query, but nothing else. The privacy notices requirements in arts 13(1)(a) and 14(1)(a) of the GDPR require the controller to provide contact details. Should not this include at least a phone number or a simple to use email system and preferably also an address? We must return to this matter when considering transparency under art.12.

4.2.3.17 Article 7(3) requires that controllers tell individuals, before they give consent, that they also have a right to withdraw consent at any time. This is repeated in the GDPR's requirements for privacy notices. The ICO *Consent Guidance* notes that this requirement is part of the requirement for consent to be informed—and suggests that the controller should also include details as to how consent can be withdrawn. Any such withdrawal does not affect the lawfulness of any processing based on consent before the withdrawal (arts 13(2)(c) and 14(2)(d)).

4.2.3.18 The EDPB suggests that, in addition to listing the identity of the controller, purposes of processing and the right to withdraw consent, information about the types of data which will be collected and used should also be included in the request for consent. If consent is requested for an international data transfer, then the controller must also inform the individual of the possible risks posed and that the data is being transferred to a country without an adequacy decision and without appropriate safeguards (art.49(1)(a)).

4.2.3.19 The GDPR contains special rules for consent and scientific research, where rec.33 provides that the requirement for consent to be "specific" does not meant that it needs to be limited to a particular study.

> "*It is often not possible to fully identify the purpose of personal data processing for scientific research purposes at the time of data collection. Therefore, data subjects should be allowed to give their consent to certain areas of scientific research when in keeping with recognised ethical standards for scientific research . . .*".

Unambiguous, clear, affirmative action

4.2.3.20 According to the ICO *Consent Guidance*:

> "*This requires more than just a confirmation that they have read terms and conditions —there must be a clear signal that they agree. If there is any room for doubt, it is not valid consent*".

In recent years we have detected a move away from asking a web-user to click agreement to "I have read and accept the conditions . . ." to a simple and doubtless more accurate if bleaker "I accept the conditions . . .".

4.2.3.21 The GDPR is not prescriptive about how this this clear consent is obtained. Recital 32 gives non-exhaustive examples:

> "*... such as by a written statement, including by electronic means, or an oral statement. This could include ticking a box when visiting an internet website, choosing technical settings for information society services* [i.e. online services] *or another statement or conduct which clearly indicates ... acceptance*".

However, "*silence, pre-ticked boxes or inactivity should not ... constitute consent*".

4.2.3.22 The ICO notes that opt-out boxes are also insufficient:

> "*The GDPR does not specifically ban opt-out boxes but they are essentially the same as pre-ticked boxes, which are banned. Both methods bundle up consent with other matters by default, and then rely to some extent on inactivity. They also increase the likelihood of confusion and ambiguity*".

4.2.3.23 Obtaining consent by including it in the small-print of long terms and conditions is also ruled out. Article 7(2) provides that:

> "*If the data subject's consent is given in the context of a written declaration which also concerns other matters, the request for consent shall be presented in a manner which is clearly distinguishable from the other matters, in an intelligible and easily accessible form ... Any part of such a declaration which constitutes an infringement of this Regulation shall not be binding*".

This is likely to mean that the controller has to seek consent in a separate section of a form which asks for agreement to terms and conditions.

4.2.3.24 There is a risk that multiple requests for consent—from terms and conditions to multiple types of processing—may lead to consumer dissatisfaction, if access to services is delayed while these multiple requests for consent are made. Recital 32 warns against this—recommending that, where requests for consent are made by electronic means, the request must not be "*unnecessarily disruptive to the use of the service for which it is provided*". The aim of this provision is to encourage user-friendly design, not to provide an excuse for not requesting consent where required. As the ICO warns:

> "*this is not an exemption and avoiding disruption does not override the need to ensure that consent requests are clear and specific. Some level of disruption may be necessary to obtain valid consent*".

4.2.3.25 Consent can be demonstrated by an individual's conduct, when sufficiently clear. In this situation, the controller would be inferring consent from the conduct. Implied consent is, therefore, still valid under GDPR. However, where a controller infers consent in this way, it may be harder for it to prove this consent at a later date and it may be more difficult for it to demonstrate that the consent was unambiguous (i.e. that the action actually demonstrated consent). Controllers seeking to rely on implied consent are likely to need to document the circumstances surrounding the consent and to have a rigorous approach to what the consent may cover to address these points.

4.2.3.26 The ICO *Consent Guidance* notes that "*this type of implied consent method would not extend beyond what was obvious and necessary*". It gives the following example:

> "*An individual drops their business card into a prize draw box in a coffee shop. This is an affirmative act that clearly indicates they agree to their name and contact number being processed for the purposes of the prize draw. However, this consent does not extend to using those details for marketing or any other purpose and you would need a different lawful basis to do so*".

The EDPB notes that where organisations wish to infer consent from an individual's actions:

> "*they must ensure that the action by which consent is give can be distinguished from other actions. Therefore, merely continuing the ordinary use of a website is not conduct from which one can infer an indication of wishes ... to signify agreement ...*
> *Example 15*
> *Swiping a bar on a screen, waiving ... in front of a smart camera, turning a smartphone around clockwise, or in a figure of eight motion may be options to indicate agreement, as long as clear information is provided, and it is clear that the motion in question signifies agreement to a specific request (e.g. if you swipe this bar to the left, you agree to the use of information X for purpose Y. Repeat this motion to confirm)...*
> *Example 16*
> *Scrolling down or swiping through a website will not satisfy the requirement of a clear and affirmative action. This is because the alert that continuing to scroll will constitute consent may be difficult to distinguish and or may be missed when a data subject is quickly scrolling through large amounts of text and such an action is not sufficiently unambiguous.*"

4.2.4 Explicit

4.2.4.1 In contrast to the general rule that consent can be implied, there are some situations where consent must be explicit. The situations where consent must be explicit are if the controller relies on consent:

- to process special category data;
- for automated decision taking which would otherwise be prohibited; or
- to transfer personal data outside the EU.

4.2.4.2 As the ICO *Consent Guidance* explains:

"The definition of consent says the data subject can signify agreement either by a statement (which would count as explicit consent) or by a clear affirmative action (which would not). Consent that is inferred from someone's actions cannot be explicit consent, however obvious it might be that they consent. Explicit consent must be expressly confirmed in words . . .
. . . Even in a written context, not all consent will be explicit. You should always use an express statement of consent".

The *Guidance* gives two examples to illustrate this point:

"A beauty spa gives a form to its customers on arrival which includes the following:

Skin type and details of any skin conditions (optional): *. . . . . .* *We will use this information to recommend appropriate beauty products. . .*

. . . another beauty spa uses the following statement instead:

Skin type and details of any skin conditions (optional): *. . . . . .* *I consent to you using this information to recommend appropriate beauty products [ ]"*

Both are written: the first produces implied consent; the second is explicit. The ICO guidance also notes that the wording must clearly refer to the particular factor for which consent is being sought. For example, to the processing of a specific type of special category data, or to the details of a decision which is to be taken automatically and what its effect may be.

4.2.5 Children

4.2.5.1 Where a controller provides an online service to children and relies on consent to justify its processing of personal data, it will need to obtain parental consent to the processing. In the UK, this rule applies to children under 13 (DPA 2018 s.9).

4.2.5.2 Recital 38 of the GDPR warns that

"Specific protection should, in particular apply to the used of personal data of children for the purposes of marketing or creating personality or user profiles and the collection of personal data with regard to children when using services offered directly to a child."

This does not mean that parental consent is always required when processing children's data in the context of online services. For example, if the processing is in the controller's legitimate interests, or is necessary to perform a contract, then there is no obligation to obtain parental consent. However, if the controller asks for consent to process personal data, then it should obtain this consent from the parent. **Chapter 14** has more information on this and on the provisions in the GDPR relating to children in general (**14.1**).

4.2.6 Consent on behalf of someone else?

4.2.6.1 The GDPR does not address this. The ICO's conclusion, is that the GDPR does not prevent this, but that "*In practice, it is likely to be difficult in most cases to verify that a third party has the authority to provide consent*" and that "*This is most likely to be appropriate in cases where the individual lacks the capacity to consent and someone else has specific legal authority to make decisions on their behalf*" (e.g. via a power of attorney).

4.2.6.2 It is not clear why the ICO considers that this should be so difficult—and when it comes to revoking consent, the ICO does not seem to see the same difficulty either:

> "*The GDPR does not prevent a third party acting on behalf of an individual to withdraw their consent, but you need to be satisfied that the third party has the authority to do so. This leaves the door open for sectoral opt-out registers or other broader shared opt-out mechanisms, which could help individuals regain control . . . It might also help to demonstrate that consent is as easy to withdraw as it was to give*".

4.2.6.3 In relation to capacity to give consent more generally, again, the GDPR contains no specific rules (save in relation to children—see **4.2.5.2**). It would therefore seem appropriate to follow general rules on capacity and the ICO suggests that "*you can assume that adults have the capacity to consent unless you have reason to believe the contrary*".

4.2.7 Format for and proof of consent

4.2.7.1 There is no requirement for consent to be obtained in any particular format: so long as the requirements above (**4.2.3**) are met, consent could be signed, given in writing electronically (by typing "agree" or ticking a box), or be given orally or by conduct, such as changing settings. The controller must, however, "*be able to demonstrate that the data subject has consented*" (art.7(1))—and it will be more difficult to demonstrate consent in the case of oral or implied consent.

4.2.7.2 The ICO's *Consent Guidance* states that records of consent should include information to demonstrate:

- who has consented (name or other relevant identifier—in an online context this could be user name or the session ID);
- when they consented (a dated document; online records including a time stamp);

- what they were told at the time (the actual statement requesting consent—with information about version numbers and dates in use, which must match the date when consent was obtained); and
- how they consented (a copy of a completed form, or the data submitted online plus time stamp to link to the relevant form).

If consent has been obtained orally, notes should be taken of the date and time and details of the conversation, including a copy of any script used. If consent is later withdrawn, then this date should also be noted.

4.2.7.3 The ICO guidance doesn't say so, but it seems reasonable that any such oral consent is, if at all possible, followed up by an email or other communication from the controller to the data subject stating what they have consented to—with of course the right to withdraw. Including a flag in a system which states consent or opt-in is not sufficient: this shows that the organisation considers that consent has been given but it is not the same as being able to demonstrate that this is, in fact, the case. These records of consent should be kept for as long as the controller relies on that consent to carry out processing. The records may also be retained after that date, to the extent necessary in connection with legal claims, or to meet a legal obligation (WP 259, s.5.1).

4.2.8 Once consent has been obtained

Revocation

4.2.8.1 Article 7(3) provides that "*The data subject shall have the right* to *withdraw his or her consent at any time*". Also, it must "*be as easy to withdraw as to give consent*". At the very least, an individual should be able to withdraw consent using the same medium as was used to give consent: an individual who gave consent by ticking a box, should have an easy online method of withdrawing consent and should not be required to write in or phone up to do this. The ICO also recommends use of preference centres, easily accessible online resources where an individual can access and update permissions. In some circumstances the use of an "unconsent" button (by analogy with unsubscribe buttons) might be appropriate and should certainly be easy to use.

4.2.8.2 Once consent is withdrawn, art.7(3) notes that "*the withdrawal of consent shall not affect the lawfulness of processing based on consent before its withdrawal*".

When an individual withdraws consent, this may not affect the lawfulness of processing which has already taken place. However, it will mean that the controller will be likely to have to delete the personal data: if the controller has justified its processing on the basis of consent, then, if consent is withdrawn, it will no longer have a lawful basis to process the data, meaning that the data should be deleted, since mere storage of the data falls within the definition of processing in art.4(2).

4.2.8.3 If a controller processes personal data for multiple purposes, only one of which is dependent on consent—for example if data are processed to fulfil a contract and for email marketing purposes—then the situation would be different. Here the controller could retain the data for the purposes which do not rely on consent but cease to carry out the processing which requires consent.

4.2.8.4 Both the ICO and the EDPB warn against trying to "switch" lawful bases for processing if consent is withdrawn:

> "*Even if you could originally have relied on a different lawful basis, once you choose to rely on consent you are handing control to the individual. It is inherently unfair to tell people they have a choice, but then continue the processing after they withdraw their consent*" (ICO *Consent Guidance*).

The fact that controllers will be likely to have to delete data if consent is withdrawn, is another reason why organisations should think carefully before seeking to rely on consent.

4.2.8.5 Sometimes this can be counter-intuitive. This is particularly true in the health context. Health care providers rely on consent to provide treatment and on implied consent to process confidential health information for direct care. In the context of medical research, sponsors carry out clinical trials after patients give consent. However, consent is unlikely to be the correct lawful basis to process health data in these situations—because the provider or sponsor would then be likely to have to delete the data if the patient withdrew consent. A healthcare provider is better advised to look to justify its processing as being necessary for diagnosis and provision of care and treatment (art.9(2)(h)) and those carrying out scientific research should look instead to processing for scientific research (art.9(j)) or processing for reasons of public health, which includes ensuring high standards of quality and safety of medicinal products (art.9(i)) (ICO *Consent Guidance*).

4.2.9 Does consent expire?

4.2.9.1 No, as the ICO notes, "*there is no set time limit for consent*". However, because consent has to be specific, as time passes, it is possible that the details of the processing change and that this may require new consent. Because of this, the ICO recommends that controllers review processing based on consent over time, to determine if the consent should be renewed.

4.2.9.2 In its *Direct Marketing Guidance*, the ICO suggests that organisations which have obtained consent from individuals to send direct marketing by email or text, must start to use the data within six months of the date of consent and that it will not be appropriate to first use the data for direct marketing after more than six months (see also **7.4.2.8**).

4.2.9.3 Sometimes, the context in which consent was obtained may also affect the period for which consent is valid. The ICO gives the following example:

> "*A gym runs a promotion that gives members the opportunity to opt in to receiving emails with tips about healthy eating and how to get in shape for their summer holiday that year.*

As the consent request specifies a particular timescales and end point – their summer holiday – the expectation will be that these emails will cease once the summer is over. The consent will therefore expire".

The ICO suggests that "*If in doubt, we recommend you consider refreshing consent every two years*"—this is, however, clearly a best practice recommendation rather than a specific requirement under the GDPR.

4.2.10 Pre-GDPR consent

Recital 171 provides that:

"*Where processing is based on consent pursuant to Directive 95/46/EC, it is not necessary for the data subject to give his or her consent again if the manner in which the consent has been given is in line with the conditions of this Regulation, so as to allow the controller to continue such processing after the date of application of this Regulation*".

Whilst it is helpful that there is no automatic need to seek new consent, the standards for consent under GDPR are such that relatively few controllers may be able to rely on this provision in practice.

4.3 NECESSITY

4.3.1. Controllers always have to ensure that the personal data they process is "*adequate, relevant and limited to what is necessary in relation to the purposes for which they are processed*" (art.5(1)(c) and **5.3.1.2**). Where controllers do not rely on the consent of the individual to process personal data, "*necessity*" has an additional significance. This is because all of the other conditions for processing require that the processing is "necessary" for the relevant purpose.

4.3.2 A similar rule applies when special category and criminal offence data are processed. If the controller processes such data other than where the individual has given explicit consent (or "ordinary" consent for criminal offence data), then in almost all cases the lawful basis for processing only applies where the processing is "necessary" for that purpose.

4.3.3 The ICO Commissioner's Guide has a helpful gloss on what "necessary" means. It states:

"*This does not mean that the processing always has to be essential. However, it must be a targeted and proportionate way of achieving the purpose. The lawful basis will not apply if you can reasonably achieve the purpose by some other less intrusive means.*

It is not enough to argue that processing is necessary because you have chosen to operate your business in a particular way. The question is whether the pro-

cessing is a [sic] *necessary for the stated purpose, not whether it is a necessary part of your chosen method of pursuing that purpose.*"

4.3.4 More guidance—and an example of how this may be applied—can be found in the CJEU case of ***Oesterreichischer Rundfunk*** (joined cases C-465/00, C-138/01, C-139/01, 2003). Among other things, the case considered the provisions in Directive 95/46/EC relating to processing "*necessary for compliance with a legal obligation*" and "*necessary for the performance of a task carried out in the public interest*".

4.3.5 Austrian law required public bodies to report details of salaries paid to certain public employees to the *Rechnungshof* (Court of Audit). The *Rechnungshof*, in turn, published reports which included details of the salaries paid to named individuals. The objective was to ensure that public bodies did not pay unreasonably high salaries, by public scrutiny of salaries paid. Employees of a public broadcaster objected—including on the basis that publication of salaries on an individual basis was not "necessary" for this purpose.

4.3.6 In considering these provisions of the Data Protection Directive, the CJEU referred to Art.8(2) of the European Convention on Human Rights. "*According to the European Court of Human Rights, the adjective 'necessary' . . . implies that a 'pressing social need' is involved and that the measure employed is 'proportionate to the legitimate aim pursued'. . .*". The CJEU remitted to the national courts the question of whether, in this case, publication of individual salaries was necessary—noting that the question arose as to whether the objective could have been met by reporting to the Court of Audit alone, or by publication of reports by the Court of Audit in a more general way (so listing the persons who were employed and some information on financial benefits, but not of the precise payments made).

4.3.7 The meaning of the term "necessary" has also been considered in a number of domestic cases and there is a good summary of these—and of the meaning of "necessary" in ***Michael Cooper v National Crime Agency*** [2019] EWCA Civ 16. Mr. Cooper had been employed by the predecessor to the National Crime Agency, the Serious Organised Crime Agency (SOCA). SOCA required that its staff maintained the highest professional standards of behaviour in and out of work. In April 2012, Mr. Cooper was charged with being drunk and disorderly in a public place and with assaulting police officer. Mr. Cooper reported this to SOCA, as he was required to do. Information about the matter was also shared by the local police force with SOCA in accordance with information sharing agreements. Mr. Cooper was aware of this and did not object to it at the time. He was subject to disciplinary proceedings, which led to his being dismissed by SOCA. Separately, he was convicted of the offences but acquitted on appeal. Mr Cooper had been punched in the same disturbance and he called a medical expert who gave evidence that his behaviour could have been caused by a head injury. The Crown Court acquitted him but, as the Court of Appeal noted, "*this was not a ringing vindication of Mr Cooper. The Court found that Mr Cooper . . . was certainly disorderly, was* *uncooperative with the police* ... [and] *was swearing appallingly in a public place* ..." [34].

4.3.8 Mr Cooper had been concerned that information obtained during the course of the disciplinary investigation would be used in the subsequent prosecution (as was indeed the case) and that this meant that he would not be able to defend himself properly in the disciplinary investigation. For this (and other reasons) he appealed against his dismissal to the Employment Tribunal and the Employment Appeal Tribunal. He also argued that the data sharing between SOCA and the local police force breached the 1998 Act and he brought separate proceedings in this regard. The Court of Appeal considered both the data protection proceedings and the employment proceedings—finding against Mr. Cooper on all of the data protection claims.

4.3.9 In relation to the meaning of "necessary", the Court of Appeal approved of the interpretation suggested by the judge at first instance—that it means "*more than desirable but less than indispensable or absolutely necessary*" [89], [90]. The Court also quoted Baroness Hale, in the case of ***South Lanarkshire Council v Scottish Information Commissioner*** [2013] UKSC 55, who suggested that "*in ordinary language we would understand that a measure would not be necessary if the legitimate aim could be achieved by something less*" [91]. In this case, the Court of Appeal concluded that there were legitimate reasons, in accordance with the 1998 Act, for SOCA to investigate Mr. Cooper's behaviour and it was "necessary" for them to obtain information about the incident from the local police in order to do this [96].

4.4 CONDITIONS FOR PROCESSING NON-SPECIAL CATEGORY DATA

4.4.1 Contractual necessity (article 6(1)(b))

4.4.1.1 This applies where "*processing is necessary for the performance of a contract to which the data subject is a party or in order to take steps at the request of the data subject prior to entering into a contract*".

4.4.1.2 This would apply where a controller processes an individual's name and address in order to deliver goods which the individual has ordered, or where a controller processes bank details of an employee in order to make salary payments.

4.4.1.3 The fact that a contract states that the controller will process personal data, or purports to reserve a right to the controller to do this, does not mean that the processing is actually necessary to perform the contract. On this WP 217 states

> "*The provision must be interpreted strictly and does not cover situations where the processing is not genuinely necessary for the performance of the contract, but rather unilaterally imposed on the data subject by the controller*".

4.4.1.4 The fact that there is a contract between the controller and the individual does not mean that *all* processing relating to this relationship can be justified on this basis. The following examples from WP 217 illustrate this—and suggest a relatively narrow interpretation of the provision by data protection authorities:

(i) a financial services company may carry out a credit reference check on an individual prior to granting a loan. This check is not genuinely made at the request of the individual – rather the processing is carried out because it is in the legitimate interests of the company;

(ii) profiling of customers to identify potential fraudulent transactions is not "necessary" to perform the contract—again, legitimate interests is likely to be more suitable (WP 29 also suggests consent or legal obligation);

(iii) sending formal reminders of outstanding obligations would be necessary to perform the contract. However, WP 29 suggests that sharing data with external debt collection agencies or processing personal data to take a customer who has not paid to court, would not be justified on the basis of performance of the contract—again, legitimate interests is suggested.

4.4.2 Legal obligation (article 6(1)(c))

4.4.2.1 This applies where

"*processing is necessary for compliance with a legal obligation to which the controller is subject*".

This does not necessarily mean an obligation set out in statute. Recital 41 notes that:

"*Where this Regulation refers to a legal basis or a legislative measure, this does not necessarily require a legislative act adopted by a parliament, without prejudice to requirements pursuant to the constitutional order of the Member State concerned. However, such a legal basis or legislative measure should be clear and precise and its application should be foreseeable to persons subject to it, in accordance with case law of the Court of Justice of the European Union . . . and the European Court of Human Rights*".

So, obligations deriving from common law would be covered—as could those imposed by regulators (WP 217, p.20). This condition would not, however, cover requirements imposed by contract (WP 217, p.19).

4.4.2.2 There are further requirements for laws which can justify processing of personal data in art.6(3) and rec.45. They must be EU or Member State laws—so a controller who is required to process personal data by the laws of another country must find another justification for this (perhaps legitimate interests, if the other requirements of that condition are met). In addition, the law should set out:

> "... *the general conditions governing the lawfulness of* ... *processing; the types of data which are subject to the processing; the data subjects concerned, the entities to and the purposes for which, the personal data may be disclosed; the purpose limitation; storage periods; and processing operations and processing procedures, including measures to ensure lawful and fair processing*...".

Data protection authorities (e.g. the Information Commissioner) are also tasked with advising on legislative measures relating to processing of personal data (art.57(c)). The requirements set out in art.6(3) and rec.45 are expressed to be relevant both to processing which is required by law and to processing necessary for tasks in the public interest. For this reason, we are going to take this condition next and defer vital interests until later (**4.4.4**).

4.4.3 Public interest tasks

4.4.3.1 This applies where "*processing is necessary for a task carried out in the public interest or in the exercise of official authority*". Section 8 of the DPA 2018 includes non-exhaustive examples of processing covered by this condition. These are largely taken from Sch.2 of the 1998 Act and cover processing of personal data that is necessary for:

"*a) the administration of justice;*
b) the exercise of a function of either House of Parliament;
c) the exercise of a function conferred on a person by an enactment or rule of law;
d) the exercise of a function of the Crown, a Minister of the Crown or a government department; or
e) an activity that supports or promotes democratic engagement".

This last item is expanded on in the Explanatory Notes, which comment that it "*is intended to cover a wide range of political activities inside and outside of election periods*", including communicating with electors, surveying, activities to increase turnout, work to support candidates or elected representatives and fundraising for these activities. The *Michael Cooper* case (**4.3.7–4.3.9**), considered the equivalent provision under the 1998 Act, noting that the term "function" has a "wide ambit" including "*actions taken to comply with any statutory duty or actions taken in order to exercise any statutory power*" [105].

4.4.3.2 This condition is *not* restricted to public bodies alone. Recital 45 notes that "*It should ... be for Union or Member State law to determine whether the controller performing a task carried out in the public interest or in the exercise of official authority should be a public authority or another natural or legal person governed by public law, or, where it is in the public interest to do so, ... by private law, such as a professional association*".

4.4.3.3 In other words, for a public interest task, one looks to EU or Member State law to see what types of entities can carry out that activity. There is a good example of this in the ICO's *Guide to GDPR*:

"Private water companies are likely to be able to rely on the public task basis even if they do not fall within the definition of a public authority in the DPA 2018. This is because they are considered to be carrying out functions of public administration and they exercise special legal powers to carry out utility services in the public interest".

The GDPR also leaves it to Member States to determine which bodies amount to public authorities. This is addressed at s.7 of the DPA 2018, which provides that the terms public authority and public body means public authorities under the Freedom of Information Act 2000 or, for Scotland, the Freedom of Information (Scotland) Act 2002. There are certain exceptions listed at s.7(3), principally including parish councils and meetings and community councils and meetings in Wales and Scotland. There is provision for secondary legislation to add to, or remove, bodies from the scope.

4.4.3.4 Section 7(2) provides that:

"An authority or body that falls within subsection (1) is only a 'public authority' or 'public body' for the purposes of GDPR when performing a task carried out in the public interest or in the exercise of official authority vested in it".

Where public authorities process personal data for purposes which are outside their public interest tasks, then they can look to legitimate interests. The ICO gives the example of a university, which *"might rely on public task for processing personal data for teaching and research purposes; but a mixture of legitimate interests and consent for alumni relations and fundraising purposes"*.

4.4.4 Vital interests

4.4.4.1 This applies where processing is *"necessary in order to protect the vital interests of the data subject or of another natural person"*. Recital 46 suggests that this would apply where *"essential for the life of the data subject or that of another person"*, although it could also cover *"monitoring epidemics* . . . [and] *humanitarian emergencies, in particular in situations of natural and man-made disasters"*. It is intended to be an emergency condition and *"should in principle take place only where the processing cannot be manifestly based on another legal basis"*.

4.4.5 Legitimate interests

Legislative provisions and guidance

4.4.5.1 Article 6(1)(f) permits processing of personal data which:

"is necessary for the purposes of the legitimate interests pursued by the controller or by a third party, except where such interests are overridden by the interests or fundamental rights of the data subject which require protection of personal data, in particular where the data subject is a child.

Point (f) of the first sub-paragraph shall not apply to processing carried out by public authorities in the performance of their tasks".

There is detailed analysis of the provision in the ICO's *Legitimate Interests Guidance* (*Lawful basis for processing: Legitimate Interests,* March 2018) and in the Opinion of the Article 29 Working Party from 2014, WP 217.

4.4.5.2 In the ***Rigas*** case (***Valsts policijas Rigas regiona parvaldes Kartibas policijas parvalde v Rigas pašvaldibas SIA 'Rigas satiksme'*** (C-13/16) EU:C:2017:336, the Court of Justice of the EU analysed the equivalent provision at art.7(1)(f) of the old Data Protection Directive. The CJEU considered that there were three elements:

- identifying the relevant interests;
- determining if the processing was necessary; and
- balancing this with the interests of the individual.

We have followed this three-part assessment in this chapter.

4.4.5.3 Public bodies and children's data are specifically called out in Art.6(1)(e)–(f). Public bodies may assume from the comment in the Article that they can never justify their processing of personal data on the basis of their legitimate interests. This is not necessarily the case and there is comment on this below (**4.4.5.4**). Section **14.1** looks in more detail at processing children's data.

Special cases: public bodies

4.4.5.4 Recital 47 explains the reason behind the restriction on public bodies relying on the legitimate interests provision: because "*. . . it is for the legislator to provide by law for the legal basis for public authorities to process personal data*".

4.4.5.5 Where a public body's tasks are set out by law, there is no need for any other lawful basis for processing—and the relevant condition would be art.6(1)(e) (processing necessary for the performance of a task carried out in the public interest or in the exercise of official authority vested in the controller). However, not all activities undertaken by a public body would fall under this condition. For example, commercial activities undertaken by universities (such as renting out accommodation to private conferences) would fall outside this. Here, the ICO's *Legitimate Interests Guidance* notes:

> "*. . . if you have other legitimate purposes outside the scope of your tasks as a public authority, you can consider legitimate interests where appropriate. This will be particularly relevant for public authorities with commercial interests*".

Determining the legitimate interests

4.4.5.6 The legitimate interests can be those of the controller itself, or of a third party. The ICO's *Legitimate Interests Guidance* states that:

"... you (or a third party) must have some clear and specific benefit or outcome in mind. It is not enough to rely on vague or generic business interests".

the GDPR talks about interests "pursued by" the controller—and the Article 29 Working Party notes that this means that there must be a *"a real and present interest (i.e. not be speculative)".*

The interests must also be "legitimate", on which the ICO notes:

"Anything illegitimate, unethical or unlawful is not a legitimate interest. For example, although marketing may in general be a legitimate purpose, sending spam emails in breach of electronic marketing rules is not legitimate".

4.4.5.7 The recitals to the GDPR include examples of processing which will, or may be, for a legitimate interest. They also suggest relevant factors to consider when assessing this in other circumstances. The recitals reference the following purposes:

- processing strictly necessary to prevent fraud (rec.47);
- processing strictly necessary to ensure network and information security, such as preventing unauthorised access to networks and denial of service attacks (i.e. overwhelming a website with activity so that is cannot be available) (rec.49) (both this and fraud prevention are described as purposes which constitute legitimate interests). By contrast, the purposes listed below are given as examples of purposes which *may* be carried out for legitimate interests (i.e. this is not pre-determined);
- sharing data within a corporate group for internal administrative purposes including processing client and employee data (rec.48); and
- processing for direct marketing (rec.47).

4.4.5.8 Not all direct marketing can be justified based on legitimate interests. For example, direct marketing by email can often require consent under the ePrivacy Directive. In that case, the specific rules of the ePrivacy Directive would take precedence and, as the ICO *Legitimate Interests Guidance* notes,

"If you have obtained consent in compliance with e-privacy laws, then in practice consent is also the appropriate basis under the GDPR. Trying to apply legitimate interest when you already have GDPR-compliant consent would be an entirely unnecessary exercise and would cause confusion for individuals".

4.4.5.9 Furthermore, under GDPR art.21(3), data subjects have a right to object to direct marketing. Clearly, where such an objection has been raised, the controller can no longer rely on legitimate interests for processing, i.e. sending direct marketing to that particular data subject. However, outside of these rules, legitimate interests can apply to direct marketing. In the context of processing data about business contacts, the ICO notes that "*it is likely that much of this type of processing will be lawful on the basis of legitimate interests*" although "*there is no absolute rule*".

4.4.5.10 If the processing is not for one of the purposes described above (**4.4.5.7**), the controller itself will have to determine whether the purpose is legitimate. The ICO notes that the condition can be of wide application as the purposes "*they include commercial interests, individual interests, or broader societal benefits*" (p.80). Relevant factors to consider are set out at rec.47; in particular, looking at whether

> "*there is a relevant and appropriate relationship between the data subject and the controller in situations such as where the data subject is a client or in the service of the controller*"

and

> "*the reasonable expectations of data subjects...including whether a data subject can reasonably expect at the time and in the context of the collection of the personal data that processing for that purpose may take place*".

The ICO notes that "*This is an objective test. The question is not whether a particular individual actually expected the processing, but whether a reasonable person should expect the processing in the circumstances*".

4.4.5.11 The ICO also warns that controllers cannot short-circuit proper consideration of legitimate interests purely by providing notice of their data processing:

> "*Although reasonable expectations is an important factor, it does not automatically determine the outcome. Simply having warned the individual in advance that their data will be processed in a certain way does not necessarily mean that your legitimate interests always prevail, irrespective of harm ...*".

4.4.5.12 The ICO *Legitimate Interests Guidance* contains other examples of processing which may be for a legitimate interest, including:

- keeping details of emergency contacts for employees at work;
- lenders sharing data with credit reference agencies, to avoid over-commitment by borrowers;
- a company sharing details of employee misconduct with legal advisers for advice on whether it is justified in dismissing the employee.

4.4.5.13 WP 217 also includes a non-exhaustive list of commonly occurring legitimate interests. Those not already mentioned are:

- exercising a right of freedom of expression;
- enforcing legal claims and debt collection;
- preventing misuse of services and money laundering;
- employee monitoring for safety or management purposes;
- whistleblowing schemes; and
- processing for historical, scientific or statistical purposes or for research purposes (including market research).

4.4.5.14 The *Rigas* case mentioned above **(4.4.5.2)** also notes that there is a legitimate interest in a third party obtaining details of someone who damaged their property in order to take legal proceedings against that person. In ***František Ryneš v Úřad pro ochranu osobních údajů*** (CJEU C-212/1311, December 2014) (a case relating to CCTV used by a private individual to monitor his property and the public space leading to his home), the CJEU considered that protection of property, health and the life of the individual's family could be legitimate interests. WP 217 also notes that the fact that processing is referenced in guidance by other (EU or Member State) regulators is also an indicator that the processing is likely to be for a legitimate interest.

4.4.5.15 The fact that an interest is legitimate in some cases does not, however, mean that the processing is automatically permissible on all occasions. Other factors such as the scale of the processing and the degree of the intrusion will be relevant (WP 217, p.26).

Is the processing necessary?

4.4.5.16 Even if a controller is seeking to achieve a legitimate purpose, it should not process personal data which is not necessary for that purpose. As the *Legitimate Interests Guidance* notes:

> "*This doesn't mean that it has to be absolutely essential, but it must be a targeted and proportionate way of achieving your purpose*".

The ICO uses the example of background screening to make this point—here the organisation must determine which checks are actually necessary for the various roles at the organisation.

The interests of the individual

4.4.5.17 A controller can only justify its processing on this basis if "*the interests or the fundamental rights and freedoms of the data subject are not overriding*" (rec.47). However, as the *Legitimate Interests Guidance* notes "*even if the processing might have a negative impact on the individual, this does not automatically mean that their interest always override yours*".

Recital 75 explains the types of risks which processing of personal data can present to individuals and this may a useful list of factors for an organisation to assess when it considers relying on legitimate interests. These include:

- risk of physical, material or non-material damage;
- discrimination;
- identity theft or fraud;
- financial loss;
- damage to reputation;
- loss of confidentiality of data or unauthorised reversal of pseudonymisation;
- being deprived of rights.

4.4.5.18 Recital 75 also reminds us that the nature of the data is also relevant—in particular if it is special category, or relates to vulnerable persons, or is processed on a very large scale so affects many individuals. Once a controller has determined the risks posed to individuals by the processing, it must then balance its interests with the interests of the individuals' and determine if the individuals' interests override the interests of the organisation. This is commonly referred to as the "balancing test" or, in the ICO's *Legitimate Interests Guidance*, the legitimate interests assessment (LIA).

4.4.5.19 By way of an example, in the direct marketing context, the ICO cites the following factors as being relevant in this balancing test (*Legitimate Interests Guidance*):

- individuals' expectations;
- the potential nuisance factor of unwanted marketing messages;
- the effect of the method and frequency of communication on more vulnerable individuals; and
- whether an opt-out was offered initially.

4.4.5.20 The ***Rigas*** case considered that whether or not the data could be accessed in public sources (para.32) was also a relevant factor in the balancing test. Much of the ***Google Spain*** case (***Google Spain SL, Google Inc v Agencia Española de Protección de Datos (AEPD), Mario Costeja González (C-131/12)***, 13 May 2014), was spent considering the balancing test between Google's interests and those of other internet users and the interests of the individual who had asked Google to delist their search results. The CJEU noted that this would be a case-by-case analysis: as a general rule, the interests of the individual would prevail, although in some cases the interests of internet users in having access to information may be more significant, in particular where the individual has a public role [81]. However, Google's economic interests in operating its search engine could never justify the serious interference with the individual rights [81].

4.4.5.21 The last point in the ICO guidance reminds that the choices offered by a controller to individuals and the safeguards it implements, may affect the balancing test. As well as rights to object, WP 217 also points to:

- technical and organisational measures to ensure that the processing does not have an impact on individuals;
- use of anonymisation, aggregation, or other privacy enhancing technologies; and
- increased transparency and rights for individuals to gain increased control over (and benefits from) their data.

Documenting the balancing test

4.4.5.22 The ICO recommends that controllers keep a record of their legitimate interests assessment. It provides a list of relevant factors to consider and a sample LIA template in *Legitimate Interests Guidance*.

Other considerations

4.4.5.23 Where an organisation relies on legitimate interests, this has an impact on individuals' rights:

- the right to portability does not apply to data processed on the basis of legitimate interests (art.20(1)(a)); and
- individuals have a right to object to processing carried out on this basis—and the organisation must draw this to their attention at the outset (art.21(1)).

It is useful to note that, once an individual objects, the balancing test tilts in favour of the individual. The controller has to cease processing unless it can demonstrate that its interests are compelling.

4.5 SPECIAL CATEGORY DATA AND DATA ABOUT CRIMINAL OFFENCES

4.5.1 The prohibition on processing special category data

4.5.1.1 Article 9(1) of the GDPR provides that processing of "special category" data (sensitive personal data) is prima facie prohibited. Article 9(2) then sets out a number of occasions when this prohibition does not apply. "Special category data" is personal data revealing racial or ethnic origin, political opinions, religious or philosophical belief, or trade union membership, and the processing of genetic data, biometric data for the purpose of uniquely identify someone, data concerning health, sex life or sexual orientation.

4.5.2 Prohibition on processing criminal offence data

4.5.2.1 The 1998 Act treated criminal offence data as one more category of sensitive personal data. This was a practical approach, but both the 1995 Directive and now the GDPR treat criminal offence data as a distinct type of data, separate from other special category data. Article 10 of the GDPR provides that

> "*processing of personal data relating to criminal convictions and offences or related security measures . . . shall be carried out only under the control of official authority or when the processing is authorised by Union or Member State law providing for appropriate safeguards for the rights and freedoms of data subjects. A comprehensive register of criminal convictions shall be kept only under the control of official authority*".

4.5.2.2 The DPA 2018 tries to push the approach of the 1998 Act into the framework of the GDPR. The DPA 2018 follows the GDPR in treating criminal offence data as a separate category of data. However, s.10(5) of the Act then provides that any of the conditions for processing special category data set out in Sch.1, Pt 2 (substantial public interest) and Pt 3 (additional conditions relating to criminal convictions, etc.) of the Act, may be used as a lawful basis to process criminal offence data—so in substance following the principles of the old 1998 Act.

4.5.3 Permitted processing of special category data

4.5.3.1 Article 9 sets out occasions when special category data can be processed. Some of these occasions apply without any need for Member State legislation (for example, processing of personal data which is necessary for legal claims). However, on other occasions (for example processing for management of healthcare), the condition only applies where the processing is carried out on the basis of Union or Member State law —here the reference to the processing in art.9 is not sufficient: there must also be an additional legislative provision governing the processing.

4.5.3.2 The DPA 2018 addresses conditions for processing special category and criminal offence data in Sch.1. Where the GDPR permits special category data to be processed for purposes—such as management of healthcare—on the basis of Union or Member State law, then Sch.1 provides the legal framework for this processing in the UK.

4.5.3.3 Most of the conditions in Sch.1 apply to both special category data and to criminal offence data. However, as these are separate concepts under GDPR, there is scope for differences in approach. Schedule 1, Pt 3 addresses this, providing that consent to process criminal offence data can be implied, not explicit; and references to processing being in the "substantial public interest" are disapplied for criminal offence data. Schedule 1, Pt 3 (para.35) also introduces an additional condition for processing, which is unique to criminal offence data (relating to administration of payment cards used in connection with child pornography.

It enables credit card companies to collect the information necessary to convict someone using a credit card for this purpose).

4.5.3.4 In this chapter, we have considered all of the conditions set out in the GDPR relating to special category data. Many of the additional conditions introduced by the DPA 2018 are only of interest to particular sectors or bodies. However, where conditions are likely of wider relevance, we have commented on them in this chapter. **Appendix 4** has a full listing of all conditions relating to processing of special category data and criminal offence data. As a preliminary matter, we have also set out some general comments on the approach taken in the DPA 2018 to special category data.

4.5.4 Processing authorised by law

4.5.4.1 Article 9(2)(g) provides that special category data can be processed, in addition to the conditions set out in the GDPR, where the processing is:

> "*necessary for reasons of substantial public interest, on the basis of Union or Member State law which shall be proportionate to the aim pursued, respect the essence of the right to data protection and provide for suitable and specific measures to safeguard the fundamental rights and freedoms of the data subject*".

Article 9(2)(g) is an enabling provision—allowing subject matter specific, or Member State specific provisions to be introduced which permit processing of special category data.

4.5.4.2 In this chapter, we have followed the structure of the GDPR, describing the conditions for processing set out in the GDPR itself, and then addressing those which the UK has chosen to introduce in addition to the GDPR.

4.5.4.3 There is also an enabling provision at art.9(4). This relates specifically to processing of "*genetic data, biometric data or data concerning health*" and it allows Member States to maintain or introduce additional conditions allowing processing of such data, or limitations, on the processing of such data. Recital 53 reminds us that one of the objectives of the Regulation is to "*provide harmonised conditions for . . . processing*" including health data. Accordingly, any conditions or limitations "*should not hamper the free flow of personal data within the Union when those conditions apply to cross-border processing of such data*".

4.5.4.4 Where personal data is processed on the basis of EU or Member State law, any such law must always adequately address data protection considerations. These are described at **4.4.2.2** above. As long as data protection requirements are addressed, the GDPR does not require that the laws relating to special category data should be focused exclusively on data protection. It would, therefore, be perfectly possible for these requirements to be set out in relevant subject matter specific laws. The UK, however, has chosen to set out all UK related laws in the DPA 2018 and s.10 of the Act provides that "*processing meets the requirement ... for a basis in the law of the United Kingdom or a part of the United Kingdom only if it meets a condition in ... Schedule 1*".

4.5.4.5 Schedule 1, Pt 1, corresponds to the provisions in art.9 of GDPR which refer to a basis in Member State law. Schedule 1, Pt 2, sets out additional substantial public interest-based processing conditions, permitted by art.9(2)(g), and Sch.1, Pt 3 contains additional provisions relating to criminal convictions.

4.5.4.6 This has the benefit of providing more certainty as to what is allowed, or not allowed, and it means that controllers can look to one place for all relevant UK conditions. However, it means that Sch.1 will (like its predecessor, Sch.3 to the Data Protection Act 1998) have to be kept up to date. Enabling provisions for this are included in s.10(6), which allows for secondary legislation to add to or remove or vary the conditions in Sch.1. In addition, in most cases, the law must also provide for "appropriate safeguards" the for individuals. Because this requirement applies to many of the conditions for processing personal data, we have considered this first below.

Appropriate safeguards

4.5.4.7 Article 9 of the GDPR provides that special category data may be processed, on the basis of EU or Member State law, for a number of purposes which are either defined in the GDPR itself, or which can be set out in other EU/Member State law. Article 9 also adds the proviso that these laws must also include "appropriate safeguards" for individuals.

4.5.4.8 Schedule 1, Pt 4 of the DPA 2018 sets out what safeguards must be in place. Somewhat confusingly, the safeguards:

- Only apply to the conditions set out in Pts 1 and 3 of Sch.1 where the particular condition states that a controller must have appropriate safeguards in place.
- Apply generally to all of the conditions in Pt 2 of Sch.1, unless the condition says that there is no requirement for appropriate safeguards to be in place.

Appendix 4, which lists all conditions for processing special category data available at January 2019, indicates if safeguards must be in place or not. Schedule 1, Pt 4, of the DPA 2018 sets out the additional safeguards, which are described below.

An "appropriate policy document"

4.5.4.9 This must explain the controller's procedures for complying with GDPR Art.5 (data protection principles) and the controller's policies as regards retention and erasure, "*giving an indication of how long such personal data* *is likely to be retained*" (para.39(b)) and must be retained by the controller, reviewed and, if necessary, updated from time to time; and be available to the Information Commissioner on request and without charge. This obligation must be met for the period of processing and for six months after processing has ceased.

An extended record of processing

4.5.4.10 Most controllers must maintain a record of processing activities under art.30 GDPR. For special category data where additional safeguards are required, the record of processing activities must also indicate which special category condition is relied on, which art.6 condition is relied on and whether the personal data are actually being retained and erased in accordance with the policies set out in the policy document and, if not, why not.

4.5.5 Conditions provided for in the GDPR

Explicit consent (article 9(2)(a))

4.5.5.1 Special category data may be processed where "*the data subject has given explicit consent to the processing of those personal data for one or more specified purposes*". EU or Member State law can "*provide that the prohibition* [on processing special category data] . . . *may not be lifted by the data subject*". In other words, Member States can stipulate that certain types of processing of special category data cannot take place *even if* the individual gives consent to this. The UK has not prohibited any processing of special category data in this way.

Employment, social security or social protection law (article 9(2)(b), DPA 2018, Schedule 1, Part 1, paragraph.1)

4.5.5.2 This applies where the processing is "*necessary for the purposes of carrying out the obligations and exercising specific rights of the controller or of the data subject in the field of employment and social security and social protection law in so far as it is authorised by Union or Member State law or a collective agreement pursuant to Member State law providing for appropriate safeguards for the fundamental rights and the interests of the data subject*".

Pursuant to paras 1(1)(b) and 2 of Sch.1, the controller must have appropriate safeguards in place.

4.5.5.3 Schedule 1, Part 1, para.1(3) of the Act references EU legislation which describes social security and social protection. The Explanatory Notes to the DPA 2018, para.617, note that this would cover a wide range of social service interventions—in connection with health care or sickness; disability; old age; survivorship; family and children; unemployment; housing; and social exclusion. Recital 52 gives the example of law relating to pensions.

4.5.5.4 The equivalent provision in the 1998 Act, permitted processing where

> "*The processing is necessary for the purposes of exercising or performing any right or obligation which is conferred or imposed by law on the data controller in connection with employment*" (Sch.3, para.2(1)).

In the ***Michael Cooper*** case (**4.3.7–4.3.9**) the Court of Appeal suggested (obiter) that this "*might well be apt to describe the (enforceable) rights and obligations of which arise under a contract*" [118].

Vital interests (article 9(2)(c))

4.5.5.5 The processing must be necessary to protect the "*vital interests of the data subject or of another natural person*". Unlike the equivalent condition for processing normal personal data (as to which see **4.4.4**: the guidance on this will also be relevant to special category data), here the data subject must be "*physically or legally incapable of giving consent*".

Associations and foundations pursuing political, philosophical, religious or trade union purposes (article 9(2)(d))

4.5.5.6 This covers associations, foundations and other not-for-profit bodies, with "*a political, philosophical, religious or trade union aim*". The condition only covers processing about "*members, former members ... or persons who have regular contact with it*" and must be "*in connection with its purposes and* [on condition] *that the personal data are not disclosed outside that body without the consent of the data subject*".

Personal data which are manifestly made public by the data subject (article 9(2)(e))

4.5.5.7 This would cover material issued to the press, or postings in social media with a public setting. The equivalent condition in the 1998 Act was considered in ***NT1 and NT2 v Google LLC and the Information Commissioner (intervenor)*** ([2018] EWHC 799 QB). The case considered requests by two individuals to Google to have conviction data about them delisted from search results (see also **6.9.2.8** on the right to erasure). Because the case concerned criminal offence data, one of the points considered was how Google could justify its processing of this type of data. The judge rejected most of Google's arguments on this point —but did consider that Google would be able to use the 1998 Act Sch.3, para.5 —"*the information contained in the personal data has been made public as a result of steps deliberately taken by the data subject*".

4.5.5.8 Warby J noted that the condition:

"A person who deliberately conducts himself in a criminal fashion runs the risk of apprehension, prosecution, trial, conviction and sentence. Publicity for what happens at trial is the ordinary consequence of the open justice principle".

4.5.5.9 Unsurprisingly, counsel for the claimants argued that the UK approach was inconsistent with the requirements of the Data Protection Directive. Warby J disagreed. He referred to the European Court of Human Rights (ECtHR) case of ***Axel Springer AG v Germany*** ((2012) 32 BHRC [83]). Here the publisher had been sanctioned for publishing information about a celebrity's arrest, conviction and sentence for possession of cocaine. The ECtHR considered this to breach the publisher's rights under art.10, noting that

"whilst reputation is protected by art.8 of the Convention, 'it cannot be relied on in order to complain of a loss of reputation which is the foreseeable consequence of one's own actions such as, for example, the commission of a criminal offence ...'".

Warby J also considered the difference in wording between the 1998 Act and the condition in the Data Protection Directive (which is identical to that in the GDPR). While he felt that the provision in the Directive used "rather obscure language" he did not think any difference was a sufficient reason to depart from his interpretation of the UK provision.

Legal claims (article 9(2)(f))

4.5.5.10 This applies where the processing is "*necessary for the establishment, exercise or defence of legal claims or whenever courts are acting in their judicial capacity*". Recital 52 notes that it applies both to matters in court and to out of court settlements.

4.5.5.11 Processing necessary in the context of legal claims is also an exemption to the restrictions on data transfers out of the EEA. As the provision is phrased in identical terms, comment on this provision is also of interest to the special category data condition. In that context, Recital 111 notes that this also applies to administrative procedures and procedures before regulatory bodies.

4.5.5.12 The Article 29 Working Party gave guidance on this phrase—in the context of data transfers—in 2007, in WP 114. Here it noted that

"this exception cannot be used to justify the transfer of all ... employee files to the group's parent company on the grounds of the possibility that such legal proceedings might be brought one day".

In other words, there must be a realistic possibility of proceedings, not theoretical possibility.

Health and social care (article 9(2)(h); DPA 2018, Schedule 1, Part 1, paragraph 2)

4.5.5.13 This applies where the processing is necessary for

"*the purposes of preventative or occupational medicine, for the assessment of the working capacity of the employee, medical diagnosis, the provision of health or social care or treatment or the management of health or social care systems and services on the basis of Union or Member State law or pursuant to a contract with a health professional and subject to the conditions and safeguards referred to in paragraph 3*".

These specific purposes are copied out in Sch.1, Pt 1, para.2(2) of the DPA 2018.

4.5.5.14 GDPR art.9(3) restricts who may carry out processing on this basis to

"*processing by or under the responsibility of a professional subject to the obligation of professional secrecy under Union or Member State law or rules established by national competent bodies or by another person also subject to an obligation of secrecy under Union or Member State law or rules established by national competent bodies*".

4.5.5.15 The condition is considerably expanded from the equivalent condition in the Data Protection Directive. It can cover areas such as occupational health, as well as processing for wider management and quality control purposes. Recital 52 references processing to "*ensure quality and cost-effectiveness of the procedures used for settling claims for benefits and services in the health insurance system*" and rec.53 which refers to processing by "*management and central national health authorities... for the purpose of quality control, management information and the general national and local supervision of the health or social care system*". However, rec.53 also emphasises that special category data may only be processed for these purposes where this is for "*the benefit of natural persons and society as a whole*".

4.5.5.16 Section 11 of the DPA 2018 makes clear which persons are permitted to rely on this condition in the UK—and this is stated to

"*include circumstances in which it* [the processing] *is carried out–*

a) *by or under the responsibility of a health professional or a social work professional, or*

b) *by another person who in the circumstances owes a duty of confidentiality under an enactment or rule of law*".

This would, therefore, include professionals where there is a professional duty of confidentiality (and various categories of health and social work professionals are listed in s.204 of the DPA 2018) as well as individuals who are subject to an equitable duty of confidentiality. The condition is stated to "include" these individuals – it is, therefore, possible that other individuals could also satisfy the appropriate person test in art.9(2)(h) if they are subject to other professional obligations of confidentiality.

Public health (article 9(2)(i); DPA 2018, Schedule,1, Part 1, paragraph 3)

4.5.5.17 This applies where processing is "*necessary for reasons of public interest in the area of public health*". The GDPR provides that this must be on the basis of Union or Member State law, which provides "*suitable and specific safeguards ... in particular professional secrecy*". Schedule 1, Pt 1, para.3 of the DPA 2018 addresses this in an identical way to the rules for processing data for health and social care purposes, although the condition does not explicitly reference social workers.

4.5.5.18 Public health could include "*serious cross-border threats to health ... ensuring high standards of quality and safety of health care and of medicinal products or medical devices*" (art.9(2)(h)). Recital 54 notes that it extends to "*all elements related to health, namely health status, including morbidity and disability, the determinants having an effect on that health status, health care needs, resources allocated to health care, the provision of, and universal access to, health care as well as health care expenditure and financing and the cause of mortality*". However, "*such processing ... for reasons of public interest, should not result in personal data being processed for other purposes by third parties such as employers or insurance and banking companies*".

4.5.5.19 While this would rule out data obtained for this purpose being used at a later date by employers, insurance or financial service providers, the condition is not limited to public authorities. Pharmaceutical companies, for example, could rely on this condition to justify processing of health data for pharmacovigilance purposes, for example, where a patient reports an adverse event.

Archiving, scientific and historical research and statistical purposes (article 9(2)(j); DPA 2018, Schedule 1, Part 1 paragraph 4)

4.5.5.20 This allows processing of special category data where necessary for archiving purposes in the public interest, scientific or historical research purposes or statistical purposes in accordance with Art.89(1) based on Union or Member State law.

4.5.5.21 The UK law is set out in both Sch.1, Pt 1 para.4 and s.19 of the DPA 2018. There are requirements that the research is in the public interest; that it must not be likely to cause substantial damage or substantial distress to a data subject; and that it must not be carried out for measures or decisions relating to particular data subjects unless it is approved medical research. **Chapter 10** contains more details on the research and statistics provisions.

4.5.6 UK-specific conditions

Consent is not a suitable condition

4.5.6.1 Many of the conditions introduced by the DPA 2018 only apply if consent would not be a suitable lawful basis for the controller. The conditions refer to this in different ways, but six scenarios recur (although, confusingly, some of the conditions include more than one of these formulations). Because these scenarios recur, we have considered them all together at the outset. **Appendix 4**, which lists all conditions for processing special category and criminal offence data and sets out which of the various consent scenarios apply to each condition.

Individual cannot give consent

4.5.6.2 In Sch.1, Pt 2, paras 18, 19, 23 and 24, one situation where the condition applies is where "*in the circumstances, consent to the processing cannot be given*". This would presumably cover occasions where the individual is incapable of giving consent—for example where the patient was unconscious or lacked mental capacity.

Tipping-off considerations

4.5.6.3 This applies where "*the processing must be carried out without the consent of the data subject because obtaining the consent of the data subject would prejudice the provision of*" the relevant service or processing. The other scenarios refer to consent generally, rather than to "*obtaining*" consent. Accordingly, it seems to be the act of seeking consent which is seen as problematic in these conditions. By way of example, this scenario is relevant to the conditions which allow processing of special category data for confidential counselling services and for the safeguarding of children and vulnerable adults.

Consent would prejudice the purpose

4.5.6.4 This applies where the processing "*must be carried out without the consent of the data subject so as not to prejudice those purposes*". This scenario does not refer to "*obtaining*" consent—so is not limited to situations where it is the act of seeking consent which is problematic. Rather this would apply to any situation where the controller must process the data to achieve the relevant purpose, irrespective of whether or not an individual has given consent or has withdrawn consent.

4.5.6.5 This scenario is referenced in only three conditions: processing to prevent or detect unlawful acts (para.10); processing for functions which protect the public against dishonesty (para.11) and processing for sports integrity purposes (para.28). The Explanatory Notes explain that the scenario applies in the following situation:

"... where seeking consent ... would prejudice those purposes, which would cover a situation where giving the data subject a choice or giving them the necessary information required for valid consent would prejudice the purpose; or where valid consent is not possible because a refusal to consent could cause detriment".

It would be unreasonable to obtain consent

4.5.6.6 This applies where: "*in the circumstances, the controller cannot reasonably be expected to obtain the consent of the data subject to the processing*". One example where this scenario is included, is where processing is necessary for regulatory requirements which involve establishing whether an individual has committed an unlawful act or been involved in dishonesty etc. (para.12). In introducing this legal basis at Committee Stage, the Minister explained that:

"the condition can be used only in circumstances where the controller cannot reasonably be expected to obtain the data subject's consent to process data — for example, where the controller processes data from sanction lists and therefore does not have contact details for individuals."

4.5.6.7 This seems to equate reasonable with practicable. If a provider knows the address of an individual, or could readily obtain it, then it may be practicable to ask for consent. However, in practice, a financial organisation making sanctions list checks would still have to undertake this check even if consent were withheld. This would mean that having to obtain consent would prejudice that organisation's ability to fulfil this purpose. Logically a broader interpretation would seem more appropriate to this scenario than that suggested by the Minister's example. However, if this broader interpretation were adopted, there would be no difference between this scenario and the one above (where a requirement for consent would prejudice the purpose). Some distinction certainly appears to be intended, given some of the conditions cite both scenarios as alternatives (for example, the safeguarding conditions (paras 18 and 19)).

It is reasonable to process personal data without the data subject's consent

4.5.6.8 Someone trying to read the DPA 2018 quickly could be forgiven for assuming that a permission to process data when it is "unreasonable to be required to obtain" consent is the same as permission for processing when this is "reasonable without obtaining" consent. However, in the scheme of Sch.1, the two concepts are different. The second scenario applies to processing which "can reasonably be carried out without the consent of the data subject". This is further defined in these conditions as:

"where the controller cannot reasonably be expected to obtain the consent of the data subject; and
the controller is not aware of the data subject withholding consent".

Further, "*the reference ... to a data subject withholding consent does not include a data subject merely failing to respond to a request for consent*" (para.9(2)).

4.5.6.9 Some of the conditions where this is relevant are processing for purposes of equal opportunities monitoring for senior roles (para.9(1)), processing to support those with disabilities or medical conditions (para.16(1)) and the insurance and occupational health conditions (paras 20 and 21).

4.5.6.10 The scenario seems designed to cover situations where consent may be difficult to obtain (i.e. processing personal data of relatives of the member of a pension scheme) or where it may be difficult to obtain valid consent under the GDPR (equal opportunities monitoring, due to the difficulty of proving freely given consent from employees). It is more protective of the individual than the "unreasonable to obtain consent" scenario, as the condition does *not* apply if the controller is aware that the individual withholds consent. It seems, therefore, that a right to object is built into the condition.

4.5.6.11 This drafting approach is odd and leads to an impractical scenario: if it is unreasonable to expect the controller to ask for consent, then presumably the controller will not ask for consent. In presenting para.9 to the Commons Committee, the Minister did not elaborate, stating only that:

> "*the processing condition will apply only until such point as it is reasonable to expect the organisation to get the potential candidate's consent to the continued processing of their racial and ethnic origin data. If the data subject gave a positive indication that she or he did not consent to the processing of such data, the controller would have to cease processing the data.*"

4.5.6.12 How can the individual have withheld consent, when there has been no request for consent and when it would be unreasonable for the controller to have tried to obtain consent in the first place? If the condition really means that individuals have a right to object (which is the only logical interpretation), then why not say this? The formulation of this condition also seems to have defeated the drafters of the Explanatory Notes to the Act, who make no attempt to explain this scenario, simply saying that it applies where "*the processing can reasonably be carried out without the consent of the data subject*".

The individual has unreasonably withheld consent

4.5.6.13 The last variation on the consent theme, is where processing is necessary in the interests of another individual and the data subject has unreasonably withheld consent. This formulation is used in two conditions which allow elected representatives to process personal data (Sch.1, Pt 2, paras 23 and 24).

Equal opportunities monitoring (Schedule 1, Part 2, paragraphs 8 and 9)

4.5.6.14 There are two conditions relating to this in the DPA 2018. The first is suitable for broad programmes covering "*groups of people*", whereas the second is designed for initiatives targeting equality with regard to racial or ethnic origin only at senior levels (so on an individual or small group basis). In each case, the aim of the programme must be to promote or maintain diversity.

4.5.6.15 The first condition, at para.8, permits processing of personal data relating to racial or ethnic origin; religious or philosophical belief; health; and sexual orientation. The processing must be necessary to identity or keep under review the existence or absence of equality of opportunity between groups of people. It must not be likely to cause substantial damage or distress to an individual. Paragraph 8(5) provides that:

> "*processing does not meet the condition in sub-paragraph (1)* [processing is necessary for equality or opportunity of treatment] *if–*
> *a)* *an individual who is the data subject (or one of the data subjects) has given notice in writing to the controller requiring the controller not to process personal data in respect of which the individual is the data subject (and has not given notice in writing withdrawing that requirement),*
> *b)* *the notice gave the controller a reasonable period in which to stop processing such data, and*
> *c)* *that period has ended.*"

The Explanatory Notes gloss this proviso by saying "*An individual can give notice in writing to the controller requiring the controller to cease processing his or her data, and the controller must cease processing within a reasonable period*".

Finally, for this group-based equality condition, the processing must not be carried out for purposes of measures or decisions with respect to a particular data subject.

4.5.6.16 The main differences between the group-based condition and the condition for senior positions are:

(1) that this prohibition on processing to take decisions relating to specific individuals does not apply, since the purpose of the processing is to identity "*suitable individuals to hold senior positions*"; and

(2) the condition is restricted to racial and ethnic origin data. The prohibition on processing which is likely to cause substantial damage or substantial distress to an individual does still apply.

4.5.6.17 It must be reasonable for the organisation to carry out the processing without consent of the individual(s). Senior positions are defined at paras 9(5) and (6) and are those of director, secretary or other corporate officer; member of a limited liability, or non-limited liability, partnership, or a senior manager. A senior manager is someone who "*plays a significant role in—*

(a) the making of decisions about how the whole or a substantial part of the organisation's activities are to be managed or organised, or

(b) the actual managing or organising of the whole or a substantial part of those activities".

Preventing/detecting unlawful acts (Schedule 1, Part 2, paragraph 10)

4.5.6.18 This applies where:

"*the processing–*

(a) is necessary for the purposes of the prevention or detection of an unlawful act,

(b) must be carried out without the consent of the data subject so as not to prejudice those purposes, and

(c) is necessary for reasons of substantial public interest."

4.5.6.19 Controllers wishing to rely on the substantial public interest processing conditions in Pt 2 must have additional safeguards in place by way of an appropriate policy document (**4.5.4.8**). Controllers who consider that it is appropriate to make a disclosure to an appropriate body for law enforcement purposes, may well not have put such a policy document in place—because this would be an exceptional occurrence for them and not something which would have been anticipated ahead of time. To cater for this, para.10(2) provides that where the disclosure is to a competent authority (i.e. a law enforcement authority), or where the processing is in preparation for such a disclosure, then there is no need for an appropriate policy document.

Regulatory requirements relating to unlawful acts and dishonesty (Schedule 1, Part 2, paragraph 12)

4.5.6.20 Regulatory requirements mean:

"*a) a requirement imposed by legislation or by a person in exercise of a function conferred by legislation, or*

b) a requirement forming part of generally accepted principles of good practice relating to a type of body or an activity".

The requirements must relate to establishing whether a person has "*committed an unlawful act, or been involved in dishonesty, malpractice or other seriously improper conduct*". In addition, the processing must be in the substantial public interest and the controller cannot reasonably be expected to obtain consent (see **4.5.6.6**). The condition covers both the person directly subject to the legislation as well as others who assist the person subject to the legislation (such as companies providing information services). This provision was specifically introduced, according to the Minister on moving her amendment, "*to allow organisations such as Thomson Reuters, and banks themselves, to screen* *customers and suppliers for criminal activities and other seriously improper conduct*".

4.5.6.21 As the Explanatory Notes expand:

"*This paragraph allows private companies (in particular in the financial services sector) to process special categories of personal data where necessary to screen against UK laws such as the Proceeds of Crime Act 2002 to help financial institutions identity customers suspected of money laundering, and this paragraph further permits processing to screen against other regulatory requirements including widely-recognised sectoral guidelines such as those promulgated by the Financial Action Task Force*".

4.5.6.22 The condition may, however, have relevance to other sectors as well. For example, the GDPR itself requires that organisations take appropriate organisational measures to protect personal data—which could extend to checking the reliability of staff in roles with access to valuable or sensitive data.

Disclosures for journalistic and other special purposes (Schedule 1, Part 2, paragraph 13)

4.5.6.23 This condition permits disclosures of special category data, where this is necessary for journalistic, academic, artistic or literary purposes with a view to—in broad terms —exposing wrongdoing by publication of the personal data. The condition is specific to the disclosure of material to journalists etc. Those undertaking the journalistic or associated processing benefit from additional, and more wide-ranging exemptions, are considered at **10.5.6**.

CHAPTER 5

Purpose Limitation and Data Quality

5.1 INTRODUCTION

5.1.1 The four data protection principles set out in GDPR art.5(1)(b) to (e) can be considered together since they describe general rules for the processing of personal data. Principles (b)-(d) apply both to the obtaining and subsequent processing of the data, and principle (e) deals with its erasure or anonymisation after its purpose is fulfilled. However, the first principle in art.5(1)(b) on purpose limitation underpins the data quality principles and needs to be considered first. It is to be noted that these principles apply only to data controllers. However, art.28(3)(g) requires that, at the end of any processing services, the processor returns or deletes the personal data. Accordingly, the guidance on deleting personal data at **5.5.6** is also of relevance to processors.

5.1.2 The Information Commissioner's *Guide to the General Data Protection Regulation (GDPR)* devotes a substantial amount of space to these principles with copious examples. We have not attempted to reproduce every single observation or example, but in the following pages give a flavour of the points raised.

5.2 THE PURPOSE LIMITATION PRINCIPLE

5.2.1 The purposes

5.2.1.1 This principle is defined as follows:

> "*Personal data shall be collected for specified, explicit and legitimate purposes and not further processed in a manner that is incompatible with those purposes*" (GDPR art.5(1)(b)).

This principle is designated in the GDPR as "purpose limitation". It requires an organisation to determine, at the outset—i.e. before processing or even obtaining the data—the purposes for which it wishes to process personal data. It then prohibits the organisation from using this data for any other purposes which are incompatible with this. The purposes are also fundamental to the data minimisation and storage limitation principles and may be argued to be no less relevant to the accuracy principle.

5.2.1.2 As a gloss on art.5((1)(b), recital 39 says in part:

> "*. . . the specific purposes for which personal data are processed should be explicit and legitimate and determined at the time of the collection of the personal data. . . .*"

It can be argued that having the purposes determined before the data is obtained is a fundamental part of privacy by design (art.25). Recital 39 also says:

> "*Personal data should be processed only if the purpose of the processing could not reasonably be fulfilled by other means . . .*"

5.2.1.3 The Commissioner in the *Information Commissioner's Guide* says:

> "*This requirement* [i.e. the purpose limitation principle] *aims to ensure that you are clear and open about your reasons for obtaining personal data, and that what you do with the data is in line with the reasonable expectations of the individuals concerned.*
> *Specifying your purposes from the outset helps you to be accountable for your processing, and helps you avoid 'function creep'. It also helps individuals understand how you use their data, make decisions about whether they are*

happy to share their details, and assert their rights over data where appropriate. It is fundamental to building public trust in how you use personal data".

It is to be noted that Commissioner is suggesting that purpose limitation is a contributor to accountability, the principle enunciated in art.5(2).

5.2.1.4 The legal basis for processing personal data will sometimes, of itself, determine the purpose of processing. For example, if a controller processes personal data on the basis of art.6(1)(c) [compliance with a legal obligation], then the law which sets out the legal obligation will be determining the purpose of processing. Similarly, where a public authority processes personal data on the basis of art.6(1)(e) [for performance of a task in the public interest or in the exercise of official authority], it will be for the relevant EU or Member State law governing the functions of the public body to determine the purposes of the processing (rec.45). Purpose limitation, in this case, is linked to the permissible functions and tasks of the public authority—as rec.50 notes, the relevant law "*may determine and specify the tasks and purposes for which the further processing should be regarded as compatible and lawful*". Article 6(2) permits Member States to elaborate more specific provisions in this area.

5.2.1.5 Data protection professionals should note that the purposes for each category of personal data will appear in the following records:

- Privacy notices (arts 13–14, **6.4**);
- Responses to subject access requests (art.15, **6.5**);
- Controllers' records of processing activities (art.30(1), **13.5.1**);
- Legitimate interests assessments (**4.4.5**);
- Data protection impact assessments (art.35, **13.6**).

5.2.1.6 As the Information Commissioner notes in the *Guide* (p. 23):

"*if you have not provided privacy information because you are only using personal data for an obvious purpose that individuals already know about, the 'specified purpose' should be taken to be the obvious purpose*".

The purposes may also need to be identified in other documents. For example, the Commissioner may ask for this in an information notice (DPA 2018 s.142; **3.4.2.5**). Any mention of purposes in publicity material, on a website, etc. must also be fully compatible with this. Any failure to ensure this would infringe the obligation to be fair and transparent (art.5(1)(a)).

5.2.1.7 The principle refers both to the collection of the data and its processing after it has been obtained. In order to ensure compliance with this principle, therefore, the data protection professional must ensure that all subsequent use of the data is consistent with the original purposes for which it was obtained. Where this is not the case, there may be a need to change the information provided to data subjects and possibly, in the case of data already collected, to obtain their consent to this other processing. Changes to records of processing under art.30 and other documentation may also flow from this, since the purpose (or purposes) will be wrong. Recall that disclosure is defined as one of the various ways data can be processed (GDPR art.4(2)). This includes "... *disclosure by transmission, dissemination or otherwise making available* ..." so unanticipated disclosures of personal data are also affected by this provision. One obvious area where this occurs, is disclosure in connection with law enforcement proceedings. This is considered at **5.2.2.4–5.2.2.7** below.

5.2.2 Changing the purposes

5.2.2.1 The purposes for which an organisation processes personal data can change. Here, art.6(4) states:

> "*Where the processing for a purpose other than that for which the personal data have been collected is not based on the data subject's consent or on a Union or Member State law which constitutes a necessary and proportionate measure in a democratic society to safeguard the objectives referred to in Article 23(1)* [restrictions (i.e. exemptions)]... *the controller shall ... ascertain whether processing for another purpose is compatible with the purpose for which the personal data are initially collected...*"

5.2.2.2 If purposes change, therefore, the controller must consider:

- if the individual has given consent to this;
- if there is an EU or member state law which permits the processing; or
- if the new processing is "compatible".

Consent

5.2.2.3 The controller can process personal data for a new purpose if the data subject gives consent to this. If the controller is already processing personal data based on the individual's consent, then the controller will need to check if that consent covers the new purpose. As art.4(11) requires that consent is "specific" and "informed" it is probably unlikely that any initial consent obtained will cover a new purpose of processing. As the *Guide* notes "*if you originally collected data on the basis of consent, you usually need to get fresh consent to ensure your new processing is fair and lawful*".

Processing permitted by EU or member state law

5.2.2.4 Article 23 allows EU and member state law to restrict (i.e. to provide for exemptions from) elements of data protection law, including purpose limitation, where this is a necessary and proportionate measure in a democratic society to protect one of the matters listed in art.23. This includes matters such as prevention and detection of crime, regulatory functions, and enforcement of civil law claims.

5.2.2.5 Schedule 2 of the DPA 2018 uses this provision. So, for example, Sch.1, Pt 1, para.2 and para.5 provide that the purpose limitation principle will not prohibit controllers disclosing personal data when this is required to prevent or detect crime or where disclosure is necessary in connection with legal proceedings. Exemptions are considered in more detail in **Ch.10**.

5.2.2.6 In this situation, the disclosure is permitted even though it is for an incompatible purpose. Because the disclosure is processing for a new and incompatible purpose, the controller must check that it has a lawful basis for the disclosure. In the case of disclosures for crime prevention purposes, rec.50, second indent, is useful. This states that:

> "*Indicating possible criminal acts or threats to public security by the controller and transmitting the relevant personal data ... to a competent authority should be regarded as being in the legitimate interest pursued by the controller. However, such transmission in the legitimate interest of the controller or further processing of personal data should be prohibited if the processing is not compatible with a legal, professional or other binding obligation of secrecy*".

5.2.2.7 The disclosure may involve disclosure of special category data, or criminal offence data, in which case the controller would also need to find a lawful basis to disclose data under art.9 of the GDPR. In the case of disclosures for purpose of prevention and detection of crime, Sch.1, Pt 2, para.10 permits necessary disclosures (**4.5.6.19**).

Assessing if a new purpose is compatible

5.2.2.8 A controller may also process personal data for a different purpose if the purpose is "compatible" with the original purpose. The fact that a purpose is new, or different, does not necessarily mean it is "incompatible" with the original purpose. Article 6(4) and rec.50 also deal with this, by providing a list of criteria to bear in mind (inter alia) in deciding whether any new processing is compatible with the old processing They are:

- any link between the purposes for which the personal data have been collected and the purposes of the intended further processing;
- the context in which the personal data has been collected, in particular the reasonable expectations of data subjects based on their relationship with the controller as to their further use;
- the nature of the personal data, and in particular whether special categories of personal data or data related to convictions and offences are processed (arts 9 and 10);

- the possible consequences of the intended further processing for data subjects; and
- the existence of appropriate safeguards in both the original and intended further processing operations, which may include encryption or pseudonymisation.

5.2.2.9 The Commissioner says:

> *"As a general rule, if the new purpose is either very different from the original purpose, would be unexpected, or would have an unjustified impact on the individual, it is likely to be incompatible with your original purpose. In practice, you are likely to need to ask for specific consent to use or disclose data for this type of purpose."*

The Commissioner goes on to give a simple example. A GP whose wife runs a travel agency cannot disclose his patient list to her so she can offer special holiday deals to patients needing recuperation. The Article 29 Working Party considered purpose limitation in its Opinion 03/2014 (WP 203). Some of the Opinion has been superseded by the provisions within GDPR. However, it does contain a useful annex with worked examples of new processing which would, or would not, be considered to be incompatible. If a data protection professional is uncertain about a particular case, it can be worth looking at this for reference.

5.2.2.10 In cases where the new purpose is compatible, rec.50 says:

> *"In such a case, no legal basis separate from that which allowed the collection of the personal data is required."*

In this regard, it is easier for an organisation to process data for a new, compatible purpose, than it is to process data for a new purpose in reliance on an exemption—where the controller must still meet a lawful basis for processing. A new, compatible, purpose is seen rather as an extension of the original lawful basis of processing.

Archiving, scientific and historical research and statistical purposes

5.2.2.11 There is a second phrase in the definition of the purpose limitation principle at GDPR art.5(1)(b):

> *"further processing for archiving purposes in the public interest, scientific or historical research purposes or statistical purposes shall, in accordance with Article 89(1), not be considered to be incompatible with the initial purposes."*

This is discussed under archiving, research and statistical processing below at **5.5.3–5.5.4**. For the moment all that need be noted is that it is automatically compatible, and no new lawful basis is needed.

5.3 THE DATA MINIMISATION PRINCIPLE

5.3.1 General

5.3.1.1 The next three principles (data minimisation, accuracy and storage retention) are all concerned with data quality. This means it is often difficult to advise an organisation as to how to implement them since an outsider can have little idea as to whether the data is of the required quality or not. A practical step for the auditor is to arrange for a sample of the data to be checked as to accuracy by the data subjects. Obviously if this idea is adopted and the responses show data quality problems, new procedures will be required to improve the overall quality. In some cases, it may be appropriate for such data to be sent to the data subjects on a regular basis.

5.3.1.2 The data minimisation principle is defined as follows:

> "*Personal data shall be adequate, relevant and limited to what is necessary in relation to the purposes for which they are processed.*" (GDPR art.5(1)(c)).

There is often a temptation to collect data which may come in useful at some time in the future. For example, the requesting of National Insurance numbers from job applicants would seem to be excessive since it will be required (with much else) only for a successful candidate and is wholly irrelevant to the selection process itself. Such squirrelling should be resisted since it is liable to fall foul of this principle. The Commissioner states roundly:

> "*. . . you should identify the minimum amount of personal data you need to fulfil your purpose. You should hold that much information, but no more. The accountability principle* [art.5(2)] *means that you need to be able to demonstrate that you have appropriate processes to ensure that you only collect and hold the personal data you need.*"

The implication of this is that you should be able to justify each piece of personal data that you ask for.

5.3.1.3 The data minimisation principle mandates that personal data must be "adequate", "relevant" and "limited to what is necessary". The GDPR does not define these terms. The Commissioner points out that these terms

> "*will depend on the specified purpose for collecting and using the personal data. It may also differ from one individual to another . . .*
> *You may need to consider this separately for each individual, or for each group of individuals sharing relevant characteristics.*"

Provided you are clear as to why this is so, there is nothing wrong with this. Thus, in a workforce of 50 people, there may be two who are registered disabled. To provide a proper work environment for the two disabled people an employer will need to know in what respects they are disabled and thus will have a lot of additional personal data (and special categories of personal data) for the disabled staff members, which will not exist for the remaining 48 non-disabled people.

5.3.1.4 The Commissioner adds:

> "*You should in particular consider any specific factors that an individual brings to your attention—for example, as part of an objection, request for rectification of incomplete data, or request for erasure of unnecessary data.*"

The Commissioner gives an example:

> "*A debt collection agency is engaged to find a particular debtor. It collects information on several people with a similar name to the debtor. During the enquiry some of these people are discounted. The agency should delete most of their personal data, keeping only the minimum data needed to form a basic record of a person they have removed from their search. It is appropriate to keep this small amount of information so that these people are not contacted again about debts which do not belong to them.*"

The Commissioner gives a further example:

> "*An employer holds details of the blood groups of some of employees. These employees do hazardous work* [steeple jacks, perhaps] *and the information is needed in case of accident. The employer has in place safety measures so it may be that this data is never needed, but it still needs to hold this information in case of an emergency.*
> *If the employer holds the blood groups of the rest of its work force, though, such information is likely to be irrelevant and excessive as they do not engage in the same hazardous work.*"

5.3.1.5 The Commissioner reminds us that sometimes the purpose of processing can be frustrated by insufficient data. She gives the example of a club which starts with a handful of members, becomes popular and grows and it becomes necessary to keep additional information about the members if their records are to be handled efficiently.

5.3.1.6 She also mentions the possibility that the insufficiency of personal data can be caused by an inadequate grasp of what is required. A request from a data subject for rectification (art.16) in the form of additional information can be a symptom of this. The Commissioner draws attention to the second sentence of art.16 on the right to rectification:

> "*Taking into account the purposes of the processing, the data subject shall have the right to have incomplete personal data completed, including by means of providing a supplementary statement*".

A controller should ensure that his file structures allow such an addendum to a record. The Commissioner also draws attention to the right to erasure at art.17(1)(a) which allows individuals to require erasure of personal data when the data is "*no longer necessary in relation to the purposes for which they were collected or otherwise processed*".

5.3.2 Opinions

5.3.2.1 The Commissioner raises one further issue in connection with data minimisation: the matter of personal opinions. An opinion can still be personal data. The DPA 2018 in Pt III on law enforcement at s.38(2) says:

> "*In processing personal data for any law enforcement purposes, personal data based on facts must, so far as possible, be distinguished from personal data based on personal assessments.*"

The latter are of course opinions, not facts. While directed at law enforcement, the rationale behind this is equally valid in other contexts and the *Guide* states that "*your records should make clear that it is opinion rather than fact*".

5.3.2.2 An opinion is not inadequate by reason of the fact that someone may disagree with it, or think it has not taken account of something they consider important. However, it is essential to ensure that records identify whether a piece of information is a fact or an opinion. Modern scholarly books, when referring to something gleaned from the internet, give a reference not only to the URL, but also the date on which this information was downloaded. A reader who follows up the reference and finds the URL no longer has this information can draw the conclusion either that this was an opinion and the website owner has changed his mind, or the circumstances have changed and the factual information identified in the past is no longer true now.

5.4 THE ACCURACY PRINCIPLE

5.4.1 This principle is defined as follows:

> "*Personal data shall be accurate and, where necessary, kept up to date; every reasonable step must be taken to ensure that personal data that are inaccurate, having regard to the purposes for which they are processed, are erased or rectified without delay.*" (GDPR art.5(1)(d)).

This reminds us of the need to keep the data up to date. Indeed, all data whether personal data or otherwise is valueless—or worse—unless it is accurate. A stock control system is unlikely to have any personal data in it, but it is still completely useless if it contains inaccuracies.

5.4.2 The GDPR has no definition of "accurate", but the DPA 2018 s.205 provides a definition:

> "*In this Act . . . 'inaccurate', in relation to personal data, means incorrect or misleading as to any matter of fact*".

The emphasis on facts means that an opinion cannot per se be inaccurate, though it may be inaccurately reported, if, for example, it is not exactly consistent as to what was stated by its author.

5.4.3 The *Guide* says:

> "*How much weight is actually placed on an opinion is likely to depend on the experience and reliability of the person whose opinion it is, and what they base their opinion on. An opinion formed during a brief meeting will probably be given less weight than one derived from considerable dealings with the individual. However, that is not really an issue of accuracy. Instead, you need to consider whether the personal data is 'adequate' for your purposes, in line with the data minimisation principle.*
> *Note that some records that may appear to be opinions do not contain an opinion at all. For example many financial institutions use credit scores to help them decide whether to provide credit. A credit score is a number that summarises the historical credit information on the credit report and provides a numerical predictor of the risk involved in granting an individual credit. Credit scores are based on a statistical analysis of individuals' personal data, rather than on a subjective opinion about their creditworthiness. However, you must ensure the accuracy (and adequacy) of the underlying data.*"

5.4.4 We may notice in passing that the Commissioner's analysis of credit scores makes them candidates for automated decision-making (art.22) which is discussed at **6.5.4.4**. What may be perfectly accurate at one time may no longer be correct at another. The Commissioner picks up this point with an example.

> "*If an individual moves house from London to Manchester a record saying that they currently live in London will obviously be inaccurate. However, a record saying that the individual once lived in London remains accurate, even though they no longer live there.*"

5.4.5 The Commissioner also comments on records of mistakes. Sometimes it is important to keep a record of something which later turns out to be incorrect. For example, a medical misdiagnosis should continue to be part of a patient's record, as well of course, as the correction to that misdiagnosis. If the misdiagnosis were to be removed it might render inexplicable a treatment that the patient had received.

5.4.6 Many issues of fact versus opinion arise where a data subject queries his/her record. If it is simply a matter of correction of a factual record (they live at number 22 not 24 on such a road), then the controller should do what the data subject asks for. Indeed, this is to comply with GDPR art.16 (rectification—see **6.6**). Where it is a matter of opinion or where absolute certainty is impossible, the record will usually record both the original details and those requested by the data subject. It is important to ensure when acquiring new software that it can deal with this. Not all software can cope with what are in effect glosses or comments on the detailed fields of a record.

5.4.7 Sometimes too there is genuine doubt about a fact. This too will often need to be kept as part of the record. In a personnel system, where an employee is reasonably thought by the employer to have committed a disciplinary offence but has protested his innocence, his file will indicate that he has been accused of the offence but has an alternative explanation.

5.4.8 Finally the Commissioner asks "Does personal data always have to be up to date?" The answer of course is: "it depends". If the purpose relies on the data being current, then it must be up to date. However where, for example, a company receives a one-off order from an individual, while they may well wish to retain a record of this transaction for some time (for accounting reasons, and because of possible complaints), they do not need to keep verifying whether the purchaser still lives at the same address.

5.4.9 The guide comments:

"*You do not need to update personal data if this would defeat the purpose of the processing. For example, if you hold personal data only for statistical, historical or other research reasons, updating the data might defeat that purpose. In some cases it is reasonable to rely on the individual to tell you when their historical data has changed, such as when they change address or other contact details. It may be sensible to periodically ask individuals to update their own details, but you do not need to take extreme measures to ensure your records are up to date, unless there is a corresponding privacy risk which justifies this.*"

And the guide gives this example:

"*An organisation keeps addresses and contact details of previous customers for marketing purposes. It does not have to use data matching or tracing services to ensure its records are up to date—and it may actually be difficult to show that the processing involved in data matching or tracing for these purposes is fair, lawful and transparent.*"

5.5 THE STORAGE LIMITATION PRINCIPLE

5.5.1 The end of processing

5.5.1.1 This principle (GDPR art.5(1)(e)) begins with the statement that:

"*Personal data shall be kept in a form which permits identification of data subjects for no longer than is necessary for the purposes for which the personal data are process (d)*".

The effect of this is that not only must a controller have in mind one or more clear purposes and keep the data for those purposes only, but there must be a clear policy of disposal of data, or at least the identifiers, at the conclusion of the last purpose. If a controller wishes to anonymise the data, the comments on the meaning of personal versus anonymous data at **1.2.3** will be relevant. This must mean both that the individual records or parts of records (fields within a record) must be disposed of (erased or de-identified) once their purpose is completed, and also that the file itself may need to be disposed of once there are no further valid records in it or the purpose for which it was created is completed.

5.5.1.2 Recital 39 softens this requirement a little, saying in part:

> "*In order to ensure that the personal data are not kept longer than necessary, time limits should be established by the controller for erasure or for a periodic review.*"

This suggests that it is not necessary always to establish an erasure date before processing. A review date may be a sensible option. In days before data protection was thought of, the Civil Service had long had a policy of marking on the front of a completed file a date for review and possible destruction. The idea was that the file would be put away, to be examined at that later date with a view to its destruction. If on examination it was felt that it should not immediately be destroyed, the clerk would record the decision and the reasons for it and mark a new date on the front of the file for review and destruction. One of the reasons why a file might not be destroyed might be that it should be kept for archival purposes—either with the intention of keeping all files of its type, or at the least some representative files of that type. This technique has much to recommend it. One reason why files get kept indefinitely is that no one can bring themselves to decide on a future date for destruction. By re-examining this decision at a later date, a sensible date can sometimes more easily be set. It should still of course mean that most files are indeed destroyed on the date set.

5.5.1.3 The Commissioner argues that:

> "*Personal data held for too long will, by definition, be unnecessary. You are unlikely to have a lawful basis for retention.*"

And, of course, retention ("storage") is itself a type of processing (art.4(2)).

She also adds that there are costs associated with unnecessary storage, and it also complicates responding to a subject access request under art.15.

5.5.1.4 The practical implications of this are that the organisation must consider, at the outset, both the purpose(s) for which the data will be processed and the date(s) when the data as a whole, or each field in the data, will no longer be processed or the event which will signify the end of the need to process personal data.

5.5.2 Determining retention periods

5.5.2.1 It will be obvious that the same data may well have different purposes which are successive, rather than simultaneous. For example, a personal contact record may eventually become a customer record when the contact actually makes a purchase. Similarly, for an employer, some data relating to an employee will still be relevant once the employee has retired and has become a pensioner. To comply with this principle, it is essential to ensure that data which may be required for the employee stage is not retained if it is irrelevant for the pension stage. For example, records of the employee's annual staff assessment by his line manager while essential for an employee would seem to be of no value for the pensioner record. Thus, an erasure may not be of a whole record but only of such fields as are no longer required. On the other hand, some data is required both for personnel purposes and pension purposes. For example, date of birth and identity of spouse or other beneficiary will still be retained for the pension stage. Another example, as we shall see, concerns data which after its original purpose is complete becomes some sort of historical archive (**10.5.7.6**). It is essential that both purposes—for example personnel and pension—are recognised at the time the data is collected in the first place.

5.5.2.2 It follows that for each record (or in some cases for each file or each item of data within record), a period for its destruction must be fixed at the time the purpose of processing is defined. The need to keep the record may expire at the end of a period of time—this is particularly the case with company records which need to be kept for a statutory period of time. In most other cases it will be on the happening of a particular event—for example, a file of job applicants is no longer required once the vacancy is filled and all possibility of a legal challenge has expired (unless the employer has additional record-keeping requirements for immigration purposes). The destruction may be of a complete file. But more usually there will be successive erasure of individual records as and when the relevant event occurs—for example a personnel file will continue, but single records will be erased as and when individual members of staff leave. The data protection professional should be in charge of assisting departments to define the period of destruction of records or whole files and of ensuring that this destruction policy is carried out thoroughly.

5.5.2.3 For most organisations, the rules as to when to destroy files whose purposes are complete are partly statutory. The statutory obligations must be considered first since there can be no question of destroying a record before its statutory period for retention has expired. This is generally dictated by the various Acts for financial records and tax records and in some cases employment legislation. To give a couple of examples, where the Working Time Regulations 1998 apply, the employer must keep associated records of working periods for a minimum of two years from the date on which they were made (reg.9). Information required for tax returns must be retained for six years under the Finance Act 1998, Sch.18, para.21. Such statutory periods will of course mean that in those cases there can be no question of disposal of relevant files until the period is completed. However once that period has been completed there must be a strong case for disposal unless there are other considerations.

5.5.2.4 Where records have no statutorily defined period for their preservation, the retention period is a matter of practical common sense in line with the purposes for which the data is required to be collected and processed. Businesses sometimes look to limitation periods for claims when they set a retention period. If the reason for keeping personal data is to address the risk of potential claims, then this is appropriate. However, if there is another purpose, this will not assist. It is therefore necessary in these cases to think carefully about the purposes. To meet the principle of accountability, which requires that an organisation can "demonstrate compliance with" the storage limitation principle (art.5(2) **13.5.1.2**), an organisation should commit to writing both the purpose(s) for which the data has been collected, the policy on preservation, both of the file as a whole and of individual records and fields within it, and the reasoning behind that policy as based on the purpose(s), together with any procedures the controller will take to ensure that personal data is securely destroyed (as to which see **5.5.6–7**). This is often referred to as a data retention policy and any table attached to it, which lists the retention periods for particular records, or types of records, is often referred to as a data retention schedule (**5.5.3**). As is seen at **5.5.4.1**, where an organisation processes special categories of data or criminal offence data, there is also sometimes a specific requirement under the DPA 2018 to do this.

5.5.2.5 A data retention policy must also take account of the need to ensure that personal data, or other records, which are relevant to litigation are not destroyed. In litigation, a party has an obligation to produce to the other side both documents on which it wishes to rely, as well as documents that adversely affect its own cause or could support the other party's cause. Sanctions for improperly deleting documents include the imposition of costs penalties or the judge drawing an adverse inference as to the facts of the case. In extreme cases, destruction of documents relevant to proceedings may even amount to contempt of court. It is, therefore, essential, to retain documents which could be relevant to legal proceedings. This duty to retain such documents applies not just during proceedings, but as soon as litigation is contemplated. This means when the party seeking to establish privilege becomes aware of circumstances rendering litigation a real likelihood, rather than a mere possibility. In a criminal context, this is not merely when an investigation begins, but when it becomes clear that there is some truth in the allegations and that prosecution is contemplated. In a civil litigation context, it is likely to be accepted that litigation is anticipated at the latest upon receipt of a letter before action or similar notice. Practice Directions applicable to the conduct of litigation (PD31B), require that legal representatives notify their clients of this obligation as soon as proceedings are contemplated. If litigation is contemplated, the company must suspend its document retention policy for documents relevant to the proceedings. This type of suspension, often referred to as a "litigation hold" borrowing from common US terminology, should identify the types of documents that must be retained and should be reviewed periodically to determine that it is still appropriate.

5.5.2.6 So far we have talked about assessing the retention period at the outset of processing, however, the restructuring of data for a new system must also be an occasion when the question is to be asked as to whether the old files (or at least any fields of data which are not to be converted over) have not completed their purpose and should be destroyed.

Special considerations for certain types of media and devices

5.5.2.7 Manual files in a filing system are also covered by data protection legislation. It goes without saying that the disposal policy for electronic data must also apply to the manual files covered by the legislation: i.e. that there must be a policy for systematic disposal as soon as the data's purpose no longer applies, and that such disposal must be thorough—destruction by shredding, burning or some other irreversible method, not just placing them in a bin to be carried away in a still legible form.

5.5.2.8 The same must go for the other types of automatically processed files to which the legislation applies, such as images (e.g. CCTV footage), though here both the mechanism for deciding when destruction of the file must take place and how the disposal is carried out are simpler—usually by overwriting with newer data in a regular cycle. Most CCTV systems allow for regular overwriting and re-use of tapes after a set number of days unless there are good reasons (e.g. suspected criminal activity) for retention.

5.5.2.9 Sound recordings are usually in a different position. It is increasingly common for organisations who conduct business by telephone to advise the customer that for purposes of elimination of doubt, as to precisely what was said, or sometimes for some other purposes such as staff training, a recording will be made. Here the mechanism for *automatic* overwriting which we have encountered with CCTV footage may be absent and a formal mechanism for assessing when the purposes no longer require the file must be instituted followed by actual destruction of the file whether by overwriting or otherwise.

5.5.2.10 Finally, bring your own device (BYOD) can present particular difficulties. This is an arrangement whereby some staff members are permitted, with safeguards, to use their own devices (mobile phones, laptops, etc) for certain types of processing of the organisation's data. The matter is discussed in much more detail at **14.3**. The deletion of the organisation's data on devices belonging to staff is a particular problem. Controllers should ask themselves how they will recover their data if the member of staff dies or is summarily dismissed. Mechanisms to enable data to be erased on remote devices would seem to be fundamental to this.

Special considerations for processing for archival, scientific or historical research or statistical purposes

5.5.2.11 The rest of the storage limitation principle at GDPR art.5(1)(e) reads:

"*Personal data may be stored for longer periods insofar as the personal data will be processed solely for archiving purposes in the public interest, scientific or historical research purposes or statistical purposes in accordance with Article 89(1) subject to implementation of the appropriate technical and organisational measures required by this Regulation in order to safeguard the rights and freedoms of the data subject*".

Article 5(1)(e) recognises that continued retention of and access to personal data after the usual retention period has expired is often a pre-requisite for the creation of archives, or the conduct of scientific or historical research or processing for statistical purposes. Article 89 requires that controllers make use of additional safeguards—in particular in relation to data minimisation, where art.89 requires that controllers anonymise data if this does not prejudice the relevant purpose, or pseudonymise data if that would allow the purpose to be achieved. Processing for these purposes is considered further in **Ch.10**.

5.5.3 Data retention schedule

5.5.3.1 The Commissioner recommends a data retention schedule be established by all except "*a small organisation undertaking occasional low-risk processing*". The schedule will:

- list the types of personal data you hold;
- describe what you use each for (the purposes);
- list how long you intend to keep each type of data, or as the GDPR helpfully says what the criteria are for erasure.

This effectively combines what was said earlier about the data retention schedule at **5.5.2.4** and recording the purposes at **5.1.2.4**.

5.5.3.2 The Commissioner not only recommends the establishment of a data retention schedule, but also that it should be monitored by regular review to ensure it is used properly. If it is consistently infringed, it may be that it is too strict, or it may be that infringers need to be brought into line. The Commissioner also suggests that if a record is not being used there may well be a case for early deletion. She also recommends anonymising records if that is appropriate.

5.5.3.3 One of the Commissioner's interesting examples (p.43) concerns a tracing agency retained by a creditor trying to locate a debtor. Once the tracing agency has located the debtor and passed this information to the creditor, there may be little reason why the agency needs to keep this data. The agency as a processor will, therefore, delete the record, whereas the creditor (controller) is operating on a different set of criteria and will keep the record until it has managed to obtain the full amount of the debt. Such a pattern of very short retention of a record by a processor in contrast to a much longer retention by a controller is not unusual. This is because the trigger for the processor's deletion will be what is specified by the controller in the processor contract, whereas the controller has other considerations (statutory requirements, or driven by the possibility of litigation, or even archiving).

5.5.4 Records of processing and appropriate policy documents

5.5.4.1 Readers may recall that there are also requirements in art.30 which deals with controllers' records of processing activities. Under art.30(1)(f) the controller is required to record:

> "*Where possible, the envisaged time limits for erasure of the different categories of data*".

For controllers which process special category data, or data about criminal offences in reliance on one of the additional conditions in Sch.1 of the DPA then there are additional requirements. In the majority of cases, these conditions require that the controller has an "appropriate policy document" in place (Sch.1, Pt 4, para.39). The appropriate policy document must set out how the controller will comply with the principles in art.5 of GDPR (transparency, purpose limitation, data minimisation, accuracy, storage limitation, integrity and confidentiality). In addition, the appropriate policy document must:

> "*explain the controller's policies as regards the retention and erasure of personal data processed in reliance on the condition, giving an indication of how long such personal data is likely to be retained*".

5.5.4.2 In other words, a retention schedule, of the kind described by the Information Commissioner at **5.5.3** above is mandatory whenever special category data is processed for many of the purposes listed in the Schedule. This would include processing of special category data for purposes required by employment law (for example, processing health data in order to pay statutory sick pay) and processing personal data in order to ensure equality of opportunity. **Appendix 4** contains a list of all conditions when special category data may be processed and indicates which of these require an appropriate policy document to be in place.

5.5.4.3 The appropriate policy document must be maintained throughout the relevant processing and for a period of six months thereafter. It must also be available to the Commissioner on request, without charge (Sch.1, Pt 4, para.4). In addition to an "appropriate policy document" controllers must also supplement their records of processing by including in them information as to the purpose of processing, the special condition in Sch.1 which is relied on and whether the personal data is actually retained and erased in accordance with the retention and erasure policies described above (Sch.1, Pt 4, para.41).

5.5.4.4 For much special category data, therefore, there is a particular focus on determining retention periods; checking they are applied in practice; and that data is securely erased at the end of that period.

5.5.5 Information for data subjects

5.5.5.1 When determining retention periods, controllers should also bear in mind that the GDPR requires that information about this is provided to data subjects, both in privacy notices and in response to a subject access request. In relation to privacy notices, arts 13(2)(a) and 14(2)(a)) require the controller to provide:

> "*The period for which the personal data will be stored, or if that is not possible, the criteria used to determine that period*".

Article 15(1)(d), dealing with subject access requests, varies it slightly, requiring the controller to provide:

> "*where possible, the envisaged period for which the personal data will be stored, or, if that is not possible, the criteria used to determine that period*".

5.5.5.2 The Article 29 Working Party's Guidelines on transparency (WP 260 recital 01) p.38) states that:

> "*The storage period (or criteria to determine it) may be dictated by factors such as statutory requirements or industry guidelines but should be phrased in a way that allows the data subject to assess, on the basis of his or her own situation, what the retention period will be for specific data/purposes. It is not sufficient for the data controller to generically state that personal data will be kept as long as necessary for the legitimate purposes of the processing. Where relevant, the different storage periods should be stipulated for different categories of personal data and/or different processing purposes, including where appropriate, archiving periods*".

To comply with this requires a considerable effort. We have provided a template privacy notice for processing of data for employment purposes in **Precedent P1**.

5.5.6 Deleting data

5.5.6.1 It is worth pointing out that on most electronic devices, deletion is a two-stage process. Usually pressing the delete button will simply remove the available pointers to the data but leave the data in situ. At this stage the data is for most purposes inaccessible and its location is freed up to be overwritten. Its true deletion will only occur when some other data (or software) is input and overwrites it—an event that may be a long way into the future. It follows that deletion of the pointers alone means that the data is still recoverable when an examination of all the device's locations takes place—something that forensic investigators are equipped to do, but which may also be within the capabilities of others. It is possible to obtain software that will automatically overwrite all the data that it deletes. Clearly full deletion is highly desirable for the purposes of authorised erasure of personal data.

5.5.6.2 Once an organisation no longer needs personal data, the data must be erased or anonymised. Erasure or anonymisation is, itself, processing of personal data and so must be carried out in a secure manner. There is brief guidance on this from the Information Commissioner in the *Guide* (p.45). On anonymisation, the guide notes that anonymisation is not the same as pseudonymisation (**1.2.3.2**) and data which has been masked, or key-coded, will still count as personal data—so the storage limitation principle will still apply. In other words, pseudonymisation is a useful measure for security and other purposes, but it doesn't meet this requirement.

5.5.6.3 On deletion, the *Guide* reminds that deletion obligations extend not just to live systems but also to back-ups, although there is an acknowledgement that it is not always possible to delete or erase all traces of personal data. The *Guide* suggests that "*the key issue is to ensure you put the data beyond use*". This concept of putting personal data "*beyond use*" is expanded on in guidance which predates the GDPR, entitled "*Deleting personal data*" (v.1.1 20140226). This also tackles archiving, where the Commissioner states (p.4) that archiving, as the information is not in live use, is less likely to have any unfair or detrimental impact on the individual. However, because the information can be retrieved, it still counts as personal data and is subject to all the usual data protection obligations. The Commissioner contrasts this with situations where deletion is particularly difficult—one example given is where the organisation intends to delete, but where the data has not yet actually been deleted (for example, where the organisation has deleted the pointers to the data but the information has not yet been overwritten). Another example is where data should have been deleted but, for technical reasons, is still held on a live system because it cannot be deleted without deleting other information held in the same batch (again, p.4). Here the Commissioner states that she will accept that organisations can put information "beyond use" (p.5) if the controller holding it:

"• *is not able, or will not attempt, to use the personal data to inform any decision in respect of any individual or in any manner that affects the individual in any way;*
- *does not give any other organisation access to the personal data;*
- *surrounds the personal data with appropriate technical and organisational security; and*
- *commits to permanent deletion of the information if, or when, this becomes possible.*"

5.5.6.4 If the controller puts personal data "*beyond use*" in this way then the Commissioner notes that she will not require data controllers to grant subject access, "*nor will we take any action over compliance with the fifth data protection principle*" (storage limitation under the 1998 Act).

5.5.6.5 There is also a further, short, online guide produced by the Information Commissioner, *Deleting your data from computers, laptops and other devices* (*https://www.ico.org.uk/your-data-matters/online/deleting-your-data* [Accessed 3 May 2019]).This looks at pros and cons of different methods for data deletion, from physical destruction (mostly effective but may invalidate the warranty and will be difficult to use with equipment without removable media unless the whole equipment is destroyed); secure deletion software (not effective on some media); restore to factory settings (depends on the manufacturer's options); use of a specialist (as good as the specialist—see also below); and formatting (not effective by itself).

5.5.6.6 If an organisation uses a contractor for the destruction of its data, it will need to note that the contractor will be a processor under the GDPR art.28 in that "erasure or destruction" is included in the GDPR's definition of "processing" at art.4(2). All the requirements for selecting, appointing and managing processors therefore apply (**13.7**). The Information Commissioner (*Deleting your data guidance*) also suggests using another method to try to delete data (such as using restore factory settings) before sending equipment to a third party, to help with the security of the equipment in transit. Furthermore, the premises where the data may be held pending its destruction may be different from the premises where the destruction takes place, and the security of the holding premises is as important as that of the destruction premises. This seems to have been a material issue in the matter of the fine levied by the Commissioner against the Brighton and Sussex University NHS Trust in 2012 (**3.4.3.45**). US standard NIST SP800-88 or HMG IS 5 for UK government contractors may be relevant.

5.5.7 Disposal of old equipment

5.5.7.1 As well as a clear policy about disposal of old records and files, there must also be a policy about disposal of old equipment. As the guidance mentioned above recognises, information which has been used on a personal computer will usually still reside for some time afterwards on the disk or in cache memory—a fact which has proved particularly useful to the police when investigating computer pornography and other offences. Therefore, unless the computer is to be disposed of by total and irreversible destruction, data must be erased if the organisation is to not be in breach of the storage limitation principle and the purpose limitation principle (in that the data will be disclosable to people who are almost certainly inconsistent with the original purposes). We may also remark that if personal data remains on a device, then almost certainly software will also remain and any inadequate erasure of the software will expose the licensee to civil action by the licensor. Operating system software and pre-loaded bundled application software can normally be transferred with the machine in accordance with s.56 of the Copyright, Designs and Patents Act 1988. However, some software licences expressly prohibit transfer of the software to a new owner. Where this is the case, the software must be removed to avoid being in breach of contract. There are programs which are claimed expressly to delete files (whether personal data or software) in such a way that they are impossible to resurrect, but such a system should only be used if the controller is satisfied that the supplier's claim to total destruction is entirely justified. This should be performed before the equipment is removed.

5.5.7.2 Alternatives to destruction include donating the equipment to a charity—often a school, especially in a third-world country. Donation to charity is an option promoted by a charity called Computer Aid International (*https://www.computeraid.org* [Accessed 3 May 2019]) who are understandably appalled at the waste in simply destroying equipment which still has many years life left in it. They undertake to wipe the hard disk completely, take full legal responsibility for this and reconfigure the computer for the new recipients. If this option is attractive then you should either use an organisation like Computer Aid International who will erase the disk for you and take legal responsibility, or else take steps to erase it yourself. However a word of warning: if you hand the equipment with one or more personal files over to some charitable body for them to destroy the file, even though they take legal responsibility, it seems to us that in such circumstances they will still be processors under the legislation ("processing" includes "erasure or destruction" (GDPR art.4(2)) acting on behalf of you as controller, exactly as a contractor destroying data alone, which means that you may still be liable to individuals if the data is not, in fact, appropriately destroyed.

5.5.7.3 The ICO has issued *IT Asset Disposal for Organisations* version 1.1. (20121101). This deals only with the data protection aspects and does not mention the software licence problems that inadequate disposal may give rise to. The Commissioner recommends (p.4) an asset disposal strategy buttressed by a risk analysis, to consider the vulnerabilities associated with each method of disposal. This document was published by the Commissioner before GDPR so this is not a full-blown data protection impact assessment (DPIA) (**13.6**), but a simpler exercise, though its findings should still be recorded in case of any query from the Commissioner or others or any claim in the future. Following that, there is good advice about engaging a contractor to handle the task. A contractor will be a processor in data protection terms, and it covers particular matters to be addressed in the processor contract with such an entity (pp.5–6), including:

- explicit direction on the services to be undertaken, and that it will act only in accordance with your (i.e. the controller's) instructions;
- an approved specification for IT asset disposal which is aligned to your disposal/security policy; and
- full details of all downstream partners (i.e. sub-contractors) involved in the service. Any downstream partner contracts should include the same data controller specification for IT asset disposal as the minimum service level to be met.

To this we can now add that the processor must comply with GDPR art.28 including art.28(4) on sub-contractors (**13.7.4.1**).

CHAPTER 6

Data Subject Rights

6.1 STRUCTURE OF THIS CHAPTER

6.1.1 Chapter III of the GDPR is dedicated to individuals' rights. These are:

- a right to information about processing of personal data (i.e. a right to receive a privacy notice) (**6.4**);
- a right to access the personal data (**6.5**);
- a right to rectify the data (**6.6**);
- a right of erasure (or "to be forgotten") (**6.9**);
- a right to "restrict" processing of personal data (**6.10**);
- a right to "port" personal data (to receive the data in a more useful format or to transfer it to another controller) (**6.7**);
- rights to object to certain data processing (**6.8**); and
- a right not to be subject to automated individual decision-making (**6.11**).

6.1.2 The GDPR addresses individual rights in the order above. However, we think it is helpful to consider them in a different order and this explains the structure of this chapter: a request for access often leads to a request to rectify personal data and, when considering how to implement portability, it is helpful to understand how it compares with subject access. The right to erasure can be triggered by an individual exercising their rights to object to processing, meaning that it is not possible to consider how to implement that right without first considering rights to object to processing. Automated individual decision-making has little in common with the other rights, so is best considered last.

6.1.3 The GDPR also contains a general principle of transparent information and communication at art.12, which applies to all of the above situations, as well as when a controller provides notice to individuals of a personal data breach (**8.4.4**). For this reason, we have considered the transparency obligation first.

6.1.4 The Information Commissioner's *Guide* contains a checklist for each type of individual right for controllers to use. **Precedent P2** contains a template policy for handling requests from individuals to exercise their rights, with template letters to individuals.

6.2 TRANSPARENCY (ARTICLE 12)

6.2.1 Introduction

6.2.1.1 The general principle of transparency is introduced in art.5, where the first data protection principle is that personal data shall be:

> "*processed lawfully, fairly and in a transparent manner in relation to the data subject . . .*".

The requirement for fair and lawful processing was already present in the old Data Protection Directive, but the requirement for processing to be "transparent" is a new requirement of the GDPR.[1] Article 12 particularises this general principle. The EDPB has adopted *Guidelines on transparency* (revised and adopted on 11 April 2018 (WP 260 rev.01)).

WP 260 (p.4) considers that there are three components of transparency:

1) requirements for privacy notices (considered later at **6.4**);
2) general requirements affecting communications with individuals about their rights; and
3) requirements which could be classed as "facilitating the exercise" of rights (such as requirements about format, identification, timing, etc).

We have followed this same structure below.

[1] Fair and lawful processing are addressed at **4.1.7**.

6.2.2 Communicating in a transparent way

6.2.2.1 As mentioned above (**6.1.3**), these principles apply whenever a controller provides information to an individual as part of a privacy notice; when the individual exercises their rights; or when the controller provides notice of a personal data breach. Article 12(1) requires that any of these communications must be:

> "*. . . in a concise, transparent, intelligible and easily accessible form, using clear and plain language, in particular for any information addressed specifically to a child*".

Given the length of the GDPR and the lack of clarity in the drafting of many of its provisions, this is a legislative case of "do as I say, not as I do". The EDPB places considerable emphasis on this provision, however, noting that "*the quality, accessibility and comprehensibility of the information is as important as the actual content of the transparency information*" (p.5). The key message is that information should be "*user centric rather than legalistic*" (p.5).

Clear and plain language: intelligible

6.2.2.2 WP 260 (p.8) notes that clear and plain language means avoiding complex structures, using definitive examples (rather than language which is vague); using the active, rather than the passive voice; and using bullets and indentations (or other visual aids) to make information easier to read than a long, continuous, section of text. "*We may use your personal data to develop new services*"; "*we may use your personal data for research purposes*"; and "*we may use your personal data to offer personalised services*", staples of many privacy notices, are all cited in WP 260 (p.9) as examples of poor practice, because the reader will not know what the services, or research, will be, or what the personalisation entails. An example of good practice is given:

> "*We will retain your shopping history and use details of the products you have previously purchased to make suggestions to you for other products which we believe you will also be interested in*".

6.2.2.3 WP 260 notes that in determining what will be intelligible, the controller should have regard to the average member of the controller's intended audience (p.7). This may mean taking additional steps if the audience is unlikely to understand more complex concepts and may mean translating into different languages, if the controller is targeting people in those languages (p.10). User testing in the relevant group may assist. Where there are two target audiences, as should be the case with material designed for children which is also to be seen by their parents, this can be quite difficult.

Easily accessible

6.2.2.4 The requirement that information should be "easily accessible" means that the individual should not have to seek it out; the information should be separate from other information (such as terms of service). WP 260 (p.8) states that in an online context this means that:

- every website should have a direct link to a privacy policy under a relevant commonly used term (for example, a link behind "privacy" would be sufficient; information contained in "legal information" link would not);
- colour schemes which make it hard to see the link are not acceptable (so black on black font, which can sometimes inadvertently happen if a publisher does not carry out sufficient testing on accessibility across different browsers);
- apps should have information available from the relevant store prior to downloading. Once installed, the information should never be more than two clicks away (e.g. there could be a privacy option in the menu functionality of the app);
- the information should be specific to the app and should not be the generic privacy policy of the publisher.

The mention of confusing colour schemes should also alert readers to the requirements of the Equality Act 2010 s.20 when providing information to people with optical disabilities such as colour blindness. Problems for with disabilities people can often be alleviated by the use of technology—for example to allow a website user to access textual information in audio form. It goes without saying that wilful failure to apply such technology will be unfair as well as non-transparent.

6.2.2.5 The EDPB also states that controllers should take account of the context or medium when determining how to make information accessible. Online, just-in-time notices (which are presented at the point when data is collected), or hover-over-notices (which display when a cursor is on a particular word) can be useful. More creative approaches will be needed for other situations, where it is less easy to display text, for example when dealing with connected devices with small screens. Here, spoken information may be useful, or inclusion of URLs which a user can then visit to obtain more information. Inclusion of information in manuals or on packaging is also suggested.

Information directed at children

6.2.2.6 The need for child-friendly language is specifically highlighted in art.12. Article 8 provides that, on some occasions, a controller will need to obtain consent from a parent in order to process a child's personal data (**14.1.2**). The EDPB notes that, even in this situation, the controller should still provide necessary information which is clear to the child: the requirement for parental consent does not override the separate obligations owed to the child (p.9).

Icons

6.2.2.7 Article 12(7) suggests that standardised icons could be used in conjunction with more traditional privacy notices in order to provide a meaningful overview of processing in a way which is more easily visible and intelligible. The Commission is given powers to introduce delegated acts relating to standard icons. This may be a useful development in the future—however, as the EDPB notes (p.26), for icons to be effective extensive user-research and testing will be needed. It may be easier to do this at an industry level; initiatives by individual controllers are likely to be more difficult to be effective.

6.3 FACILITATING THE EXERCISE OF INDIVIDUAL'S RIGHTS

6.3.1 Introduction

6.3.1.1 Article 12(2) provides that the controller must "*facilitate the exercise of data subject rights*". The remaining obligations set out in art.12 can be seen as ways of particularising this over-arching obligation to take pro-active steps to assist individuals.

6.3.2 Form and format

6.3.2.1 The 1998 Act required that individuals had to provide notice in writing to exercise their rights. This is no longer the case under the GDPR and the DPA 2018: there is no format requirement. Some organisations under the 1998 Act tried to get data subjects to use a standard form for a subject access request. The use of such forms under the 1998 Act was not enforceable and that remains the case under the GDPR. A data subject can of course be invited to use a standard form but cannot be compelled to do so.

6.3.2.2 The GDPR contains provisions which aim to ensure that information is provided to individuals in a format which is useful to them. Under art.12(3) if an individual makes a request electronically, the response has to be provided in electronic format and rec.59 emphasises that the controller should "*provide means for requests to be made electronically, especially where personal data are processed by electronic means*". This could be a privacy portal—or, less sophisticated, an ability to send an email to a privacy mail-box, which is made clear on relevant sites and apps.

6.3.2.3 Article 12(1) also provides that, where an individual so requests, the relevant information should be provided orally. This might be helpful to some blind or partially sighted data subjects (see above for the Equality Act). In this case, art.12 notes that there may be a need for the individual to prove their identity by other means. WP 260 notes that this reference to checking identity is not relevant to the pro-active obligation to provide privacy notices which, after all, are usually provided before or at the point that personal data are collected, so that the identity of the individual does not need to be proved. WP 260 contains additional recommendations on providing information orally:

- The controller should provide mechanisms for the individual to re-listen to a pre-recorded message;
- The controller should ensure it has a record of any request for information to be provided orally; how the individual's identity was verified (where relevant); and the fact that information was provided in this way. Unless this is done, in the event of a later complaint, the controller will struggle to be able to demonstrate that it has met its obligations.

6.3.3 Identifying individuals

6.3.3.1 Controllers should always take reasonable steps to check the identity of an individual who wishes to exercise the rights granted under the GDPR: failure to do so may mean a breach of security obligations, as personal data may be released to someone other than the data subject (a breach of confidentiality), or may be erased, or modified etc. incorrectly (a breach of data integrity). This is implicit in the obligation on the controller to take technical and organisational measures to protect personal data but is not spelt out as a specific step to take under art.12. Article 12(6) does, however, provide that:

> "*. . . where the controller has reasonable doubts concerning the identity of the natural person making the request referred to in Articles 15 to 21* [data subject rights], *the controller may request the provision of additional information necessary to confirm the identity of the data subject*".

6.3.3.2 A common example of this will be requests for data gathered by CCTV cameras, since, unless the controller knows what the data subject looks like, it will be unable to identify the relevant data. A prudent controller might at the same time invite the data subject to define the time when the data subject might have been in the vicinity of the CCTV cameras, though if the data subject declines to provide such information, the controller cannot refuse to act unless the request can be reasonably considered excessive or disproportionate (for which see **6.5.3.17** below).

6.3.3.3 The controller should not request excessive or disproportionate information, as a way of discouraging requests, however, and rec.57 provides that:

> "*Identification should include the digital identification of a data subject, for example through authentication mechanism such as the same credentials, used by the data subject to log-in to the on-line service offered by the data controller*".

6.3.3.4 A controller should not seek to build in extra identity checks in registration processes solely in anticipation of possible requests by individuals to exercise their rights at a later date. Article 11 addresses this situation, noting that:

> "1) *If the purposes for which a controller processes personal data do not or do no longer require the identification of a data subject by the*

controller, the controller shall not be obliged to maintain, acquire or process additional information in order to identify the data subject for the sole purpose of complying with this Regulation.

2) *Where, in cases referred to in paragraph 1) of this Article, the controller is able to demonstrate that it is not in a position to identify the data subject, the controller shall inform the data subject accordingly, if possible. In such cases, Articles 15 to 20 shall not apply except where the data subject, for the purpose of exercising his or her rights under those articles, provides additional information enabling his or her identification*".

6.3.3.5 In effect, art.11 creates a sub-category of personal data: information which is identifiable enough so as to be subject to the rules of the GDPR, but not so identifiable as to mean that a controller can safely respond to individual rights requests. The exception in art.11(2) is designed to mean that a controller cannot refuse to accept additional information, presented by the individual, if this would make compliance possible.

6.3.3.6 Article 11 only refers to exemptions from arts 15–20. There is no exemption from art.22 (automated individual decision-making): this makes sense, as this provision is not a right which the individual has to contact the controller to exercise, but a prohibition on using this type of processing. There is also no exemption from art.21 (rights to object to certain types of processing). This is more difficult—if a controller cannot identify the individual purporting to object to processing, how can the controller be confident that the request is properly authorised? The drafting is also curious given that art.12(2) specifically says:

> "*In the cases referred to in Article 11(2), the controller shall not refuse to act on the request of the data subject for exercising his or her rights under Articles 15 to 22, unless the controller demonstrates that it is not in a position to identify the data subject*".

As art.12(2) clearly refers to all individual rights, the point is probably academic: if a controller cannot sufficiently identify an individual, then it does not have to respond to their request; however, the burden of proving that this is the case falls on the controller.

6.3.3.7 The case of ***Azra Sabados v Facebook Ireland*** [2018] EWHC 2369 (QB) shows the importance of correctly checking the identity of individuals before acting on their instructions. The claimant had been in a long-term relationship with a musician in Bosnia, who died during a medical procedure. The relationship was also long-distance, and the claimant and her former partner used Facebook to share much information. The information related both to the claimant and her partner. Facebook received and acted on a request to delete the partner's Facebook content; it refused to reveal the identity of the person making the request to the claimant but said that it would have been the executor of the partner's affairs or a close family member. The claimant did not accept this, arguing that the family treated her as the wife of the deceased, and alleged that the request was likely to have been improperly authorised. The judge accepted that the claimant had an arguable case of breach of the 1998 Act and misuse of private information and ordered Facebook to reveal the identity of the individual who had requested deletion to the claimant.

6.3.4 Timing

6.3.4.1 Article 12(3) provides that the controller must "*provide information on action taken on a request under Articles 15 to 22 to the data subject without undue delay and in any event within one month of receipt of the request*".

The one-month period is, therefore, a long-stop: in some circumstances it may be appropriate to comply more quickly than this.

6.3.4.2 Section 205 of the DPA 2018 provides that "month" has the meaning set out in the relevant EU Regulation (3 June 1971). Article 3 of this provides that the date on which a notice is received is discounted; the month starts on the next day and runs until the same day of the following month (i.e. 20 to 20). If the second month does not contain that date, then the last date of the month is taken as the relevant date (relevant for periods starting on the 29, 30, or 31 of the month). Finally, where the last day of the month is a public holiday, or the weekend, then the month ends at the end of the next working day after the public holiday or weekend. However, no allowance is made for any public holidays which occur in the middle of the month.

6.3.4.3 Article 12(3) provides that this period may be extended by two further months, where necessary taking into account the complexity and number of requests. If the controller relies on this, then it must inform the individual at the end of the period, together with details of the reasons for the delay.

6.3.4.4 The case of ***AB v Ministry of Justice*** [2014] EWHC 1847 (QB) is an interesting example of damages being awarded because of a failure by the Ministry of Justice (MoJ) to provide personal data pursuant to a subject access request within the required period. The claimant was a solicitor who regularly handled cases involving individuals' interactions with Government departments and public bodies. In this capacity he made many requests for information under freedom of information and data protection legislation. The claimant also made a subject access request relating to information processed by MoJ about him after the death of his wife. There was a delay of between 17 months and 6 years in the MoJ providing all personal data processed. The claimant had been particularly concerned to receive the material as he believed some of it might be distressing and he wished to ensure it was destroyed. The judge noted that he had no evidence about the claimant's health or mental state, but he made an award of £2,250 for distress caused by the delay.

6.3.5 Providing reasons

6.3.5.1 Article 12(4) provides that:

> "*If the controller does not take action on the request of the data subject, the controller shall inform the data subject without delay and at the latest within one month of receipt of the request of the reasons for not taking action and on the possibility of lodging a complaint with the supervisory authority and seeking a judicial remedy*".

Article 12(4) does not say whether this only applies where the controller declines to comply at all with an individual's request, or if the obligation is also relevant where a controller complies in part, but not in full. Given the over-arching obligation on the controller to "facilitate" the individual's exercise of their rights, the latter interpretation seems preferable: unless an individual knows that the controller has not fully complied with the request, they will find it harder to challenge the controller's approach.

6.3.5.2 It also means that a data subject who has received no response from a controller within the month can immediately take action, either by reminding the controller or indeed going straight to the Commissioner as supervisory authority.

6.3.6 Costs and exemptions for excessive or unreasonable requests

6.3.6.1 The 1998 Act used to allow controllers to charge a modest amount for handling access requests. This has now been removed by the GDPR, as art.12(5) provides that all individual rights must be met "*free of charge*". There is an exception to this where requests are "*manifestly unfounded or excessive, in particular because of their repetitive character*". Here, art.12(5) leaves it to the discretion of the controller whether he refuses to act on the request, or whether he processes the request, but subject to the individual paying a fee. Where the latter is chosen, the fee must be "*reasonable . . . taking into account the administrative costs of providing the information or communication or taking the action requested*".

6.3.6.2 In the EDPB guidance on portability (p.15) the EDPB notes that this refers to the situation where there are repeated requests from the same data subject and where the costs of dealing with that one individual would be manifestly excessive: the controller cannot argue that, because of the total volume of requests it receives, it would be excessive for it to have to comply. If a controller wishes to rely on this, the onus is on it to demonstrate that the derogation applies.

6.3.6.3 The DPA 2018 s.12(1) permits the Secretary of State to prescribe what fees may be payable to controllers in these situations. As the GDPR makes clear any such fees must be "*reasonable . . . taking into account the administrative costs*" of the controller.

6.3.6.4 Section 12(2) authorises the Secretary of State to make Regulations to:

> "*(a) require controllers of a description specified in the regulations to produce and publish guidance about the fees they a charge in reliance of those provisions; and*
>
> (b) *specify what the guidance must include.*"

6.4 RIGHT TO BE INFORMED (ARTICLES 13 AND 14)

6.4.1 Introduction

6.4.1.1 The 1998 Act contained an obligation on controllers to tell individuals how the controller would use their data (commonly referred to as a privacy notice). The provisions recognised that there would be slightly different rules for controllers who obtained information directly from the individual and controllers who obtained the information indirectly. In GDPR, these provisions have been turned into rights for individuals to be informed about processing. In addition to the EDPB guidance in WP 260 and the Commissioner's *Guide,* there is also a guidance note from the Commissioner just on this: *The right to be informed* (v.1.1.101, 28 March 2018). This collates information from across the GDPR on privacy notices and replaces the *Privacy Notices Code of Practice*, issued by the Commissioner under the 1998 Act and now withdrawn from the Commissioner's website. There is a sample privacy notice (describing processing of personal data about employees) at **Precedent P1**.

6.4.2 Collecting information directly from individuals (article 13)

6.4.2.1 When a controller collects personal data directly from an individual, the content of the privacy notice is set out in art.13. As the required content of a privacy notice is nearly identical, irrespective of whether the information is collected directly, or indirectly, we have considered content common to both types of privacy notice at **6.4.5** below, after first looking at the separate rules for directly and indirectly collected personal data.

6.4.2.2 Where a controller collects personal data directly from the individual, art.13(1) requires the controller to provide the privacy notice at the time when personal data are collected. There is only one exemption: where the data subject already has this information (art.13(4)). WP 260, para.56, notes that, for this exemption to apply, the individual must have *all* of the privacy notice information. If there are any gaps, then the supplemental information must still be provided. If the exemption applies, the EDPB also advises controllers to document where and how this information was provided to the individual.

6.4.3 Collecting information indirectly (article 14)

6.4.3.1 When the controller has not collected the personal data directly from the data subject then the controller must provide the information within a reasonable period but, at the latest, within one month, having regard to the specific circumstances in which the data are processed (art.14(3)(a)). This one-month period can be curtailed in two situations: if the controller communicates with the individual, or if the controller envisages disclosing the personal data to another recipient (which can include persons within the same organisation (**1.3.6**)). In these situations, the privacy notice must be provided to the individual at the latest at the point of communication or disclosure as applicable.

6.4.3.2 As with directly collected data, there is an exemption where the individual already has all the information required. There are also exemptions if:

- the provision of the information proves impossible or would involve disproportionate effort or would seriously impair the controller's ability to achieve its purposes (art.14(5)(b));
- obtaining or disclosing the information is expressly laid down by EU or Member State law to which the controller is subject and which provides appropriate measures to protect the data subject's legitimate interests (art.14(5)(c)); or
- The data must remain confidential subject to an obligation of professional secrecy, including statutory secrecy, regulated by EU or Member State law (art.14(5)(d)).

6.4.3.3 There are also detailed exemptions to the obligations to provide a privacy notice (when the controller collects personal data directly and indirectly) in the DPA 2018 (**10.3** and **10.4**).

Impossibility, disproportionate effort, seriously impair objectives

6.4.3.4 We have seen that art.14(5)(b) includes three separate exemptions. The first is when it would be impossible to provide the privacy notice. In WP 260 (para.59), the EDPB notes that this is an all or nothing exemption—it either applies, or it doesn't. The EDPB considers that it rarely applies in practice.

6.4.3.5 The next exemption is where provision of the notice would involve "disproportionate effort". Article 14(5)(b) goes on to provide that this is the case:

> "*... in particular for processing for archiving purposes in the public interest, scientific or historical research purposes or statistical purposes, subject to the conditions and safeguards referred to in Art.89(1) ...*"

Recital 62 notes that the number of data subjects, the age of the data and the relevant safeguards adopted should all be taken into consideration when assessing this. The EDPB suggests (para.61) that the statement that this exemption should apply "*in particular*" when processing for research purposes etc. means that this exemption should not be routinely relied on in other cases. This seems overly narrow: the fact that the exemption is particularly likely to apply in this situation should not affect whether it can apply in other cases. The EDPB gives an example of hospital admittance forms including details for next of kin and notes that, given the volume of data processed, it would be disproportionate for the hospital to have to provide privacy notices to them. ICO has a similar example (p.33 of the *Right to be Informed* guidance) of schools collecting emergency contact details. In practice, it seems that both the EDPB and the Commissioner interpret this provision somewhat more generously than the EDPB comment on research would suggest.

6.4.3.6 The final exemption in this article is where meeting the obligation to provide notice would make it impossible for the controller to achieve the objectives for which it processes personal data or would seriously impair its ability to achieve these objectives. The EDPB gives the obvious example here (p.32) that this would allow a financial services provider not to provide a privacy notice to someone it suspects of money laundering offences, if this would tip-off the individual and make it impossible for the financial services provider to process personal data for this purpose effectively.

6.4.3.7 Where a controller intends to rely on these exemptions, it must take appropriate measures to protect the data subject's interests, which as a minimum includes making a privacy notice publicly available (for example, by means of a privacy policy posted on a website) (art.12(5)(b)). The Information Commissioner also suggests considering use of pseudonymisation, minimising the data collected and processed—and conducting a data protection impact assessment. Indeed, as mentioned at **13.6.1.12**, the Commissioner also requires a DPIA to be conducted if an organisation believes it is exempted from having to provide a privacy notice to individuals.

Obtaining or disclosure is laid down by law

6.4.3.8 Here the EDPB gives the example of tax authorities, which may be obliged by law to obtain information from employers. Where this is the case, there is no need for them to provide notice to individuals.

6.4.3.9 The exemption only applies to organisations which do not collect information directly from the data subject—so the employer would not be able to benefit from this exemption. In addition, the law must contain appropriate measures to protect the data subject's legitimate interests.

Secrecy

6.4.3.10 The EDPB gives the example of a patient providing details of other family members who have experienced a particular disease, to his or her medical practitioner, as an example of when this exemption would apply: in this example, the health care professional would not need to provide a privacy notice to the individuals (this may also be a case of impossibility—he won't necessarily know whether they are alive or dead, or if alive, where they are to be found).

6.4.4 Overall change from the 1998 Act

6.4.4.1 The GDPR is much more demanding than the 1998 Act. Where privacy notices had to be provided, the 1998 Act provided that they could either be provided to individuals or made "*readily available*" (Sch.1, Pt II, para.2). The disproportionate effort derogation was interpreted more widely. There was also an exemption (at s.34) for bodies, such as Companies House or HM Land Registry, which are obliged to make information available to the public. The equivalent exemption under the DPA 2018 (at Sch.2, Pt 1, para.5) only applies where compliance would prevent the organisation from complying with its statutory obligations, and it is hard to see how providing a notice would prevent these bodies from their statutory obligation to make certain information publicly available.

6.4.4.2 Not only are notices more likely to be required under the GDPR, but, as is seen below, the content is much more extensive. These requirements do not just apply to new processing of personal data: rec.171 provides that processing which was already underway when the GDPR was adopted should be brought into conformity with the Regulation by 25 May 2018—a point emphasises by the EDPB on p.5 of WP 260.

6.4.5 Content of privacy notices

6.4.5.1 The content to be included in privacy notices is set out below, showing how this compares for directly collected personal data and indirectly collected personal data. WP 260 also contains detailed recommendations in relation to each of these requirements. In many cases these are extensive and will lead to very thorough privacy policies, which will be difficult to keep up to date and their detail may be to the detriment of ease of understanding. Many of the EDPB's comments are stated to be recommendations, suggesting that they seem that as matters of good practice, rather than strict legal requirement. Where we consider that a comment is a recommendation or suggestion, rather than strict requirement, we have made this clear.

Requirement	Direct? Art.13	Indirect? Art.14	Comment
Identity and contact details of controller and, where applicable (i.e. the controller is not in the EEA), the controller's representative	✓	✓	WP 260 recommends allowing different forms of communication (e.g. online, postal, phone) At present many websites give minimal or no information as to how they may be contacted. In that connection it may be noted that rec.59 expressly says "*The controller should also provide means for requests to be made electronically . . .*" The word "also" implies this should not be the only mechanism.

Contact details for the data protection officer (DPO)	✓	✓	This does not need to include the actual name of the DPO (title and other contact details would be sufficient)
Purposes and legal basis for processing	✓	✓	Should cover the lawful basis under both arts 6 and 9 (the latter if special category data is processed) and the lawful basis for processing any criminal offence data. The EDPB suggests that this means citing any applicable EU or Member State laws which justify the processing
If the controller processes personal data on the basis of legitimate interests, the interest which are pursued must be specified	✓	✓	The EDPB also suggest—as a matter of best practice—including information from the balancing test which was carried out to determine that this processing could take place (**4.4.5.22**)
Categories of personal data processed	N/A	✓	
Recipients (or categories) of personal data	✓	✓	Covers persons within the controller's organisation, not just third parties. The EDPB recommends naming actual recipients wherever possible as this is most meaningful; if this is not possible, then the EDPB recommends describing the activities carried out; the industry, and sector of the recipient and the location of the recipients. The Commissioner's *Guide* emphasises this as a particularly important obligation if an organisation is involved in selling personal data (i.e. is a list broker) (p.98).

If transfers to third countries are anticipated; whether an adequacy decision is in place or not; what other safeguards are used and where these are available or where a copy can be obtained	✓	✓	The EDPB recommends citing the specific article in the GDPR on which the controller relies and naming each third country (for more on data transfers, see **Ch.9**).
Storage period or, if not possible, criteria used to determine the period	✓	✓	The EDPB considers that it is not sufficient simply to state that personal data will be kept as long as necessary for the legitimate purpose(s) of the processing. This should be at the level of different categories of personal data or different purposes of processing. The EDPB recommends that archival periods are also specified where possible. (For more on retention periods, see **5.5**).
Rights of data subjects to access, rectification, erasure, restriction, objection and portability.	✓	✓	Information should be specific to the processing and include a summary of what the right includes, how the individual can exercise it and any limitations to the right. Note that the right to object must be drawn to the individuals' attention at the time of first communication with the individual and must be presented clearly and separately from other information
Where processing is based on consent, the right to withdraw consent at any time	✓	✓	Noting that it should be as easy to withdraw consent as to give it (art.7(3))

Right to lodge a complaint with a supervisory authority	✓	✓	The information should, according to the EDPB, go on to explain that the individual has a right to complain in the Member State of their habitual residence, place of work, of any alleged infringement of the GDPR
Whether there is a statutory or contractual requirement to provide the information; whether it is necessary to enter into a contract; or whether it is otherwise obligatory; and the consequences of not providing the information	✓	N/A	This could be done by online forms indicating which fields are required and explaining the consequence of not completing this
The source of the data, including whether this is a publicly accessible source	N/A	✓	The specific source should be provided unless this is not possible (note the GDPR does not refer to categories here). If this cannot be provided then information about the nature (public/private/ industry sector) should be given. Again, the Commissioner's *Guide* emphasises this as particularly important where an organisation buys-in marketing data. Recital 61 says "*Where the origin of the personal data cannot be provided to the data subject because various sources have been used, general information should be provided.*"

The existence of automated decision-making, including profiling, together with information as to the logic used, the significance and envisaged consequences of the processing for the individual	✓	✓	
Where the data is to be further processed for a purpose other than the original one for which the data were obtained, a statement of that other purpose and any relevant further information	✓	✓	

6.4.5.2 Although neither the EDPB chart nor arts 13 and 14 mention this, if personal data is processed by joint controllers, art.26(2) also requires that the "*essence of the arrangement*" between them is made clear—in particular which controller the individual should contact to exercise their rights (**1.3.4.7**). For organisations which use Binding Corporate Rules to provide adequate protection for personal data transferred out of the EEA (**9.5.5.12**), these also impose additional requirements in relation to privacy notices.

6.4.5.3 WP 260 acknowledges that there is a tension between the list of information which has to be provided to individuals and the obligation to provide information in a succinct, clear and intelligible form. The EDPB notes that layering cannot be used as a way of making it more difficult for the individual to find content, so there should be clear links to the later information, or a way for the individual to read it all in one go, if they so wish; further the information in the layers should be consistent.

6.4.5.4 The EDPB pushes all of this back to controllers as a challenge they have a duty to tackle. The EDPB recommends (p.19) use of layering to help deal meet this challenge. The most important information could be presented in an initial layer, with the rest of the detail available later. The EDPB suggests that the most important information would be:

- purposes of processing;
- identity of controller;
- data subject rights;

- details of processing which will have the most impact or be the most surprising for the individual.

6.4.6 Updating the information provided

6.4.6.1 Articles 13(3) and 14(4) provide that if a controller intends to process personal data for a new purpose, the controller must provide individuals with all the information required under arts 13 and 14. This has to be done "prior to" the further processing starting. EDPB notes that the information should be provided sufficiently early as to allow the data subject time to take action (such as ceasing to use a service, or objecting to processing)[2]. Controllers should remember that the purpose limitation principle is also relevant here—providing that personal data collected for one purpose cannot subsequently be used for an incompatible purpose, unless the controller obtains the individuals' consent or an exemption applies (**5.2**). WP 260 emphasises that the obligation to provide an updated privacy notice does not override purpose limitation: if processing is incompatible it should not be undertaken at all. Instead, these articles are dealing with the situation where the controller is engaging in further, compatible, processing.

6.4.6.2 The GDPR does not contain any other provisions relating to updating privacy notices. However, the EDPB, in WP 260, states that it considers that there is a requirement to update notices and to communicate significant or material changes to individuals—this follows from the over-arching principles of transparency and accountability.[3] Examples of material changes would be a change to the identity of the controller or the ways in which individuals can exercise their rights; examples of minor changes would be stylistic or grammatical changes. The EDPB recommends providing notice in such a way as to ensure that individuals notice the new policy, so an email (not combined with marketing information) or new landing page on a website dedicated to this, are recommended. Notices should, again, be provided in sufficient time as to allow individuals to consider the changes and to exercise their rights if they wish to do so.

6.5 RIGHT OF ACCESS

6.5.1 Overview of access rights

6.5.1.1 Article 15 of the GDPR obliges data controllers to provide, on request, specified information to individuals in respect of whom they process personal data. This includes confirmation as to whether the controller processes personal data, a copy of all information processed (subject to a number of limited exceptions), together with supplemental information, such as descriptions of the purposes for which the information is to be processed and to whom it is likely to be released. Individuals are entitled to all information about themselves falling within the definition of "personal data"—accordingly, the right extends

---

2 WP 260, para.48.

3 WP 260, pp.16 and 17.

to manual records if they form part of a filing system (**1.2.5.3**) as well as video, photographic and audio records, and completely unstructured personal data held by public authorities (**10.2.5**).

6.5.1.2 It can be expensive and time-consuming for an organisation to respond to an access request. With the very short timescales prescribed by the GDPR it is important that the organisation has clear and efficient procedures in place that allow access requests to be identified and that set out who should handle subject-access requests, and what they have to do. The time and expense involved must not be underestimated. In addition, a controller will need a well thought through plan and evidence of how this plan was applied, where the controller wishes to rely on one of the exemptions to subject access under the GDPR or the DPA 2018. The Information Commissioner issued a *Subject Access Code of Practice* under the 1998 Act[4] (the "*Subject Access Code*"). The Commissioner's Office has advised us that it intends to update this and re-issue it as guidance, rather than a code of practice and the *Code* was removed from the Information Commissioner's website during September 2018. However, as the *Subject Access Code* contains more detailed guidance than the GDPR *Guide*, much of which remains relevant to the GDPR and the DPA, and as we have not yet seen the proposed new guidance, we have referred to the *Code* throughout this section. There are also detailed templates for each stage of a subject access request as part of the template individual rights policy at **Precedent P2.**

6.5.2 Initial response to a subject-access request

Form of request

6.5.2.1 There is no requirement for an access request to be made in any particular format. There is also no requirement for the request to state that it is a subject access request, or for it to mention the GDPR or the DPA 2018[5]. As the Commissioner's *Guide* notes:

> "*This presents a challenge as any of your employees could receive a valid request. However, you have a legal responsibility to identify that an individual has made a request to you and handle it accordingly. Therefore you may need to consider which of your staff who regularly interact with individuals may need specific training to identify a request.*
> *Additionally, it is good practice to have a policy for recording details of the requests you receive, particularly those made by telephone or in person . . .*"

---

4 Subject Access Code of Practice, version 1.2.

5 Controllers which are public authorities, subject to FOIA, may find that individuals make requests for their own personal data incorrectly referencing that Act. The *Subject Access Code* (p.17) suggests that public authorities simply treat the request as a request under data protection legislation and notes that it will not expect authorities to explain that they have rejected the request under FOIA (as they would technically be required to do).

6.5.2.2 In practice, many requests will be made electronically. Where this is the case, the controller must provide the response to the access request in a "*commonly used electronic form*" unless the individual requests otherwise (art.15(3)). The GDPR encourages controllers to facilitate easy electronic access. Recital 59 notes that "*the controller should also provide means for requests to be made electronically, especially where personal data are processed by electronic means*" and rec.63 also suggests subject access portals, as a form of best practice, whereby the controller "*should be able to provide remote access to a secure system which would provide the data subject with direct access to his or her personal data*". For larger organisations, which are likely to receive a large number of access requests, investing in a self-serve portal is likely to be the most efficient way of dealing with subject access requests. Where this is not an option, developing a subject access request form will be useful because, as the *Guide* notes, this can make it easier to recognise access requests and can make it easier to guide the individual to providing the information which the controller will need to locate the personal data requested. The controller must still accept requests made which do not use a standard form. Indeed, as the *Guide* and the *Subject Access Code*, note, a request could even be made by social media. Organisations often set up contact email addresses which are included on web-pages or apps. However, as new sites are developed and as organisations change, it is easy for such addresses to be overlooked. Controllers should ensure that all methods for communicating with the organisation are checked for subject access (and other data subject) requests.

Identification of the data subject

6.5.2.3 As with all other requests from individuals, the organisation should take reasonable steps to check the identity of the individual making the access request (**6.3.3**). This is particularly important with access requests to ensure that the organisation does not inadvertently provide personal data to someone other than the data subject, which would amount to a personal data breach. The *Subject Access Code* emphasises that these checks should be reasonable and notes that where an organisation has an ongoing request with the individual, so that the identity of the personal making the request is obvious, the controller should not request unnecessary additional information (p.23). The level of checks could be affected by the possible harm and distress that would be caused by inappropriate disclosure of information (p.24).

Requests made by agents

6.5.2.4 An individual may appoint an agent to make a subject access request on their behalf. Historically, this has tended to be a solicitor making a request on behalf of a client, or a parent making a request on behalf of a child. However, The GDPR has led to the creation of companies (such as Chommy and One Thing Less) offering to make automated access and other individual rights requests on behalf of the individual. There is nothing to stop an individual from appointing an agent to do this. However, the controller must check that the agent does have this authority. Where a solicitor makes a request on behalf of a client, the controller is entitled to assume that the solicitor has appropriate authority (***Guriev v Community Safety Development (UK) Ltd***, 6 April 2016 [2016] EWHC 643 (QB), [33]). In other cases, the controller should ask for evidence of authority, such as a letter from the individual or a power of attorney.

6.5.2.5 There can be special considerations when the request concerns a child. Section 208 of the DPA 2018 contains rules applicable to the exercise of rights by children in Scotland. It states that a child will have capacity to exercise rights under the legislation when he or she "*has a general understanding of what it means to exercise the right*"; a child of 12 or over is presumed to have this understanding. Although this provision is specific to Scotland, considering the level of understanding of the child is generally good advice and is recommended by the Commissioner in the *Guide*. The *Guide* notes that:

> "*If you are confident that the child can understand their rights, then you should usually respond directly to the child. You may, however, allow the parent to exercise the child's rights on their behalf if the child authorises this, or if it is evident that this is in the best interests of the child.*
> *What matters is that the child is able to understand (in broad terms) what it means to make a subject access request and how to interpret the information they receive as a result of doing so. When considering borderline cases, you should take into account, among other things:*
>
> - *the child's level of maturity and their ability to make decisions like this;*
> - *the nature of the personal data;*
> - *any court orders relating to parental access or responsibility that may apply;*
> - *any duty of confidence owed to the child or young person;*
> - *any consequences of allowing those with parental responsibility access to the child's or young person's information. This is particularly important if there have been allegations of abuse or ill treatment;*
> - *any detriment to the child or young person if individuals with parental responsibility cannot access this information; and*
> - *any views the child or young person has on whether their parents should have access to information about them*".

Fees

6.5.2.6 Under the 1998 Act, controllers were able to charge a small (£10) fee for handling subject access requests. This is no longer the case under the GDPR and DPA 2018: responses have to be provided free of charge (art.12(5)). If the controller receives requests which are "*manifestly unfounded or excessive, in particular because of their repetitive character*" then, under art.12(5)), the controller has a choice as to whether or not to reject the request or a charge a fee. If a fee is charged, the GDPR says in art.12(5)(a) that it must be reasonable taking into account administrative costs of providing the information.

6.5.3 Finding the data

6.5.3.1 Once the controller has confirmed the identity of the individual making the access request, it must carry out a search for the individual's personal data. The results of any audit will be useful for this (**12**) as will the record of processing activities which the controller must maintain (**13.5**). Any search is likely to need to take account of:

- central applications that use personal data (for example applications maintained by the IT department);
- personal data applications processed for the controller by a processor;
- local personal data applications maintained by specific divisions or individuals;
- any email and other correspondence;
- individual databases—there should be a list of any bespoke software used by individuals in the organisation. There should also be a general statement/reminder of the need to check contact systems such as Microsoft Access;
- those individuals/divisions of the business that are likely to hold relevant manual records (**1.2.5.3**)—this is likely to include supervisors and team leaders; and
- those individuals/divisions of the business that are likely to hold photographic, CCTV, video or audio records.

6.5.3.2 The person responsible for the search should contact the IT department, and any other division of the business responsible for running central applications and ask them to provide a copy of all information relating to the applicant. The same goes for those responsible for the personal data applications mentioned above, they should also make a similar request of any processors. They should then contact other individuals and divisions, as necessary, to ensure that relevant data of the types listed above are searched. Where an organisation has appointed data protection co-ordinators in different business divisions, a standard memo could be sent to them asking them for their co-operation. Samples of such notes are set out at **Precedent P2.**

6.5.3.3 Where data is shared between two or more controllers (joint controllers), the agreement between the controllers should have identified which controller(s) process which parts of the personal data. It may be that one or more additional controller should also be asked to help here. It may in any event be the case that the same data subject has simultaneously exercised his right against more than one of them, as he is entitled to do under art.26(3).There has been considerable debate in the courts as to the extent of a controller's obligation to carry out searches and there is also detailed guidance from the Information Commissioner on how to treat certain types of records. This is summarised below.

Assistance in locating the data

6.5.3.4 The 1998 Act (s.7(3)) used to provide that where a controller reasonably required information from the data subject in order to locate the personal data requested, and where the controller had requested this, that the controller did not have to provide the personal data unless and until this additional information was provided. The GDPR contains a similar provision at rec.63:

> "*Where the controller processes a large quantity of information concerning the data subject, the controller should be able to request that, before the information is delivered, the data subject specify the information or processing activities to which the request relates*".

6.5.3.5 The provision under the GDPR is arguably narrower than that under the 1998 Act: organisations are assumed to be able to locate personal data in the ordinary course of events; it is only where there are large quantities that assistance may be required. The Information Commissioner's *Subject Access Code* (p.21) also emphasises that the ability to search for and locate information is a basic expectation of controllers:

> "*Given that subject access has been a feature of data protection law since the 1980s, your information management systems should facilitate dealing with SARs. They should allow you to easily locate and extract personal data in response to subject access requests. Systems should be designed to allow for the redaction of third party data where this is deemed necessary*".

Nevertheless, where CCTV data is concerned, unless the controller already has a good picture of the data subject, it can hardly make any meaningful search. It is therefore reasonable to ask for a photograph.

Processors

6.5.3.6 The obligation to respond to an access request applies to the controller, not the processor. As a processor should only process personal data on the instructions of the controller (**1.3.5.3**), it should forward any access request which it receives to the controller for instructions. Controllers may be dependent on assistance of the processor to handle an access request. The contract between the controller and the processor must include an obligation on the processor to offer assistance to the controller in dealing with individual rights. It would also be desirable to require the processor to inform the controller immediately if by some chance the processor were to receive a subject access or other data subject request in respect of the processed personal data. Response to the data subject must all be done within the usual time limits—so it will be important to have turnaround times in the contract with the processor which facilitate this.

Emails

6.5.3.7 The *Subject Access Code* (p25) notes that:

> "*The contents of emails stored on your computer systems are, of course, a form of electronic record to which the general principles above apply.*"

Controllers often find emails difficult to deal with, as searches can produce very large volumes of documents, which have been sent to or from, or which refer to the individual. This highlights the importance of adopting (and implementing) appropriate data retention and destruction policies (to avoid over retention of emails in the first place) and systems which can allow for filing and searching.

6.5.3.8 There are practical difficulties in searching just by surname or even by first name and surname. In ***Ittihadieh v 5-11 Cheyne Gardens RTM Co Ltd and others*** [2017] EWCA Civ 121 (a case to which we shall return) Lewison LJ said:

> "*... in the case of a wide-ranging SAR, a simple search of a computerised system (for instance a server, or a personal e-mail account) by reference to a surname or a forename of the data subject is highly likely to reveal a mass of material, particularly if the search terms are used disjunctively. If the data subject has a common name, say 'Smith' or 'Patel', the search may retrieve data which have nothing to do with the data subject at all. It may be necessary to refine the search, or it may be necessary for a human being to review the material to decide whether the named individual is indeed the data subject...* [101]".

In fact, it is worse than this. The data subject may be referred to as Mr So-and-so, or by his first name, or by a nick-name, or by his job title, and any of these may be misspelled.

6.5.3.9 The ***Deer*** case (***Dr Cecile Deer v University of Oxford and University of Oxford v Dr Cecile Deer;*** joined with ***Ittihadieh v 5–11 Cheyne Gardens and other respondents and the Information Commissioner as Intervener*** [2017] EWCA Civ 121) is a good example of the scale of the email problem. Dr Deer had been engaged in litigation with the University of Oxford for eight years relating to alleged victimisation because of a sex discrimination claim. Dr Deer made two subject access requests and then brought proceedings against the University alleging it had failed to respond to these requests properly. By the time the University had carried out the searches required by the initial proceedings, it had reviewed over 500,000 emails and other documents at a cost of £116,116 [26]. The University originally asked relevant employees to search their own email accounts. Dr Deer's claim was initially considered by Recorder Hancock QC and he ordered the University to search its central server and the servers of four specific departments or faculties: this shows the difficulty of relying on searches carried out by employees and suggests that a central search will be more effective.

6.5.3.10 Letters (on paper as opposed to emails) exhibit similar problems. It may be thought in general they will be outside the legislation unless they are in a filing system, but of course these days almost all letters start by being processed on a computer, before being printed out and signed. So almost inevitably they will be available.

Archives, back-ups and deleted material

6.5.3.11 The *Commissioner Code* (p.25) highlights the difficulty of dealing with emails in archived systems:

> "*For the avoidance of doubt, the contents of an email should not be regarded as deleted merely because it has been moved to a user's 'Deleted items' folder. It may be particularly difficult to find information to which a SAR relates if it is contained in emails that have been archived and removed from your 'live' systems. Nevertheless, the right of subject access is not limited to the personal data which it would be easy for you to provide, and the disproportionate effort exception . . . cannot be used to justify a blanket refusal of a SAR . . .*".

The *Subject Access Code* gives useful additional guidance on this (pp.30–31)

- "*information is archived because, although you wish to remove it from your live systems, you decide to retain a copy in case it is needed in the future*" it follows that a controller must be able to retrieve it in response to an access request (although doing so may be more complex than for live data);
- Back-up date is also covered. However, "*it is reasonable to consider whether there is any evidence that the back-up data differs materially from that which is held on the 'live' systems and which has been supplied to the requester. If there is no evidence that there is any material difference, the Information Commissioner would not seek to enforce the right of subject access in relation to the back-up records*";
- Deleted information—if information has been permanently discarded and there is no intent to access it again, then this falls outside the scope of an access request. The fact that it may be technically possible to recreate the data (e.g. with forensic assistance) does not mean this is required for a subject access request.

Bring Your Own Device (BYOD)

6.5.3.12 An organisation only has an obligation to search for and provide copies of data in respect of which it is the data controller. According to the *Subject Access Code* (p.32) an organisation would not normally have a responsibility to search personal equipment used by staff. However, the situation may be different if the organisation permits them to use such equipment for work purposes—for example, as part of a Bring Your Own Device (BYOD) policy. In this case such devices/information would be in scope and the organisation would have to be able to meet its obligations to individuals. This would likely have an impact on the way such devices can be used—for example, it may mean that work "containers" should be used to facilitate compliance (see **14.3** for more on BYOD).

Drafts

6.5.3.13 This was considered in ***Deer*** [156]:

> "*If she had already had the final version and the personal data did not differ from the personal data contained in the draft then I agree that she would not have been entitled to any further information. Otherwise, she would prima facie have been entitled to the personal data contained in the draft*".

Complaint files

6.5.3.14 The Information Commissioner has issued a note on *Access to information held in complaint files* (version 2, September 2011). This has useful guidance (and worked examples) on when information generated by a complaint will be personal data relating to the complainant, when it may also be personal data relating to another person and when it becomes non-personal information about the organisation's policies and procedures—which will not be personal data even though it is included in a complainant's file and may be relevant to their complaint.

6.5.3.15 It can sometimes be difficult to know whether information generated in a professional capacity at work is personal data—and there is useful comment on this in the guidance as well, based on the example of work produced by a company lawyer:

> "*Originally the advice related to the various issues the lawyer had given advice about. At that stage it did not relate to the lawyer himself, and he was certainly not the subject of it. Later on, the lawyer's boss collated all the advice the lawyer had given in a file about him, because he was concerned about the standard of the advice being given. At this point, the focus of the information changed from the issues the lawyer has dealt with to the lawyer himself—the collection of information started to relate to him. In addition, the lawyer is identified as the author of the advice, it records his personal opinions and therefore it has become his personal data*".

Changes in the data during searching

6.5.3.16 The Commissioner's *Guide* notes that a subject access request "*relates to the data held at the time the request was received*". However, the Guide notes that if the data will be routinely amended or deleted during the period when the request is being handled, then it would be acceptable to send out the data as so edited. Controllers should, however, remember that s.173 of the DPA 2018 makes it an offence to alter or destroy etc. personal data with the intent of stopping it being provided in response to an access request (see **3.2.4.16**).

Disproportionate effort

6.5.3.17 It will be apparent from the commentary so far that it can be a significant undertaking for an organisation to locate all of an individual's personal data. A number of cases have now considered to how much effort an organisation must go before this becomes disproportionate and no longer required. This is also summarised in the *Subject Access Code* which states (p.45):

> "... *in assessing whether complying with a SAR would involve disproportionate effort ... you may take into account difficulties which occur throughout the process of complying with the request, including any difficulties you encounter in finding the requested information.*
> *This approach accords with the concept of proportionality in EU law, on which the DPA is based. When responding to SARs, we expect you to evaluate the particular circumstances of each request, balancing any difficulties involved in complying with the request against the benefits the information may bring to the data subject, whilst bearing in mind the fundamental nature of the right of subject access.*
> *In order to apply the exception, the burden of proof is on you as data controller to show that you have taken all reasonable steps to comply ...*
> *We consider it good practice for you to engage with the applicant, having an open conversation about the information they require. This might help you to reduce the costs and effort that you would otherwise incur in searching for the information*".

6.5.3.18 As Lewison LJ stated in *Deer* [103]:

> "... *the implied obligation to search* [implied because this is not stated in the legislation] *is limited to a reasonable and proportionate search ... the result of a search does not necessarily mean that every item of personal data relating to an individual will be retrieved as a result of such a search ... Accordingly, the mere fact that a further and more extensive search reveals further personal data relating to that individual does not entail the proposition that the first search was inadequate*".

As the Commissioner notes, the burden of proof here is on the controller. Accordingly, it will be important for the controller to demonstrate that it had an appropriate approach to searching (for example, that it identified relevant systems, or custodians of emails; that it identified suitable search terms) and that it executed this properly in practice (so retaining copies of instructions given to search for material and notes of any sampling or review of data undertaken). As Lady Justice Arden put it, in another Court of Appeal case considering subject access (***Dawson-Damer v Taylor Wessing LLP, the Information Commissioner as Intervener*** [2017] EWCA Civ 74),

> "*TW must produce evidence to show what it has done to identify the material and to work out a plan of action. It has singularly failed to do this and so has not discharged the onus on it*".

Does it make a difference if the request is linked to litigation?

6.5.3.19 In many of the cases mentioned above, the applicant was engaged in litigation with the controller. Controllers can be reluctant to provide information in response to an access request where they feel that the individual will use this to fuel a separate dispute. Recital 63 of the GDPR states that an individual should have a right of access "*in order to be aware of, and verify, the lawfulness of the processing*". In some cases, the courts had looked at the equivalent provision in the Directive and argued that if there was some other, collateral, motive for making the request, that this may justify a controller in not responding to the request. It is now clear from the ***Dawson-Damer*** case (and others) that this is not correct. In this case, the appellants were beneficiaries under a Bahamian Trust. The trustees had appointed the majority of the trust funds to new trustees to hold for the benefit of other beneficiaries, excluding the appellants. The appellants challenged this arrangement. They also made subject access requests to Taylor Wessing LLP, which acted for the trustee of one of the trusts. Arden LJ roundly dismissed arguments that the access requests were improper because they may be made for non-data protection purposes [91], [107] and [108]:

> "*Confining the scope of subject access rights by reference to purpose is an unprincipled restriction of the section 7 right and will result in complex litigation in an attempt to determine the 'true' purpose of any application. There is no reason why having a collateral purpose should disqualify a data subject from relief.*
> *We have been shown nothing in the DPA [1998] or the Directive which limits the purpose for which a data subject may request his data, or provides data controllers with the option of not providing data based solely on the requester's purpose. . . .*
> *. . . It would be odd if the verification of data was always in practice a complete aim in itself which excludes all others. . .*"

The case vindicates the approach taken in the *Subject Access Code*, where the Commissioner states roundly (p.55):

> "*you may not refuse to supply information in response to a SAR simply because the information is requested in connection with actual or potential legal proceedings. The DPA contains no exemption for such information*".

Reviewing the material: what can (or must) be withheld?

6.5.3.20 Once the data protection professional, or other person responsible for the access request, has located the information to be provided to the applicant, they will need to review it themselves, or to arrange for others to review it. This review is necessary to ensure that information is not released in inappropriate circumstances where data protection legislation would either allow, or require, the information to be withheld. There are two general exemptions under the GDPR itself, which we consider first (**6.5.3.25**). These are supplemented by more case-specific exemptions introduced under the DPA 2018. Some of the exemptions under the DPA 2018 will be of relevance only to selected organisations. As a result, we have not discussed them in further detail in the chapters of the book. However, organisations would be advised to look at the full list in **Appendix** before reviewing material in response to an access or other individual rights request. **Chapter 10** contains information on more frequently used exemptions—and the exemptions of most relevance to subject access requests are considered below. Before we look at the specific exemptions themselves, however, it is important to consider general limitations on exemptions—both which arise from general principles of EU law and from the particular wording of the DPA 2018.

Exemptions are to be construed narrowly

6.5.3.21 There is a general principle of EU law that exemptions from data protection legislation should be interpreted narrowly, as summarised in ***Institut professionnel des agents immobiliers v Geoffrey Englebert*** (C-473/12) EU:C:2013:715 at [39]:

> "*According to settled case-law, the protection of the fundamental right to privacy requires that derogations and limitations in relation to the protection of personal data must apply only in so far as is strictly necessary . . .*".

This principle has also been considered in UK cases relating to subject access—for example it is cited in ***Dawson-Damer***.

6.5.3.22 Many of the exemptions in the DPA 2018 (and in the earlier UK data protection legislation) only apply "*to the extent that*" releasing the information "*would be likely to prejudice*" the specific purpose of the exemption. In these situations, the exemption cannot be relied upon as a blanket exemption from compliance. The case of ***Baker v Secretary of State for the Home Office*** [2001] 10 WLUK 2; [2001] U.K.H.R.R. 1275 is relevant here. In this case, Mr Baker applied to the Security Service and asked it to advise whether it processed personal data in respect of which he was the data subject. The Service gave him a non-committal reply, in accordance with its policy that it would "neither confirm nor deny" whether relevant data existed. The Service had invoked the national security exemption (s.28 of the 1998 Act) and in accordance with s.28(2) had sought and relied upon a certificate issued by the Secretary of State for the Home Office exempting it from the requirement to inform applicants whether or not it had processed information relating to them. Mr Baker appealed under s.28(4), arguing that such a policy was unreasonable and that under s.28(5) the certificate should be quashed. Whilst it might be reasonable to refuse to release information on the grounds that this would be prejudicial to national security, it was not reasonable to operate a blanket policy refusing to inform all applicants whether any data relating to them were processed. The Information Tribunal (predecessor of the present General Regulatory Chamber, **1.3.8.17**) agreed with the applicant and concluded that the certificate was too wide. The Tribunal suggested that it would not be unreasonable for the Tribunal to consider applications on an individual basis to see if there was a need to claim exemption.

6.5.3.23 The case of ***R. (on the application of Lord) v Secretary of State for the Home Department*** ([2003] EWHC 2073) is also relevant here. This related to a Category A life prisoner, who sought to obtain access to the full reports prison staff had compiled as part of the review of his status, as opposed to the summarised "gist" provided by the prison. The Home Office argued, inter alia, that s.29 provided it with a blanket exemption from the obligation to release such reports, because of the risk that, in certain cases, information might be released which would prejudice the prevention or detection of crime. Munby J confirmed that s.29 would only be relevant if, in the particular case at hand, there was a risk of prejudice. This would, however, allow the controller to take into account whether disclosure in the particular case would cause a "chilling effect" on the activities protected by the exemption more generally.[6] He also considered that the term "likely"

> "*connotes a degree of probability where there is a very significant and weighty chance of prejudice to the identified public interests. The degree of risk must be such that there 'may very well' be prejudice to those interests, even if the risk falls short of being more probable than not*" [100].

6.5.3.24 The exemptions may also prove to be quite time-limited. For example, whilst an organisation may be entitled to rely on the management forecast exemption (**6.5.3.40**) to avoid disclosing information relating to a potential redundancy exercise or outsourcing at the time the exercise is being contemplated, once the management exercise has been concluded and the redundancy policy has been carried out or abandoned, it will be very hard for the organisation to show that releasing information that it has kept about this would prejudice its ability to complete its management forecasting.

Manifestly unfounded or excessive requests (article 12(5))

6.5.3.25 As with all individual requests (**6.3.6.1**), a controller may refuse to act on a request which is manifestly unfounded or excessive, in particular because of its repetitive character. This being so, it would seem reasonable that a controller

[6] On this, ***Lord*** is quoted approvingly in ***Guriev*** [49].

faced with a repeat request from the same data subject might arguably have to provide only any personal data about the data subject which had changed from, or was additional to, whatever had already been provided.

Rights and freedoms of others (article 15(4))

6.5.3.26 This article provides that "*the right to obtain a copy ... shall not adversely affect the rights and freedoms of others*". Recital 63 goes on to note that this includes

> "*trade secrets or intellectual property and in particular the copyright protecting the software. However, the result of those considerations should not be a refusal to provide all information to the data subject*".

The exemption is specific to provision of a copy—rather than to the wider obligation to confirm if personal data are being processed. Given the statement in rec.63, a controller which wishes to rely on this may need to consider what information can be provided to the data subject so as to allow the data subject some information as to what is processed—a summary of the personal data processed, or a sample, may be possible approaches.

6.5.3.27 A particular aspect of the protection of the rights and freedoms of others is provided by the third-party information provisions at DPA 2018 Sch.2, Pt 3, paras 16 and 17. The information covered by the subject-access request may reveal the identity of another individual, either directly, because the individual is named, or indirectly because the applicant will know independently that the information could only relate to a certain person. In this situation there could be a conflict between the applicant's rights to information and the third party's rights to privacy. Accordingly, the DPA 2018 provides that the data controller need not provide information in response to the subject access request unless:

- the third party has given their consent; or
- it is reasonable to release the information without consent.

6.5.3.28 If the information can be anonymised to protect the identity of the third party, then this should be done and the information released (para.16(1)). However, the data controller must have regard to any other identifying information which they believe is reasonably likely to be in or to come into the applicant's possession; it may not be sufficient to remove the third party's name if the third party's identity will be obvious to the applicant from the context. For example, even if the name of the author of the reference (e.g. a line manager) is blacked out, it may still be obvious to the data subject who was in a position to write the reference. If the third party is a limited company, or other legal individual, then para.16 does not apply (although art.15(4) may assist). However, if the information relates to another individual, then the balancing test set out above applies. The DPA 2018 sets out further guidance on this balancing test at para.16(3). This states that, in assessing whether it is reasonable to release information without consent that one must have regard, in particular, to:

- the type of information that would be disclosed;
- any duty of confidentiality owed to the third party;
- any steps which the data controller has taken in order to seek consent;
- whether the other individual is capable of giving consent; and
- any express refusal of consent by the other individual.

6.5.3.29 Where the information relating to the third party is health data, educational data or social work data and relates to the third party in a professional capacity, then para.17 provides that it will be reasonable to release the information without consent (**10.2.2.7**).

6.5.3.30 Finance and staffing data was considered in ***Deer*** (mentioned above [158] and [159]). The University's budget contained Dr Deer's date of birth and length of service. A list of staff members contained her grade, salary and evaluation. This data was personal data relating to Dr Deer—but the other information in the budget and list of staff members was not. (The limitation in respect of educational data applies only to state schools as defined in DPA 2018 Sch.3 para.14., so would not apply to Dr Deer's colleagues at the University.) Emails were considered in ***Rudd v Bridle*** [2019] EWHC 893 (QB). Here, Warby J. noted that whether or not information about correspondents (the senders or recipients of emails which contain personal data about the data subject) will also amount to personal data relating to that data subject, will be fact-specific [111]. In making the factual determination in that case, the judge considered whether it was easy to understand what was written about the data subject without knowing to whom the relevant email was sent [116].

6.5.3.31 The *Subject Access Code* (p.39) offers additional guidance on this balancing test. It notes that there will generally be a relationship of confidentiality in medical, employment, legal, financial and counselling relationships. However, the fact that information is labelled "confidential" will not be conclusive. The *Code* does, though, note (p.39) that

> "*in most cases where a duty of confidence does exist, it will usually be reasonable to withhold third party information unless you have the third-party individual's consent to disclose it*".

The *Code* suggests that it may not always be appropriate to seek consent—in particular if doing so would involve the disclosure of personal data about the requester to the third party (p.38)—and lists additional factors to be considered, beyond those listed in the DPA 2018 itself. These are whether the information is generally known to the individual making the request (in which case, disclosure is more likely to be reasonable) and the importance of the information to the requester (p.39). The Commissioner's guidance on complaints files suggests that the fact that data is a professional and objective opinion is also relevant (p.10) and reduces the interests of the third party in having information withheld.

6.5.3.32 The third-party information provisions have been considered in some detail by the Court of Appeal in the *GMC* case (***Dr B v The General Medical Council*** 28 June 2018 [2018] EWCA Civ 1497). Dr B was a GP who had treated P and diagnosed P with cancer of the bladder. P complained to the GMC about Dr B's treatment, claiming that Dr B's incompetence led to a delay of about one year in the diagnosis of his cancer. The GMC commissioned an independent expert to prepare a report as part of its investigations and the report concluded that Dr B's care did fall below the standard expected—but not seriously below—and that most reasonably competent GPs would not have suspected bladder cancer given the particular information available at the time. The GMC decided not to take further action against Dr B. Dr B was given a copy of the report, but it was not provided to P—who made a subject access request to obtain it. The GMC consulted Dr B, following the third-party information provisions under the 1998 Act. Dr B objected to disclosure, but the GMC considered that, in all the circumstances, it would be reasonable to release the report notwithstanding. Dr B then applied to court to prevent disclosure. At first instance, the judge agreed with Dr B. The Court of Appeal (in a majority judgment) considered that the GMC's decision to release the report was reasonable and should stand.

6.5.3.33 The Court of Appeal confirmed that the third-party information provisions are evenly balanced [70] and "*there is no sound basis for saying that one should load the exercise at the outset in favour of either the objector or the requester*". However, if having considered all the relevant factors, there were to be a "*perfect equilibrium with nothing to choose between them, in that situation . . . this would be a presumption of the weak, tie-breaker type . . . It is not a significant or substantive presumption to be applied at the outset*".

6.5.3.34 The Court of Appeal also considered whether the fact that information may be used in litigation against the third party was relevant. Here, the majority decision agreed that this was a relevant factor—although the judges disagreed as to the weight to be given to this. Sales LJ noted that [45]

> "*I should not be understood to mean that in mixed data cases, an intention to litigate represents an inevitable bar to release of information. However, it seems to me that the judge was correct in thinking this is a significant matter to be weighed in the balance . . .*".

Arden LJ, however, placed less emphasis on this [99]

> "*it is simply a factor to be weighed in the balance by the data controller. There could be exceptional cases where the data controller concludes that the litigation motive outweighs every other consideration, as where the person requesting mixed data is a vexations litigant or wishes to bring further litigation of a kind that has been held previously to be an abuse of the court . . .*".

6.5.3.35 The Court of Appeal also noted [87] that its role is not to substitute its decision for that of the controller, but to determine if the controller had taken a reasonable decision. Sales LJ also suggested [83] that, in some situations, where the reasons for being concerned about disclosure were because of the use which the requester may make of the information (for example, further posting the information to damage the reputation of the third party), then

"*it might be reasonable ... to make disclosure of the information if there can be appropriate assurance that no wider dissemination of the information will occur...* [such as] *giving a binding contractual undertaking to the data controller or the objector or both ... To be clear, I do not think that this would usually be an appropriate course to try to restrict a requester from using information sought by means of a SAR in litigation thereafter. Later use in litigation is not something which is illegitimate in itself, so far as the subject access regime is concerned*".

The case is helpful in many ways—and its advice for controllers could be summarised as:

- act reasonably to balance all relevant factors;
- take account of the interests of both parties;
- if the scales are completely evenly-balanced, then withhold.

Legal professional privilege (Schedule 2, Part 4, paragraph 19)

6.5.3.36 Information need not be supplied if a claim to legal professional privilege could be made in respect of the information in legal proceedings of if the Scots law equivalent applies. The *Subject Access Code* (p.55) has a helpful gloss on privilege:

"*In broad terms, the former applies only to confidential communications between client and legal adviser, and the latter applies to confidential communications between client, professional legal adviser or a third party, but only where litigation is contemplated or in progress*".

6.5.3.37 In ***Dawson-Damer*** [39], Arden LJ stated that the identically worded exemption under the 1998 Act would apply only to legal proceedings in the UK. Perhaps to address this point, the DPA 2018 specifically extends the predecessor exemption under the 1998 Act, so that the exemption now also applies to "*information in respect of which a duty of confidentiality is owed by a professional legal adviser to a client of the adviser*".

6.5.3.38 In ***Dawson-Damer*** and ***Deer***, the Court considered the extent to which a controller should have to search through materials where it was likely that legal privilege would apply. In ***Deer*** [102], the Court of Appeal concluded that where all material would be covered by legal professional privilege, then there would be no obligation to search the material. However,

> "*plainly this only applies to the extent that personal data are covered by legal professional privilege. If some personal data are covered by legal professional privilege and others are not, the data controller will have to carry out a proportionate search to separate the two*".

In ***Deer*** the University was able to show that it had considered the scope of the request and applied it to certain categories of data requested by the applicant. In ***Dawson-Damer***, Taylor Wessing could not show what it had done to identify the material or to determine a plan of action: procedures and evidence are important.

6.5.3.39 Lastly, when a controller claims that material is exempt on grounds of privilege, it should expect the courts to take a cautious approach to this

> "*given that, unusually, the legal advisers to a party claiming privilege are judges in their own client's cause . . . For this reason, the evidence should be specific enough to show something of the deponent's analysis of the purpose for which the documents were created, something which it is possible to do without disclosing the substance of that which the claim for privilege is designed to protect*".[7]

Management forecasts (Schedule 2, Part 4, paragraph 22)

6.5.3.40 Data controllers will hold personal data that they use for management forecasting and planning. This information need not be disclosed in response to a subject-access request to the extent that this would prejudice the data controller's ability to conduct its business. An example would be if a data controller was considering making staff redundant and was processing personal data to decide which staff to make redundant and what redundancy payments would be due, or if a data controller was processing personal data in relation to a proposed outsourcing. The data controller would not be obliged to make this information available in response to a subject-access request to the extent that this would prejudice the data controller's ability to carry on this planning.

Negotiations (Schedule 2, Part 4, paragraph 23)

6.5.3.41 Information need not be provided in response to a subject access request where:

(1) the information consists of records of the data controller's intentions in relation to negotiations with the data subject; and

(2) provision of this information would prejudice the conduct of those negotiations.

So, for example, information on intended salary rises need not be provided prior to the negotiation of the rise. However, information about a pay rise which was

[7] ***Guriev*** [52].

not negotiable would not enjoy this exemption, though it might still possibly be exempt under the management forecasts exemption).

Confidential references (Schedule 2, Part 4, paragraph 24)

6.5.3.42 A data controller is not obliged to provide a copy of a reference given in confidence in connection with the actual or potential education, training, employment, placement or appointment of the data subject or provision of services by the data subject.

6.5.3.43 The 1998 Act only covered references given by the data controller—meaning that references were not exempt while in the hands of the recipient. As it is likely to be the case that all references are held by both the writer (controller) and the recipient, this distinction was frankly peculiar and the ICO recommended in the *Employment Practices Code* (2.9.3) making them equally disclosable. This difficulty has been removed by the DPA 2018. The *Subject Access Code* (p.50) emphasises that references must have been given in confidence for this to apply.

Exam scripts (Schedule 2, Part 4, paragraph 25)

6.5.3.44 Although this exemption may only be relevant to certain controllers, we have included it because it has the effect of countering much of a CJEU decision on subject access, ***Nowak v Data Protection Commissioner*** (C-434/16) EU:C:2017:994. The exemption provides, firstly, that information recorded by candidates in an exam is exempt, i.a. from subject access. Secondly, the exemption alters the timescales by which an organisation must respond to an access request. Where the personal data consist of marks or other information processed to determine exam results or in consequence of determining this, then the response to the access request is due on the earlier of 40 days after the exam results are made public, or five months after the question arises as to whether the controller has to disclose personal data. (This rather curious phrasing presumably means five months from the date on which request is made). The exemption contains a definition of exam (which is wide) and of publication (which is either general publication or to the candidate).

6.5.3.45 In ***Novak*** a would-be accountant had passed many of his accountancy exams but had repeatedly failed an open-book exam. He unsuccessfully challenged the decision of the accountancy board and then made a subject access request for his exam scripts. The CJEU determined that the candidate's responses were his personal data [51] (the questions answered were not) and so would be accessible under a subject access request. Because the DPA 2018 continues the exemption for exam scripts already provided by the 1998 Act, the question raised by ***Nowak*** will be academic in the UK in any event.

6.5.4 Issuing the information to the applicant

6.5.4.1 Once the data protection professional or other person handling the request has made appropriate checks as to the applicant's identity and checked all the material that they have collated against the various exemptions in the GDPR or the DPA 2018, the data protection professional should issue the material to the applicant.

Data not documents

6.5.4.2 Article 15(3) of the GDPR provides that the controller must provide "*a copy of the personal data undergoing processing*". This is more prescriptive than the equivalent requirement under Directive 95/46, where art.12 merely gave the individual a right to require the "*communication to him in an intelligible form of the data undergoing processing*". This requirement was considered in a case where asylum seekers in the Netherlands made subject access requests to obtain information held in the administrative minutes relating to their cases (***YS v Minister vor Immigratie, Integratie en Assiel*** and another joined case (C-1141/12; C-372/12) EU:C:2014:2081). The CJEU considered that art.12 did not require a copy of the data to be provided—the right could be met in other ways, for example:

> "*it is sufficient for the applicant for a residence permit to be provided with a full summary of all of those data in an intelligible form, that is a form which allows him to become aware of those data and to check that they are accurate and processed in compliance with that directive, so that he may, where relevant exercise the rights conferred on him by . . . that directive*".

6.5.4.3 This change in wording will be of little effect in the UK, as the 1998 Act (s.8(2)) already required the controller to meet its obligations by providing a copy of the information in permanent form (unless this would involve disproportionate effort or the individual agreed otherwise). The obligation to provide a copy of the personal data is *not* the same as an obligation to provide copies of documents in which the personal data is contained (although those making subject access requests do frequently ask for copies of documents). The *Subject Access Code* (p.43) encourages organisations to provide documents (as this is often more meaningful for the individual and sometimes easier for the organisation), but notes that this is not required:

> "*Subject access provides a right to see the information contained in personal data, rather than a right to see copies of the documents that include the information. You may therefore provide the information in the form of transcripts of relevant documents (or of sections of documents that contain the personal data), or by providing a print-out of the relevant information from your computer systems. Although the easiest way to provide the relevant information is often to supply copies of original documents, you are not obliged to do so*".

6.5.4.4 In ***Deer***, Lewison LJ noted [93] that:

> "*It seems from many of the reported cases (as well as these two appeals) that individuals who make SARs are, in truth, looking for copy documents. They*

are in my judgment aiming at the wrong target ... Accepting as I do that a person's name is his personal data, it does not follow that every piece of information in a document in which is name appears is his personal information. In such a case it would, in my judgment, be enough for the data controller to inform the data subject that, for instance, his name is consistently recorded as 'Charles Pooter' and his address as 'The Laurels, Brickfield Terrace, Holloway' in a specified number of documents between particular dates. There would be no obligation to disclose the documents themselves".

6.5.4.5 Similarly, in ***Guriev*** [47], Warby J noted that "*the requirement to provide a copy of the data in 'permanent form' can be satisfied by the provision of redacted copy documents, but that is not the only way. Another is a transcript of the data. Moreover it is only personal data that must be disclosed*".

6.5.4.6 Where material collated in response to a subject access request contains a mixture of non-personal (for example, commercially sensitive data), personal data which can be provided and personal data where an exemption applies, then the individual dealing with the access request needs to decide how the personal data will be provided: one option would be to redact the information which is not being provided, but an alternative approach would be to copy just the personal data elements into another document which is then provided to the applicant. A controller taking this route would have to be careful not to omit information which is material to the applicant and which is their personal data—in the example given in ***Deer***, knowing that the individual's name is held in a document consisting of debtors, or of individuals to be awarded a prize, would likely also be the individual's personal data.

Explanatory material

6.5.4.7 As explained above at **6.5.1.1**, the data protection professional must do more than simply put a large pile of computer printouts in the post, or on a USB stick, to the applicant. He/she must confirm if information is being processed, explain what information is processed and why, together with details of the types of organisation to whom the data will be disclosed and, where available, from whom it has been obtained. Any codes or abbreviations must also be provided.

6.5.4.8 A few years back a correspondence in a national paper discussed abbreviations used by GPs. One such was a habit of a doctor in Lincoln putting GEFL on patients' records meaning "Good enough for Lincoln"—the point being that the doctor considered the symptoms more or less bogus. A prudent controller should be on the look-out for initials like this which at best would be very embarrassing if they fell to be disclosed and explained to the relevant data subjects.

6.5.4.9 More explanatory material has to be provided than was the case under the 1998 Act. Under art.15(1), a controller must explain:

- the purposes of processing;
- the categories of personal data processed;

- the recipients or categories of recipients to which personal data have been or will be disclosed (noting that "recipients" does not just mean third parties, but also divisions or persons in the controller's organisation), with information about recipients in third countries and the safeguards used to protect the personal data being provided as well. It will be apparent that here as in the case of rectification, etc. (**6.6.5**) the controller needs to keep a record of all recipients or at the very least all categories of recipients;
- the envisaged retention period—or where this is not possible, the criteria used to determine the period;
- the individual's right to rectification or erasure, or restriction, or to object to processing;
- the right to lodge a complaint with the Information Commissioner;
- where data are not collected direct from the individual any information as to their source (which, in ***Rudd v Bridle*** (**6.5.3.30**) was considered to mean the actual source, a reference to a category would not be sufficient [123]); and
- whether significant decisions are being taken which rely on entirely automated decision—making techniques, including profiling (**6.11**), and, at least in those cases, information about the logic involved and the significance and likely consequences of such processing for the individual.

6.5.4.10 Consumer credit organisations must note that under DPA 2018 s.13 their responses to SARs must apply only to

> "*personal data relating to the data subject's financial standing, unless the data subject has indicated a contrary intention.*"

Their responses must also

> "*be accompanied by a statement informing the data subject of the data subject's rights under section 159 of the Consumer Credit Act*".

6.5.4.11 This information is very similar to the information that has to be provided in a privacy notice (**6.4.5**). While an organisation may use the privacy notice to help inform the reply to the individual, a reply which merely cross refers to this, or copies this verbatim, risks being too generic—as a practical point, if an access request has been triggered by a particular concern or complaint (as often seems to be the case), then provision of generic information which does not address the points of concern can compound the individual's concerns. If an organisation is likely to receive a large number of subject-access requests, it may well be worthwhile preparing a "playbook" which contains sample answers for typical requests, to minimise the burden of doing this on a case by case basis.

6.5.4.12 Article 12(1) requires the controller to provide the information in intelligible and easily accessible form. If the controller uses codes or abbreviations, this will mean providing a glossary. The *Guide* helpfully explains that this means taking account of what will be understandable by the average person, not necessarily this applicant—although the GDPR does require that particular account is taken of the needs of children. The *Subject Access Code* (p.43) in a similar vein explains that explanation is not the same as translation, which would not be required by data protection legislation (although other legislation, such as Welsh language legislation, may require this). The *Code* (p.23) also reminds that, separate from data protection legislation, there may be a requirement for an organisation to make reasonable adjustments for a disabled person to make an access request—for example, by providing material in large print, email or audio format.

Explaining if the request has not been fulfilled

6.5.4.13 Under the 1998 Act, there was no obligation for an organisation to explain whether or why it had not complied with an access request. Accordingly, the controller could simply revert to saying that it had provided all the information to which the applicant was entitled (which could be read as code for, we have withheld some information but will not explain why).

6.5.4.14 Article 12(4) provides that:

> "*If the controller does not take action on the request of the data subject, the controller shall inform the data subject without delay and at the latest within one month of receipt of the request of the reasons for not taking action and on the possibility of lodging a complaint with the supervisory authority and seeking a judicial remedy*".

It is not clear if this simply applies where the controller rejects a request completely (for example, because it is manifestly unfounded), or if this also extends to providing information about the fact that the request has not been met in full (because exemptions have applied). The Information Commissioner's *Guide* simply repeats the text of the GDPR without guidance on this point. Given the general obligation for the controller to provide information in response to individual's rights in a "transparent" manner (art.12(1)) and for the controller to "*facilitate the exercise of data subject rights*", a wider reading of this provision would seem more appropriate, but the point remains to be determined.

Dealing with requests where the applicant dies before the request is fulfilled

6.5.4.15 In this situation, the *Subject Access Code* (p.25) suggests that the controller check with the personal representatives as to whether they wish the data to be provided or not. However, in principle the *Code* suggests that the request must be honoured. This approach now seems incorrect after the decision of the Upper Tribunal (Administrative Appeals Chamber) in ***Campbell v Secretary of***

State [2018] UKUT 372 (AAC). The case related to a subject access request under the 1998 Act, but the principle determined—that the right is a purely personal right which does not survive death—would seem equally applicable to the GDPR.

6.5.5 Offences linked to subject access

6.5.5.1 Organisations should be aware of two subject-access request related criminal offences. The first is at s.173 of the DPA 2018 and applies if an organisation receives a subject access request or a portability request and then alters or otherwise conceals information with a view to avoiding having to provide it to the data subject. This is considered in more detail at **3.2.4.16**. The other offence is that of "enforced subject access"—this means forcing a data subject to make a subject access request and to share the results with you, as a condition of offering them employment or providing services to them. Where access requests are made in this way, it means that spent convictions, for example, will be revealed inappropriately. Accordingly, this type of practice is criminalised by s.184 of the DPA 2018 and more details of the scope of the offence and the defences are set out at **3.2.4.1**.

6.6 RECTIFICATION

6.6.1 The right of access is closely linked to the right to rectify incorrect personal data. Article 16 provides that:

> "*The data subject shall have the right to obtain from the controller without undue delay the rectification of inaccurate personal data concerning him or her. Taking into account the purposes of the processing, the data subject shall have the right to have incomplete personal data completed, including by means of providing a supplementary statement*".

6.6.2 Inaccuracy is not defined in the GDPR, but s.205 of the DPA 2018 provides that data will be inaccurate if it is "*incorrect or misleading as to any matter of fact*".

6.6.3 The right is for data to be corrected "*without undue delay*". This could, therefore, be faster than the one-month period at the end of which the controller has to revert to the data subject (art.12(3)) and **6.3.4**).

6.6.4 The reference to updating incomplete personal data with a supplementary statement might, for example, be relevant where a controller makes a decision on the basis of information provided by an individual at a certain date. The individual may want to update this information at a later date, and it may be important for the organisation to have both correct records about the individual's current situation and of the information which was originally submitted by the individual. If this is the case it is essential that the software allows for a comment field to accommodate this. It is in any case generally helpful for all personal data software to provide this.

6.6.5 Where a controller rectifies inaccurate personal data then, as with data which has been erased or restricted, the controller must notify each recipient to whom the personal data have been disclosed of the rectification (art.19). Recipients do not just mean external third parties—they are defined at art.4(9) as "*a natural or legal person, public authority, agency or another body, to which the personal data are disclosed, whether a third party or not . . .*". Accordingly, it follows that, to be able to comply with this obligation, a controller must keep records of the external parties, and internal departments, with whom personal data is shared. The controller does *not* have to provide this notice if it would prove impossible or involve disproportionate effort. If the data subject so requests, then the controller must inform the individual about the recipients—presumably so that the individual can then contact them to check that the request has been implemented, or to request them to cease processing or to erase or restrict the data which has had to be corrected, erased, or restricted.

6.6.6 The Commissioner's *Guide* contains useful guidance on the difficult situations which can arise where records contain mistakes and opinions. On the former, the *Guide* notes

> "*It may be possible to argue that the record of the mistake is, in itself, accurate and should be kept. In such circumstances the fact that a mistake was made and the correct information should also be included in the individual's data*".

The *Guide* goes on to include an example of mis-diagnosis of a medical condition to explain this. It will be important to keep the record of this in order to explain the subsequent treatment provided: the records correctly record the mis-diagnosis but should also make clear the correct diagnosis which was obtained later.

6.6.7 On disputed opinions, the *Guide* takes a similar approach:

> "*Opinions are, by their very nature, subjective, and it can be difficult to conclude that the record of an opinion is inaccurate. As long as the record shows clearly that the information is an opinion and, where appropriate, whose opinion it is, it may be difficult to say that it is inaccurate and needs to be rectified*".

6.6.8 The *Wozencroft* case (*P v Wozencroft* [2002] EWHC 1724 (Fam)) is a good example of a case under the 1998 Act where the courts rejected an inappropriate attempt by an individual to use his right to rectify incorrect data to try to overturn other decisions and proceedings. The background to the case lies in acrimonious proceedings under the Children Act 1989. The claimant P had applied under the Children Act for a residence or contact order in respect of his daughter. In the course of these proceedings, a psychiatric report had been prepared which was extremely critical of P. P's application for residence or a contact order was unsuccessful. P unsuccessfully tried to appeal against the Children Act proceedings. When this failed, he contacted the psychiatrist and asked for all papers relating to his case. The psychiatrist refused to supply the papers on the grounds that, in his view, he was not the data controller and hence had no obligation to provide access. In the view of the psychiatrist, the person who instructed him, the Children and Family Court Advisory and Support Service (CAFCASS), was the data controller. P applied to Court for an order requiring the psychiatrist to provide access to the papers. P was quite candid that he required access in order to support an application under the Act to require the psychiatrist to "correct" his inaccurate and prejudicial report. In this case Black J concluded robustly that the Act was wholly inappropriate for the issues raised. The judgment concluded that it would be an abuse of process to allow P to use the Act to supplement rights granted to him under the Children Act. Black J made it clear that the Court had discretion as to whether or not it would make any of the order sought under the Act. In this case, the Court declined to make any of the orders sought.

6.7 RIGHT TO DATA PORTABILITY

6.7.1 Introduction

6.7.1.1 This is a new right introduced by the GDPR. There is detailed guidance on the right both in the Commissioner's *Guide* and in *Guidance on the right to data portability* revised and adopted by WP 29 on 5 April 2017 (WP 242) and since approved by the EDPB.

6.7.1.2 We have taken this right out of the order suggested in Ch.III of the GDPR, because we think it is helpful to consider it next to subject access. Portability only applies to personal data in certain situations and there are exemptions from the right: however, it is important to remember that individuals will still have rights to access all of their personal data (and, if they make a request electronically, in a commonly used electronic format), so even when portability does not apply, subject access may well still apply.

6.7.2 What does "portability" mean?

6.7.2.1 Article 20(1) explains that this is a right to receive personal data:

- in a structured, commonly used and machine-readable format (art.20(1));
- which should be interoperable (rec.68); and
- to have the data transmitted direct to another controller "without hindrance" from the original controller (art.20(1)) and, where technically feasible, by having the data transmitted direct from one controller to another (art.20(2)) however, this does not create an obligation on controllers to adopt or maintain processing systems which are technically compatible (rec.68).

6.7.2.2 In addition, art.20(3) says that exercise of the right is to be without prejudice to the individual's right of erasure—in other words, as rec.68 makes clear, where an individual asks for data to be ported, this does *not* mean that the controller should also erase the data: if it is still needed to perform a contract, the original controller should still continue to process the data for this purpose.

6.7.2.3 The Commissioner's *Guide* has guidance as to what the terms at art.20(1) and rec.68 mean:

- structured means that software must be able to extract specific elements of the data—so a spreadsheet where data is organised in rows and columns would meet this requirement;
- machine-readable—means that data can be automatically read and processed by computer—and data which is structured will also often be machine-readable;
- commonly used simply means widely-used and well-established. However not all commonly used formats are structured and machine readable (for example, pdf would not be);
- interoperable means that the data is in a format so that it can be exchanged between different systems and be understandable to both. The Commissioner's *Guide* takes the view that interoperability is best practice but not mandated; WP 242 pushes more strongly for interoperability as a requirement.

CSV and XML files or data in JavaScript Object Notation would meet these requirements (although these are not the only appropriate formats). The *Guide* refers controllers to the Open Data Handbook[8] for more guidance as to what these terms mean and for examples and details of relevant standards.

6.7.2.4 WP 242 notes that the requirement that data can be ported "*without hindrance*" would encompass barriers such as fees, provision of obfuscated datasets or requirements for recipients to be accredited by the original controller (p.15). WP 242 also emphasises the need for the ported data to be usable—for example, this may require data to be produced at a high level of abstraction to avoid the constraints of internal or proprietary formats (p.17) or may require the controller to provide metadata (for example, providing dates or times when emails have been sent or received as well as the content of an in-box) to preserve functionality of the ported data (p.18).

6.7.2.5 It is clear from the above commentary, that meeting portability requirements could impose significant burdens on controllers. The Information Commissioner's *Guide* notes that this includes responsibility for security of data which is being transmitted to the individual or the new controller: for this reason, the *Guide* and WP 242 recommend controllers use secure methods of transmission, such as secure file transfer sites, or develop APIs, to facilitate secure direct transfer of personal data. The *Guide* does, however, make clear that controllers are *not* responsible for the acts of the recipient of the ported personal data.

[8] A resource designed for government and civil society on open data and available at *opendatahandbook.org*.

6.7.3 When does it apply?

6.7.3.1 Portability only applies to personal data which is processed "*by automated means*", so there is no obligation to port paper records held in a filing system. In addition:

- the processing must be based on consent or processing necessary to perform a contract with the individual or to take steps at the request of the data subject prior to entering into a contract (i.e. the grounds for processing must either be art.6(1)(a), art.9(2) or art.6(1)(b); and
- the data must be personal data which "*he or she has provided to a controller*".

6.7.3.2 WP 242 gives the examples of a playlist or titles of books downloaded as examples of personal data which would meet the first criterion. It notes that, in a financial services context, this would mean that data processed as part of the bank's obligation to prevent and detect money laundering would not have to be provided (p.8).

6.7.3.3 The second criterion has the potential to significantly restrict the scope of portability: the example of the email in-box above highlights this. If this only extends to the content of the message which a user sends to the email provider, or (arguably) the replies which the recipient provides to the provider to store, but not automatically generated data about time and date of sending, then the individual's ability to make use of the ported data is significantly reduced. It is no surprise, therefore that the Information Commissioner and the EDPB take an expansive and purposive approach to interpretation here. In the *Guide* the Commissioner states that:

> "*It* [the meaning of data provided to a controller] *is also personal data resulting from observation of an individual's activities (e.g. where using a device or service).*
> *This may include:*
>
> - *history of website usage or search activities;*
> - *traffic and location data; or*
> - *'raw' data processed by connected objects such as smart meters and wearable devices*".

6.7.3.4 The provision does not, however, include inferred or derived data although the Commissioner even recommends providing this as a matter of good practice. The EDPB also notes that if a controller is subject to sector specific legislation which includes portability obligations, that these would apply instead of the GDPR provisions: the example given in WP 242 (pp.8 and 9) is the provision in the Payment Services Directive providing for portability of banking account history to account information service providers.

6.7.4 Raising awareness of portability

6.7.4.1 As portability is a new right, individuals may be less aware of it. Controllers are, of course, required to include information in their privacy policies which explains to individuals what their rights are under the GDPR. In addition, as a matter of good practice, WP 242 (p.13) recommends that controllers should mention this right when individuals close accounts.

6.7.5 Exemptions

6.7.5.1 Data portability does not apply to controllers whose lawful basis for processing is art.6(1)(e)—i.e. processing necessary for the performance of a task carried out in the public interest or in the exercise of official authority vested in the controller. Article 20(4) also provides that the right of portability "*shall not adversely affect the rights and freedoms of others*"—offering an exemption in this situation.

Trade secrets and intellectual property rights

6.7.5.2 The language at art.20(4) is identical to that at art.15(4) in relation to subject access requests: the right "*shall not adversely affect the rights and freedoms of others*". Recital 63 specifically notes that this includes trade secrets and intellectual property rights, and this is also referred to as being relevant to portability in WP 242 (p.12).

Data relating to multiple data subjects

6.7.5.3 Article 20(4) is also relevant if the data to be ported relates to more than one individual—as may often be the case. Again, the approach of the EDPB and the Commissioner to this is purposive, driven by a desire to avoid the exemption being so widely interpreted as to mean that the right is of little value. WP 242 notes that "*data controllers should not take an overly restrictive interpretation*" to this provision (p.9).

6.7.5.4 The ICO's rule of thumb (p.130 of the *Guide*) is as follows:

> "*Generally speaking, providing data to the individual making the portability request should not be a problem, assuming that the requester provided this data to you within their information in the first place. However, you should always consider whether there will be an adverse effect on the rights and freedoms of third parties, in particular when you are transmitting data directly to another controller.*
> *If the requested data has been provided to you by multiple data subjects (e.g. a joint bank account) you need to be satisfied that all parties agree to the portability request. This means that you may have to seek agreement from all the parties involved*".

6.7.5.5 Where the service offered by the controller to the individual inevitably involves processing personal data about others—for example, a webmail service which will include a directory of contacts—then the EDPB also suggests (p.11) that the controller should, on request, transfer all such data included in the service to the new provider. The EDPB suggests that if the new controller uses the third-party data for other purposes (i.e. beyond fulfilling the contract with the data subject) then this would present risks to the third parties. Accordingly, in the example about the webmail service,

> "*to prevent adverse effects on the third parties involved, the processing of such personal data by another controller is allowed only to the extent that the data are kept under the sole control of the requesting user and is only managed for purely personal or household affairs*".

6.7.5.6 The EDPB's approach is to read art.20(4) as a restriction on the new controller, rather than as an exemption for the controller providing portability. This is an ingenious approach to the problem that the exemption to portability, protecting third parties, may mean that the right cannot effectively be exercised. However, it is not clear that this interpretation is correct and, even if it were to be correct, it would raise other problems—in particular where the receiving controller is not itself subject to the GDPR. The EDPB suggests that those providing portability and those receiving ported data should look at "*leading practices*" to implement tools to allow data subjects to select what data should be ported and to allow third parties to give consent to this. This seems destined to be a difficult area for controllers.

6.7.6 Position of the organisation receiving data

6.7.6.1 There is no obligation on controllers to receive personal data—so controllers should decide if this is something they wish to do, or not. Both the EDPB and the ICO *Guide* (p.135) emphasise that a controller which receives ported data must then comply with all elements of the GDPR in respect of such data: accordingly, it will need to ensure it has a lawful basis for processing and that the data is relevant and not excessive. It will also need to ensure that any processing of data about other individuals can be justified.

6.7.7 Industry developments

6.7.7.1 The practical, technical and legal complexities of portability mean that co-operation between controllers who are likely to receive portability requests and/or the ported data is essential. An important development in this regard has been the launch of the Data Transfer Project: a collaboration between Google, Microsoft, Twitter and Facebook, to develop tools to facilitate data transfer between service providers.[9] Industry specific developments are also possible—for example, banks should be aware of the longstanding midata initiative.[10]

---

[9] See *http://datatransferproject.dev*.

[10] See *http://www.pcamidata.co.uk/*.

6.8 RIGHTS TO OBJECT TO PROCESSING

6.8.1 Introduction

6.8.1.1 The GDPR grants individuals three distinct rights to object to processing: for direct marketing related purposes; where processing is carried out because this is for someone's legitimate interests or for a public or official task; or for processing for research and statistical purposes. Individuals often object to other processing, sending requests to controllers to cease all processing of personal data relating to them: however, the GDPR grants no such broad right. The right to object to processing of personal data for direct marketing purposes is considered at **7.3.1**. Each of the other relevant rights is considered below.

6.8.2 Right to object to processing based on legitimate interests or public task lawful basis

6.8.2.1 Article 21(1) grants individuals a right to object to processing of personal data where the processing is based on art.6(1)(e) or (f). By way of reminder:

- art.6(1)(e) applies to processing which is "*necessary for a task carried out in the public interest or in the exercise of official authority vested in the controller*"; and
- art.6(1)(f) applies to processing which is "*necessary for the purposes of legitimate interests pursued by the controller or by a third party, except where such interests are overridden by the interests or fundamental rights and freedoms of the data subject which require protection of personal data, in particular where the data subject is a child*".

6.8.2.2 The right to object to direct marketing is an absolute right—individuals can exercise it without having to demonstrate any reason and there are no exemptions to it. The right to object to processing based on 6(1)(e) and (f) is more limited: it applies only where there are "*grounds relating to* [the data subject's] ... *particular situation*". As the *Guide* notes, this may include (but is not limited to) situations where the individual can show that the processing is likely to cause them damage or distress. If an individual can meet this requirement, the controller must then go on to consider if it can demonstrate "*compelling legitimate grounds for the processing which override the interests, rights and freedoms of the data subject*" or if the processing is "*for the establishment, exercise or defence of legal claims*": if either of these situations applies, then there is no obligation to stop processing the personal data. In addition to these exemptions, there are additional exemptions under the DPA 2018 (see **Ch.10**) as well as the exemption under art.12(5) for requests which are manifestly unfounded or excessive (**6.3.6**).

6.8.2.3 Where an organisation processes personal data because this is necessary for its, or a third party's legitimate interests, then the organisation will already have carried out a balancing test, or legitimate interests assessment, in order to consider whether the individual's interests may outweigh its, or the third parties, interests (**4.4.5.22**). The assessment needed under art.21(1) is similar. However, the positions of the controller and the data subject are reversed: when a legitimate interests assessment is carried out, the controller may proceed to process personal data unless the individual's interests outweigh its interests; here the controller must cease to process personal data unless it can demonstrate that its interests are "*compelling*". This is a higher standard—and suggests not merely that the scales must be tipped in favour of the controller, but that the controller's interests must be particularly important.

6.8.3 Right to object to processing for scientific or historical research or statistical purposes

6.8.3.1 The GDPR introduces additional flexibility for controllers who wish to process personal data for scientific or historical research or for statistical purposes (**10.5.7**). In return, however, the GDPR introduces a new right for individuals to object to such processing[11]. Like the right to object to processing based on art.6(1)(e) or (f), the right only applies on grounds relating to the individual's particular situation. Article 21(6) provides that the right does not apply if "*the processing is necessary for the performance of a task carried out for reasons of public interest*"—for example, this may mean that organisations carrying out research for public health purposes, for example, may not have to stop processing. This is, of course, in addition to the usual exemptions at art.12(5) and in the DPA 2018 (**Ch.10**).

6.8.3.2 The provisions in the GDPR and the DPA 2018 relating to objections to processing for scientific and historical research and to processing for statistical purposes and to erasure of data processed for such purposes are somewhat convoluted:

- Article 21(6) provides that individuals can object to such processing, on grounds relating to his or her particular situation, unless the processing is necessary for performance of a public interest task.
- Most research will be justified on the basis of art.6(1)(e) or (f)—so introducing the right for individuals to object under art.21(1)—again on grounds relating to their particular situation—this time, unless the controller can demonstrate compelling legitimate grounds which override the individual's interests.
- Article 17(3)(d) provides that when an individual asks for data to be erased, there is an exemption for scientific or historical research, statistical purposes and archiving in the public interest, in so far as the right to erasure is likely to "*render impossible or seriously impair the achievement of the objectives of that processing*".

[11] The GDPR provisions relating to scientific and historical research and statistical purposes usually also reference archiving purposes in the public interest. However, the right to object does not extend to archiving.

- Schedule 2, Pt 6, para.27 of the DPA 2018 provides an exemption from, amongst other things, art.21(1) (but *not* from the right to object to processing for research and statistical purposes) where application of the right would prevent or seriously impair achievement of the research or statistical purposes. For this to apply, the safeguards in art.89 and s.19 of the DPA 2018 must be followed and the results of the processing must not be made available in a form which identifies the individual.

6.8.3.3 The net effect of these provisions is that organisations carrying out research which is necessary for a task carried out in the public interest will be exempt from objections to processing and are also likely not to have to implement erasure requests. Organisations carrying out other research are more likely to have to stop processing personal data (as they would be less likely to be processing data for a task carried out in the public interest), but they may not have to erase the data already collected if this would seriously impair the achievement of the objectives of the processing (for example if this could undermine the statistical validity of processing which has already taken place). The provisions are difficult to reconcile.

6.8.4 Making the rights easier to exercise

6.8.4.1 Article 21(4) provides that the rights to object to processing set out at sub-article 1 (relating to art.6(1)(e) and (f)) and sub-article 2 (direct marketing and profiling related to direct marketing) must be explicitly drawn to the attention of data subjects, at the latest at the time of first communication with the individual. The rights must be presented clearly and separately from other information—so cannot be buried in small print, or even in a privacy policy. Instead there should be a separate section of any data collection form or marketing email which explains the rights. This obligation to draw individuals' attention to their rights to object at the outset does not apply to processing for research or statistical purposes. However, as the lawful basis for such processing is likely to be art 6(1)(e) or (f), in any event, the distinction seems unimportant. In addition, as the ICO *Guide* notes the organisation would also have to include this information in its privacy policy.

6.8.4.2 Article 21(5) provides that "*in the context of the use of information society services*" (i.e. online services), data subjects may exercise their rights to object "*by automated means using technical specifications*". This seems to be an attempt to introduce a requirement for publishers to respect initiatives such as do not track (i.e. a signal included in a request for a web-page sent by a user's browser which instructs the publisher not to track the user).[12]

---

12 See also *https://eff.org>issues>do-not-track*.

6.9 RIGHT OF ERASURE

6.9.1 Introduction

6.9.1.1 The right to erasure is neatly summarised in rec.65 of the GDPR:

"*A data subject should have the right to have personal data concerning him or her rectified and a 'right to be forgotten' where the retention of such data infringes this Regulation or Union or Member State law to which the controller is subject*".

6.9.1.2 The right only applies in certain situations and, even in these situations, there are exemptions. Where the right applies and data is erased, there are also obligations to notify third parties, who are processing the data, that it has been erased. Each of these points is considered below. First, though, we consider what the obligation to erase data may mean.

6.9.2 Erasing data

6.9.2.1 Article 17(1) of the GDPR provides that individuals have a right to obtain, and the controller has an obligation to implement, erasure of personal data "without delay". The usual provisions of art.12 apply, meaning that the controller must inform the data subject of the actions taken in response within one month, although this period may be extended by two further months where complexity and number of requests make this necessary (**6.3.4.3**).

Backup systems

6.9.2.2 A controller will typically process personal data in both live systems and backups retained for business continuity purposes. The data held on backups will be over-written after a set period of time, usually some months. It will be difficult and expensive for a controller to have to restore back-up data in order to implement an erasure request. The Information Commissioner's *Guide* addresses this difficult topic briefly. The *Guide* states that, in principle, an erasure request will also extend to data held in backup systems. However, the *Guide* also states that the actual steps:

"*will depend on your particular circumstances, your retention schedule (particularly in the context of its backups), and the technical mechanisms that are available to you . . .*

It may be that the erasure request can be instantly fulfilled in respect of live systems, but that the data will remain within the backup environment for a certain period of time until it is overwritten.

The key is to put the backup data 'beyond use', even if it cannot be immediately overwritten. You must ensure that you do not use the data within the backup for any other purpose, i.e. that the backup is simply held on your systems until it is replaced in line with an established schedule . . .".

6.9.2.3 The *Guide* also states that if the data is not all erased, the controller should make clear to individuals what will happen to their data, including in respect of back-up systems. The conclusion in the *Guide* is based on an assumption that, because the data will not be put to live use, it is reasonable to allow a longer period for erasure to take place. In order to rely on this, an organisation would need to ensure, if it *does* revert to backup systems, that it has a separate record of erasure requests which had been implemented in the live system but not in the backup, so that these could be implemented as soon as the backup is put into use. Much the same might happen to other regularly overwritten data, such as CCTV records or voicemail. It will usually be far easier to wait for the regular overwrite than try and find the data subject's record out of sequence.

6.9.2.4 This section of the *Guide* refers to guidance issued by the Information Commissioner under the 1998 Act on deletion of data—*Deleting personal data* v.1.1—which is where the Commissioner expands on what she means by putting data "beyond use". *Deleting personal data* also has guidance on what deletion means, noting that:

> "*There is a significant difference between deleting information irretrievably, archiving it in a structured, retrievable manner or retaining it as random data in an un-emptied electronic wastebasket*" (p.4).

6.9.2.5 It is fairly obvious that neither of the latter two options (archiving or moving to a deleted folder) will amount to deletion (or to erasure). But it is also usually the case that simply pressing the delete button or emptying a deleted folder does not actually remove the data. All it does is to remove the pointers to the data (thereby making it very hard to use, and also allowing later data (not necessarily in any way connected with the "deleted" data) to overwrite it. In practice it may be many weeks or even months before the data is actually overwritten and thus obliterated. The guidance states that the Commissioner will adopt a "*realistic approach*" to information which has been "deleted", with no intent that it should be used again, but where the data "*may still exist in the electronic ether*".

6.9.2.6 The guidance also considers the situation of data which

> "*should have been deleted, but is still held on a live system because, for technical reasons, it is not possible to delete this information without also deleting other information held in the same batch*".

The guidance suggests that, in this situation, the Commissioner will accept that the data has been put beyond use (and will not require further steps—for example insisting on subject access to the data, or more permanent deletion), provided that the controller:

- is not able to, or will not in practice attempt to use, the personal data in any way;
- does not give others access to the personal data;

- surrounds the data with appropriate technical and organisational security; and
- commits to permanent deletion of the information of or when this becomes possible (p.5).

6.9.2.7 Of course, this guidance note was written before the advent of the GDPR (its objective is to give guidance on meeting the fifth data protection principle under the 1998 Act, the storage limitation principle), and the section on putting data beyond use is difficult to reconcile, in its entirety, with the GDPR—which, via the concept of privacy by design at art.25, requires controllers to "*integrate the necessary safeguards into the processing to meet the requirements of the Regulation*". The suggestions made in *Deleting personal data* seem closer to the GDPR's concept of restriction (**6.10**).

Search engines

6.9.2.8 The right to erasure has gained fame (or notoriety, depending on your perspective) as a result of the ***Google Spain*** case (***Google Spain SL, Google Inc v AEPD, Mario Costeja Gonzalez*** (C-131/12) EU:C:2014:317). This case sets out how search engines should comply with the right and influenced the provisions in the GDPR. The case concerned Mr. Costeja, who objected to the fact that newspaper articles about an auction of his property, in connection with repayment of social security debts, continued to be returned in responses to internet searches on his name, 16 years after the relevant events took place. Mr Costeja complained to the Spanish data protection authority (AEPD), who declined to take any action against the newspaper because of journalistic exemptions but ordered Google to delist these results. Google objected to the order and the case was referred by the Spanish courts to the CJEU. The CJEU's decision was that individuals did have a "right to be forgotten": they could require search engines to delist results relating to them. The CJEU confirmed that search engines were data controllers, responsible for the processing of personal data involved in their operations. The CJEU also confirmed that the effect of search engines was to make information about individuals ubiquitous, so that this was a serious interference with individuals rights which could not be justified by the economic interests of the search operator alone [81]. The CJEU acknowledged that internet users also have a right to receive information and that this interest has to be balanced against the privacy and data protection rights of the person to whom the search result relates (even if Google's economic interests do not count in this balance) [81]. The CJEU noted that, as a general rule, privacy and data protection rights would override the interest of internet users, but that, in specific cases, this balance would depend on the nature of the information in question—in particular its sensitivity for the individual's private life and on the interest of the public in having the information, in particular, whether the individual plays a role in public life. The CJEU concluded that this meant that where a search is made on the basis of a person's name, the results which are to be forgotten should not be included in the search results [88].

The obligation is specific to searches made by reference to the individual's name: a search made in a different way might still reveal the material in respect of which a right to be forgotten request has been made.

6.9.2.9 The *Google Spain* judgment does *not* mean that the publisher of the underlying pages must remove the material—the publisher's obligations and the search engine's obligations should be considered separately and there may be separate reasons which would justify material remaining on the publisher's site (para.88). A different CJEU decision (*Camera di Commercio, Industria, Artigianato e Agricoltura di Lecce v Salvatore Manni* (C-398/15) EU:C:2017:197), shows how this may lead to a different outcome. The facts of *Manni* have some similarity with those of *Google Spain*, as Mr Manni complained about the continued availability of information showing his role as sole director and liquidator of a company which had become insolvent. He complained that the continued availability of this information caused difficulties for a different company, of which he was also the sole director. However, in this case, Mr Manni sought to have the reports removed from the relevant Chamber of Commerce, which was obliged to publish such details. The CJEU recognised that there was a legitimate interest in this type of information being available about those who run limited companies. It also recognised that the variety of limitation periods across the EU meant that it was difficult to set one period after which such information would cease to be useful and concluded that it was a matter for Member States to determine whether or not bodies which publish such information should be required to consider requests by individuals, such as Mr Manni, to limit access to these records.

6.9.2.10 Following the *Google Spain* decision, the Article 29 Working Party Issued *Guidelines on the implementation of the Court of Justice of the European Union judgment on 'Google Spain & Inc v AEPD and Mario Costeja Gonzalez'* (adopted on 26 November 2014 under document number WP 225). WP 225 summarised WP 29's approach to the judgment and sets out common criteria to be applied by data protection authorities in handling complaints by individuals that search engines had not appropriately implemented their requests to be forgotten. WP 225 notes that although individuals outside the EU could, in theory, make requests to be forgotten to Google's EU establishments, data protection authorities would prioritise complaints where there is an EU nexus (for example, where the individual is an EU citizen or resident). WP 225 does, however, state that the delisting requirement should apply globally—in other words it is not sufficient to delist search results on EU-focused domain names (such as .uk or .fr), but that the delisting should also be reflected in all domains worldwide including .com domains (p.3). This requirement is the subject of a further reference to the CJEU (*Google LLC v CNIL* (C-507/17)).

6.9.3 When does the right to erasure apply?

6.9.3.1 *Google* and *Manni* predated the GDPR. We now have a more complete view of the rules to be applied. The right to erasure applies when one (or more) or of the following grounds, listed at art.17(1) of the GDPR, applies:

"*a)* *the personal data are no longer necessary in relation to the purposes for which they were collected or otherwise processed;*

b) *the data subject withdraws consent on which the processing is based according to point a) of Article 6(1)* [lawful basis for processing; consent] *or point (a) of Article 9(2)* [special category data; explicit consent to process], *and where there is no other legal ground for processing;*

c) *the data subject objects to the processing pursuant to Article 21(1) and there are no overriding legitimate grounds for the processing, or the data subject objects to the processing pursuant to Article 21(2)* [direct marketing]*;*

d) *the personal data have been unlawfully processed;*

e) *the personal data have to be erased for compliance with a legal obligation in Union or Member State law to which the controller is subject;*

f) *the personal data have been collected in relation to the offer of information society services* [online services] *referred to in Article 8(1)* [child's consent]".

6.9.3.2 Most individuals who ask for data to be erased are unlikely to be sufficiently well-versed in data protection law as to explain which ground they consider justifies their request. As the controller must "facilitate" the exercise of individual's rights, the first thing the controller must do when it receives a request for erasure (and when it has confirmed the identity of the requester) is to consider which, if any, provision under art.17(1) is relevant. In some situations, the ground will be obvious, but in others, the controller may need to revert to the individual to ask for more information in order to establish if the right could apply.

6.9.3.3 On the last provision in art.17(1), rec.65 explains that the "*right is relevant in particular where the data subject has given his or her consent as a child and is not fully aware of the risks involved by the processing, and later wants to remove such personal data, especially on the internet. The data subject should be able to exercise that right notwithstanding the fact that he or she is no longer a child*".

6.9.3.4 Article 17(1)(c) links to art.21, which grants individuals rights to object to processing in some situations. The right to object is limited to situations where processing is for direct marketing or profiling related to direct marketing, or where the processing is justified on the basis that it is necessary for the performance of a task carried out in the public interest or in the exercise of official authority vested in the controller (art.6(1)(e)) or is necessary for purposes of the legitimate interests pursued by the controller or a third party, so long as those interests are not overridden by the interests of the data subject (art.6(1)(f)). In our experience, many individuals who contact a controller and ask for their data to be deleted really also intend to object to further processing by the controller. Where an organisation carries out direct marketing or relies on arts 6(1)(e) or (f) to process personal data, it would be sensible for it to assume that the individual is also objecting to further processing, or at the very least to check this with the individual.

6.9.4 Exemptions

6.9.4.1 Article 17(3) provides that the right to erasure does not apply:

"*... to the extent that processing is necessary:*

a) *for exercising the right of freedom of expression and information;*
b) *for compliance with a legal obligation which requires processing by Union or Member State law to which the controller is subject or for the performance of a task carried out in the public interest or in the exercise of official authority vested in the controller;*
c) *for reasons of public interest in the area of public health in accordance with points h) and i) of Article 9(2) as well as Article 9(3)* [special categories of personal data processed by a professional subject to an obligation of secrecy];
d) *for archiving purposes in the public interest, scientific or historical research purposes or statistical purposes in accordance with Article 89(1) in so far as the right referred to in paragraph 1 is likely to render impossible or seriously impair the achievement of the objectives of that processing; or*
e) *for the establishment, exercise or defence of legal claims*".

6.9.4.2 In addition to these exemptions which are specific to the right to erasure, the general provisions at art.12(5) (relating to requests which are manifestly unfounded or excessive (**6.3.6**)), and art.11 (relating to situations where the controller cannot sufficiently identify the individual) apply, as do the exemptions set out in Schs 2 and 3 to the DPA 2018 and considered in **Ch.10**.

Freedom of expression and information

6.9.4.3 The 1995 Directive left to Member States the way they should provide a balance between data protection and freedom of expression. While the GDPR again mandates Member States to do this, it also sets out a specific exemption from the right to erasure on this basis.

6.9.4.4 ***Google Spain*** confirmed that when a search engine presents search results, its processing is based on the legitimate interests condition—the legitimate interests being both Google's and those of the internet users who have an interest in receiving information. The CJEU considered that these interests could, in some cases, outweigh those of the data subject. Accordingly, ***Google Spain*** also provides guidance as to the way freedom of expression and information and the right to erasure should be balanced. The Annex to WP 225 lists factors which WP 29 considered relevant in balancing the legitimate interests of internet users in receiving information about the data subject, and the privacy interests of the data subject. These factors are: whether the individual has a public role (which WP 29 interpreted as including carrying out a regulated profession); whether the information relates to the individual as a minor; accuracy; relevance of the information and whether it is excessive and accurate and up to date; whether any of the information concerns special category data; whether continued listing causes prejudice to the data subject or puts him or her at risk; the context of the original publication (in particular, if it was published for journalistic, literary or artistic purposes, or if there was a legal obligation to make material public); and, lastly, if the information concerns criminal offences. On the latter point, WP 225 noted that Member States take different approaches to the legality of publishing data about criminal offences and to the principle of rehabilitation (which has links to the concept of a right to be forgotten); accordingly, this was an area where there would be divergence in treatment of complaints about delisting requests.

6.9.4.5 The criteria in WP 225 were applied by the UK courts in ***NT1, NT2 v Google LLC and The Information Commissioner*** [2018] EWHC 799 (QB). This concerns two joined cases—NT1 was convicted of criminal conspiracy in connection with the business activities of a property company with which he was involved. The conviction was spent and he sought to have search results relating to it delisted by making a right to be forgotten request to Google. He also engaged a reputation management company to try to drown-out the adverse search results by posting articles about him; the articles contained exaggerated and unsubstantiated claims about his professional life. Warby J found him to be an unattractive witness, who did not recognise his own former wrongdoing. Warby J refused to require delisting, noting that continued availability of the search results about NT1 was justified because he still had a limited public role and was attempting to mislead via the reputation management articles. NT2 had also been convicted—for hacking and phone tapping linked to attempts to find the source of actions against a controversial company with which he was involved. The conviction was also spent. By contrast with NT1, Warby J found NT2 to be a reliable witness. The Judge did order delisting—inaccuracy of the linked information was relevant, as was the fact that the individual had not sought to mislead the public as to his past and was operating in a different field where there was no need to warn others about his past. Google also sought to argue that it could rely on the UK specific exemptions for the special purposes (i.e. journalism) at s.32 of the 1998 Act. However, Warby J rejected this on the basis that Google was not processing solely (if at all) for the special purposes.

6.9.5 Notifying others

6.9.5.1 Where a controller has to implement an erasure request, it may also have to advise others of this. This is relevant if the controller has made the personal data public, where art.17(2) provides that the controller must take reasonable steps, including technical measures, to inform controllers which are processing the data (in particular by way of links to the data, or copies or replicas of the data) that the individual has requested erasure. This is particularly likely to apply to data posted, or linked to, online—with rec.66 noting that the provision is "*to strengthen the right to be forgotten in an online environment*". The steps required will depend on available technology and cost of implementation but might include posting online an equally prominent correction.

6.9.5.2 In addition to this specific provision, art.19 is also relevant, which requires the controller to notify each recipient to whom the personal data has been disclosed—unless this proves impossible or would involve disproportionate effort.

6.10 RESTRICTION

6.10.1 What is restriction?

6.10.1.1 The right to restriction is a new right introduced by the GDPR. At the date of writing (September 2018), there is no dedicated opinion on the right from the EDPB, so controllers have little assistance in interpreting the provisions.

6.10.1.2 Article 4(3) defines restriction as "*the marking of stored personal data with the aim of limiting their processing in the future*". Article 18(2) provides that, where processing has been restricted, it can still be stored, but cannot be processed in any other way without the individual's consent, or

> "*for the establishment, exercise or defence of legal claims or for the protection of the rights of another natural person or for reasons of important public interest of the Union or of a Member State*".

The principle, therefore, is that the data is put beyond live use, save for the limited situations permitted by art.18(2).

6.10.1.3 Recital 67 offers illustrative examples of what restriction may mean, suggesting that methods of restriction could include:

> "... *temporarily moving the selected data to another processing system, making the selected data unavailable to users, or temporarily removing published data from a website. In automated filing systems, the restriction of processing should in principle be ensured by technical means, in such a manner that the personal data are not subject to further processing operations and cannot be changed. The fact that the processing of personal data is restricted should be clearly indicated in the system*".

6.10.1.4 The idea that data may be stored, but not otherwise put to live use, sounds similar to the notion of putting data "beyond live use" which is discussed in guidance on deletion of data issued by the Commissioner under the 1998 Act (**5.5.6.3**). These suggestions in this guidance as to what the controller must do to put data beyond live use may, therefore, also be useful reference points (although that guidance does not talk about this being "clearly indicated in the system", which must not be overlooked).

6.10.1.5 When processing is restricted, the controller must inform the individual before lifting the restriction (art.12(3)), presumably to give the individual an opportunity to challenge this. As processing of restricted data (other than for the purposes listed at **6.10.1.2** above) may only take place with the consent of the individual, and as consent must be specific, an individual could give consent to request a restriction for one particular act of processing, but not for another. In addition, as with rectification and erasure, the controller must notify recipients of the data that it has been restricted (**6.9.5.1**).

6.10.2 When does restriction apply?

6.10.2.1 The right to restriction only applies in certain situations: two of these are linked to disputes between controller and data subject; two apply where the data subject requires the controller to restrict data, rather than to delete the data.

6.10.2.2 The first two cases apply where:

- the data subject contests the accuracy of personal data and applies for a period which enables the controller to verify the accuracy of the personal data (art.18(1)(a); or
- the data subject objects to processing pursuant to art.21(1) (processing for purposes which are in the controllers or a third party's legitimate interests, or for a task in the public interest, or the exercise of official authority), and applies until the controller can determine whether its grounds for processing override those of the individual (art.18(1)(d).

6.10.2.3 Most individuals are unlikely to be aware that they have a right to "restrict" processing of personal data. If an individual asks a controller to stop processing their data, or disputes the accuracy of the data, the individual would probably not expect the organisation to carry on using the data during the period while the organisation assesses that request. For this reason, the Information Commissioner's *Guide* suggests that

> "*as a matter of good practice you should automatically restrict the processing whilst you are considering its accuracy or the legitimate grounds for processing the personal data in question*".

6.10.2.4 The second two cases apply where:

- the processing is unlawful, but where the data subject "*opposes the erasure of the personal data and requests the restriction of their use instead*" (art.18(1)(b)); or
- the controller no longer needs the personal data itself, but the data is required by the data subject for establishment, exercise or defence of legal claims (art.18(1)(c)).

6.10.2.5 It is difficult to imagine how the first of these can come about: why would the data subject prefer restriction to erasure? The last provision is more interesting. Deletion of personal data is, itself, processing; therefore, if processing is restricted, an organisation must ensure that the data is not deleted unless the individual is notified of this.

6.10.3 Exemptions

6.10.3.1 There are no special exemptions to the right of restriction within the GDPR. However, as usual, the provisions relating to requests which are manifestly unreasonable or excessive at art.12(5) (**6.3.6**) and the exemptions in the DPA 2018 (**Ch.10**) may be available.

6.11 PROFILING AND AUTOMATED DECISION-MAKING

6.11.1 Introduction

6.11.1.1 The GDPR contains provisions relating to profiling and automated decision-making.

- Profiling is the automated evaluation of factors relating to an individual.
- Automated individual decision-making is automated processing which produces legal or similarly significant effects for an individual, with no human involvement.

6.11.1.2 Automated individual decision-making is, therefore, more serious for an individual. It will often involve processing, but this isn't inevitable. The EDPB gives the example of speeding fines generated automatically from speed cameras, as a case of automated individual decision-making which does not involve profiling (WP 251, p.8). As the Commissioner's *Guide* notes:

"*Automated individual decision making and profiling can lead to quicker and more consistent decisions. But if they are used irresponsibly there are significant risks for individuals*".

6.11.1.3 Article 70(1)(f) of the GDPR provides specially that the EDPB can issue guidelines, recommendations and best practices for permitted uses of automated individual decision-making and rec.70 notes that the guidance can also be issued in relation to profiling. The EDPB has already done this, amending and adopting *Guidance on automated individual decision-making and profiling* on 6 February 2018 (WP 251, rev.01).

6.11.2 Profiling

Meaning of profiling

6.11.2.1 Profiling is defined at art.4(4) as:

"*... any form of automated processing of personal data consisting of the use of* *personal data to evaluate certain personal aspects relating to a natural person, in particular to analyse or predict aspects concerning that natural person's performance at work, economic situation, health, personal preferences, interests, reliability, behaviour, location or movements*".

6.11.2.2 The EDPB notes that "*the use of the word 'evaluating' suggests that profiling involves some form of assessment or judgement about a person*" (WP 251, p.7). However, the profiling has to relate to a particular person: as the EDPB notes:

"*. . . a business may wish to classify its customers according to their age or gender for statistical purposes and to acquire an aggregated overview of its clients without making any predictions or drawing any conclusion about an individual. In this case, the purpose is not assessing individual characteristics and is therefore not profiling*".

6.11.2.3 Profiling is a form of processing of personal data and so, as the EDPB notes, all the requirements of the GDPR apply to it. However, we think the points highlighted below are worth particular note.

Transparency

6.11.2.4 We have explained at **6.4.5.1**, when a controller provides a privacy notice to an individual, the controller must include additional information where the controller intends to make use of automated individual decision-making. Articles 13 and 14 refer specifically to this obligation applying to use of automated individual decision-making. However, rec.60, seems to refer to a more general obligation, stating that "*the data subject should be informed of the existence of profiling and the consequences of such profiling*". The EDPB guidance is inconsistent as to whether information should *always* be provided about profiling, as opposed to being provided only when this is linked to automated individual decision-making. Page 17 of WP 251 states that this information should always be given, whereas, at p.25, the EDPB suggests that this is a matter of good practice. If a controller justifies its profiling on the basis of legitimate interests or performance of a task in the public interest, or uses profiling for purposes of direct marketing, then the controller probably should provide specific information about its use of profiling. This is because there is a right to object to processing in both of these scenarios—and art.21(4) requires the controller to draw this right to the individual's attention—which would necessarily include explaining that the controller carries out some form of profiling.

Right to object

6.11.2 As mentioned at **6.8.2**, art.21(1) grants individuals a right to object to profiling where the legal basis for the processing is art.6(1)(e) or (f) (performance of a task in the public interest or in the exercise of official authority, or relying legitimate interests). In addition, art.21(2) grants individuals a right to object to "*profiling to the extent that it is related to . . . direct marketing*".

Accountability

6.11.2.6 The general principle of accountability at art.24(1) applies to profiling as to all other types of processing and will require the controller to "*ensure and be able to demonstrate that processing is performed in accordance with the Regulation*". The GDPR's requirements for data protection impact assessments (arts 35–36) and data protection officers (arts 37–39) can be seen as prescriptive methods of achieving accountability. Use of profiling may make it more likely that these are necessary, as explained below.

6.11.2.7 Article 35(1) requires that data protection impact assessments are carried out where processing is likely to result in a "*high risk*" to individuals, taking into account "*new technologies, and . . . the nature, scope, context and purposes of processing*". Profiling is called out in the GDPR precisely because it may pose a risk to individuals, so—depending on the particular facts—it may well satisfy this test. It is also specifically called out in the examples of processing which will require a data protection impact assessment, at art.35(3)(a):

> "*systematic and extensive evaluation of personal aspects relating to natural persons which is based on automated processing, including profiling, and on which decisions are based that produce legal effects concerning the natural person or similarly significantly affect the natural person*".

6.11.2.8 The reference to legal effects or similarly significant effects replicates the description of automated individual decision-making. However, there is no requirement here for the decision to be *entirely* automated. Systematic and extensive profiling, which may significantly affect people, must, therefore, go through a data protection impact assessment even if there is human involvement in the ultimate decision.

6.11.2.9 If a controller or processor uses profiling for one of its core activities and on a large scale, then, it will need a DPO: one of the thresholds for appointing a DPO is where the

> "*core activities of the controller or the processor consist of* processing *operations which, by virtue of their nature, their scope and/or their purposes require regular and systematic monitoring of data subjects on a large scale*" (art.37(1)).

6.11.3 Automated individual decision-making

The prohibition on automated individual decision-making

6.11.3.1 Article 22(1) provides that:

> "*The data subject shall have the right not to be subject to a decision based solely on automated processing, including profiling, which produces*

> *legal effects concerning him or her or similarly significantly affects him or her*".

The decision must be based "solely" on automated processing. However, WP 251 (p.21) notes that

> "*the controller cannot avoid the Article 22 provisions by fabricating human involvement. ... To qualify as human involvement, the controller must ensure that any oversight is meaningful, rather than just a token gesture ...*".

6.11.3.2 Recital 71 uses the examples of online decisions to refuse credit, or e-recruiting practices. As examples of decisions in scope of art.22, WP 251, notes that (p.21)

> "*a legal effect requires that the decision ... affect someone's legal rights, such as the freedom to associate with others, vote in an election, or take legal action. A legal effect may also be something that affects a person's legal status or their rights under a contract*".

Examples given include cancelling a contract, a decision relating to a social benefit such as child or housing benefit or refusing admittance to a country. WP 251 notes that similar significant effects would mean that the effects must be "*sufficiently great or important to be worthy of attention*".

The EDPB suggests that this means the decision must have the potential to significantly affect the circumstances, behaviour or choices of those affected, to have a prolonged or permanent impact or to lead to exclusion or discrimination. Examples are given of decisions which could fall into that category, if they affect:

- financial circumstances—e.g. eligibility for credit;
- access to health services;
- an employment opportunity; or
- access to education.

6.11.3.3 Many organisations will make use of targeted advertisements online, whereby ads are only shown to individuals who meet certain criteria (such as having viewed the particular product before or having visited sites which suggest an interest in products of that type): would this amount to a similarly significant effect? Here the EDPB suggests not (p.22), although such processing would be profiling and would have to meet all other requirements of the GDPR and the e-Privacy Directive. WP 251 suggests that factors which would push such online profiling into the scope of art.22 would be:

- level of intrusiveness (including tracking across different sites, devices and services);

- the expectations and wishes of the individual;
- how the ad is delivered; and
- any use of knowledge of vulnerabilities of the individuals being targeted.

6.11.3.4 WP 251 suggest that differential pricing (whereby different visitors to the same site are shown different prices or offers for similar services, based on their perceived price sensitivity) may fall within art.22 if it results in prohibitively high prices effectively barring someone from certain goods or services (p.22).

6.11.3.5 Article 22 is drafted as a "right" for the individual. Other rights created by the GDPR—of access, correction, portability, etc—have to be exercised by the individual and the controller does not have to comply with them unless and until the individual contacts him to exercise his right. However, notwithstanding the choice of the word "right" in art.22, the provision is better seen as a prohibition on use of significant automated decisions. This is implicit in rec.71, which notes that such types of processing "should be allowed" in certain limited cases (**6.11.3.8**); the inference being that the processing is not allowed at all in other cases. This is also the approach taken by the EDPB, which notes that:

> "*Art.22(1) establishes a general prohibition for decision-making based solely on automated decision making based solely on automated processing. This prohibition applies whether or not the data subject takes an action regarding the processing of their personal data*" (p.19).

Permitted uses of automated decision-making

6.11.3.6 It can take as little as a couple of minutes to obtain certain types of insurance online: this is only possible because of automated individual decision-making assessing the consumers risk and premium. It follows that there must be exceptions, when such processing is permitted. These are set out at art.22(2), which provides that the prohibition at art.22(1) does not apply if the decision:

> "*a)* *is necessary for entering into, or performance of, a contract between the data subject and a data controller;*
> *b)* *is authorised by Union or Member State law to which the controller is subject and which also lays down suitable measures to safeguard the data subject's rights and freedoms and legitimate interests; or*
> *c)* *is based on the data subject's explicit consent*".

Explicit consent is straight forward. The other conditions benefit from some additional comment.

6.11.3.7 The fact that a controller could, in theory, reach a decision without an entirely automated decision (but in a much slower way, after vast expenditure of resource) does *not* rule out reliance on art.22(1)(a). WP 251 (p.23) notes that:

> "*routine human involvement can sometimes be impractical or impossible due to the sheer quantity of data being processed . . . The controller must be able to show that this type of processing is necessary, taking into account whether a less privacy-intrusive method could be adopted*".

The EDPB then gives the example of an organisation advertising a role, which receives tens of thousands of applications—and which, as a result, would have to use automated means to sift out irrelevant applications.

6.11.3.8 Recital 71 gives examples of processing for fraud and tax-evasion monitoring and prevention purposes, conducted in accordance with standards or regulations of Union institutions or oversight bodies, and of processing to ensure the security and reliability of a service offered by a controller. Many controllers will want to undertake monitoring for fraud and security purposes and to block apparently fraudulent or suspicious transactions. Examples of law which could justify such processing would be the *FCA Handbook* (i.e. its requirements for regulated entities to establish appropriate systems and controls); Chapters 4 and 5 of the Payment Services Directive (2015/2366), requiring processing by payment service providers for prevention and detection of fraud and to manage operational and security risks and the Directive on security of network and information systems, in relation to operators of essential services and digital service providers (EU 2016/1148).

6.11.3.9 There is also helpful comment on art.22(2)(b) at para.115 of the Explanatory Notes. These comment that:

> "*the GDPR does not require the law to expressly provide that a decision can be made based solely on automated processing . . . It is enough that automated processing is a reasonable way of complying with a requirement, such as a regulatory obligation or licence condition. Such obligation may be provided in general terms, such as a requirement to maintain fraud and financial crime detection systems*".

6.11.3.10 Section 14 of the DPA 2018 sets out safeguards which apply when controllers rely on art.22(2)(b). These are that the controller must, as soon as reasonably practicable, notify the data subject in writing that a decision has been taken solely based on automated processing. The individual then has one month from the date they receive the notice, to ask the controller to reconsider the decision or to take a new decision which is not based on automated processing. The controller, in turn, has a period of one month to comply and to inform the individual of the steps it has taken to comply and the outcome of doing this. The general provisions in art.12 relating to transparency etc., are stated to apply to this provision. There is also scope for secondary legislation to be adopted, by affirmative resolution, to introduce additional safeguards.

Special category data and children

6.11.3.11 Article 22(4) provides that permitted decisions shall not be based on special categories of data unless the individual has given explicit consent, or the processing is necessary for reasons of substantial public interest, on the basis of Union or Member State law, in accordance with art.9(2)(g). Suitable safeguards to protect individuals' interests are required. The requirement for explicit consent adds nothing to the basic requirement for any automated individual decision-making justified on this basis. The main impact of this article, therefore, is that controllers justifying use of automated individual decision-making based on legal requirements must ensure that the processing is in the substantial public interest.

6.11.3.12 Recital 71 provides that automated individual decision-making "*should not concern a child*". Whilst it is right that controllers take special care when processing personal data about children, banning any automated individual decision-making could be counter-productive. In this instance, the EDPB is happy to take account of the fact that this is a recital, and to conclude that this means that this is not an absolute prohibition. Instead it should be seen as indicative of a high bar which must be met before such decision-making can be implemented (WP 251, p.28).

Safeguards

6.11.3.13 Where controllers use automated individual decision-making because this is authorised by law, the law must ensure sufficient safeguards for the individual. Article 22(3) introduces a requirement for safeguards where the processing is based on explicit consent or contractual necessity. Article 22(3) provides that these must include "*at least the right to obtain human intervention on the part of the controller, to express his or her point of view and to contest the decision*".

6.11.3.14 There are further provisions at rec.71, second indent, although these read as provisions which should be adopted for all automated individual decision-making. These are:

- to use appropriate mathematical or statistical procedures for any modelling;
- to implement appropriate technical and organisational measures to minimise risk of error and factors leading to inaccuracy;
- to secure the personal data; and
- to prevent discriminatory effects on grounds of one of racial or ethnic origin, political opinion, religion or beliefs, trade union membership, genetic or health status, or sexual orientation.

6.11.3.15 The Annex to WP 251 also suggests the measures below, in addition to safeguards already listed above:

- regular quality assurance checks to ensure fair treatment and non-discrimination;
- algorithmic auditing (i.e. checking that algorithms are performing as intended);
- third party audit (where the processing could have a high impact on individuals);
- contractual assurances of audit and testing for use of any third-party algorithms;
- data minimisation measures; and
- use of anonymisation or pseudonymisation techniques where possible.

Transparency

6.11.3.16 Individuals will only be able to exercise rights to put their own point of view, to contest decisions, and to ask for human review if they know that decisions have been taken using automated individual decision-making. Accordingly, a key safeguard is letting individuals know that such a technique has been used. This is a key feature in privacy notices (arts 13(2)(f) and 14(2)(g)) and the same information must also be given if an individual makes a subject access request (art.15(1)(h)).

6.11.3.17 The GDPR provides that the individual must be told about

> "*the existence of automated decision-making, including profiling, referred to in Article 22(1) and (4)* [i.e. significant solely automated decisions] *and, at least in those cases, meaningful information about the logic involved, as well as the significance and the envisaged consequences of such processing for the data subject*".

6.11.3.18 The general requirements for transparency at art.12 apply, requiring the information to be clear and readily understandable. WP 251 (p.31) suggests that:

> "*Instead of providing a complex mathematical explanation about how algorithms or machine-learning work, the controller should consider using clear and comprehensive ways to deliver the information to the data subject, for example:*
>
> - *the categories of data that have been or will be used in the profiling or decision-making process;*
> - *why these categories are considered pertinent;*
> - *how any profile used in the automated decision-making process is built, including any statistics used in the analysis;*

- *why this profile is relevant to the automated decision-taking process; and*
- *how it is used for a decision concerning the data subject*".

Some of these requirements sound quite onerous—but there is a good example on p.26 of WP 251 to show how this could be done:

> "*An insurance company uses an automated decision-making process to set motor insurance premiums based on monitoring customers' driving behaviour. To illustrate the significance and envisaged consequences of the processing it explains that dangerous driving may result in higher insurance payments and provides an app comparing fictional drivers, including one with dangerous driving such as fast acceleration and last-minute braking.*
> *It uses graphics to give types on how to improve these habits and consequently how to lower insurance premiums*".

Exceptions

6.11.3.19 The usual exceptions for manifestly unfounded or excessive requests, set out at art.12(5) of the GDPR apply here. The GDPR does allow other derogations to be introduced—however, none of the exceptions in Schs 2–4 apply to the rules on automated individual decision-making.

Key points for the data protection professional

6.11.3.20 Any use of profiling or automated individual decision-making by the controller needs careful review—to ensure that the correct information is provided to individuals; to ensure that appropriate reviews are undertaken; and that appropriate safeguards are put in place if needed.

6.11.3.21 The DPO may find the following short list of key points useful:

- identify occasions where the controller uses:
  - profiling;
  - automated decisions with significant effect (either solely based on automated processing, or partially based on this).
- ensure you have mechanisms to alert you to new processing, or to changes in processing, which start to use such processing, or which could change the significance of, or safeguards used in, existing processing;
- consider if the processing means that a data protection impact assessment is necessary—and use the impact assessment to ensure that automated individual decision-making is only carried out if it meets the requirements and has the safeguards described above;
- for organisations without a data protection officer, consider if it means a data protection officer should be appointed;

- check there are periodic processes to monitor accuracy and non-discrimination.
- ensure your privacy notices tell people:
    - about their rights to object to profiling for direct marketing or based on legitimate interests;
    - if you make significant decisions using automated individual decision-making (in a way which lets them understand the key factors considered and how they can challenge this);
- if you use automated individual decision-making, ensure you allow people to challenge any decisions made. This may impact on the timing for other business processes—for example, if a controller uses this automated short-listing technology it should not finish the process of appointments before the time allowed in its safeguards for appeals has expired.

CHAPTER 7

Direct Marketing

7.1 INTRODUCTION

7.1.1 All, or almost all, organisations will process personal data for direct marketing purposes. This processing must comply not just with the GDPR (which contains specific provisions relating to direct marketing), but also with significant additional legislation, the Privacy and Electronic Communications (EC) Directive Regulations 2003 (SI2003 No.2426) (as subsequently amended and often referred to as the PECR). This additional legislation is the focus of this section. We also cover the various guidance notes on direct marketing issued by the Information Commissioner, in particular:

- *Direct Marketing* (version 2.3);
- *Guide to Privacy and Electronic Communications Regulations* (available at *http://www.ico.org.uk/for-organisations/guide-to-pecr* [Accessed 7 May 2019]);
- *Companies receiving unwanted marketing* (version 1) (available at *http://www.ico.org.uk/media/1537/companies-receiving-unwanted-marketing.pdf [Accessed 7 May 2019]*); and
- *Guidance on political campaigning* (version 3.1).

7.1.2 Readers should note that the provisions on direct marketing must be kept under review. First, the DPA 2018, at s.122, mandates the Information Commissioner to prepare a code of practice on direct marketing. This is to give "practical guidance" on meeting the requirements of the legislation, as well as to give such other guidance as the Commissioner thinks appropriate to promote good practice. Once approved by Parliament (see **1.3.8.10**), the code will be admissible in proceedings and courts and tribunals; the Information Commissioner herself will also have to have regard to its provisions. On 12 November 2018, the Information Commissioner launched a call for views; the first stage in consulting on this new code.

Second, the European Commission has proposed that the Directive which the PECR implement (Directive 2002/58/EC) (as amended) should be replaced. More information about this proposal is included at **7.7**, at the end of this section.

7.2 MEANING OF DIRECT MARKETING

7.2.1 The DPA 2018 defines "direct marketing" at s.122(5) as:

> "*the communication (by whatever means) of advertising, or marketing material which is directed to particular individuals*".

As the *Direct Marketing* guide notes at para.37:

> "*The key element of the definition is that the material must be directed to particular individuals. Indiscriminate blanked marketing – for example, leaflets delivered to every house in an area, magazine inserts, or adverts shown to every person who views a website – will not therefore fall within this definition of direct marketing*".

The definition is still very wide. In particular, there is no requirement that it contains an offer for sale and the Commissioner takes the view that it "*includes promoting an organisation's aims and ideals*". This would include political campaigning (confirmed by the Information Tribunal in ***Scottish National Party v Information Commissioner (EA/2005/0021)***) as well as fund-raising by charities (*Direct Marketing* guide, para.46).

7.2.2 The *Guide to PECR* accepts that

> "*routine customer service messages do not count as direct marketing – in other words, correspondence with customers to provide information they need about a current contract or past purchase (e.g. information about service interruptions, delivery arrangements, product safety, changes to terms and conditions, or tariffs)*".

Merely including general branding or logos in such messages will not make them count as marketing. However, if they include promotional material aimed at getting customers to buy extra products or services or to renew contracts which are coming to an end, then that will amount to marketing.

7.2.3 The *Direct Marketing* guide also accepts (para.38) that market research is not the same as direct marketing. However, any attempt to disguise marketing as a survey or market research would still be caught by the rules. This would include research which also promotes products or services, or which results in respondents' details being provided for future sales or marketing use.

7.3 GDPR PROVISIONS RELATING TO DIRECT MARKETING

7.3.1 Right to object to direct marketing

7.3.1.1 Article 21(2) grants individuals a right:

"*to object at any time to processing of personal data concerning him or her for such marketing, which includes profiling to the extent that it is related to such direct marketing*".

Article 21(3) then provides that where individual objects, "*the personal data shall no longer be processed for such purposes*".

7.3.1.2 Organisations often address requests from individuals not to receive marketing by having a suppression, or do-not-market list, and by ensuring that any postal, email or telephone marketing campaigns are run against this list, so that individuals who have objected do not receive marketing material. However, the rights granted under the GDPR are wider than this—as an individual can object not just to receiving the direct marketing, but to *any* processing for direct marketing purposes. Recital 70 explains that this means both "*initial or further processing, at any time*". Article 21(2) also highlights that the right allows an individual to object to profiling related to direct marketing. Profiling means "*any form of automated processing of personal data . . . to evaluate certain personal aspects relating to an individual*" (see also **7.5.6.7** below). Controllers often analyse the information they know or can infer about their customers, in order to decide which groups of customers should receive direct marketing offers. The right to object to profiling for purposes related to direct marketing means that controllers must ensure that the data of individuals who object to this is not used for this purpose, in addition to ensuring that the individuals do not receive direct marketing themselves.

7.3.1.3 In a UK context, the breadth of the predecessor provision in the 1998 Act was highlighted in the ***Robertson*** case (***Robertson v City of Wakefield and Home Office*** [2001] EWHC Admin 916). Mr Robertson objected to the fact that, if he registered on the electoral roll, his details would be available to third parties who would use it for marketing purposes. (The case predated—and indeed caused the introduction of—the edited versus full electoral roll). The electoral registration officer did not himself use the data for direct marketing purposes, but it was clear that third parties obtaining the lists did use them for this purpose. The judge confirmed that s.11 of the 1998 Act covered an organisation's own direct marketing and situations where the organisation "*anticipates*" use for direct marketing, including by others.

7.3.1.4 Individuals who object to direct marketing sometimes ask an organisation to delete their data, instead of (or as well as) objecting to direct marketing. If an organisation implements an erasure request, then it may also delete the record of the fact that the individual does not want to receive direct marketing: if the organisation buys-in a marketing list in future, then the organisation will not be able to honour the individual's request. As explained at **6.9.4** (individual rights) the right to erasure is not absolute. In this example, an organisation would likely be justified in retaining the minimal information needed for suppression purposes. This would be necessary to allow the organisation to meet the individual's objection to receiving direct marketing and art.11(3)(b) allows information to be retained, notwithstanding an erasure request, where this is necessary for compliance with a legal obligation, under EU or Member State law, where the law requires processing of personal data. This is also the approach which the Information Commissioner recommends. At p.55 of the *Direct Marketing* guide the Commissioner says:

> "*Note that individuals may ask an organisation to remove or delete their details from a database or marketing list. However, in most cases organisations should instead follow the marketing industry practice of suppressing their details.*
> *Rather than deleting an individual's details entirely, suppression involves retaining just enough information to ensure that their preferences are respected in the future. Suppression allows organisations to ensure that they do not send marketing to people who have previously asked them not to, as there is a record against which to screen any new marketing lists. If people's details are deleted entirely, there is no way of ensuring that they are not put back on the database. Deleting details might also breach industry-specific legal requirements about how long to hold personal data*".

Timing for dealing with objections

7.3.1.5 Objections to direct marketing should be dealt with as soon as possible and, in any event, within one month from receipt of request. This follows from provisions in the GDPR, the Information Commissioner's *Direct Marketing* guide and the *Code of Practice for the Use of Personal Data* adopted by the Federation of European Direct and Interactive Marketing (FEDMA) (available at *http://www.fedma.org/work-areas/self-regulation [Accessed 7 May 2019]).*

7.3.1.6 Article 21(3) of the GDPR provides that where an individual objects to processing for direct marketing purposes, the personal data "*shall no longer be processed for such purposes*", without stipulating a time period. Article 12(3) sets out general rules for dealing with individual rights—where the controller must provide information on the action taken "*without undue delay and in any event within one month of receipt of the request*". One month may be reasonable for implementing an opt-out request relating to postal mailings, where there are longer lead times for printing and posting. However, in the context of email or text marketing, or online advertising, it is hard to see why an organisation would need this amount of time—and individuals are likely to be frustrated if they receive repeat direct marketing within this period. Organisations should, therefore, note that the obligation is to revert not just within one month but "*without undue delay*".

7.3.1.7 The FEDMA direct marketing codes reflect this distinction, with para.5.1.2 of the main code allowing four weeks to implement an opt-out request, whereas the electronic communications annex, at para.2.7, refers to requests being implemented "promptly" and "within a reasonable period of time". This is also the approach taken in the Information Commissioner's *Direct Marketing* guide which requires opt-out requests to be dealt with "*as soon as possible*" (p.38).

7.3.2 Providing information to individuals

7.3.2.1 Individuals must be told about these rights—and the information must be explicitly brought to their attention and be presented "*clearly and separately from any other information*" at the latest at the time of first communication with the individual (art.21(4)). This suggests a clear, discrete, opt-out, separate from any other terms and conditions, ideally as part of a registration page or similar.

7.3.2.2 Privacy notices provided under arts 13 and 14 (**6.4**), must also include information about the purposes for which the controller processes personal data (which will include direct marketing) and about the rights to object to processing (where it is justified on the basis of legitimate interests), or to withdraw consent (if this is the legal basis for processing). The *Direct Marketing* guide emphasises the importance of fairness in drafting privacy notices (p.7), noting that organisations must not do anything with personal data which individuals would not reasonably expect (or that would cause the individual unjustified harm)—and that organisations must tell people, in particular, if they will share their data with others, where the guide suggests that consent will usually be required.

7.3.3 Lawful basis for processing

Legitimate interests

7.3.3.1 As explained at **6**, controllers may only process personal data where there is a lawful basis for the processing. One such lawful basis, at art.6(1)(f) is where the processing is necessary for the legitimate interests of the controller or a third party and does not cause unwarranted prejudice to the interests of individuals—in particular where the data subject is a child (see also **14.1**). Recital 47 notes that:

> "*The processing of personal data for direct marketing purposes may be regarded as carried out for a legitimate interest*".

This is clearly helpful in recognising that direct marketing is accepted as a legitimate interest. Controllers who wish to justify their processing on this basis should then go on and consider whether this interest would be overridden by the rights and freedoms of individuals, ideally documenting this in a legitimate interest assessment (**4.4.5.22**). For organisations who wish to undertake direct marketing by email, using cookies or similar technology, using automated calls, or faxes, then the situation is more complex, due to the additional provisions of the PECR, which require consent for such marketing (see **7.4.2** below).

Consent

7.3.3.2 Where organisations do rely on consent for direct marketing, then the requirements in the GDPR relating to consent apply. These are summarised at **4.2.3**. Key points are that consent has to be freely given, specific, informed and active (art.4(11)). Pre-ticked boxes are specifically mentioned as being invalid (rec.32). The controller must also be able to "demonstrate" consent (art.7(1)). If consent is included in a document which contains other provisions, then the request for consent must be clearly distinguishable from those provisions and in clear and plain language (art.7(2)). In considering if consent is freely given, utmost account is to be taken of any term which makes provision of a service or performance of a contract conditional on consent which is not actually necessary to perform the contract (art.7(4)). If the controller will use the data for different processing operations (e.g. for email marketing and for sharing with others), then the individual should be able to give consent to each type of processing separately; if they are all combined into one request for consent it will be presumed not to be freely given (rec.43). Further, for consent to be informed, people must know the identity of the controller (rec.42) who is relying on the consent. In a marketing context, therefore, this means:

- separate consent to direct marketing (not hidden in small print);
- ideally set out in the registration process;
- opt-in boxes to be used (not pre-ticked);
- separate boxes for different processing activities (e.g. own marketing versus sharing data with others and for different media for marketing);
- be clear to whom consent is given;
- do not make consent to marketing a condition of providing the goods or services;
- make clear that the individual can change his or her mind at any time (arts 13(2)(c) and 14(2)(d)).

7.3.3.3 Suitable wording could be as follows:

> *Localgrocery.co.uk* would like to keep in touch with news and offers. Tick
>
> [ ] if youd like to hear from us by email
>
> [ ] if you'd like to hear from us by text
>
> [ ] if you'd like us to share your information with local companies who will send you grocery offers by post.
>
> You can change your mind at any time. For more information about how *Localgrocery.co.uk* uses your informaiton, see our privacy policy.

7.3.3.4 In 2015, the Information Commissioner took action against the Universities and Colleges Admissions Service (UCAS), for failure to obtain "freely given" consent (summarised in *Direct Marketing* guide, pp.20 and 21). The UCAS form asked applicants to untick three boxes, if they did not want to receive marketing from commercial companies by email, post and text. However, the wording meant that if an applicant unticked these boxes, they would also not receive information about career opportunities, education providers or health information. The Commissioner concluded that this meant that applicants would feel obliged to allow UCAS to use their information for commercial purposes, because of the risk that they would otherwise miss out on important information. This meant that the consent would not be fairly given. In the light of the GDPR's prohibition on pre-ticked boxes, this would now also be problematic.

7.3.3.5 Where organisations obtain consent in order to meet the requirements of the PECR then readers should note that there is some debate as to whether the GDPR consent requirements should be read across into those Regulations. This uncertainty arises because of art.95 of the GDPR, which provides that:

> "*This Regulation shall not impose additional obligations on natural or legal persons in relation to processing in connection with the provision of publicly available electronic communications services in public communications networks in the Union in relation to matters for which they are subject to specific obligations with the same objective set out in Directive 2002/58/EC*".

7.3.3.6 The intent of this provision is to make clear that where the ePrivacy Directive contains specific rules on a topic, as a piece of sector specific legislation, those rules should apply; there should not be double legislation in the same area. A good example of where this saving provision is needed is in relation to reporting of personal data breaches by public communications service providers, which follow the special rules in the ePrivacy Directive, not the general rules in the GDPR (see **8.4.5**). However, in the case of the rules on consent for direct marketing, the ePrivacy Directive specifically states that the definitions in Directive 95/46/EC are to apply—and art.94 of the GDPR provides that all references to that Directive are to be interpreted as replaced by the Regulation. So the ePrivacy Directive does not contain specific obligations on consent, rather it defers to the rules in the main legislation. This is the approach of the Information Commissioner in the *Guide to PECR*, which specifically states that "*existing PECR rules continue to apply, but using the new GDPR standard of consent*". For UK organisations, this has been put beyond doubt by the Data Protection, Privacy and Electronic Communications (Amendments etc) (EU Exit) Regulations 2019, regulation 8 of which amends the PEC Regulations to state that consent "*corresponds to the data subject's consent in the GDPR . . .*".

7.3.4 Other provisions in the GDPR

Organisations must, of course, comply with all other provisions in the GDPR. However, as these apply to all processing of personal data in general and are not specific to direct marketing, we have not listed them again here.

7.4 PRIVACY AND ELECTRONIC COMMUNICATIONS (EC DIRECTIVE) REGULATIONS (PECR)

7.4.1 Scope of the PECR

7.4.1.1 As the *Guide to PECR* explains clearly:

> "*The Privacy and Electronic Communications Regulations (PECR) sit alongside the Data Protection Act and the GDPR. They give people specific privacy rights in relation to electronic communications.*
> *There are specific rules on:*
> - *marketing calls, emails, texts and faxes;*
> - *cookies (and similar technologies);*
> - *keeping communications services secure; and*
> - *customer privacy as regards traffic and location data, Itemised billing, line identification, and directory listings*".

7.4.1.2 Certain provisions of the PECR only apply to the providers of electronic communications services or the electronic communications networks by means of which these services are provided. For example, there are security obligations on service providers and obligations to ensure the confidentiality of communications. There are also provisions relating to itemised billing, the use of calling and connected line identification (i.e. the facility to see the phone number of the person calling you on your telephone before you decide whether or not to take the call), on automatic call forwarding and in relation to directories of subscribers. The PECR also regulate the use of traffic data and location data. Traffic data is the information that allows an electronic communications network to transmit a communication and bill for it. This would include information about call route, duration and time. Location data is information processed in an electronic communications network that, as the name suggests, tells the service provider where the user is located. The PECR set out when service providers may use traffic and location data. As these provisions are only of relevance to some organisations, a detailed consideration of them is outside the scope of this work. However, the provisions dealing with breach of personal data security are discussed at **8.4.5**. The provisions dealing with direct marketing and cookies are widely relevant and are considered below.

7.4.1.3 Before turning to the detail of the PECR, it is worth looking at key definitions which are used throughout the Regulations. These are:

"subscriber" who is "*the person who is party to a contract with a provider of public electronic communications services for the supply of such services*";

a "corporate subscriber" (any form of body corporate or entity which has a legal personality distinct from those of its members—which would include a limited company, a Scots law partnership, or an LLP);

an "individual" (that is a living individual, or an unincorporated body of individuals—such as a club);

a "user" who is "*any individual using a public electronic communications service*"; and

a "public electronic communications service" which is "*a service consisting in, or having as its principal feature, the conveyance by means of an electronic communications network of signals, except in so far as it is a content service* [services which provide or edit content]" and which is "*provided so as to be available for use by members of the public*".

So, provision of fixed line or mobile telephone, email, or provision of internet access to the public, would all be public electronic communications services. The person who has the contract for the supply of such services will be the subscriber (either a corporate subscriber or an individual subscriber) and the individual making use of the services will be the user.

7.4.1.4 The Regulations set out different rules for direct marketing, depending on the medium used and whether the marketing is being sent to an individual, or corporate, subscriber, or (in the case of cookies and similar technology), whether it affects a user as well as a subscriber. These rules are considered below. It is important to remember that these rules apply *in addition* to the general right to object set out above.

7.4.1.5 Appendix 5 contains a table which summarises the rules which apply to different direct marketing media. The Information Commissioner has also produced a useful direct marketing checklist which can be used for all direct marketing other than online marketing. This is available at *https://ico.org.uk/media/1551/direct-marketing-checklist.pdf*.

7.4.2 Email marketing

7.4.2.1 Regulation 22 applies to use of email for direct marketing sent to individual subscribers. It provides that:

> "*a person shall neither transmit, nor instigate the transmission of, unsolicited communications for the purposes of direct marketing by means of electronic mail unless the recipient of the electronic mail has previously notified the sender that he consents for the time being to such communications being sent by, or at the instigation of, the sender*".

7.4.2.2 The Regulation, therefore, introduces a consent requirement for email marketing. The rule also applies to SMS and some other forms of messages, because "*electronic mail*" is defined as:

"*any text, voice, sound or image message sent over a public electronic communications network which can be stored in the network or in the recipient's terminal equipment until it is collected by the recipient and includes messages sent using a short message service*" (i.e. SMS).

The Information Commissioner considers that the requirements for consent here are even stricter than the general rules on consent. In the *Direct Marketing* guide, the Commissioner comments, at p.23, that:

- the requirement that the recipient has "*notified the sender*" and that the consent is for messages "*being sent by the sender*" means that consent must be notified to the organisation actually sending the direct marketing, making it difficult to rely on consent given to a third party unless the recipient "*intended for their consent to be passed on to the organisation doing the marketing*". The *Guide to PECR* states "*You must make checks to ensure that the consent is valid and specifically identifies you. Generic consent covering any third party is not enough*";
- the reference to consent "*for the time being*" suggests that it must be clear from the context that this is ongoing consent, not consent for a one-off marketing message; and
- the requirement that the recipient consents "*to such communications*" means that the consent must be specific to the type of communication—so consent to receive phone calls will not cover emails or texts.

7.4.2.3 This requirement that the consent specifically and clearly covers the legal entity which will be relying on the consent to send direct marketing will also affect corporate groups, where one entity may initially interact with the customer and obtain consent, but where other entities in the group wish to send direct marketing. Here the *Direct Marketing* guide (para.87) notes that

"*organisations cannot infer consent just because consent was given to a similar organisation, or an organisation in the same group. It must have extended to the organisation actually sending the message as well*".

The *Direct Marketing* guide also makes clear (p.27) that contacting individuals by email or text to ask for their consent to future marketing messages is itself a message, sent by electronic mail, for purposes of direct marketing—so is itself prohibited by the PECR.

7.4.2.4 The requirements under the PECR are in addition to the requirements under the GDPR. This matters when an organisation sends direct marketing by email to individuals working for companies (so *individual@companyname.com*). The PECR rules relating to consent to send direct marketing by email to individual subscribers will not apply. However, the individuals would still have rights to object to processing under the GDPR (see **7.3.1**).

The soft opt-in

7.4.2.5 Regulation 22(3) allows email marketing to be sent without consent where:

> "*a) that person has obtained the contact details of the recipient of that electronic mail in the course of the sale or negotiation for the sale of a product or service to that recipient;*
>
> *b) the direct marketing is in respect of that person's similar products and services only; and*
>
> *c) the recipient has been given a simple means of refusing (free of charge except for the costs of transmission of the refusal) the use of his contact details for the purposes of such direct marketing, at the time that the details were initially collected, and, where he did not initially refuse the use of the details, at the time of each subsequent communication*".

The provision allows email marketing on an opt-out basis to an organisation's customers, or those with whom it has negotiated. The exemption is narrow: it only applies to *that* person's direct marketing (so it would not cover group companies) and the goods and services must be "*similar*". As the Information Commissioner notes, in the *Direct Marketing* guide (p.18) this may be difficult for not-for-profit organisations—e.g. fund-raising by charities—because there will not have been a sale, or negotiation for a sale, to their supporters.

7.4.2.6 In the *Direct Marketing* guide, the Information Commissioner also emphasises that opting-out must be easy (p.42):

> "*It must be simple to opt-out. When first collecting a customer's details, this should be part of the same process (e.g. online forms should include a prominent opt-out box . . .). In subsequent messages, we consider that the individual should be able to reply direct to the message, or click a clear 'unsubscribe' link. In the case of text messages, organisations could offer an opt-out by sending a stop message to a short code number: e.g. 'text STOP to 12345'. The only cost should be the cost of sending the message.*"

Buying-in lists

7.4.2.7 As explained at **7.4.2.2** above, the requirement in the PECR that the customer must notify the sender of the email marketing of their consent makes it more difficult to use bought-in lists, where someone else has collected the customer's consent. Recital 42 re-enforces this provision, as it requires that "*for consent to be informed, the data subject should be aware at least of the identity of the controller and the purposes of the processing . . .*".

7.4.2.8 The Information Commissioner's guidance is that bought-in lists can still be used, but only where it is clear that the consent obtained is intended to cover the actual party sending the email marketing. The *Direct Marketing* guide, p.31, states:

"*Organisations must therefore make rigorous checks as to how and when consent was obtained, by whom, and what the customer was told. It is not acceptable to rely on assurances of indirect consent without undertaking proper due diligence, in order to demonstrate consent if challenged. Organisations must ensure that consent was validly obtained, that it was reasonably recent, and that it clearly extended to them or organisations very closely fitting their description . . .*".

On the requirement that consent be recent, p.35 of the *Direct Marketing* guide states:

"*As a general rule of thumb, if an organisation is making contact by phone, text or email for the first time, we recommend that it does not to* [sic] *rely on any indirect consent given more than six months ago . . . we accept there may be some very specific cases where the circumstances clearly indicate that the person would expect to start receiving marketing at a certain later date (e.g. consent to receive offers on seasonal products or annually renewable insurance services)*".

7.4.2.9 Pages 52 and 53 have a checklist of due diligence questions to use when buying-in marketing lists:

- "*Who compiled the list? When? Has it been amended or updated since then?*
- *When was consent obtained?*
- *Who obtained it and in what context?*
- *What method was used – e.g. was it opt-in or opt-out?*
- *Was the information provided clear and intelligible? How was it provided – e.g. behind a link, in a footnote, in a pop-up box, in a clear statement next to the opt-in box?*
- *Did it specially mention texts, emails or automated calls?*
- *Did it list organisations by name, by description, or was the consent for disclosure to any third party?*
- *Has the list been screened against the TPS or other relevant preference services? If so, when?*
- *Has the individual expressed any other preferences -e.g. regarding marketing calls or mail?*
- *Has the seller received any complaints?*
- *Is the seller a member of a professional body or accredited in some way?*"

Viral marketing

7.4.2.10 Viral marketing is the term used for direct marketing where a marketer asks its customers to help it 'spread' its message. There are two ways of doing this: 1) asking customers to forward an offer directly to their friends and contacts; or 2) asking customers to send the organisation details of their friends so that the organisation can send them marketing. Both options are problematic so far as email marketing is concerned and the *Guide to PECR* notes that viral marketing cannot be used as a way of getting around the PECR. If an organisation asks customers to send direct marketing then it will be 'instigating' the messages; if it sends the marketing itself, then it will be sending the direct marketing: both arrangements only work if the recipients have given consent to receive direct marketing. This can be an area of tension between the privacy professional and the marketing team, because viral marketing is an effective method of lead generation and is often popular with customers who like to be able to recommend a good deal or an offer to a friend. The *Direct Marketing* guide (para.164) reflects this tension, with the guide making clear it would "*advise against this type of viral marketing*" because of the difficulties of obtaining valid consent, but goes on to say that:

> "*organisations who do this must at the very least clearly explain that the contact should only provide someone else's details with that person's consent, and that the person may be told who provided their details. They should also provide a privacy notice to the new contact as soon as possible unless it would be disproportionate to do so*"

(see **6.4.3.4** for comments on this exemption which, under the GDPR, is very hard to use). The Information Commissioner also notes that offering incentives to the customer to recommend friends may make it more likely that the customer will not act in the other person's best interests. In other words, if the discount or other reward offered to a customer is too good, the customer will likely suggest contact details for people who have not given consent. Even if an organisation follows The Information Commissioner's advice, and asks its customers just to send contact details for friends who have said they would like to receive offers, it is difficult to see how the organisation will be able to meet the requirement, at art.7(1) of the GDPR, that the controller must be able to "demonstrate" that the data subject has given consent.

No disguises

7.4.2.11 Regulation 23 prohibits the sending, or instigating the sending of, direct marketing by email where the identity of the sender has been concealed or disguised; where there is no valid unsubscribe address; or where the email itself would breach the Electronic Commerce (EC Directive) Regulations 2002, or would encourage the recipient to visit a website which does not comply with those Regulations.

7.4.3 Phone marketing

7.4.3.1 The rules on phone marketing are clearly summarised in the *Guide to PECR*, as follows:

> "*The rules on live marketing calls are in regulation 21 and 21A. In short, you must not make unsolicited live calls:*
>
> - *to anyone who has told you they don't want your calls;*
> - *to any number registered with the TPS* [telephone preference service] or CTPS [corporate telephone preference service], *unless the person has specifically consented to your calls – even if they are an existing customer; or*
> - *for the purpose of claims management services, unless the person has specifically consented to your calls.*
>
> *You must always say who is calling, allow your number (or an alternative contact number) to be displayed to the person receiving the call, and provide a contact address or freephone number if asked*".

There is more detail on preference services at **7.4.6** below.

7.4.3.2 The requirement for claims management companies to have consent to make calls was introduced by the Financial Guidance and Claims Act 2018 (s.35(2)). Claims management services are defined broadly at reg.21A(4) and (5) and cover:

- any kind of claim for compensation or other remedy or relief, whether by way of legal proceedings, a statutory or voluntary compensation scheme, or a voluntary undertaking; and
- services offering advice, representation, making inquiries, referrals or introductions, or financial services and assistance, in connection with a claim.

The provision would, for example, cover callers offering to make claims for compensation for personal injury, or refunds of payment protection insurance, or to check if someone is eligible for a refund. Claims management companies must also comply with the Conduct of Authorised Persons Rules 2013.

7.4.3.3 The Privacy and Electronic Communications (Amendment) (No.2) Regulations 2018 (SI 2018/1396) introduce similar restrictions in relation to cold calls about pensions. These Regulations prohibit cold calls about pensions unless:

- the individual has given consent; or
- the individual is an existing client and would reasonably expect to receive calls. Furthermore, the caller must be the trustee or manager of an occupational, or personal, pension scheme, or be FCA authorised.

7.4.4 Automated calls

7.4.4.1 The *Guide to PECR* also has a clear summary of the rules on automated calls, explaining that these:

> "*are in regulation 19, and are stricter. You must not make an automated marketing call – that is, a call made by an automated dialling system that plays a recorded message – unless that person has specifically consented to receive this type of call from you. General consent for marketing, or even consent for live calls, is not enough – it must specifically cover automated calls . . .*
> *All automated calls must include your name and a contact address or free phone number. You must also allow your number (or an alternative contact number) to be displayed to the person receiving the call*".

The automated sending of faxes or emails does not amount to an automated calling system (the separate rules on faxes and emails would apply to this). Neither does the definition cover power dialling—that is automated dialling of target numbers, for connection to a call centre operator, if the subscriber picks up the phone.

7.4.4.2 This provision was included to deal with concern at the possible rise of technology previously found in the US. This technology allows a telephone number to be dialled automatically and a recorded message advertising the product to be played. This has the unfortunate effect that the person called cannot hang up—as it is the person making the call who has to end the call for the line to be cleared. There have been a number of cases in the US where individuals were allegedly unable to make emergency calls, as a result of their lines being engaged because of these automated messages.

7.4.5 Fax marketing

7.4.5.1 The Privacy and Electronic Communications Regulations also contain rules on direct marketing by fax. Although few, if any, organisations still carry out direct marketing in this way, we have included this for the sake of completeness. Regulation 20 provides that organisations need consent to send direct marketing by fax to individual subscribers; corporate subscribers are given a right to object to direct marketing sent by fax. Both corporate and individual subscribers are able to register with the fax preference service to object to receiving direct marketing sent by fax (**7.4.6.6**). An organisation sending fax marketing must also ensure that each communication includes the organisation's name and address or freephone number (reg.24(2)).

7.4.6 Preference services

7.4.6.1 The sections of the PECR relating to phone and fax marketing both refer to preference services (sometimes called do-not-call registers, or Robinson lists). The rules on this are set out at regs 26 and 25 of the PECR.

Telephone preference service (TPS)

7.4.6.2 Regulation 26 provides that the Information Commissioner must maintain a list of numbers where the subscriber has objected to receiving unsolicited direct marketing calls. There are separate lists for individual subscribers (the TPS) and corporate subscribers (the Corporate Telephone Preference Service or CTPS). Regulation 26(5) allows the Commissioner to make arrangements for someone else to discharge this obligation on her behalf and the TPS is run by the Telephone Preference Service Ltd. This is a subsidiary of the Direct Marketing Association (UK) Ltd (DMA), which also operates other preference services. The DMA liaises with marketers to try and resolve complaints about the scheme, however it is not responsible for enforcing the rules in the PECR. Instead, it passes complaints to the Information Commissioner, on a periodic basis, for her Office to review.

7.4.6.3 The arrangements for the TPS and the CTPS are very similar. However, corporate bodies that wish to object to receiving calls must provide notice in writing and the CTPS must send them an annual reminder, within 28 days of the anniversary of their registration, that they have objected to receiving unsolicited direct marketing calls by phone.

7.4.6.4 Regulation 21(1) provides that unsolicited direct marketing calls must not be made to numbers which are on the register. Regulation 21(3) provides that this rule will not be breached where the number was placed on the register within the last 28 days—an organisation which wishes to make direct marketing calls, must ensure that it checks the register at least 28 days prior to the relevant calls being made. Organisations must pay a fee to use the register, and this is to be set at a level so as to ensure the costs of the scheme are met. Organisations wishing to use the service can do so at *https://corporate.tpsonline.org.uk [Accessed 7 May 2019]*.

7.4.6.5 Regulation 21(4) provides that the prohibition on calling a number which has registered with the scheme does not apply where the subscriber has notified the caller that, notwithstanding any registration with the preference service, they do not object to receiving unsolicited direct marketing calls. This provision ensures that businesses are entitled to call potential customers who happen to have registered with the TPS, but where the customer does, actually, want to hear from them. There is a risk that less scrupulous marketers will try to abuse the carve-out —for example, by including provisions in the small-print stating that, by making a purchase the customer is taken to have notified the business that they do want to hear from the organisation by phone. The Information Commissioner addresses this at p.37 of her *Direct Marketing Guidance* noting that:

> "*Opt-in consent is always best. If an organisation wants to rely on another type of action (e.g. signing up for a service) as notification that the customer does not object, the wording must be very clear and prominent so that the customer will reasonably expect that organisation's marketing calls. There should also be a simple means for them to opt out.*

Example
'By signing up to this service, you agree to us contacting you by phone to tell you about our other products and services.
If you do not want to receive calls, please tick here [ ].'"

Other preference services

7.4.6.6 The fax preference service is provided for in reg.25. The provisions are very similar to those for the telephone preference service.

7.4.6.7 The DMA also operates the Mail Preference Service (for those who prefer not to receive direct mail by post) and the Baby MPS, for parents who have suffered a miscarriage or bereavement of a baby in the first few weeks of life and who do not want to receive baby related mailings. Unlike the TPS, CTPS and FPS, there is no specific requirement in legislation to check these preference services. However, it is a requirement for organisations which are members of the Direct Marketing Association, under the DMA's Code. There is also a strong argument that the GDPR also requires this. Organisations sending direct marketing must have a lawful basis for their processing of personal data (see **7.3.3**). This will either be that prospects have given consent, or that the direct marketing is necessary for the organisation's legitimate business interests. In order to rely on this legitimate interest provision, an organisation must consider whether its interests are overridden by the interests of individuals. It seems highly likely that, where individuals have registered with a well-known preference service, that their interests in having their wishes respected would override those of the marketer.

7.5 COOKIES

7.5.1 Introduction

7.5.1.1 The PECR also contain rules on the use of cookies and similar technologies. As the Information Commissioner's *Guide to PECR* explains:

> *"A cookie is a small text file that is downloaded onto 'terminal equipment' (e.g. a computer or smartphone) when the user accesses a website. It allows the website to recognise that user's device and store some information about the user's preferences or past actions".*

Organisations use cookies, amongst other reasons:

- to make online shopping carts work (so that a check-out page of a website knows what good have been selected by the visitor);
- to remember preferences about a user (such as language choices) to personalise services;
- to remember log-in credentials on a secure site;

- to gather analytics about their websites or apps (to see if the site is working properly, or which sections of the site are most attractive to visitors); and
- to undertake personalised marketing by building up a profile of a user's interests and actions and using this to serve adverts which are linked to these interests.

7.5.1.2 There is guidance about the rules on cookies in the Information Commissioner's *Guide to PECR* and in the Information Commissioner's specific *Cookies Guidance* (version 3 May 2012). The Article 29 Working Party has also issued guidance on cookies: in particular *Opinion 04/2012 on Cookie Consent Exceptions* (WP 194), *Working Document 02/2013 providing guidance on obtaining consent for cookies* (WP 208) and *Opinion 09/2014 on the application of Directive 2002/58/EC to device fingerprinting* (WP 224). The *Guidelines on consent under Regulation 2016/679* revised and adopted by WP 29 on 10 April 2018 and affirmed by the EDPB are also relevant. Lastly, as is explained below (**7.5.3**), the rules on cookies are also often relevant when data is collected via mobile apps and there is additional guidance on apps, issued by the Information Commissioner (*Privacy in mobile apps*, December 2013, version 1) and by the Article 29 Working Party (*Opinion 02/2013 on apps on smart devices*, WP 202).

7.5.2 The consent rule

7.5.2.1 Regulation 6 of the PECR provides that:

"*. . . a person shall not store or gain access to information stored, in the terminal equipment of a subscriber or user unless the requirements of paragraph (2) are met.*

(2) The requirements are that the subscriber or user of that terminal equipment—

(a) is provided with clear and comprehensive information about the purposes of the storage of, or access to, that information; and

(b) has given his or her consent.

(3) Where an electronic communications network is used by the same person to store or access information in the terminal equipment of a subscriber or user on more than one occasion, it is sufficient for the purposes of this regulation that the requirements of paragraph (2) are met in respect of the initial use.

(3A) For the purposes of paragraph (2), consent may be signified by a subscriber who amends or sets controls on the internet browser which the subscriber uses or by using another application or programme to signify consent.

(4) Paragraph (1) shall not apply to the technical storage of, or access to, information—

(a) for the sole purpose of carrying out the transmission of a communication over an electronic communications network; or

(b) *where such storage or access is strictly necessary for the provision of an information society service requested by the subscriber or user.*"

7.5.2.2 As explained at **7.5.1.1** above, cookies are text files which are stored on the user's computer or other device (the "terminal equipment" referred to above), so they are caught by this rule requiring provision of information and consent. The rule applies to storage of *any* information—irrespective of whether it contains personal data. As the *Guide to PECR* notes:

"*although cookies that process personal data give rise to greater privacy and security risks than those that process anonymous data, PECR apply to all cookies*".

7.5.3 What types of technology are covered?

7.5.3.1 The rules are broadly written and as the *Guide to PECR* notes:

"*... the same rules apply to any similar technologies – such as Local Stored Objects (sometimes called Flash cookies) – and can also cover other types of technology, including apps on smartphones, smart TVs or other devices*".

By way of example, the Article 29 Working Party Opinion on device fingerprinting (WP 244), referred to above, looks in detail at when attempts to use other information from or about connected devices in order to recognise users again (such as a combination of information about the browser, plug-ins and screen size) will be subject to the cookie rules. It concludes that in many cases they will be covered. In this section, although we refer to cookies for convenience, we do also mean any other similar technology.

7.5.4 Exceptions

7.5.4.1 The cookie-consent rule does not apply to cookies which are used solely to transmit communications over an electronic communications network (for example, technology which is used to allow data to be transferred in the intended order, by numbering data packets) or to cookies which are "strictly necessary" to provide an information society service (i.e. an online service) requested by the subscriber or user. Opinion WP 194 considers these exemptions in detail, noting that the exemption must be strictly applied.

7.5.4.2 Web-teams often distinguish between:

- session cookies (which expire when a browsing session is terminated) and permanent cookies (which persist); and
- first-party cookies (which are read by the publisher of the site) and third-party cookies, which are placed on behalf of and read by a different entity (often an organisation involved in online advertising).

Session cookies and first-party cookies are less intrusive than persistent and third-party cookies. This sometimes leads to an assumption amongst the web-team that the exemptions for strictly necessary cookies in the PECR cover those types of cookies. However, as is apparent from the wording of the rule, this is not the case. As WP 194 explains:

> "*'first party' session cookies are far more likely to be exempted from consent than 'third party' persistent cookies. But while these characteristics may serve as an initial indicator to prioritise compliance actions, they are not sufficient alone to establish if a cookie* [is exempt]" (p.5).

7.5.4.3 According to Opinion WP 194, cookies will only be "strictly necessary" for a service the user has requested where, "*if cookies are disabled, the service will not work*". The fact that a free site is supported by advertising revenue, so that use of cookies for advertising (even just to allow payments to be made to the advertiser, rather than for targeting purposes) is what allows the content to be offered for free, does not make these cookies strictly necessary—"*This requirement for consent naturally extends to . . . cookies used for the purpose of frequency capping, financial logging, ad affiliation, click fraud detection, research and market analysis, product improvement and debugging, as neither of these purposes can be considered to be related to a service or functionality of an information society service <u>explicitly requested by the user</u> . . .*" (p.10).

7.5.4.4 WP 194 contains detailed analysis of cookies which likely will, or will not, be exempt. Cookies it considers will likely be exempt are:

- user-input cookies for the duration of a session (e.g. shopping cart functionality)
- authentication cookies for the duration of a session (e.g. used for online banking)
- user-centric security cookies, used to detect authentication abuses, for a limited persistent period
- multimedia content player session cookies, such as flash player cookies, for the duration of the session
- load balancing session cookies, for the duration of the session
- user interface customisation persistent cookies for the duration of a session (or slightly more)
- third-party social plug-in content sharing cookies, for logged in members of a social network.

7.5.4.5 Most website publishers will use website analytics (such as Google Analytics or Omniture) in order to analyse the performance of their websites.

Here, WP 194 suggests that analytics which are of low intrusiveness should be treated as exempt, even though they do not meet the criteria in the PECR:

> "... *the Working Party considers that first party analytics cookies are not likely to create a privacy risk when they are used by websites that already provide clear information about these cookies in their privacy policy as well as adequate privacy safeguards. Such safeguards are expected to include a user friendly mechanism to opt-out from any data collection and comprehensive anonymization mechanisms that are applied to other collected identifiable information such as IP addresses*".

However,

> "*first party analytics should be clearly distinguished from third party analytics, which use a common third-party cookie to collect navigation information related to users across distinct websites, and which pose a substantially greater risk to privacy*" (all p.10).

So, websites using basic, first party, analytics cookies may not need consent—but they will still need to tell visitors that such cookies are used and to offer an opt-out method. It is also worth noting that the Information Commissioner's *Guidance on Cookies* does not comment on this distinction, suggesting that consent should be obtained for all analytics (p.9).

7.5.5 Obtaining consent

7.5.5.1 Regulation 6 provides that cookies may not be placed until the subscriber or user is given "*clear and comprehensive information*" about the purposes of the cookies and until consent is given.

Browser settings

7.5.5.2 Readers may recall the reference to browser settings in reg.6 and wonder if this may meet the consent requirement. Browsers contain settings which allow users to block certain types of cookies and to delete cookies which have been set. The regulation suggests that organisations may be able to infer consent from browser settings—but only where the subscriber "*amends or sets controls on the internet browser*".

As the Information Commissioner's *Guidance on cookies* notes (p.16):

> "*At present, most browser settings are not sophisticated enough for websites to assume that consent has been given to allow the site to set a cookie. For consent to be clearly signified by the browser settings it would need to be clear that subscribers had been prompted to consider their current browser settings and, had either indicated in some way they were happy with the default, or have made the decision to change the settings* ...".

EU guidance on valid consent

7.5.5.3 Working Document WP 208 sets out guidance on what a publisher will need to do to obtain consent in a way which "*would be legally compliant for a website that operates across all EU Member States*" (p.2). It concludes that the following will be needed:

- specific information: about the exact purpose of processing must be provided;
- timing: consent should be given before the processing starts;
- active choice: consent should be unambiguous and active;
- freely given: there should be a real choice for the user, with no risk of significant negative consequences if they do not consent.

Providing specific information would, for example, mean explaining that cookies will be used:

- to allow the publisher to understand which parts of the site are attractive to visitors and perform well; and
- to allow an individual's interests to be remembered, so that the site can be personalised to reflect these interests in future. (This may mean displaying certain content or products in preference to others).

It could also mean providing information about the organisations responsible for the cookies, if they are third party cookies.

7.5.5.4 WP 208 suggests that active behaviour

> "*means ... one that is based on a traceable user-client request towards the website, such as clicking on a link, image or other content on the entry webpage etc. The form of these types of user requests are such that the website operator can be confident that the user has actively requested to engage with the website (assuming the user is fully informed) does therefore indeed consent to cookies and that the action is an active indicator of such consent. In any case it must be clearly presented to the user, which action will signify consent to cookies ... the information should be present on the website and not disappear until the user has expressed his/her consent... Additionally, only a click to a 'more information on cookies' link cannot be deemed consent, due to the fact that the user explicitly requested only for more information. Absence of any behaviour cannot be regarded as valid consent*".

7.5.5.5 This requirement for clear, active, unambiguous consent is also repeated in the *Guidelines on consent under Regulation 2016/679* (WP 259 rev.01) which notes (in example 16) that:

"Scrolling down or swiping through a website will not satisfy the requirement of a clear and affirmative action. This is because the alert that continuing to scroll will constitute consent may be difficult to distinguish and/or may be missed when a data subject is quickly scrolling through large amounts of text and such an action is not sufficiently unambiguous".

So websites should either ask the visitor to click on an 'agree' button to show consent or, if clicking on something on the site is to be used to demonstrate consent, then the cookie overlay or banner needs to state this clearly—and needs to be so prominent that the point cannot be missed.

7.5.5.6 Readers may wish to refer to the ICO's own website as an example of how consent can be obtained. The ICO has a cookie control overlay in the bottom left hand side of the website. The overlay is shown below, along with the more detailed panel which is revealed if you click information and settings. If you click on 'cookies we use', there is additional information about the actual cookies used and how to adjust browser settings.

Cookie control x
We have placed cookies on your device to help make this website better.
You can use this tool to change your cookie settings. Otherwise, we'll assume you're OK to continue.
I'm fine with this
Information and settings
About this tool

Cookie control x
We have placed cookies on your device to help make this website better.
You can use this tool to change your cookie settings. Otherwise, we'll assume you're OK to continue.
Some of the cookies we use are essential for the site to work.
We also use some nonessential cookies to collect information for making reports and to helo us improve the site. The cookies collect information in anonymous form.
To control third party cookie, you can also adjust your browser settings.
Turn cookies off
I'm fine with this

Information Commissioner's Office guidance

7.5.5.7 WP 208 is designed to meet the requirements of all EU Member States. It follows that its recommendations are the highest standard. The Information Commissioner's *Guidance on cookies* is more flexible in some places. In particular, the Commissioner's *Guidance* (p.7) accepts that obtaining consent before cookies are placed is difficult and suggests that "wherever possible" consent should be obtained before cookies are placed but *"where this is not possible at present websites should be able to demonstrate that they are doing as much as possible to reduce the amount of time before the user receives information about cookies and is presented with options"*.

7.5.5.8 The ICO *Guidance on cookies* also has commentary on whether consent should be obtained from the subscriber or the user, noting that as the Regulations refer to consent from subscriber or user, without making clear whose wishes prevail, there is some uncertainty on this point (p.10). In fact, this is resolved by the Directive that the PECR implement, which provides that cookies can only be placed where "*the subscriber or user concerned has given his or her consent*"—so the key question is, whose privacy is affected? If the tracking affects the user only, then consent should be obtained from the user; conversely if it affects the subscriber, it should be from the subscriber; and if it affects both, then consent of both would be needed. For most organisations who use cookies on websites for marketing and analytics, then the only person affected by this is the person browsing the website (i.e. the user): the fact that a different household member may be party to the contract with the internet service provider is not relevant.

7.5.5.9 In some cases, a website publisher will place cookies for its own purposes. However, on other occasions, the publisher will place "third-party cookies"—which will allow information to be read by another organisation. This is often the case for cookies used for advertising. For example, a shop may partner with an advertising technology (ad-tech) company and agree to place cookies on its shop website on behalf of the ad-tech company. This allows the ad-tech company to recognise someone who has visited the shop's website and viewed a particular item (say a bale of towels) when that person then visits a different website (for example a news website), with which the ad-tech company also works. The ad-tech company is then able to place an advert for the same bale of towels on the news website. The *Guidance on cookies* looks at who has responsibility for obtaining consent in this type of situation. It notes (p.13) that:

"The Regulations do not define who should be responsible for complying with the requirement to provide information about cookies and obtain consent. Where a person operates an online service and any use of cookies will be for their purposes, it is clear that person will be responsible for complying with this Regulation.

The person setting the cookie is therefore primarily responsible for compliance with the requirements of the law. Where third-party cookies are set through a website both parties will have a responsibility for ensuring users are clearly informed about cookies and for obtaining consent. In practice it is obviously considerably more difficult for a third party who has no direct interface with the user to achieve this . . . Third parties setting cookies, or providing a product that requires the setting of cookies, may wish to consider putting a contractual obligation into agreements with web publishers to satisfy themselves that appropriate steps will be taken to provide information about the third-party cookies and obtain consent".

7.5.5.10 This is exactly what many ad-tech providers do. For example Google's EU user consent policy (available at *http://www.google.com/about/company/user-consent-policy*.html [Accessed 7 May 2019]) requires that those using Google products must obtain legally valid consent to use cookies and the collection, sharing and use of personal data for personalization of ads. This consent must also clearly identify each party that may collect, receive or use end-users' personal data as a consequence of use of the Google product. There is more information on cookies and advertising at (**7.5.6**) below. Lastly, the *Guidance on cookies* has a helpful FAQ addressing how the rules apply to intranets: they do not. This is because the "user" is a person using a public electronic communications service and, when a user makes use of an intranet, this is unlikely to be accessed via a public electronic communications service (p.28). This will be relevant to organisations which use intranets in the workplace.

Can access to a site be made conditional on the user accepting cookies?

7.5.5.11 Many news sites are only able to offer free access to content because of the advertising revenue they get from the sites. Such sites need to use cookies—either to facilitate targeted advertising or, even for non-targeted advertising, to ensure that ads are not repeatedly served to the same person, and for anti-fraud and attribution purposes (i.e. to prove that ads have been viewed by real persons, not robots, and to ensure that fees are allocated to the right advertisers). Are such sites able to insist that visitors accept cookies if they want the free content?

7.5.5.12 WP 208 states (p.5) that users should have a "*real and meaningful choice*" regarding cookies, noting that "*the user should retain the possibility to continue browsing the website without receiving cookies*" and that

> "*it is thus recommended to refrain from the use of consent mechanisms that only provide an option for the user to consent, but do not offer any choice regarding all or some cookies*".

It also notes (p.6) that public sector services must not make sites conditional on accepting non-essential cookies and that "*users should also be offered a real choice regarding tracking cookies*".

7.5.5.13 The provisions in the GDPR relating to consent could strengthen the view that "cookie walls" are not permissible. In particular, the provision at art.7(4) that suggests when assessing whether consent is freely given,

> "*utmost account shall be taken of whether . . . the . . . provision of a service is conditional on consent to the processing of personal data which is not necessary for the performance of the contract*"

and at rec.42 that consent should "*not be regarded as freely given if the data subject . . . is unable to refuse or withdraw consent without detriment*".

7.5.5.14 There are difficult policy objectives at stake here: on the one hand, 'take it or leave it' requests for consent achieve little for the individual; however, on the other hand, an overly strict approach may lead to free sites barring visitors from the EU, because such sites cannot be operated on a commercial basis. Based on unofficially reported decisions, it seems that—at the moment—different data protection authorities take different views on this. The Information Commissioner's Office was reported as concluding that news sites which offer subscription-based, but cookie-free content, versus free content which is ad-supported based on cookies, do not comply with the GDPR (*http://www.iapp.org/news/a/ico-tells-washington-post-it-offers-invalid-cookie-consent-under-gdpr* [Accessed 7 May 2019]). However, the Austrian data protection authority has concluded that this model is valid, because the user does receive a recognisable advantage (free content) if they choose to accept ads and cookies (see *https://mobil.derstandard.at/2000093057312/Datenschutzbehoerde-STANDARD-Angebot-entspricht-DSGVO?ref=article* [Accessed 7 May 2019 (unfortunately, we have only found this considered in German)]).

7.5.5.15 This topic is one of the points considered in the proposed changes to the ePrivacy legislation, (see **7.7** below), where the European Parliament's report on the draft Regulation on Privacy and Electronic Communications proposes a prohibition on cookie-walls (Art.8(1)(1b)).

7.5.6 Cookies and advertising

7.5.6.1 Online advertising depends on use of cookies. Cookies allow advertisers and those working with them to recognise a user. Amongst other things, this allows advertisers to ensure that the same advert is not shown repeatedly to the same user, to measure the number of unique users who have seen an advert (which can affect how much the advertiser pays) and, for online behavioural adverts, by allowing ad-tech companies to collect information about what is of interest to a user online, so that corresponding adverts can be served. Online advertising seems to attract a large number of acronyms and industry specific terminology. The previous Information Commissioner prepared a *Personal Information Online Code of Practice* (*http://www.ico.org.uk/media/fororganisations/documents/1591/personal_information_online_cop.pdf* [Accessed 7 May 2019]). This contains a good, user-friendly summary of how online advertising works (p.19 and onwards)—although the code predates both the GDPR and the PECR, so must be supplemented with later guidance. There is also useful guidance (written for consumers) at *http://www.youronlinechoices.com/uk/about-behavioural-advertising [Accessed 7 May 2019]* and a useful jargon-buster prepared by UK trade body, Internet Advertising Bureau UK, at *http://www.iabuk.com/jargon-buster [Accessed 7 May 2019].*

7.5.6.2 The requirement to obtain consent, to a GDPR standard, to place and read cookies poses challenges to all involved in online advertising:

- Ad-tech companies often do not have a direct relationship with the user. Instead the publisher of the website, or the developer of the app will have this relationship. This means that the ad-tech company is dependent on the publisher to obtain consent for it. This can cause difficulties, given the requirement under art.7(1) that the controller must be able to demonstrate consent.

- Recital 42 provides that, for consent to be informed, the user must know the identity of the organisation relying on consent: one publisher can often work with multiple ad-tech companies (10, 20 or more ad-tech partners is not uncommon), the identities of which must all be provided.
- Consent must be informed—the industry is complex, with multiple entities that share data with each other, often bidding in real-time for the option to display an ad to a user. If industry body IAB UK has a jargon-buster page on its website this shows the challenge facing those who need to provide clear, readily understandable explanations to website visitors.

These challenges have led to two industry-led, self-regulatory, initiatives.

European Advertising Standards Alliance Best Practice Recommendation (BPR)

7.5.6.3 This was developed by the European Advertising Standards Alliance (EASA) in response to the cookie consent requirements introduced by the changes to Directive 2002/58/EC. It is available at *http://www.easa-alliance.org/sites/default/files/EASA%20Best%20Practice%20Recommendation%20on%20Online%20Behavioural%20Advertising_0.pdf [Accessed 7 May 2019]*.

7.5.6.4 The BPR is directed to the ad-tech industry, rather than to publishers. It covers organisations which engage in online behavioural advertising, on sites which they (or their corporate group) do not themselves control. In other words, if company A serves targeted ads on its own website, or a website operated by a group company, then the BPR does not apply. However, if company A engages an ad-tech company to advertise its products on completely unconnected websites, then the BPR would apply to the ad-tech company. The BPR focuses on transparency and an easy way for consumers to object to online behavioural advertising. The BPR seeks to raise user awareness by requiring that online targeted ads all contain a small icon (an 'i' in a triangle), which the user can click on to learn more. More information must also be included in privacy policies. *Youronlinechoices.com* (see **7.5.6.1** above) was developed to provide information to consumers and to provide an easy way for them to opt-out of receiving targeted ads by participating companies. The BPR helps to raise awareness of targeted advertising, but—by itself—it does not meet the requirements in the PECR for informed consent for use of cookies. This has also been emphasised by WP 29 in *Opinion 16/2011 on EASA/IAB Best Practice Recommendation on Online Behavioural Advertising* (WP 188) which concludes that "*Adherence to the EASA/IAB Code . . . does not result in compliance with the current e-Privacy Directive . . .*".

Transparency and Consent Framework (TCF)

7.5.6.5 The TCF (*https://advertisingconsent.eu/* [Accessed 7 May 2019]) was developed by IAB Europe in response to the challenges described above. It aims to help publishers and ad-tech providers by providing a way in which consent can be coded into the communication from the user's device (so allowing consent to be passed by the publisher to the ad-tech company). Recording consent in this way will only work if publishers and ad-tech companies have a common understanding of what any particular request for consent covers. Accordingly, the TCF also includes a standard list of purposes and features for which consent can be requested. It also encompasses a list of approved vendors, who agree to follow the framework, so that publishers can ask for consent for participating ad-tech companies.

7.5.6.6 As at the date of writing (January 2019), two high profile complaints have been made in relation to the TCF and advertising:

- Brave complaint (*https://brave.com/adtech-data-breach-complaint* [Accessed 7 May 2019])—complaints lodged in September 2018 with the Irish Data Protection Commissioner and the UK Information Commissioner. These allege sharing of data between ad-tech companies, without any or sufficient control and without always requiring user consent; and
- Privacy International (*https://privacyinternational.org/advocacy-briefing/2434/why-weve-filed-complaints-against-companies-most-people-have-never-heard-and* [Accessed 7 May 2019])—complaints made to the Information Commissioner, the Irish Data Protection Commissioner and the French data protection authority, the CNIL. Three complaints were filed—one against Acxiom and Oracle (the data brokers complaint); one against Experian and Equifax (the credit reference complaint) and one against Criteo, Quantcast and Tapad (the ad-tech complaint).

On 21 January 2019, the French data protection authority fined Google €50 million in relation to deficiencies in obtaining consent as a result of the first complaint (*https://www.cnil.fr/en/cnils-restricted-committee-imposes-financial-penalty-50-million-euros-against-google-llc* [Accessed 7 May2019]).

7.5.6.7 In addition to the WP 29 Opinion specifically addressing the EASA BPR (considered at **7.5.6.4** above), the WP 29 adopted an Opinion on online behavioural advertising in 2010 (WP 171). Its more recent *Guidelines on Automated individual decision-making and Profiling for the purposes of Regulation 2016/679* (WP 251 rev.01) also address online behavioural advertising. The Working Party noted that the GDPR distinguishes between profiling, decisions taken on the basis of profiling, and automated individual decision-making, with the latter being most restrictively controlled. Automated individual decision-making will be relevant where the decision has a legal or similarly significant effect, but, according to WP 29 and as affirmed by the EDPB:

"*In many typical cases the decision to present targeted advertising based on profiling will not have a similarly significant effect on individuals, for example an advertisement for a mainstream online fashion outlet based on a simple demographic profile: 'women in the Brussels region aged between 25 and 35 who are likely to be interested in fashion and certain clothing items*'" (p.22).

7.5.6.8 The WP 251 rev.01 Opinion notes that targeted adverts may involve automated individual decision making if they are particularly intrusive; ignore individuals wishes and expectations; or use knowledge of the vulnerabilities of the individuals targeted; or are delivered in a particular way (p.22). Where this is relevant, then such decision making will be prohibited unless it is carried out with explicit consent and with appropriate safeguards in place. There is more information about automated individual decision-making at **6.11**.

7.5.6.9 Organisations using online behavioural advertising must not only comply with the rules on cookies—they must also have a lawful basis to process personal data (see **Ch.4** and **7.3.3** on lawful basis). The only relevant lawful bases will be consent, or that the processing is necessary for the purposes of the legitimate interests of the controller (or others) which are not overridden by the interests of the individuals. Here, WP 251 rev.01 considers that

"*it would be difficult for controllers to justify using legitimate interests as a lawful basis for intrusive profiling and tracking practices for marketing or advertising purposes, for example those that involve tracking individuals across multiple websites, locations, devices, services or data brokering*" (p.16).

7.5.7 Checklist

7.5.7.1 Organisations using cookies will need to consider the following:

1) Do you know for what purposes cookies will be used?

   (a) Strictly necessary

   (b) Functional (e.g. remembering preferences)

   (c) Analytics

   (d) Social media

   (e) Advertising

   And if you are placing third party cookies, do you know details of the third parties?

2) Draft a cookie policy, or a section in your privacy policy, which explains theses purposes; which provides the identity of relevant third parties; and which explains how users can give or withdraw consent.

3) Prepare an overlay or banner which explains why cookies are used and

what the user must do to give consent (for example, ticking an agree button, or making clear that proceeding with the site will be consent).

4) Ensure that the overlay or banner is sufficiently prominent and does not disappear unless and until the user has demonstrated consent. If possible, avoid placing cookies until the user has demonstrated consent.

5) If you allow advertising cookies to be used, consider following the Transparency and Consent Framework (TCF).

6) If you work with third parties (for analytics or advertising), ensure that the appropriate contract terms are in place (for example, if the third party is a processor, then this should include terms required by art.28 (**13.7.4**)). If the third party places obligations on you (for example, requirements to obtain consent for specified purposes of processing, such as obtaining location data), ensure you meet this obligation.

7) Ensure the above steps are in place for all of your organisation's websites and apps and that the information given in the overlay and policy remains accurate when there are technical changes.

7.6 ENFORCEMENT

7.6.1 Enforcement by the Information Commissioner

The law

7.6.1.1 The Information Commissioner enforces the PECR. However, her powers are not those under the DPA 2018. Instead, the Commissioner's enforcement powers remain those under the 1998 Act, at Pt V, ss.55 A to E and Schs 6–9 of that Act. Although the DPA 2018 repeals the 1998 Act, Sch.20, para.58 provides that these provisions of the 1998 Act remain in force, as needed for the PECR. In particular, this means that the Information Commissioner's ability to impose monetary penalties is still subject to the previous limit of £500,000 and a penalty can only be imposed where there is a "serious" breach of the PECR, although there is no longer a requirement for the Commissioner to prove "substantial" damage or distress as was previously the case.

7.6.1.2 The PECR do contain some special enforcement provisions. First, reg.31A gives the Information Commissioner power to require communications providers to provide her with information where this is necessary for her to investigate compliance (for example, for her to see who has been making calls). There is a right of appeal for communications providers to the Tribunal at reg.31B.

7.6.1.3 Secondly, with effect from 17 December 2018, the PECR were amended (by the Privacy and Electronic Communications (Amendment) Regulations 2018 (SI 2018/1189), so as to allow the Information Commissioner to impose a monetary penalty directly on the management team of companies or other corporate persons, where the breach of the PECR is due to management action or inaction. This allows the Information Commissioner more effective powers to tackle rogue operators who flagrantly breach the PECR and who liquidate companies used for illegal direct marketing once a fine and an enforcement notice have been imposed, then commence trading through a different company instead. The fines can be imposed on directors, managers, the company secretary of other similar officers or members who manage the corporate body, where the breach of the PECR took place with their consent or connivance or was attributable to their neglect.

7.6.1.4 Because the DPA 2018 repeals the 1998 Act, it is difficult for the reader to find the legislation setting out the Information Commissioner's enforcement powers in relation to the PECR. The copies of the 1998 Act which are available at (*https://www.legislation.gov.uk/ukpga/1998/29/contents [Accessed 7 May 2019]*) either show the latest amended text of the 1998 Act (where most sections have been deleted as they have been repealed) or the version of the 1998 Act as originally enacted (which does not contain later amendments to the legislation, including, significantly, the Commissioner's power to impose monetary penalties). To view the relevant legislation, readers should select 'latest available' and then 'show timeline of changes': this allows the reader to view the 1998 Act as it was prior to the repeal of the majority of the legislation by the DPA 2018.

Enforcement in practice

7.6.1.5 Enforcement of the PECR has been a high priority for the Information Commissioner, who receives high numbers of complaints from individuals about direct marketing. By way of example, the Information Commissioner released a "trend report" on the action taken in October 2018 (available at *https://ico.org.uk/action-weve-taken/nuisance-calls-and-messages [Accessed 7 May 2019]*) and this shows that there were 15,772 concerns reported during October, with the Information Commissioner having 103 cases under investigation. As a result, the Information Commissioner has also imposed a large number of monetary penalties on organisations breaching the PECR. Due to the volume of monetary penalties, it is not possible to cover them all. However, we think the following are useful examples:

- £400,000 fine for Keurboom Communications Ltd in May 2017 which made 99.5 million automated calls without consent, triggering more than 1,000 complaints—a good example of a large fine for flagrant breach of the PECR.
- £60,000 fine for Everything DM Ltd in September 2018. Everything DM Ltd acted as a list broker, selling lists compiled by others to those wishing to send direct marketing. It also offered a service whereby it sent direct marketing out. Everything DM Ltd argued it was just the middle-man, acting as a processor in between those who compiled the lists and those using them. ICO disagreed (para.18), concluding that Everything DM Ltd obtained lists for its own purposes, which were either to sell the lists on

or to use the lists to send direct marketing itself; that it had discretion as to how the lists were used and was a controller. ICO also concluded that it had not carried out appropriate due diligence to check for consent from those receiving emails.

- £80,000 fine for Moneysupermarket.com Ltd in July 2017, which sent emails advising about changes to terms and conditions and its privacy policy. The email was sent to opted-out customers and, for these customers, also had a substantial section explaining that they were opted-out and were missing out on offers and inviting them to visit a preference centre to change their preferences. This was held to be an email sent for purposes of direct marketing. One recipient complained: this is not unusual and many of the monetary penalties issued by the Information Commissioner are in response to a very small number of complaints.
- Xerpla Ltd successfully challenged a monetary penalty notice before the First-tier Tribunal (Appeal Reference: EA/2017/0262, decision dated 14 August 2018 and promulgated on 20 August 2018). Xerpla sent emails to individuals who had signed up to receive offers on two websites that it ran. The offers sent to the subscribers were wide-ranging. The Commissioner had imposed a penalty of £50,000 arguing that Xerpla did not have valid consent to send the emails. The Tribunal disagreed, finding that consumers had given valid consent; it was clear that they would get a wide-range of offers and the small number of complaints (14 out of a mailing of over 1.25 million emails) was consistent with this. The Tribunal also noted [41] that there is a qualitative difference between receiving direct marketing from an organisation with which a consumer has voluntarily established a relationship and from third parties where this is not the case (suggesting that parties relying on indirect consent may be better targets for higher fines than those who have a direct consumer relationship).

7.6.2 Enforcement by individuals

7.6.2.1 Regulation 30(1) provides that

> "*any person who suffers damage by reason of any contravention of any of the requirements of these Regulations by any other person shall be entitled to bring proceedings for compensation from that other person for that damage*".

Regulation 30(2) provides for a defence, where the defendant can show that they had taken such care, as was reasonable in all the circumstances, to comply with the requirement.

7.6.2.2 The DPA 2018 provides (at s.168 in relation to the GDPR and at s.169 in relation to other elements of the DPA 2018) that "damage" includes distress and other non-material damage. These definitions do not apply to the PECR. However, as was mentioned at **3.3.1.11**, in ***Google Inc v Vidal-Hall,*** the Court of

Appeal concluded that "damage" should be given its natural and wide meaning, including both material and non-material damage [76]. Accordingly, claims for compensation under the PECR could also include claims for distress without any financial damage.

7.6.2.3 There have been a number of successful actions in the courts against spammers. In one, a businessman based in Alderney successfully sued a company called Media Logistics in the English Courts for unwanted spam ("Spammers to Pay £300 in Damages" *The Times*, 28 December 2005; Helen Hart, "Cutting down on spam", (2006) 150 *S.J.* 9, p.290). The claimant tracked down the source of the spam using the IP address and found they were UK-based (Scotland). He wrote to them asking for an apology and information as to how they had obtained his data. Media Logistics complied only with the first of these requests. The claimant chose to limit his damages so as to obtain a speedy and successful claim in the County Court. His action in Colchester County Court won £270 plus £30 costs.

7.6.2.4 Another case was brought in the Small Claims Court by an Edinburgh-based businessman against an Oxfordshire company called Transcom. The damages were slightly more satisfactory than the earlier case—the claimant won £750 for a single item of spam (Tom Young, "Courts put price on unsolicited email", *Computing*, 15 March 2007, p.14).

7.6.2.5 The case of ***Microsoft Corp v Paul Martin McDonald*** [2006] EWHC 3410 (Ch) takes a different line. In September 2006, Microsoft obtained summary judgment against the Manchester spammer—reputedly to the tune of £45,000. Microsoft had set up unprotected "unmanned" email addresses within its Hotmail system, for the express purpose of attracting and identifying spam. The defendant was not in fact the transmitter of the spam but a collector of addresses which he then sold on to spammers. His defence was, at first, that he was not a spammer. This was refuted by the wording of reg.22(2) which states that:

> "*a person shall neither transmit, nor instigate the transmission of, unsolicited communications.*"

The defendant was clearly an instigator and as such caught by the Regulations. The defendant's allegation that the websites receiving his spam had been set up expressly to receive spam and so had opted in under the Regulations was also not accepted. Finally, he suggested that Microsoft was not in a position to launch an action against him on behalf of its subscribers. The wording of reg.30(1) talks of:

> "*A person who suffers damage by reason of any contravention . . . by any other person shall be entitled to bring proceedings for compensation from that person for that damage.*"

This was held to be sufficiently wide to allow Microsoft to bring the action, given the costs that Microsoft incurred in setting up systems to combat spam. To complete the defendant's discomfiture, Microsoft asked for, and was granted, in addition to the damages, an injunction against the defendant, even though injunctions were not mentioned as a remedy in the Regulations.

7.7 REPLACEMENT OF DIRECTIVE 2002/58/EC

7.7.1 Recital 173 of the GDPR instructs the Commission to review Directive 2002/58/EC "*in particular in order to ensure consistency with this Regulation*". On 10 January 2017, the Commission duly published a proposal for a Regulation of the European Parliament and of the Council concerning the respect for private life and the protection of personal data in electronic communications and repealing Directive 2002/58/EC (Regulation on Privacy and Electronic Communications (2017/0003 (COD)).

7.7.2 The proposed Regulation on Privacy and Electronic Communications aligns rules with the GDPR (for example, removing breach reporting rules (**8.4**), which are now addressed by the GDPR, and setting out GDPR-style revenue-based fines and providing for the co-ordination and consistency mechanisms to apply). Of particular relevance to this chapter, it also proposes remedying two areas of Directive 2002/58/EC which no longer effectively protect individuals.

- First, it notes that its rules need to take account of technological change (p.2):

  > "*consumers and businesses increasingly rely on new internet-based services enabling inter-personal communications such as Voice over IP, instant messaging and web-based e-mail services, instead of traditional communications services. These Over-the-Top communications services (OTTs) are in general not subject to the current Union electronic communications framework, including the ePrivacy Directive. Accordingly, the Directive has not kept pace with technological developments, resulting in a void of protection of communications conveyed through new services*".

- Second, it re-assesses the cookie consent rule (p.5) which

  > "*failed to reach its objectives as end-users face requests to accept tracking cookies without understanding their meaning . . . The cookie consent rule is over-inclusive, as it also covers non-privacy intrusive practices, and under-inclusive, as it does not clearly cover some tracking techniques . . .*".

7.7.3 The proposed Regulation suggested extending the email consent or soft opt-in rule to cover unsolicited direct marketing sent by all electronic communications services (although the rules on phone, automated calling and fax marketing would remain as they are). The proposed modification of the rules on cookies are at arts 8 and 10: the consent requirement would be retained, but the exemptions from the consent requirement would be extended to cover "*web audience* *measuring*" (i.e. analytics) in certain circumstances. The difficulties posed by repeated pop-ups which users do not want to read and do not understand would be addressed by requiring those who build software permitting electronic communications (i.e. browser manufacturers) to tell end-users about privacy settings and to require users to consent to a setting. In others words, users would be asked to make active choices about privacy at the outset, meaning that ad-tech companies and website publishers and app developers would then have the option of relying on this initial choice.

7.7.4 The European Parliament adopted its report (i.e. its position) on the proposed Regulation relatively promptly on 23 October 2017 (*http://www.europarl.europa.eu/doceo/document/A-8-2017-0324_EN.html* [Accessed 7 May 2019]). However, it has proved harder for Member States to reach an agreement in the Council of Ministers and, as of December 2018, no agreement has been reached, meaning that trialogue—where the final text of the Regulation will be agreed and adopted—cannot start. The timing of and final text of the proposed Regulation is, therefore, unclear.

7.7.5 Meanwhile, there is now a newly adopted Directive of the European Parliament and the Council establishing the European Electronic Communications Code (Recast) (Directive 2018/1972) (EECC). This also tackles the concern that more services need to be regulated than traditional telecommunications service. Recital 15 of this notes that end-users must be protected when using "*functionally equivalent services*" *and* a new definition of "*electronic communications service*" is adopted at art.2(4), which now includes an "*interpersonal communications service*", being:

> "*a service normally provided for remuneration that enables direct interpersonal and interactive exchange of information via electronic communications networks between a finite number of persons, whereby the persons initiative or participating in the communication determine its recipient(s) and does not include services which enable interpersonal and interactive communication merely as a minor ancillary feature that is intrinsically linked to another service*" (art.2(5)).

7.7.6 Interestingly, the EECC also explicitly recognises that users "pay" for services with their data—with rec.16 noting that the requirement for services to be provided "for remuneration" would include provision of data as

> "*the concept of remuneration should therefore encompass situations where the provider of a service requests and the end-user knowingly provides personal data within the meaning of* [the GDPR] . . . *The concept of remuneration should therefore also encompass situations in which the end-user is exposed to advertisements as a condition for gaining access to the service, or situations in which the service provider monetises personal data it has collected* . . .".

7.7.7 The EECC must be implemented into national law by 21 December 2020. When the EECC is effective, this will automatically affect some provisions of Directive 2002/58/EC—for example, the rules requiring confidentiality of communications and restricting use of traffic and location data by providers of electronic communications services will apply to more providers. However, it will not solve the difficulty of cookie consent, nor will it clearly widen the rules on email marketing to cover wider types of communication such as instant messaging.

7.8 OTHER RELEVANT RULES FOR DIRECT MARKETING

7.8.1 Direct marketers must also comply with other laws and codes, which overlap with the GDPR and the PECR. The Information Commissioner's *Direct Marketing Guidance* contains a useful list of relevant regulation (pp.10–11). We have also provided a short summary of key areas of overlap below. Organisations must also be alert to the contractual requirements placed on them—for example by Google, where they use Google's ad services (see above) or the requirements of other ad-tech companies, and of Apple and Google if they wish to have apps available in the App Store or Google Play.

7.8.2 Ofcom

7.8.2.1 Ofcom has a policy on abandoned or silent calls, which has been issued under the Communications Act 2003 (available at *https://www.ofcom.org.uk/consultations-and-statements/category-2/silent-calls* [Accessed 7 May 2019]). These are the result of call centres using automating calling systems, whereby numbers are called automatically and only transferred to a member of staff when the call is answered. Inaccuracies in the technology can lead to abandoned or silent calls—for example, if calls are made when there are insufficient staff available or when the technology inaccurately concludes that the call is being picked up by an answer-phone. Among other things, Ofcom's rules require call centres to ensure that no more than 3% of live calls lead to abandoned calls and that a brief recorded message must be played when the line is picked up, which contains the identity of the company responsible for the call and a number which the caller can use to object to receiving further calls. The rules also stipulate that the recorded message cannot itself be used for marketing purposes. Ofcom can impose a penalty of up to £2 million for persistent misuse of networks or services.

7.8.3 Phone-paid Services Authority

7.8.3.1 This body regulates content, goods and services charged to a phone-bill. Its Code of Practice is also relevant where direct marketing will be sent by, or where a response to direct marketing will be routed by, premium rate mobile (see *https://psauthority.org.uk/for-business/code-guidance-and-compliance* [Accessed 7 May 2019]).

7.8.4 Consumer Protection from Unfair Trading Regulations 2008 (Unfair Trading Regulations)

7.8.4.1 Making persistent and unwanted solicitations by telephone, fax, email or other remote media unless this is justified to enforce a contractual obligation is automatically regarded as an unfair commercial practice. Engaging in unfair commercial practices is an offence under these Regulations and can lead to a fine or to imprisonment for up to two years, depending on the way the offence is prosecuted. There are parallel rules regulating advertising to business (the Business Protection from Misleading Marketing Regulations 2008).

7.8.5 The CAP Code

7.8.5.1 This is the Code that (amongst other things) sets out the requirement for adverts to be legal, decent, honest and truthful. Its full name is the UK Code of Non-broadcast Advertising and Direct & Promotional Marketing and it is available at *https://www.asa.org.uk/codes-and-rulings/advertising-codes/non-broadcast-code.html [Accessed 7 May 2019]*. As the full name applies, it excludes adverts and broadcasts, but covers other forms of marketing—including emails, texts, direct mail, posters, online advertisements and an organisation's own website content. The Code is enforced by the Advertising Standards Authority (ASA), which is a self-regulatory body. Sanctions for non-compliance include the adverse publicity associated with publication of an adverse ASA ruling, or can include other members withdrawing services or discounts or refusing to make space available for ads. The ASA can also ultimately refer instances of non-compliance to Trading Standards.

7.8.5.2 Most of the Code is concerned with the content of marketing communications. However, s.10 addresses the Use of Data for Marketing: this repeats the relevant requirements of the GDPR and the PECR for direct marketing. The Code also contains provisions relating to direct marketing and children. As at December 2018, the relevant provisions of s.10 dealing with children (10.15–10.17 inclusive) are still subject to consultation. However, organisations should note that other sections of the CAP Code relating to children (i.e. non-data sections), apply to children under 16. This includes a supplemental help note on mobile marketing (available at *https://www.asa.org.uk/resource/mobile-marketing.html* [Accessed 7 May 2019]), which provides that verifiable and explicit consent from a parent must be obtained before sending direct marketing via mobile to a child. This rule is, therefore, stricter than that under the GDPR or the PECR. Another interesting point to note in this help note relates to one-off messages to individuals to ask for consent to send direct marketing. The Information Commissioner considers that requests for consent to direct marketing cannot be sent—because such requests are, themselves, unsolicited communications for direct marketing purposes. However, the help note takes a more flexible line, suggesting that:

> "*A consumer who has not completed or negotiated a sale but has in some other way actively formed a relationship with the marketer, e.g. by interactive voting*

or responding to a prize promotion, may be sent one mobile communication asking for explicit consent to use their data for direct marketing purposes. Unless the consumer responds positively to that message, the marketer should not send any further direct marketing messages".

CHAPTER 8
Security

8.1 SECURITY AND DATA LOSS

8.1.1 Article 5(1)(f) of the GDPR states that personal data shall be:

"*processed in a manner that ensures appropriate security of the personal data, including protection against unauthorised or unlawful processing and against accidental loss, destruction or damage, using appropriate technical or organisational measures ('integrity and confidentiality')*".

Chapter IV s.2 of the GDPR (arts 32–34) elaborates on this.

8.1.2 The Commissioner points out in the Information Commissioner's *Guide* that the terms 'confidentiality', 'integrity', and 'availability' constitute the 'CIA triad', such that if any one of the three is compromised, there can be serious consequences for the controller and the data subjects. Security measures should guarantee all three.

8.1.3 In addition to a general requirement to keep the personal data safe there are now also procedures to be adopted in the event of a data breach, involving notifying the Commissioner and possibly also the data subjects (**8.4**).

8.2 APPROPRIATE TECHNICAL AND ORGANISATIONAL MEASURES

Assessment of risk

8.2.1 Article 32 is headed "Security of processing" and begins:

> "*(1) Taking into account the state of the art, the costs of implementation and the nature, scope, context and purposes of processing as well as the risk of varying likelihood and severity for the rights and freedoms of natural persons, the controller and the processor shall implement appropriate technical and organisational measures to ensure a level of security appropriate to the risk, including inter alia as appropriate:*
>
> *(a) the pseudonymisation and encryption of personal data;*
>
> *(b) the ability to ensure the ongoing confidentiality, integrity, availability and resilience of processing systems and services;*
>
> *(c) the ability to restore the availability and access to personal data in a timely manner in the event of a physical or technical incident;*
>
> *(d) a process for regular testing, assessing and evaluating the effectiveness of technical and organisational measures for ensuring the security of the processing.*
>
> *(2) In assessing the appropriate level of security account shall be taken in particular of the risks that are presented by processing, in particular from accidental or unlawful destruction, loss, alteration, unauthorised disclosure of, or access to personal data transmitted, stored or otherwise processed.*"

8.2.2 The first thing to notice is that the processor is coupled with the controller as having an obligation to keep the personal data secure—a point we return to below at **8.2.7**.

8.2.3 Articles 32(1)–(2) require a balancing act between several different criteria: the technical development of security measures ("state of the art"), their cost, the nature of the personal data, its scope, its context, the purposes and the risk. The controller or processor then should, to comply with arts 32(1)–(2), be aware of and consider the latest technical developments for security, together with the cost of such measures. "Latest" does not imply that unproven techniques should be introduced. The Commissioner's repeated appeals to "best practice" are appropriate here. Overall, the controller or processor must ensure "*a level of security appropriate to the risk*". We look first at the provisions in the GDPR relating to assessment of risk, followed by the provisions in the GDPR relating to particular security measures.

Risk

8.2.4 Article 32(2) draws specific attention to security risks—from accidental or unlawful destruction, loss, alteration, unauthorised disclosure of or access to personal data, whether transmitted, stored or otherwise processed. However, the GDPR also suggests that wider types of 'risk' should be considered. Recital 75 notes that:

> "*could lead to physical, material or non-material damage, in particular: where the processing may give rise to discrimination, identity theft or fraud, financial loss, damage to the reputation, loss of confidentiality of personal data protected by professional secrecy, unauthorised reversal of pseudonymisation, or any other significant economic or social disadvantage; where data subjects might be deprived of their rights and freedoms or prevented from exercising control over their personal data; where personal data are processed which reveal racial or ethnic origin, political opinions, religion or philosophical beliefs, trade union membership, and the processing of genetic data, data concerning health or data concerning sex life or criminal convictions and offences or related security measures; where personal aspects are evaluated, in particular analysing or predicting aspects concerning performance at work, economic situation, health, personal preferences or interests, reliability or behaviour, location or movements, in order to create or use personal profiles; where personal data of vulnerable natural persons, in particular of children, are processed; or where processing involves a large amount of personal data and affects a large number of data subjects*".

This long list should be seen by controllers and processors as a list of factors which would suggest that a higher level of security is required. Of course, a higher level of security is not the only consideration—and rec.76 goes on to note that "*likelihood and severity of the risk*" should be considered, by reference to the nature, scope context and purposes of processing. The risk should be "*evaluated on the basis of an objective assessment*".

8.2.5 Any audit carried out by the organisation should have identified the likely areas where higher risk processing takes place. Such areas may also require Data Protection Impact Assessments (DPIAs) in order to evaluate the risk (**13.6**). At the other end of the scale, if any data can realistically be considered trivial and if the level of security is to be reduced for that data, a record of this assessment, together with the reasons for considering it trivial or at least less important, will be desirable. This is obviously problematic and if in any doubt whatever, a controller should avoid labelling any data trivial and consider only two classes of personal data: "normal" and "higher security".

8.2.6 The relevant section of the organisation's security strategy will thus need to take into account any documented separate risk assessment either by a DPIA or otherwise. Risk assessment should be something that a good IT department has constantly in mind.

8.2.7 We have seen that art.32(1) requires processors to take some responsibility for appropriate security measures. What is "appropriate" for the processor, may be different from what is "appropriate" for the controller. To take two examples, some processors may have more expert technical knowledge than some controllers; some controllers may be better placed to appreciate particular risks posed by the nature of the personal data they process. Indeed, processors are very often not in the best position to evaluate risk themselves, but it is reasonable that they should usually be given the controller's evaluation of risk and tailor their security measures accordingly, in consultation with the controller. This does not prevent the processor from suggesting a different security measure that may not have occurred to the controller, if they think it is desirable. Article 32(1) speaks of the controller and the processor implementing appropriate security measures.

Technical and organisational measures

8.2.8 The GDPR art.32(1) and elsewhere suggests taking "*appropriate technical and organisational measures*" for security. The word "organisational" might cover physical security such as locked doors and filing cabinets, as well as arrangements for dealing with staff and other organisations, whereas "technical" security suggests firewalls, encryption, etc. The *Guide* suggests for physical security looking at such factors as:

"• *the quality of doors and locks, and the protection of your premises by such means as alarms, security lighting or CCTV;*

• *how to control access to your premises, and how visitors are supervised;*

• *how you dispose of any paper or electronic waste; and*

• *how you keep equipment, particularly mobile devices, secure.*"

The consideration of physical security first seems a useful start. There is a danger of getting carried away by the technical wheezes and ignoring the obvious.

8.2.9 For technical security ("cybersecurity") the *Guide* suggests looking at:

"• *system security – the security of your network and information systems, including those which process personal data;*

• *data security – the security of the data you hold within your systems, e.g. ensuring appropriate access controls are in place and that data is held securely;*

- *online security – e.g. the security of your website and any other online service or application that you use; and*
- *device security – including policies on Bring-your-own-device (BYOD) if you offer it.*" (see **14.3**).

8.2.10 The *Guide* adds:

"*Whatever you do, you should remember the following:*
- *your cybersecurity measures need to be appropriate to the size and use of your network and information systems;*
- *you should take into account the state of technological development, but you are also able to consider the costs of implementation;*
- *your security must be appropriate to your business practices. For example, if you offer staff the ability to work from home* [which may or may not include BYOD (**14.3**)], *you need to put measures in place to ensure that this does not compromise your security; and*
- *your measures must be appropriate to the nature of the personal data you hold and the harm that might result from any compromise*".

8.2.11 The controller and/or processor should clearly take into account the specific measures called out by art.32 itself. These are:

- pseudonymisation and encryption;
- the ability to ensure ongoing confidentiality, integrity and resilience of processing systems and services;
- the ability to restore availability and access to personal data in a timely manner in the event of a physical or technical incident (i.e. resilience); and
- a process for regularly testing, assessing and evaluating the effectiveness of technical and organisational measures for ensuring security.

8.2.12 The Information Commissioner places particular stress on encryption, which as we have seen was head of the GDPR's list of measures in art.32(1)(a). On encryption the *Guide* says:

"*The ICO has seen numerous incidents of personal data being subject to unauthorised or unlawful processing, loss, damage or destruction. In many cases, the damage and distress caused by these incidents may have been reduced or even avoided had the personal data been encrypted.*
It is also the case that encryption solutions are widely available and can be deployed at relatively low cost.
It is possible that, where data is lost or destroyed and it was not encrypted,

regulatory action may be pursued (depending on the context of each incident)".

The Information Commissioner has published both in-brief and detailed guidance on encryption. It recommends encryption for data both in transit and at rest—and also explains the limitations to encryption (for example, the need to ensure security of keys and that secure encrypted communication channels do not protect the security of data before or after receipt of transmission). Given the Commissioner's strong statement that encryption can often mitigate the impact of personal data breaches and that failure to encrypt will often lead to enforcement action, organisations should ensure that they are familiar with this guidance. It is also likely to be the case that technical guidance like this will need to be updated fairly frequently and readers should always seek out the up-to-date version.

8.2.13 Password management is not mentioned in art.32(1), but is also an area of focus for the Information Commissioner, where specific guidance has been issued. The Commissioner highlights:

- key challenges of using passwords—in particular, that individuals tend to use passwords which are easy to remember and, therefore, insecure and that security measures to counter this (minimum length etc.) can be counter-productive as they lead individuals to re-use passwords, due to the difficulty of remembering them;
- as a result organisations should consider if a password is actually the most appropriate choice;
- passwords must be stored securely and protected against theft and brute force (i.e. guessing) attacks;
- passwords must be entered securely; and
- passwords must be appropriately strong (e.g. minimum 10 characters with possible use of special characters)—but this should be balanced with point one, above.

Again, controllers and processors should be read the guidance in full.

8.2.14 This book is not a manual of security measures and it would be impertinent of us to recommend any particular security techniques for all data controllers or processors, beyond the specific factors highlighted in the GDPR itself. As has been seen from the guidance on encryption and passwords above, much information is available from the Information Commissioner. The *Guide to GDPR* contains a listing of other guidance produced by the Commissioner in this area (*https://ico.org.uk/for-organisations/guide-to-data-protection/guide-to-the-general-data-protection-regulation-gdpr/security* [Accessed 8 May 2019]) as well as links to the Government's Cyber Essentials scheme and sector-specific initiatives, such as the Payment Card Industry Data Security Standards. The Commissioner states in her *Guide* that, where an industry has its own security requirements, though they may not necessarily equate to GDPR compliance,

> "*the ICO will nevertheless consider these carefully in any considerations of regulatory action. It can be the case that they specify certain measures that you should have, and that those measures contribute to your overall security posture*"

and the *Guide* gives the example of the Payment Card Industry Security Standard (*http://www.pcisecuritystandards.org* [Accessed 8 May 2019]) and adds:

> "*... if you process card data and suffer a personal data breach, the ICO will consider the extent to which you have put in place measures that PCI-DSS requires particularly if the breach related to a lack of a particular control or process mandated by the standard*".

8.2.15 Codes of conduct and certification could be particularly useful to give the organisation itself, or others who deal with it, re-assurance that it has taken appropriate technical and organisational measures. The GDPR itself recognises this, noting—at art.32(3), that:

> "*adherence to an approved code of conduct or an approved certification mechanism ... may be used as an element by which to demonstrate compliance with the requirements set out in ... this Article*".

Any such codes or certification schemes would have to be approved under the terms of the GDPR. As the date of writing, no such codes or certifications exist. However, this is clearly an area for organisations to keep under review (see also **13.1.28**).

8.2.16 In the Checklist of Audit questions in **12.5.1** we have list of security questions to be considered, which readers may find helpful. The list is not exhaustive and technical experts' advice should be taken for particular circumstances.

8.2.17 Readers should also note that privacy by design (**13.8.2**) is also important to ensure appropriate technical and organisational measures are implemented. This means both building in security measures throughout the processing to ensure end-to-end security, but also considering if all planned personal data processing is actually necessary. The famous data loss in 2008 by HM Revenue and Customs was because the data was sent to the National Audit Office on a CD and there was apparently no mechanism to strip out all the personal identifiers: there was unnecessary processing of personal data, as well as a personal data breach.

8.3 EMPLOYEES

8.3.1 The GDPR at art.32(4) says:

> "*The controller and processor shall take steps to ensure that any natural person acting under the authority of the controller or the processor who has access to personal data does not process them except on instructions from the controller, unless he or she is required to do so by Union or Member State law*".

This is a recognition that inevitably personal data will be disclosed to staff in an organisation. Such disclosure must be limited to relevant staff on a need-to-know basis if it is not to fall foul of the data minimisation principle (art.5(1)(c)), since disclosure is one of the ways in which data can be processed (art.4(2)) and disclosure to someone who has no need to know must be at variance with that principle (**5.3**).

8.3.2 The ICO's *Guide* notes that staff training is "vital" to ensure compliance with art.32(4). The Information Commissioner suggests initial and refresher training, covering:

- the organisation's obligations as a controller (or, presumably, processor);
- what is expected of staff—including the fact that deliberate unauthorised access to or disclosure of personal data may be a criminal offence;
- proper procedures to identify those trying to access personal data;
- the dangers of people trying to obtain data by deception; and
- any restrictions placed on personal use of systems.

8.3.3 The Morrisons case (**3.3.1.19**) shows the risk of liability to an organisation posed by a disaffected employee. In the light of this case, organisations should consider not just training, but also assessment of trustworthiness at interview stage, and monitoring of access to systems which include significant amounts of personal data. Clearly any such assessments and monitoring must, themselves, be conducted in a way which respects data protection legislation.

Processors

8.3.4 An assessment of appropriate technical and organisational measures, must also consider the suitability of processors who will process personal data on the controller's behalf. Where the organisation is itself a processor, this would include any sub-processors.

8.3.5 The 1998 Act used to list selection and appointment of processors as one element of the security principle set out in that Act. The controller's relationship with its processor is no longer seen just as an element of data security: instead, under art.28 of the GDPR, the controller has to ensure that the processor can meet *all* the requirements of the GDPR (so including, but not limited to, security).

8.3.6 Security is still an important element of this, though, and the Information Commissioner's *Guide* notes that

> "*the GDPR's security requirements also apply to any processor you use ... you must choose a data processor that provides sufficient guarantees about its security measures; your written contract must stipulate that the processor takes all measures required under Article 32 – basically, the contract has to require the processor to undertake the same security measures that you would have to take if you were doing the processing yourself ...*".

The requirements for selecting and managing processors are considered at **13.7.**

8.4 PERSONAL DATA BREACHES

8.4.1 Introduction

8.4.1.1 The high-profile data breaches in the UK (and elsewhere) have focused attention on the need for organisations to anticipate and plan for data breaches, to allow them to contain the breach, minimise the impact on those affected, and return to normal operations more quickly. This has also led to the introduction of requirements to notify breaches to supervisory authorities and, on some occasions, to affected individuals. The obligation to notify the Information Commissioner and individuals is placed on the controller. There are separate obligations placed on processors and these are considered at **13.7.**

8.4.1.2 The GDPR has devoted arts 33 to 34 to data breach. Article 33 states what has to be done in the event of a data breach so far as concerns the supervisory authority. Article 34 covers relations between the controller involved in the data breach and the data subjects. The provisions in the GDPR were closely modelled on breach reporting requirements under the PECR (**7.4**). At the moment, these are still in force for providers of public electronic communications services and they are considered at **8.4.5.5**. We also consider the *Guidelines on Personal data breach notification under Regulation 2016/679* adopted by the Article 29 Working Party (WP 250 rev.01) and guidance from the Information Commissioner on personal data breach reporting, available as part of the Commissioner's *Guide*.

8.4.2 Definition of data breach

8.4.2.1 Article 4(12) provides that:

> "*'personal data breach' means a breach of security leading to the accidental or unlawful destruction, loss, alteration, unauthorised disclosure of, or access to, personal data transmitted, stored or otherwise processed.*"

WP 250 rev.01 (p.7) explains that personal data breaches can be categorised according to classic information security principles, as:

> "*'Confidentiality breach' – where there is an unauthorised or accidental disclosure of, or access to, personal data.*

'Integrity breach' – where there is unauthorised or accidental alteration of personal data.
'Availability breach' – where there is an accidental or unauthorised loss of access to, or destruction of, personal data".

The Working Party refers to art.32, which sets out the obligation to ensure security of processing, and states that controllers must have appropriate measures to be able to "*restore the availability and access to personal data in a timely manner in the event of a physical or technical incident*" to show why an availability breach is one type of personal data breach.

8.4.2.2 WP 250 rev.01 p.9 uses the example of ransomware—where a malicious attacker makes personal data unavailable to the controller (for example, by encrypting it) and will only release the data in return for payment—as an example of an availability breach. WP 250 rev.01 also comments (p.8) that it may be less obvious when loss of availability may be a breach, noting that a permanent loss of availability of data (for example, if data is encrypted but the key is lost) will be a personal data breach, but that temporary loss of availability during planned system maintenance will not be a personal data breach, because this is not a breach of security (also p.8).

8.4.3 Notification to the Information Commissioner

When is the controller 'aware of' the breach?

8.4.3.1 Article 33(1) says:

"*In the case of a personal data breach, the controller shall without undue delay and, where feasible, not later than 72 hours after having become aware of it, notify the personal data breach to the supervisory authority competent in accordance with Article 55, unless the personal data breach is unlikely to result in a risk to the rights and freedoms of natural persons. Where the notification to the supervisory authority is not made within 72 hours, it shall be accompanied by reasons for the delay.*"

The controller has 72 hours, from the point at which the controller became aware of the breach, to report the personal data breach. It is, therefore, important to note when this happens and any procedures addressing personal data breaches must ensure that the timings of events are noted. When the controller reports the personal data breach to the Information Commissioner, or another supervisory authority, the controller will have to provide this information, so this is another reason for noting the time.

8.4.3.2 WP 250 rev.01 accepts that an unverified concern that there may have been a personal data breach is not the same thing as knowledge of a breach. It considers that:

"*... a controller should be regarded as having become 'aware' when that controller has a reasonable degree of certainty that a security*

> *incident has occurred that has led to personal data being compromised"* (p.11);

and that

> "*. . . the controller may undertake a short period of investigation in order to establish whether or not a breach has in fact occurred*" (p.11).

However, this period of investigation needs to be brief: the GDPR places a responsibility on organisations to have the technical and organisational measures in place so as to be able to respond to breaches and to make this determination promptly. This is emphasised by rec.87, which states:

> "*It should be ascertained whether all appropriate technological protection and organisational measures have been implemented to establish immediately whether a personal data breach has taken place and to inform promptly the supervisory authority and the data subject*".

8.4.3.3 There are useful worked examples in WP 250 rev.01:

"1. *In the case of a loss of a USB key with unencrypted personal data it is often not possible to ascertain whether unauthorised persons gained access to that data. Nevertheless, . . . such a case has to be notified as there is a reasonable degree of certainty that an availability breach has occurred: the controller would become 'aware' when it realised the USB key had been lost.*
2. *A third party informs a controller that they have accidentally received the personal data of one of its customers and provides evidence of the unauthorised disclosure. As the controller has been presented with clear evidence of a confidentiality breach then there can be no doubt that it has become 'aware'.*
3. *A controller detects that there has been a possible intrusion into its network. The controller checks its systems to establish whether personal data held on that system has been compromised and confirms this is the case. Once again, as the controller now has clear evidence of a breach there can be no doubt that it has become 'aware'.*
4. *A cybercriminal contacts the controller after having hacked its system in order to ask for a ransom. In that case, after checking its system to confirm it has been attacked the controller has clear evidence that a breach has occurred and there is no doubt that it has become aware*" (p.11).

Risk

8.4.3.4 A controller does not have to report where the personal data breach is "*unlikely to result in a risk to the rights and freedoms of individuals*". The provisions at art.34 dealing with notice to data subjects give the example of encryption (if effectively deployed) as a measure which may effectively protect personal data so that there is no need to notify individuals. WP 250 rev.01 gives the same example when discussing notification to supervisory authorities (p.19), stating:

> "*A breach that would not require notification to the supervisory authority would be the loss of a securely encrypted mobile device, utilised by the controller and its staff. Provided the encryption key remains within the secure possession of the controller and this is not the sole copy of the personal data then the personal data would be inaccessible to an attacker. This means the breach is unlikely to result in a risk to the rights and freedoms of the data subjects in question. If it later becomes evident that the encryption key was compromised or that the encryption software or algorithm is vulnerable, then the risk to the rights and freedoms of natural persons will change and thus notification may now be required*".

There is further consideration of risk at **8.4.4.1** below.

Delayed reporting

8.4.3.5 In the immediate aftermath of a suspected personal data breach, a controller will be busy trying to remedy the breach, as well as gathering the information needed to report to the Information Commissioner. The words "where feasible" and "without undue delay" will come as a relief to many. In fact, the GDPR also adds (art.33(4):

> "*Where, and in so far as, it is not possible to provide the information at the same time, the information may be provided in phases without undue further delay.*"

8.4.3.6 In other words, the controller must communicate as much of the information required as possible within 72 hours of discovering a data breach, and may continue to pass further information to the Commissioner as and when it comes to light. WP 250 rev.01 suggests (p.16) that this may be particularly useful where a controller experiences multiple breaches over a short period of time, where the breaches are similar in the nature of the data and the impact on individuals, but where there are different causes. Here the Working Party suggests that the controller may need time to investigate the extent of the breaches and may choose to make one, more meaningful, notification. The Working Party does note that if the breaches were *not* similar (so if they concerned different types of personal data, breached in different ways), then notifications should not be bundled and should proceed in the normal way.

To whom does the controller report?

8.4.3.7 For many readers, the answer will be straightforward: the Information Commissioner. However, if the personal data breach affects "cross-border processing" then the answer is more complex. "Cross-border processing" is processing of personal data which either:

1) takes place in the context of multiple EU establishments of the controller or processor, or
2) only takes place in the context of the activities of one establishment, but which could substantially affect data subjects in more than one Member State.

Where there is cross-border processing, the controller must notify its "lead supervisory authority" (**1.4.3.2**), which is determined by looking at where its "main establishment" is. These points are considered at **1.4.3** and **9.5.5.21**. If a controller does not have an EU establishment, then it should have appointed a "representative" in an EU Member State (**2.2.5**). In this case, WP 250 rev.01 suggests that the controller notify the supervisory authority in the Member State where the representative is based (p.18).

How to report in the UK

8.4.3.8 Controllers can either report by phone (the number is currently 0303 123 1113) —suitable if the controller would like advice from the Information Commissioner's staff (and does not mind what can often be a long queue)—or online (form available at *https://ico.org.uk/for-organisations/report-a-breach/personal-data-breach* [Accessed 8 May 2019]). There is a separate link for NHS bodies to report breaches, via the Data Security and Protection Incident Reporting Tool.

Article 33 mandates that notice of a data breach should "at least":

"*(a) describe the nature of the personal data breach including where possible, the categories and approximate number of data subjects concerned and the categories and approximate number of personal data records concerned;*
(b) communicate the name and contact details of the data protection officer or other contact point where more information can be obtained;
(c) describe the likely consequences of the personal data breach;
(d) describe the measures taken or proposed to be taken by the controller to address the personal data breach, including, where appropriate, measures to mitigate its possible adverse effects."

8.4.3.9 In practice, the Commissioner requires more information. For example, the personal data breach report form asks organisations for the following information:

- if this is an initial report or follow up report (if the latter, then the ICO case reference number should be provided);
- what has happened;
- if the breach was caused by a cyber incident (and if yes, whether confidentiality, integrity and/or availability of systems has been affected, the impact on the organisation and the recovery times);

- how and when the breach was discovered and when the breach happened (date and time are required);
- what categories of personal data were included (special category data must be listed; as must identifiers and identification data, economic and financial data, official documents, location data, genetic or biometric data and conviction and offence data);
- numbers of affected records and affected data subjects;
- categories of data subjects (for example, employees, customers);
- potential consequences of the breach;
- whether it is very likely, likely, neutral, unlikely, very unlikely or unknown whether individuals will experience significant consequences;
- whether individuals involved in the breach have received data protection training in the past two years;
- if there has been a delay in reporting, why;
- what remedial actions have been taken;
- whether data subjects have been notified;
- whether other organisations have been notified (e.g. other regulators or the police);
- information about the organisation reporting including contact details for the data protection officer or other senior person responsible for the incident.

8.4.3.10 There is also a mechanism for a follow-up report which, in particular, should describe any measures in place before the breach with the aim of preventing a breach of this nature. The ICO may also have asked for additional information on receipt of the original notification. For NHS organisations, the ICO has a separate procedure called the Data Security and Protection Incident Reporting Tool. Health and social care organisations should have registered for the Data Security and Protection Toolkit.

8.4.4 Notification of personal data breaches to data subjects

8.4.4.1 Article 34 sets out the obligations here. The obligation to communicate with data subjects arises only where:

"*the data breach is likely to result in a high risk to the rights and freedoms of data subjects*" (art.34(1)).

8.4.4.2 Under art.34(3), even then the controller need not communicate the data breach to the data subjects if any of the following apply:

"*(a) the controller has implemented appropriate technical and organisational protection measures, and those measures were applied to the personal data affected by the personal data breach, in particular those that render the personal data unintelligible to any person who is not authorised to access it, such as encryption;*

(b) the controller has taken subsequent measures which ensure that the high risk to the rights and freedoms of data subjects referred to in paragraph 1 is no longer likely to materialise;

(c) it would involve disproportionate effort. In such a case, there shall instead be a public communication or similar measure whereby the data subjects are informed in an equally effective manner."

This last point applies if the numbers of data subjects are huge and contacting them individually is impossible. The threshold for notification to data subjects is, therefore, higher than for notification to supervisory authorities—reflecting the fact that, as the Information Commissioner noted in guidance under the 1998 Act, *Guidance on data security breach management* (version 2.1, 12 December 2012), there is a danger in 'over notifying'.

8.4.4.3 In order to determine whether to notify individuals and/or data subjects, therefore, the controller must consider the risk posed by the personal data breach. WP 250 rev.01 devotes considerable space to looking at questions of risk assessment. There is also a useful annex to WP 250 rev.01 (pp.31–33) with worked examples. First, it reminds readers that if a DPIA (**13.6**) was carried out in relation to the processing, then risk would have been considered there: documentation relating to DPIAs should, therefore, remain accessible and should be consulted. Second, WP 250 rev.01 suggests that controllers consider (pp.24–25):

- the type of breach (e.g. a confidentiality breach will pose different risks to an availability breach);
- the nature, sensitivity and volume of personal data; the ease with which individuals could be identified (if identification is very difficult, this will affect risk);
- the severity of the consequences for individuals (including whether the data is in the hands of a malicious actor, or a trusted individual);
- any special characteristics of the individual (e.g. any particular vulnerabilities) or of the controller (e.g. a data breach involving a medical organisation may pose a higher risk than a breach involving the subscription list of a newspaper);
- the number of affected individuals; and any other relevant factors.

8.4.4.4 Recital 85 is also relevant in assessing the types of risk posed by a data breach—stating that a personal breach may result in:

"... *physical, material, or non-material damage to natural persons such as loss of control over their personal data or limitation of their rights, discrimination, identity theft or fraud, financial loss, unauthorised reversal of pseudonymisation, damage to reputation, loss of confidentiality of personal data protected by professional secrecy or any other significant economic or social disadvantage to the natural person concerned* ...".

8.4.4.5 The comments in WP 250 rev.01 about the nature of any third party who has, or had, access to the personal data, are interesting. WP 250 rev.01 notes (p.25) that:

"*This may occur, for example, where personal data is sent accidentally to the wrong department of an organisation, or to a commonly used supplier organisation. The controller may request the recipient to either return or securely destroy the data it has received. In both cases, given that the controller has an ongoing relationship with them, and it may be aware of their procedures, history and other relevant details, the recipient may be considered 'trusted'. In other words, the controller may have a level of assurance with the recipient so that it can reasonably expect that party not to read or access the data sent in error, and to comply with its instructions to return it. Even if the data has been accessed, the controller could still possibly trust the recipient not to take any further action ... In such cases, this may be factored into the risk assessment the controller carries out following the breach – the fact that the recipient is trusted may eradicate the severity of the consequences of the breach ... this in turn may remove the likelihood of risk ... thus no longer requiring notification* ...".

8.4.4.6 A controller should not be blasé about such incidents: they are still personal data breaches and care should be taken to try and prevent them (for example, by more secure messaging processes). However, the comments in WP 250 rev.01 are extremely helpful in avoiding the need to notify every internal misaddressed email.

8.4.4.7 Where there is an obligation to communicate with the data subjects, art.34(2) says the breach and its implications must be described in clear and plain language and the controller must provide a contact point for data subjects, explain the likely consequences of the breach, any remedial measures, and any recommended ways whereby the data subjects can themselves mitigate the effect of the breach—e.g. by changing their password.

8.4.4.8 Where a controller has not communicated information about the breach to the data subjects, the Commissioner, under art.34(4),

"*having considered the likelihood of the personal data breach resulting in a high risk, may require it* [the controller] *to do so or may decide that any of the conditions referred to in para 3 are met*" (the conditions in **8.4.4.2** above).

8.4.4.9 In some cases, a controller may have involved law enforcement agencies in a breach and may have been asked by them not to notify individuals, because this could prejudice ongoing investigations. This is anticipated by the GDPR, where rec.86 notes that communications with data subjects should be made "*in close co-operation with the supervisory authority, respecting guidance provided by it or by other relevant authorities such as law-enforcement authorities*".

Processors and joint controllers

8.4.4.10 So far, we have only considered the reporting obligations on controllers. In relation to processors, art.33(2) says: "*The processor shall notify the controller without undue delay after becoming aware of a personal data breach*".

Such a provision must be catered for by an appropriate condition in the processor contract (art.28(3)(f) **13.7.4**). Processors should note that, whereas controllers have to consider the risk posed by the breach before they report, there is no such qualification for processors, who, by implication therefore should seem to report all breaches, so that the controller is able to take a decision on risk. Reporting of every incident in this way may be difficult both for the processor and the controller: this may be an area where the parties wish to agree certain parameters in the contract, for example, requiring periodic reporting of incidents which fall within certain low risk parameters.

8.4.4.11 WP 250 rev.01 suggests (p.13) that the controller will be considered to be "aware" of the breach once the processor has informed it of the breach. The controller should, therefore, ensure that any notices provided under the terms of a contract with a processor are passed on promptly to the appropriate person internally: a dedicated point of contact for breach reports would be advisable for all but the smallest organisations. The GDPR does not specifically address the position of joint controllers. However, WP 250 rev.01 suggests that the usual provisions for joint controllers should apply: namely, the "arrangement" between the joint controllers should determine which controller will take the lead on, or be responsible for, breach reporting (p.13)—see also **13.7.5**.

Record keeping

8.4.4.12 Even if a breach does not have to be reported to the Commissioner because it is unlikely to pose a risk to data subjects, the controller must still keep a record of the breach. Article 33(5) says:

> "*The controller shall document any personal data breaches, comprising the facts relating to the personal data breach, its effects and the remedial action taken. That documentation shall enable the supervisory authority to verify compliance with this Article.*"

The rationale for this documentation is presumably so that the organisation can see if there is a pattern to breaches, which should be remedied, and to allow the

Commissioner to see this—and to check if the organisation is taking the right decision as to when breaches should be reported and when they need not be reported.

8.4.4.13 The GDPR does not specify for how long such records should be retained. The obligation to keep a record of personal data breaches is also found in the older provisions addressing breach reporting by providers of public electronic communications services (**8.4.5**). Here, the Commissioner's guidance on *Notification of PECR security breaches* (v.2.2) states that the Commissioner will keep these logs for two years, although providers may need to keep them longer for their own business purposes (para.46). This suggests that a retention period of at least two years is advisable.

Involving the data protection officer (DPO)

8.4.4.14 The provisions at arts 33 and 34 do not state that the controller, or processor, has to involve any data protection officer (**13.2**) in personal data breaches. However, as WP 250 rev.01 notes (pp.27 and 28) this would clearly be advisable: there is a general obligation to involve the DPO in "*all issues which relate to the processing of personal data*" (art.38(1)). Furthermore, the DPO is to be the point of contact for individuals and supervisory authorities and their details must be included in any notice to supervisory authorities or individuals. Involving the DPO at an early stage would, therefore, be advisable.

Sanctions for not reporting personal data breaches

8.4.4.15 Failure to report a personal data breach—either to the Information Commissioner or to individuals—could attract a penalty of up to 2% of worldwide turnover, or €10 million whichever is the higher (art.83(4)(a); see also **3.4.3.31**). WP 250 rev.01 pp.9–10 notes that failure to report a breach could be indicative of other failings—for example, a failure of underlying security measures and, in that case, a supervisory authority could fine both for the failure in security measures and for the failure to notify the breach. There is a good example of a fine for late breach reporting under the 1998 Act: Uber was fined £385,000 by the Information Commissioner over a data breach—and one of the factors contributing to the size of the fine was the fact that Uber delayed reporting the incident to those affected for a year (*https://ico.org.uk/about-the-ico/news-and-events/news-and-blogs/2018/11/ico-fines-uber-385-000-over-data-protection-failings* [Accessed 8 May 2019]).

8.4.5 Breach notification: communications service providers

8.4.5.1 As mentioned at **3.4.1.3, 8.4.1.2** and **8.4.4.13**, the PECR contain express obligations requiring public electronic communications service providers to keep a log of and to notify personal data breaches. The log must contain:

- the facts surrounding the breach;

- the effects of that breach; and
- remedial action taken.

8.4.5.2 The record-keeping and notification requirements are very similar to those under the GDPR. This is not surprising as the GDPR took account of lessons learned under this regime. The main differences are:

- all breaches have to be reported to the Information Commissioner (there is no risk threshold);
- the timescales for reports are faster—24 hours; and
- the threshold for reporting to individuals is lower—reports should be made if they will be adversely affected, as opposed to the GDPR standard of 'high risk'.

8.4.5.3 The obligation to report *all* breaches to the Information Commissioner, irrespective of seriousness and irrespective of use of technical protection measures, is clearly impractical for providers and the Commissioner alike. Accordingly, the Commissioner's guidance contains some more practical suggestions:

- first, a comment that the Commissioner will be unlikely to take action over any failure to report breaches where personal data has been effectively protected by encryption (p.6);
- secondly, a statement that the Commissioner "accepts" that it will not be feasible to report all breaches in 24 hours, with follow up within three days (para.26); and
- thirdly, a suggestion that providers send in their breach reports on a monthly basis, even though this is not required by the PECR (para.43).

The Commissioner has a standard form and breach notification email address for providers.

8.4.5.4 Lastly, a provider who fails to comply with the requirements to notify breaches, is at risk of a fixed monetary penalty of £1,000 from the Information Commissioner.

Other reporting obligations

8.4.5.5 Readers should note that there are now a multitude of security incident reporting obligations. For personal data, there are the obligations under the GDPR and the PECR described above. For law enforcement authorities, there are also separate obligations on notifying data breaches to the Commissioner and/or data subjects in DPA 2018 ss.67–68 (considered at **15.1**).

8.4.5.6 Some organisations may also be subject to breach reporting obligations linked to the nature of their business, rather than to personal data. Operators of essential services or digital service providers have reporting obligations under the NIS Directive, and providers of trust services, have reporting obligations under the eIDAS Regulation (**1.3.8.1**). Regulated financial service providers may have to notify the Financial Conduct Authority—and there can also be contractual obligations—for example for insurers, professional bodies, or providers of payment cards or payment processing services. The ICO's guidance on breach reporting contains a useful summary of where such obligations occur. Organisations should ensure that they know the obligations which will be applicable to them: as a matter of law, professional obligations, or contract.

8.4.6 Compliance by organisations

8.4.6.1 All this results in a major undertaking for controllers and communications service providers organisations. To comply we suggest they must:

- establish a team (the breach team) to deal generally with incidents and notices under the GDPR, the PECR or other requirements and in particular to act swiftly in the event of a data breach. Notifications have to be "without undue delay" and often within specified time limits;
- the breach team must work closely with (or even be part of) the organisation's IT security team, and know and understand all the existing security measures and be able to suggest ways in which they may be improved;
- the breach team must understand any immediate requirements and points of contact—for example, if there is a need to involve law enforcement agencies, this should be done at an early stage, in case this affects later conduct of the matter; if the organisation has insurance, insurers should also be involved at an early stage, as the policy may have restrictions on choice of legal advisers or other specialist service providers;
- if external consultants are to be involved, then the organisation should consider if they should be instructed by lawyers, with a view to obtaining advice on potential claims and litigation—which may be protected by privilege (**10.4.1.1**);
- The breach team will need to familiarise themselves with guidance from the Information Commissioner and WP 250 rev.01;
- they must enable the Commissioner on demand to audit their security arrangements;
- they must set up the record of personal data breaches;
- notifying the Commissioner is one thing, but the breach team will also need to establish how all or a significant number of data subjects can be notified. Can it be by email, bearing in mind that most anti-spam software quickly suppresses all messages to large numbers of recipients? There is also a risk that sending notices of this kind by e-mail, may increase the credibility

of scam-emails sent to individuals, which purport to advise of a security breach (typically at a bank) but which in reality are phishing exercises, trying to persuade individuals to reply with valuable personal data. If the organisation deals with individuals in multiple countries, then translations will also be required—as may call-centres. For large organisations, it may be helpful to have contracts in place ahead of time with specialist service providers who can guarantee capacity and turnaround times in the event of a significant incident;

- a further point outside the regulations needs to be addressed. A breach by a service provider could be a major event and one which would attract a lot of adverse publicity. The breach team should consider the publicity aspects and have in place mechanisms to ensure they work swiftly and efficiently with the organisation's publicity people;
- lastly, as with all crisis response mechanisms, the breach team should test its arrangements ahead of time.

CHAPTER 9
Data Transfer

9.1 THE RESTRICTION ON DATA TRANSFERS

9.1.1 Many organisations—even quite small businesses—will transfer personal data overseas, especially if they make use of cloud computing, or software as-a-service solutions, where the organisation's personal data is processed by a third party, often in a data centre in another country. If the data is transferred outside the European Economic Area (EEA) (which comprises the Member States of the EU together with Norway, Iceland and Liechtenstein), the data transfer restrictions in arts.44 – 49 of the GDPR are relevant. (We discuss the difference between the EU and the EEA at **1.4.1.4**). The eurospeak term for such non-EEA jurisdictions is "third country".

9.1.2 The GDPR recognises that data transfers are important commercially—but insists that this should not be at the expense of appropriate protection for the data. Accordingly, arts 45–49 set out rules for data transfer. The basic principle is set out in rec.91 and art.44 which provide as follows:

> "*Flows of personal data to and from countries outside the Union and international organisations are necessary for the expansion of international trade and international co-operation. . . . However, when personal data are transferred from the Union to controllers, processors or other recipients in third countries, or to international organisations, the level of protection of natural persons in the Union by this Regulation should not be undermined . . .*" (rec.91)
> "*Any transfer of personal data which are undergoing processing or are intended for processing after transfer to a third country or to an international organisation shall take place only if, subject to the other provisions of this Regulation, the conditions laid down in this Chapter are complied with by the controller and processor, including for onward transfers of personal data . . .*" (art.44).

The Chapter referred to is Ch.V of the GDPR, comprising arts 44–50.

9.1.3 Before looking at the provisions in arts 45–47 which set out the conditions under which transfers can be made, or art.49 which sets out derogations (i.e. exemptions) to the restriction on data transfers, it is important to realise just how broad the restriction is and how many types of data transfer it covers.

9.2 TYPES OF DATA TRANSFER

9.2.1 The data protection professional must be alert to the fact that personal data can be transferred in many different ways. The data protection audit should reveal what types of personal data an organisation transfers, to which countries, and why. The most obvious way in which personal data is transferred outside the EU, is where there is a bulk transfer of data on a regular basis. This will happen if, for example, an organisation is part of a larger corporate group that processes all its human resources data in the US because the HR application is stored on servers in the US. Organisations may also make bulk transfers of personal data outside the EU, where they use a data processor that is located elsewhere. A typical example here would be an organisation that has appointed a Canadian company to carry out all its bulk email marketing on its behalf. In order for this arrangement to work, the organisation will transfer its email marketing lists to the Canadian supplier on a regular basis. Back-up arrangements are often in countries in other time-zones to take advantage of cheap power and low competing usage on the servers or other equipment to which the data is sent.

9.2.2 An organisation is also likely to transfer personal data if it posts personal data on the Internet, or on an intranet, that is, or is intended to be, accessed from outside the EU. This would, for example, cover organisations which put biographies of key individuals on their websites. The impact of the data transfer principle on the internet has been considered by the CJEU in the case of ***Bodil Lindqvist*** (C-101/01) EU:C:2003:596; [2004] Q.B. 1014. The case concerned a member of a Swedish Church, who set up web pages with information about the Church, information about Mrs Lindqvist herself and about some of her fellow parishioners (including the fact that one was on medical leave with an injured foot). Mrs Lindqvist had not notified her colleagues about the web pages or obtained their consent. The CJEU held, unsurprisingly, that the information posted included personal data, and the item about the injured foot was special category personal data. It also considered whether the posting of the information on the web pages would automatically involve a transfer of personal data outside the EU. Mrs Lindqvist used a Swedish company to host the pages: in this situation the Court concluded that the mere accessibility of the information in a third country would not amount to a "data transfer".

9.2.3 The fact that Mrs Lindqvist used a Swedish company to host the web pages and that the site was aimed at the local community means that the case is of limited application. If Mrs Lindqvist had used a company outside the EU to host the website, or if the website was designed to have more international appeal, then the outcome could have been different. This is the approach taken in the Information Commissioner's *Guide* which notes:

> "*If you load personal data onto a UK server which is then available through a website, and you plan or anticipate that the website may be accessed from outside the EEA, you should treat this as a restricted transfer*".

9.2.4 The *Guide* has other examples of what will—and will not—be a transfer. For example, art.44 applies to data "*which are intended for processing after transfer*"—as the Commissioner notes:

> "*You are making a restricted transfer if you collect information about individuals on paper, which is not ordered or structured in any way, and you send this to a service company located outside of the EEA to:*
> - *put into digital form; or*
> - *add to a highly structured manual filing system relating to individuals.*
>
> *Example:*
> *A UK insurance broker sends a set of notes about individual customers to a company in a non-EEA country. These notes are handwritten and are not stored on computer or in any particular order. The non-EEA company adds the notes to a computer customer management system. This is a restricted transfer*".

9.2.5 The restriction does not, however, prohibit transfers of personal data where the data physically passes outside the EU, but where no substantive processing operation is performed on the data. In other words, "transfer" does not mean the same as "transit". For example, if one individual in the UK sends an email to another individual in the UK, the sender has no control over the route by which the email will travel. The email may well be routed through the US or other non-EU countries. The Commissioner makes clear that

> "*... If personal data is just electronically routed through a non-EEA country but the transfer is actually from one EEA country to another EEA country, then it is not a restricted transfer*".

The clarification can be less useful than it appears at first sight. For example, an organisation may have its email server in Japan, so that all emails transit through Japan. However, if the organisation also has an email archiving or journaling system, whereby emails passing through the server are copied and stored, then this would count as substantive processing and so transfer, not transit. The organisation would need to assess how to justify this, based on the options below.

9.2.6 Lastly, but perhaps most importantly, the Information Commissioner takes the view that the GDPR only applies to what the Commissioner calls "restricted transfers"—that is, transfers to a person outside the EU and to whom the GDPR does not apply. It is implicit from this that if the legislation *does* apply to the recipient, that the transfer is not restricted, and the considerations described in this chapter do not apply. This would be the case if, for example, a company and its parent company, both offer goods and services to individuals in the EU—so that the legislation applies directly to the parent company (**2.2.1.21**). If the company transfers customer data to the parent, then this would not be a restricted transfer, since the parent is already subject to the legislation. Thus, the transfer is not considered as being from the EU to an unregulated jurisdiction, but from one entity regulated by the GDPR to another GDPR-regulated entity. The Commissioner's *Guide* states:

> "*You are making a restricted transfer if:*
> - *the GDPR applies to your processing of the personal data you are transferring.... In general, the GDPR applies if you are processing personal data in the EEA, and may apply in specific circumstances if you are outside the EEA and processing personal data about individuals in the EEA;*
> - *you are sending personal data, or making it accessible, to a receiver to which the GDPR does not apply, usually because they are located in a country outside the EEA; and*
> - *the receiver is a separate organisation or individual. The receiver cannot be employed by you or by your company. It can be a company in the same group*".

9.2.7 Where an organisation wishes to transfer personal data overseas, there can be a temptation to focus straight away on arts 44–49. However, before we move on and look at how personal data can be transferred, we must emphasise that meeting data transfer requirements is only one element of compliance: when considering data transfers, the data protection professional must ensure that they do not overlook the need to ensure that the transfers meet the other requirements of the legislation. For example, is it necessary to transfer the data at all (privacy by design **13.8.2**); if the transfer is to a controller, what is the lawful basis for the transfer? (**4.1**); what have individuals been told about the transfer (transparency **6.4.5**); and has the transfer been documented (**13.5.1.2**). If the organisation transferring the data is a processor, has the controller instructed (or authorised) the processor to make the transfer (**9.4.5.4, 13.1.1.4**) and do the processor's records of processing reflect the transfer (**13.5.1.2**).

9.2.8 The remainder of this chapter looks at how personal data can be transferred outside the EU in compliance with the legislation. Many of the rules in the GDPR were influenced by one case—***Schrems v Data Protection Commissioner & Digital Rights Ireland*** (C-362/14) EU:C:2015:627—so we start with a summary of that case before looking at the rules in more detail.

9.3 THE *SCHREMS* CASE

9.3.1 At the time of the case, Mr Maximillian Schrems was an Austrian law student. He had been a Facebook user since 2008. As a Facebook user based in Austria, Mr Schrems' contract for use of Facebook was with Facebook's Ireland establishment, safely within the EU. However, data from Facebook Ireland was transferred to and processed by Facebook Inc in the US (outside the EU). The EU Commission has the power to identify aspects of non-EU jurisdictions as being sufficiently compliant with EU data protection legislation, such that transfers can safely be made to such approved jurisdictions. Facebook Inc participated in the EU–US Safe Harbor programme (an adequacy agreement between the EU Commission and the US authorities, explained below at **9.4.2**) and relied on this to provide adequate protection for the transferred EU data. Mr Schrems complained to the Irish Data Protection Commissioner about this transfer of personal data; he asked the Commissioner to suspend this transfer of personal data, citing in particular the revelations made by Edward Snowden about the activities of the US intelligence services. The Irish Commissioner declined to investigate—on the basis that the Commission's Safe Harbor decision left him no remit to reach any conclusion about the adequacy of the Safe Harbor arrangement. Mr Schrems challenged the Commissioner's decision via the High Court, which noted that the essence of Mr Schrems' complaint was that Safe Harbor itself was unsatisfactory—a view which the Irish High Court shared—and which therefore referred to the European Court the question of whether a supervisory authority (the Irish Data Protection Commissioner) was absolutely bound by the Commission decision, or whether the authority could or should undertake its own investigation of the matter.

9.3.2 The CJEU decision concluded that Commission's adequacy decisions could not exclude supervisory authorities such as the Irish Commissioner from having oversight over data transfers [54]; the Commission's Safe Harbor decision purported to do this and was therefore invalid [92]–[94]; in addition, an adequacy decision must contain reasoned findings concluding that a third country in fact ensures adequate protection for personal data, either by reason of its domestic law or international commitments, in a way which is essentially equivalent to the protections guaranteed in the EU [96]; the Commission's Safe Harbor decision did not state that the US ensured an adequate level of protection and for this reason also was invalid [98].

9.3.3 In addition to—at a stroke—invalidating one of the main methods used by organisations to transfer data to the US, the CJEU judgment also made a number of other comments relevant to future adequacy decisions. These are as follows:

- if a person makes a claim to a supervisory authority in relation to an adequacy decision, the authority has to be able to consider that claim [54];
- ultimately, only the CJEU has the authority to determine that an adequacy decision is invalid—accordingly, such a claim may lead to a reference to the CJEU for it to take a decision [64]–[65];
- the law in the third country has to be considered either by reference to domestic law or to the international commitments given by the country and this has to be "essentially equivalent" to the protections in the European Union [73], although the mechanisms used to protect data may be different [74];
- the level of protection may change over time so there is an obligation on the Commission to keep decisions under review [76]–[77];

- the Commission's discretion when reviewing adequacy is limited and should be applied in a strict manner [78];
- self-certification is not, per se, inconsistent with adequacy. However, the reliability of such a system will depend on effective detection and supervision mechanisms [81];
- Safe Harbor was limited solely to commercial organisations—public authorities did not have to comply with the Safe Harbor principles [82] and Safe Harbor also stated that its principles would be limited if required for national security interests [84]; however, the Commission decision did not make any findings about the rules relevant in these cases [88]–[89] and the Commission's own later papers suggested that the US rules were deficient as there was no means of redress for EU individuals [90]; and
- legislation which permits public authorities to have access to the content of electronic communications on a generalised basis must be regarded as compromising the essence of the right to respect for private life [94] and legislation which provides no possibility for legal remedies does not respect the essence of the fundamental right to judicial protection [95].

9.3.4 Having looked at the ***Schrems*** decision, we can now turn to look at how and when the GDPR permits data transfers. The GDPR anticipates

- transfers covered by an "adequacy decision" (art.45);
- transfers where appropriate safeguards are in place (art.46), which may include binding corporate rules (art.47);
- transfers which use an exemption ("derogation") for a specific situation.

9.3.5 The GDPR sets out a hierarchy for addressing data transfers: adequacy decisions apply first; appropriate safeguards can be used where there is no adequacy decision; lastly if there is no adequacy decision or appropriate safeguard then derogation may be considered. We have followed this structure.

9.4 ADEQUACY DECISIONS

9.4.1 Introduction

9.4.1.1 Organisations may transfer personal data to a recipient in a country in respect of which there is a formal decision that the country offers adequate protection. The GDPR provides that the European Commission will make this decision. Article 45(1) provides that:

> "*A transfer of personal data to a third country or an international organisation may take place where the Commission has decided that the third country, a territory or one or more specified sectors within that third country, or the*

international organisation in question ensures an adequate level of protection. Such a transfer shall not require any specific authorisation".

9.4.1.2 Article 45(8) provides that the Commission has to publish—both in the *Official Journal* and on its website—a list of such adequacy decisions and art.45(9) provides that adequacy decisions taken under the equivalent provision of Directive 95/46/EC remain valid unless and until they are amended, replaced or repealed. The Commission list of adequacy decisions is available at *https://ec.europa.eu/info/law/law-topic/data-protection/data-transfers-outside-eu/adequacy-protection-personal-data-non-eu-countries_en* [Accessed 8 May 2019].

9.4.1.3 At the date of writing, Commission adequacy decisions are in place in relation to: Andorra, Argentina, Canada (but only in respect of organisations to whom Canada's Personal Information Protection and Electronic Documents Act (PIPEDA) applies), Faroe Islands, Guernsey, Israel, Isle of Man, Japan, Jersey, New Zealand, Switzerland, Uruguay and the United States Privacy Shield Framework (**9.4.2**). These countries are collectively often described as White List countries. The Commission is in talks with South Korea about such a decision.

9.4.2 Privacy Shield

9.4.2.1 The EU–US Privacy Shield replaced Safe Harbor, which was invalidated by the CJEU in the ***Schrems*** case. The European Commission decision on Privacy Shield was adopted on 12 July 2016 (Commission Implementing Decision (EU) 2016/1250 of 12 July 2016 pursuant to Directive 95/46/EC of the European Parliament and of the Council on the adequacy of the protection provided by the EU-US Privacy Shield, OJ L207, 1 August 2016). The Privacy Shield consists of a series of principles, which participating organisations commit to follow. These principles include recourse, enforcement and liability mechanisms—including a commitment to arbitration. The Commission decision also takes account of commitments given by the US Department of Commerce (which administers the scheme in the US) and correspondence from the US, explaining enforcement mechanisms and safeguards, limitations and practices relating to national security, signals intelligence, law enforcement and public interest purposes. The full Commission decision runs to 112 pages, but the principles can be read more easily on the US Department of Commerce's site: *https://www.privacyshield.gov/EU-US-Framework [Accessed 8 Mary 2019].*

9.4.2.2 The Privacy Shield only covers organisations which have chosen to join the framework by self-certifying their compliance, making a public commitment to comply and being accepted by the US Department of Commerce. There is a parallel framework which applies to transfers of personal data from Switzerland to the US. Organisations can participate in the EU–US shield, the Swiss–US shield, or both. Organisations can decide to participate for all, or just some, of their data processing (for example, an organisation could decide to participate just in respect of its HR data processing, or just in respect of data collected online). The first thing an organisation must do, therefore, when wanting to transfer personal data in reliance on the Privacy Shield, is to check if the recipient is actually on the list of participants and if the scope of the recipient's participation matches what the organisation needs. The list includes details about the scope of the participant's involvement (i.e. EU and/or Swiss and types of personal data) and is available at *https://www.privacyshield.gov/list*.

9.4.2.3 The exporting organisation will also need a commitment from the importing organisation to notify it if it ceases to participate in Privacy Shield and, in that case, to put in place alternative arrangements to ensure adequacy which are acceptable to the exporting organisation. The adequacy of the Privacy Shield has already been referred to the CJEU, and we mention below that Privacy Shield is assessed annually as to its continued adequacy, so contractual terms must also deal with the possibility that Privacy Shield itself may disappear. As there is a pending challenge to standard data protection clauses (another method used to transfer personal data, see **9.5.6**), this type of fall-back provision is generally advisable in any agreement relating to the transfer of personal data. There are sample data transfer clauses in **Precedent P4**.

9.4.2.4 As we discuss in **Ch.13**, whenever a controller appoints a processor to process personal data for it, the parties must put in place terms which meet the requirements of art.28 of the GDPR. Organisations which transfer personal data to a processor which participates in Privacy Shield will, of course, also need to do this. This is also made clear in the Privacy Shield framework itself, where supplemental principle 9 reminds that a contract will always be required in this situation.

9.4.2.5 The Privacy Shield was designed to meet the requirements set out by the Court of Justice in the ***Schrems*** case and under Directive 95/46/EC. The Privacy Shield principles, therefore, correlate to the provisions of the, now repealed, Directive and do not address the additional requirements introduced by the GDPR. So, by way of example, there are no provisions in the Privacy Shield relating to parental consent or to data portability. The Privacy Shield will, therefore, have to be amended to take account of these additional requirements.

9.4.2.6 This re-writing of the Privacy Shield, to upgrade it for the GDPR, is not the same as the annual review of the Privacy Shield Framework. Article 4 of the Commission Decision commits the Commission to reviewing the Privacy Shield adequacy decision on an annual basis. The Commission's second review was published on 19 December 2018. It made recommendations for actions but concluded that Privacy Shield was still adequate.

9.4.3 Mechanism for the Commission to make other adequacy decisions

9.4.3.1 The Commission is able to decide that other countries, territories, or sectors within a country, offer 'adequate' protection where the guarantees for personal data which are offered are 'essentially equivalent' to those ensured in the EU (rec.94). Article 45(2) spells out that the Commission (or the Secretary of State) must take account of:

- the relevant laws in that country—this includes data protection rules, but rules concerning public security, defence, national security and criminal law and the ability of public authorities to access data must also be considered, as well as whether there are "*effective and enforceable data subject rights and effective administrative and judicial redress for the data subjects whose personal data are being transferred*";
- rules for the onward transfer of personal data to another third country or international organisation;
- the existence of an effective and functioning independent supervisory authority, which can enforce the rules and can assist data subjects and co-operate with EU supervisory authorities; and
- the international commitments entered into by the country which relates to personal data (which rec.95 notes could include whether the country has acceded to Council of Europe Convention 98 for the Protection of Individuals with regard to the Automatic Processing of Personal Data and the Additional Protocol to that Convention).

These provisions clearly restate the requirements spelt out in the *Schrems* case. On 28 November 2017, the Article 29 Working Party adopted a document intended to give guidance on assessing adequacy (Adequacy Referential (updated), WP 254)).

9.4.3.2 Before the Commission can take an EU adequacy decision, it has to consult the European Data Protection Board (rec.95). A committee, representing the Member States then votes on the proposed decision and (unless any Member State votes against the decision) the Commission can then adopt the decision. This procedure, known as the "examination procedure" is set out in Regulation (EU) No.182/2011. The Commission must monitor developments which could affect adequacy decisions on an ongoing basis (art.45(4)) and must carry out a periodic review of each adequacy decision, on the timescales set out in each adequacy decision (but at least every four years) (art.45(3)). If this review or monitoring process means that a country or territory no longer offers adequate protection, then the Commission must suspend, amend or repeal the decision (art.45(5) and the Commission is able to enter into consultations with third countries to remedy any deficiencies (art.45(6)). If a decision is suspended, amended or repealed, this is stated to be "without retro-active effect" (art.45(5)): in other words, transfers which have already been carried out are not made illegal as a result of any revocation.

9.4.4 Data transfers pursuant to other international agreements

9.4.4.1 Organisations may also transfer personal data outside the EU if the transfer is pursuant to an international agreement entered into by the EU or a Member State. This is referenced in rec.92 which states that:

"*This Regulation is without prejudice to international agreements concluded between the Union and third countries regulating the transfer of personal data*

> *including appropriate safeguards for the data subjects. Member States may conclude international agreements which involve the transfer of personal data to third countries or international organisations, as far as such agreements do not affect this Regulation or any other provisions of Union law and include an appropriate level of protection for the fundamental rights of the data subjects*".

Article 96 further provides that:

> "*International agreements involving the transfer of personal data to third countries or international organisations which were concluded by Member States prior to 24 May 2016, and which comply with Union law as applicable prior to that date, shall remain in force until amended, replaced or revoked*".

9.4.4.2 The EU has entered into agreements with Australia, Canada and the US in relation to the transfer of passenger name records (the airline booking information which carriers require for commercial purposes, but which is also important to detect and prevent serious crime and terrorism). There is also an agreement between the EU and the US relating to the processing and transfer of financial messaging data. More information on these agreements is available at the European Commission website: *https://ec.europa.eu/info/law/law-topic/data-protection/data-transfers-outside-eu/transfer-air-passenger-name-record-data-and-terrorist-finance-tracking-programme_en.*

9.4.4.3 Member State specific agreements would cover agreements to share data with other countries for tax purposes—for example, this would cover the agreement between the UK and the US relating to the US's Foreign Account Tax Compliance Act (FATCA) (*https://www.treasury.gov/resource-center/tax-policy/treaties/Documents/FATCA-Agreement-UK-9-12-2012.pdf*).

9.4.4.4 These agreements must themselves meet the requirements of EU law: the agreement between the EU and Canada relating to the transfer of passenger name record data was, for example, challenged on this basis with the CJEU issuing an Opinion stating that the agreement was incompatible with the Charter of Fundamental Rights of the European Union (26 July 2017, Opinion 1/15).

9.5 APPROPRIATE SAFEGUARDS

9.5.1 Introduction

9.5.1.1 Article 46(1) provides that:

> "*In the absence of a decision pursuant to Article 45(3)* [Commission adequacy decision], *a controller or processor may transfer personal data to a third country or an international organisation only if the controller or processor has provided appropriate safeguards, and on condition that enforceable data subject rights and effective legal remedies for data subjects are available*".

Article 46 then goes on to set out these "appropriate safeguards", which include data transfer agreements and binding corporate rules.

9.5.1.2 Article 46(1) states that these safeguards should only be used "*in the absence of a decision pursuant to Article 45(3) . . .*". If an adequacy decision is in place then these safeguards will not be required. The drafting could also be read as suggesting that, if an adequacy decision is in place, these safeguards are not available—for example, if a recipient participates in Privacy Shield, this should be relied on in preference to either using a data transfer agreement or relying on binding corporate rules if the organisation has those in place.

9.5.1.3 Article 46(1) states that the transfer may take place if there are appropriate safeguards in place "*and on condition that enforceable data subject rights and effective legal remedies for data subjects are available*". The equivalent provision at art.26 of Directive 95/46/EC does not contain this statement, which has clearly been added to reflect the requirement spelled out in ***Schrems*** that there must be effective remedies available to EU individuals whose data has been transferred outside the EU. In the case of transfers to the US, the EU-US Privacy Shield framework included creation of an Ombudsperson Mechanism to investigate complaints from EU individuals about access to their data by US intelligence agencies—the Ombudsperson has this role in relation to transfers generally, not just transfers to Privacy Shield recipients (paras 111–124 of Commission Implementing Decision (EU) 2016/1250).

9.5.2 Safeguards where no supervisory authority authorisation is required

9.5.2.1 Organisations may transfer personal data on the basis of one of the safeguards listed in art.46(2):

a) a legally binding and enforceable agreement between public authorities or public bodies;

b) binding corporate rules (see **9.5.5**);

c) standard data protection clauses adopted by the Commission (**9.5.4**);

d) standard data protection clauses adopted by a supervisory authority and then approved by the Commission;

e) an approved code of conduct pursuant to art.40 plus binding and enforceable commitments from the organisation in the third country to apply these safeguards; or

f) an approved certification mechanism pursuant to art.42, again, together with binding and enforceable commitments from the organisation in the third country to apply these.

The ability to rely on codes of conduct or certification in relation to data transfers is an innovation by comparison to Directive 95/46. Codes and certification are considered further in **Ch.13**. As at the date of writing, no codes or certification schemes have yet been approved.

9.5.3 Safeguards where supervisory authorisation is still required

9.5.3.1 By contrast, if an organisation wishes to use one of the safeguards listed in art.46(3), authorisation from the relevant supervisory authority *is* still required. These safeguards are:

a) contractual clauses between the organisation and the recipient (that is, clauses which have not already been approved as described at **9.5.2** above); or

b) provisions in administrative arrangements between public authorities or public bodies, which include enforceable and effective data subject rights. (The Commissioner's *Guide* (p.237) notes that this is a new option introduced by the GDPR and that, at the date of writing, there are no approved administrative arrangements yet in use. The Commissioner promises more details about this option in due course).

Organisations wishing to avoid potentially time-consuming discussions with supervisory authorities should, therefore, make sure to use pre-approved clauses and these are discussed below.

9.5.4 Standard data protection clauses

9.5.4.1 As mentioned above, art.46(2)(d) allows the Commission to approve standard data protection clauses—sometimes also called standard contractual clauses or model clauses. As a matter of contract law, these require the recipient to provide adequate protection for personal data. Article 26(4) of Directive 95/46/EC contained an equivalent provision and the Commission approved four sets of clauses under this (although one approval has been revoked and organisations can no longer now enter into this set of clauses). The clauses approved by the Commission under Directive 95/46/EC remain valid (art.46(5))(although rec.96 does require the Commission to review them "*within a reasonable time*").

9.5.4.2 One of the main drawbacks to using standard data protection clauses under Directive 95/46/EC was that, in many Member States, the transfer still had to be authorised by that Member State's supervisory authority or a copy of the actual clauses used had to be deposited with the supervisory authority. For organisations operating in many Member States, this quickly became a time-consuming bureaucratic exercise. As art.46(2) provides that these safeguards can be used "*without requiring any specific authorisation*" this procedure is abolished by the GDPR.

9.5.4.3 Readers should note that Directive 95/46/EC referred to these pre-approved transfer agreements as "standard contractual clauses", whereas the GDPR refers to them as "standard data protection clauses", instead using the term "contractual clauses" to mean ad-hoc clauses which have to be approved on a case by case basis by the relevant supervisory authority. Many sources, such as the Europa website, still refer to them as standard contractual clauses, and we have felt obliged to continue to use this term when referring to such websites or other written material. It would have been helpful if the GDPR had continued to use the same terminology as the earlier Directive.

9.5.4.4 For many organisations wishing to transfer personal data outside the EU, to a country which is not "adequate", these standard clauses will often be the best (or often, only) method which can be used to make the transfer lawful. For this reason, we consider these standard data protection clauses in some detail.

9.5.4.5 There are two different "flavours" of clauses. The first is for use when data is transferred from one controller to another (commonly referred to as C2Cs); the second is for use when a controller transfers personal data to a processor located outside the EU (C2Ps). Organisations will need to consider which variety of standard data protection clauses (or standard contractual clauses as the Europa website calls them) is appropriate to them. Where personal information is transferred outside the EU to a service provider, the second type of contractual clauses for processors will probably be appropriate. Where, however, the importer is free to use the personal data for its own purposes, the first standard contractual clauses for controllers should be used.

9.5.4.6 The Commission has issued decisions in relation to four sets of Standard Contractual Clauses (i.e. standard data protection clauses) which can be found at *http://ec.europa.eu/justice/policies/privacy/modelcontracts/index_en.htm.*

C2C	**C2P**
C2C Set I (ref 2001/497/EC)	Old C2P (ref 2002/16/EC) (now repealed)
C2C Set II (ref C 2004/5271)	C2P (ref C 2010/593)

9.5.4.7 The Standard Contractual Clauses all follow a similar structure:

- they oblige the exporting company, inter alia, to confirm that it has complied with national data protection legislation until transfer and to assist with compliance enquiries;
- the clauses then set out obligations on the data importer to comply with EU style data quality obligations and restrictions, to confirm that it is not subject to any local laws that would preclude this, to assist with compliance queries and to submit to audits by the data exporter and the supervisory authority for the Member State in which the exporter is established;
- the clauses also grant third-party rights to data subjects, so that they can enforce certain provisions of the clauses themselves;
- the clauses for data processors do not require the data processor to comply

with all EU-style data quality obligations and restrictions. Instead, there are obligations placed on the processor to comply with the security arrangements specified by the exporter and set out in one of the annexes to the clauses.

Controller to Controller clauses

9.5.4.8.1 The European Commission originally adopted a set of C2C clauses in 2001 (C2C Set I). These original clauses provide that the data exporter must accept joint and several liability with the importer for the way in which the importer uses the personal data. Although the clauses do contain an indemnity from the data importer to cover this liability, the provision often meant that the clauses were not considered suitable for use in arms' length commercial arrangements and C2C Set I has not been widely used because of this. The International Chamber of Commerce, CBI and other business organisations initiated their own form of standard contractual clauses (Set II). On December 27 2004, the EU Commission approved these.

9.5.4.9 One significant difference between Set I and Set II of the C2C standard contractual clauses is the method by which individuals can pursue remedies against the importer and exporter. As mentioned above, in Set I, the exporter is jointly and severally liable with the importer for the importer's use of exported personal data. Set I also allows individuals whose rights have been breached to take action directly against the data importer. By contrast, Set II requires that the data subject must first take action against the data exporter. The data subject is only able to enforce rights against the data importer if the data exporter does not take action within a reasonable period (which Set II suggests, in normal circumstances, would be one month). Under Set II, the data exporter is *not* jointly and severally liable with the data importer for the importer's acts. However, the data exporter is incentivised to carry out appropriate due diligence on the party to whom it transfers personal data. Under clause III(b) a data subject can proceed against a data exporter if the data exporter has failed to use reasonable efforts to determine that the importer is able to satisfy its obligations under the contract and the onus is on the exporter to show that it did make reasonable efforts.

9.5.4.10 These arrangements for liability should now be considered together with the provisions in the GDPR on liability, at art.82. Article 82(4) provides that where more than one controller (or a controller and processor) is involved "*in the same processing*", they can be held liable for the entire damage, recouping compensation paid from the other controller separately. Where parties to the standard contractual clauses are involved in "*the same processing*", therefore, the more preferable terms on liability in the Set II standard contractual clauses are academic, as the GDPR effectively produces the same terms as those set out in the Set I clauses.

9.5.4.11 Another significant difference between Set I and Set II is the ability to derogate from core data protection principles. Both Set I and Set II contain a set of data protection principles, which the data importer has to agree to follow. (As an alternative, the importer could also agree to comply with data protection law which applies in the Member State where the exporter is based or could agree to comply with the provisions of an adequacy decision if the importer is based in that country but is not covered by the decision). However, Set I states (Appendix 2) that:

> "*These data protection principles should be read and interpreted in the light of the provisions (principles and relevant exceptions) of Directive 95/46/EC. They shall apply subject to the mandatory requirements of the national legislation applicable to the data importer which do not go beyond what is necessary in a democratic society on the basis of one of the interests listed in Article 13(1) of Directive 95/46/EC, that is, if they constitute a necessary measure to safeguard national security, defence, public security, the prevention, investigation, detection and prosecution of criminal offences or of breaches of ethics for the regulated professions, an important economic or financial interest of the State or the protection of the data subject or the rights and freedoms of others*".

There is no such statement in the Set II standard contractual clauses – so Set I gives more flexibility to derogate from the principles in appropriate and important cases.

Controller to Processor clauses

9.5.4.12 The Commission adopted a set of Controller to Processor standard contractual clauses in 2002. However, in February 2010, the European Commission adopted a Decision revoking this authorisation and authorising new standard contractual clauses for the transfer of personal data to processors located outside the EU. The Decision applied from May 15 2010. One change introduced by the 2010 C2Ps is to set out a method by which the importing processor may, in some circumstances, sub-contract elements of its processing activities to other processors (sub-processors), also established in third countries (this was not possible under the earlier version). A statement from the Commission said:

> "*According to the newly adopted Decision, where a data importer (processor) intends to subcontract any of its processing operations performed on behalf of the EU data exporter (controller), it must first obtain the prior written consent of the data exporter . . . The written contract will impose the same obligations on the sub-processor as those imposed on the data importer under the standard contractual clauses*".

9.5.4.13 Controller-processor contracts concluded before May 15 2010 remain in full force and effect for as long as the transfers and data processing activities described in the contract remain unchanged and personal data covered by the contract continues to be transferred. Any amendments to the existing contractual arrangement, however, mean that the controller and processor must enter into a new contract on the basis of the 2010 C2Ps.

9.5.4.14 Controllers appointing a processor must also ensure that the contract with the processor meets the requirements of art.28 of the GDPR, in addition to meeting data transfer requirements. The C2P standard contractual clauses were drafted so as to meet the requirements for appointing processors under Directive 95/46/EC. Although they contain most of the provisions required by art.28, they do not contain all of the provisions. Controllers will, therefore, need to include a small number of additional provisions. These are set out in **Precedent P4**.

9.5.4.15 One particular difference between art.28 and the C2P standard contractual clauses is in relation to sub-contracting. Clauses 5(h) and 11(1) of the standard contractual clauses provide that the importer must have notified the exporter as to the existence of the sub-processor and obtained the exporter's written consent to the sub-processing. Article 28(2) of the GDPR also provides that the controller must authorise any sub-processing, but also allows for "general written authorisation", pursuant to which:

> "*the processor shall inform the controller of any intended changes concerning the addition or replacement of other processors, thereby giving the controller the opportunity to object to such changes*".

Changes to the standard contractual clauses

9.5.4.16 Where parties to a data processing agreement have agreed a general authorisation for sub-processing, an equivalent change will need to be agreed to the standard contractual clauses. Standard contractual clauses cannot be used if they are amended (a point stressed on p.235 of the Commissioner's *Guide*). However, rec.99 makes clear that this principle should:

> "*... prevent controllers or processors neither from including the standard data protection clauses in a wider context, such as a contract between the processor and another processor, not from adding other clauses or additional safeguards provided that they do not contradict, directly or indirectly, the standard contractual clauses ... Controllers and processors should be encouraged to provide additional safeguards via contractual commitments that supplement standard protection clauses*".

9.5.4.17 It seems clear that agreeing to a "general authorisation" for sub-processing will be treated as a procedural clarification, rather than an impermissible contradiction of the standard contractual clauses. By way of example, Microsoft includes this 'clarification' to the standard contractual clauses in its terms with enterprise customers—and asked the Article 29 Working Party to confirm that this would be acceptable, which the Working Party did (see *https://www.microsoft.com/en-us/TrustCenter/Compliance/EU-Model-Clauses* and *https://ec.europa.eu/*

justice/article-29/documentation/other-document/files/2014/20140402_microsoft.pdf).

9.5.4.18 All versions of the standard contractual clauses require that the clauses be made available to data subjects on request (for example, see clause 4(c) of the Set I C2C clauses). Accordingly, even though rec.99 suggests that standard contractual clauses could be included in a wider commercial agreement, parties may find it easier to sign them separately, so as to minimise the risk of needing to disclose other commercial terms to individuals.

Challenges to standard contractual clauses

9.5.4.19 We have already read about the challenge brought by Mr. Schrems to the Safe Harbor programme, which led to its invalidation by the CJEU (**9.3**). Following this decision, Facebook (in common with many other businesses who had relied on Safe Harbor) put in place standard contractual clauses to address its data transfers to the US. Mr. Schrems has also complained to the Irish Data Protection Commissioner about the transfers made to Facebook Inc in reliance on the standard contractual clauses, arguing that the factors which led the CJEU to conclude that Safe Harbor was invalid should also mean that the Irish Commissioner should suspend data transfers to the US which are made in reliance on the standard contractual clauses. The Irish High Court considered that the earlier ***Schrems*** decision meant that the CJEU itself should determine the matter and made a reference to the CJEU. A useful summary of the state of the proceedings is available on the Irish Data Protection Commission website at *https://dataprotection.ie/docs/Explanatory-Memoranda-on-the-Litigation-concerning-Standard-Contractual-Clauses/1709.htm*. At the date of writing, the case has not yet been listed for hearing by the CJEU. The case has the potential to be enormously disruptive to business: readers should, therefore, keep the use of standard contractual clauses under review and ensure that, wherever possible, any agreements which include data transfer provisions also include further assurance provisions requiring the parties to work together to suspend data transfers, or put in place alternative protections for personal data, in the event that standard contractual clauses are invalidated (see **Precedent P4**).

9.5.5 Binding corporate rules (BCRs)

9.5.5.1 Binding corporate rules (BCRs) facilitate the transfer of personal data within a group. The group must have legally binding rules addressing data protection and these rules are then revised by supervisory authorities, prior to approval by the European Data Protection Board for those organisations who need their binding corporate rules to be approved across the EU.

9.5.5.2 There are two types of binding corporate rules:

Controller Binding Corporate Rules	Used where the personal data being transferred is the group's 'own' personal data (that is, where entities within the group are controllers for the personal data)
Processor Binding Corporate Rules	To be used where the personal data being transferred is being processed on behalf of one or more controllers outside the group

9.5.5.3 The Commission published a list of organisations whose BCRs were approved under Directive 95/46/EC. This is available at *https://ec.europa.eu/info/law/law-topic/data-protection/data-transfers-outside-eu/binding-corporate-rules_en#listofcompanies* [Accessed 8 May 2019].

Binding corporate rules approved under art.47 will, in due course, presumably be publicised on the decisions page of the European Data Protection Board (EDPB). As at the date of writing, no such decisions have been published.

Requirements

9.5.5.4 Binding corporate rules must meet the requirements set out in art.47, which are expanded upon in papers by WP 29. The most useful of these papers are:

- checklists for controllers and processors (WP 256 rev.01 [adopted on 28 November 2017 and revised and adopted on 6 February 2018] and WP 257 rev.01 [also adopted on 28 November 2017 and revised and adopted on 6 February 2018]). These set out in table format the required contents for binding corporate rules for controllers and processors respectively; and
- standard application forms which must be completed and submitted to data protection supervisory authorities (WP 264 for controllers and WP 265 for processors [both adopted by WP 29 on 11 April 2018]).

9.5.5.5 In the event of a query as to how a particular topic should be addressed, we also sometimes find it useful to refer back to the original WP 29 paper which introduced the concept of BCRs, WP 74, *Working Document on transfers of personal data to third countries: Applying Article 26(2) of the EU Data Protection Directive to Binding Corporate Rules for International Data Transfers* (adopted on 3 June 2003). WP 74 is available in the archive of WP 29 papers from November 2016 and earlier, available at *https://ec.europa.eu/justice/article-29/documentation/index_en.htm* [Accessed 8 May 2019]. The other WP 29 papers mentioned above are available at the WP 29 newsroom at *https://ec.europa.eu/newsroom/article29/news-overview.cfm* [Accessed 8 May 2019]. Key elements which must be addressed in the rules are summarised below.

Scope of the binding corporate rules

9.5.5.6 The BCRs must describe the structure of the group. Each must also list (and provide contact details for) the members of the group which are covered by the BCR (arts 47(1)(a) and 47(2)(a)). Binding corporate rules are most often used by companies which are majority- or wholly-owned by the same parent company. However, they are also available for use by other forms of a group of undertakings, or a group of enterprises, engaged in a joint economic activity. A group of undertakings could mean any group where one undertaking can exert dominant influence over the others—by "*ownership, financial participation or the rules which govern it or the power to have personal data protection rules implemented*" (rec.35 and art.4(19)). This could, for example, include situations where a company has a minority stake but where, as a result of a shareholders' agreement, it has power to control decisions relating to processing of personal data.

9.5.5.7 The BCRs must also describe the data transfers (or sets of transfers) to which they apply, as well as the categories of personal data, the categories of data subjects, the type of processing and the purposes of processing and the countries to which the personal data will be transferred (art.47(2)(b)).

9.5.5.8 A group can choose the scope of its BCRs. It could, therefore, choose to apply for approval of BCRs which just apply to certain types of personal data and transfers (such as transfers of human resources data). It may also choose to restrict its BCRs to personal data transferred from the European Union—or, at the other extreme, to adopt rules which apply to all processing of personal data within the group. This scope must be set out both in the BCRs and in the application form.

Enforceability of binding corporate rules

9.5.5.9 The BCRs must be binding on every member of the group. They must also confer enforceable rights on data subjects (art.47(1)(a)). The usual method of making the rules binding within the group is to use an intra-group agreement, or unilateral declaration. The group must also ensure its employees are bound by the rules.

9.5.5.10 The BCRs must state that individuals can enforce the rules, by way of third-party rights which are expressly granted to data subjects. In practice, it will be difficult for individuals to take action against members of a group outside the EU. That being so, the BCRs must provide for an entity in the EU to be responsible for remedying the acts of group members outside the EU and for paying compensation in the event of a breach of the rules. For corporate groups setting up BCRs for data transfers from the EU, this entity could be the EU headquarters of the group or, failing that, an entity to which the group delegates the responsibility for ensuring compliance and which agrees to accept this liability. The EU entity is then liable unless it can prove that the other members are not responsible for the relevant event (art.47(2)(f)). As an alternative, if one entity cannot be liable in this way, all EU entities exporting data can agree to be liable for breaches of the BCRs by group members which received data from the exporting entity (WP 256 rev.01, p.9).

9.5.5.11 Groups using BCRs must also accept that an individual can bring proceedings in a place convenient to him or her. This will either be his place of habitual residence, or (for complaints to a supervisory authority), place of work or alleged infringement; or (for claims brought at court), before a member state where the controller or processor has an establishment (art.47(2)(e)).

9.5.7 The BCRs must explain how the group will make individuals aware of the rules—including their rights to enforce the rules and to compensation for breaches of the rules—and information as to how these rights can be exercised (arts 47(2)(g) and (e)). The group must also explain the actual data protection principles themselves and must make sure the clause relating to liability must be provided to individuals (WP 256 rev.01, p.3). Data protection authorities consider that this information must be provided "*in full and a summary will not be sufficient*" (WP 256 rev.01 p.9). As GDPR art.12 also requires that communications with data subjects should be in "clear and plain language", it is helpful to bear in mind, while drafting the BCRs, that large parts of them will have to be provided verbatim to individual data subjects.

Complying with the data protection principles

9.5.5.13 The BCRs must set out how the group meets the core data protection principles: transparency, fairness and lawfulness, purpose limitation, data minimisation and accuracy, storage limitation, processing of special categories of data, security, restriction on transfer and onward transfer (i.e. rules covering data transfers to other organisations not covered by the BCRs); and how the group addresses accountability: records of processing, data protection impact assessments, privacy by design and by default. The wording and definitions of the BCRs key principles must be consistent with the GDPR (WP 256 rev.01 p.17).

Making the rules effective in practice

9.5.5.14 The GDPR contains an accountability principle—that an organisation must be responsible for and be able to demonstrate compliance (art.5(2)). This has always been central to BCRs, which must set out:

- details of the person in charge of monitoring compliance (which could be the data protection officer) (art.47(2)(h));
- arrangements for training (art.47(2)(n));
- data protection audits (internal or external) and other arrangements for verifying compliance. These must include:

  —methods to ensure corrective actions are implemented;

  —the results of the audit are provided to the data protection officer, or other responsible person;

—and to the board of the controlling undertaking;

—and to be made available to the competent data protection authority on request (the Information Commissioner for the UK) (art.47(2)(j)); and

- a complaints procedure (art.47(2)(i)). WP 29 requires this is handled by an independent person or function.

Co-operation with the supervisory authority

9.5.5.15 Members must agree to co-operate with, and (as set out in the WP 29 papers) to agree to follow the advice of, data protection authorities. For the UK that is the Information Commissioner (art.47(2)(l)).

Conflicting legal requirements

9.5.5.16 Article 47(2)(m) also requires the BCRs contain commitments to report to the competent supervisory authority (for UK-approved BCRs, the Information Commissioner) if a member of the group is subject to legal requirements in a non-EU country which could have a substantial effect on the guarantees provided by the BCRs. The WP 29 papers provide more detail on this requirement, including setting out what the group should do if it is subject to secrecy requirements which conflict with the obligation to notify the competent data protection authority (WP 256 rev.01, s.6.3 and WP 257 rev.01 s.6.3).

Processor binding corporate rules

9.5.5.17 Processor BCRs contain some differences from controller BCRs—reflecting the differing obligations between controllers and processors under the GDPR.

- Processor BCRs must also address the relationship between the processor and the controller. There must be a contract or other legal act, binding the processor with regard to the controller (as required by art.28(3)) and this agreement must also reference the processor BCRs (WP 257 rev.01, para.1.4).
- Processor BCRs must be enforceable by the controller customer—so third-party rights must also extend to the controller customer, allowing it to enforce both against the group member responsible for any breach as well as against the entity in the group within the EU which has responsibility for and liability for compliance (**9.5.5.10**).
- Individuals' rights to enforce processor BCRs are more complex. Where processors have direct obligations under the GDPR, individuals can take action against the processor group directly. However, for other elements of the GDPR, BCRs should provide that individuals may only take action

against the processor group if the controller customer has disappeared or ceased to exist or is insolvent.

- The processor is not subject to all of the data protection principles—instead there are commitments on the processor group to help and assist the controller to comply with these principles.
- Processor BCRs reflect the principles in GDPR arts 28(2) and (4) that subprocessing is only possible with prior written approval of the controller, and on the basis that the processor remains liable for the acts of the subprocessor, and that the same obligations are flowed down to it (see also **13.7.4** where art.28 is addressed).

Approvals process

9.5.5.18 For UK-only BCRs, the Commissioner can approve BCRs. The approvals process for EU BCRs is described in the *Working Document Setting Forth a Co-Operation Procedure for the approval of 'Binding Corporate Rules' for controllers and processors under the GDPR* adopted by the WP 29 on 11 April 2018 (WP 263 rev.01).

Identify the binding corporate rules' lead authority

9.5.5.19 An applicant has to first identify, and apply to, a supervisory authority which will act as its lead authority (BCR Lead). WP 263 rev.01 (p.3) lists the relevant criteria as follows:

- location of the Group's European headquarters (if any);
- location of the company within the Group with delegated data protection authority;
- location of the company which is best placed (in terms of management function, administrative burden etc) to deal with the application and to enforce the BCRs;
- the place where most decisions relating to personal data processing (or at least data transfers) are taken;
- the member state in the EU from which most or all transfers outside the EU will take place.

9.5.5.20 WP 29 notes that they will give most weight to the first factor (location of headquarters). However, WP 29 also notes (again p.3) that these are "*not formal criteria*". They are relevant factors which will be considered by supervisory authorities, which decide, amongst themselves which authority will be the lead. Another factor is whether choosing a different authority would be helpful "*for speeding up the procedure (e.g. taking into account the workload of the originally requested SA* [supervisory authority]*)*". Binding corporate rules can be complex arrangements and dealing with them makes a significant demand on a supervisory authority's time—which is implicit in this comment. An applicant needs to be aware of this.

9.5.5.21 Some of the criteria above sound similar to those which are used to assess which is the "main establishment" of a controller or processor. As explained at **1.4.3.14**, this is relevant where there is "cross border processing" of personal data, as the supervisory authority for the "main establishment" of the controller or processor will be the authority responsible for liaising with the controller or processor, and all concerned supervisory authorities, with a view to adopting a consensus decision. In particular, the references to the location of the organisation's headquarters, the place where decisions are made and the place where most processing activities take place (here the relevant activities being data transfers), are all relevant to identifying the "main establishment".

9.5.5.22 However, the two concepts are not the same. Identifying which entity will be the main establishment, and hence which authority will be the lead authority, is a question of fact and law, whereas here supervisory authorities emphasise their discretion in determining who will handle an application. It is also quite possible (as explained at **1.4.3.14**) for an organisation *not* to have an EU-based main establishment—for example if its headquarters and all significant decisions are taken outside the EU—but the organisation could still implement BCRs. WP 29 also notes that the two concepts are different noting (p.2) that "*The 'BCR Lead' is generally distinct from the 'OSS* [one stop shop] *Lead*'".

9.5.5.23 Because the criteria are flexible, it is important that an applicant checks with the supervisory authority which it wishes to act as its lead—it would be advisable to approach the authority before making a formal application, to check if the authority would be willing to act as BCR Lead. It would also be sensible to ask the authority about its workload. Once an applicant has identified which authority is likely to be suitable to act as the BCR Lead, it should complete and submit Pt 1 of the standard BCR application forms. Here, the group explains how the criteria above apply to it. The suggested BCR Lead then circulates Pt 1 of the form to other concerned authorities and asks them to confirm if they have any objection to the suggested authority acting as the BCR Lead. Authorities will be consulted if the applicant also has a presence in their member state or of individuals in their member state are likely to be substantially affected by the data processing. Concerned authorities have two weeks to raise any objection (WP 263 rev.01, para.2.1).

Review of binding corporate rules and application forms

9.5.5.24 The BCR Lead will review the completed checklist, standard application form and the other documents submitted with the application (for example, the BCRs themselves, any intra-group agreement used to make them binding, and the supporting materials used to show how the group will implement the BCRs, keep them maintained, train staff on compliance and explain the BCRs to individuals). Once the BCR Lead considers that the relevant requirements are met it will circulate the document to one or two additional supporting authorities.

These will be selected from the authorities who are concerned with the application (**9.5.7.23**)—and whether one or two authorities are selected will depend on the number of authorities which are concerned with the application and the capacity of authorities to review applications (WP 263 rev.01, para.2.2). The BCR Lead and the supporting authorities will then work with the applicant to produce materials which the authorities agree are satisfactory. To facilitate this review process, materials should be submitted both in the language of the BCR Lead and in English (wherever this is allowed under the relevant Member State law) (WP 263 rev.01, para.2.9).

Approval by the European Data Protection Board using the co-operation procedure

9.5.5.25 Once the BCR Lead and supporting authorities consider that an application is satisfactory, then it will proceed to review and (hopefully) approval via the co-operation procedure described at art.60 and **1.4.3.4**. Concerned authorities have four weeks to comment. Once the BCR Lead is confident that all comments have been addressed then it sends a final draft to the EDPB for it to issue an Opinion approving the BCRs, in accordance with art.64(1)(f). To allow for this review process, the applicant must translate the final BCR documentation into the languages of all concerned authorities (if any changes are made to the BCRs as part of the final approval process, then the approved BCRs must also be translated) (again, WP 263 rev.01, para.2.9).

Ongoing maintenance

9.5.5.26 The BCRs must identify a person to keep track of changes—either to the members of the group or to the rules themselves (art.47(2)(k)). New members can, therefore, be added—however data must not be transferred to new members in reliance on the BCRs until the new member is able to comply with the rules in practice (WP 256 rev.01, section 5.1).

9.5.5.27 An annual update must be provided to the competent supervisory authority. In addition, up to date copies of the rules and of the members bound by them must be provided to the authority or to individuals on request. If a more significant change is made—that is, which could affect the protection offered by the BCRs, then this must be discussed promptly with the competent data protection authority. Such a change would need to be separately authorised and could not be tackled via the annual update process.

9.6 DEROGATIONS

9.6.1 Derogations generally

9.6.1.1 An organisation may find that it is important for it to be able to transfer personal data, but that it cannot use any of the mechanisms outlined above—for example, because the recipient is in a country which does not benefit from an adequacy decision, or because the transfer is urgent and there is no time to implement standard contractual clauses. In this type of situation, the organisation may find an answer in the derogations (exemptions) set out in art.49. These are intended to be used as a last resort, where the other mechanisms described above are not available but where the GDPR nonetheless recognises that, in this specific situation, the transfer ought to be able to take place. This 'last resort' attitude is apparent in the introductory wording to art.49, which provides that the conditions can be used:

> "*In the absence of an adequacy decision or of appropriate safeguards pursuant to Article 46 . . .*".

Recital 111 also provides that two of the derogations (contractual necessity (**9.6.3**) and transfers linked to legal claims (**9.6.5**)) are only available "*where the transfer is occasional*"—again, limiting the derogations to exceptional situations.

9.6.1.2 The available derogations are all considered below. The WP 29 has also issued *Guidelines on Article 49 of Regulation 2016/679* (adopted on 6 February 2018) (WP 262) and we refer to this throughout.

9.6.2 Consent

9.6.2.1 Article 49(1)(a) provides that personal data can be transferred where:

> "*the data subject has explicitly consented to the proposed transfer, after having been informed of the possible risks of such transfers for the data subject due to the absence of an adequacy decision and appropriate safeguards*".

Article 49(3) further provides that where a public authority processes personal data in the exercise of its public powers, that this condition is not available.

9.6.2.2 The GDPR distinguishes between ordinary consent (which can, for example, provide a lawful basis for processing normal personal data) and explicit consent (which can provide a lawful basis for processing special categories of data). This is one of the occasions where the consent must be explicit. The WP 29, in its *Guidelines on consent under Regulation 2016/679* (WP 259 rev.01 p.18), notes that explicit refers to the way consent is obtained from the individual: it means that the individual must expressly confirm consent; the possibility of inferring consent (for example, from sufficiently clear conduct) is ruled out.

9.6.2.3 The GDPR provides a high standard for consent, which we have considered at **4.2**. All of these requirements apply here. The WP 29 notes, in particular, that the requirement for consent to be "specific" means that information about the particular data transfer, or set of data transfers must have been provided to the individual: it will not, for example, be possible to ask individuals to consent in general terms to data transfers to third countries (WP 262, para.1.2). WP 262 also states that the organisation must have told the individual about all the recipients, or categories of recipients and all the countries, as well as the fact that the country or countries have not been considered by the European Commission to offer an adequate level of protection. Article 49(1)(a) specifically requires that information about "risks" should be provided. Here WP 262 (p.8) notes that this will be case specific, but could include information as to whether or not there is a supervisory authority in that country, the fact that data protection principles are different and that individuals may not have the same data subject rights as they do in the EU. Lastly, but perhaps most importantly, consent can be revoked. This alone is likely to limit the occasions when organisations can rely on this derogation.

9.6.3 Contractual necessity

9.6.3.1 There are two relevant derogations under art.49:

- Article 49(1)(b) which applies where "*the transfer is necessary for the performance of a contract between the data subject and the controller or the implementation of pre-contractual measures taken at the data subject's request*"; and
- Article 49(1)(c) which applies where the transfer is "*necessary for the conclusion or performance of a contract concluded in the interest of the data subject between the controller and another natural or legal person*".

As with consent, this derogation is not available to public authorities when they transfer data in the course of exercising their public powers.

9.6.3.2 The Information Commissioner's *Guide* gives the example of a hotel booking to illustrate the difference between the two conditions: the first would cover transfer of the bill-payer's details to a hotel outside the UK or the EU where they are booking a holiday; the second the transfer of their family's details.

9.6.3.3 The derogation only applies where the transfer is "necessary". The WP 29, in WP 262 (p.4) notes that this does not assist if the only reason transfers are necessary is because, for business purposes, the data exporter has chosen to centralise its payment or human resources functions in a particular location outside the UK or the EU: this would be a matter of convenience, not necessity.

9.6.3.4 Recital 111 applies to this derogation—meaning that it is only applicable where the transfer is "occasional". This is very limiting—and is a restrictive factor which was not present in relation to the equivalent derogation in Directive 95/46/EC. As the WP 29 notes in WP 262 (p.9), repeated and systematic transfers will not be able to meet this constraint. The Information Commissioner, in the *Guide,* notes that this would affect transfers such as the transfer to the hotel mentioned above: if the travel agent regularly arranged for customers to travel to this particular hotel, the travel agent would instead need to consider an alternative safeguard, most likely standard data protection clauses.

9.6.4 Important reasons of public interest

9.6.4.1 This applies where "*the transfer is necessary for important reasons of public interest*" (art.49(1)(d)).

Recital 112 gives examples of the kinds of interests which this may cover:

> "*cases of international data exchange between competition authorities, tax or customs administrations, between financial supervisory authorities, between services competent for social security matters, or for public health, for example in the case of contact tracing for contagious diseases or in order to reduce and/or eliminate doping in sport*".

9.6.4.2 WP 262 notes that the condition can also apply to private bodies as long as the interest is public, but that (p.11):

> "*... it is not sufficient that the data transfer is requested (for example by a third country authority) for an investigation which services a public interest of a third country which, in an abstract sense, also exists in EU or Member State law. Where for example, a third country authority requires a data transfer for an investigation aimed at combatting terrorism, the mere existence of EU or member state legislation also aimed at combatting terrorism is not as such a sufficient trigger to apply Article 49(1)(d) to such a transfer. Rather ... the derogation only applies when it can also be deduced from EU law or the law of the member state to which the controller is subject, that such data transfers are possible for important public interest purposes including in the spirit of reciprocity for international co-operation*".

In other words, this is not an enlightened recognition of the importance of transfers which may be of public interest to another country—but also an attempt to push reciprocal data sharing arrangements with the EU.

9.6.4.3 Another example of where this may apply is given later in rec.112—this is transfers to international humanitarian organisations which are accomplishing tasks under the Geneva Conventions or complying with international humanitarian law—although the recital notes that this could also satisfy the requirements for the condition relating to vital interests (**9.6.6**).

9.6.5 Legal claims

9.6.5.1 Article 49(1)(e) applies where the transfer is "*necessary for the establishment, exercise or defence of legal claims*". It is clear from the recitals and from WP 262 that this is not just intended to cover court procedures. Recital 111 notes that, in addition to judicial procedures, this would cover "*administrative or ... out of court procedure, including procedures before regulatory bodies*". WP 262 (p.12) suggests that it could be used to cover transfers for investigations relating to anti-trust law, corruption, insider trading or similar situations, as well as pre-trial discovery procedures, or merger clearance. However,

> "*the derogation cannot be used to justify the transfer of personal data on the grounds of the mere possibility that legal proceedings or formal procedures may be brought in the future*".

9.6.5.2 The "occasional" requirement in rec.111 applies to this condition and there is also a requirement that the transfer is "necessary". Here WP 262 (p.13) notes that organisations should always consider if the claims could be met by the supply of anonymous, or pseudonymous data and, if that is not the case, then only the set of personal data which is actually necessary should be disclosed.

9.6.5.3 Organisations should also be aware of art.48 and recital 115. These are concerned with:

> "*third countries* [that] *adopt laws, regulations and other legal acts which purport to directly regulate the processing activities of natural and legal persons under the jurisdiction of the Member States. This may include judgments ... or decisions of administrative authorities in third countries requiring a controller or processor to transfer or disclose personal data*" (rec.115).

Article 48 then provides that:

> "*Any judgment of a court or tribunal and any decision of an administrative authority of a third country requiring a controller or processor to transfer or disclose personal data may only be recognised or enforceable in any manner if based on an international agreement, such as a mutual legal assistance treaty, in force between the requesting third country and the Union or a Member State, without prejudice to other grounds for transfer pursuant to this Chapter*".

9.6.5.4 These provisions are concerned with non-EU laws which purport to have extra-territorial effect and to require EU organisations to comply with them by providing personal data. Because art.48 relates to the recognition and enforcement of judgments, arts 81 and 82 of the Treaty on the Functioning of the EU (TFEU) are relevant (judicial co-operation in criminal and civil matters). The UK is only bound by these matters if it opts in to them—and the UK has decided not to opt-in here (see statement of Baroness Neville-Rolfe on 4 February 2016, ref. HLWS500 [note that—because of the date of the statement—the article references in that statement do not correspond to the numbers in the final text of the GDPR]. Readers should also note that when this was considered by the relevant Commons Select Committee, the Committee disagreed with the Government's conclusion: *https://publications.parliament.uk/pa/cm201516/cmselect/cmeuleg/342-xxiv/34218.htm* [Accessed 8 May 2019]).

9.6.5.5 Article 48 states that it is "*without prejudice to other grounds for transfer pursuant to this Chapter*". The concern of art.48, therefore, is not to ban transfers made pursuant to non-EU requirements automatically, but to make clear that an organisation should not assume that the transfer of personal data is justified on this basis: it must separately consider how it ensures adequate protection for the data being transferred. The WP 29 emphasise this in WP 262, noting that:

> "*Article 48 and the corresponding recital 115 provide that decisions from third country authorities, courts or tribunals are not in themselves legitimate grounds for data transfers to third countries. Therefore, a transfer in response to a decision from third country authorities is in any case only lawful, if in line with the conditions set out in Chapter V* [i.e. the data transfer rules in the GDPR]".

9.6.5.6 Suitable conditions under art.49 could be important reasons of public interest or necessity for establishment, exercise or defence of legal claims. Recital 115 points to public interest, noting that

> "...*Transfers should only be allowed where the conditions of this Regulation for a transfer to third countries are met. This may be the case, inter alia, where disclosure is necessary for an important ground of public interest recognised in Union or Member State law to which the controller is subject*".

9.6.5.7 The equivalent condition to the legal claims ground and the important public interest ground under the 1998 Act were considered in the case of ***Re Bernard L Madoff Investment Securities LLC*** [2009] EWHC 422. The case concerned the investigation into the alleged fraud by the Madoff companies. A trustee in bankruptcy had been appointed by the New York court. The liquidators of the group's UK subsidiary asked the court for a declaration that they could transfer relevant information to the US trustee in bankruptcy, given that the US was not considered to provide adequate protection for personal data. Lewison J had no difficulty in concluding that it was in the public interest that large-scale complex fraud should be investigated and that the transfer was necessary for this (in line with Sch.4, para.4(1) of the 1998 Act). He also concluded that this would likely involve legal proceedings and be required to establish legal rights, so would also satisfy paras 5(1)(a) and (c) of Schedule 4 of the 1998 Act.

9.6.6. Vital interests

9.6.6.1 Article 49(1)(f) applies where the transfer is:

> "*necessary in order to protect the vital interests of the data subject or of other persons, where the data subject is physically or legally incapable of giving consent*".

WP 262 (p.13) notes that this would cover transfers of personal data in the case of a medical emergency.

9.6.7 Public registers

9.6.7.1 Article 49(1)(g) allows transfers of data from public registers. The condition applies in two situations:

(1) Where "*according to Union or Member State law* [the register] *is intended to provide information to the public and which is open to consultation . . . by the public in general*"; and

(2) To registers which, again according to Union or Member State law, can be consulted by "*any person who can demonstrate a legitimate interest*"—so the second condition would cover registers which are accessible only to qualifying individuals.

9.6.7.2 In accordance with art.49(2) the transfer must not involve the entirety of the register and, if the register is only accessible to those with a legitimate interest, then the transfer must also be to such persons or at their request. As the WP 29 note (WP 262, p.14) adds that the condition is restricted to public registers, so it would not cover private sector databases, such as credit reference agencies.

9.6.8 Transfers for compelling legitimate interests with appropriate safeguards

9.6.8.1 Article 49(1) also introduces an additional derogation, not previously present in Directive 95/46/EC. This is available where:

- none of the other adequacy arrangements, safeguards or derogations apply;
- it is necessary for a "compelling legitimate interest" of the controller, which is not overridden by the interests or rights or freedoms of the data subject;
- the transfer is not repetitive and involves only a limited number of data subjects; and
- where the controller has assessed all the circumstances surrounding the transfer and has, on the basis of this assessment, provided suitable safeguards for the transfer.

9.6.8.2 The WP 29 notes that these safeguards could, by way of example, include requirements to delete the data as soon as possible, restrictions on the purposes for which the data could be used, or transfer of pseudonymised or encrypted data (WP 262, p.17). Recital 113 notes that in considering the risks, the controller should pay particular attention to the nature of the data, the duration and purpose of the transfer, as well as the situation in the importing country and any country of final destination (if this is not the importing country).

9.6.8.3 It will be seen from the restrictions and requirements listed above that it will not be easy to rely on this condition. In order to allow supervisory authorities check how the condition is being used, there is also a requirement in art.49(1) to notify the supervisory authority that the condition has been used, as well as a requirement to document the fact and the safeguards used in records of processing maintained under art.30 (art.30(1)(e) and 30(2)(c) and see **13.5.1.2.** on accountability). As well as doing this, the controller must also notify the individuals concerned about the transfer—and what the compelling interests were which made the transfer necessary. The condition may introduce some welcome flexibility for emergency situations. However, the requirements will mean that it can only be rarely used—as, indeed, is the intent.

9.7 MEMBER STATE SPECIFIC RESTRICTIONS ON DATA TRANSFERS

9.7.1 Those subject to the GDPR should note art.49(5) which provides that:

"*In the absence of an adequacy decision, Union or Member State law may, for important reasons of public interest, expressly set limits to the transfer of specific categories of personal data to a third country or an international organisation*".

9.7.2 Where an organisation wishes to transfer personal data to a recipient in a country which benefits from an adequacy decision, therefore, EU and Member State law may not restrict this. However, in other situations—either where safeguards such as standard contractual clauses would be used, or where derogations would be relied on, then the transfer could be blocked by other laws. Any such laws must be notified to the European Commission. The WP 29 notes that 'blocking statutes' would fall within this provision (WP 262, p.12). This topic is considered further in the WP 29's *Working document 1/2009 on pre-trial discovery for cross border civil litigation* (adopted on 11 February 2009) which gives the example of the French Penal Law No.80–538 which prohibits disclosure of information outside France for use in foreign judicial or administrative proceedings in the absence of an international treaty or agreement—as a result of which a French lawyer was convicted for complying with a request from the US courts to disclose information relevant to US litigation (p.5; fn.3).

9.8 BREXIT

9.8.1 The effect of the Withdrawal Agreement

9.8.1.1 If the UK leaves the EU on the basis of the Withdrawal Agreement (**0.15**), there will be no change to the current situation for the duration of the transitional period. The UK must allow free-flows of personal data to the EU and the EU must allow free-flows of personal data to the UK during this period. The political declaration says that the Commission aims to adopt a UK adequacy decision by the end of 2020. In the event that an adequacy decision is not agreed, then art.71 of the Withdrawal Agreement commits the UK to continue to apply EU law on protection of personal data to personal data which was transferred to the UK before the end of the transitional period. This commitment would not, however, extend to the co-operation and consistency mechanism in the GDPR (**1.4.3**).

9.8.2 *The effect of a no-deal Brexit*

9.8.2.1 In the event of a no-deal Brexit, the UK will immediately become a "third country", meaning that transfers of personal data from the EU to the UK will need to comply with the adequacy arrangements described in this chapter.

9.8.2.2 UK-based organisations will still be able to transfer personal data freely to the EU. Transitional arrangements to be set out in Sch. 21, Pt 3 of the DPA 2018 will provide that transfers made to any of the following, all listed at para.5(1), will be regarded as adequate:

- an EEA state;
- Gibraltar;
- a Union institution, body, office or agency set up by, or on the basis of, the Treaty on the European Union, the Treaty on the Functioning of the European Union or the Euratom Treaty;
- an equivalent institution, body, office or agency set up by, or on the basis of, the Treaties establishing the European Economic Area.

As mentioned above, this is a transitional provision and can be amended by secondary legislation.

9.8.2.3 UK-based organisations will still need to ensure adequacy for personal data transferred elsewhere. Here, the UK GDPR and amendments to the DPA 2018 will carry forward provisions for dealing with adequacy which are very similar to those in the GDPR. The UK GDPR will provide that the Secretary of State will make adequacy decisions and have the obligation to publish the UK specific list of adequate countries. The DPA 2018 will be amended to introduce ss.17A and 17B which address UK adequacy decisions. Such decisions are to be made by way of secondary legislation, subject to the negative resolution procedure. Section 17B will contain an obligation on the Secretary of State to review adequacy decisions at least every four years. Schedule 21, Part 3, of the DPA 2018 sets out that existing adequacy decisions will also apply to the UK, post-Brexit. Paragraphs 4 and 5 will provide that transfers can also be made from the United Kingdom in reliance on these EU adequacy decisions, provided that the decisions have not been repealed or suspended by the EU. This mechanism only applies to adequacy decisions which were in force at the point of Brexit. In the case of the Privacy Shield, US organisations which participate in Privacy Shield and which want their certifications to cover transfers of personal data must amend their public commitment of compliance to state that it includes the UK (*https://www.privacyshield.gov/article?id=Privacy-Shield-andthe-UK-FAQs*). The provision is intended to be transitional and the Secretary of State is to be given powers to repeal or amend this arrangement, in whole or in part (DPA 2018 s.17B). If the UK is to keep broadly in step with EU Member States, it must be hoped that the Secretary of State's list of approved jurisdictions will continue to look exactly like the EU's White List.

9.8.2.4 Similarly with standard data protection clauses (**9.5.4**). Instead of standard contract clauses approved by the Commission, such clauses may be specified in regulations made by the Secretary of State via an amendment to s.17C(b) DPA 2018 adopted by the Information Commissioner under an amended s.119A DPA 2018). Amended section 119A of the DPA 2018 will sets out the procedure for the Information Commissioner to approve new standard contractual clauses, which she considers provide appropriate protection for transfers of personal data. Before doing this, the Information Commissioner must consult trade associations, data subjects and persons who appear to the Commissioner to represent the interests of data subjects. Any documents specifying new clauses must be laid before Parliament for approval on a negative resolution basis. The Commissioner must also publish documents issued under s.119A and keep approved clauses under review.

9.8.2.5 Amendments to the DPA 2018 at Sch. 21, Pt 3, paras.7 and 8 will provide that standard contractual clauses can still continue to be used for data transfers from the UK post-Brexit. Paragraph 6 will address continued validity of "*transfer of personal data made under arrangements entered into before exit day*", that is, data transfers where the standard contractual clauses were entered into before Brexit. Paragraphs 2–4 will address entering into the standard contractual clauses after Brexit and provide that if the arrangement would have been valid, from a GDPR perspective, pre-Brexit, then it will continue to be acceptable post-Brexit. Paragraphs 3 and 4 will clarify that, post-Brexit, parties to the standard contractual clauses can, if they so wish, amend the clauses to introduce changes which reflect Brexit, although there is no obligation to make these changes. Two examples of these changes are given – replacing references to Commission adequacy decisions with references to regulations made under the DPA 2018, and changing references to transfers of personal data outside the EU, to refer to transfers of personal data outside the UK. Either the Secretary of State, by regulations, or the Information Commissioner are able to disapply this saving provision for the standard contractual clauses; in either case, such a decision must be laid before Parliament (para.8).

9.8.2.6 Amendments to Schedule 21, Part 3, para.9 of the DPA 2018 will provide that binding corporate rules which had been approved by the Information Commissioner before Brexit and which provided appropriate protection for personal data in accordance with GDPR requirements will continue to provide adequate protection for personal data post-Brexit. Any changes made to approved binding corporate rules which are purely Brexit-related and do not alter the effect of the binding corporate rules will not prejudice this approval (paras.9(3) and (4)). The Information Commissioner will be able to withdraw authorisation for binding corporate rules (para.9(5)). The UK GDPR will provide that the BCR applicant must have an entity in the UK which is responsible for remedying breaches of the BCRs and paying compensation.

9.8.2.7 Amended section 18(1) of the DPA 2018 will allow the Secretary of State to introduce secondary legislation setting out circumstances in which transfers of personal data to third countries will, or will not be considered to be necessary for important reasons of public interest.

9.8.2.8 The Data Protection (EU Exit) Regulations will disapply art.48 in the UK GDPR. Article 48 will, however, still be relevant to organisations which are subject to the laws of other Member States and—post-Brexit—to any attempt by UK courts or administrative authorities to issue decisions which purport to require the release of data by organisations subject to the GDPR.

9.8.2.9 Lastly, amendments to s.18(2) of the DPA 2018, will allow the Secretary of State to specify where transfers cannot take place based on adequacy regulations.

CHAPTER 10
Special Cases

10.1 INTRODUCTION

10.1.1 Elsewhere in this book, we have set out the way in which data protection legislation will apply to the majority of organisations. However, the legislation makes provisions for a number of special cases where the usual arrangements do not quite apply. These are the subject of this chapter and **Ch.15**.

10.1.2 These special cases fall into four categories:

- special types of records, which, by virtue of the content of the record, or the nature of the organisation processing the record, must be handled differently from other records. (This covers health data and health records, education data, and social services data, together with unstructured personal data held by public authorities, which is covered by the Freedom of Information Act 2000 (FOIA data in this chapter));
- processing for certain special purposes (such as journalism or research) which are exempted from various provisions of the data protection legislation;

- processing carried out by competent authorities for law enforcement purposes; and
- processing by the intelligence services.

In relation to these last two categories, the GDPR does not apply at all, but the DPA 2018 contains bespoke rules in Pts 3 and 4 and in associated Schedules. As these provisions will apply to fewer organisations, we have set out commentary on them in the last chapter of this book, **Ch.15**. Paragraph **15.2.8.3** also discusses the exemptions relating to processing for national security or defence purposes, which can apply to other organisations.

10.2 SPECIAL TYPES OF RECORDS

10.2.1 Introduction

10.2.1.1 Most of the provisions relating to special types of records only apply to certain organisations—e.g. schools or local authorities. However, the provisions relating to health data and health records apply to any organisations that process health data or health records. For example, a sick note is produced by a health professional—so a company which receives a sick note when a member of staff is off work will process data concerning health and a health record.

10.2.2 Health data and health records

10.2.2.1 The DPA 2018 distinguishes between "data concerning health" and "health records". Data concerning health is a wider concept—and organisations which process data concerning health need to take special steps when dealing with subject access requests, in order to avoid releasing information to the individual which may cause serious harm. "Health records" are created by health professionals. There are special rules to prevent individuals being required to use subject access rights to obtain health records and provide the records to third parties—for example, to potential employers or insurers.

Data concerning health

10.2.2.2 Data concerning health is defined at DPA 2018 s.205 as

> "*personal data relating to the physical or mental health of an individual, including the provision of health care services, which reveals information about his or her health status*".

10.2.2.3 The special arrangements for subject access are set out in DPA 2018 Sch.3, Pt 2, paras 5 and 6. Before releasing information in response to a subject access request, organisations that hold data concerning health must consider whether releasing the information would cause serious harm to the physical or mental health of the data subject or another individual. It may be difficult for someone who is not a health professional to make this decision. Accordingly, para.6(1) provides that where the data controller is not a health professional, it must always consult with the appropriate health professional before releasing information. According to Sch.3, Pt 2, para.2, the appropriate health professional is the person who is currently, or was most recently, responsible for the diagnosis, care or treatment of the individual and to which the records relate. An opinion provided by a health professional must have been provided within six months of the date on which the controller intends to rely on it. There are special arrangements that relate to child support, social security and war pension functions carried out by the Secretary of State, who can obtain medical opinions from another health professional.

10.2.2.4 Organisations need not go through this prior consultation process if they are satisfied that the information has already been seen by the individual (for example because it is a medical report that has already been provided to the individual by the medical practitioner) or is otherwise already known to the individual.

10.2.2.5 In addition to this special procedure, which will be of relevance to any organisation that processes data concerning health, there are a number of more esoteric subject-access provisions relating to data concerning health. First, at Sch.3, Pt 2, para.3, there is a broad exemption from all data subject rights (other than in relation to automated decision taking), from the requirement to provide a privacy notice and from the corresponding provisions of art.5 for certain reports and evidence provided to a court and processed by a court in proceedings relating to young persons where, under the rules of court, the court may withhold information from the data subject. Secondly, at para.4, there is an exemption that is designed to prevent the release of data concerning health to, for example, a parent against the wishes of a child. This provides that where an access request is made by someone with parental responsibility for a child, or someone appointed by a court to manage the affairs of the data subject, then the information is exempt from subject access if the individual either expressly indicated that it should not be released, or if this would have been the individual's expectation.

Health records

10.2.2.6 Health records are defined at s.205(1) of the DPA 2018 as any record which:

> "*(a) consists of data concerning health, and*
> *(b) has been made by or on behalf of a health professional in connection with the diagnosis, care or treatment of the individual to whom the data relates.*"

Health professionals are listed at s.204 of the Act. The list is extensive and includes medical practitioners, nurses, midwives, pharmacists, speech-therapists and so forth. Health records are most likely to be held by hospitals, GP surgeries and so forth—although the rules on health records apply irrespective of who holds the record.

10.2.2.7 There are special rules—at Sch.2, Pt 3, para.17—relating to third-party information. This is information which, were it to be released in a subject access request, would identify, or allow a data subject to identify, another individual. The usual provisions in the DPA 2018 oblige the data controller to balance the applicant's right under the DPA 2018 with the privacy rights of a third party (as to which, see **6.5.3.27**). However, where the third-party information is contained in a health record, there is no ability to withhold third-party information where the third party concerned is a health professional who has compiled or contributed to the record or who has been involved in the diagnosis, care or treatment of the data subject. It is worth noting that the information could still be withheld under the serious harm provisions (**10.2.2.3**), if releasing the information would be likely to cause serious harm to the health-professional—for example by putting them in danger.

10.2.2.8 Organisations who wish to know about the health of actual or prospective employees, contract staff or members of the public to whom they may provide goods, facilities or services should also be aware of ss.185 and 184 of the DPA 2018. These sections prohibit organisations from requiring individuals to exercise subject access rights to obtain health records, which must then be made available to the organisation as a precondition to employment, or the provision of goods or services. Section 185 states that a term or condition of contract is void if it purports to require an individual to exercise his or her subject access rights to obtain a health record and to supply all, or part of, the information from the health record to another person. Section 184 makes it an offence for a person to require another party to exercise their subject access rights to obtain certain types of records (including health records) and to provide some or all of the information from that record to them in connection with recruitment of an employee, or continued employment, or a contract for services, or providing goods, facilities or services to a member of the public. This practice is known as "enforced subject access" and is covered in more detail at **3.2.4.1**. Advice on how to handle staff health records is also in Pt 4 of the *Employment Practices Code*.

10.2.2.9 Organisations handling health records should note that the DPA 2018 is not the only legislation relevant in this area. The Access to Health Records Act 1990, although mostly repealed by the Data Protection Act 1998, survives in limited form so as to allow the representatives of a deceased patient rights of access to that patient's records—in contrast to data protection legislation which is concerned only with the rights of living individuals. Furthermore, organisations who require medical records for insurance or employment purposes should be aware of the Access to Medical Reports Act 1988, which by s.3 requires the consent of individuals for the use of medical reports for insurance or employment purposes, and by s.4 gives individuals a right of access to medical reports about themselves prepared for those purposes, before they are submitted to the relevant (prospective) insurance company or employer.

10.2.3 Educational data

10.2.3.1 Educational data is addressed in Sch.3, Pt 4. It is defined in the Schedule and, in broad terms, covers records of information about current or former pupils processed by (or on behalf of) state funded, grant-aided, or independent schools in England, Wales and Northern Ireland or by an education authority in Scotland. It does not include information processed by a teacher solely for the teacher's own use.

10.2.3.2 The special arrangements for providing access to educational data are similar to those that apply to health data. There are, therefore, exemptions that relate to information processed in the context of certain court proceedings, information that would be likely to cause serious harm to the data subject or another person, and there are modifications of the usual third-party information provisions. There are also special provisions where education records originated from the Principal Reporter in Scotland and where an individual is not entitled to receive the data from the Principal Reporter. To the extent that educational data comprises health data, the special arrangements for health data and records apply.

10.2.4 Social work data

10.2.4.1 Social work data are personal data processed by a range of bodies listed in Sch.3, Pt 3, para.8 (these range from local authorities, through to NHS Trusts and the courts). Again, such data has a special access regime that allows information to be withheld where it is processed in the course of certain court proceedings, where releasing the information would be likely to cause serious harm to any person, or where the person making the request has parental authority or has been appointed by a court to manage the individual's affairs and the information was provided in the expectation that it would not be released to such a person. There are also special provisions where social work data originated from the Principal Reporter in Scotland and where the data subject is not entitled to receive the data from the Principal Reporter. Where social work data includes educational data or data concerning health, then the special provisions for those types of data apply in priority.

10.2.5 Freedom of Information Act data

10.2.5.1 The Freedom of Information Act 2000 (FOIA) provided in broad terms for public access to much recorded information held by public authorities (FOIA data). Unlike data protection legislation, FOIA applies irrespective of whether the information is processed automatically or in a structured filing system. Where a person makes a request for personal data relating to him or herself, then the FOIA provides that that request is to be handled under data protection legislation. To facilitate this, the FOIA amended the Data Protection Act 1998 to provide that it would also extend to manual unstructured personal data held by a public authority. However, the FOIA also introduced substantial exemptions into the 1998 Act for FOIA data, to avoid public authorities being subject to unreasonable obligations in relation to such unstructured data.

10.2.5.2 This approach is continued, with DPA 2018 s.21(2) providing that Ch.3 of the DPA 2018 applies to manual unstructured processing of personal data held by an FOIA public authority.

10.2.5.3 Section 24 then introduces broad exemptions from most data protection obligations. The exemptions are so extensive that it is easier to say what obligations remain than to set out the exemptions themselves. The exemptions mean that public authorities are subject, in relation to FOIA data, only to the following obligations:

- access rights (art.15);
- obligations to ensure that data is accurate and where necessary kept up to date and rights of rectification (art.5(d) and art.16);
- obligations to erase or restrict data (arts 17, 18 and 19) and to object to processing of personal data for direct marketing or research and statistical purposes (arts 21(2) and (6));
- obligations on controllers and processors in arts 24–39 of the GDPR (contracts with processors and joint controllers, data protection by design and by default, records of processing, security and breach reporting, data protection impact assessments, data protection officers); and
- the enforcement powers of the Information Commissioner and the rights of individuals to seek judicial remedies (Pts 5 and 6 of the DPA 2018).

The criminal offences set out in the DPA 2018 also apply, other than the offences of unlawful obtaining (s.170) and re-identification of de-identified data (s.171).

10.2.5.4 Section 24(3) makes clear that employees of public authorities do not acquire greater data protection rights than their private sector counterparts: all the remaining individual rights, and the controller and processor provisions and the rules in the GDPR for special cases (Ch IX) are disapplied. Section 24(5) also provides that a public authority is not obliged to comply with an access request in relation to FOIA data unless the request contains a description of the actual data sought. Nor need it comply if the cost of doing so would be likely to exceed the appropriate limit set by the Secretary of State. The Freedom of Information and Data Protection (Appropriate Limit and Fees) Regulations 2004 (SI 2004/3244) currently set this limit at £600 for public authorities listed in Sch.1 to FOIA and £450 for other public authorities. These Regulations also set out how costs are to be calculated.

10.2.5.5 Lastly, s.25 contains additional exemptions for FOIA data used in longstanding historical research. Where such research was already underway immediately before 24 October 1998, and where the processing is not carried out for the purpose of measures or decisions with respect to a particular data subject, or in a way that causes or is likely to cause substantial damage or substantial distress to a data subject, then there are additional exemptions from the data accuracy principle (art.5(1)(d) of the GDPR) and the rights to rectification and erasure (arts 16 and 17).

10.3 EXEMPTIONS UNDER THE GDPR

10.3.1 The GDPR addresses exemptions in four places:

1) in art.23 (restrictions);
2) in art.6(3) (adaptations to GDPR, where processing is based on Member State law or is necessary for a task in the public interest);
3) Chapter IX (Special Cases); and
4) within Chapter III (Rights of the Data Subject).

10.3.2 Exemptions under article 23

10.3.2.1 Article 23 allows Member States to introduce exemptions to all individual rights, to the obligation to give notice of a data breach to individuals and to the data protection principles of art.5 "*in so far as its provisions correspond to the rights and obligations provided for in Articles 12 to 22*". Most obviously, this would allow an exemption to the obligation to process personal data "*in a transparent manner*" at art.5(1)(a), which is linked to the notice obligations and to access under arts 12–15.

10.3.2.2 These rights may be restricted where the restriction "*respects the essence of the fundamental rights and freedoms and is a necessary and proportionate measure in a democratic society*" to safeguard one of a number of permitted purposes listed in art.23. These purposes include national security, defence, and public security, prevention and detection of crime, other important objectives of general public interest (including economic interests), protection of the rights and freedoms of the data subject or of others and enforcement of civil law claims.

10.3.2.3 There is limited case law on what "*respecting the essence of the right*" actually means. The European Data Protection Supervisor, in a guide to EU institutions on factors to consider when data protection rights are restricted, glosses the phrase helpfully as "*whether the right is in effect emptied of its basic content* ...".[1] In the ***Digital Rights Ireland*** case (joined cases, ***Digital Rights Ireland Ltd*** [C-293/12] and ***Kaerntner Landesregierung*** [C-594/12] EU:C:2014:238), the CJEU considered that Directive 2006/24/EC (the Data Retention Directive) *did* respect the essence of the right, because it did not permit access to content of communications and required communications data to be stored securely. In ***Maximillian Schrems v Data Protection Commissioner, joined party Digital Rights Ireland Limited*** (C-362/14) EU:C:2015:650, the CJEU noted that legisla-

1 *EDPS, Assessing the necessity of measures that limit the fundamental right to the protection of personal data: A Toolkit*, 11 April 2017, p.4.

tion which authorises public authorities to have access to content of electronic communications on a generalised basis would compromise the essence of the fundamental right to respect for private life and that legislation providing no legal remedies for an individual who wanted access to their data, or to rectify or erase their data, would breach the essence of the right to effective judicial protection.

10.3.2.4 Article 23(2) provides that legislation introducing exemptions should, where relevant, contain provisions addressing purposes of processing, categories of processing or of personal data, the scope of the restrictions, safeguards to prevent abuse or unlawful access or transfer, specification of the controller (or category of controller), storage periods and other applicable safeguards, measures addressing the risks to the rights to individuals, and rights for individuals to be informed about the restrictions unless this would prejudice the purpose of the restriction.

10.3.3 Adaptations under article 6(3)

10.3.3.1 Article 6(3) is concerned with lawfulness of processing when relying on legal obligations laid on the controller (art.6(1)(c)) or tasks carried out in the public interest or in the exercise of official authority vested in the controller (art.6(1)(e)). The only provisions which can be limited under art.23 are individuals' rights. However, art.6(3) contains a more general right for Member States to "*adapt the application of rules of this Regulation*".

10.3.3.2 Article 6(3) allows Member States to set out

> "*general conditions concerning the lawfulness of processing by the controller; the types of data ... the data subjects concerned; the entities to, and the purposes for which, the personal data may be disclosed, the purpose limitation; storage periods ...*".

The law must "*meet an objective of public interest and be proportionate to the legitimate aim pursued*".

10.3.4 Specific situations under Chapter IX

10.3.4.1 Chapter IX (arts 85–91) of the GDPR contains "*Provisions relating to specific processing situations*" where Member States can adopt rules—including exemptions. Article 85 requires Member States to reconcile the competing considerations of data protection and freedom of expression. The other provisions are left to Member State discretion. The UK has made use of provisions at art.86 (public access to official documents), art.89 (archiving, scientific and historical research and statistical purposes) and art.90 (obligations of professional secrecy, **10.5.7**).

10.3.5 Special exemptions linked to data subject rights

10.3.5.1 Lastly, there are detailed exemptions linked to particular data subject rights. For example, art.15(4) provides that the right to obtain a copy of data "*shall not adversely affect the rights and freedoms of others*". Similarly, there are exemptions from the right to erasure for processing which is necessary for freedom of expression and information, for compliance with a legal obligation or performance of a task in the public interest, for public heath purposes, for purposes of archiving in the public interest, scientific or historical research or statistical purposes or for establishment, exercise or defence of legal claims (art.17(3)).

10.3.5.2 Because these exemptions are specific to individual rights, they are considered in connection with the right to which they apply in **Ch.6**. Whilst the UK is a member of the EU these exemptions will apply and be available to controllers directly, even though they are not written out in the DPA 2018. It is, therefore, important for controllers to be aware of these provisions. For ease of reference, **Appendix 6** contains a chart listing all exemptions available at the date of writing.

10.4 EXEMPTIONS UNDER THE DATA PROTECTION ACT 2018

10.4.1 Structure of exemptions

10.4.1.1 The exemptions to the GDPR are introduced at s.15 of the Act. The exemptions are divided into separate Schedules, and Parts of Schedules, based on a combination of which provision in the GDPR allows the exemption to be introduced; what substantive provisions in the GDPR the exemption addresses; and its subject-matter. This approach—and the long and detailed nature of the Schedules—can make it difficult for practitioners to know where to look to check if an exemption may be available. The chart below may assist with this.

Area	Detail	Source of ability to derogate in the GDPR	DPA 2018 reference
Misc. exemptions from most individual rights and some other provisions of the GDPR	Crime and taxation; immigration; disclosures required by law or in connection with legal proceedings	art.6(3) and art.23(1)	Sch.2, Pt 1
Misc. exemptions from most individual rights	Functions protecting the public or regulatory functions; audit; Bank of England; parliamentary privilege; judicial appointments and legal proceedings; crown honours	art.23(1)	Sch.2, Pt 2

<table>
<tr><td>Exemptions from access and notice</td><td>Legal privilege; self-incrimination; corporate finance; management planning; negotiations; confidential references; exam scripts and marks</td><td>art.23(1)</td><td>Sch.2, Pt 4</td></tr>
<tr><td>Special provisions for subject access</td><td>Data relating to other individuals</td><td>art.23(1)</td><td>Sch.2, Pt 3</td></tr>
<tr><td>Health, social work and education data
Child abuse data</td><td>Special rules relating to withholding health, social work and education data either from the data subject or from someone making a request on behalf of the data subject
Withholding child abuse data from someone making the request on behalf of the child.</td><td>art.23(1)</td><td>Sch.3</td></tr>
<tr><td colspan="2">Freedom of expression and information</td><td>art.85(2)</td><td>Sch.2, Pt 5</td></tr>
<tr><td colspan="2">Research, statistics and archiving</td><td>art.89(2) and (3)</td><td>Sch.2, Pt 6</td></tr>
<tr><td colspan="2">Provisions to accommodate other laws that prohibit disclosure to the individual</td><td>art.23(1)</td><td>Sch.4</td></tr>
<tr><td colspan="2">National security and defence</td><td>The GDPR itself does not apply. However, the applied GDPR does apply, necessitating the exemptions in the adjacent right-hand column</td><td>ss.26, 27 and 28</td></tr>
</table>

10.4.2 "To the extent that" and "would be likely to"

10.4.2.1 Controllers should note that most of the exemptions only apply where compliance with the DPA 2018 would prejudice the particular purpose protected by the exemption. For example, the crime prevention exemption does not entitle an organisation to argue that, as its sole purpose is the prevention of crime, all of its activities are exempt from the DPA 2018. Instead, the organisation must consider each subject-access, or other, request that it receives and decide whether, on the facts of each particular case, it should comply with the request. This restriction is introduced by the phrase "to the extent that", absent the exemption, compliance with the Act "would be likely to prejudice" the particular purpose the exemption protects. These phrases are considered at **6.5.3.22**.

10.4.2.2 The implication for controllers is that whilst the exemptions might be useful in particular cases, they should not build their compliance policies and procedures on an assumption that an entire department's activities will always be exempt from the provisions of the Act. On the rare occasions where exemptions are not limited in this way, we have mentioned this.

10.4.3 Types of exemptions

Subject access-only provisions

10.4.3.1 The narrowest exemptions in the DPA 2018 are the provisions allowing personal data to be withheld only from a subject access request (i.e. from arts 15(1)–(3) of the GDPR) where the data:

- relates to data concerning health, social work records or educational records, where release of the material would be likely to cause serious harm to an individual (Sch. 3 Pt 2, paras 5–6; Sch. 3, Pt 3, para.11 and Sch.3, Pt 4, para.19) (**10.2.2.3**); or
- relates to information as to whether a child or vulnerable adult is or has been at risk of child abuse, where the request is made by someone with authority for the child or adult and where release of the data is not in the victim's best interests (Sch.3, Pt 5).

10.4.3.2 In addition, there are exemptions from those articles and from art.5 (data protection principles) "*so far as its provisions correspond to the rights and obligations provided for in Article 15(1) to (3)*" would prejudice the rights of another individual (Sch.2, Pt 3 para.16(1)) (**6.5.3.27**) or where disclosure is prohibited by one of a number of specified enactments (Sch.4). This covers the third party information provisions (**6.5.3.26**) and disclosures which are prohibited by legislation relating to human fertilisation and embryology, adoption records and reports, statements of special educational need, parental order records and reports and information provided by the Principal Reporter in children's hearings in Scotland.

Subject information provisions

10.4.3.3 The next group of exemptions are those which apply to the obligations to give notice to individuals (in arts 10 and 14 of the GDPR) and to subject access rights. The DPA 1998, at s.27(2), used to refer to this group of provisions as the "*subject information provisions*"—the idea being that sometimes prejudice is specifically caused by the need to confirm to people that you process their personal data, either pro-actively, or reactively in response to a subject access request. We have continued to use this phrase, although it is not used in the DPA 2018, because it neatly conveys the scope of these exemptions.

10.4.3.4 Like the other groups of exemptions in the DPA 2018, this exemption also applies to "*Article 5 so far as its provisions correspond to the right and obligations provided for in the* [subject information] *provisions*" (Sch.2, paras 1(a)(x); 2(3)(d); 3(3)(d); 4(2)(g);4(4)(d); 6(j); 18(d); Sch.3(1)(i); Sch.4(1)(b)). As per the table above, this covers matters such as legal privilege, self-incrimination, confidential references and information held for management planning purposes and negotiations with the data subject.

Other individual rights

10.4.3.5 There are also some purposes which benefit from exemptions from almost all individual rights, not just the subject information provisions. These exemptions also apply to art.16 (rectification), art.17 (erasure), art.18 (restriction), art.19 (notifying others about erasure and restriction), art.20 (portability) and art.21 (objections to processing). In addition, there are again, exemptions from art.5 in so far as its provisions correspond to these obligations.

10.4.3.6 These exemptions apply to processing for the purposes of functions which protect the public or for regulatory functions; audit; the Bank of England; parliamentary privilege; judicial appointments and legal proceedings; and crown honours—as well as to processing for purposes of freedom of expression and information. There are also exemptions from some of the additional individual rights (but not all) for processing for immigration purposes and research, statistics and archiving purposes. The DPA 2018 does not contain any exemptions from individuals' rights under the GDPR in relation to automated decision-making, even though such exemptions could have been introduced under art.23. For more on this, see **6.11**.

Non-disclosure provisions

10.4.3.7 The widest exemption covers all of the subject information provisions and other individual rights, as well as "*Article 5(1)(a) (lawful fair and transparent processing), other than the lawfulness requirements set out in Article 6;* [and] *Article 5(1)(b)(purpose limitation*" (Sch.2, Pt 1, para.1(b)).

10.4.3.8 By way of example, this exemption will be relevant if a controller processes personal data for employment purposes, but wishes to, or is obliged to, co-operate with a body such as the Department for Work and Pensions in connection with an investigation into benefits fraud which involves its employees. The controller will process personal data for the purpose of staff administration; providing data to an investigatory body for prevention and detection of crime is (potentially) a different and incompatible purpose. Article 5(1)(b) of the GDPR ("*personal data shall be collected for specified, explicit and legitimate purposes and not further processed in a manner that is incompatible with those purposes* . . .") may prohibit disclosure of data for this purpose. However, this exemption would allow the controller to disclose data. Again, we think the description used for this exemption at s.27(3) of the 1998 Act (the "non-disclosure provisions") is apt and continue to use this. The scope of the exemption is slightly narrower than that under the 1998 Act, which also covered the third, fourth and fifth data protection principles (data quality and storage limitation (art.5)).

10.4.3.9 This exemption only applies to disclosures which are required by law or in connection with legal proceedings or for crime and taxation purposes and to processing for reasons of freedom of expression and information. There are special rules on purpose limitation in relation to processing for research, statistics and archiving (**10.5.7.14**).

Notice of data breaches

10.4.3.10 Lastly, art.23(1) also allows Member States to introduce restrictions on the obligation at art.34(1) and (4) of the GDPR to notify individuals of personal data breaches. The DPA 2018 Sch.2 para.2 only allows an exemption from this in very limited situations: where there is processing for crime prevention and taxation purposes (Sch.2, para.2), if this would be required to avoid infringing parliamentary privilege (Sch.2, para.10) and for purposes of freedom of expression or information. (Sch.2, para.26(9)(c)).

10.5 THE EXEMPTIONS

10.5.1 The DPA 2018 Schs 2–4 contain a long list of exemptions, some of which will apply to relatively few organisations. In this chapter we have concentrated on exemptions which will be of wider relevance. However, **Appendix 6** contains a list of all exemptions applicable to the GDPR and applied GDPR as at the date of writing (February 2019).

10.5.2 Crime and taxation (Schedule 2, Part 1, paragraphs 2 to 4)

10.5.2.1 The exemptions apply where personal data are processed for:

"a) *the prevention or detection of crime,*
b) the apprehension or prosecution of offences, or
c) the assessment or collection of a tax or duty or an imposition of a similar nature . . .".

There are three different exemptions. The first (Sch.1, Pt 1, para.2(1)) is an exemption from the subject information provisions, other data subject rights (other than automated decision taking) and non-disclosure provisions. There is also an exemption from the obligation to notify individuals of personal data breaches. This exemption applies whenever personal data are processed for the above purposes, to the extent that compliance with these provisions would be likely to prejudice any of the matters listed.

10.5.2.2 The second exemption (para.2(2)) applies where a controller processes personal data for these crime or taxation provisions and where another controller (controller 2) then obtains the data from the first controller, in order to discharge statutory functions. In its guidance on the equivalent provision in the 1998 Act[2], the Information Commissioner gave the example of the Independent Police Complaints Commission (IPCC) receiving information from the police to show where this may apply. In this situation, controller 2 (i.e. the IPCC) can rely on an exemption—but only from the subject information provisions—to the same extent that the first controller (the police force) could rely on this exemption. A data subject could not, therefore, use a subject access request to obtain information from the IPCC where that same information had originally been held by the police and where the police would be entitled to withhold the information because disclosure would prejudice their ability to prevent or detect crime.

10.5.2.3 The last exemption (para.3) applies where government departments, local authorities or other authorities administering housing benefit apply risk assessment systems in order to assess taxes, duties or similar, or to prevent, detect, apprehend or prosecute offenders in connection with unlawful claims for payment of, or use of, public money. It is an exemption from subject information provisions and means that if such bodies have applied a classification to an individual as a result of a risk assessment system, then this classification does not have to be released.

10.5.2.4 Although the controller needs to demonstrate that compliance with the relevant data protection provisions would be likely to cause prejudice, this does not need to be prejudice to a *particular* investigation; it is also possible to establish prejudice if there will be a "chilling effect" on the ability to pursue these purposes more generally. This was considered in the ***Zaw Lin*** case ***(Zaw Lin v Commissioner of Police of the Metropolis*** [2015] EWHC 2484 (QB)), where the claimants were on trial in Thailand, facing the death penalty, on charges of murdering two British tourists. The claimants had alleged that they confessed under torture and this led to an independent investigation of the process by the Metropolitan police. Information was provided by the Thai authorities on the basis that it would be shared with the victims' families but not further. The claimants made a subject access request to the police. Green J accepted the argument of the police that releasing the information would have a chilling effect on similar international investigations in future. However, he only concluded this after having inspected the relevant data, and having determined that, having done this, there was nothing of real value to the claimants in the data.

10.5.2.5 The cases above all turn on the prejudice caused by releasing data.

---

[2] *Using the crime and taxation exemptions* (version 1), p.9.

In the *Robert Gaines-Cooper* case (***Robert Gaines-Cooper v Commissioners for HM Revenue and Customs (HMRC)***, [2017] EWHC 868), HMRC suggested (at [63]) that the exemption would be engaged because the sole investigator working on the investigation into the tax affairs of the claimant was having to divert her time into dealing with the subject access request. The Judge only mentions this claim in passing, because no further evidence was submitted by HMRC on the point. Whilst creative, the argument is problematic as it would create an incentive for organisations not to invest in the systems and people necessary to meet their data protection obligations.

10.5.2.6 This exemption is in very similar terms to the equivalent exemption under the 1998 Act, so the ICO guidance on this exemption will still be relevant. In the guidance, ICO notes that

> "*the crime and taxation exemptions are based on the purpose for which the personal data is being processed not on the type of organisation doing the processing*".[3]

Accordingly, controllers could rely on the exemption at Sch.2, Pt 1, para.2(1) to allow them to disclose information to law enforcement bodies or HMRC without tipping off the individual concerned, or in situations when the disclosure would otherwise amount to processing for an "incompatible purpose".[4]

10.5.2.7 As the same ICO guidance notes (p.11), the exemption allows disclosure but does not require it. The controller choosing to provide personal data would be responsible for demonstrating that compliance with data protection requirements would prejudice the particular purpose. For this reason, ICO advises (para.37) that:

> "*The exemption should only be applied to the extent that it is necessary to do so to avoid prejudicing the crime and taxation purposes. This means that the data controller making the disclosure must do as much as it can to comply with the usual requirements of the DPA. A data controller should only disclose the information that is necessary for the purposes, and should not assume that all the data they hold is exempt. Speculative requests for personal data, especially about large numbers of people, are unlikely to meet the tests for necessity and prejudice*".

In case of uncertainty, a controller may be better advised to require the relevant authority to obtain an appropriate order requiring it to release personal data.

10.5.2.8 A controller can only rely on the exemption in relation to *criminal* proceedings, not civil (although the exemption at Sch.2, Pt 1, para.5 may apply

---

3 *Using the crime and taxation exemptions* (version 1), p.2.

4 In the case of ***R. v Bhatti (Waqar)*** [2015] EWCA Crim 1005, the police investigated the claimants in relation to alleged immigration fraud. In this context, they obtained a credit report from Experian, which disclosed the data in reliance on s.29 of the Data Protection Act 1998. The Court of Appeal rejected the claimants' argument that this was an improper method of circumventing the Police and Criminal Evidence Act 1984.

there). In the *Guriev* case (*Guriev v Community Safety Development (UK) Ltd* [2016] EWHC 643 (QB)), a company offering security and investigative services, Community Safety Development (CSD), run by former police staff, was employed to conduct an investigation in relation to the claimants. The claimants made a subject access request to CSD. CSD claimed—amongst other matters—that s.29 of the 1998 Act applied so as to avoid disclosure of the information. Warby J rejected this; partly because insufficient evidence of prejudice had been provided, but also because such details as had been provided suggested that the primary aim of CSD's client was the pursuit of civil remedies for an alleged theft [40].

10.5.3 Immigration (Schedule 2, part 1, paragraph 4)

10.5.3.1 This applies where personal data is processed for purposes of maintaining effective immigration control, or to investigate or detect activities that would undermine maintenance of effective immigration control. Personal data processed for these purposes is exempt from the subject information provisions and from some (but not all) of the additional subject rights. Exemptions extend to the right to erasure (art.17), the right to restriction (art.18) and the right to object (art.21).

10.5.3.2 There is also an exemption (at para.4(4)) where a controller (controller 1) discloses information to another controller (controller 2) which can benefit from the above exemption. This exemption for controller 1 is from subject information provisions only and applies to the same extent that controller 2 would be exempt. There was no equivalent provision in the 1998 Act.

10.5.4 Information required to be disclosed by law (Schedule 2, Part 1, paragraph 5)

10.5.4.1 There are three separate exemptions, from the subject information provisions and all other data subject rights except for automated decision taking, as well as from the non-disclosure provisions.

10.5.4.2 The first, 5(1) applies to "*information that the controller is obliged by an enactment to make available to the public*". This would, therefore, cover personal data contained in public registers, such as Companies House, as well as any personal data released by public authorities pursuant to the Freedom of Information Act 2000. The equivalent exemption under the 1998 Act (s.34) specifically carved out FOIA disclosures. However, s.34 was a broader exemption which also covered the fourth data protection principle (data quality). It would have been inappropriate for public authorities to be relieved of obligations to ensure that personal data were accurate and up to date, just because the data had been released pursuant to a FOIA request. As there is no longer any exemption from this provision, the limitation has been removed.

10.5.4.3 The earlier exemption was also absolute—with no need for a controller to demonstrate that compliance with the provision would cause prejudice. As the exemption applied to all subject information provisions (including the obligation to provide a privacy notice), this meant that organisations responsible for public registers did not have to provide data protection notices to individuals. It is difficult to see why providing such notices would prejudice the ability of such organisations to publish such registers: presumably they will now have to provide such notices. The 1998 Act also stated that the equivalent exemption applied irrespective of whether the information was made available "gratuitously or on payment of a fee". This is not included in the DPA 2018.

10.5.4.4 The second exemption applies where disclosure of personal data is required by enactment, rule of law or order of a court or tribunal (para.5(2)).[5] The third (para.5(3)) applies where disclosure of the personal data:

> "• *is necessary for the purpose of, or in connection with, legal proceedings (including prospective legal proceedings);*
> • *is necessary for the purpose of obtaining legal advice; or*
> • *is otherwise necessary for purposes of establishing, exercising or defending legal rights.*"

10.5.4.5 Cases relating to the equivalent exemption under the 1998 Act, s.35, make clear that neither the controller nor the data subject has to be a party to the particular legal proceedings that are in question. In ***Totalise Plc v Motley Fool Ltd and Interactive Investor Ltd*** [2001] EWCA Civ 1897; [2002] 1 W.L.R. 1233, an individual calling himself Zeddust made defamatory statements about Totalise on bulletin boards run by Interactive Investor and The Motley Fool. Totalise asked the bulletin board owners to release details of Zeddust's identity in order that it could consider taking proceedings against Zeddust. Both Interactive Investor and The Motley Fool refused on the grounds that this might place them in breach of the Act and duties of confidentiality owed to Zeddust under their standard terms and conditions. Totalise proceeded to obtain a court order requiring Interactive Investor and The Motley Fool to disclose Zeddust's identity. Most of the case focused on who should bear the responsibility for costs in orders of this nature. However, the case also makes clear that s.35 of the 1998 Act would have allowed either of the bulletin board owners to disclose information to Totalise upon request without breach of the Act on the basis that Totalise required the information in connection with legal proceedings it was considering initiating.

10.5.4.6 ***Golden Eye (International) Ltd v Telefonica UK Ltd*** [2012] EWCA Civ 1740 also considered s.25 of the 1998 Act. This related to an application by the claimants requiring the defendant (trading as O2) to release details of its subscribers which the claimant believed had infringed copyright in pornographic films where it either owned the copyright or had rights to pursue infringement of copyright. The Court of Appeal cited earlier cases concluding that rights to property are to be balanced with rights to privacy:

---

[5] When making such orders, Civil Procedure Rules mean that the court or tribunal must itself consider the rights of the affected individuals (***Durham CC v D*** [2012] EWCA Civ 1654) and, in the context of Norwich Pharmacal Orders, ***Rugby Football Union v Viagogo Ltd*** [2012] UKSC 55.

neither should be given priority over the other [19]. In this case, the court noted that the subscribers were consumers, many would be on low incomes without access to legal advice, especially the specialist advice needed to deal with claims of copyright infringement, and any approach alleging infringement would be likely to cause them significant embarrassment [20]. Nonetheless, the court concluded that it was appropriate for Telefonica to release details of the subscribers.

10.5.5 Processing by controllers discharging certain functions to protect the public (Schedule 2, Part 1, paragraph 7)

10.5.5.1 This exemption applies to the subject information provisions and other data subject rights (except automated decision taking). It applies to personal data processed for one of the following functions:

- designed to protect members of the public against financial loss due to dishonesty, malpractice or other seriously improper conduct by, or the unfitness or incompetence of, persons involved in financial services, or to protect the public against financial loss due to dealing with individuals who have been made bankrupt;
- designed to protect members of the public against other dishonesty, malpractice, seriously improper conduct or other unfitness or incompetence;
- designed to protect against mismanagement etc. of charities;
- designed to secure health and safety and welfare of persons at work, or to protect the health and safety of others as a result of the actions of persons at work;
- designed to protect members of the public against maladministration by or failures in public services provided by public bodies, by the Parliamentary Commissioner for Administration or other listed bodies; or
- The Competition and Markets Authority when protecting the public, including by regulating anti-competitive agreements or conduct which is an abuse of a dominant position.

The first four categories cover functions conferred by enactment; a function of the Crown, a Minister of the Crown or a government department, or which is of a public nature and is exercised in the public interest. There are other exemptions, covering narrower public interest functions, listed in **Appendix 6**.

10.5.5.2 Again, the ICO's Guidance on *Regulatory Activity*—s.31 of the 1998 Act (version: final) will continue to be helpful, as the provisions of the DPA 2018 closely follow those of the 1998 Act. The guidance has useful comment on the provision in the exemption relating to functions "*of a public nature . . . exercised in the public interest*".

Here the ICO notes (p.3) that:

"*The paragraph is concerned with functions of a public nature exercised by a variety of watchdogs whose regulatory role is recognised by both the general public and the sector that they oversee. Such regulators may be established by statute or as a result of formal agreement of the participants in their sector of business*".

10.5.5.3 However, this provision is not wide enough to cover complaints departments:

"*Most organisations have an internal complaints procedure to investigate and report on how the organisation has carried out its primary functions. In addition, most organisations will have disciplinary procedures for dealing with inappropriate behaviour by staff. These procedures are not the primary activity or function of the organisation and are therefore not regulatory activities covered* [by the exemption] . . .".

10.5.5.4 The ICO also notes that the exemption may be engaged when a controller passes personal data to a regulatory body which then relies on the exemption:

"*Although an organisation would not normally consider this exemption . . . this exemption may become relevant if the information is referred to the regulator or copied to a regulator in order to assist in the performance of its formal regulatory functions. If the regulator can withhold personal data in response to a subject access request because it is likely to prejudice the discharge of its regulatory function the originating organisation will also be able to do the same. Failure by the originating organisation to withhold data might allow a data subject (who would be refused access to the data if he approached the regulator) to circumvent the provisions of the DPA* [1998] *by simply obtaining the data from the originating organisation instead. It is therefore important that organisations are cautious with information being used by regulatory bodies to carry out their functions* . . .".

10.5.6 Freedom of expression and information

10.5.6.1 Article 85 of the GDPR places an obligation on Member States to:

"*reconcile the right to the protection of personal data pursuant to this Regulation with the right to freedom of expression and information, including processing for journalistic purposes and the purposes of academic, artistic or literary expression*".

Article 85(2) goes on to provide that Member States shall provide for exemptions from all elements of the Regulation (Ch.II [principles], Ch.III [rights of the data subject], Ch.IV [controller and processor], Ch.V [transfers to third countries], Ch.VI [supervisory authorities], Ch.VII [co-operation and consistency] and Ch.IX [special situations]), "*if they are necessary to reconcile the right to the protection of personal data with the freedom of expression and information*".

10.5.6.2 There has long been tension between privacy and data protection considerations and the press. The *News of the World* phone hacking scandal led to the Leveson Inquiry into the culture, practices and ethics of the press. The Report of Pt 1 of the Leveson Inquiry was published in 2014. On 1 March 2018, the Culture Secretary, Mr Matt Hancock, MP, announced to the House of Commons that Pt 2 of the Inquiry (into unlawful or improper conduct within the media and the police and the role of politicians and public servants in this) would not take place. This announcement coincided with the passage of the 2018 Data Protection Bill through the House of Commons—and meant that much of the debate in the House of Commons on the Data Protection Bill focused on the sections of the Bill addressing freedom of expression, as well as wider discussions on the Leveson Inquiry.

10.5.6.3 The DPA 2018, at ss.174–179 and Sch.2 Pt 5, introduces very broad exemptions to facilitate freedom of expression. Where personal data are processed:

- for the "special purposes";
- with a view to publication of journalistic, academic, artistic or literary material; and
- the controller reasonably believes that publication of the material would be in the public interest

then there are sweeping exemptions from most of the substantive provisions of the GDPR, to the extent that the controller reasonably believes that the application of those provisions would be incompatible with the special purposes. The DPA 2018 also restricts the enforcement powers of the Information Commissioner and the ability of individuals to bring proceedings before the courts and includes special defences to some of the criminal offences under the DPA 2018. The Act (s.124) also requires the Information Commissioner to adopt a Code of Practice on data protection and journalism and requires both the Information Commissioner and the Secretary of State to undertake regular reviews in relation to journalism and the media. These provisions are all considered in turn below.

The special purposes

10.5.6.4 The special purposes are defined[6] as "*one or more of the following:*

a) *the purposes of journalism;*

---

[6] There are separate definitions, for Sch.2, Pt 5 (exemptions) at para.26(1) of that Schedule and, in relation to Pt 6, (Enforcement), at s.174. The definitions refer to the paragraph (26), and the Part (Part 6 of the Act) respectively. They are, however, identical.

b) *academic purposes;*

c) *artistic purposes;*

d) *literary purposes*".

"*Academic purposes*" was not in s.32 (the equivalent provision) in the 1998 Act and so widens the scope of the exemption. It derives from art.85(1) of the GDPR.

10.5.6.5 Recital 153 states that:

> "*In order to take account of the importance of the right to freedom of expression in every democratic society, it is necessary to interpret notions relating to that freedom, such as journalism, broadly*".

This broad approach has been followed both in CJEU and domestic case law. In the case of ***Tietosuojavaltuutettu v Satakunnan Markkinapörssi Oy & Satamedia Oy*** (C-73/07) EU:C:2008:727, the CJEU was, amongst other things, asked to consider the journalistic purposes exemption under art.9 of the 1995 Data Protection Directive. In Finland, details of personal taxes paid are made public and Markkinapörssi had collected and published this data in the newspapers for a number of years. The case concerned a new service which Markkinapörssi and Satamedia wished to run, whereby published information about individuals' tax payments would be sent by text message to anyone who wished to pay for such information. The CJEU was asked to confirm if this public domain data was still protected by data protection legislation (it was) and if the journalistic purposes exemption at art.9 of the Directive could apply. The CJEU confirmed that, in principle, the exemption for journalistic purposes could apply to this, although whether it did, in fact, apply was a matter for the Finnish courts to determine.

10.5.6.6 The Court noted that:

> " . . . *the exemptions and derogations provided for in Article 9 of the* [95/46/EC Data Protection] *Directive apply not only to media undertakings but also to every person engaged in journalism*
> . . . *the fact that the publication of data within the public domain is done for profit-making purposes does not, prima facie, preclude such publication being considered as an activity undertaken 'solely for journalistic purposes'*;
> *A degree of commercial success may even be essential to professional journalistic activity;*
> . . . *account must be taken of the evolution and proliferation of methods of communication and the dissemination of information. As was mentioned by the Swedish Government in particular, the medium which is used to transmit the processed data, whether it be classic in nature, such as paper or radio waves, or electronic, such as the internet, is not determinative as to whether an activity is undertaken 'solely for journalistic purposes';*
> *It follows from all of the above that activities such as those involved in the*

main proceedings, relating to data from documents which are in the public domain under national legislation, may be classified as 'journalistic activities' if their object is the disclosure to the public of information, opinions or ideas, irrespective of the medium which is used to transmit them. They are not limited to media undertakings and may be undertaken for profit-making purposes."

The case of ***Sergejs Buivids v Datu valsts inspekcija*** (C-345/17) 14 February 2019 (and see **10.5.8.4**) also confirms that journalistic activities can be carried out in a wide variety of ways: there is no need for the exception to be limited to professional journalists. Distribution of material online (in that case via YouTube) could amount to journalistic activity, although the exemption cannot be pushed so far as to mean that all material published online is therefore exempt [55], [57], [58]. The CJEU also summarised criteria, mentioned in ***Satamedia***, which should be taken into account in determining whether processing is for journalistic activities. These are:

- whether the processing contributes to a debate of public interest;
- the degree of notoriety of the person affected;
- the subject of the news report;
- the prior conduct of the person;
- the content, form and consequences of publication; and
- the manner and circumstances in which the information was obtained and its veracity [66].

10.5.6.7 *The Law Society v Kordowski* [2011] EWHC 3185 (QB) is an example of how a non-traditional media organisation could rely on the exemption. The case concerned the website, "Solicitors from Hell", set up by an individual to name and shame law firms. The judge considered that this could (in theory) benefit from the equivalent exemptions at s.32 of the 1998 Act:

"*Today anyone with access to the internet can engage in journalism at no cost. If what the defendant communicated to the public at large had the necessary public interest, he could invoke the protection of journalism . . .*".

The fact that the exemption extends to literary and artistic purposes, makes it wider still—allowing it to cover pure entertainment as well as news.

10.5.6.8 Although journalistic processing may be a wide concept, it is not wide enough to cover processing by search engines. In the ***Google Spain***[7] case, the CJEU had to consider the request by Mr Costeja for Google to delist him from its search results. The CJEU noted that search engines play an important role in

[7] ***Google Spain SL v Agencia Española de Protección de Datos (AEPD) and Mario Costeja González*** (C-101/12) EU: C: 2014:317. See also **6.9.2.8**.

making information readily available. However, the CJEU concluded that they could not benefit from exemptions for journalistic purposes:

> *"the processing by a publisher of a web page consisting in the publication of information relating to an individual may, in some circumstances, be carried out 'solely for journalistic purposes' and thus benefit by virtue of Article 9 of Directive 95/46, from derogations from the requirements laid down by the directive, whereas that does not appear to be so in the case of the processing carried out by the operator of a search engine"*[85].

Solely processed for journalistic purposes

10.5.6.9 ***Google Spain*** only considered journalistic purposes very briefly, and it is not clear from this brief reference if the CJEU concluded that Google could not rely on the provision because Google was not processing for journalistic purposes at all, or because this was not the *sole* purpose of its processing.

10.5.6.10 As far as search engines themselves are concerned, the distinction may not be significant. In ***NT1 & NT2 v Google LLC*** [2018] EWHC 799 (QB) Warby J, after having discussed ***Google Spain***, concluded robustly that search engines do *not* engage in processing for journalistic purposes at all, stating:

> "*... the concept* [of journalism] *is not so elastic that it can be stretched to embrace every activity that has to do with conveying information or opinions. To label all such activity as 'journalism' would be to elide the concept of journalism with that of communication. The two are plainly not the same, and I do not consider that Google's own activity can be equated with journalism*" [98].

Processing with a view to publication

10.5.6.11 Schedule 2, Pt 5, para.26(2) provides that the exemption only applies where "*the processing is being carried out with a view to the publication by a person of journalistic, academic, artistic or literary material*". "*Publish*" is defined at s.205(1) as meaning to "*make available to the public or a section of the public*".

10.5.6.12 In ***NT1 v Google***, Google argued that, under the 1998 Act, this phrase could extend not just to the actual publisher but to others—as long as the processing was with a view to publication by someone. In Google's case it argued that its processing was for journalistic purposes because it enabled others to access journalistic content—and so was undertaken "with a view to publication" by the original media sources. Warby J accepted that this phrase could extend to others, beyond the publisher. For example, "*processing by a printer to which a newspaper has outsourced its production might qualify*". However, Warby J roundly rejected any argument that this could apply to Google itself:

> "*... when Google responds to a search on an individual's name by facilitating*

access to journalistic content about that individual, this is purely accidental, and incidental to its larger purpose of providing automated access to third party content of whatever nature it may be, that it has identified and indexed and meets the search criteria specified by a user. That is a commercial purpose which, however, valuable it may be, is not undertaken for any of the special purposes, or 'with a view to' the publication by others of journalistic material within s.32(1)(a). Such processing is undertaken for Google's own purposes which are of a separate and distinct nature" [100].

10.5.6.13 In the ***Campbell v Mirror Group Newspapers Ltd*** [2002] EWCA Civ 1373, the courts considered whether "with a view to publication" meant that s.32 of the 1998 Act only offered an exemption up until the moment of publication. The Court of Appeal had no difficulty in dismissing this argument as absurd:

"*. . . it would seem totally illogical to exempt the data controller from the obligation, prior to publication, to comply with provisions which he reasonably believes are incompatible with journalism, but to leave him exposed to a claim for compensation under s.13 the moment that the data have been published. For these reasons we have reached the conclusion that, giving the provisions of the sub-sections their natural meaning and the only meaning that makes sense of them, they apply both before and after publication*" [120], [121].[8]

10.5.6.14 In the Report on the Leveson Inquiry, the Information Commissioner was tasked with publishing good practice guidelines on the application of data protection to the press. The Information Commissioner published *Data Protection and Journalism: A Guide for the Media,* v1.0, 4 September 2014, in response to this. In this, the Commissioner helpfully summarises the effect of the ***Campbell*** decision as follows:

"*As long as the information was originally collected and used with the ultimate aim of publication, the exemption can protect the media both before and after publication*" (p.32).

The Commissioner also notes:

"*This doesn't mean the organisation must be aiming to publish the personal data in question at that time for that particular story. Personal data can be retained with a view to it being used in a different story or in updating a story that has been already published. As long as the ultimate aim is to publish a story (or for someone else to publish it), all the background information collected, used or created as part of a journalist's day-to-day activities could*

[8] The Court of Appeal decision was overturned by the House of Lords. However, this was based on decisions about confidentiality. The House of Lords did not comment on data protection, so the Court of Appeal's comments on this point still stand.

also be exempt, even if those details are not included in any final article or programme – and even if no story is actually published or broadcast" (p.31).

Publication would be in the public interest

10.5.6.15 The exemption applies where "*the controller reasonably believes that the publication of the material would be in the public interest*" (para.26(2)(b)). Further:

> "*In determining whether publication would be in the public interest the controller must take into account the special importance of the public interest in the freedom of expression and information*" (DPA 2018 Sch.2 para.26(4).
> "*In determining whether it is reasonable to believe that publication would be in the public interest, the controller must have regard to any of the codes of practice or guidelines listed in sub-paragraph (6) that is relevant to the publication in question*" (Sch.2 para.26(5)).

Sub-paragraph 6 references the *BBC Editorial Guidelines*, the *Ofcom Broadcasting Code* and the *Editors' Code of Practice*. There is provision for this list to be amended by secondary legislation.

10.5.6.16 The exemption gives significant freedom to the media—specifically recognising the special importance of freedom of expression and allowing this to be determined by the controller, acting reasonably. Both of these points are addressed in the Information Commissioner's *Guide for the media*, which states:

> "*We recognise that there is an inherent public interest in freedom of expression itself, regardless of the specific content of the story. It is in the public interest to have a free and independent media informing the public about current events and providing information of general interest to the audience. We therefore accept that there will be a public interest in the full range of media output, from day-to-day stories about local events to celebrity gossip to major public interest investigations*" (p.34).
> "*... the exemption requires only a reasonable belief. This gives much more leeway than other exemptions ... In other words, the DPA respects the media's independent decisions on the public interest, and doesn't disregard them lightly. The ICO does not have to agree that publication is in the public interest, as long as the intended publisher's belief is a reasonable one*" (p.35).
> "*Any consideration of what is in the public interest must involve an element of proportionality—it cannot be in the public interest to disproportionately or unthinkingly interfere with an individual's fundamental privacy and data protection rights*".

10.5.6.17 This will have to be assessed on a case by case basis. The fact-specific nature of the test is also shown in the ***Naomi Campbell*** case, where the House of Lords concluded, in a majority 3:2 decision, that publication of certain information relating to Naomi Campbell's treatment by Narcotics Anonymous for drug addiction was in the public interest, but publication of accompanying pictures was not.

The controller reasonably believes that the application of those provisions would be incompatible with the special purposes

10.5.6.18 The special purposes provision does not exempt all processing from data protection considerations—only where the controller reasonably considers that compliance is not possible. Again, this is left to the controller's consideration, acting reasonably. The controller is given significant discretion—and responsibility—in relation to the special purposes. The controller will only be able to rely on the exemptions where it has applied its mind to the provisions and considered them. This point was considered in the case of ***NT1 v Google:***

> "*Each of* [DPA 1998] *s.32(1)(b) and (c) has a subjective and an objective element: the data controller must establish that it held a belief that publication would be in the public interest, and that this belief was objectively reasonable; it must establish a subjective belief that compliance with the provision from which it seeks exemption would be incompatible with the special purpose in question, and that this was an objectively reasonable belief . . . There is no evidence that anyone at Google ever gave consideration to the public interest in continued publication of the URLs complained of, at any time before NT1 complained*" [102].

The exemptions for freedom of expression

10.5.6.19 If a controller satisfies the above requirements in respect of the special purposes, then it is exempted from the following GDPR provisions in the DPA 2018.

Reference	Scope
Chapter II Principles	
art.5(1)(a)–(e)	Principles relating to processing
arts 6, 9 and 10	Lawful basis for processing personal data and special category data; restrictions on processing criminal conviction data
arts 7 and 8	Requirements for consent and parental consent for certain information society services
art.11	Provisions relating to processing which does not require the controller to identify the individual
Chapter III Data subject rights	
arts 10–21	There are exemptions from all data subject rights except the right not to be subject to an automated decision

Chapter IV Controller and processor	
arts 34(1) and (4)	Obligation to report personal data breach to the individual
art.36	Obligation to consult the Commissioner if a DPIA reveals unmitigated risks in relation to high risk processing
Chapter V data transfers to third countries	
art.44	The prohibition on transfer
Chapter VII co-operation and consistency	
arts 60 to 62	Co-operation
arts 63 to 67	Consistency

10.5.6.20 The exemption from the co-operation and consistency mechanisms is in line with rec.153, which provides that:

> "*Where such exemptions or derogations differ from one Member State to another, the law of the Member State to which the controller is subject should apply*".

10.5.6.21 The DPA 2018 Sch.2 Pt 5 para.3 states:

> "*The listed GDPR provisions do not apply to the extent that the controller reasonably believes that the application of those provisions would be incompatible with the special purposes*".

It is unclear how this will apply to the exemption from the co-operation and consistency mechanism: will the controller have to wait for the mechanism to have taken its course, and for a decision to have been adopted, in order for the controller to be able to show that the applying the eventual decision will be incompatible with the special purposes? It is difficult to see how a controller could ever demonstrate that it 'reasonably' believes the application of a decision taken via the consistency mechanism to be incompatible with the special purposes before it knows what will be required of it under a decision. However, it also seems illogical to require a lengthy decision-making process to be followed, when the controller may not be bound by the eventual decision in any event.

10.5.6.22 In addition to the exemptions set out in Sch.2, Pt 5, para.26, controllers should also recall the provisions of Sch.1, Pt 2, para.13 (**4.5.6.23**). This condition allows special category data to be disclosed (for example, to an investigative journalist) where this is carried out for the special purposes, with a view to the publication of personal data relating to the commission of unlawful or other improper acts and where the disclosure is necessary for reasons of substantial public interest and the controller reasonably believes that publication of the personal data would be in the public interest.

10.5.6.23 The exemptions are so extensive, it may be helpful for controllers to see what data protection obligations cannot be disapplied in favour of the special purposes. These are all obligations which could be characterised as relating to accountability, as summarised below:

Provision	Summary
art.24	Controller to adopt measures to ensure and to be able to demonstrate compliance
art.25	Controller to implement data protection measures by design and by default
art.26	Joint controllers to allocate responsibility
art.27	Appointment of representatives by controllers not established in the EU
arts 28 and 29	Provisions relating to appointment and activities of processors
art.30	Records of processing activities
art.31	Obligation to co-operate with supervisory authorities
arts 32 and 33	Security of processing and reporting personal data breaches to the Information Commissioner
art.35	Obligation to undertake data protection impact assessments (but no obligation to consult the Information Commissioner)
arts 37 to 39	Appointment of a data protection officer

Special arrangements for the special purposes relating to enforcement and court proceedings

10.5.6.24 Where personal data are processed for the special purposes, then there are restrictions on the enforcement and investigatory powers of the Information Commissioner, as well as limitations on court actions which could restrict publication. In many cases, no action can be taken unless and until the Information Commissioner has first reached a decision as to whether or not the processing is for the special purposes. Accordingly, we have considered this provision first, followed by the restrictions on the Commissioner's powers, then special arrangements for court proceedings and special defences to some of the criminal offences under the DPA 2018.

Determination by the Commissioner as to the special purposes

10.5.6.25 The DPA 2018 s.174(3) provides that the Commissioner:

"*may make a written determination, in relation to the processing of personal data, that*

a) *the personal data is not being processed only for the special purposes;*

b) *the personal data is not being processed with a view to the publication by a person of journalistic, academic, artistic or literary material which has not previously been published by the controller*".

The drafting does not make clear whether the sub-paragraphs are cumulative or independent. Logically, a determination either that personal data are not being processed only for the special purposes, or that personal data are not being published with a view to publication should be sufficient, as failure to satisfy either of these requirements would affect the public interest in freedom of expression. This was also the approach taken in the 1998 Act. If the Commissioner makes such a determination, then she must give written notice of this to the controller and processor, including details of rights of appeal under s.162 (s.174(4) and (5)). The notice is not effective until any appeals have been determined, or if the determination (or an appeal from that determination) is not appealed, the period allowed for appeal has expired (s.174(6)).

Restrictions on the Information Commissioner's powers as to the special purposes

10.5.6.26 The Commissioner's powers to investigate and to take enforcement action are all restricted where personal data are processed for the special purposes, as set out below.

Power	Ref.	Restriction
Investigatory		
Ability to require provision of information by information notice	s.143	May not give an information notice unless: a) a s.174 determination has taken place; or b) the Commissioner has reasonable grounds for suspecting that a s.174 determination could be made and the information is required in order to make that determination

Ability to carry out an assessment, including entering premises and viewing information and equipment	s.147(5)	May not give an assessment notice with respect to processing of personal data for special purposes
Powers of entry and inspection	Schs 15, para.3	Judge may not issue a warrant unless a s.174 determination has taken place
Enforcement		
Ability to require steps to be taken, or to refrain from taking steps by an enforcement notice[8]	s.152	May not serve a notice unless: 1) a s.174 determination has been made; and 2) the High Court has granted leave for the notice to be given. The court may only grant leave if it is satisfied that the Commissioner has reason to suspect that the failure in respect of which the notice is being served is of substantial public importance and the controller or processor has been given notice of the application for leave, unless (in accordance with the rules of court), the case is urgent.
Ability to issue a penalty notice for breach of a substantive data protection provision	s.156 (1) and (2)	

Special arrangements for special purposes processing in court proceedings

10.5.6.27 Section 176 of the DPA 2018 provides that the court must stay proceedings for a claim to compensation under s.169 or for a compliance order under s.167, where the proceedings relate, wholly or partly, to personal data processed for the special purposes. The provision can be invoked in response to a claim by a controller or processor, or where it appears to the court, that personal data to which the proceedings relate:

> "*a)* *is being processed only for the special purposes,*
> *b)* *is being processed with a view to the publication by any person of journalistic, academic, artistic or literary material, and*

9 There is no restriction on the Commissioner's ability to issue an enforcement notice requiring charges to be paid under s.137.

c) has not previously been published by the controller."

Under s.176(2), material published in the last 24 hours is disregarded.

10.5.6.28 The stay is effective until a determination by the Information Commissioner under s.174 takes effect, or until the claim is withdrawn. In ***Stunt v Associated Newspapers Limited and the Information Commissioner*** [2018] EWCA Civ 1780, the Court of Appeal was asked to consider the equivalent wording under s.32(4) of the 1998 Act and to decide whether the requirement for a stay would apply whenever a controller asserted that any of the personal data to which the proceedings related is held with a view to the intended publication of new material in the future. The Court of Appeal rejected this argument in favour of a purposive approach whereby a stay would not be granted in cases relating to material which has already been published and the processing which culminated in that publication ([64] and [68]). The Court of Appeal also specifically noted that this interpretation would be in line with the provisions at s.176 of the DPA 2018.

10.5.6.29 Notwithstanding the decision of the Court of Appeal in ***Stunt***, as will be apparent from the comments above, proceedings involving the special purposes may take a considerable period. Where a stay is relevant, there is a right for the publisher to appeal against any determination by the Commissioner and the determination will not be effective until all appeals are concluded, or the period allowed for appeal has expired. Rosemary Jay, in *Data Protection Law & Practice*, p.556, noted that the equivalent provisions in the 1998 Act meant that

> "*an individual who wishes to use the Act to take action against the press will need deep pockets, a robust constitution and preferably a favourable life expectancy*".

10.5.6.30 In ***Stunt*** the claimant argued that the effect of the equivalent provisions in the 1998 Act was so draconian as to mean that the Act mis-implemented the Data Protection Directive. At first instance, Popplewell J agreed that the provision would produce lengthy delay and his succinct summary of the difficulties is quoted by the Court of Appeal:

> "*The upshot is that once a data controller has made a claim that the two conditions in s.32(4) are fulfilled, the data subject cannot compel the Commissioner to embark upon a s.45 exercise, which if it takes place at all may well involve a lengthy process in which the data subject is largely a spectator, with the result that the stay is itself either permanent or of lengthy duration*" [40].

10.5.6.31 However, Popplewell J at first instance, and the majority in the Court of Appeal, rejected the claimant's argument that this mis-implemented the Directive, noting that the this restriction on pre-publication restraint was within the margin of manoeuvre allowed to Member States, that the very availability of pre-publication restraint for data protection breaches would have a chilling effect on freedom of expression and the availability of damages later may be a sufficient protection. However, the Court of Appeal noted that the disagreements between the members of the court would make a reference to the CJEU appropriate, although, at the date of writing, the terms of the reference are not yet available.

Assistance and guidance by the Information Commissioner in cases involving the special purposes

10.5.6.32 If, notwithstanding these challenges, an individual does wish to engage in court proceedings relating to processing for the special purposes, then they may apply to the Commissioner for assistance in those proceedings, under s.175. The Commissioner may only grant assistance where the case involves a matter of substantial public interest and must notify both the applicant and the other party in the proceedings that assistance is being provided. The assistance could include paying the applicant's costs or indemnifying the applicant in relation to the liability to pay costs in relation to the proceedings. There are provisions for the Commissioner to recover these expenses from costs or sums payable to the applicant in the proceedings.

10.5.6.33 Lastly, under s.177, the Commissioner must produce and publish guidance about the steps that an individual may take if they consider that an organisation involved in journalism is failing to comply with data protection legislation. The guidance must include details about relevant complaints procedures (explaining who runs the scheme, the scope of the scheme and how a complaint may be made), as well as the powers of the Commissioners and the courts in relation to such complaints. The guidance must be published by 23 May 2019.

Criminal offences

10.5.6.34 Where a person obtains, processes or discloses personal data for the special purposes, with a view to publication by a person of journalistic, academic, artistic or literary material and in the reasonable belief that, in the particular circumstances, the relevant act was justified as being in the public interest (s.170(3)(3)(c) and s.171(2)(4(c)), then this is a defence to proceedings under s.170 for unlawful obtaining or disclosure of personal data or to the new offence, at s.171, of re-identification of de-identified personal data.

Codes of practice and ongoing reviews of data protection and the media

10.5.6.35 We have already mentioned that the Leveson Report instructed the Information Commissioner to produce guidance on data protection and the media. This is written into the DPA 2018 at s.124, which requires the Commissioner to prepare a code of practice which contains:

> "*a)* *practical guidance in relation to the processing of personal data for the purposes of journalism in accordance with the requirements of the data protection legislation, and*
>
> *b)* *such other guidance as the Commissioner considers appropriate to*

> *promote good practice in the processing of personal data for the purposes of journalism*".

This *Code* will, therefore, replace the Commissioner's existing *Guide*. The Commissioner is instructed to consult when drawing up the *Code* and to ensure that the *Code* takes into account both the interests of data subjects and others and the special importance of the public interest in freedom of expression and information (s.124(5)). As with other statutory codes, the *Code* must be submitted by the Secretary of State to Parliament, which, if it wishes, is able to vote not to approve the code. For more information on the status of codes, see **1.3.8.10**.

Ongoing reports on the special purposes

10.5.6.36 As mentioned, the provisions in the DPA 2018 relating to the media were subject to intense debate in Parliament. To ensure that an effective balance is struck between the two interests of data protection and freedom of expression, the DPA 2018 requires two periodic reviews to be undertaken.

10.5.6.37 The first is a review to be undertaken by the Commissioner of the extent to which the processing of personal data for the purposes of journalism complies with the legislation and good practice in each part of the UK. The review must be undertaken, initially, in respect of the first four years of the Act's application and, thereafter, for subsequent five-year periods. The first report must be commenced sometime in the period December 2022 to May 2023 and must be completed within 18 months. The report is to be submitted to the Secretary of State and then to Parliament and to the devolved parliament and assemblies.

10.5.6.38 The second report, required by s.179, is to be prepared by the Secretary of State, or someone appointed by him and is to consider the effectiveness of alternative dispute resolution procedures by non-broadcast media organisations. This report is to be completed by 23 May 2021 and is to be repeated every three years. Again, a copy of the report is to be provided to Parliament and to the devolved administrations.

10.5.7 Research, statistics and archiving

10.5.7.1 Controllers that process personal data for archival purposes or for scientific or historical research or statistical purposes are given more flexibility under the GDPR as regards purpose limitation and data retention periods. The GDPR also allows Member States to permit processing of special categories of data for these purposes and to introduce exemptions to data subject rights. The UK has taken advantage of these provisions. All of these provisions depend on appropriate safeguards being followed—both as set out in the GDPR itself and also in the DPA 2018. This section considers:

- what types of processing are covered by these provisions;
- what safeguards must be followed;

- the special rules in the GDPR;
- the additional special rules in the DPA 2018.

Which processing is covered?

10.5.7.2 Article 89 refers to processing "*for archiving purposes in the public interest, scientific or historical research purposes or statistical purposes*". Each of these purposes is further clarified in recitals.

Archiving

10.5.7.3 Not all processing for archival purposes can benefit from these provisions: it must be in the public interest. This is further emphasised by rec.158 which refers to "records of public interest" where there is a legal obligation on the body running the archive to "*acquire, preserve, appraise, arrange, describe, communicate, promote, disseminate and provide access to records of enduring value for general public interest*". However, the recital does make clear that these can be public authorities, or public or private bodies. Examples are given of archives which provide information on political behaviour under former totalitarian state regimes, genocide, war crimes and crimes against humanity, including the Holocaust in particular.

Historical research

10.5.7.4 There is only brief comment on this in rec.160, which notes that this should include "research for genealogical purposes".

Scientific research

10.5.7.5 Recital 157 emphasises the importance of research, referring to the important role played by registries, which mean that

> "*researchers can obtain new knowledge of great value with regard to widespread medical conditions ... research results obtained through registries provide solid, high-quality, knowledge which can provide the basis for the formulation and implementation of knowledge-based policy, improve the quality of life for a number of people and improve the efficiency of social services ...*".

As a result, rec.159 notes that scientific research should be "*interpreted in a broad manner*"—covering both "*fundamental research, applied research and privately funded research*". Reference is made to art.179(1) Treaty on the Functioning of the European Union (TFEU) which sets out the EU's objective of achieving a European Research Area —and this again makes clear the broad scope of research, referring to the role of undertakings, small and medium sized enterprises as well as research centres and universities.

10.5.7.6 An example may assist. From about 1760 to 1832 several thousand voyages for the East India Company between the UK and India or China took place and almost all the captains' logs ("Journals") for this period survive and are in the British Library. These afford much information about the ships, their crew and passengers. But they are also of interest to meteorologists since they provide expertly gathered information as to weather and sea conditions in the Indian Ocean over several decades, for comparison with more recent records as to the warming or cooling of the planet. Thus, a record made for business purposes may prove to have great value not only as a historical record but also as a record of scientific observation. The GDPR is right to deal with archiving and historical and scientific records together.

10.5.7.7 Recital 159 provides that

> "*specific conditions should apply in particular as regards the publication or otherwise of disclosure of persona data in the context of scientific research purposes. If the result of scientific research in particular in the health context gives reason for further measures in the interest of the data subject, the general rules of this Regulation should apply in view of those measures*".

These points are addressed in the safeguards set out in s.19 of the DPA 2018.

Statistical purposes

10.5.7.8 Recital 162 notes that

> "*Statistical purposes mean any operation of collection and the processing of personal data necessary for statistical surveys or for the production of statistical results. Those statistical results may further be used for different purposes, including a scientific research purpose. The statistical purpose implies that the result of the processing for statistical purposes is not personal data, but aggregate data, and that this result or the personal data are not used in support of measures or decisions regarding any particular natural person*".

Recital 162 also notes that Union or Member State law should set out appropriate safeguards for processing of personal data for statistical purposes. Where official national or EU statistics are concerned, then rec.163 points to Regulation (EC) No. 223/2009 which sets out general rules for such statistics.

10.5.7.9 Processing for statistical purposes used to be relevant only to a limited number of controllers. However, the increasing availability of large data sets has meant that many organisations now analyse personal data to see what lessons can be learnt from this. This has led the Information Commissioner to prepare a detailed report on *Big data, artificial intelligence, machine learning and data protection* (v2.2). As well as describing what each of these terms means and working through how they are affected by data protection requirements, the report also recommends (p.97) six key safeguards for use of big data. These are:

- consider if analysis can be carried out without personal data;
- be transparent about processing of personal data for this purpose;

- use privacy impact assessments (the more general concept of determining privacy impact, of which data protection impact assessments are one type);
- implement privacy by design;
- use ethical principles;
- implement auditable machine learning algorithms to check the basis of decisions and to check for bias and errors.

Safeguards for archiving, etc

10.5.7.10 Certain safeguards are set out in art.89; others in s.19 of the DPA 2018. Article 89 focuses on ensuring that "*technical and organisational measures are in place in particular in order to ensure respect for the principle of data minimisation*". The article further requires that pseudonymisation, and anonymisation, must be used if the purposes of processing can still be fulfilled if these techniques are used.

10.5.7.11 This presupposes that the type of scientific or historical processing is known when the data has been archived or otherwise collected. This may not always be so. However, in some cases the data subjects will all be dead when the processing of the archive takes place.

The DPA 2018 sets out additional safeguards, broadly in line with those which applied under the 1998 Act. These are that:

- the processing must not be "*likely to cause substantial damage or substantial distress to a data subject*"; and
- the processing must not be carried out for the purpose of "*measures or decisions with respect to a particular data subject, unless the purposes for which the processing is necessary include the purposes of approved medical research*".

10.5.7.12 Approved medical research is further defined at s.19(4) and includes medical research approved by a research ethics committee. The definition of approved medical research can be amended by secondary legislation. The processing of personal data as part of a clinical trial will result in measures or decisions being taken with regard to a particular data subject. The reference to approve medical research is, therefore, necessary to ensure that such trials can rely on the scientific research condition for their processing of personal data. Recital 156 makes clear that the GDPR is not intended to override other relevant legislation—in particular clinical trials legislation—which continues to apply to scientific research.

10.5.7.13 Schedule 19 to the DPA 2018 (minor and consequential amendments) contains amendments to numerous other legislative provisions which allow for certain data sets (primarily the electoral register) to be used for research purposes, by requiring the safeguards in the GDPR and the DPA 2018to be applied to such processing.

Special provisions under the GDPR

Purpose limitation

10.5.7.14 Where personal data are processed for research purposes then art.5(1)(b) of the GDPR provides that purpose limitation does not apply:

> "*further processing for archiving purposes in the public interest, scientific or historical research purposes or statistical purposes shall, in accordance with Article 89(1), not be considered to be incompatible with the initial purposes*".

Recital 50 further notes that in this case "*the legal basis provided by Union or Member State law for the processing of personal data may also provide a legal basis for further processing*". It is not entirely clear from these provisions whether this just absolves the controller from needing a separate legal basis under art.6 or whether this also extends to the additional conditions for processing of special category data under art.9.

Retention periods

10.5.7.15 Article 5(1)(e) provides that

> "*personal data may be stored for longer periods insofar as the personal data will be processed solely for archiving purposes in the public interest, scientific or historical research purposes or statistical purposes in accordance with Article 89(1)*".

Special provisions under the DPA 2018

Conditions for processing special category data

10.5.7.16 Article 9(2)(j) of the GDPR provides that special category data may be processed if the processing:

> "*is necessary for archiving purposes in the public interest, scientific or historical research purposes or statistical purposes in accordance with Article 89(1) based on Union or Member State law which shall be proportionate to the aim pursued, respect the essence of the right to data protection and provide for suitable and specific measures to safeguard the fundamental rights and interests of the data subject*".

The provision is enabling, allowing other laws to permit processing of special category data for these purposes. The DPA 2018 follows up on this, with Sch.1, Pt 1, para.4 permitting processing of special category data for these purposes, provided that the safeguards in art.89(1) and s.19 are followed and provided that the processing is in the public interest. The GDPR only refers expressly to the public interest in connection with archiving (presumably on the basis that this is not necessary for the other purposes, which are accepted to be always in the public interest). However, the DPA 2018 extends this condition to processing for any of these purposes.

10.5.7.17 Controllers should remember that this condition will only allow them to process special category data without consent for data protection purposes. Other laws may still require the controller to obtain consent—for example, the law of confidentiality, or the Clinical Trials Regulation (Regulation (EU) No. 536/2014), which, rec.161 reminds, continues to apply for purposes of consenting to participation in such trials. As controllers have to explain the lawful basis for processing of personal data in their privacy notices, controllers will likely end up with informed consent documents for participation in a trial, which will include data protection language where the lawful basis for process is stated to be scientific research (not consent). See **4.2.8.5** for further comment on this.

10.5.7.18 The quid pro quo for this ability to process special category data for research purposes is a specific right to object to such processing. This is set out in art.21(6) which provides that:

> "*Where personal data are processed for scientific or historical research purposes or statistical purposes pursuant to Article 89(1), the data subject, on grounds relating to his or her particular situation, shall have the right to object to processing of personal data concerning him or her, unless the processing is necessary for the performance of a task carried out for reasons of public interest*".

Accordingly, organisations running medical registries or archives relating to former totalitarian regimes, are likely to be exempt from this right to object, whereas private sector controllers processing personal data for scientific research are likely to be subject to this right.

Exemptions for processing for research purposes

10.5.7.19 The GDPR art.89(3) provides that Union or Member State law may introduce exemptions from data subject rights

> "*in so far as such rights are likely to render impossible or seriously impair the achievement of the specific purposes, and such derogations are necessary for the fulfilment of those purposes*".

Where processing is both for research purposes and other purposes, then art.89(4) provides that the exemption shall only apply to the research purpose.

10.5.7.20 Article 89(2) introduces this possibility to derogate for scientific, historical research and statistical processing. Article 89(3) does the same for processing for archival purposes. The two conditions are nearly identical, covering access, rectification, restriction and rights to object—save that the ability to derogate for archival purposes can also extend to portability and the obligation to provide notice of rectification and erasure to each recipient to whom data have been disclosed.

10.5.7.21 The UK takes advantage of this provision in Sch.2, Pt 6, para.26. This provides an exemption from access rights; rectification and restriction of processing. Paragraph 26(2)(d) also provides an exemption from the right to object to processing set out at art.21(1) of the GDPR—that is processing which is based on legitimate interests or which is carried out to perform a task carried out in the public interest. There is no exemption from the right to object set out at art.21(6) —that is to object to processing for research purposes. Again, the safeguards in art.89(1) and s.19 must always be followed for the exemption to be available. In addition, so far as processing for research and statistics is concerned, the exemption is only available provided that "*the results of the research or any resulting statistics are not made available in a form which identifies a data subject*".

10.5.8 Domestic purposes

10.5.8.1 The 1998 Act stated, at s.36, that personal data processed by an individual only for personal, family, or household affairs, were exempt from the most of that Act. Personal data processed for domestic purposes are similarly exempt from current data protection legislation, although, because of the way the legislation operates, there is no need for an express derogation.

10.5.8.2 Article 2(2)(c) of the GDPR provides that the Regulation does not apply to processing of personal data "*by a natural person in the course of a purely personal or household activity*". For so long as the UK is an EU Member State, the GDPR has direct effect in the UK. It follows that there is no need for an exclusion in the DPA 2018, as processing for this purpose is not covered by the Regulation in the first place. Part 3 of the DPA 2018 sets out data protection principles which apply to processing by competent authorities for law enforcement purposes (**15.1**) and Pt 4 sets out the principles which apply to processing by the intelligence services (**15.2**). Again, such principles cannot possibly apply to processing for domestic purposes, so there is no need for an exemption. The Information Commissioner is, however, at s.142, given powers to serve information notices on individuals in order to determine if their processing is for purely personal or household activities or not.

10.5.8.3 There has been litigation on the equivalent provision under the Data Protection Directive. The CJEU first considered this in the case of ***Bodil Lindqvist*** (also discussed in **9.2.2** in connection with data transfer abroad). The case concerned a member of a Swedish Church, who set up web pages with information about the Church, information about Mrs Lindqvist herself and about some of her fellow parishioners (including the fact that one was on medical leave to an injured foot). The CJEU held that information posted was personal data. The Court was asked to decide whether the processing was exempt on the basis that it was carried out by a natural person for exclusively personal or domestic purposes. The Court held that the processing here was for church purposes, but that, in any event, the domestic purposes exemption:

"*... must be interpreted as relating only to activities which are carried out in the course of private or family life of individuals, which is clearly not the case with the processing of personal data consisting in publication on the internet so that those data are made accessible to an indefinite number of people*" [47].

10.5.8.4 The ***Bodil Lindqvist*** case dates from 2003 and readers may wonder if this s conclusion would be the same today, given the use of social media. Recital 18 of the Regulation provides that household activities

"*could include correspondence and the holding of addresses, or social networking and online activity undertaken within the context of such activities. However, this Regulation applies to controllers or processors which provide the means for processing personal data for such personal or household activities*".

The recital also notes that for this provision to apply, the processing must have "*no connection to a professional or commercial activity*". So, use of social media is not necessarily inherently incompatible with processing for personal or household activities. However, the exemption will be interpreted strictly and widespread publication to the world at large will still not be exempt. These points were considered in 2019 in ***Sergejs Buivids v Datu valsts inspekcija,*** (C-345/17, 14 February 2019), where the CJEU was faced with the case of an individual who was arrested, secretly videoed police officers while he was arrested, and then posted this footage on YouTube. Mr. Buivids argued either that the processing should be covered by the domestic purposes exemption, or that it should be seen as processing for journalistic activities (**10.5.6.6**). The CJEU noted that because processing for domestic activities falls completely outside data protection law, the exemption must be interpreted strictly [41]. The CJEU also followed ***Lindqvist*** in noting that publication of data online to an unrestricted number of people is not covered by this exemption [43].

10.5.8.5 The conclusion in ***Lindqvist*** that processing for Church-related purposes is not covered by this provision was also re-affirmed by the CJEU in 2018 in the case of ***Tietosuojavaltuutettu intervening parties: Jehovan todistajat—uskonnollinen yhdyskunta,*** (C-25/17, EU:C:2018:551). This related to processing by the Jehovah's Witnesses religious community, where one argument raised was that such processing fell outside the scope of the Data Protection Directive because it was for domestic purposes. The CJEU flatly rejected this, at para.42, noting that

"*As the Court held, Article 3(2), second indent, of Directive 95/46 must be interpreted as covering only activities that are carried out in the context of the private or family life of individuals. In that connection, an activity cannot be regarded as being purely personal or domestic where its purpose is to make the data collected accessible to an unrestricted number of people or where that activity extends, even partially, to a public space and is accordingly*

> *directed outwards from the private setting of the person processing the data in that manner (see, to that effect, judgments of 6 November 2003,* ***Lindqvist,*** *C-101/01, EU:C:2003:596, para.47; of 16 December 2008,* ***Satakunnan Markkinapörssi and Satamedia,*** *C-73/07, EU:C:2008:727, para.44; and of 11 December 2014,* ***Ryneš,*** *C-212/13, EU:C:2014:2428, paras 31 and 33)".*

Preaching is, by definition, an activity which is "directed outwards" so cannot be covered by the exclusion.

10.5.8.6 The case of ***František Ryneš v Úřad pro ochranu osobních údajů*** (C-212/13 EU:C:2014:2428) related to an individual whose property had been subject to vandalism. To protect it, he installed a home CCTV surveillance system. The CJEU concluded that this could not benefit from the domestic purposes provision, because the CCTV system was not limited to his property and extended to images of people in a public space and:

> "*to the extent that video surveillance . . . covers, even partially, a public space and is accordingly directed outwards from the private setting of the person processing the data in that manner, it cannot be regarded as an activity which is purely 'personal or household*".

10.5.8.7 The principle has also been considered in some UK cases. In ***Ittihadieh v 5–11 Cheyne Gardens RTM Co Ltd*** [2017] EWCA Civ 121, the Court of Appeal rejected an attempt to apply ***Ryneš*** so broadly that an individual's complaints about neighbours in the same block of flats would fall outside of the domestic purposes exemption, concluding that:

> "*activities relating to the management of a private block of flats in which the putative data controller resides (including the processing of his neighbour's personal data in so far as they concern matters arising from or relating to the management of that block) fall within the scope of the exemption because they directly concern his private life and also directly concern his household*" [76].

However, in ***Law Society v Kordowski*** [2011] EWHC 3185 (QB), Tugendhat J roundly dismissed suggestions from the then Information Commissioner that the individual running the blog, "Solicitors from Hell", would be within the domestic purposes exemption.

10.5.8.8 Finally, there is some helpful guidance from the ICO in *Social networking and online forums—when does the DPA apply?* v1.1 20140226. The Guidance says that the domestic purposes exemption can be invoked only by individuals; an organisation cannot use it (p3). Groups of individuals need to be considered carefully. Sometimes an informal group of friends can over time morph into a club. To start with there may be informal exchange of messages between friends. But once the group becomes a club, the processing is for an organisation and the domestic purposes exemption is not applicable. The ICO is of the view that it depends on the purposes: an individual processing personal data on behalf of a club, for example, is outside the domestic purpose exemption. The purposes of that processing will be the club's not the individual's. Processing a Christmas card list is prima facie domestic purposes, but if a sole trader uses their Christmas card list to advertise their services, then they lose the domestic purposes exemption.

PART II

The Data Audit

CHAPTER 11
Preparations for Audit

11.1 ROLE AND SCOPE OF AUDIT

11.1.1 The only way to be sure that you are processing your various files about identifiable human beings (data subjects) in compliance with the legislation is by actual examination. If you do not know what you have you cannot be sure you are processing it compliantly. All files which contain any personal data must be identified and questions asked as to where that data comes from, how it is gathered, how it is processed, how it is corrected when necessary, how it is disclosed, where (if anywhere) else it goes to, how long it is kept, and how and when it is finally deleted. To do this the organisation needs a data audit.

11.1.2 A data protection officer in particular (**1.3.7, 13.2**) needs to be satisfied that they understand all the items that go to make up the personal data which must be handled at all times in a fully compliant way. So too must a data protection professional in charge of the day-to-day management of data protection.

11.1.3 So the audit should be concerned not only with the personal data files but also compliance: the mechanisms to ensure that the legislative requirements are at all times observed. **Part II** of this book deals with the audit, before moving on to consider compliance and accountability. By the end of the audit the organisation should know what personal data it "owns", what, if any, data it processes on behalf of others, whether its personal data is at all times fully compliant with the legislation, whether it has in place mechanisms to reinforce that, and whether those mechanisms are likely to be sufficient to ensure continued compliance in the future.

11.1.4 On completion of the audit, improvements to the way data is handled can be implemented (**Ch.13**). A data audit like any other audit is a snapshot of an organisation's activity at a particular time. It does not by itself guarantee continued compliance, even though it may uncover nothing contrary to the legislation.

11.1.5 By its nature the audit needs to delve into every part of the organisation. Personal data which is handled perfectly correctly in one department may be used very improperly in another department. For example, the sales team may follow the requirements of the legislation in dealing with customer data, while the marketing team may be unaware of the full implications of the legislation and recklessly ignoring it. It is also the case that not all the data will be computer files or information on the web. Certain types of manual files, information such as CCTV and sound recordings (e.g. voice mail) are also within the ambit of the legislation (**5.5.2.8, 6.9.2.3**) and need to be considered, as well as non-automated public sector records, if any (**1.2.5.6**). In examining what happens to data, consideration must also be given to its receipt from, and transmission outside, the organisation, whether with trading partners (suppliers, dealers and distributors, for example), regulatory or Government bodies, other marketing organisations and also the public; and whether transmitted as a computer file, on the web, by email, written letter, in the press, as a video image or a sound recording, or even disclosed internally—for example as a telephone call. As we shall see (**Ch. 9**), the precise relationship between the UK organisation and those organisations outside the UK to whom it transmits personal data—whether as contractors, partners, subsidiaries or branches—may also be crucial.

Scope of the audit

11.1.6 We speak in this chapter of an organisation's audit, but the audit may be of only part of an organisation, and indeed if the organisation is a large one it may well be simpler to audit each department in turn. The danger to watch out for is where data is transferred from one department to another. To guard against missing this, again scrutiny as to source and destination of data is vital. As part of the preparations for an audit a decision will have to be taken as to whether to audit the entire organisation or whether some more limited audit of part of the organisation is more appropriate.

11.1.7 So far, we have spoken about an audit of data protection within an organisation. In this book we have also touched on the Privacy and Electronic Communications Regulations (PECR) which overlap with data protection, share the same regulator (the Information Commissioner), but derive from separate legislation (**7.4**). The question must arise whether compliance with this also should be audited.

11.1.8 The Information Commissioner's Office (ICO) conduct data protection assessments which are effectively audits (**3.4.2.14**ff). They also conduct audits of compliance with the PECR and have published a useful paper about this: *Audit: a guide to ICO privacy and electronic communications regulations audits* v2.0 May 2014 (referred to as *Audit: a guide*). It is directed at electronic communications providers (*Audit: a guide* para.1.1) and specifically mentions PECR reg.5 which is concerned with the security of public electronic services (p.15 Appendix A). As such it lies outside this book. However, general compliance with the PECR by controllers and processors seems to us desirable and something which should be covered.

11.1.9 Another aspect to be clarified at the outset is precisely what legislation the audit is being conducted under:

- GDPR (the EU or UK variant);
- law enforcement processing under DPA 2018 Pt 3 (**15.1**); and
- intelligence services processing under DPA 2018 Pt 4 (**15.2**).

Timing of the audit

11.1.10 Even if you have had an audit fairly recently, if it was before 25 May 2018 there are aspects of the GDPR which may cause you to look again. The new requirements for consent comprise one example (**4.2**).

11.1.11 We have said that the audit will be a snapshot of the personal data processed by the organisation at a particular time. Organisations change all the time. A snapshot of something moving tends to be a blur. It follows that the snapshot should be done expeditiously.

11.1.12 One further point: the audit will need to be done again from time to time, not only as the organisation changes, but also as the law develops. The GDPR and the DPA 2018 are new pieces of legislation and it is reasonable to expect a bedding-down process over the next year or two.

11.1. 13 The end product of the audit should be a written report. This should be an analysis of what personal data the organisation processes, whether, and if so to what extent, the organisation is non-compliant or at risk of being non-compliant, and how future compliance can be achieved and maintained (**Pt III**).

11.2 WHO SHOULD CONDUCT THE AUDIT?

11.2.1 The choice is between:

- your own in-house staff;
- outside consultants; or
- the ICO.

In-house audit

11.2.2 The choice of in-house staff has the merit that it should be inexpensive. But the immediate question is who among your in-house staff? Should it be HR? or IT? Or someone else? Above all you must consider whether they have the necessary data protection knowledge. There is a danger that your in-house auditing staff may have insufficient experience of data protection—or of auditing. There is also a danger of delay in completing the audit as the auditing staff will have other duties and may be summoned back to the day job by some crisis. There is also a risk of in-house auditing staff thinking they already know it all, since they will be fully conversant with the organisation. Worse still they may try to cover up or gloss over failings in particular parts of the organisation. Finally, it must be admitted that auditing can ruffle feathers. This may result in an in-house team of auditors either pulling their punches or leaving permanently damaged relationships.

Audit by consultants

11.2.3 Outside consultants will cost money. But against that, outside auditors should be data protection professionals with relevant experience (ask them about it). They will bring fresh eyes to the organisation. They will be less likely to be bamboozled or intimidated. They will be interested in completing the audit swiftly. Finally, any treading on corns can be blamed on the auditors who will soon have gone, and there should be no permanent damage to relationships in the organisation.

11.2.4 An audit can uncover both good practices—which are to be encouraged—and bad practices, which are to be rectified. The fact that an organisation was aware of bad practices and areas of non-compliance at a particular date could be useful information for those considering later action against the company if those problems have not been rectified. One way of minimising this risk is to ensure that the audit is undertaken by a lawyer, with its conclusions given as legal advice to the organisation, so that the recommendations may benefit from legal professional privilege.

Audit by the Information Commissioner's Office

11.2.5 Finally there is the ICO. Their website tells us

> "*An audit provides an assessment of whether your organisation is following good data protection practice. We believe that audits provide a key role in assisting organisations in understanding and meeting their data protection obligations. The audit looks at whether you have effective policies and procedures in place and whether you are following them and includes recommendations from the ICO on how to improve.*
> *You benefit from the data protection knowledge and experience of our audit team, at no expense to your organisation. It is an opportunity for your staff to discuss relevant data protection issues with the members of the ICO's audit team.*"

11.2.6 The ICO describe their methods:

> "*Following agreement of a scope of work, which is formally documented in a letter of engagement, we:*
> *Carry out an off site check of policies and procedures;*

Carry out an on site check of procedures in practice;
Provide a report which outlines good practice and any areas of improvement, with practical recommendations to help you to address these where appropriate;
Write an executive summary which we can publish on our website with your consent
Carry out a follow up review approximately six months after audit."

11.2.7 This is the point to mention the ICO's statutory duties in this area. GDPR art.58(1) gives supervisory authorities (i.e. the ICO) the power "*(b) to carry out investigations in the form of data protection audits*". DPA 2018 s.129 reinforces this in the form of:

> "*the power, with consent of the controller or processor, to carry out an assessment of whether the controller or processor is complying with good practice in the processing of personal data.*
> *(2) The Commissioner must inform the controller or processor of the results of such an assessment.*"

11.2.8 Good practice is defined in DPA 2018 s.128:

> "'*good practice in the processing of personal data' means such practice in the processing of personal data as appears to the Commissioner to be desirable having regard to the interests of data subjects and others, including compliance with the requirements of the data protection legislation.*"

It will be noted that good practice is not confined to legislative compliance —a point amplified by the ICO Guidance on audits:

> "*The good practice activities we have listed are not necessary to ensure compliance. However, they are things which we have observed work well in practice and positively impact the organisation's ability to comply with the legislation we are responsible for.*"

11.2.9 The ICO aim to complete a report in 30 days. But they also say:

> "*As we can audit only a limited number of organisations each year, we want to share our findings so others can learn from them. We have therefore published a number of reports detailing some of the good practice and areas for improvement we have seen.*"

So they may not be willing to take your particular job on at the time when you want it.

11.2.10 In summary, the ICO are:

- free;

- very experienced;
- if you follow the ICO's guidance, you can never be criticised even if they were to be found subsequently to be wrong;
- but they have a very slightly different agenda;
- and may not be able to undertake the audit when you want it, though they will do it expeditiously if and when they start;
- you may be reluctant to expose your organisation's shortcomings to the regulator—or allow the ICO to publish details of your organisation on their website;
- you will virtually be obliged to comply with any recommendations they make, however expensive or onerous.

11.3 PROCEDURES TO BE PUT IN PLACE BEFORE THE AUDIT

11.3.1 A recurrent theme of **Pt II** of this book is the putting in place of management structures to facilitate compliance, and a key part of this is the need for the compliance strategy to have the full support of the Board (**13.2.3.7**). Whether or not your existing mechanisms for handling data protection have the support from the Board, you should certainly ensure that the audit process enjoys that support. Only with that support can your auditors get at the truth about your handling of personal data. The only way their report will be of any real value to your organisation is if its findings are addressed to the Board and the Board takes full note of them. This means that the Report from the auditors at the end of their study should be seen and discussed by the Board. Even if the organisation already has a data protection officer, who would probably be the person to deal with the day-to-day relations with the auditors, the ultimate responsibility of the Board is paramount.

11.3.2 It is of course very much in the Board's interest to take a leading part in all this since as we have seen (**3.2.1**) they and other senior officers can potentially be personally liable for failures in data protection.

11.3.3 It follows that if the auditors have the support of the Board, the staff will need to be aware of the purpose of the audit and the necessity of compliance. They should be informed in advance of the audit and its purpose and instructed to make all information asked for readily available to the auditors. Any union representation or other formal mechanism for consultation with staff should also be used.

11.3.4 All existing data protection procedures, codes, strategies, and regulatory frameworks (however incomplete), instructions in staff handbooks or an intranet, should be put at the disposal of the auditors before they start. Other documents might include all staff recruitment and appointment literature and procedures, and any scripts used in call centres. The provision of all these documents will help the auditors to see where compliance is most likely to be weak and ensure that such areas are thoroughly investigated.

11.3.5 The auditors will also wish to see any processor contracts which the organisation is a party to, whether the organisation is the controller or the processor. Following this there may be a need for the auditors to talk to the other party in such processor contracts—i.e. the processor(s) if the organisation is a controller, and the controller(s) if the organisation acts a processor. If there are joint controllers they may need to talk to other joint controllers. There may also be a need to talk to any other external organisations to whom the commissioning organisation discloses personal data.

11.3.6 The GDPR provides for a good deal of documentation to be kept by each controller or processor. All this should be made available to the auditor before the audit begins. It includes such items as:

- legitimate interest assessments under art.6(1)(f);
- the records to demonstrate data subject consents under art.7(1);
- privacy notices under arts 13–14;
- records of the arrangements between two or more joint controllers (art.26);
- records of processing activities in GDPR art.30;
- any Data Protection Impact Assessments (DPIAs) carried out according to GDPR arts 35–36;
- documentation to determine whether or not to appoint a data protection officer (art.37);
- appropriate policy document if special category personal data is processed in accordance with one of the conditions in Sch.1 under DPA 2018.

11.3.7 The auditors will also need to understand the organisation generally and will want an organogram or other document showing the structure of the organisation and its constituent parts, the names and contact details of key staff, and the geographical distribution of staff functions.

11.3.8 Another group of documents for the auditors should include any communications to or from the ICO, or the police insofar as they relate to data protection, an idea of the incidence of data subject and other requests and rights under GDPR arts 13–22 and full details of any personal data breaches which have occurred and were reportable to the Commissioner under art.33, as well as access to the record of personal data breaches which were not reported, so as to allow assessment of the approach to reporting.

11.3.9 Like any other external consultants, the auditors should be given all necessary facilities at the organisation: a room, desks, parking places, appropriate access to the organisation's network, etc.

11.3.10 The auditors themselves will also be processing personal data when they conduct the audit, in that they will inevitably have disclosed to them some of the personal data which the organisation controls. Whether external auditors are controllers or processors will depend on the nature of the organisation conducting the audit and the level of discretion afforded to the auditors. Where the auditors are data processors, then it will be necessary that the contract for the audit should comply with requirements relating to appointment of processors which are discussed in more detail in **13.7**. In particular, the commissioning organisation should follow GDPR art.28 and satisfy itself as to the security of the auditors, the reliability of the staff proposed to carry out the audit, ensure the contract is made or evidenced in writing, and that the auditors act only on the (written) instructions of the organisation, etc.

11.3.11 The Board should also hold itself in readiness to receive the report. They will need to cross-examine the auditors as to their analysis and any recommended actions. Any such actions will, once agreed, need to be implemented as swiftly as is practicable, to avoid any risk of non-compliance. A delay in implementation will not make the problems go away. Indeed, a data breach or other incident which occurs between the receipt of the report and any action being taken on the basis of the report will be particularly embarrassing.

CHAPTER 12

The Audit

12.1 RECORDS AND THEIR PROCESSING

12.1.1 The purpose of this chapter is to enable the reader to proceed with an audit of their organisation's processing of personal data and collect the right information to assess compliance. As a result, this chapter will necessarily cross-refer as appropriate to material treated at greater length later elsewhere in the book.

12.1.2 The first task will be to identify all personal files or other data which the organisation processes. The reader should be aware that computer files are not the whole story—there may also be certain manual records to be considered, as well as such things as CCTV, audio tapes, voicemail, tachograph records, etc. (**6.9.2.3**). For all but the smallest organisation, it will not be possible to examine each file and see precisely how it is processed, from its first collection or obtaining till its final destruction or indefinite retention as an archive. Instead the auditor will need to examine representative samples of the various files. The GDPR in art.4(2) defines "processing" extremely widely, to include not only such obvious things as retrieval, consultation, use and various types of disclosure, but also the collection, recording or storing of the data at one end of its life and erasure or destruction at the other, not to mention its organisation, adaptation or alteration. There is quite literally nothing you can do with data which is not defined by the GDPR as processing of one kind or another (**1.2.5**).

12.1.3 The files cannot show all the information. The auditor will need to talk to members of staff in all or most of the divisions which handle the files, and also any contractors who handle the organisation's personal data since these will be prima facie processors (**13.7**). Similarly, the auditor will need to consider the personal data the organisation handles on behalf of others, since, in this case, the organisation itself will be the processor for one or more external controllers. If any personal data is shared with other organisations (i.e. there are two or more controllers processing the same or overlapping sets of personal data), whether sent to them or received from them, that data too will need to be examined. The auditor should also obtain copies of any contracts that set out the terms on which the data is processed or shared or, if an organisation's core business is as a processor and there are too many contracts to review them all, copies of precedent services agreements and samples of customer contracts. Data will need to be pursued across more than one department of the organisation as different people see or use the data or modify it in some way or erase it. The information given to the auditor as to how the files are processed (in the widest sense of that word) will need to be checked for accuracy against the files themselves. The data auditor will need to determine if there is a lawful basis for the processing (**Ch.4**) and consider the data protection principles, plus accountability (art.5) discussed in more detail in **Ch.13**, as well as to determine whether the organisation can meet the rights granted to individuals, including checking what information is given to individuals (**Ch.6**), its obligations of security and accountability and its obligations when dealing with other controllers and processors (**13.7**).

12.1.4 The auditor should also check on the existence, use and enforcement of any policies and procedures within the organisation relating to personal data. For example, inappropriate disclosure of data is a common concern for anyone with large volumes of customer data e.g. call centres. It may amount to a breach of security—possibly even severe enough to incur a penalty. There is also a risk of liability for the organisation concerned if disclosure causes damage, or distress to the individual (**3.2.2**).

12.1.5 It will be necessary to consider where data is transferred, both within the organisation and outside (i.e. a transfer of personal data from outside into the organisation, or from the organisation to some person or organisation outside). As we have seen the rules on the transfer of personal data to "third countries" require certain safeguards in the transfer of data abroad (**Ch.9**). Even if the data does not go abroad but is transferred wholly within the UK or other approved country or territory, it is essential to know to whom it is going to be accessible and for what purposes (**5.2.2**), if we bear in mind that disclosure is included within the definition of processing (art.4(2)). It is also essential to ensure that any processing of this data by the recipients is consistent with the purposes for which the data was collected in the first place.

12.1.6 We mentioned the Privacy and Electronic Communications Regulations

(PECR) at **7.4** above. Much of PECR is concerned with what electronic communications providers should do. As such it lies outside this book. But regs 19 (automated calling systems) and 20–24 (direct marketing)—all discussed at **7.4**—apply to any controller and might, if the organisation wished, be covered by the data protection audit.

12.1.7 In due course the data auditor will need to consider the various exemptions from one or more provisions of the legislation (discussed in detail in **Ch.10**), to see whether the organisation is free under an exemption to do, or omit to do, something which would otherwise infringe data protection legislation.

12.2 DATA SUBJECTS

12.2.1 It may be useful to start by considering throughout the organisation who are the data subjects? Who are the identifiable living individuals about whom the organisation may have and process data? There will almost certainly be staff. There may also be lists of ex-staff, either for the purposes of providing a pension for them, or for some other purpose. Then there may also be any of applicants, volunteers, temporary staff, office holders, spouses of staff, etc. A school will have governors as well as the teaching staff. There will also usually be customers or clients, though how these are defined may be hard to decide. Are a school's customers the parents or the pupils? What of a flourishing old pupils' association? And then there may be records of visitors to the building. There may be other business partners, or the staff of another organisation with which your organisation comes in contact.

12.2.2 Beyond ordinary customers there may be a larger mailing list of people who are not necessarily customers or clients at any one time, though they may (or may not) have been so in the past and possibly may be so in the future. Cookies will have picked up data about casual web browsers who come upon the organisation's website. They may not be identified by name, but their use is still regulated by data protection legislation (**7.5**). There may also be members of the public—for example, video footage for security purpose of all who pass in front of the main entrance of the organisation.

12.2.3 It is of course possible that an individual may move from being a supplier to be a member of your own organisation or vice versa. However, as these examples make clear, in many organisations people on a marketing list can become customers and may then return to the marketing list, staff may become pensioners, and so forth, so at all times one should be on the watch out for different files which still refer to the same data subjects. A file labelled "Customers" for example may not necessarily be the full story. The same person may be both staff and a customer—and perhaps also on the video security tapes. This is important not only from the point of view of the audit, but it will also be vital when it comes to handling swiftly and efficiently data protection enquiries such as data subject access under GDPR art.15 (**6.5**), where the same data subject may be referred to in more than one file.

12.2.4 For each type of data subject, the auditor will need to find out what data or fields of data exist, what the purpose of the data is, where each field of the data comes from, the extent to which the data subject has himself or herself willingly provided the data and understands the processing of that data which is to take place, how that data is combined with other data, how it is manipulated, how it is printed out or displayed or otherwise disclosed, to whom it is disclosed, how that data is corrected or amended from time to time, to whom else, within the organisation or outside, the data is transferred, and how and when the data is ultimately deleted.

12.2.5 Sometimes data about people is processed where it is claimed that the data does not refer to individuals, but only records information about non-identifiable groups. Examples of this are surveys of opinion and censuses, where we learn that 76% of a given group of people are of a particular view. It will be recalled that personal data is defined in the GDPR art.4(1) as

"*any information relating to an identified or identifiable natural person*"

and this is further delimited by rec.27 which says:

"*This Regulation does not apply to the personal data of deceased persons*...".

Thus, if the data is about a living individual who cannot be identified at all, the data is not personal data so far as the legislation is concerned and therefore not subject to the provisions of the legislation. GDPR rec.26 gives some guidance on this (**1.2.2**). Where such data is encountered, extreme care must be taken to ensure it is in fact not personal data. The points to check for to determine whether data are personal are its capture, and what subsequent combinations of data there are or could be.

12.2.6 First as to such data's capture, it may be useful to consider the decennial census, whereby householders fill in forms for each household. Such forms clearly contain data about living individuals who are identifiable. Yet when the data is published, the information is solely in the form of statistics (as in for example Office for National Statistics, *2011 Census: Detailed Characteristics for England and Wales*, March 2011 *https://www.ons.gov.uk/peoplepopulationandcommunity/populationandmigration/populationestimates/bulletins/2011census/2013-05-16* [Accessed 26 May 2019]), and all the personal details have been stripped way. Clearly the statistical report itself cannot be personal data, but what of the household forms (formerly called 'enumerators' forms")? Equally clearly they are personal data.

12.2.7 When an auditor encounters survey information and is satisfied that the personal elements which identify living individuals have been completely stripped out, they should check whether the personal information has been completely de-coupled from the statistical information. For example, in clinical trials a sponsoring company only receives patient data from which the patient's name and address has been removed. Instead a number will identify the patient. The clinician conducting the trial will retain the link between name and number. However, the sponsoring company must be able to access this link—for example, for safety reasons. In this example, the data is not *truly* anonymous, as the identifying link could be re-established. This is referred to as pseudonymous data and as such it is still subject to data protection legislation. There is more discussion of anonymous and pseudonymous data at **1.2.3**. (An auditor should also always check to see whether the data originally collected was personal data and if so what has happened to that in terms of storage, disclosure, etc.) Was it destroyed as personal data (i.e. to take the Census example were the household forms destroyed?), once the statistical data had been extracted? If not, that remaining personal data will still need to be accounted for. We may notice in passing that there is a new offence under the DPA 2018 s.171 of "Re-identification of de-identified personal data", discussed in more detail in **3.2.3**.

12.2.8 Another danger with survey data is that an individual may nevertheless be identifiable even though no "formal" identifiers (e.g. name and address) have been collected. If a firm keeps ethnic monitoring data as to the racial origin of its staff, such data is clearly "special categories of personal data" (formerly called "sensitive personal data") as defined within GDPR art.9(1), and as such subject to more stringent safeguards which are dealt with in **1.2.4**. Such data may be published in statistical form with all personal details stripped away. But if there is only one person within the organisation who is "Asian (Chinese)", the anonymity is not sufficient to protect that individual from identification. In other words where the sample is very small or where the combination of pieces of information is very specific, it may nevertheless identify a person, albeit in a way which was not intended. It will always be essential to examine such statistical data for inadvertent identifications of this sort. Such identifications will bring the data fully within the orbit of the legislation. This was the issue in the ***Common Services Agency*** case [2008] UKHL 47 (**1.2.3.5**).

12.3 FILES

12.3.1 Computer files

12.3.1.1 Computer files must be our starting point for the audit since these are for the most part defined and should be known to the IT department who presumably have to provide support to users. It may be simplest to get from the IT department a list of all software applications known to them, which should be sufficient for the main corporate files, and those who in the organisation "own" each file or application. Then as each "owner" is interviewed by the auditor, they can be questioned as to "their" files. However, it will be borne in mind that there are likely also to be other files which are not known to or supported by the IT department. These include not only the manual or other non-electronic or at least non-IT files (**1.2.5**), but also private files which an individual may have on his own laptop or other device. For example, a member of staff may have put together a file in Access or some similar format about the firm's sports club, which only he handles and uses. It is essential to check that there are not any of these private files which have not been examined by the auditor. As a practical tip, a glance at the icons on the member of staff's screen can sometimes identify a private piece of software or a file which is not supported by the IT department but is being used for a private file. However, there will also be many which use perfectly standard supported software (e.g. Excel) for unofficial files.

12.3.1.2 Another area to watch is the use of apps. These typically may process such things as:

- registration data;
- device data (either the device ID or advertising ID);
- software development kits (SDKs) allowing information to be shared with advertising partners; and
- data collected via the app as to contact or location.

If any non-official software is encountered, then quite apart from the examination of any personal data processed by the app or other non-standard software, there must also be a question of whether this is a matter that the IT department need to know about. In many organisations, staff are not allowed to upload onto the organisation's devices software or apps not authorised by the IT department. It might be argued that this lies outside the audit, but as it could be a source of weakness in the security of the data, there is a strong case for it to be reported to the organisation. An audit contractor will need to know in advance what to do about such software and whether it needs to be reported to the IT department. It also potentially raises the issue of monitoring staff—a matter we discuss in more detail in the next paragraph.

12.3.1.3 If the organisation permits BYOD (Bring Your Own Device, whereby staff members use their own devices for the organisation's processing—explained at **14.3**), then use of these devices will also have to be considered. This raises a potential problem, since each device will have on it data belonging to the staff member alone. Such an examination by the organisation or a contractor working on its behalf immediately becomes a form of monitoring of the staff by the organisation, and must be squared with the law, authorised by the organisation, and understood and agreed by the staff members (**14.2**). A contractor should not undertake this without the express contractual authorisation of the organisation and a strong indemnity.

12.3.1.4 Another area of difficulty is email and for that matter letter and memo files, which are not single files but a series of more or less interlinked files held on the organisation's (or its IT service provider's) servers, and also very often retained on the computers (desktop, laptop or server) on which the email has been composed or stored. In most organisations many emails so retained will probably not be on the organisation's business, but be personal to the individual member of staff (**14.2.2**). We note that in some organisations such private emails are kept in separate files and systems for each member of staff. For audit purposes the auditor will have to take a view on how in general emails are retained by the organisation, either centrally or by the individual senders or recipients, and what the organisation's policy is as to private emails (**14.2.2.2**), and how if at all emails are monitored (**14.2.3**). Again, an auditor will need authorisation.

12.3.1.5 The despatch of emails to destinations outside the EU is also important for consideration of transfers to third countries which relates to data going abroad (**Ch.9**). A more interesting example is the use of "cloud computing", where personal data is sent to a service company for processing. The company may be within the EU or it may be elsewhere—e.g. in the US. Such cases should be noted. So too should the possibility that the data going abroad may be in an attached file rather than the email itself.

12.3.1.6 The organisation's website and apps are specific areas for examination since by definition data on them will to a degree be disclosed and hence processed outside the organisation and thus invoke security aspects (**Ch.8**) and may also be available to go abroad and involve the issue of transfers to third countries (**Ch.9**). For many organisations this may be no problem if the website does not contain any personal data, but a number of these will still collect personal data via cookies (**7.5**). All these cases will need thorough investigation. A common example of personal data on the internet is a series of profiles of key staff. But there are other types of personal data on the internet. Social networking sites and other many-to-many or one-to-many social media and other internet publication sites which often have little control over, or supervision of, the content or destination of data can be a particular danger, as was shown by the case of ***Godfrey v Demon Internet Ltd*** [2001] Q.B. 201. This was a case of defamation over the internet rather than data protection. But even in 2001 it showed the dangers of publicising material over the internet. The courts under the defamation law in force at that time interpreted this as being publicised each time the data is accessed, and thus publicised many times in many jurisdictions, with calamitous results for the owner of the web page.

12.3.1.7 However, if the data is only on an intranet (i.e. internal to the organisation), the crucial questions will be not only whether that data is personal data, but also whether it goes outside the EU (**Ch.9**) and if so to which countries. Does the organisation have branches or staff or users outside the EU?

12.3.1.8 If the organisation collects data from individuals from the web—e.g. by requiring customers to input their data—it is essential to ensure that the data is collected in full compliance with the legislation. Firstly, as regards security (**Ch.8**) and fair processing (**4.1.7**), the organisation should check that all those whose details appear are aware of this. Failure to check would amount to a breach of the transparency principle, as well potentially as of arts 44–50 (transfers of personal data outside the EEA; **Ch.9**).

12.3.1.9 This is also likely to be the time when the privacy notice (art.13) is first made available to the data subject. Full compliance with art.13 at this point is essential (**6.4**). The examination of the user interface for the prospective customer is also the time to validate observance of PECR regs 20–24 (**7.4**).

12.3.1.10 A particular class of personal data derived from the web is a "cookie". Cookies are pieces of data sent back to the user's computer from a website he has visited. Their purpose can be to assist the website owner (and perhaps also the user) by making it easier for the user to access the website again and they may also remember user preference and other details about the visit. The data protection implications of cookies are discussed in detail at **7.5.** The auditor needs to be aware of their existence and should seek the IT department's help in deciding whether the organisation uses cookies and if so which ones, and for each one how, for what purpose, and what kind of data (personal or otherwise) they contain.

12.3.1.11 It should be noted that the various non-manual types of files which record photographic, video and/or audio material, discussed in **6.9.2.3,** can also be stored and processed by computer and may also therefore be identified in the audit and should be handled accordingly. There are also other non-manual files which, while not in every instance suitable for direct input to a computer, come under the legislation because they are "*the processing of personal data wholly or partly by automated means*" (GDPR art.2(1)).

The tachograph in a lorry which records the hours the vehicle is used by a particular driver is an example. So too is CCTV for security purposes. The auditor should be on the lookout for files in non-computer and non-office environments.

12.3.2 Manual files

12.3.2.1 All public authority manual records (whether structured or unstructured) are covered by the legislation and so will need to be considered by an auditor. (**1.2.5.6**). For all other controllers, apart from computer files, the GDPR also refers to non-computer manual files. Those which come under the legislation are defined at **1.2.5**. Filing systems must be

> "*any structured set of personal data which are accessible according to specific criteria, whether centralised, decentralised or dispersed on a functional or geographical basis*" (GDPR art.4(6)).

which means that a file whose data is held in different locations can still be considered structured; in other words, files do not lose their structure simply because they are held in different locations.

12.3.2.2 This definition would include data which is alphabetically arranged or accessed by data subject, i.e. the individual, or by some characteristic of the individuals within the file, such as by department of an organisation and within each department by order of seniority like the old *Army Lists*. Where data is not structured in any way it would seem that the data is outside the scope of the legislation since GDPR rec.15 says:

> "*Files or sets of files, as well as their cover pages, which are not structured according to specific criteria, shall not fall within the scope of this Regulation*".

So, totally unstructured data would seem to be in the clear. However, as the *Jehovah's Witnesses* case (C-25/17) EU:C:2018:551 (**1.3.4.4**) makes clear, the bar to be included in the legislation is quite low.

12.3.2.3 The auditor should therefore be on the lookout for such files in their investigations, and of course equally watch where, as may happen, the personal data in such a manual file is used either within another manual file or in a computer file—matters which are easily managed in these days of easy copying or scanning. The auditor should ask for a sample of *any* records of personal data, so they can form their own conclusions as to whether they are caught by the legislation or not. The auditor should also remind those interviewed that they may hold such files *both* in relation to customers *and* in relation to staff whom they manage.

12.3.2.4 We should also remind the reader that non-paper files, provided they fulfil the other criteria for a filing system, may be caught by the legislation—such as X-rays, tissue samples, etc. Alternatively, since they are usually created by NHS Trusts they may be considered as public authorities' records (**1.2.5.6**). There is also biometric material such as fingerprints, iris scans, etc. now increasingly used for granting or withholding access to places and systems. This is now expressly included in the definition of special categories of personal data in accordance with GDPR art.9. All these need to be considered.

12.3.2.5 The GDPR states: "*This Regulation applies to the processing of personal data wholly or partly by automated means*" (GDPR art.2(1)). This means that the case of ***Johnson v the Medical Defence Union*** [2007] EWCA Civ 262, which sought to distinguish between data wholly processed or only partly processed by automated means (**1.2.5.2**) is no longer relevant.

12.3.3 Photographic and video files

Scanned documents

12.3.3.1 Personal data may be scanned into a computer file, as well as entered in character form. Many organisations such as insurance companies who receive written forms filled in by their customers often find it easier to scan in the form and keep it as a visual image than try to transcribe it with the possibility of error in transcription vitiating the data. Such visual files which include personal data—i.e. data about an identifiable living individual—are still squarely within the ambit of the legislation.

Photographs and films

12.3.3.2 So too are photographs of individuals, since at least to those who know the individual, it is perfectly possible to identify the individual from the photograph. Many organisations keep photographs of staff in personnel files. Where they do so, these are likely to be caught by the legislation. As noted at **1.2.5.3**, X-rays are also covered by this definition, provided that they are labelled to identify the data subject.

12.3.3.3 We have seen that the GDPR defines what we may loosely call "computer data" in broad terms as "*the processing of personal data wholly or partly by automated means*" (GDPR art.2(1)). As has been noted at **1.2.5**, this definition is sufficient to catch other kinds of automatic processing besides that of ordinary computers. In particular automatic video (e.g. CCTV) and audio (e.g. voice mail) are caught by the Act and must be considered. Photographs or films of identifiable living people will also be covered by the legislation.

CCTV footage and other visual personal data

12.3.3.4 CCTV footage is collected by many organisations. Prima facie such data is likely to be covered by the legislation. In addition to the Commissioner's own CCTV code of practice, *In the picture: A data protection code of practice for surveillance cameras and personal information* (October 2014), there is a separate code from the Surveillance Camera Commissioner. *The Surveillance Camera Code of Practice* (June 2013) was issued under s.30 of the Protection of Freedoms Act 2012.

12.3.3.5 Where video conferencing or Skype have been used in an organisation, then these too engage the legislation and must be accounted for. The conditions of use described in **12.3.4** below in respect of recording of telephone calls, etc. apply here.

12.3.3.6 Much CCTV data is routinely erased (overwritten) after an elapsed period unless there is any good reason for its retention—e.g. there is reason to think an untoward or suspected criminal event may have been recorded. The auditor will need to be satisfied that the period before erasure is no longer than is necessary, and that when data is kept beyond the usual erasure period, it is because it genuinely fulfils the criteria for such retention, and the data is at all times kept secure, and not disclosed to unauthorised persons.

12.3.4 Audio files

12.3.4.1 Audio files also come under the legislation, since they relate to identifiable living persons. As to how the legislation applies, the purposes for which the data is created are the crucial issue. Common requirements for audio files include:

- records of conversations which have contractual force, such as telephone quotations for insurance;
- staff training; and
- voicemail records.

12.3.4.2 Records of conversations where a contract was being formed so as to establish precisely what was said by whom are a perfectly proper use of audio recordings. There are usually only two people involved: the prospective customer and the representative of the company, and it is in both parties' interest that there should be a clear understanding of what was said. The auditor should note the existence or absence of such data, the identity of persons to whom disclosure can be made, how the data is stored, how long the data is kept, etc., and also the ease with which an individual record can be located for the purposes of giving the data subject access to their own record. Provided the customer has been warned in advance of the need for and purpose of such recording, there can be no objection to it in general since it complies thereby with the transparency principle (see **6.2**), and further that the processing of the data (i.e. its replaying by the company's staff) is necessary for the performance of a contract to which the data subject is a party (GDPR art.6(1)(b)). Alternatively, under GDPR art.6(1)(f) the controller may be able to argue that the processing is necessary for the purposes of legitimate interests pursued by the controller, and there is no prejudice to the interests or fundamental rights or freedoms of the data subject—see **4.4.5**. The usual conditions attach to the questions of the person to whom disclosure can be made, how the data is stored, how long the data is kept, etc.

12.3.4.3 A second common reason for creating such data is for staff training. If the recording is purely for training, there must be a strong case for not recording or at least not preserving those parts of the call which identify the customer, by name, address or otherwise. The advantage of this is that if the data subject of the recording cannot be identified, the data will not be personal data under the legislation (GDPR art.2(1)). If the data's identifying features are completely stripped out in this way, it would seem to follow that the data does not come under the legislation and can safely be ignored by the auditor.

12.3.4.4 Voice mail similarly comes under the legislation if only because the caller is invited to give as a minimum their name and phone number, and so the data subject is thereby identifiable. It is also likely to be the case that the voice mail is for a particular phone extension and thus directed for an individual member of the organisation's staff. In many organisations voice mail is not kept indefinitely but is routinely erased a short set period after the recipient has heard the message. As always, the auditor will concern themselves with the way the data is collected, stored, used and erased and how easy it is to identify a particular person (data subject)'s record.

12.3.4.5 Thus in general, the auditor will need to find where and how these recordings are kept, who has access, to whom they are disclosed, whether they are copied or transcribed into another medium (e.g. a paper or computer transcript), how easy it will be to locate a particular data subject, for how long the recordings are kept, and how they are erased.

12.3.5 Biometric data

12.3.5.1 The GDPR art.4(14) defines biometric data as follows:

> "*'biometric data' means personal data resulting from specific technical processing relating to the physical, physiological or behavioural characteristics of a natural person, which allow or confirm the unique identification of that natural person, such as facial images or dactyloscopic* [finger print] *data.*"

It also includes patterns of veins in the eye. Sometimes voice prints which capture and compare the unique sounds (not words, but voice pitch, timbre, etc) can be used for identification. If such data is used for the purpose of uniquely identifying an individual, then it is special category personal data under art.9. It may come to an auditor's attention when it is used to identify those permitted to have access to a particular part of a building. The auditor will need to take note of such records and, as always, their processing (including disclosure and ultimate erasure), their retention and ease of access.

12.3.6 Other automatically processed data

12.3.6.1 We have already mentioned tachographs, the "spy in the cab" which records when and where long-distance lorry drivers have been driving a particular vehicle. A related technology is increasingly now offered by insurance companies, whereby a recorder in a vehicle picks up poor driving patterns, such as sudden braking, driving above the speed limit (picked up by geo-location), etc. If a driver can be seen to be driving well, their premiums can be reduced. The use of the technology depends on an agreement between a driver and their insurer. But there are other less high-tech systems that must also be considered here. Old-fashioned clocking-in machines which register the time of arrival or departure of staff must also be covered. So too must much medical equipment recording patient data such X-ray equipment, ultrasound scans, etc.

12.4 PROCESSING

12.4.1 General

12.4.1.1 The auditor will be looking at how the data is processed, bearing in mind the wide range of meanings of "processing" in GDPR art.4(1). In the case of computer programs, processing will include the entry, manipulation, correction, erasure of the data, and any kind of display on a screen, printer or otherwise. In the case of display, the auditor will need evidence as to whether anyone with a computer can see the data or whether it is by pass-word or otherwise protected so that only authorised personnel can see it or amend it. For manual files, establishing precisely how the data is processed may be a little harder since there is no identifiable piece of program code which says precisely what is done with the data. Here the issue may often be one of security: who has access to a filing cabinet for example; is the cabinet kept locked? If not, can anyone get at it? etc. When the data is finally erased is it simply tipped into a waste paper basket, probably eventually destined to blow around on some rubbish tip? Or, is it shredded or otherwise destroyed completely? If destruction is by a contractor, what are the security arrangements (discussed at **5.5**)? For CCTV and sound recordings, the issues will probably include the cycle of re-use of tapes in a regular time table, so that each day's recording is overwritten after a certain number of days unless there is a strong reason such as the investigation of a crime for preserving the tape longer.

12.4.1.2 The compliance structure will be of particular interest to the auditor. Does the organisation have to appoint a data protection officer (DPO)? This is covered by arts 37–39 of the GDPR (**1.3.7, 13.2**). If so, who is the DPO and how do they relate to the data protection staff and structure of the organisation? Is it the case that the organisation does not have to appoint a DPO, but has voluntarily decided to do so? Are the DPO's safeguards and duties the same as they would be for a mandatory DPO? If not how do they differ? What are the consequences of any such a difference?

12.4.1.3 The GDPR requires certain types of record keeping—e.g. under art.30. Another example is the requirement under art.7(1) for the controller to be able to *demonstrate* that it has the consents it claims to have. Who is responsible for this? Are these records in fact kept?

12.4.1.4 What Data Protection Impact Assessments (DPIAs) have been conducted (**13.6**)? What were the circumstances of each? If there was a DPO, did the DPO offer advice on each as required by GDPR art.35(2)?

12.4.2 Processing data abroad

12.4.2.1 A particular matter to consider is the processing abroad of data. This arises, for example, in the case of the location of a call centre abroad, though it will readily be understood that it can arise in other circumstances also, some of which have been touched on: email (**6.5.3**), internet (**9.2.2**), possibly intranet (**12.3.1**). A discussion of the whole question of transfer of personal data outside the EU belongs in **Ch.9**. For the moment the auditor will wish to consider whether personal data goes outside the EU and if so with what if any safeguards (contractual or technical) and methods to ensure adequacy there are, and where, why and to whom it is disclosed outside the EU.

12.5 CHECKLIST OF AUDIT QUESTIONS

12.5.1 The auditor in looking at the organisation and its data should ask the following about the organisation's data.

Extent of audit

- Is this an audit for pure data protection purposes?
- ... or does it include PECR regs 19–24?
- ... or does it include elements of Law Enforcement in which case DPA 2018 Pt 3 is relevant?
- ... or does it include elements of Intelligence Services in which case DPA 2018 Pt 4 is (possibly also) relevant?
- What parts of the organisation and its files and systems have been audited and why?
- Are they likely to be sufficient to give an indication of the organisation's overall compliance or otherwise?

Classes of data audited

- computer?
- BYOD?
- email?
- other letter/memo files?
- internet?
- apps?
- intranet?
- manual (filing system)?
- public authority data?
- video (scanned images, CCTV, photographic, film)?
- audio (contract, training, voicemail)?
- biometrics?
- other (e.g. tachograph)

Types of personal data—for each type consider:

- Is the data personal or not?
- If, "yes", is the data special category (formerly sensitive) personal data or data about criminal offences?
- Is any of the data confidential? (e.g. medical/financial information). If so, what are the consequences and risks of this and what are individuals told about this?
- Is there any significant automated decision-making involving the data, as defined in GDPR art.22? If so, what are the consequences of this and what are individuals told about this?
- Does the organisation consider that it processes pseudonymous or anonymous data? Are the labels correctly applied?
- Are there any cookies or other device identifiers? If so, how are they used?

Types of data subject— for each type consider

- staff;
- retired staff;
- staff spouses or other family members;

- job applicants;
- members of the public?
- customers;
- prospective customers;
- visitors?
- business contacts; these may include
  - sole traders or partnerships, who are identifiable individuals and so data subjects; or
  - managers or other individual office holders in those corporate bodies the organisation has contacts with;
  - if the organisation has contracts with children, how is age assessed?
  - other?

Lawfulness of processing—for each type consider

- What is the basis of processing this data?

"Owner" of the data—for each type consider

- Who is the controller?
- Any "private" files—
  - on BYOD devices? or
  - on the organisation's devices?
- How are private emails handled?
- What, if any, of the data is processed by a processor?
- What data is received from another organisation or individual?
- What data is shared with one or more other organisations or individuals?
- Does the organisation process data itself on behalf of other controllers, as a processor? If so what processing for whom? Does the organisation collaborate with others to process personal data so that it may be a joint controller?

Purposes of the processing, data quality and data destruction—for each type consider

- How and why is the data collected?
- What information is given to individuals about this, how and when?

- How well does the data's use match the purposes for which it is collected?
- Does the organisation carry out direct marketing? If so, how?
- How does it handle "preference" services (TPS, CTPS, FPS)?
- To whom is it disclosed or shared?
- What or who ensures the data's accuracy?
- Is it sampled for accuracy?
- What are the consequences if data is inaccurate?
- How is it kept up to date?
- How long is it kept?
- What happens to it when it is no longer used?
- What are the criteria for its destruction?
- Is it in fact destroyed: if so, who does this and how do they do it?
- any archiving of personal data?

Contracts—for each type consider

- Data processing contracts?
  - Any cloud contracts?
  - Any social media contracts?
- Data sharing contracts?
- Contracts involving data outside the EU?
- Fair obtaining warranties

Security of data—for each type consider:

- Organisational security;
- Staff security;
- What standards of accreditation does the organisation have?
- System security—e.g. passwords, firewalls, etc.;
- What of portable media (laptops, memory sticks, CDs, etc) and what system of security does each have (encryption?);
- BYOD security?
- How is old equipment disposed of?

- Procedures for sending secure faxes—and emails—for special categories of personal data?
- Procedures for sending sensitive or financial material by post
- Any use of wireless transmission ("wi-fi")?
- Security of processors;
- How were they selected?
- Was their security checked?
- How is this guaranteed by the processor and documented?
- Is there any ongoing review process?
- Have the contracts for such processors been updated to address supplemental GDPR terms?

Data breach

- Who is in charge on the detection of a data breach?
- Who will constitute his/her team?
- Are procedures in place to advise the Commissioner of any notifiable data breaches?
- . . . and for advising data subjects?
- . . . and documenting data breaches in accordance with GDPR art.33(5)?

Sending outside EEA – for each type consider

- Files?
- Emails?
- carried on laptops or other portable devices
- Internet material?
- Intranet material?
- Cloud computing or use of SaaS or other outsourced data processing where the provider may use facilities outside the EU.

Cookies and device IDs

- Which?
- Whence each one?

- How intrusive each one?
- How described in the Cookie statement?

12.5.2 At **5.5.4** we mentioned the need to have mechanisms in place to ensure that the legislation is at all times observed and suggested the auditor should see these before beginning work (**11.3.6**). We return to these mechanisms in detail in **Chs 4, 5**, etc, but during the audit process the extent to which the organisation has such mechanisms and procedures in place should be investigated alongside the data itself. The questions to be asked include:

People

- Who is in charge of data protection?
- What resources do they have?
- How are they supported by senior management?
- What if any disciplinary action has been taken in respect of data protection?
- Is the organisation of a type to require to have a DPO?
- Does it in fact have a DPO?
- Where in the hierarchy does the DPO fit?
- Has the ICO been notified of this appointment?

Processes and procedures

- What industry/trade association guidance is available?
- What published processes and procedures are there in respect of personal data?
- What are the procedures for DPIAs?
- Do staff know when a DPIA is necessary?
- How are policies and procedures brought to the attention of staff and others?
- How are they enforced?
- How are they updated?
- Who is responsible for this?
- How do they fit into the organisation's structure?

Training

- what training is provided for staff
- . . . and to which staff. . .
- . . . at what time?
- What refresher courses?
- How are staff kept up to date?

Records

- legitimate interest assessments under GDPR art.6(4);
- the records to demonstrate data subject consents under art.7(1);
- Privacy notices under arts 13–14;
- records of joint processing of the same or overlapping sets of data by two or more controllers (art.26);
- records of processing activities in art.30;
- records of personal data breaches (art.32);
- any data protection impact assessments carried out according to arts 35–36;
- documentation to determine whether or not to appoint a DPO (art.37);
- appropriate policy document where special category personal data is processed in accordance with one of the conditions in Schedule 1 of DPA 2018.

Relations with the ICO

- Has the organisation paid its fee under DPA 2018 s.137?
- Who is responsible for this?
- Is it up to date?
- If the organisation has a DPO, has the ICO been informed?
- Has the organisation notified the ICO of a data breach?
- Has the organisation ever received a notice from the ICO?
- Any other contact with the ICO?

Relations with others

- Any contact with any other regulator in respect of personal data?
- Or the police?
- Any data protection-based litigation?

Data subjects' rights

- What procedures are in place to deal with requests in connection with data subject rights?
- How has this worked so far?
- Any problems with identifying a particular individual in the data?

Codes and certification

- Are the Commissioner's Codes followed?
- If so which? At the time of writing we are awaiting codes, but the first ones will doubtless become available shortly, and when they do, they should of course be taken fully into consideration (**1.3.8**).
- Is certification used? If so, give details. Again, at the time of writing we are awaiting developments (**1.3.8**).

12.6 INTERPRETING THE RESULTS OF THE AUDIT

12.6.1 The auditor will at the end of the audit have extensive information based on the foregoing questions. Its interpretation will be based on the matters discussed earlier in this book and the reader should apply the key recommendations in the chapters to their own data to see from this how the organisation can establish, improve and maintain its compliance.

12.6.2 Following this and by marking up the results of the audit in this way the auditor should produce a list of recommendations as to how individual files and data protection generally are handled. The main conclusions should be presented to the Board or other commissioning body. The detailed conclusions should be presented to the organisation by department or even in respect of a particular file, rather than on the basis of the individual part of the legislation infringed, since an action list will need to be drawn up for each organisational unit. It will also enable the organisation to identify the less compliant parts of the organisation.

12.6.3 Finally, a mechanism to keep the organisation compliant must be identified. This is an issue of governance and must be addressed in the Report. This is also addressed in the subsequent chapter on accountability (**Ch.13**).

PART III

Data Protection Compliance

CHAPTER 13

Compliance and Accountability

13.1 STRATEGY FOR COMPLIANCE AND ACCOUNTABILITY

13.1.1 The importance of accountability

13.1.1.1 Once an organisation has completed a data protection audit and knows what personal data it handles, it will need to adopt a strategy to ensure that any risks highlighted by the audit are addressed and that it remains fully compliant with the legislation. One of the changes introduced by the GDPR is that it specifically requires compliance to be addressed, via a new principle at art.5(2):

> "*The controller shall be responsible for, and able to demonstrate compliance with, paragraph 1* [the principles of fair and lawful processing, purpose limitation, data minimisation, accuracy, storage limitation and integrity and confidentiality] *('accountability')*".

As we shall see, this obligation is then repeated and expanded in art.24.

13.1.1.2 This chapter is all about accountability. Readers should note that the accountability principle in arts 5 and 24 only applies to controllers. However, processors must also take steps to ensure they comply with the legislation and many of the specific accountability measures mandated by the GDPR apply both to controllers and to processors.

13.1.1.3 The importance of accountability and the advantages of compliance are set out in the Information Commissioner's *Guide*:

> "*Why is accountability important?*
> *Taking responsibility for what you do with personal data, and demonstrating*

the steps you have taken to protect people's rights not only results in better legal compliance, it also offers you a competitive edge. Accountability is a real opportunity for you to show, and prove, how you respect people's privacy. This can help you to develop and sustain people's trust.
Furthermore, if something does go wrong, then being able to show that you have actively considered the risks and put in place measures and safeguards can help you provide mitigation against any potential enforcement action. On the other hand, if you can't show good data protection practices, it may leave you open to fines and reputational damage."

13.1.1.4 The GDPR prescribes certain key elements of an organisation's accountability and compliance strategy:

1) appointing a data protection officer where necessary (art.37 and **13.2**);
2) keeping records of processing activity (art.30 and **13.5**);
3) undertaking data protection impact assessments for any processing which is likely to pose a high risk to individuals (arts 35 and 36, and **13.6**); and
4) assessing and managing arrangements with processors (or for processors, with sub-processors), putting contracts in place, and ensuring that arrangements with joint controllers allocate responsibility for compliance, especially as regards individual rights (arts 27, 28 and 26 and **13.7**).

The GDPR also refers more generally to adopting policies, training and audit. In this chapter, we have addressed the specific requirements first, with more general discussion of policies, training and other measures last.

13.1.1.5 The accountability and compliance strategy should not only ensure that the organisation complies with the legislation now; but, in addition, it should build in procedures and checks to ensure that a culture of compliance is generated, so that any changes the organisation makes to its processing will also be compliant with the legislation. Again, this is also something with the GDPR mandates as art.24(1) notes that "*Those measures shall be reviewed and updated where necessary*".

13.1.1.6 The accountability and compliance strategy will need to address how each division of the organisation complies with the legislation. Accountability has to be specific and relevant

"*taking into account the nature, scope, context and purposes of processing as well as the risks of varying likelihood and severity for the rights and freedoms of natural persons*" (art.24(1)).

Recital 75 in particular has a long list of risks ("*physical, material or non-material damage*") which the controller must guard against. They include:

"discrimination, identity theft or fraud, financial loss, damage to the reputation, loss of confidentiality of personal data protected by professional secrecy, unauthorised reversal of pseudonymisation, or any other significant economic or social disadvantage; where data subjects might be deprived of their rights and freedoms or prevented from exercising control over their personal data; where personal data are processed which reveal racial or ethnic origin, political opinions, religion or philosophical beliefs, trade union membership, and the processing of genetic data, data concerning health or data concerning sex life or criminal convictions and offences or related security measures; where personal aspects are evaluated, in particular analysing or predicting aspects concerning performance at work, economic situation, health, personal preferences or interests, reliability or behaviour, location or movements, in order to create or use personal profiles; where personal data of vulnerable natural persons, in particular of children, are processed; or where processing involves a large amount of personal data and affects a large number of data subjects".

Recital 76 continues:

"The likelihood and severity of the risk to the rights and freedoms of the data subject should be determined by reference to the nature, scope, context and purposes of the processing. Risk should be evaluated on the basis of an objective assessment, by which it is established whether data processing operations involve a risk or a high risk".

13.1.1.7 Where a division has many collections of personal data, each collection of personal data held will need to be addressed. These issues are considered in this chapter. Readers will also want to cross refer to **Ch.6** which focuses specifically on compliance strategies for responding to data subjects' enquiries, **Ch.7** which focuses on direct marketing, and **Ch.14** which considers some special difficulties relating to monitoring, Bring Your Own Device (BYOD) and processing of personal data relating to children.

13.1.2 Codes and certification

13.1.2.1 Organisations will also want to consider if there are codes of conduct or any certification which may assist them in compliance. Article 24(3) notes that these may be useful methods for demonstrating compliance with the GDPR. These are introduced at arts 40 and 42 respectively.

Article 40(1) provides that codes of conduct are

"intended to contribute to the proper application of this Regulation, taking account of the specific features of the various processing sectors and the specific needs of micro, small and medium-sized enterprises".

They can be drawn up by "*associations and other bodies representing categories of controllers or processors*". Article 40(2) provides an illustrative list of the areas which could be covered by a code of conduct, ranging from identifying legitimate interests pursued by controllers in specific contexts through to dealing with the exercise of data subject rights.

Article 42(1) provides that certification mechanisms, seals and marks, are "*for the purpose of demonstrating compliance with this Regulation of processing operations by controllers and processors*". Certification does not replace compliance obligations and art.42(4) provides that it "*does not reduce the responsibility of the controller or the processor for compliance with this Regulation*".

Certifications are to be issued for a maximum of three years (art.42(7)).

13.1.2.2 Accordingly, codes of conduct are intended primarily as ways for an organisation to help itself to comply, addressing particular requirements of an industry or sector, whereas certification is a way of demonstrating compliance to others. In practice, this distinction is not clear-cut: if a controller knows that a processor meets a particular code of conduct, for example, this may also be a useful indicator to the controller that the processor has invested time and effort in addressing data protection requirements. Both codes of conduct and certification can also, when combined with binding and enforceable commitments, be used as ways to meet data transfer requirements (under arts 46(2)(e) and (f) respectively; see **9.5.7**).

13.1.2.3 In addition to the above type of codes (codes of conduct), DPA 2018 ss.121–127 require the Commissioner to produce codes of practice including:

- data sharing code;
- direct marketing code;
- age-appropriate design code; and
- data protection and journalism code.

DPA 2018 s.128 may also require the Commissioner to produce other as yet unidentified codes. At the time of writing the Commissioner has embarked on consultation for two new codes. For the age-appropriate design code she has issued a lengthy consultation document (*https://ico.org.uk/about-the-ico/news-and-events/news-and-blogs/2019/04/ico-launches-consultation-on-code-of-practice-to-help-protect-children-online* [Accessed 17 June 2019]) covering the headings of:

- Best interests of the child;
- Age-appropriate application;
- Transparency;
- Detrimental use of data;
- Policies and community standards;
- Default settings;

- Data minimisation; and
- Data sharing.

For the data protection and journalism code, she states that she wants to build on her old Code under the 1998 Act (*Data protection and journalism: a guide for the media*) and has issued a brief Call for Views (*https://ico.org.uk/about-the-ico/ico-and-stakeholder-consultations/ico-call-for-views-on-a-data-protection-and-journalism-code-of-practice* [Accessed 17 June 2019]). Both documents have a deadline of late May 2019.

13.1.2.4 Both codes of conduct and certification depend on the credibility of the way they are approved and monitored on an ongoing basis and the GDPR provides guidance on this, with further guidance having been provided by the Article 29 Working Party and the European Data Protection Board (EDPB). As most organisations are unlikely to want to develop their own codes of conduct or certification mechanisms, we do not propose to go into detail on this. The most important point for readers to note is that, at the date of writing, no codes of conduct or certification mechanisms have yet been approved under these provisions. However, several are under development and on 12 February 2019, the EDPB adopted draft Guidelines on Codes of Conduct and Monitoring Bodies under Regulation 2016/679 for consultation. The draft Guidelines set out the criteria against which codes of conduct will be assessed and how they will be approved. The EDPB is obliged to publish all approved codes and certification mechanisms (arts 40(11) and 42(8)), so data protection professionals should keep this possibility under review.

13.2 THE DATA PROTECTION OFFICER

13.2.1 Appointment of a data protection officer

13.2.1.1 We have already touched on this at **1.3.7.** We must now address the detail of this post. The data protection officer (DPO) figures prominently in the GDPR arts 37–39 as follows:

- art.37—when a DPO must be appointed and the requirements the DPO must meet;
- art.38—the position of the DPO in the organisation;
- art.39—the tasks of the DPO.

The matter is also illuminated by the Article 29 Working Party *Guidelines on Data Protection Officers* (WP 243 rev.01). The first page of this makes clear the importance of the DPO:

> "*Before the adoption of the GDPR, the WP29 argued that the DPO is a cornerstone of accountability and that appointing a DPO can facilitate compliance and furthermore, become a competitive advantage for business*" (p.4).

When must a data protection officer be appointed?

13.2.1.2 GDPR art.37(1) says all controllers and processors must designate a DPO where:

> "*(a) the processing is carried out by a public authority or body, except for courts acting in their judicial capacity;*
> *(b) the core activities of the controller or the processor consist of processing operations which, by virtue of their nature, their scope and/or their purpose, require regular and systematic monitoring of data subjects on a large scale; or*
> *(c) the core activities of the controller or the processor consist of processing on a large scale of special categories of data pursuant to Article 9 or personal data relating to criminal convictions and offences referred to in Article 10*".

13.2.1.3 Accordingly, not all organisations need to appoint a DPO. Instead, the article limits this to organisations which undertake processing which is likely to pose a higher risk. The relevant criteria are considered below. Once an organisation determines that it must appoint a DPO, or once it appoints one voluntarily, then, as WP 243 rev.01 notes: "*The DPO . . . is designated for all the processing operations carried out by the controller or processor*"(p.6) not just for the higher risk processing described in art.37. Article 37(4) allows Member States to set additional lists of categories of controllers or processors who must appoint data protection officers. The UK has not done this in the DPA 2018.

Public authorities and bodies

13.2.1.4 As explained at **4.4.3.3**, the GDPR leaves it to each Member State to determine who they regard as a public authority or body. The DPA 2018 s.7 follows the definition of public authority in the Freedom of Information Act 2000 and the Freedom of Information (Scotland) Act 2002, with power reserved to the Secretary of State to specify other bodies. English parish councils, Welsh and Scottish community councils and similar bodies are however excluded from the definition.

Core and large-scale activities

13.2.1.5 The second and third tests in art.37(1) only apply where processing is part of the "core activities" of the controller or processor and where it is "large scale". Recital 97 notes that:

> "*In the private sector, the core activities of a controller relate to its primary activities and do not relate to the processing of personal data as ancillary activities*".

The Article 29 Working Party, in WP 243 rev.01, paraphrases core activities as "*the key operations necessary to achieve the controller's or processor's goals*" or "*activities where the processing of the data forms an inextricable part of the controller's or processor's activity*" (p.7).

13.2.1.6 WP 243 rev.01 provides helpful examples (p.7):

- a hospital must process health records in order to provide care;
- a security company's surveillance of a shopping centre. In this example, the processing of personal data is inextricably linked to surveillance;
- on the other hand, paying staff and running standard IT support activities is usually ancillary not core. However, the Information Commissioner's *Guide* notes that for organisations which specialise in doing just this, the analysis would be different:

> "*For most organisations, processing personal data for HR purposes will be a secondary function to their main business activities and so will not be part of their core activities.*
> *However, an HR service provider necessarily processes personal data as part of its core activities to provide HR functions for its client organisations. At the same time, it will also process HR information for its own employees, which will be regarded as an ancillary function and not part of its core activities*".

"Large scale" is considered in relation to data protection impact assessments (**13.6**) at rec.91, where initiatives "*which aim to process a considerable amount of personal data at regional, national or supranational level and which could affect a large number of data subjects*" is given as an example of large-scale processing. However, conversely,

> "*the processing of personal data should not be considered to be on a large scale if the processing concerns personal data from patients or clients by an individual physician, other health care professional or lawyer*".

13.2.1.7 As the Article 29 Working Party notes, "*the recital provides examples at the extremes of the scale . . .; there is a large grey zone in between these extremes*" (p.7, fn.14). The factors which the Working Party suggests should be considered are self-evident rather than enlightening. Consider:

- the number of data subjects or their proportion of the whole;
- the volume of data or range of different items;
- the duration or permanence of processing;
- the geographical extent of processing.

13.2.1.8 WP 243 rev.01 does, though, give some further examples of large-scale processing:

- patient data in a hospital;
- data on individuals' travel on a public transport system;
- geo-location of customers in an international fast food chain for statistical purposes;
- customer data processed by an insurance company or bank in the regular course of business;
- behavioural advertising by a search engine;
- traffic etc. data processed by telephone or internet providers

Regular and systematic monitoring of data subjects

13.2.1.9 The Article 29 Working Party reminds us that rec.24 discusses monitoring (when considering the territorial scope of the GDPR), noting that

> "*it should be ascertained whether natural persons are tracked on the internet . . ., particularly in order to take decisions concerning her or him or for analysing or predicting her or his personal preferences, behaviours and attitudes*".

Online monitoring would seem to be clearly covered by art.37(1)(c), but the Working Party emphasises (p.8) that other forms of monitoring should also be considered.

13.2.1.10 WP 243 p.8 para.2.1.4 provides further definitions:

Regular:

- ongoing or occurring at particular intervals for a period;
- recurring or repeated at fixed times;
- constant or periodic.

Systematic:

- occurring according to a system;
- pre-arranged, organised or methodical;
- taking place as part of a general plan for data collection;
- carried out as part of a strategy.

The Article 29 Working Party also includes a list of activities which may constitute regular and systematic monitoring:

- operating a telecommunications network;
- email retargeting;

- data-driven marketing activities;
- profiling or scoring for risk assessment;
- location tracking—for example by mobile apps;
- loyalty programs;
- behavioural advertising;
- health monitoring by wearable devices;
- CCTV;
- connected devices such as smart meters in cars or other home automation.

Of course, an organisation would still have to engage in these activities as part of its "core activities" and on a "large scale" in order to be obliged to appoint a DPO.

13.2.1.11 The condition relating to large-scale processing of special categories of data or criminal conviction and offence data is straight-forward.

13.2.1.12 WP 243 says (p.5, para.2.1):

"*Unless it is obvious that an organisation is not required to designate a DPO, the WP29 recommends that controllers and processors document the internal analysis carried out to determine whether or not a DPO is appointed, in order to be able to demonstrate that the relevant factors have been taken into account properly*".

This forms another example of the record-keeping required of controllers and processors, which we discuss at **13.5.3**.

Relationship between controllers' and processors' data protection officers

13.2.1.13 If a controller has to appoint a DPO, its processor is not necessarily required to appoint a DPO. And vice versa: the test is to be applied separately for each. In some cases, it may well be the case that a processor is more likely to meet the requirements for processing to be for its "core activities" and to be "large scale" than for its clients to meet this requirement. The Working Party (p.9) gives the example of a small family business which uses website analytics through a processor who does the like for several companies. The family business does not have to appoint a DPO, as its activities are not large scale. However, the processor may well need to appoint a DPO.

Voluntary data protection officers

13.2.1.14 The GDPR art.37(4) makes clear that controllers or processors which are not obliged to appoint a DPO, may nevertheless appoint one voluntarily. WP 243 p.3, para.2.1 adds:

"*When an organisation designates a DPO on a voluntary basis, the same requirements under Articles 37 to 39 will apply to his or her designation, position and tasks as if the designation had been mandatory*".

The purpose behind this is obviously to ensure that if someone is referred to as a DPO everyone will at once know what their job is. To have DPOs with different functions would lead to confusion. This also means that voluntarily appointed DPOs must be free from conflicts of interest and cannot be dismissed or penalised because of the way they perform their role (**13.2.3**): organisations should ensure they can meet these requirements before appointing a DPO on a voluntary basis. In cases where the analysis of whether an organisation needs to appoint a DPO (**13.2.1.12**) is finely balanced, it may well be desirable to appoint one anyway.

13.2.2 Qualifications and other requirements for the data protection officer

13.2.2.1 The remainder of art.37 sets out details of the qualifications and other requirements relating to the appointment of a DPO. GDPR art.37(5) says:

"*The data protection officer shall be designated on the basis of professional qualities and in particular, expert knowledge of data protection law and practices and the ability to fulfil tasks referred to in Article 39*".

Recital 97 notes that "*the necessary level of expert knowledge should be determined in particular according to the data processing operations carried out and the protection required for the personal data processed by the controller or the processor*".

So, what is needed will be dependent on the particular organisation. WP 243 rev.01 notes that there is little detail in the GDPR on the required level of expertise, but, in the view of the Article 29 Working Party, it should include (p.11):

- expertise in national and European data protection laws and an in-depth understanding of the GDPR;
- knowledge of the business sector and of the organisation of the controller;
- knowledge of the processing operations carried out as well as the information systems and data security and data protection needs of the controller;
- in the case of a DPO for a public authority, the DPO should have a good knowledge of the administrative rules and procedures of the organisation; as well as;
- integrity and high professional ethics (p.12).

13.2.2.2 It may be difficult to find an internal, or external, candidate who fulfils all of these requirements: where this is the case, training may be needed, or support from others in the organisation who can fulfil certain of the requirements better. There is more detail on the support the organisation must provide to the DPO at **13.2.3** below.

Data protection officers working for multiple organisations

13.2.2.3 Article 37(2) allows a group of undertakings to appoint a single DPO "*provided that a data protection officer is easily accessible from each establishment*". Article 37(3) likewise allows several public authorities to appoint one DPO.

13.2.2.4 WP 243 rev.01 p.10, comments on the meaning of "accessible". It notes that because the DPO has to be a point of contact for data subjects (art.38(4) and supervisory authorities (art.39(1)(e)), this means that the DPO will need to be able to communicate in the languages used by data subjects of the authority. If the individuals cannot do this themselves, the organisation will need to provide support to the DPO to assist them in this. Accessibility can be physical, or via a hotline or other secure communication. The Working Party (p.11) also suggests that:

> "*To ensure that the DPO is accessible, the WP29 recommends that the DPO be located within the European Union, whether or not the controller or processor is established in the European Union*".

It seems likely that most supervisory authorities and individuals will try to contact a DPO by phone or email, so the advantage of a physical presence in the EU seems over-stated. We query also how many data subjects would want to travel even to a different Member State to consult the DPO, again re-enforcing online and phone contact. Even the Working Party seems to acknowledge that this recommendation may go somewhat far, as it acknowledges (seemingly grudgingly) that:

> "*... it cannot be excluded that, in some situations where the controller or the processor has no establishment within the European Union, a DPO may be able to carry out his or her activities more effectively if located outside the EU*" (p.11).

Employee or service provider?

13.2.2.5 GDPR art.37(6) says the DPO "*may be a staff member of the controller or processor, or fulfil the tasks on the basis of a service contract*".

Here, WP 243 rev.01 notes that, where this is the case:

> "*For the sake of legal clarity and good organisation and to prevent conflicts of interests for the team members, the Guidelines recommend to have, in the service contract, a clear allocation of tasks within the external DPO team and to assign a single individual as a lead contact and person 'in charge' of the client*" (p.23).

The Working Party also suggests (p.24) that there may be a conflict of interests if an external DPO is asked to represent the controller or processor before the courts in data protection cases.

Publishing the details of the data protection officer

13.2.2.6 Article 37(7) provides that the controller or processor must publish the contact details of the DPO and communicate them to the supervisory authority. The DPO's contact details must be included in privacy notices (arts 13(1)(b) and 14(1)(b) **6.4**). Here, the Working Party suggests that multiple points of contact should be included (so email and phone, as well as physical address). However, the DPO's name does not necessarily have to be publicised (p.13), although the Working Party recommends that this is made clear to staff. By contrast, the actual name of the DPO should be notified to supervisory authorities. In the UK, details of the DPO can be added to the notification form (**13.5.2**). Lastly, although the Working Party does not mention this point, processors must include details of the name and contact details for their controller customers' DPOs in their records of processing (art.30(2)(a)) and joint controllers must also include the name and contact details for other joint controllers in their records of processing (art.30(1)(a)) —so organisations must be pro-active in requesting this information in relevant contracts. Where an organisation is not obliged to appoint a DPO and in fact has not appointed one voluntarily, it is still good practice to have clear identification of the lead data protection professional in the organisation in these cases.

13.2.3 The data protection officer's position in the organisation

13.2.3.1 GDPR art.38 deals with the DPO's position in the organisation:

"(1) The controller and the processor shall ensure that the data protection officer is involved, properly and in a timely manner, in all issues which relate to the protection of personal data".

13.2.3.2 This is enlarged upon in WP 243 rev.01, para.3, which speaks of "*the early involvement of the DPO*", and continues (para.3.1):

"Ensuring that the DPO is informed and consulted at the outset will facilitate compliance with the GDPR, ensure a privacy by design approach and should therefore be standard practice within the organisation's governance. In addition, it is important that the DPO be seen as a discussion partner within the organisation and that he or she is part of the relevant working groups dealing with data processing activities within the organisation.
Consequently, the organisation should ensure, for example, that:

- *The DPO is invited to participate regularly in meetings of senior and middle management.*

- *His or her presence is recommended where decisions with data protection implications are taken. All relevant information must be passed on to the DPO in a timely manner in order to allow him or her to provide adequate advice.*
- *The opinion of the DPO must always be given due weight. In case of disagreement, the WP29 recommends, as good practice, to document the reasons for not following the DPO's advice.*
- *The DPO must be promptly consulted once a breach or another incident has occurred.*"

13.2.3.3 Article 38 continues:

"*(2) The controller and processor shall support the data protection officer in performing the tasks referred to in Article 39* [DPO duties] *by providing resources necessary to carry out those tasks and access to personal data and processing operations, and to maintain his or her expert knowledge*".

13.2.3.4 If the DPO is to have all the expertise and skills suggested by the Working Party, and to be accessible to individuals and authorities in multiple languages, then support from the organisation will be essential. WP 243 rev.01 pp.13–14 comments that this means management should:

- provide active support (from senior management—e.g. at board level) for the DPO;
- provide sufficient time for the DPO to fulfil their duties—particularly important if the DPO has other duties;
- provide the necessary financial resources, infrastructure, staff, etc for the DPO. If a team is provided, tasks should be apportioned between them;
- apprise staff officially of the DPO's role;
- give access for the DPO to (for example) HR, legal, IT, etc services within the organisation; and
- provide continuous training for the DPO. (We discuss at **13.4** how the DPO and data protection professionals can keep up to date in data protection law.)

Independence of the data protection officer

13.2.3.5 Article 38(3) provides that:

"*The controller and processor shall ensure that the data protection officer does not receive any instructions regarding the exercise of those tasks. He or she shall not be dismissed or penalised by the controller or processor for perform-*

ing his tasks. The data protection officer shall directly report to the highest management level of the controller or the processor".

In this connection, WP 243 pp.14–15 draws attention to rec.97:

"*. . . such DPOs should be in a position to perform their duties and tasks in an independent manner*".

So, controllers and processors should not tell the DPO what result should be achieved, or how to investigate a complaint, or whether to consult the Commissioner.

13.2.3.6 WP 243 p.15 points out that the ability of a company to penalise its DPO is only prohibited if such penalties are imposed as a result of the DPO doing their job. So, for example, the DPO cannot be dismissed for warning that a type of processing is risky, though they might still be dismissed for embezzlement or sexual harassment. The definition of penalties can include absence or delay of promotion, prevention of career advancement, or denial of staff benefits. A penalty need not be carried out to be unlawful. The threat of such a penalty itself is also unlawful. WP 243 goes on to say that the better the guarantees against unfair dismissal, the more independent the DPO can be.

13.2.3.7 WP 243 rev.01 (p.15) explains that direct reporting to senior management (such as the board of directors) is important to ensure that they are aware of the DPO's advice and recommendations. It gives an example of direct reporting as drafting of an annual report. It seems that the GDPR means that the DPO should have the ability to report to the board for data protection purposes—not that the DPO should report to the board for line management purposes (such as approval of holidays and like matters). In this book we call the Director or other senior officer who is the DPO's link to management at the highest level as the "responsible board member". The responsible board member may or may not also be the DPO's pay and rations line manager.

13.2.3.8 Article 38(6) is related to art.38(3). It provides that:

"*The data protection officer may fulfil other tasks and duties. The controller or processor shall ensure that any such tasks and duties do not result in a conflict of interests*".

This means that the post of DPO need not be a full-time job. Some DPOs will be general compliance officers dealing with other matters as well. Like art.38(3) the second part of this provision is designed to ensure the independence of the DPO. WP 243 rev.01 includes examples of positions where conflicts would seem likely and where, therefore, persons filling these roles would seem to be ineligible to act as the DPO (p.16):

"*As a rule of thumb, conflicting positions within the organisation may include senior management positions (such as chief executive, chief operating, chief financial, chief medical officer, head of marketing department, head of Human Resources or head of IT departments) but also other roles lower down in the organisational structure if such positions or roles lead to the determination of purposes and means of processing*".

13.2.3.9 WP 243 p.16 also recommends that organisations (or at least those which are larger) should:

- identify positions incompatible with DPO's duties;
- draw up internal rules to this effect;
- include a more general explanation of conflicts of interests;
- declare that the DPO has no such conflict by way of raising awareness of this; and
- ensure that job descriptions and any internal rules reflect this.

13.2.3.10 Lastly, art.38 provides:

"*(4) Data subjects may contact the data protection officer with regard to all issues related to processing of their personal data and the exercise of their rights under this Regulation.*
(5) The data protection officer shall be bound by secrecy or confidentiality concerning the performance of his or her tasks, in accordance with Union or Member State law".

Readers will note that one of the tasks of the DPO is to co-operate with, and be the point of contact for, the supervisory authority (**13.2.4.5**) and may wonder how the DPO's duty of confidentiality fits in with this role. It would seem odd if a DPO who may wish to seek advice from the Commissioner was not able to do so because of this duty of confidentiality. Unsurprisingly, the Article 29 Working Party (p.12) sees the confidentiality obligation as a duty owed to those who express concerns to the DPO, as it will allow them to raise concerns without fear. By contrast (p.18), "*the obligation of secrecy/confidentiality does not prohibit the DPO from contacting and seeking advice from the supervisory authority*".

13.2.4 The data protection officer's task

13.2.4.1 The tasks of a DPO are described in art.39:

"*(1) The data protection officer shall have at least the following tasks:*
(a) to inform and advise the controller or processor and the employees who carry out processing of their obligations pursuant to this Regulation and to other Union or Member State data protection provisions.
(b) to monitor compliance with this regulation, with other Union or

Member State data protection provisions and with the policies of the controller or processor in relation to the protection of personal data, including the assignment of responsibilities, awareness-raising and training of staff involved in processing operations, and the related audits".

13.2.4.2 WP 243 p.17 comments on *(b)* above. Monitoring could include:

- collecting information to identify processing;
- analysing and checking compliance; and
- informing, advising, issuing recommendations to the controller or processor.

13.2.4.3 Data Protection Impact Assessments (DPIAs) to analyse risk in processing are described below at **13.6**. Article 39(1) continues that the DPO's tasks are also "*(c) to provide advice where requested as regards the data protection impact assessment and monitor its performance pursuant to Article 35*".

Article 35(2) on data protection impact assessment states: "*The controller shall seek the advice of the data protection officer, where designated, when carrying out a data protection impact assessment*". (There is no mention of the processor since the obligation to conduct a data protection impact assessment only applies to the controller).

13.2.4.4 WP 243 rev.01 pp.16–17 recommends that the controller carry out any DPIA, but the DPO must be asked;

- whether or not the controller should carry out the DPIA;
- what methodology to use;
- whether the DPIA should be resourced in-house or outsourced;
- what safeguards exist to mitigate any risk to the rights and interests of data subjects; and
- finally, whether the DPIA was correctly carried out.

13.2.4.5 Article 39(1) continues its list of DPO duties:

"*(d)* *to cooperate with the supervisory authority* [i.e. the Commissioner].
(e) *to act as the contact point for the supervisory authority* [i.e. the Commissioner] *on issues relating to processing, including prior consultation referred to in Article 36 and to consult, where appropriate, with regard to any other matter*".

Article 36(1) requires prior consultation with the supervisory authority/Commissioner where

"*... a data protection impact assessment under Article 35 indicates that the processing would result in a high risk in the absence of measures taken by the controller to mitigate the risk*".

(Other supervisory authority/DPO liaison is prescribed elsewhere in the GDPR—e.g. in art.33(3)(b) on notification of a data breach (**8.4.3**)).

13.2.4.6 Article 39(2) says:

> "*The data protection officer shall in the performance of his or her tasks have due regard to the risk associated with processing operations, taking into account the nature scope, context and purposes of processing*".

The comment of WP 243 rev.01 p.18 on this is that DPOs should prioritise their activities and focus on higher data protection risks.

13.2.4.7 WP 243 p.18 also draws attention to the controller's duties of record-keeping under art.30(1) and the processor's record-keeping duties under art.30(2). The Working Party notes that the list of tasks for the DPO in art.39 is non-exhaustive: it may be convenient for the DPO to be in charge of these activities as well. If the DPO is not in charge of these activities, then the DPO should certainly have ready access to the record of processing activities. We discuss this further at **13.7**.

Liability of the data protection officer's task

13.2.4.8 Although the DPO is tasked with informing and advising the controller or processor on data protection matters, responsibility for compliance rests with the organisation, not the DPO himself or herself. At p.17, WP 243 rev.01 states clearly:

> "*Monitoring of compliance does not mean that it is the DPO who is personally responsible where there is an instance of non-compliance. The GDPR makes clear that it is the controller, not the DPO, who is required to 'implement appropriate technical and organisational measurers to ensure and to be able to demonstrate that processing is performed in accordance with this Regulation' (Article 24(1)). Data protection compliance is a corporate responsibility of the data controller, not of the DPO*".

13.3 OTHER DATA PROTECTION PROFESSIONALS

13.3.1 All organisations should appoint one individual with responsibility for data protection in the organisation: this is the first step in a compliance strategy. However, some organisations may not need a DPO and may not wish to appoint one on a voluntary basis (for example, because they cannot meet the requirements associated with a GDPR-style DPO). In this situation, an organisation should be careful not to designate the person it does task with the responsibility as a "data protection officer". As WP 243 rev.01 notes (p.6):

> "*In this case it is important to ensure that there is no confusion regarding their title, status, position and tasks. . . . it should be made clear, in any communications within the company, as well as with data protection authorities, data*

subjects, and the public at large, that the title of this individual or consultant is not a data protection officer".

13.3.2 Larger organisations will often find that one DPO cannot fulfil all the tasks placed on them by the GDPR, so that others need to be appointed to assist them. Again, care should be taken to avoid holding out these individuals as the DPO. We have used the term "data protection professional" throughout this book to refer to someone who has a role in management of data protection, but who is not the DPO.

13.4 SOURCES OF ADVICE ON DATA PROTECTION

13.4.1 It will be apparent that the DPO, the data protection professional, and their staff, and in some cases any responsible board member need to keep abreast of data protection issues. The most important source of guidance will continue to be the ICO (*http://www.ico.org.uk* ([Accessed 10 May 2019]). The ICO has a wealth of information about data protection, including codes of practice and other guidance, all downloadable free of charge (**1.3.8.2.3**). They can also send publications by post. The ICO also publishes news items about data protection, and these may be accessed as a daily live feed or in a monthly form. We recommend the daily service for the DPO and data protection professionals. Finally, the ICO is also able to provide answers to queries about data protection via its Helpline 0303 123 1113.

13.4.2 The next most useful source of knowledge is the EDPB. It can be found at *https://edpb.europa.eu* [Accessed 10 May 2019]. In providing papers and guidance they are following in the steps of their predecessor under the old legislation, the Article 29 Working Party, many of whose more recent papers are also directly concerned with the GDPR, and some that have been issued have even been updated post-May 2018. They can most easily be found at *https://ec.europa.eu/newsroom/article29/news-overview.cfm* [Accessed 10 May 2019].

13.4.3 There are a large number of other organisations that comment on data protection issues. One of the most useful is the Society for Computers and Law (*http://www.scl.org* [Accessed 10 May 2019]). As its name suggests, it is involved in all aspects of IT law, but data protection is probably the largest single IT-related area of law that it deals with. It has specialist groups including a Privacy and Data Protection Group. It publishes a weekly newsletter with links to papers, cases, etc. It also publishes a glossy magazine six times a year, and provides conferences and courses at all levels. It is UK-based and most (but by no means all) of its events are in London. It is an educational charity, with lower academic and concessionary rates, and free membership for students.

13.4.4 We may also mention the International Association of Privacy Professionals (*https://iapp.org* [Accessed 10 May 2019]). Whereas the Society for Computers and law is primarily a UK-centred organisation the IAPP takes a wider international view and often has helpful news of developments in other jurisdictions, including the EU. It has regular newsletters, local discussion groups and conferences. The data protection professional should also consider if there are suitable codes of conduct or certification which may assist the organisation (**1.3.8.3, 13.1.2**).

13.5 RECORDS OF PROCESSING

13.5.1 Records required by the GDPR

13.5.1.1 Article 30 GDPR requires that controllers and processors each keep records of their processing activities. The records must be in writing (which could be in electronic form) (art.30(3)) and must be available to the supervisory authority on request (art.30(4)). Where the controller or processor has a representative, because it has no establishment in the EU, but is subject to the extra-territorial scope of the GDPR under art.3(2)(**2.2**), then the representative must also maintain these records.

13.5.1.2 The obligations placed on controllers and processors differ slightly, reflecting their different obligations. So, the controller is obliged to keep a record of all "*activities under its responsibility*" (which would include processing carried out by a processor), whereas a processor must keep details of "*all categories of processing activities carried out on behalf of a controller*". Of course, a processor will also be a controller when it processes personal data for its own purposes—for example, for HR and business development purposes, so, in this case, the processor would keep two types of records of processing. The details of the records are set out at art.30(1) for controllers and art.30(2) for processors and can be summarised as set out below.

<table>
<tr><th></th><th>Controller</th><th>Processor</th></tr>
<tr><td>Name and contact details of the organisation, plus details of any representative and any data protection officer</td><td>✓
Must also include the same details for any joint controller</td><td>✓
Must also include these details for each controller on whose behalf data is processed</td></tr>
<tr><td>Purposes of processing</td><td>✓</td><td rowspan="3">N/A
Instead, the processor must note the categories of processing carried out on behalf of each controller</td></tr>
<tr><td>Description of the categories of data subjects and the categories of personal data</td><td>✓</td></tr>
<tr><td>Categories of recipients to whom personal data have been disclosed—including whether they are in third countries or not, or are an international organisation</td><td>✓</td></tr>
</table>

Where applicable, details of transfers of personal data to third countries, including identifying the country and, if transfers are made on the basis of compelling legitimate interests – see **9.5.5.13**) for further details of this.	✓	✓
Where possible, envisaged time limits	✓	N/A
Where possible, a general description of the technical and organisational security measures	✓	✓

13.5.1.3 The Information Commissioner has prepared template forms in Excel format of records of processing for each of controllers and processors. These are available at:

https://ico.org.uk/for-organisations/guide-to-data-protection/guide-to-the-general-data-protection-regulation-gdpr/documentation/how-do-we-document-our-processing-activities/#how5 [Accessed 24 May 2019]

13.5.1.4 These also usefully contain sample content, so that the organisation can see the level of detail the Information Commissioner expects. If one takes managing employees as an overall purpose, then the Commissioner has separate entries for payroll processing; maintaining the personnel file; and recruitment. This gives an idea of level of detail required for purposes. Similarly, for categories of data subjects, the Commissioner distinguishes between employees, and successful and unsuccessful candidates. On the description of security measures, the Commissioner merely notes "encrypted storage; access controls". The Commissioner's template documents contain additional information which is not mandated by the legislation: this is clearly marked so that organisations can choose to include this or not. Organisations should, however, recall that if they process special category data in reliance on most of the additional conditions for processing set out in Sch.1 to the DPA 2018 that their record of processing activities *must* include, in addition to the items listed above, details of the lawful basis relied on under art.6 and under Sch.1 and information as to whether such data is being retained and erased in accordance with the "appropriate policy document" which has to be adopted to set out the safeguards for use of special category data.

13.5.1.5 Recital 82 notes that the record of processing activities is to be maintained "*in order to demonstrate compliance with this Regulation*" and that it must be available to the supervisory authority on request "*so that it might serve for monitoring those processing operations*" which the organisation carries out, or for which it is responsible. It follows that the record of processing activities cannot be completed and then forgotten: an organisation must ensure that it is kept up to date. Suitable strategies would be ensuring that staff know to alert the data processing professional when they are changing elements of processing, or introducing new personal data processing, so that the record can be kept up to date and/or with periodic checks as to its accuracy by way of audit.

13.5.1.6 These records do not need to be compiled by an organisation employing fewer than 250 people unless the processing is likely to result in a risk the rights and freedoms of data subjects; the processing is not occasional; or the processing includes special categories of data as referred to in art.9(1) or personal data relating to criminal convictions and offences referred to in art.10.

13.5.1.7 Although rec.13 states that:

> "*To take account of the specific situation of micro, small and medium-sized enterprises, this Regulation incudes a derogation for organisations with fewer than 250 employees with regard to record-keeping.*"

the exemption in art.30(5) is so limited as to mean that almost no organisation would be able to rely on it. This point was underlined by the Article 29 Working Party *Position Paper on the derogations from the obligation to maintain records of processing activities pursuant to Article 30(5) GDPR* (no reference number but available at *https://ec.europa.eu/newsroom/article29/item-detail.cfm?item_id=624045* [Accessed 24 May 2019]). This notes that the exemption does not apply when the processing is likely to result in "a risk" to individuals, not necessarily a high risk and that the requirements are cumulative—so that any repeat or regular processing will mean that the organisation cannot satisfy the "not occasional" requirement. As the Working Party noted:

> "*... a small organisation is likely to regularly process data regarding its employees. As a result such processing cannot be considered 'occasional' and must therefore be included in the record of processing activities*".

However, other processing activities which *are* occasional do not have to be included. The reason we have included details of this exemption right at the end of the section on records of processing reflects the fact that it will very rarely be of any use.

13.5.2 Controller's registration with the Information Commissioner

13.5.2.1 Under the 1998 Act, data controllers were required to notify the Information Commissioner that they processed personal data and pay an annual fee. Controllers also had to provide the Commissioner with a description of the processing of personal data which they undertook. This description of each controller's processing activities was available online on the ICO website. Indeed, the original title of the Information Commissioner, as the Data Protection Registrar, shows that the primary role of the Commissioner was originally linked to the maintenance of this public register of data controllers.

13.5.2.2 The GDPR has swept all this away. Recital 89 begins:

> "*Directive 95/46/EC provided for a general obligation to notify the processing of personal data to the supervisory authorities. While that obligation produces administrative and financial burdens, it did not in all cases contribute to improving the protection of personal data. Such indiscriminate general notification obligations should therefore be abolished, and replaced by effective procedures and mechanisms which focus instead on those types of processing operations which are likely to result in high risk to the rights and freedoms of natural persons by virtue of their nature, scope, context and purposes...*".

The rest of this and the succeeding recitals are concerned with data protection impact assessments and the appointment of data protection officers, which are seen as approaches better suited to targeting higher-risk processing.

13.5.2.3 So far as the UK was concerned, the fees paid as part of notification funded the ICO's data protection activities, and the abolition of notification means a shortfall. This problem is addressed in DPA 2018 s.137 which states that;

> "*(1) The Secretary of State may by regulations require controllers to pay charges of an amount specified in the regulations to the Commissioner.*
> *(2) Regulations under subsection (1) may require a controller to pay a charge regardless of whether the Commissioner has provided, or proposes to provide, a service to the controller*".

13.5.2.4 The Data Protection (Charges and Information) Regulations 2018 (SI 2018/480) (the "Charges Regulations"), which also came into force on 25 May 2018, specify the controller's annual fees to the ICO. The fees are in three tiers: for "micro organisations", for small and medium organisations, and for large organisations. Charities and small occupational pension schemes are also in tier 1 (regs 2, 3(1)).

Staff nos		Turnover	Annual fee
≤ 10	or	≤ £632,000	£40
> 10 but ≤ 250	or	> £632,000 but ≤ £36M	£60
> 250	and	> £36M	£2,900

13.5.2.5 The Information Commissioner regards all controllers as eligible to pay the tier 3 fee, unless and until they notify her otherwise. Helpfully, there is an online assessment tool available at *http://ico.org.uk* [Accessed 13 May 2019] which organisations can use to work out which tier they are in.

13.5.2.6 Small occupational pension schemes are very small: fewer than twelve members (reg.2(6)), and they are further defined in reg.4 of the Occupational and Personal Pension Schemes (Consultation of Employers and Miscellaneous Amendment) Regulations 2006 (SI 2006/349).

13.5.2.7 For the purposes of calculation, a member of staff includes any employee, worker within the meaning given in s.296 of the Trade Union and Labour Relations Act 1992, office holder, or partner. Numbers of staff are averaged by

"*(a) ascertaining for each completed month of the data controller's financial year the total number of persons who have been members of staff of the data controller in that month,*
(b) adding together the monthly totals, and
(c) dividing by the number of months in the data controller's financial year". (reg.1(2)).

13.5.2.8 For Public Authorities the tier they fall into is calculated solely on the basis of number of staff (reg.3(3)). The definition of "public authority" is defined by the Freedom of Information Act 2000 or the Freedom of Information (Scotland) Act 2002, as appropriate, and thus is not the same as the definition in DPA 2018 s.7 which excludes parish and community councils (**13.2.1.4**).

13.5.2.9 The Charges Regulations provide for exemptions for some organisations. The Information Commissioner provides a useful gloss on this as follows:

"*You don't need to pay a fee if you are processing personal data* ***only*** *for one (or more) of the following purposes:*

- *staff administration*
- *advertising, marketing and public relations*
- *accounts and records*
- *not-for-profit purposes*
- *personal, family or household affairs*
- *maintaining a public register*
- *judicial functions*
- *processing personal information without an automated system such as a computer*".

There are limitations on some of these categories. For example, the reference to advertising and marketing only covers an organisation carrying out marketing in respect of its *own* business: if it does this as a service for others, the exemption does not apply (Charges Regulations, Sch.1, para.2(2)(e)). The staff administration provision works in a similar way. However, the fact that an organisation discloses data in the course of legal proceedings, as required by law, to prevent or detect crime or to apprehend or prosecute offenders, or to allow for assessment or collection of taxes does not take an organisation outside the exemption. Again, the Information Commissioner has a helpful self-assessment tool on her website.

13.5.2.10 If a controller has to pay the charge, there are a variety of ways to pay—although a modest incentive by way of a £5 discount is provided for payment by direct debit. The controller will need to provide its name and address, staff numbers and turnover information (so that the charge can be confirmed). It must also provide a point of contact to deal with queries on the form, and (if different) a point of contact for other regulatory queries and (again, if different) details of its DPO. The Commissioner maintains a register of controllers who have paid the charge. Where a DPO has been appointed, the details of the DPO will also be included unless the DPO has asked for his or her details to be kept private. Controllers should note that the Information Commissioner can issue a fixed penalty to controllers who should have paid the charge but have not done so (**3.2.6**). The maximum penalty is £4,350. In the first months since the legislation came into force, the Commissioner has been assiduous in following up on this.

13.5.3 Other records to be kept under the legislation

13.5.3.1 The GDPR prescribes that "*records of processing activities*" have to be maintained. However, an organisation will actually have to keep records of far more than this if it is to be compliant with the legislation. The Commissioner's *Guide* contains a short list of other documents:

- information needed to populate privacy notices (such as details of the lawful basis for processing; their legitimate interests etc);
- records of consent
- controller—processor contracts;
- location of personal data;
- DPIA reports (see below);
- records of personal data breaches;
- appropriate policy documents.

In practice, we think the list is far longer than this—by way of example, in the section earlier on DPOs, data protection authorities recommend that if a DPO is not appointed, that a note is kept of the reasons. If a DPO is appointed, then there will be an appointment letter or terms of reference. At **13.5.1.2**, we have included checklists of documents which will often be necessary for compliance. For ease of reference, we have done this for controllers and for processors.

13.6 DATA PROTECTION IMPACT ASSESSMENT (DPIA)

13.6.1 Introduction

13.6.1.1 Although privacy impact assessments were not mentioned in the 1998 Act, they are not a new thing. For many years now, successive Information Commissioners have been recommending an analysis of what the privacy implications are for a particular business practice or initiative involving personal data, in the form of a Privacy Impact Assessment (PIA). This was formulated into a *Privacy Impact Assessment Handbook* v2.0, followed in 2014 by *Conducting privacy impact assessments code of practice*. This has now been taken a stage further in the GDPR with art.35 on data protection impact assessment (DPIA). There is guidance in the article on which types of processing may be sufficiently risky as to require a DPIA to be conducted and also on how to conduct a DPIA.

13.6.1.2 The bibliography on DPIAs is extensive. The two initial sources of reference for data protection professionals, which we quote in our commentary, are

- Article 29 Working Party *Guidelines on Data Protection Impact Assessment (DPIA) and determining whether processing is 'likely to result in a high risk' for the purposes of Regulation 2016/679* WP 248 rev.01, 4 October 2017 (WP 248).
- The ICO guidance on *Data Protection Impact Assessments (DPIAs)* designed "*to sit alongside our* Guide to the GDPR"[1] and covering:
  - What is a DPIA?
  - When do we need to do a DPIA?
  - How do we do a DPIA?
  - Do we need to consult the ICO?
- Examples of processing 'likely to result in high risk' (*ICO DPIA guidance*)

These documents, in turn, reference additional sources of guidance for the reader who wants to know more.

When is a data protection impact assessment required?

13.6.1.3 The GDPR makes it clear that DPIAs are needed for evaluating risky processing. Article 35(1) says:

> "*Where a type of processing <u>in particular using new technologies,</u> and taking into account the <u>nature, scope, context and purposes</u> of the processing, is <u>likely to result in high risk</u> to the rights and freedoms of natural*

[1] This document is obviously intended to form part of the ICO *Guide*, but it has not yet been incorporated into the *Guide* and at present it is in a form with neither page numbers nor paragraph numbers.

> *persons, the controller shall, prior to the processing, carry out an assessment of the impact of the envisaged processing operations on the protection of personal data. A single assessment may address a set of similar processing operations that present similar risks*" (emphasis added).

Data protection impact assessments are required by the GDPR for all high-risk processing. WP 248 rev.01 notes that this primarily concerns risks to individuals' data protection rights, but is not exclusively concerned with this, and could also involve:

> "*other fundamental rights such as freedom of speech, freedom of thought, freedom of movement, prohibition on discrimination, right to liberty, conscience and religion*" (p.6).

13.6.1.4 Article 35(3) specifies three sample cases when a DPIA must be undertaken. The first is:

> "*(a) a systematic and extensive evaluation of personal aspects relating to natural persons which is based on automated processing, including profiling* [which it will be recalled includes processing to analyse or predict aspects concerning a natural person's performance at work, economic situation, health, personal preferences, interests, reliability, behaviour, location or movements (art.4(4))], *and on which decisions are based that produce legal effects concerning the natural person or similarly significantly affect the natural person*".

The *ICO DPIA guidance* gives further guidance on this:

> "*In short, it is something that has a noticeable impact on an individual and can significantly affect their circumstances, behaviour or choices.*
> *A legal effect is something that affects a person's legal status or legal rights. A similarly significant effect might include something that affects a person's financial status, health, reputation, access to services or other economic or social opportunities*".

ICO DPIA guidance also reminds that:

> "*Decisions that have little impact generally could still significantly affect more vulnerable people, such as children*".

13.6.1.5 The second case (art.35(3)(b)) is:

> "*processing on a large scale of special categories of data referred to in Article 9(1), or of personal data relating to criminal convictions and offences referred to in Article 10*".

The Article 29 Working Party has commented on the meaning of "large scale" in the context of the threshold at which a DPO must be appointed. The same considerations are relevant here and they are discussed at **13.2.1.5**.

The last case (art.35(3)(c)) is:

"*a systematic monitoring of a publicly accessible area on a large scale*".

Again, the comments of the Article 29 Working Party on this point, referenced at **13.2.1.6** are relevant.

13.6.1.6 The examples in art.35(3) are non-exhaustive: any processing which is likely to result in a high risk triggers the need for a DPIA. It is important to note that the test is not whether the processing *will* pose a high risk, but whether it is *likely* to pose a high risk. If there is doubt, then a DPIA may be needed to determine the point. Accordingly, WP 248 rev.01 states that:

"*. . . where it is not clear whether a DPIA is required, the WP29 recommends that a DPIA is carried out nonetheless as a DPIA is a useful tool to help controllers to comply with data protection law*".

13.6.1.7 WP 248 rev.01 provides nine additional criteria (pp.9–11) to assist controllers in determining if a DPIA is needed. These may be summarised as follows:

1) *Evaluation or scoring*. This includes profiling and predicting, such as the screening by a financial institutions of customers against a credit reference database or against a money-laundering or counter-terrorist financing; or a biotechnology company offering genetic tests to assess and predict health risks; or a company building behavioural or marketing profiles on usage or navigation on its website.

2) *Automated decision-making with legal or similar significant effect*. Such as processing which may lead to the exclusion of some individuals. Conversely "*processing with little or no effect on individuals does not match this specific criterion*".

3) *Systematic monitoring including data collected through networks*. This is because the data subjects may not be aware of who is collecting their data or how it will be used and may not be able to avoid the processing.

4) *Sensitive data or data of a highly personal nature*. This includes special category data under art.9 and data on convictions, etc under art.10. However, it can also include other personal data such as data affecting confidentiality or financial data. Recital 75 lists among other things:

   a. "*. . . discrimination, identity theft or fraud, financial loss, damage to the reputation, loss of confidentiality of personal data protected* *by professional secrecy, unauthorised reversal of pseudonymisation, or any other significant economic or social disadvantage . . .*".

5) *Data processed on a large scale.* To determine this it is relevant to consider:

   (a) the numbers of data subjects or their proportion of the whole;

   (b) the volume of data or range of different data items;

   (c) the duration or permanence of the processing; and

   (d) the geographical extent of the processing.

6) *Matching or combining datasets.* For example, when they originate from different operations and are combined in ways which exceed the reasonable expectations of the data subjects.

7) *Data concerning vulnerable data subjects (rec.75).* In this case there is likely to be a greater imbalance between the controller and the data subject, which puts the latter at a disadvantage in defending their rights. Such people could include children, mentally ill persons, asylum seekers, the elderly, patients, etc. Employees are also mentioned.

8) *Innovative use or applying new technological or organisational solutions.* Novelty itself may imply a risk—possibly of an unknown nature. The "Internet of Things" may affect individuals' daily lives and privacy and therefore require a DPIA. *ICO DPIA guidance* mentions AI, neuro-measurement and connected vehicles as examples in this context.

9) *When the processing itself "prevents data subjects from exercising a right or using a service or a contract"* (art.22, rec.91). For example, a bank screening customers against a credit reference database when considering whether to offer them a loan.

13.6.1.8 It will be seen that these criteria are not mutually exclusive. WP 248 (p.11) adds:

> "*In most cases, a data controller can consider that a processing meeting two criteria would require a DPIA to be carried out. In general, the WP29 considers that the more criteria are met by the processing, the more likely it is to present a high risk . . . and therefore to require a DPIA, regardless of the measures which the controller envisages to adopt.*
> *However, in some cases, **a data controller can consider that a processing meeting only one of these criteria requires a DPIA***" (original emphasis).

13.6.1.9 WP 248 pp.11–12 offers several examples. Two will suffice:

- The gathering of public social media data for generating profiles ticks boxes 1, 5 and 4.

- The use of a camera to monitor driving behaviour on motorways, using intelligent video analysis of individual cars and automatic number plate recognition, ticks boxes 3 and 7.

Again WP 248 resorts to bold on p.12 to emphasise:

> "***a processing operation may correspond to the above mentioned cases and still be considered by the controller not to be 'likely to result in a high risk'. In such cases, the controller should justify the reasons for not carrying out a DPIA, and include/record the views of the DPO***".

13.6.1.10 Article 35(4) requires each supervisory authority to make a list of processing operations that necessitate a DPIA. Where the list includes processing operations which

> "*are related to the offering of goods or services to data subjects or to the monitoring of their behaviour in several Member States, or may substantially affect the free movement of personal data within the Union*",

then art.35(6) provides that the list must be submitted to the EDPB, under the consistency mechanism (**1.3.8**).

13.6.1.11 Much of the first few months of the EDPB's existence has been taken up with looking at lists submitted by supervisory authorities, including our own Information Commissioner, and commenting on them. The Information Commissioner has amended the initial list, to reflect comments made by the EDPB.

13.6.1.12 *ICO DPIA guidance* contains the Commissioner's list of additional types of processing in respect of which a DPIA must be carried out. The Commissioner, reflecting guidance given to her by the EDPB, distinguishes between criteria which will always trigger the need for a DPIA and criteria which will only trigger the need for a DPIA if they are combined with at least one other test mentioned in WP 248 rev.01. By way of example, biometric data is included in the Commissioner's list—so use of biometric data about children, would trigger the need for a DPIA as this involves a vulnerable group. We have indicated with an '*' the criteria which have to be combined with WP 248 rev.01 in this way. The Commissioner's criteria are:

1. innovative technology*;
2. denial of service;
3. large-scale profiling;
4. biometrics*;
5. genetic data (other than that processed by a health professional to provide direct care)*;

6. data matching;
7. invisible processing: this refers to cases where data was not obtained from the data subject and where art.14 provides an exemption from the obligation to provide a privacy notice where this would be impossible or require disproportionate effort*;
8. tracking—either of location or behaviour*;
9. targeting children or other vulnerable persons—this includes use of their data for marketing, profiling or other automated decision-making including any offers of online services to children;
10. risk of physical harm—that is where a personal data breach could "*jeopardise the* [physical] *health or safety of individuals*". (The use of square brackets is in the original).

13.6.1.13 Controllers in the UK must, therefore, refer both to the list in WP 248 rev.01 and to the Commissioner's list. If necessary, they must also be aware of the criteria for conducting DPIAs in other Member States. Lastly, they should also remember that these criteria are aids to assist in determining if processing is likely to pose a high risk: if the controller considers that its processing is not covered by these criteria but is still likely to pose a high risk to individuals, then a DPIA should still be conducted.

When is a data protection impact assessment not required?

13.6.1.14 Where processing is *not* likely to result in a high risk to the rights and freedoms of natural persons, then art.35(1) will not apply and a DPIA will not be required. In the same way supervisory authorities have to provide lists of processing which *will* require a DPIA, the GDPR allows supervisory authorities to provide lists of processing where a DPIA will *not* be required (art.35(5)). This list is left to the discretion of the supervisory authority. At the moment, the Information Commissioner has not issued such a list, although *ICO DPIA guidance* notes that the Commissioner may do so in future.

13.6.1.15 Readers may recall that art.35(1) provides that a

> "*single assessment may address a set of similar processing operations that present similar high risks*".

If the nature, scope, context and purposes of a particular initiative are very similar to the processing for which a DPIA has been carried out (art.35(1)), no further DPIA will be needed. Recital 92 also notes:

> "*... There are circumstances under which it may be reasonable and economical for the subject of a data protection impact assessment to be broader than a single project, for example where public authorities or bodies intend to estab-*

lish a common application or processing platform or where several controllers plan to introduce a common application or processing environment across an industry sector or segment or for a widely used horizontal activity".

Accordingly, WP 248 rev.01 notes that:

"*A single DPIA could be used to assess multiple processing operations that are similar in terms of nature, scope, context, purpose, and risks*".

WP 248 rev.01 (p.7) notes that this could be appropriate where multiple local authorities conduct a single DPIA concerning use of CCTV. The Working Party also notes (p.8) that a supplier of a particular platform or product may publish a DPIA for the platform or product. In this case, controllers would need to carry out a DPIA for their own specific implementation—but this could be informed by the central product DPIA.

13.6.1.16 Sometimes an organisation may process personal data to implement a government objective. If a DPIA was carried out to assess the implications of the over-arching objective then, in some situations, a further DPIA may not be needed. This is set out at art.35(10) which states:

"*Where processing pursuant to point (c)* [processing is necessary to comply with a legal obligation] *or (e)* [processing is necessary for a task in the public interest or the exercise of official authority] *of Article 6(1) has a legal basis in Union law or in the law of the Member State to which the controller is subject, that law regulates the specific processing operation or set of operations in question, and a data protection impact assessment has already been carried out as part of a general impact assessment in the context of the adoption of that legal basis, paragraphs 1 to 7 shall not apply unless Member States deem it to be necessary to carry out such an assessment prior to processing activities*".

13.6.1.17 Article 36 is also relevant here. Article 36(4) provides that where a Member State prepares a proposal for a law which relates to processing of personal data, then the Member State must consult the supervisory authority on the law. Article 36(5) then links to the last sentence of art.35(10) quoted above, noting that—even when a supervisory authority has been consulted, the law which is eventually adopted may still require controllers to consult with, and obtain prior authorisation from, the supervisory authority where the processing relates to a task carried out in the public interest. Social protection and public health are given as non-exhaustive examples of where this may be appropriate.

13.6.1.18 WP 248 rev.01 also addresses the question of existing processing: is a DPIA required for this? It states (p.13) that there is no requirement to conduct a DPIA in relation to existing processing unless there has been a change of risks, taking into account the nature, scope, context and purposes of processing. The Working Party suggests a change might occur

- by the use of new technology, or
- a change in the purposes, or
- because "*the organisational or societal context for the processing activity has changed, or*
- *new categories of data subjects have become vulnerable to discrimination.*"

This also reminds us of another, important, point: the controller must keep processing under review, so as to determine, on an appropriate ongoing basis, either if a DPIA should be initiated, or if an existing DPIA should be re-assessed.

13.6.1.19 If a controller determines that a DPIA is not necessary, then it should document this. If it has a DPO, it should consult the DPO on this point. Failing to undertake a DPIA when one is needed may make it more likely that the controller's use of non-compliant processing exposes individuals to unnecessary risk. It is also a breach of the legislation by itself for which a fine could be imposed, whereas no one will ever be penalised for undertaking a DPIA which was not necessary. As long as the organisation has the resources to conduct the DPIA, it will be better to err on the side of caution and have too many DPIAs.

13.6.2 Data protection impact assessment practicalities

Timing

13.6.2.1 Article 35(1) provides that a DPIA must be carried out "*prior to the processing*". By building privacy into the structure of a new system there is a much better chance both of avoiding privacy errors, and also of continuing to comply even when the system is changed in the future to meet changing business, legislative or other requirements. As WP 248 rev.01 notes:

> "*The DPIA should be started as early as is practicable in the design of the processing operation even if some of the processing operations are still unknown. Updating the DPIA throughout the lifecycle project will ensure that data protection and privacy are considered and will encourage the creation of solutions which promote compliance...*
> *The fact that the DPIA may need to be updated once the processing has actually started is not a valid reason for postponing or not carrying out a DPIA. The DPIA is an on-going process, especially where a processing operation is dynamic and subject to ongoing change.* ***Carrying out a DPIA is a continual process, not a one-time exercise***" (original emphasis) (p.14).

This statement reflects art.35(11) which provides that "where necessary", the controller should review whether processing is performed in compliance with any relevant DPIA, and states that this should certainly happen when there is a change of risk.

Who must be involved?

13.6.2.2 The DPIA is to be carried out by the controller—as the entity which determines the purposes and the means of the relevant processing. However, art.28(3)(f) requires that

> "*... the processor... assists the controller in ensuring compliance with the obligations pursuant to Articles 32 to 36* [which include art.35 on DPIAs] *taking into account the nature of the processing and the information available to the processor*".

So, although the processor does not have a direct obligation to conduct a DPIA, it must nevertheless be prepared to assist the controller in any DPIA, insofar as it (the processor) has the necessary information. In some cases, the processor may need to play a considerable part in the DPIA and this is also apparent from art.36 (2), which provides that where the controller has to consult a supervisory authority following a DPIA, that the authority may provide advice to, or exercise its powers against, the controller or any relevant processor.

13.6.2.3 Where a controller has appointed a DPO, art.35(2) provides that the controller must seek the advice of the DPO. The GDPR does not prescribe the input to be given by the DPO, but *ICO DPIA Guidance* states that the DPO should:

> "*provide advice on:*
>
> - *whether you need to do a DPIA;*
> - *how you should do a DPIA;*
> - *whether to outsource the DPIA or do it in-house;*
> - *what measures and safeguards you can take to mitigate risks;*
> - *whether you've done the DPIA correctly; and*
> - *the outcome of the DPIA and whether the processing can go-ahead.*
>
> *You should record your DPO's advice on the DPIA. If you don't follow their advice, you should record your reasons and ensure you can justify your decision.*
>
> *DPOs must also monitor the DPIA's ongoing performance, including how well you have implemented your planned actions to address the risks*".

13.6.2.4 Article 35(9) suggests taking into account the views of data subjects or their representatives (e.g. trade unions) "where appropriate". The article goes on to acknowledge that this can be done in a way so as to avoid "*prejudice to the protection of commercial or public interests or the security of the processing operations*".

ICO DPIA guidance puts the point even more strongly, recommending that "*you should seek and document the views of individuals (or their representatives) unless there is a good reason not to*". ICO goes on to suggest that this may mean designing a consultation process—including a public consultation process or market research. It may be time-consuming to do this properly—and require expertise which the controller does not have in-house, hence the ICO's question, in the list of topics for the DPO to address, as to whether there is a need to outsource some elements of the DPIA. The Commissioner also recommends documenting if the controller's decision differs from the views of the individuals who have been consulted.

Content of the data protection impact assessment

13.6.2.5 The DPIA is described in detail in art.35(7). It must contain at least:

"*(a) a systematic description of the envisaged processing operations and the purposes of the processing, including, where applicable, the legitimate interest pursued by the controller;*
(b) an assessment of the necessity and proportionality of the processing operations in relation to the purposes;
(c) an assessment of the risks to the rights and freedoms of data subjects referred to in paragraph 1 [i.e. the data subjects to whom the processing poses a high risk]*; and*
(d) the measures envisaged to address the risks, including safeguards, security measures and mechanisms to ensure the protection of personal data and to demonstrate compliance with this Regulation taking into account the rights and legitimate interests of data subjects and other persons concerned".

13.6.2.6 On assessing necessity and proportionality, *ICO DPIA guidance* poses two key questions:

"*Do your plans help to achieve your purpose?*
Is there any other reasonable way to achieve the same result?"

On assessing risks, *ICO DPIA guidance* looks to the list of risks set out in rec.75 of the GDPR, suggesting that the controller should:

"*In particular, look at whether the processing could contribute to:*

- *inability to exercise rights (including but not limited to privacy rights);*
- *inability to access services or opportunities;*
- *loss of control over the use of personal data;*
- *discrimination;*
- *identity theft or fraud;*
- *financial loss;*
- *reputational damage;*
- *physical harm;*
- *loss of confidentiality;*
- *re-identification of pseudonymised data; or*

- *any other significant economic or social disadvantage.*

You should include an assessment of the security risks, including sources of risk and the potential impact of each type of breach (including illegitimate access to, modification of or loss of personal data)".

13.6.2.7 *ICO DPIA guidance* suggests a classic information security approach to risk assessment, whereby the controller assesses likelihood and severity of possible harm, whereby:

> "*Harm does not have to be inevitable to qualify as a risk or a high risk. It must be more than remote, but any significant possibility of very serious harm may still be enough to qualify as a high risk. Equally, a high probability of widespread but more minor harm may still count as a high risk*".

The Commissioner suggests a structured matrix to assess risk, where severity of impact is plotted on one axis and likelihood of harm on the other. This is classic risk analysis, whereby most prudent people will avoid a quite likely but unpleasant event (high-risk), but also avoid an event whose likelihood (risk) is low but whose consequences could be very serious.

13.6.2.8 *ICO DPIA guidance* also suggests points to consider for risk mitigation:

> "*Against each risk identified, record its source. You should then consider options for reducing that risk. For example:*
>
> - *deciding not to collect certain types of data;*
> - *reducing the scope of the processing;*
> - *reducing retention periods;*
> - *taking additional technological security measures;*
> - *training staff to ensure risks are anticipated and managed;*
> - *anonymising or pseudonymising data where possible;*
> - *writing internal guidance or processes to avoid risks;*
> - *using a different technology;*
> - *putting clear data-sharing agreements into place;*
> - *making changes to privacy notices;*
> - *offering individuals the chance to opt-out where appropriate; or*
> - *implementing new systems to help individuals to exercise their rights*".

13.6.2.9 *ICO DPIA Guidance* also reminds that the controller can take into account the costs and benefits of each measure when deciding if it is appropriate. Lastly, art.35(8) notes that, if there is a relevant code of conduct (**1.3.8.9**) with which the controller or any relevant processor complies, then this is a relevant factor which should be taken into account in assessing the impact of the processing operations.

13.6.2.10 During the above process, the controller will have identified risks and mitigating actions. At the end of the process, the controller should conclude and document if the risks have been eliminated, reduced or accepted and what the overall level of residual risk is. This—together with input from any DPO—will then determine if the controller must consult the Information Commissioner (see **13.6.2.13** below). The Commissioner also recommends publishing the DPIA—although she notes that this is a matter of good practice, to promote transparency and accountability, and is not required under the legislation.

13.6.2.11 The Information Commissioner has published a template form to use for DPIAs. Controllers do not have to use this, but it is often helpful to see a template, even if a controller decides not to follow every element of it. It is at: *https://ico.org.uk/media/about-the-ico/consultations/2258461/dpia-template-v04-post-comms-review-20180308.pdf* [Accessed 24 May 2019]. The French data protection authority, the CNIL, has also made available open-source software for conducting DPIAs, which we have found useful. This is available here: *https://www.cnil.fr/en/open-source-pia-software-helps-carry-out-data-protection-impact-assesment* [Accessed 13 May 2019]. Much CNIL material on this is available in English including a template at *https://www.cnil.fr/sites/default/atoms/cnil-pia-2-en-templates.pdf* [Accessed 24 May 2019].

13.6.2.12 If a controller prefers to use a different template, or to develop its own DPIA template, it should check that it meets the "criteria for an acceptable DPIA" set out by the Article 29 Working Party at annex 2 of WP 248 rev.01. We think it is helpful to set this out in full.

"*A systematic description of the processing is provided (Article 35(7)(a)):*

- *nature, scope, context and purposes of the processing are taken into account (recital 90);*
- *personal data, recipients and period for which the personal data will be stored are recorded;*
- *a functional description of the processing operation is provided;*
- *the assets on which personal data rely (hardware, software, networks, people, or paper transmission channels) are identified;*
- *compliance with approved codes of conduct is taken into account (Article 35(8));*

necessity and proportionality are assessed (Article 35(7)(b)):

- *measures envisaged to comply with the Regulation are determined (Article 35(7)(d) and recital 90) taking into account:*
  - *measures contributing to the proportionality and the necessity of the processing on the basis of:*
    - *specified, explicit and legitimate purpose(s) (Article 5(1)(b));*
    - *lawfulness of processing (Article 6);*
    - *adequate, relevant and limited to what is necessary data (Article 5(1)(c));*
    - *limited storage duration (Article 5(1)(e));*

- *measures contributing to the rights of the data subjects:*
  - *information provided to the data subject (Articles 12, 13 and 14);*
  - *right of access and to data portability (Articles 15 and 20);*
  - *right to rectification and to erasure (Articles 16, 17 and 19);*
  - *right to object and to restriction of processing (Article 18, 19 and 21);*
  - *relationships with processors (Article 28);*
  - *safeguards surrounding international transfer(s) (Chapter V);*
  - *prior consultation (Article 36).*

risks to the rights and freedoms of data subjects are managed (Article 35(7(c)):

- *origin, nature, particularity and severity of the risks are appreciated (cf. recital 84) or, more specifically, for each risk (illegitimate access, undesired modification, and disappearance of data) from the perspective of the data subjects;*
  - *risk sources are taken into account (recital 90);*
  - *potential impacts to the rights and freedoms of data subjects are identified in case of events including illegitimate access, undesired modification and disappearance of data;*
  - *threats that could lead to illegitimate access, undesired modification and disappearance of data are identified;*
  - *likelihood and severity are estimated (recital 90);*
- *measures envisaged to treat those risks are determined (Article 35(7)(d) and recital 90);*

interested parties are involved:

- *the advice of the DPO is sought (Article 35(2));*
- *the views of data subjects or their representatives are sought, where appropriate (Article 35(9))".*

Consultation with the Information Commissioner

13.6.2.13 Article 36(1) provides as follows:

"*The controller shall consult the supervisory authority prior to processing where a data protection impact assessment under Article 35 indicates that the processing would result in a high risk in the absence of measures taken by the controller to mitigate the risk*".

This obligation to consult only arises if the controller has not been able to mitigate the identified risks. Although the drafting in art.36 is not clear on this point, it is clarified in rec.84, which notes that where:

"*... processing operations involve a high risk which the controller cannot mitigate by appropriate measures in terms of available technology and costs of* *implementation, a consultation of the supervisory authority should take place prior to the processing*".

13.6.2.14 Article 36(3) provides that when the controller consults, it must provide the supervisory authority with the following:

- where there is one or more processor and/or more than one controller, an analysis of the respective responsibilities of the various controllers or processors—art.36(3) notes that this may be particularly relevant for groups of undertakings;
- the purposes and means of the intended processing;
- the measures and safeguards to protect the data subjects;
- the contact details of the DPO if there is one;
- the DPIA itself; and
- any other information requested by the supervisory authority.

13.6.2.15 The procedure as to what happens once a controller consults the Information Commissioner is set out in art.36(2) and in the *ICO DPIA Guidance*. First, the Commissioner will acknowledge receipt of the DPIA. Her Office will revert within 10 days to confirm if they will accept the DPIA. As the *ICO DPIA guidance* notes, the Commissioner "*expects the percentage* [of DPIAs] *sent to us to be small*"—so the Commissioner will presumably reject DPIAs which do not rise to the level of risk set out in art.35. Where the Commissioner rejects the DPIA, she will provide reasons for this.

13.6.2.16 After this, the Commissioner has up to eight weeks under art.36(2) to consider the DPIA and to revert with written advice. This period can be extended by a further six weeks—and if the Commissioner thinks this is necessary, she must advise the controller of this within one month of receipt of the DPIA. If the Commissioner needs more information from the controller, these periods are suspended until such time as the information is provided. If the processing involves cross-border processing, the Commissioner will need to co-operate with other supervisory authorities in the EU. In this case, the 14-week maximum period will not apply. At **1.3.8.3**, we set out more details of the process and timing.

13.6.2.17 At the end of this process, the Information Commissioner may confirm that the controller has sufficiently mitigated the risk; or she may recommend additional mitigating steps. As art.36(2) makes clear, however, the Information Commissioner may use any of the powers granted to her by data protection legislation. As *ICO DPIA Guidance* states, this could include an official warning, requiring limits to the processing, or banning the processing. Although the guidance does not mention it, a fine could also be imposed if the process reveals deficiencies in existing processing. There is no mechanism to appeal a decision from the Information Commissioner at the end of this process—although a controller could seek judicial review if it considers that the Commissioner has acted unreasonably. Consultation with the Information Commissioner, therefore, is not to be undertaken lightly. Controllers should seek to mitigate risks themselves wherever possible and should ensure that they are fully prepared before consulting the Information Commissioner.

13.7 RELATIONS WITH PROCESSORS AND OTHER CONTROLLERS

13.7.1 Introduction

13.7.1.1 Any organisation processing personal data will need to deal with other organisations. A controller will need to deal with processors it may wish to appoint (and vice versa). A controller may also need to deal with other controllers in relation to personal data processing—for example, if it wishes to acquire a list of customers to use for marketing purposes. The GDPR contains specific provisions which have to be addressed to govern relations between controllers and processors and between joint controllers. The previous Information Commissioner adopted a *Data sharing code of practice* which looked more generally at what organisations should do whenever they wished to disclose personal data to another organisation. This section addresses these requirements. As a preliminary point, readers should note that these requirements and recommendations apply whenever personal data is shared by one entity with another—including within a corporate group. By way of example, a controller which arranges for a different group company to process personal data for it (for example, to host personal data), may have more assurance as to the standards which the processor will follow—but a contract between the controller and processor will still be required, in just the same way as it would with any external organisation. A new data-sharing code is promised by DPA 2018 s.121, but as yet we have no details.

13.7.2 Relations with processors

13.7.2.1 It will be recalled that a processor is defined as "*the natural or legal person, public authority, agency or other body which processes personal data on behalf of the controller*" (GDPR art.4(8)). An example is a payroll service whereby A works out the pay, tax and other deductions of pay for the staff in B's company and then remits the data so processed back to B for them to pay their staff accordingly. Another example is where back-up or other server activity is provided remotely by a third party instead of having a server physically on the customer's premises. Software can also be provided in this way whereby the user—rather than mounting the software on his own computer—sends his data to an internet site ("the cloud") where it is processed by a contractor and the results sent back to him. Most cloud providers, including providers of Software as a Service, would consider themselves processors.

13.7.3 Processor selection

13.7.3.1 GDPR art.28(1) says:

> "*Where processing is carried out on behalf of a controller, the controller shall use only processors providing sufficient guarantees to implement appropriate technical and organisational measures in such a manner that processing will meet the requirements of this Regulation and ensure the protection of the rights of the data subject*".

Technical and organisation measures are usually considered as security measures (**8.2**). However, the drafting here makes clear that the controller must not just consider the security obligations to be met by the processor—but how all aspects of the processing to be undertaken by the processor will meet the requirements of the GDPR, especially as regards individuals' rights. The controller must now ensure that it selects a processor who will comply with the obligations as to security must also check that the processor carries these out. As the Information Commissioner's *Controllers and Processors* notes:

> "*Controllers shoulder the highest level of compliance responsibility . . . You are also responsible for the compliance of your processor(s)*".

Article 28(5) suggests the use of codes or certification (arts 40 and 42, **1.3.8**) to provide proof of compliance.

13.7.4 Processor contracts

13.7.4.1 Article 28(2)–(4) describes the processor contract. First, there is a ban on the processor sub-contracting to other processors. The reason is obvious. A contract between the controller and the processor is straightforward enough, but if the processor starts to sub-contract there is likely to be uncertainty as to what extent the new sub-contractor is bound in obligation to the controller:

> "*(2) The processor shall not engage another processor without prior specific or general written authorisation of the controller. In the case of general written authorisation, the processor shall inform the controller of any intended changes concerning the addition or replacement of other processors, thereby giving the controller the opportunity to object to such changes*".

The contract between the controller and the processor must have a clause positively preventing the processor from sub-contracting, except with the prior written agreement of the controller. As the quote above shows, this authorisation could be given in general terms, as long as there is a mechanism for the controller to review new sub-processors.

13.7.4.2 In the event that such prior written permission from the controller to allow the processor to engage another processor is forthcoming, art.28(4) specifies that this new processor must provide the same safeguards and security measures to the same standard as are required in the original processor contract between the controller and the first processor. The Information Commissioner's guidance on *Contracts and liabilities between controllers and processors* (*https://ico.org.uk/for-organisations/guide-to-data-protection/guide-to-the-general-data-protection-regulation-gdpr/contracts-and-liabilities-between-controllers-and-processors-multi* [Accessed 13 May 2019]) notes that

> "*The wording of these obligations do not need to exactly mirror those set out in the contract between the controller and the processor, but should offer an equivalent level of protection for the personal data*".

Further, once a sub-processor is appointed:

> "*Where that other processor fails to fulfil its data protection obligations, the initial processor shall remain fully liable to the controller for the performance of that other processor's obligations*" (art.28(4)).

13.7.4.3 Article 28(3) prescribes both the format and content of the clauses that should go into a processor contract:

> "*Processing by a processor shall be governed by a contract or other legal act under Union or Member State law, that is binding on the processor with regard to the controller and that sets out the subject matter and duration of the processing, the nature and purpose of the processing, the type of personal data and categories of data subjects and the obligations and rights of the controller. The contract or other legal act shall stipulate, in particular, that the processor:*
>
> *(a)* *processes the personal data only on documented instructions from the controller, including with regard to transfers of personal data to a third country or an international organisation, unless required to do so by Union or Member State law to which the processor is subject; in such a case, the processor shall inform the controller of that legal requirement before processing, unless that law prohibits such information on important grounds of public interest;*
> *(b)* *ensures that persons authorised to process the personal data have committed themselves to confidentiality or are under an appropriate statutory obligation of confidentiality;*
> *(c)* *takes all the measures pursuant to Article 32* [security measures];
> *(d)* *respects the conditions referred to in paragraphs 2 and 4 for engaging another processor* (**13.7.4.1** above);
> *(e)* *taking into account the nature of the processing, assists the controller by appropriate technical and organisational measures, insofar as this is possible, for the fulfilment of the controller's obligation to respond to*

requests for exercising the data subject's rights laid down in Chapter III [rights of the data subject];

(f) *assists the controller in ensuring compliance with the obligations pursuant to Articles 32 to 36* [security, data breach and data protection impact assessments] *taking into account the nature of the processing and the information available to the processor;*

(g) *at the choice of the controller, deletes or returns all the personal data to the controller after the end of the provision of services relating to processing, and deletes existing copies unless Union or Member State law requires storage of the personal data;*

(h) *makes available to the controller all information necessary to demonstrate compliance with the obligations laid down in this Article and allow for and contribute to audits, including inspections, conducted by the controller or another auditor mandated by the controller*".

13.7.4.4 An addendum to this lengthy article requires that the processor:

"*shall immediately inform the controller if, in its opinion, an instruction infringes this Regulation or other Union or Member State data protection provisions*".

13.7.4.5 Most of the contents of art.28(3) are self-explanatory, However, some provisions are worth extra comment.

First, it is worth noting that the contract must set out

"*the subject matter and duration of the processing, the nature and purpose of the processing, the type of personal data and categories of data subjects*".

In other words, it is not possible to append a set of standard data processing terms to another commercial agreement: the data protection terms must actually describe, in some detail, *what* the processing is.

13.7.4.6 Second, the requirement that there must be a contract (or other legal act) which is "*binding on the processor with regard to the controller*" can be problematic for groups of companies. Corporate groups often find that there are multiple controllers in the group (either separate or joint) who all make use of a common processor. For example, one payroll processor may be appointed on behalf of multiple employing entities in the group. The parties may be keen to avoid a series of direct processing agreements:

- first, this may be administratively cumbersome (in terms of arranging for signature by multiple controllers);
- second, it may cause commercial difficulties for the processor, which may want to streamline the instructions it receives from the group—for example, taking all instructions from a central HR team.

The wording of art.28(3) itself seems to leave open a more creative approach to contracts —direct contracts, a series of sub-contracts (where members of a corporate group appoint one company as a processor, with permission to sub-contract to the payroll provider), or third-party rights—could all leave the processor bound to the controller. Unfortunately, the Information Commissioner's guidance on *Contracts and liabilities between controllers and processors* is inconsistent on this point, saying at one point that the article could be complied with

> "*not only by a direct contract between the controller and the processor, but also by other legally binding contractual arrangements... provided the processor is ultimately bound, as a matter of contract law, to each controller in respect of the particular processing*"

but later on saying that "*the controller and processor must be party to the contract*".

13.7.4.7 Third, the requirement to "*delete or return all the personal data to the controller after the end of the provision of services relating to processing*" can cause practical problems: a processor may well have set periods after which personal data is over-written and it will be difficult for it to delete data immediately on termination. Here the Information Commissioner's guidance (again on *Contracts and liabilities between controllers and processors*) states that:

> "*We appreciate the practical reality that it may not be possible for data in backups or archives to be deleted immediately on termination of a contract. Provided appropriate safeguards are in place, such as the data being put immediately beyond use, it may be acceptable that the data is not deleted immediately if the retention period is appropriate and the data is subsequently deleted as soon as possible, e.g. on the processor's next deletion/destruction cycle*".
> See also **5.5.6–5.5.7** on deletion.

13.7.4.8 Lastly, it is worth noting that the mandatory terms for controller-processor contracts do not address cost or commercial matters. Discussion of such matters is, of course, a major part of the discussion between controllers and processors, with processors wanting to ensure that they can recoup costs of dealing with large numbers of individual rights requests and controllers considering that processors should build their systems in such a way as to ensure that these requirements can be addressed at no additional cost. Precedent controller-processor contract terms are included at **Precedent P3**. There is also a possibility for either the EU Commission or a supervisory authority to lay down standard clauses applicable to processor contracts (arts 28(5)-(8)).

13.7.4.9 Article.28(9) requires the processor contract or other legal act to be in writing, including in electronic form. A letter—or even an exchange of emails—may be sufficient. It is surprising how many cases arise where a processor contract is not in writing. Often this can happen when both controller and processor belong to the same organisation. One example is the Yahoo! case. On 21 May 2018, Yahoo! were fined £250,000 by the Commissioner for a serious breach (news item on the ICO website of 12 Jun 2018). The breach took place on the servers of Yahoo Inc! which was found to be a data processor for Yahoo! UK Services Ltd, even though there was:

- no written contract;
- no instructions from Yahoo! UK Services to Yahoo! Inc as to steps to be taken to safeguard the data; and in particular
- no monitoring to protect data subjects' credentials and no investigation prior to effecting a very large data transfer.

13.7.5 Joint controllers

13.7.5.1 Article 26(1) GDPR provides that "*where two or more controllers jointly determine the purposes and means of processing, they shall be joint controllers*". As we saw at **1.3.4**, the CJEU has determined that:

- an administrator of a Facebook fan page will be a joint controller with Facebook: although Facebook determines much of the detail of the processing, the administrator determines the demographic data which will be collected from the fan page; and
- the Jehovah's Witnesses community is a joint controller with its members, because the community organised and encouraged its members to collect data about individuals visited.

13.7.5.2 Where there are joint controllers, art.26(1) provides that they must

> "*determine their respective responsibilities for compliance with the obligations under this Regulation, in particular as regards the exercising of the rights of the data subject and their respective duties to provide the information referred to in Articles 13 and 14*" [privacy notices].

This must be done "*by means of an arrangement between them*"—so whereas a controller must use a contract (or other "legal act") to bind a processor, the arrangements between joint controllers could be more informal, although there is nothing to stop joint controllers using contracts for this purpose. The ICO's old *Data sharing code of practice* (May 2011) is to be superseded by a new code under DPA 2018 s. 121 (see **13.7.5.4–13.7.5.5**). But the old *Code* devoted s.8 to describing what should go into a data sharing contract, and it is reasonable to think the new code will give equal prominence to this.

13.7.5.3 The particular reference to individuals' rights in art.26(1) suggests that the focus of any joint controller arrangement should be in ensuring that relations with the data subject are handled smoothly. This is re-enforced by art.26(2) which notes that the arrangement "*shall duly reflect the respective roles and relationships of the joint controllers vis-á-vis the data subjects*". Article 26(1) states that this must be done in a "transparent manner" and art.26(2) requires that "*the essence of the arrangement shall be made available to the data subject*": some part of this document or arrangement, or perhaps a summary of its key provisions, must be provided to individuals. The arrangement may also designate a contact point for individuals (art.26(1)), although individuals may exercise their rights against each of the controllers (art.26(3))—so the provision of a point of contact is intended to facilitate contact for individuals, not to restrict their rights.

13.7.5.4 The *Information Commissioner's Guide* states that:

> "*all joint controllers remain responsible for compliance with the controller obligations under the GDPR. Both supervisory authorities and individuals may take action against any controller regarding a breach of those obligations*".

The *Guide* seems to suggest that joint controllers will be jointly and severally liable for each other's acts. However, the actual provisions of the GDPR are more nuanced than this. Article 26(3) makes clear that an individual can pursue rights against either joint controller. However, liability for compensation is addressed separately at art.82. The provisions of art.82(2) state that "*any controller involved in processing shall be liable for the damage caused by the processing which infringes this Regulation*" and art.82(4) makes clear that:

> "*Where more than one controller or processor, or both a controller and a processor, are involved in the same processing . . . each controller . . . shall be held liable for the entire damage in order to ensure effective compensation of the data subject*".

Article 82(3) provides that:

> "*A controller or processor shall be exempt from liability . . . if it proves that it is not in any way responsible for the event giving rise to the damage*".

So far as compensation is concerned, therefore, whenever there are multiple controllers involved in the processing—joint or not—each can be liable. However, each can avoid liability if they can prove they are not responsible. As far as the Commissioner's powers are concerned, there is no reference to joint liability and, in relation to fines, supervisory authorities are specifically required to consider "*the degree of responsibility of the controller or processor*" (art.83(2)(d)). We consider that the Commissioner's comment is either misleading or wrong. Perhaps the matter will be reviewed in the ICO's forthcoming Data sharing code (DPA 2018 s.121).

13.7.5.5 The point has been addressed (in the context of Directive 95/46/EC) briefly in the ***Facebook fan*** case (**1.3.4.2**), where the CJEU noted that

> "*the existence of joint responsibility does not necessarily imply equal responsibility of the various operators involved in the processing of personal data. On the contrary, those operators may be involved at different stages of that processing and to different degrees, so that the level of responsibility of each of them must be assessed with regard to all the relevant circumstances of the particular case*" [43].

The responsibilities of joint controllers are also one of the key questions referred to the CJEU in the ***Fashion ID*** case (C-40/17) EU:C:2018:1039 .

Whereas art.28 provides very detailed guidance as to what must be included in a contract between controller and processor, art.26 says very little about the content of the arrangement between joint controllers. It is possible that the code of practice on data sharing, which the Commissioner must produce under DPA 2018 s.121 may provide further guidance on this. Unless and until this is available, we have found it helpful to start by setting out provisions out in a table format, with the key provisions of the GDPR summarised in rows, and with a separate column for each controller to specify the extent to which it can meet that obligation, or that it is dependent on another controller to meet the obligation. This focuses discussion on how the joint controllers need to collaborate to meet individual's rights and ensures that requirements are not overlooked. For an example see **Precedent P6.**

13.7.6 Other data sharing and arrangements between organisations

13.7.6.1 As mentioned at **13.7.4–13.7.5**, the GDPR prescribes how to address arrangements between controllers and processors, and between joint controllers. However, organisations will often have arrangements with other controllers relating to personal data. The previous Information Commissioner, in response to a requirement under the 1998 Act, adopted a *Data sharing code of practice* to give guidance on this. This *Code* had a very wide remit, with examples ranging from anti-fraud data sharing initiatives set up by public bodies and retailers, through to a GP sending information about a patient to a hospital and a retailer providing details to a payment processing company. The *Code* covered:

- lawfulness of sharing data—with specific focus on the public sector ensuring they have the power to share data (as well as the need to meet a lawful basis for processing under data protection legislation);
- considering the benefits and risks of sharing (i.e. proportionality);
- fairness and transparency;
- security of arrangements;
- governance (ensuring a senior person is responsible; undertaking a privacy impact assessment; and documenting arrangements via an agreement or protocol);

- meeting individual rights;
- things to avoid (including a reminder of the need to ensure accuracy of data before it is shared and to check compatibility of systems and formats to avoid corruption of data);
- powers of and penalties available to the Information Commissioner;
- notification requirements (now largely redundant—see **13.5.2**); and
- freedom of information considerations (for those in or dealing with public authorities).

These headings overlap almost entirely with points which a controller would have to consider when undertaking a DPIA. The new code which the Commissioner is obliged to produce under s.121 DPA 2018 must contain "practical guidance" on the sharing of personal data. To do this the Commissioner will need to re-assess the scope of the Code, given the overlap with the content of DPIAs, and decide where most value can be added. Guidance on data sharing agreements, whether between joint or separate controllers, would, however, still be useful.

13.8 POLICY AND PROCEDURES

13.8.1 Policy

13.8.1.1 Policies are mentioned specifically as an element of accountability, in art.24(2), which states:

> "*Where appropriate in relation to processing activities, the measures referred to in paragraph 1* ["technical and organisational measures to ensure and be able to demonstrate that processing is performed in accordance with this Regulation"] *shall include the implementation of appropriate data protection policies by the controller*".

13.8.1.2 The organisation will need to get its policy or policies on data protection in place and supported throughout the organisation.

This also signals clearly to all in the organisation that data protection is to be taken seriously and has support at the highest level. In the event of any complaint or request by a data subject under the legislation, the evidence that an organisation has clear written and enforced procedures for compliance may also help to make the organisation's case with the Commissioner or the courts.

13.8.1.3 Recital 74 notes that the measures to be adopted for accountability (which include policies) "*should take into account the nature, scope, context and purposes of the processing and the risk to the rights and freedoms of natural persons*". Policy and procedure documents are likely to be a mix of department-specific policies, and policies and procedures that operate across the organisation. For example, an organisation is likely to have to adopt specific procedures for each department to ensure that it complies with the data protection legislation. However, much of the policy is likely to operate across an organisation—principally for matters such as how to deal with data subject enquiries, security, transborder data flows, etc.

13.8.1.4 The need for transparency is stressed in the GDPR, especially in rec.58, and art.12 which require all dealings with individuals to be "*in a concise, transparent, intelligible and easily accessible form, using clear and plain language* . . .".

Transparency is discussed in more detail at **6.2.** in connection with data subjects' rights. Although this obligation applies in relation to interactions with data subjects, its principles could helpfully be applied to internal policies and procedures as well. The clearer they are the better.

13.8.1.5 A data protection policy is likely to address the following:

- target audience—to whom the policy will be distributed or is relevant;
- significance of data protection in the organisation:
    - a statement as to the organisation's goals as regards data protection (for example to comply with the legislation or to achieve good practice beyond the legislation). The policy should include an explanation of the key principles of the legislation and—at a high level—how the organisation will comply with them; and
    - statement of senior management's commitment to data protection;
    - a statement as to the law of confidence and its bearing on personal data. (This is not a data protection point, but it is entirely reasonable to remind staff of their obligations under the law of confidence at the same time as telling them how to comply with data protection);
    - links to other policies (such as quality management, ISO 9000 and security, ISO27001;
- organisational structure:
    - a description of the organisation's hierarchy;
    - details of the DPO (if any) and their contacts;
    - details of the data protection professional and their contacts;
    - the relationship between the DPO and the data protection professional;
    - high level description of data protection training available to staff;
    - list of the current versions of business-specific or department-specific policies;
    - commitment to audit/assessment procedures;
    - consequences for individual members of staff of non-compliance;

- the role of the supervisory authority (the Information Commissioner); and
- administrative matters such as document author or owner, review arrangements and version number.

13.8.2 Procedures

13.8.2.1 The Audit (**Ch.12**) will have identified among other things all groups of staff who handle personal data. For each such group there must be laid down procedures for how this is to be done—not necessarily a separate procedure for each, but no group should be without clear guidance as to how to comply with the legislation while performing their duties. Such groups of staff might include:

- those with contact with customers, including sales, after-sales, service, customer relations, accounts, etc.;
- those with contact with prospective customers, including marketing and the internet;
- those with contact with suppliers, including purchasing, accounts, etc;
- those with contact with the public at large—security, advertising, the internet;
- those with contact with staff and prospective staff, and sometimes also their families—human resources, the organisation's intranet;
- those who deal with any processor or data sharing contracts;
- those who work at least part of the time from home; and
- all staff who use or have access to email as part of their duties.

These examples are in no way intended to be exhaustive—each organisation will have its own variations. Each such group may include a mixture of staff with those who have direct contact with data subjects either face to face or by telephone, mail or other means, and those who do not have face-to-face dealings with data subjects, but handle their records. Each of these groups and types of staff within each group will have to have its ways of handling personal data spelled out in detail. Where the same staff member belongs to more than one group, they will be expected to comply with the policies and procedures for each group they are involved with.

13.8.2.2 For all processing which a department carries out, the data protection professional should ideally conduct an analysis, based on the audit result and any other necessary information, as to how the relevant department meets all aspects of the legislation as discussed throughout this book. **Precedent P5** contains a sample policy which may be adapted.

13.8.2.3 These policies and procedures should take account of best practice as set out in the ICO codes of practice and other guidance (**1.3.8**) and any art.40 codes of conduct (**13.1.2**). Data protection officers and data protection professionals must be alert to the fact that other sources of good practice which address data protection in whole or in part, but which may not have the Commissioner's blessing have nevertheless been devised by trade organisations and others—sometimes in consultation with the Commissioner's Office. It would be impossible to list all such documents, but as an example consider the *Guide to archiving personal data* issued by The National Archives in August 2018 (*http://www.nationalarchives.gov.uk/documents/information-management/guide-to-archiving-personal-data.pdf* [Accessed 13 May 2019]). The *Guide* is fully up to speed with the GDPR and the DPA 2018. The foreword by the Information Commissioner is of particular interest since she qualified as an archivist before becoming involved with data protection.

13.8.2.4 The DPO will also need to be kept fully informed of these policies and procedures and will be likely to wish to contribute to them. The DPO's views must be afforded the greatest attention and any failure to agree with the DPO should certainly be brought to the attention of the Board and if it persists must be recorded.

Privacy by design

13.8.2.5 So far, we have discussed accountability measures such as record keeping, appointing responsible personnel and adoption of policies. The GDPR, at art.25(1) goes beyond this by requiring that the controller must:

> "*. . . implement appropriate technical and organisational measures, such as pseudonymisation, which are designed to implement data protection principles, such as data minimisation, in an effective manner and to integrate the necessary safeguards into the processing in order to meet the requirements of this Regulation and protect the rights of data subjects*".

This is referred to as "privacy by design" and is the requirement that controllers build their systems and processes in a way which facilitates compliance with data protection legislation.

13.8.2.6 Article 25 sees this as a risk-based requirement, as the controller must undertake this:

> "*Taking into account the state of the art, the cost of implementation and the nature, scope, context and purposes of processing as well as the risks of varying likelihood and severity for rights and freedoms of natural persons posed by the processing . . .*"

13.8.2.7 Article 25 specifies that the controller must consider this *both* at the time when the means of processing are determined and at the time of processing itself—so recognising that there can be changes between system design and roll-out, which may affect data protection risks; available solutions may also change.

The reader will note that the assessment required for privacy by design is similar to the risk-based assessment required when determining the technical and organisational measures necessary for security purposes (**8.2**).

13.8.2.8 Article 25 mentions data minimisation and pseudonymisation—the process whereby identifiers are removed and held separate and secure—as an example of privacy by design. Recital 78 also mentions transparency as a privacy by design feature:

> "*transparency with regard to the functions and processing of personal data, enabling the data subject to monitor the data processing, enabling the controller to create and improve security features*".

The recital also encourages producers of products (who may not be the ultimate controller or processor) to follow privacy by design principles and encourages the principle to be reflected in public tenders.

13.8.2.9 Article 25(2) introduces the concept of privacy by default:

> "*The controller shall implement appropriate technical and organisational measures for ensuring that, by default, only personal data which are necessary for each specific purpose of the processing are processed*".

The article goes on to note that the obligation applies

> "*to the amount of personal data collected, the extent of their processing, the period of their storage and their accessibility. In particular, such measures shall ensure that by default personal data are not made accessible without the individual's intervention to an indefinite number of natural persons*".

13.8.2.10 The example of privacy settings in social media, to which the last sentence refers, is a good way of explaining privacy by default; settings should be left at private, unless and until a user chooses to allow more open access to content —for example by selecting access by "friends of friends", or the public.

13.8.2.11 If the data protection professional is to embed privacy by design and by default into the organisation, they will need to develop a close working relationship with those responsible for new systems, databases and procedures—this will mean working closely both with IT and with the business sponsors for new initiatives. Procedures, guidance and training will be essential—as will a process for reviewing initiatives for new systems. Data protection impact assessments could serve this purpose, but because these are designed for processing likely to pose a high risk they require a significant amount of time and effort to complete. It may not be realistic to complete a DPIA for all new initiatives, where risk may be lower. Instead, an organisation may need a less time intensive new system review process, which includes guidance to developers and business sponsors on privacy enhancing options, and which asks questions to identify areas of higher risk where a full DPIA can be conducted.

13.9 PROMULGATION

13.9.1 A climate of compliance

13.9.1.1 By now it will be apparent that the influence of the GDPR and Data Protection Act 2018 are pervasive throughout business. To comply with the legislation, the organisation will need to ensure that compliance is understood by staff at various levels and it is essential that a climate of compliance is fostered. To do this will require the message of data protection to be got across to staff at every level and in a variety of ways. These ways could include:

- formal training;
- inclusion of data protection issues in staff notices and intranets and
- staff handbooks;
- contracts of employment.

These are separately considered in the sections that follow.

13.9.2 Training

13.9.2.1 The staff who are identified as likely to handle personal data or be in contact with data subjects will need to be trained. In part this will be dictated by the procedures which have been identified for each. The training in the procedures can deal with the data protection aspects along with the other aspects such as security. But it is also highly desirable that the staff have at least some understanding of data protection (**Chs 6–13**) so that they correctly identify and handle any new situation with which they may be faced. It is also sometimes the case that staff are, because of staff shortages or for other reasons, obliged to undertake duties for which they have received less training than would normally be the case. The chances of a disaster in the data protection field is much reduced if the staff have a good grasp of the fundamentals of data protection.

13.9.2.2 It is therefore recommended that the staff be given a general course in data protection before they are trained in the specific procedures which apply to their particular job. It is also the case that training in the general requirements for data protection, divorced from procedural training, allows staff from different divisions to be trained simultaneously which is easier to organise (a whole division is not completely closed down for training), and allows the staff, when discussing in the training session the impact of the legislation, to appreciate its wider scope than just their own specific work. Moreover, for the future, training in data protection fundamentals and the organisation's data protection policy can form part of an induction course for all new staff. It should be added that training material is available from the Office of the Information Commissioner, both directly and via the internet.

13.9.3 Staff notices and intranets

13.9.3.1 The mechanisms that organisations use to get a message across to their staff will vary and can include any or all of notice boards, internal memos, internal emails and organisational intranets. Whatever the mechanism the organisation should use it to get the message across—again and again.

13.9.3.2 Most organisations of any size or complexity used to have a staff handbook, which set out clearly the organisation's commitment to various types of good practice such as promotion of certain staff qualifications, adhesion to certain standards, technical, legal or moral. Nowadays this is more likely to form part of the intranet. Whatever its format, this is an ideal place to include policies and procedures about data protection. In particular the principles in GDPR art.5 might form a major part of this (see **Ch.5** Data Quality and **13.1.1** above etc. The staff handbook can then set out the organisation's attitude to enforcement [**13.10**]).

13.9.4 Contracts of employment

13.9.4.1 Finally, the member of staff's contract of employment might reasonably contain a clause to the effect that they will obey data protection legislation as set out in the organisation's policy on data protection. The job applicant should be given a copy of all the policies and procedures on data protection which are likely to be relevant to them, including private use of email, on BYOD, etc. and requested to read them carefully before agreeing to take up any position in the company. The list of policies and procedures should be named in their contract. This could also include provisions requiring them to keep personal data confidential both during their employment and after they have left (**8.2.9**). This will help to impress on the member of staff that data protection is taken seriously in the organisation. It will also enable the organisation to insist on the observance of data protection legislation and confidentiality generally as to the organisation's affairs, even after the member of staff has left the organisation's employ. In the event that an ex-member of staff divulges personal data gained from their employment about another individual, failure to have insisted on such a clause might lay the organisation open to a charge of contravening the GDPR art.32 (on security).

13.9.4.2 Similar considerations will apply to temporary and contract staff. This will be buttressed by agreements with their parent organisations (e.g. a temporary staff bureau) who will usually be processors and covered by appropriate clauses in their contracts. In our experience many such bureaux have a general confidentiality clause but do not always have sufficient recognition of data protection issues.

13.10 ENFORCEMENT

13.10.1 In formulating its policies on data protection, the organisation will have to consider what sanctions are appropriate for infringement of any policy. Utterly gross violations might well merit dismissal. For example, DPA 2018 s.170 would be infringed by a policeman who used the Police National Computer system to obtain personal data about someone and then sell it to an enquiry agent, for purposes unconnected to the detection or prevention of any crime. At the other end of the scale, a failure to observe the requirements of the legislation in some trivial matter (say, failing by a few days to delete a record beyond its retention period) might earn no more than a mild rebuke. The organisation will therefore need to keep a sense of proportion about violations and have a variety of sanctions against staff who knowingly infringe the legislation and its policies.

13.10.2 Part of the data protection professional's duties will be to detect infringements and advise the Human Resources Department and the offender's line manager as to the heinousness or otherwise of the infringement and its effects. More culpable infringements might include (among others):

- laying the organisation (and possibly also individuals within it (DPA 2018 s.198, **3.2.1.1**)) open to criminal proceedings (**3.2**);
- laying the organisation open to civil proceedings (**3.3.1**);
- laying the organisation open to a penalty (DPA 2018 s.155, **3.4.3.17**), an enforcement notice (s.149, **3.5.3.3**) or special purposes information notice (s.143, **3.4.3.12**) or other unwelcome communication from the Information Commissioner;
- causing the organisation to fall foul of and be disciplined by any Regulator—not just the ICO but also for example the Financial Conduct Authority (**3.5.1.1**).
- causing the organisation to lose business by reason of an infringement;
- causing any damage or distress to a customer, supplier, other member of staff or other person;
- causing the organisation public embarrassment or disgrace (**3.5.2**).

13.10.3 Whatever sanctions are considered; the organisation will doubtless take the view that a gross enough violation could result in dismissal and will wish to warn the staff that such a sanction cannot be discounted. The various mechanisms chosen to promulgate the organisation's commitment to the legislation (**13.9**) must also give some idea at least of the maximum sentence which can be incurred. The organisation will also wish to advise its Trade Union or other staff representation body of this.

CHAPTER 14

Advanced Compliance and Accountability

Note: This chapter brings together three different matters which give rise to special consideration under the GDPR—children, monitoring, and Bring Your Own Device (BYOD) arrangements. Many controllers may have no need to study any of them, but for those who are involved with one or more of them, all raise particular aspects of accountability.

14.1 CHILDREN

14.1.1 Introduction

14.1.1.1 The GDPR contains provisions requiring organisations who offer online services directly to children to obtain consent from the person with parental authority in some situations. These provisions are described at **4.2.5**.

14.1.1.2 However, this is not the only consideration for those processing personal data of children. Recital 38 states generally that:

> "*Children merit specific protection with regard to their personal data, as they may be less aware of the risks, consequences and safeguards concerned and their rights in relation to the processing of personal data*"

so it is perhaps not surprising that there are a number of provisions in the GDPR which explicitly require organisations to consider children's interests. The DPA 2018 also contains specific provisions—in particular the requirement, at s.123, for the Information Commissioner to develop an age-appropriate design code of practice.

14.1.1.3 The Information Commissioner has issued guidance, *Children and the GDPR*, (22 March 2018/25 May 2018). This addresses all of the points above, as well as commenting on other provisions of the GDPR where special care is needed. *Children and the GDPR* (p.8) defines children as anyone under 18. Some of the advice relates to children at lower ages. We refer to the *Children and the GDPR* guide throughout this section and recommend that every data protection professional involved in processing of children's data read this.

14.1.2 Consent for online services

14.1.2.1 Article 8 of the GDPR provides as follows:

> "1. *Where point (a) of Article 6(1) applies* [consent as lawful basis for processing], *in relation to the offer of information society services directly to a child, the processing of the personal data of a child shall be lawful where the child is at least 16 years old. Where the child is below the age of 16 years, such processing shall be lawful only if and to the extent that consent is given or authorised by the holder of parental responsibility over the child.*
> *Member States may provide by law for a lower age for those purposes provided that such lower age is not below 13 years*".

As we have seen at **4.2.5**, in the UK the age limit is 13 (DPA 2018 s.9).

Online services provided directly to children

14.1.2.2 "Information society service" is a term used in the E-Commerce Directive (Directive (EU) 2015/1535), where it is defined as "*any service normally provided for remuneration, at a distance, by electronic means and at the individual request of a recipient of the services*". Remuneration includes ad-funded services and the definition is likely to include most online services. As *Children and the GDPR* notes (p.23):

> "*It generally includes websites, apps, search engines, online marketplaces and content services such as on-demand music, gaming and video services and downloads. It does not include traditional television or radio transmissions that are provided via general broadcast rather than at the request of an individual*".

14.1.2.3 We refer to "information society services" in this section as "online services". The GDPR's parental consent rules only apply where the online service is provided "directly" to the child. In *Children and the GDPR* (p.24), the ICO notes that this means that online services which are offered through an intermediary, such as a school, are not offered "directly" to the child. The Commissioner is also of the view (p.24) that "directly" implies an online service offered to all users (children or not) without distinction as to age, or where any age distinctions expressly allow some users under the age of 18.

14.1.2.4 The ICO takes a broad view of when services will be offered directly to a child (p.24). This would include:

- sites which specifically state they are for children;
- sites which do not state this, but have children as their target audience;
- as well as sites which are available to everyone.

Controllers cannot evade the provisions merely by stating that the site is only for those over 18—here the Commissioner states that, in the event of a complaint, she may look for evidence that this limit is actually applied in practice—for example taking into account processes designed to limit access and what users are told about this (p.24). Controllers which 'age-gate' their sites (i.e. which ask for age before allowing access to the site) should do so in a way which minimises the amount of personal data collected—for example, they do not actually need to know the age of the person using the site, just that they are over 13 (p.25).

How do you know you are dealing with a child?

14.1.2.5 A fundamental difficulty which arises with online services is that the controller often cannot know for certain whether or not he is dealing with a child. The Commissioner recommends (p.13):

"• *designing your processing so that it provides sufficient protection for children;*

- *putting in place proportionate measures to prevent or deter children from providing their personal data;*
- *taking appropriate actions to enforce any age restrictions you have set; or*
- *implementing up-front age verification systems*".

Age-verification systems are in a very grey area and there is at present no satisfactory method of online verification. Some controllers simply ask the individual who is online whether they are over 18 (or whatever age is relevant), but it is not easy to devise any mechanism whereby an IT-savvy 12-year-old cannot simply click 'Yes' and continue on the website.

14.1.2.6 The matter has been highlighted by s.14 of the Digital Economy Act 2017. This makes it an offence to provide pornographic material online on a commercial basis to anyone under 18. Section 16 of the Act requires the appointment of an Age-Verification Regulator and their powers are set out ss.18–21. The British Board of Film Classification has been suggested as the Regulator. The assumption is that age-verification will not be performed by the online commercial pornography sites, but by trusted third parties.

Until such time as a satisfactory mechanism can be devised to meet these objections, implementation of that part of the Digital Economy Act must be problematic, and there also remains a fundamental data protection difficulty for many controllers providing online material.

Lawful basis for processing

14.1.2.7 Organisations who are dealing with children do not always need to get consent from someone with parental authority. This is only required where a site relies on consent as the lawful basis for its processing of personal data. If an organisation processes personal data because this is necessary to fulfil a contract with the individual, or because this is in its or a third party's legitimate interests, for example, then the parental consent requirement will not apply. There are, however, also points to note when relying on either of either of these lawful bases to process children's data (see **14.1.3.6** below).

14.1.2.8 A further point to note is that rec.38 states that consent from the person with parental responsibility is also not needed for preventive or counselling services offered directly to children and this point is explicitly confirmed in s.9(b) of the DPA 2018.

When can children give valid consent?

14.1.2.9 Article 8 of the GDPR allows Member States to set the age at which children can give valid consent. The age cannot be below 13 and if no age is selected, then the default age will be 16. Section 9 of the DPA 2018 provides that children who are 13 and over can give valid consent. Some other Member States have set different ages, and some have left the default age of 16 in place. The Information Commissioner states (p.24) that

> "*This means that ISS* [information society service – i.e. online service] *providers that have an establishment anywhere within the European Union (EU) need to respect the differing age limits of the different Member States. In practice, this may mean that the child needs to select, or confirm, which country they are in each time they provide your ISS with their personal data, so that you know which age limit to apply. If you have an establishment anywhere in the EU the ICO expects you to respect the UK age limit when you process the personal data of UK based children*".

14.1.2.10 The Commissioner remarks (p.16) that one of the requirements for consent under the GDPR (art.4(11)) is that it must be "informed", and if a child has not got the capacity to understand the implications of the collection and processing of their personal data, any apparent consent cannot be informed and so is invalid. If you cannot form a clear view as to whether the child has or has not understood such implications, the Commissioner suggests: "*you should at least take into account the age of the child and the complexity of what you are expecting them to understand*".

To assist in this analysis, a data protection impact assessment (DPIA [**13.6**]) may be advisable (*Children and the GDPR*, p.25).

14.1.2.11 Under the Age of Legal Capacity (Scotland) Act 1991 s.2, a child of 12 in Scotland is considered to have "capacity". There is no such presumption under English law.

Obtaining consent

14.1.2.12 Children aged 13 and over are able to give consent themselves (provided of course that all the requirements for consent are present); where consent from someone with parental authority is required, then the organisation must use "reasonable efforts" to verify that that person does have parental authority. There is no "reasonable efforts" provision in relating to checking that someone is 13 or over and so capable of providing valid consent. However, the Commissioner notes (at p.25) that, in the event of a complaint, she will take into account if the organisation has made reasonable efforts to verify the age of the child. The Commissioner notes (p.26) that age verification mechanisms should themselves comply with privacy by design principles and that controllers should seek to minimise collection of 'hard identifiers' such as passport scans or credit card details.

14.1.2.13 Where an organisation needs consent from someone with parental authority, then the GDPR does recognise that the controller may not readily be able to confirm this—instead a "reasonable efforts" provision is included, "taking into account available technology" (art.8(2)). The Commissioner recognises that it may not be easy for controllers to check who holds parental responsibility for a child (p.26). Over time, the Commissioner suggests that technology may make verification of this easier. However, until solutions to this become available, the Commissioner suggests that it may be sufficient to check that someone is an adult and then to accept that individual's confirmation that they have parental responsibility for a child. What is appropriate may depend on the nature of the online service. For example, the Commissioner notes that where a child wants to sign up to an email newsletter from a band, it may be sufficient simply to ask the user to confirm that they are old enough to give consent themselves, or to provide a tick box for a parent to confirm consent, or to ask the child to provide the parent's email address, with a request for consent being sent to the parent. For services which pose more risk (the Commissioner gives the example of unmoderated chat functionality), an organisation may have to do more to prove the child is old enough to give consent or to prove that any adult providing consent has parental responsibility for the child.

Withdrawing consent and erasing data

14.1.2.14 If a child withdraws consent which either the child or someone with parental responsibility has given, the controller will no longer have a lawful basis for processing the data and so should cease processing. In this situation, the individual could also make a request for their data to be erased. Article 17 (the right to erasure) specifically provides for a right to erasure where: "*the personal data have been collected in relation to the offer of information society services referred to in Article 8(1)*" (i.e. online services provided directly to a child).

14.1.2.15 Recital 65 explains that:

> "*That right is relevant in particular where the data subject has given his or her consent as a child and is not fully aware of the risks involved by the processing, and later wants to remove such personal data, especially on the internet. The data subject should be able to exercise that right notwithstanding the fact that he or she is no longer a child*".

The Article 29 Working Party, in its Guidelines on Consent (WP 259), notes that the fairness and accountability principles (GDPR art.5) mean that a controller must inform children that they have a right to withdraw consent given by a parent on their behalf (p.27). It is difficult to see how controllers can comply with this recommendation if they do not collect the child's actual date of birth.

14.1.3 Other provisions relevant to children in the GDPR

How old is a child?

14.1.3.1 The provisions relating to online services deal with children 13 and over, or under 16 (depending on what age a particular Member State has selected). However, data protection legislation refers to children in other places—and here the relevant age is not 13 but 18 (*Children and the GDPR* p.8). This will be particularly relevant to provisions relating to marketing or profiling: controllers may not need parental consent when they deal with teenagers, but they still need to have regard to the other provisions in the GDPR dealing with children.

14.1.3.2 We have noted at **14.1.2.11**, that a child's "capacity" in Scotland starts at 12. Those dealing with children in Scotland should also note s.208 of the DPA 2018 which provides that whenever there is a question as to whether someone aged under 16 has capacity to exercise their rights or give consent, that a child aged 12 or over is to be presumed to have sufficient age and maturity as to be able to do this. On its face, this appears to conflict with the rules on children's consent under art.8. This is clearly not the intent and para.603 of the Explanatory Notes states that it has to be read in conjunction with art.8, so that Scottish 12-year olds are treated the same way as others so far as online services are concerned.

Privacy by design

14.1.3.3 The Commissioner recommends that any organisation which processes personal data take account of any associated risks or requirements during the design phase (p.11). She also recommends consultation with children or taking account of views of experts or child's rights advocates (p.13). The Commissioner more than once recommends that organisations conduct a data protection impact assessment (DPIA **13.6**) whenever they intend to process children's personal data, as a good way of helping to assess and mitigate risk (pp.11, 25). Under the GDPR, the Commissioner is able to issue a list of processing when a DPIA *must* be conducted: the Commissioner's list includes processing using children's data for marketing, profiling, or other automated decision making, and offering online services directly to children (p.12). The Commissioner is also of the view that in designing systems the views of children themselves should also be sought (p.13), and quotes UNICEF in support of this.

Transparency

14.1.3.4 Article 12, which sets out the general obligation to communicate clearly etc. with individuals, states that the requirement for communications to be intelligible, easily accessible and to use clear and plain language applies "*in particular for any information addressed specifically to a child*". The Commissioner (p.12) suggests three simple actions for all controllers to ensure that children and their parents are aware of data protection risks, consequences, safeguards and rights:

- "*telling them* [children and their parents] *what you are doing with their personal data;*
- *being open about the risks and safeguards involved; and*
- *letting them know what to do if they are unhappy*".

The Commissioner recommends (p.38) taking account of the needs of the particular age group—and if children of any age group could read the notice, then either to have different versions, or to make sure the youngest age group can understand the notice. Diagrams, cartoons, graphics and videos are recommended (but see below). The Commissioner also notes that the fact that a controller may have obtained consent from someone with parental authority does *not* alter the fact that child-friendly information should be provided.

> "*children do not lose their rights as data subjects to transparency just because consent has been given by a holder of parental responsibility*" (p.38).

14.1.3.5 In practice, websites that are legitimately aimed at children will also find themselves having to engage with parents. Fulfilling GDPR requirements for transparency in art.12 in such a way that information in a privacy notice under GDPR arts.13 and 14 can be understood and assimilated by both 11-year-olds and adults is tricky. The Commissioner (p.4) recommends for privacy notices the use of

> "*child friendly ways of presenting privacy information, such as: diagrams, cartoons, graphics and videos, dashboards, layered and just-in-time notices, icons and symbols*".

However, when providing any information in this form, a controller should also consider how intelligible it will be to a parent.

Legal basis for processing

14.1.3.6 We have already seen that, for online services, there are special considerations when a controller justifies its processing of personal data based on consent. There are also points to consider *whenever* a controller relies on consent and if it relies on legitimate interests or contractual necessity as the legal basis for processing.

Consent

14.1.3.7 A controller must always consider if a child has "capacity" to give valid consent. This means deciding if the child has sufficient understanding. As mentioned above at **14.1.2.11**, for children in Scotland there is a presumption that children 12 and over do have capacity. There is no such presumption for children in other parts of the UK; instead the controller must rely on its own judgment.

Contractual necessity

14.1.3.8 Controllers may justify their processing on art.6(1)(b)—that the processing is necessary for performance of a contract with the data subject. This could also be relevant for online services—for example, registration data or payment data may be processed on this basis. Page 17 of the *Children and the GDPR* guide has a good summary of the relevant considerations here:

> "*The legal age of capacity to enter into contracts is 16 in Scotland (with some exceptions which allow contracts with children younger than this). In the rest of the UK there is no definite age at which a child is considered to have the legal capacity to enter into a contract. The basic rule is that children over the age of 7 are generally able to enter into contracts, but (with some exceptions) the contracts they make may be 'voidable'. This means that you can't hold the child to what they have agreed to, or enforce the terms of the contract against them – they can effectively cancel the contract at any time. If the contract is voided then you do not have a lawful basis for processing their personal data*".

Legitimate interests

14.1.3.9 Controllers often also justify their processing on the basis that the processing is in their, or a third party's, legitimate interests and does not cause unwarranted prejudice to individuals. The legitimate interests condition, art.6(1)(f) specifically calls out that this balancing must be undertaken "*in particular where the data subject is a child*". As the Commissioner notes at p.20:

> "*you . . . have a responsibility to protect them from risks that they may not fully appreciate and from consequences that they may not envisage. . . . You should be able to demonstrate that you have prioritised their interests over your own where this is needed*".

14.1.3.10 However, legitimate interests as a basis for lawfulness of processing is often not available to public authorities (GDPR art.6(1)(f) and paragraph following) (**4.4.5.4**). They will have to find another art.6(1) basis—often it will be art.6(1)(c) or (e):

> "*processing . . . necessary for compliance with a legal obligation to which the controller is subject.*"
> "*processing . . . necessary for the performance of a task carried out in the public interest or in the exercise of official authority vested in the controller*".

In these cases the public authority as controller must point to authorising EU law or UK law to which it is subject (art.6(3)).

Capacity to exercise other rights

14.1.3.11 If a child has capacity (as set out above, **14.1.2.9**), then they will be able to exercise data protection rights—such as to make a subject access request—themselves. Where this is not the case, then the Commissioner states that: "*it will usually be in their best interests to allow an individual with parental responsibility to act on their behalf*" (p.9). In the case of health, social work, and educational records and child-abuse data, there are exemptions in Sch.3 to the DPA 2018, where providing the information would be likely to cause serious harm or would not be in the best interests of the child. The Commissioner also recommends (p.41) looking at any duty of confidence owed to the young person, the consequences of providing the information and any detriment to the child if the information is not provided, and the views of the child about providing the information.

14.1.3.12 The Commissioner remarks (p.13) that the concept of best interests comes from art.3 of the United Nations Convention on the Rights of the Child, and adds:

> "*Although it* [the Convention] *is not directly referenced in the GDPR it is something that the Commissioner will take into account when considering compliance, and that you should consider when making decisions about the processing of children's personal data. It states that:*
>
> > *'In all actions concerning children, whether undertaken by public or private social welfare institutions, courts of law, administrative authorities or legislative bodies, the best interests of the child shall be the primary consideration'*".

Automated individual decision-making, profiling and marketing

14.1.3.13 As we have seen at **6.11**, the GDPR distinguishes between:

- automated individual decision-making—which is where a decision is based solely on automated processing and where the decision produces legal or similarly significant effects (art.22); and
- profiling—which is any form of automated processing which uses personal data to evaluate personal aspects about someone—such as performance at

work, economic situation, health, personal preferences, interests, reliability, behaviour, location or movements (art.4(4)).

Automated individual decision-making will often involve profiling—although it does not have to do so. Profiling is a wider concept than automated individual decision-making, and would cover processing which has less significant impacts on individuals.

14.1.3.14 Automated individual decision-making can only be used in limited situations set out in art.22. Recital 71 further provides that "*such measures should not concern a child*". Automated individual decision-making is not necessarily a bad thing—for example, automated monitoring of a health condition, so as to adjust the level of medication or trigger urgent intervention by a health-care professional, may be extremely important and this kind of processing should be available to children. Recitals in EU legislation can aid interpretation but do not have the same force as the articles. Accordingly, the Information Commissioner suggests (p.32) that this is not meant to prohibit use of automated individual decision-making for children, but to suggest that it should generally be avoided and, if used, that suitable measures should be in place to protect the interests of the children. It would seem that the onus will be on the controller to justify any decision of this kind.

14.1.3.15 Recital 38 states that:

> "*. . . specific protection should, in particular, apply to the use of personal data of children for the purposes of marketing or creating personality or user profiles . . .*".

The Information Commissioner notes that studies have shown that children can be particularly susceptible to marketing online, through social media, games and apps, because they have less understanding of the motivation behind the processing and are more easily influenced (p.33). The Commissioner concludes that, as a result, while profiling for purposes of targeted advertising may not generally amount to automated individual decision-making (see **6.11.3.12** for comments on this), it is more likely to amount to this if the data subjects are children. If the marketing may have this type of effect, then "*we would advise you to think very carefully before you proceed with the processing*" (p.33).

14.1.3.16 On direct marketing more generally, the Commissioner refers controllers to Advertising Standards Authority guidance, which prohibits marketing directed to children which may result in physical, mental or moral harm, which would exploit children, or which would encourage poor nutritional habits or an unhealthy lifestyle. Although the Commissioner does not refer to it, the Interactive Advertising Bureau (IAB) Europe's EU Framework for Online Behavioural Advertising is also relevant here (*https://www.iabeurope.eu/policy/iab-europe-eu-framework-for-online-behavioural-advertising* [Accessed 13 May 2019]). This prohibits creation of segments which are specifically intended to target children who are 12 and under (Principle IV.A). This is a self-regulatory framework for IAB members. It does not apply to all online advertising—in particular it does not when a publisher targets its own site visitors—rather it applies when third parties are involved (for example, when information from one site is used to target visitors on another site) (**7.5.6.3**). The conclusion for advertisers is to follow the CAP Code and avoid online behavioural advertising targeted at children—certainly those under 13; possibly for those between 13 and 18: here consider whether they are likely to be unduly susceptible to the advertising.

Cookies

14.1.3.17 Consent can also be relevant when organisations make use of cookies online (see **7.5**). One obvious question is whether the requirement to obtain consent from someone with parental authority also applies to consent given to place cookies: this would be very difficult to deal with. This is dealt with briefly by the Information Commissioner. At p.27 she notes that consent to use cookies:

> "... *is not quite the same as consenting to the processing of personal data in GDPR terms. However, it remains the case that for consent to be valid the person providing it must understand what they are consenting to. This means that you need to take proportionate measures, taking into account the risks inherent in technology being used, to ensure that a child providing their own consent is competent to do so*".

For organisations with websites aimed at children, the most straight-forward approach would be only to use cookies which do not need consent—for example, those which are strictly necessary to deliver the requested content (see **7.5.4**).

Age-appropriate design code

14.1.3.18 Section 123 of the DPA 2018 mandates the Commissioner to prepare:

> "*a code of practice which contains such guidance as the Commissioner considers appropriate on standards of age-appropriate design of relevant information society services which are likely to be accessed by children*".

The section relates to online services accessed by children in general—not just those accessed by children under 13, so it could have a wide scope—although preventive and counselling services are specifically excluded at s.123(7). There is also no requirement for the services to be offered "directly" to the child, so the scope could also be wider in this regard. The Commissioner issued a call for evidence to support the creation of such a code, which closed on 19 September 2018. In the call for evidence, the Commissioner emphasised that her code would focus on matters within the Commissioner's remit—i.e. the processing of personal data, rather than other considerations. The Commissioner has published a draft of the code of practice for consultation, with the consultation period closing on 31 May 2019. The code applies to providers of information society services which are likely to be accessed by under-18s. It sets out 16 key principles which must be taken into account when designing and operating such services. These are to take into account:

- the best interests of the child;
- age appropriate application of the standards;
- transparency;
- avoiding detrimental use of data;
- upholding policies and community standards;
- ensuring high privacy default settings;
- ensuring data minimisation;
- avoiding data sharing;
- limiting use of geolocation;
- having appropriate parental controls;
- minimising profiling;
- not using nudge techniques;
- following rules for connected toys and devices;
- providing online tools;
- conducting DPIAs; and
- having appropriate governance and accountability to ensure and demonstrate compliance.

14.1.4 Other provisions relevant to children in the DPA 2018

Representative bodies

14.1.4.1 As mentioned at **3.3.1.19**, the GDPR and the DPA 2018 make provision for claims to be brought by representative bodies—these are bodies created for charitable or public purposes, which are active in the field of protecting individuals' data protection rights. Section 189 requires the Secretary of State to review the operation of these provisions—in particular, to consider whether the provisions should be extended to allow children's rights organisations to exercise rights of data subjects and whether such bodies should be permitted to do this without being authorised to do so by the relevant data subjects (at the moment, representative bodies must be authorised by data subjects to bring proceedings).

Additional condition for processing

14.1.4.2 Lastly, for controllers who process special categories of data relating to children, DPA 2018 Sch.1 sets out certain additional conditions for processing for such data. Schedule 1, Pt 2, para.18 permits processing of special category data about children (and other individuals at risk), if this is needed to protect the individual from neglect or harm, or to protect their well-being. The processing must be in the substantial public interest and it must not be appropriate to try and obtain consent (for example, because this would not be reasonable or because this would prejudice the ability to achieve the purpose). Other conditions in Sch.1 and in the GDPR may, of course, also be relevant to the processing of special category data about children even though the conditions do not specifically refer to this. These are all considered at **6.11.3.11**.

14.2 MONITORING

14.2.1 Monitoring at work

14.2.1.1 Most organisations will want to monitor their staff for purposes ranging from:

- checking traffic on the system with a view to seeing whether greater bandwidth or other upgrade is necessary;
- monitoring usage of IT systems for security purposes, either to stop viruses and malware getting into the organisation, or to stop valuable information getting out;
- checking compliance with company rules prohibiting sending of offensive material or accessing pornography;
- checking the spending of excessive amounts of time on private use;
- checking calls being made by staff to ensure that appropriate quality standards are maintained;
- investigating the use of harassing or bullying emails or telephone calls;
- to prevent trade secrets being sent outside the organisation to unauthorised persons;
- videoing staff outside the workplace to check that they are not sick;
- checking that telephone staff working to a script stick to the script;
- recording telephone conversations of contractual value (e.g. in the insurance business); to
- CCTV in the staff carpark to detect/prevent crime.

It is arguable that an ordinary machine which validates and records the times workers clock in is a form of monitoring at work.

14.2.1.2 Monitoring will usually involve personal data of staff being processed—so that the monitoring must comply with data protection legislation. Monitoring also has the potential of being highly intrusive and leading to decisions being taken on an automated basis which could lead to serious consequences for the staff concerned. For this reason, there is detailed guidance from data protection authorities on employee monitoring:

- in the UK, the Information Commissioner published the *Employment Practices Code*[1], Pt 3 of which is dedicated to employee monitoring. The *Code* will need to be updated to take account of the GDPR and other changes in legislation but, until this is done, still offers useful guidance; and
- there is guidance from the Article 29 Working Party, in Opinion 2/2017 on data processing at work (WP 249) (which updates an earlier Opinion from 2001). WP 249 provides a useful survey of a whole variety of different types of monitoring—ranging from email and IT usage monitoring, through to more advanced data loss prevention monitoring and next generation firewalls, as well as more case specific monitoring, via in-vehicle monitoring or use of wearable technology.

The sections of the GDPR which look at accountability requirements for higher risk processing (data protection impact assessments **13.6** and appointment of data protection officers **13.2.1**) also specifically refer to monitoring.

14.2.1.3 Monitoring which involves communications services (so monitoring calls, emails or internet usage) must also comply with the sector specific communications privacy rules—in the UK set out in the Investigatory Powers Act 2016 (IPA 2016). Lastly, monitoring of staff will also usually engage their right to privacy under art.8 of the European Convention on Human Rights.

14.2.2 Monitoring and privacy

14.2.2.1 The European Convention on Human Rights (ECHR) and the case law of the European Court of Human Rights (ECtHR) are a good place to start when considering monitoring. The cases clearly highlight key requirements—and pitfalls. These requirements in turn meet many of the provisions of data protection legislation and other relevant legislation (the IPA 2016) and secondary legislation made under it.

14.2.2.2 Article 8 of the ECHR provides that:

> "1. *Everyone has the right to respect for his private and family life, his home and his correspondence.*

---

[1] The *Code* has been revised several times already. The present version is November 2011. There is also some *Supplementary Guidance* to the *Code* which amplifies much of the *Code*. This too should be consulted.

> 2. *There shall be no interference by a public authority with the exercise of this right except such as in accordance with the law and is necessary in a democratic society in the interests of national security, public safety or the economic well-being of the country, for the prevention of disorder or crime, for the protection of health or morals, or for the protection of the rights and freedoms of others*".

Article 8 refers to the acts of public authorities. In fact, it has a wider impact than this: the UK has an obligation to ensure that individuals' right to privacy is respected generally, not just by public authorities, and employees (or others) can raise breach of privacy in claims against their employers (or others), irrespective of whether the defendant is a public authority or not. **Appendix 1** has more background on the ECHR and the Human Rights Act 1998. When considering art.8, the ECtHR looks at whether there is an interference with privacy and, if there is, whether it is in accordance with the law, pursued for a legitimate aim and whether the interference was proportionate to the aim pursued.

14.2.2.3 The leading ECtHR case to consider employee monitoring is that of ***Bărbulescu v Romania*** (App No.61496/08 5 September 2017[2]). Mr Bărbulescu was employed as a sales engineer by a private Romanian company. He was required to create a Yahoo! Messenger account to deal with customer enquiries. Work rules prohibited the use of work equipment for private purposes. There was no formal notice that use of IT equipment would be monitored, although the company had sent a later circular to staff where this was indirectly and briefly mentioned. The company recorded Mr Bărbulescu's messages over a short period and complained to him that he was using equipment for private purposes. When Mr Bărbulescu denied this, the company produced a 45-page transcript of private messages sent to his brother and fiancée. Mr. Bărbulescu was then dismissed.

14.2.2.4 The ECtHR concluded that:

- article 8 of ECHR was applicable—communications via Yahoo! Messenger were covered by the protections for private life and correspondence;
- the employee still had a right to respect for private life at work, even though the employer had prohibited all private use of work equipment—"*an employer's instructions cannot reduce private social life in the workplace to zero*" [80];
- the State (here Romania) had an obligation to ensure that monitoring was proportionate and to provide procedural guarantees against arbitrariness. The ECtHR noted that this was an area affected by rapid technical developments [121], but it listed the following relevant factors:

  – notice to the employee—covering the fact that the employer might take measures to monitor to communications and that these

[2] This was an appeal to the Grand Chamber of the ECtHR. There was an earlier case with the same parties heard on 12 January 2016. Its findings were overturned by the Grand Chamber.

measures were, in fact, being taken. The notice should be given before monitoring started and should be clear about the type of monitoring [121(i)];

- the extent of the monitoring and the degree of intrusion—in particular distinguishing between monitoring the flow of communications and monitoring their actual content (the latter being more intrusive). The period of monitoring, geographical scope of monitoring and number of people who had access to the results would also be relevant to assess intrusiveness [121(ii)];
- whether the employer had provided legitimate reasons to monitor—and to access actual content, the latter requiring weightier justification [121(iii)];
- whether a less intrusive monitoring system would have been possible—in particular, whether the content of communications had to be accessed [121(iv)];
- the consequences of the monitoring for the individual; was the monitoring used to achieve the intended purpose [121(v)];
- whether there were adequate safeguards for the employee—in particular relating to access to content, where the employee should have been notified in advance that this could happen [121(vi)].

14.2.2.5 At the time of ***Halford v United Kingdom*** [1997] I.R.L.R. 471, Ms Alison Halford, the most senior female police officer in England, was in dispute with her employer, Merseyside Police Authority, and was provided by Merseyside Police with two phones at work—one for police duties and one for her private use, so that she could communicate with her legal advisers (this was before the days of mobile phones). The employer abused the system and the calls on the private line were intercepted by Merseyside Police without the knowledge or consent of Ms Halford. At that date, the UK law on interception of communications only applied to interception over a *public* telecommunication system; the Merseyside Police argued that they had intercepted calls over a private telecommunication system. The ECtHR held that the calls made by Ms Halford were protected by art.8 and that the actions of the Merseyside police could not be said to be made "in accordance with the law" as there was no relevant UK law.

14.2.2.6 In ***Libert v France*** (588/13), [2018] ECHR 185, the French national railway, SNCF, dismissed an employee after finding images of pornographic files and forged certificates on his work computer. The ECtHR held that there was no violation of art.8—in this case the employer had a legitimate aim (ensuring that employees were using work equipment in accordance with company rules) and French law had appropriate rules to protect privacy, which stipulated that private files must be opened in the employee's presence, and could not be opened surreptitiously. In this case, the files were stored on a drive used to store work documents. Although they had been labelled "personal data", the French court had concluded that this was not sufficiently clear as to mean that the documents should be treated as private; instead it could have meant that the employee considered these to be work related files being processed personally by this employee.

14.2.2.7 In ***Koepke v Germany*** (420/07), a supermarket cashier was dismissed for theft, following covert video surveillance carried out by the employer. The ECtHR held that the employer had a legitimate interest (protecting its property) and that the monitoring had been proportionate (for a limited two-week period and only covering the area near the cash desk, with limited access to the data). The information had also only been used for the specific operation for which it was obtained.

14.2.2.8 The ECtHR cases show that privacy laws *do* permit monitoring of employees. However, the monitoring has to be carried out carefully:

- be clear what the objective is at the outset
  - and if this objective is legitimate: protecting company property and enforcing company rules can be legitimate; snooping on legal advice being given to your employees will not be;
- consider how the monitoring will be undertaken: is this proportionate? Is there a way to achieve the objective by carrying out less, or even no, monitoring?
  - will sampling achieve your objective?
  - can you monitor for a limited period?
  - or can you limit the physical area being monitored or the people being monitored?
  - can you achieve your objective by looking at the volume of communications, or the recipients or destination of communications, rather than looking at content?
  - can you limit who will have access to the communications?
- if you are monitoring to enforce company policies or rules, have these rules been clearly communicated?
- and have you told your employees that they may be monitored and given enough information so that they understand what this will mean? In particular, if the content of communications will be monitored, do they realise this and understand why?

14.2.3 Monitoring and the Investigatory Powers Act 2016

Interception of communications over telecommunication systems

14.2.3.1.1 We have seen that, in the *Halford* case (**14.2.2.5**), the ECtHR concluded that monitoring of communications over private networks in the UK could not be carried out "in accordance with law", because the UK laws at that date only regulated monitoring of public communication systems. The Regulation of Investigatory Powers Act 2000 was enacted, amongst other purposes, to address this deficiency. The current legislation addressing this point is the Investigatory Powers Act 2016.

14.2.3.2 The IPA 2016 applies to "interception" of "communications" over "telecommunication systems". A telecommunication system (s.261(13)) means

> "*a system . . . that exists . . . for the purpose of facilitating the transmission of communications by any means involving the use of electrical or electromagnetic energy*".

A telecommunication system can either be:

- a public system (if it is offered or provided to the public or a substantial section of the public in any part(s) of the United Kingdom) (s.261(9)); or
- a private telecommunication system (any telecommunication system which is *not* public, but which is attached to the public telecommunication system in the UK) (s.261(14)).

A communication (s.261(2)) includes "*anything comprising speech, music, sounds, visual images or data of any description*" as well as the signals which impart things between people or apparatus.

14.2.3.3 Interception is defined at s.4. It includes "*monitoring transmissions made by means of the system*" where the effect of this is to make "*content of the communication available . . . to a person who is not the sender or intended recipient of the communication*". The definition covers interceptions which make content available to someone else:

- while the communication is being transmitted (s.4(4)(a));
- while the communication is being stored in or by the system (both before and after transmission) (s.4(4)(b)); or
- as a result of the communication being diverted or recorded, whilst it is being transmitted or stored, so that the content can be made available to someone after that time (s.4(5)).

The following would all fall within the definition:

- listening in to calls at a call-centre, or recording them to listen to later;
- monitoring the content of staff emails in real time;
- looking at the content of staff emails which have been saved for later access;
- or looking at content in other forms of messages (instant messages,

recorded Skype calls), either in real time, or when they have been recorded to be accessed and reviewed later.

Sanctions for interception

14.2.3.4 Section 3 of the IPA 2016 makes it an offence intentionally to intercept a communication in the UK without lawful authority. This applies to transmissions using:

- a public telecommunication system;
- a public postal service; and
- a private telecommunication system—unless the interception is carried out by a person with the right to control the operation or use of the system, or has the express or implied consent of that person (s.3(2)).

14.2.3.5 It follows that there is no criminal offence when an employer monitors emails or phone calls over the employer's *own* system. The case of ***Clifford Stanford*** provides a cautionary tale here (*https://www.theguardian.com/technology/2005/sep/15/guardianweeklytechnologysection.uknews* [Accessed 13 May 2019]). Clifford Stanford was one of the co-founders of Redbus Interhouse. He arranged to covertly monitor the emails of a fellow director, in the hope of finding material relevant to a boardroom dispute. Although Stanford was a deputy chairman of the company, this did not mean that he had authority to intercept the company's emails for a personal dispute. He was given a six-month prison sentence, suspended for two years, and fined £20,000[3]. Even where the employer itself does authorise the monitoring, the employer must still have "lawful authority" to do this—because s.8 of the IPA 2018 provides that an employer who intercepts communications, in the UK, over its own network can still incur civil liability, to the sender, or the recipient, or intended recipient of the communication.

Lawful authority

14.2.3.6 For most organisations, "lawful authority" will mean ensuring that the monitoring is for a purpose permitted by, and is otherwise carried out in accordance with, the Monitoring and Record-Keeping Regulations (**14.2.3.8**). "Lawful authority" would also include:

- interception pursuant to a warrant under the IPA 2016 or a court order;
- interception carried out by the provider of the system for administrative or enforcement purposes (ss.45–48 IPA 2016);
- interception by specified institutions (prisons, psychiatric hospitals and immigration detention facilities) (ss.49–51); and

[3] This was under s.1(3) of the Regulation of Investigatory Powers Act 2000 which had similar wording as to "a person having the right to control the operation or use of a private telecommunication system".

- interception pursuant to overseas requests (s.52).

However, these are unlikely to be relevant to most readers. Interception is also carried out with lawful authority if one party to the communication consents and the interception is authorised under the Regulation of Investigatory Powers Act 2000 (s.44(2)), or if the sender *and* intended recipient have each consented. In most situations, it is likely to be difficult for an employer to obtain consent of each party to the communication, so this would seem to be relevant in rare situations only.

Monitoring and record-keeping regulations

14.2.3.7 Monitoring also has lawful authority if it is carried out in accordance with regulations made under s.46. This section allows the Secretary of State to make regulations which authorise interception by businesses (and others) for monitoring and record-keeping purposes. The regulations only cover "*legitimate practices reasonably required for the purpose*" (s.46(2)) and can allow businesses to intercept communications

> "*by means of which transactions are entered into in the course of the relevant* [business] *activities* [or] *other communications relating to the relevant activities or taking place in the course of the carrying on of those activities*" (s.46(2)(a) and (b)).

The regulations only authorise interceptions carried out using the businesses own telecommunication apparatus, or services provide to the business (s.46(3)). The regulations do not just cover businesses, they can also cover government departments, public authorities and persons fulfilling functions conferred on them by or under enactment (s.46(4)).

14.2.3.8 The relevant regulations are the Investigatory Powers (Interception by Businesses etc. for Monitoring and Record-Keeping Purposes) Regulations 2018 (SI 2018/356) ("Monitoring and Record-Keeping Regulations"). The Regulations repeat the limiting factors set out in the IPA 2016 and described above. Regulation 3 also lists the purposes for which communications can be monitored or recorded. These are:

- to establish facts;
- to ascertain compliance with regulatory or self-regulatory practices or procedures which apply to the system controller, or another person who is supervised by the system controller;
- to ascertain or demonstrate standards which have to be achieved by persons using the system in the course of their duties;
- in the interests of national security (specified organisations only);
- to prevent or detect crime;

- to investigate or detect unauthorised use of the system; and
- to secure the effective operation of the system.

In addition, communications can also be monitored (but not recorded) to determine if they are relevant communications (reg.3(3)) and if this is required by a confidential counselling or support service, offered on free of charge and on an anonymous basis (reg.3(4)).

14.2.3.9 The interception must be carried out with the express consent of the person who has the right to control the operation of the system (reg.3(1)(a)). Those wanting to monitor staff should, therefore, make sure that authorisations to monitor are appropriately documented. In addition, the system controller must have made all reasonable efforts to inform every person who may use the telecommunication system (reg.4(1)(c))—a requirement which overlaps with those considered in relation to the ECHR above. Organisations would typically monitor communications in order to prevent viruses or other damage entering the system; to check for unauthorised use of the system; to enforce company policies; or to check quality of call-centre staff or other communications. All of these purposes fit clearly within those described above. They also include purposes which the ECtHR has considered to be legitimate interests of the employer (**14.2.2.4–14.2.2.7**).

14.2.4 Monitoring and the GDPR

Data protection impact assessments

14.2.4.1 Article 35 of the GDPR requires that an organisation carry out a data protection impact assessment DPIA (**13.6**) where "*processing is likely to result in a high risk to the rights and freedoms of natural persons*". Article 35(2) provides that this will

> "*in particular be required in the case of:*
> *a) a systematic and extensive evaluation of personal aspects relating to natural persons which is based on automated processing, including profiling, and on which decisions are based that produce legal effects concerning the natural person or similarly significantly affect the natural person*".

14.2.4.2 Employee monitoring will often involve automated processing, including profiling. And it will often lead to decisions which significantly affect individuals—including disciplinary proceedings and dismissal. Recitals 71 and 75 also specifically highlight risks in the workplace, with rec.71 noting that automated processing to evaluate individuals would include processing "*in particular to analyse or predict aspects concerning the data subject's performance at work*" and rec.75 noting that analysis of personal aspects at work could pose a risk to individuals' rights. Organisations should, therefore, conduct a data protection impact assessment in relation to any employee monitoring. The WP 29 Guidelines on Data Protection Impact Assessments (WP 248 rev.01) note (p.13) that DPIAs do not have to be carried out in respect of processing which had started before the GDPR came fully into force. Data protection impact assessments are, however, useful processes to follow to ensure that relevant requirements are met so organisations should consider using them even for existing forms of employee monitoring. This has also been long-standing advice from the Information Commissioner, whose *Employment Practices Code* has for many years recommended undertaking Privacy Impact Assessments before conducting employee monitoring. WP 248 rev.01 notes that monitoring is an area that can change quickly, as new technologies become available and are adopted by information security teams and others (p.14). For this reason, it is also a good idea to repeat DPIAs relating to employee monitoring on a periodic basis (p.14)—and to set the next review date when the DPIA is concluded.

Content of the data protection impact assessment

14.2.4.3 Article 35(7) provides that the assessment must contain at least:

- a systematic description of the monitoring, the purposes of the monitoring and, if the controller relies on legitimate interests as the lawful basis for the processing, what the interest is that the controller pursues (this will be likely to overlap with the purpose of processing);
- an assessment of the necessity and proportionality of the processing, in relation to the purpose;
- an assessment of the risks to individuals;
- measures to address these risks, safeguards, security measures, mechanisms to ensure protection of personal data and to demonstrate compliance with the GDPR.

The need to consider the purpose of the monitoring, whether it is legitimate, whether the monitoring is necessary and proportionate and to ensure appropriate safeguards will all be familiar from the requirements spelt out by the Grand Chamber of the ECtHR in ***Bărbulescu***. The DPIA must set out how the monitoring will comply with the GDPR. We have already mentioned: purpose, purpose limitation, notice to individuals, limited access, and other elements of proportionality (**14.2.2**).

14.2.4.4 The *Employment Practices Code* suggests that, to be proportionate, employers should seek to target the monitoring where possible—for example, only monitoring departments or employees where there have been complaints; using spot checks instead of continual monitoring; and automating analysis of monitoring, rather than having other employees (who may be known to those being monitored) conduct the monitoring (p.61). The *Code* also notes that continuous video and audio monitoring is particularly intrusive and will rarely be justifiable (p.72). The *Supplementary Guidance* to the *Code* suggests that such monitoring could possibly be justified when used in refineries or nuclear facilities, or, moving to an entirely different setting, in precious stone dealerships (p.53).

The *Code* also emphasises the need for particular care when monitoring employees out of the office as this is more intrusive (p.70). The Article 29 Working Party Opinion, WP 249 also emphasises this point, noting that homeworking and Bring Your Own Device (BYOD) policies raise particular challenges: employees will be working in a way where at least some of the employer's usual physical and security checks will not be applied, which may lead to a desire to carry out more monitoring, however, monitoring out of the work place and on private devices is also more intrusive. Bring Your Own Device is considered in further detail at **14.3**.

14.2.4.5 Before embarking on any monitoring, it will be worthwhile to form some estimate of the amount of data that the monitoring will produce and then to take a realistic view as to how that data will be reviewed and—if human review is needed—by whom. A monitoring exercise that generates mountains of data probably cannot be examined in detail because there simply are not enough people with the time to review it might just as well not have been collected in the first place. Monitoring should always be sharply focused to produce the minimum data to establish whatever is being sought. This accords with the GDPR's data minimisation principle (art.5(1)(c), **5.3**) and is also likely to mean that the investigation can be concluded swiftly. Sampling may well be better than trying to ferret out every last instance of whatever is being sought.

14.2.4.6 Measures to address risks to individuals could include:

- allowing employees to make representations before taking action on any findings from monitoring (Employment Practices Code, p.67);
- blocking or redirecting suspicious traffic, and advising the employee that this has been done, rather than having a third party review it (WP 249, p.13);
- providing unmonitored equipment for private use—perhaps equipment which is not connected to work networks and so where its use poses less security risks (WP 249, p.13);
- allowing individuals to label appointments or messages as private, so that the content of these will not be reviewed (WP 249, p.15).

Other elements of compliance with the GDPR which must be considered and which have not so far been mentioned are:

- the need for a lawful basis for processing (**Ch.4**). For most organisations this will likely be legitimate interests (**4.4.5**). For public authorities, it may be that the processing is necessary for performance of a task carried out in the public interest (**4.4.3**). In some cases, the organisation may be able to demonstrate that the monitoring is necessary for compliance with a legal obligation to which it is subject (**4.4.2**);
- where the monitoring could involve processing of special category data, or criminal offence data, then an additional lawful basis for processing will

be needed (**4.5.3**). As the *Employment Practices Code* notes, this could be the case if communications between employees and occupational health departments are monitored (p.57). The *Code* notes that this will be particularly intrusive and discourages organisations from doing this: it will also be difficult for an organisation to find an appropriate lawful basis for processing;

- ensuring appropriate retention periods are set for the results of the monitoring (**5.5**);
- ensuring that the organisation can meet requests from individuals to exercise their rights (**Ch.6**), for example, to access the results of the monitoring (**6.5**), or to object to it (**6.8**);
- ensuring that there are sufficient staff to evaluate whatever data the monitoring produces;
- the need to include the monitoring in the record of processing activities (**13.5**);
- if processors (or joint controllers) are involved, the need to have appropriate contract terms in place and policed (**13.7**);
- if data transfers take place, adequate protection for the data must be provided (**Ch.9**).

Consultation

14.2.4.7 Article 35(9) provides that the controller must "*where appropriate ... seek the views of data subjects or their representatives on the intended processing*". It seems to us that it would be appropriate to consult with employees when monitoring is to be carried out—especially (but not only) if there are formal employee representatives. This is recommended in WP 249 (p.14) and, indeed, in some countries (albeit not in the UK), it is mandatory to consult before rolling out employee monitoring initiatives.

14.2.4.8 In any event, if the objective of the monitoring involves any suspected failure to comply with the organisation's rules, the ***Bărbulescu*** case (**14.2.2.3**) shows that a key issue of enforcement is whether the individual was adequately warned about the possibility of the monitoring. If an organisation has a DPO, then the DPO should also be consulted about the DPIA (art.35(2)) and—if the DPIA reveals unmitigated risks—then the Information Commissioner should also be consulted (art.36).

Covert monitoring

14.2.4.9 Sometimes organisations may wish to carry out monitoring of staff without notifying them of this – for example, if there are suspicions of theft from offices, then covert CCTV may be useful to establish who is responsible for this. There is useful guidance on this in the *Employment Practices Code*.

It emphasises that:

- covert monitoring should only be used in exceptional circumstances where there are grounds for suspecting criminal activity or equivalent malpractice and should be authorised by senior management (p.73);
- the monitoring should be for a limited period and should stop when the investigation has ended (p.73);
- if private investigators are used, then appropriate contract terms should be included, ensuring that data protection obligations are met (p.74);
- covert monitoring which include audio-visual equipment should not be used in private places (toilets, private offices) unless there is a suspicion of serious crime – this would be serious enough to consider involving the police (although they do not actually have to be involved (p.75 and Supplementary Guidance p.53);
- the information gathered from the investigation should not be used for anything else unless it shows evidence of malpractice which is so serious that no employer could reasonably be expected to ignore it (p.75).

Data protection officers

14.2.4.10 Monitoring is also relevant to the requirement, in art.37 of the GDPR, to appoint a data protection officer (**13.2.1**). Article 37(1)(b) provides that a DPO must be appointed where:

> "*the core activities of the controller or the processor consist of processing operations which, by virtue of their nature, their scope, and/or their purposes, require regular and systematic monitoring of data subjects on a large scale*".

14.2.4.11 For smaller organisations, the "large scale" requirement may make it immediately obvious that monitoring their staff will not trigger the need to appoint a DPO. For larger organisations, where monitoring could be large scale (**13.2.1.6**), rec.97 is relevant. This states that "*the core activities of a controller relate to its primary activities and do not relate to the processing of personal data as ancillary services*". The Article 29 Working Party's *Guidelines on Data Protection Officers* (WP 243 rev.01) comment that core activities should be seen as the key operations necessary to achieve the controller or processor's goals; activities which all organisations carry out, such as paying their employees or having standard IT support activities, would not be regarded as "core" (p.7). WP 243 noted that whether or not an activity is "core" or not, may depend on the nature of the organisation—so security may not normally be a core activity, however, where a private security company engages in surveillance, this would be a core activity for the security company (p.7).

14.2.4.12 On this basis, there should be no need for employers who carry out large scale, basic monitoring for information security purposes, to appoint a DPO purely because of this monitoring. The situation would be different, though, for a company providing security monitoring services to the employer: this would be a core activity of the specialist security company and, if the processing was on a large scale, a DPO would have to be appointed.

Supplemental member state laws

14.2.4.13 The last provision in the GDPR which relates specifically to employee monitoring is at art.88. This article allows Member States to introduce specific rules relating to the processing of employees' personal data in the employment context and art.88(2) notes that such rules could include measures relating to "monitoring systems at the work place". Organisations who operate in multiple member states and who wish to monitor employees must, therefore, check for additional local legal requirements.

14.3 BRING YOUR OWN DEVICE (BYOD)

14.3.1 Introduction

14.3.1.1 In the 1990s it was the case that employers tended to have sophisticated IT equipment which their employees lacked, so the burning issue was the extent to which the employees could use the company's facilities for their own private use. This was particularly the case with email, where employees regularly used the firm's email service for private and sometime even illegal purposes of their own, with the consequence that prudent employers had to regulate this. Today the boot is on the other foot: almost all employees have mobiles, tablets, laptops, etc. which they use more or less all day and find it seriously inconvenient to have to switch to the firm's devices. Another factor is the increase in home-working not only by the self-employed but also by company employees. This use by employees (and others) of their own device for the organisation's processing is known as Bring Your Own Device (BYOD).

14.3.1.2 The advantages are considerable. The employee is likely to be a fluent user of the new technology. They can use it not only at home but while commuting to work, on the way to a business meeting, or in a hotel in some distant location. Properly used, it can be argued that BYOD can increase the productivity of staff. There is also likely to be greater job-satisfaction. The constant habit of glancing at the device many times a day, so far from being a distraction, can now be harnessed to the company's benefit.

Risks of Bring Your Own Device

14.3.1.3 However there are difficulties which data protection brings to light and these must be addressed. The ICO, in early 2013, noticed the trend and issued guidance entitled *Bring your own device (BYOD)* —referred to hereafter as *BYOD*. This identifies the main risks as security-related, although risks to the employee's privacy and some other data protection risks are also identified.

14.3.1.4 The threat to security is obvious: as the employer does not own the device, it has significantly less control over it. For much of the time, the device will not be on the organisation's premises. The Commissioner says in *BYOD* (para.3, original emphasis):

> ***"It is important to remember that the data controller must remain in control of the personal data for which he is responsible, regardless of the ownership of the device used to carry out the processing".***

14.3.1.5 The Commissioner has imposed several fines on organisations whose staff, using BYOD, have failed to safeguard the personal data. For example, in October 2012 Greater Manchester Police allowed officers to take home unencrypted memory sticks so they could work on files on their own devices at home. A memory stick was stolen from an officer's home, despite the fact that a similar breach had occurred in September 2010. Greater Manchester Police were fined £120,000. In the next paragraph we outline the main risks identified in *BYOD.* Unless and until these risks are addressed, the default position for any organisation must be to ban BYOD, since the risks are considerable. Any ban should be clearly brought to the attention of staff with appropriate disciplinary sanctions. Once the organisation has worked through the points identified in the remainder of this section, and any other risks it identifies from BYOD, then it will need a policy document setting out the constraints on, and requirements associated with, BYOD. The policy will also need to give some idea of what the sanctions for failure to be abide by the policy might be. The policy will also need to state that the data is the company's and the company must have a right to have the device made available to them at will, including requiring the member of staff to surrender the device to the organisation's IT department at short notice—for example, so as to check for compliance with the policy or with other policies and to investigate a suspected personal data breach or other security incident.

14.3.1.6 More detailed risks include the following:

- the loss of a device is not just a personal problem for the staff, but also now involves the organisation who may have to report a data breach to the Commissioner under art.33. This means the staff must report any suspected loss to the organisation immediately (even if it subsequently turns out not to be a data breach) to leave enough time for the organisation to report to the Commissioner within 72 hours;
- malware on the staff member's device;
- an employee's own family members may see some of the personal data;
- staff should be aware that if BYOD is to be permitted, it will to an extent mean that the organisation must have access to the staff devices and see what processing takes place and the organisation may even on occasions find itself looking at staff members' private data (*BYOD* para.31). The

implications for staff monitoring must be considered—a tricky area (**14.2**). Some staff may be reluctant to permit this;

- staff should be aware of the necessity for keeping security fully up to date (*BYOD* para.32);
- particular attention will need to be paid to what happens to the device and the data on it when a member of staff leaves, or even dies. If nothing is organised, it may prove difficult for the organisation to recover its own data or put the data beyond use.

14.3.1.7 At **14.3.3** below we discuss the possibility of monitoring staff as a result of the introduction of BYOD. This may engage s.3 of the Investigatory Powers Act 2016. There is also (depending on the exact circumstances) a possible need for a data protection impact assessment (DPIA). If such an assessment is required it must of course be completed and any lessons learned from it before BYOD is initiated. The question of staff monitoring is discussed in more detail at **14.2**.

14.3.1.8 As an alternative to BYOD, organisations may wish to consider not using the staff's personal devices, but instead making devices belonging to the organisation available to staff purely for the organisation's own software and data. This still means staff can and doubtless will work away from base—e.g. at home, or away on a business trip. This will probably be less popular with staff but has significant advantages. These include:

- the risk of malware must be reduced;
- it should be easier for staff to keep the device secure and in particular away from family members;
- there should be no need for the organisation to monitor staff's use of a personal device;
- if the device is lost everything can be more easily deleted remotely (a point we return to);
- it will be less objectionable for the organisation to recover the device if necessary, in any event if everything has been deleted, recovery becomes less urgent.

Notwithstanding these advantages we expect that most organisations will go for full BYOD using staff members' own devices and the rest of this section, assumes this is the case.

14.3.2 Security considerations

14.3.2.1 As the Commissioner notes, with BYOD, "*security of the data is . . . a primary concern*" (para.4). The security risks can be divided into:

- the security of the device itself
- storage solutions associated with the device
- transfer of data to the device
- loss of control of the device.

Each of these is considered below. As *BYOD* notes, at para.9, there is an important preliminary question, as to what personal (or indeed other) data can or will be processed on a personal device: approaches which are acceptable for one type of data, may not be acceptable for another type.

Security of the device

14.3.2.2 An organisation would assess the security of devices which it planned to acquire. In just the same way, the organisation will need to consider which devices are acceptable for use in a BYOD programme. The greater the number of types of device, the heavier the burden on IT: this is likely to be a limiting factor on how many devices can be accommodated in a BYOD programme. The organisation will need to consider factors such as password strength, encryption, etc. and the security of the operating system. If too many attempts at a password are tried, the device (or at least the data) should automatically lock. The IT department should issue a list of devices and operating systems on which they have done due diligence and whose security and other arrangements they have inspected and approved. If a data protection audit is taking place, a survey of staff usage of their own devices could form part of it. It is not impossible that the auditors may find that some staff have already jumped the gun and are using their own devices on the organisation's data.

14.3.2.3 The Commissioner notes that staff devices often have interfaces such as Wi-Fi or Bluetooth, to allow the device to connect easily with other devices such as printers. However, this may also pose a security risk and organisations may need to require such interfaces to be disabled (para.26). It seems doubtful if all staff members would agree to that. More realistically the Commissioner suggests training for staff in assessing the security of Wi-Fi in hotels etc. In fact, in some cases the security may be non-existent. The only possible security is in the firewall etc. on the device and even that may not be enough. There can be a particular danger of Wi-Fi in (say) internet cafés where the person at the next table may be able to intercept your data. Organisations will wish to assess this for themselves before agreeing to put their personal data on the device. (para.27).

14.3.2.4 *BYOD* also notes that security of the device may be dependent on updates provided by the manufacturer of the device, or the communications provider, rather than the manufacturer of the operating system—and may not be made available for all devices either at all, or in a timely way. This makes it harder to manage security over a wide range of devices—but the Commissioner is clear that this is not an acceptable excuse: this type of vulnerability must not put personal data processed on individual devices at risk (para.32). This also suggests that any approved list of devices and operating systems will need to be kept under review and employees may need to be required to cease using a device if it is no longer approved.

14.3.2.5 The organisation will also probably need to limit the downloading of apps to prevent staff members as far as possible from installing apps from untrusted or unverified sources (*BYOD* para.34).

14.3.2.6 The security measures above will be of little use if employees allow other friends or family members to use a device which contains work data: if a private device is to be used, then use by others should be prohibited. Alternatively, data could be maintained within a ring-fenced section of the device (for example a specific app with container-based working), which has appropriate security to verify the employee trying to use the app (*BYOD* para.18).

14.3.2.7 The organisation should also require the staff member to notify the IT Department when they wish to use a different device. If the new device is a replacement for the old one, the old device should be surrendered to the IT department for them to delete the data. Replacement of the old device will usually mean that that old device is now obsolete. Even if it is not, the data and any software provided by the organisation will need to be deleted.

Storage considerations

14.3.2.8 A BYOD initiative may lead to personal data being processed:

1) on the device;
2) in the cloud (private, community or public depending on the applications or software used); or
3) on a server within the organisation's own IT network, or other private cloud (*BYOD* para.13). There could also be a combination of the above locations.

14.3.2.9 If data is processed on the device, then the organisation must consider back-up arrangements. Ideally these should be provided by the organisation itself (or via its processor) and they should be automatic. If back-up is not to be provided by the organisation, check what back-up arrangements the staff member wants to use. Unauthorised public clouds may be dangerous. Any subcontracting—e.g. by use of cloud storage—must be approved by the organisation. Automatic backing up on a cloud must also be suspect, unless the organisation has assessed the storage provider and satisfied itself that its access to data is appropriate (*BYOD* para.28). This point is not just relevant to back-up of data, but is also relevant to any cloud-based services which staff may use, which lead to the service provider having access to the organisation's data. There will also be a potential problem when staff leave in ensuring that the back-up versions of data generated by them also need to be deleted. There is also the additional risk that the data may be accessed not just by the service provider, but (potentially) by law enforcement authorities with jurisdiction over the service provider (*BYOD* para.24).

14.3.2.10 The mention of automatic back-up or saving needs further consideration. If the saving is left to the staff member, "Murphy's Law" will ensure that just when it matters most, the data has not been properly saved. If the saving is done automatically, this problem is dealt with. When a device is lost, the organisation's data on it can be deleted, remotely or otherwise, with no loss of data to the organisation. It also means that the organisation can prescribe where the data is saved—for example to the organisation's own servers or their own cloud service company.

14.3.2.11 In some circumstances it may be possible to have all the processing initiated from staff devices taking place on the organisation's servers. The staff devices would be reduced to the status of dumb terminals. This would mean that the staff would (subject to authentication) be able to see and manipulate the data from their devices, but they would not actually have the data resident on their devices. This has the advantage that if a staff device is lost, the wiping of the software would be sufficient to put the data beyond use, but the integrity of the data (including any very recent updates) would not be compromised. This would also eliminate the risk identified in BYOD para.44 of a member of staff copying data and then inadvertently pasting that data inappropriately (for example in an email or a social media post). Indeed, any copying by the staff member should if possible be avoided.

Data transfer of the personal data to staff devices

14.3.2.12 The Commissioner identifies this stage as involving a significant level of risk (para.20). A particular risk is to security in case of a 'man-in-the-middle' attack or other type of interception. The Commissioner goes on (para.22):

> "*Forcing all traffic through an encrypted channel such as VPN* [Virtual Private Network], *or HTTPS* [HyperText Transfer Protocol Secure] *for individual services, can offer some security when using an un-trusted connection. However, if you are offering a VPN connection back through the corporate network you should be mindful of any internet monitoring software you have in operation, especially during periods of personal use. If the device sends data via non-corporate systems (for example a public email service) then there is limited opportunity to audit activity*".

It should be explained that a virtual private network (VPN) is a non-physical connection of systems whether via a cloud or other transmission system. On HTTPS, readers will be familiar with the "http" system which stands for HyperText Transfer Protocol and covers the way most of us access the internet; with the suffix "Secure" and usually involves an encrypted transfer. The Commissioner flags that techniques to ensure security can, of themselves, compromise privacy, a point considered at **14.2** .

14.3.2.13 The use of USB drives and the like to transfer the data to the device is subject to the usual risks: effective encryption is essential. The Commissioner also reminds that safe and secure deletion of data on the media is important, once the transfer is complete.

Loss of control of the device

14.3.2.14 An organisation should already have a policy for what to do if its own devices are lost (**8.4**): it should also consider what it will do if staff lose personal devices which have been used as part of a BYOD programme.

14.3.2.15 The organisation will need to set out procedures if the staff member suspects a personal (or other) data breach. These procedures should not wait till the staff member has further investigated in case there has not been a breach after all. The 72-hour deadline for the organisation to report the breach to the Commissioner under art.33 is far too tight to allow any delay. Members of staff should be trained to understand that a personal data breach does not just mean loss of a device: if there is a hacking attack or other malware or if the device breaks or becomes locked or is otherwise unable to process the personal data, the staff member must also report this to the organisation immediately. Here the Commissioner notes that most devices allow for remote deletion of data on demand, via mobile device management solutions (*BYOD* para.30). These often depend on devices being pre-registered—so this would need to be considered in the development of any BYOD policy. Such remote wiping solutions can also lead to *all* data on the device being wiped. One way of avoiding this is to ensure that work data is ring-fenced, i.e. placed in a secure container, so that only that data is deleted. If this is not possible, then staff must be told that one consequence of using their devices as part of a BYOD programme will be the deletion of personal data in the event that the device is lost.

14.3.2.16 These procedures will also likely need to be extended to other situations where the employee will hand over control of the device to another party—for example, if the device is sent to a third party or the manufacturer, for diagnosis or support purposes. Here, the controller's IT department may well require that the organisation's personal data be deleted before the device goes to the manufacturer and then that the data be reloaded again after the repair is complete (*BYOD* para.35).

14.3.2.17 The need to erase data remotely also arises when the staff member leaves—or dies. When staff leave they can be asked to surrender the device so that all the organisation's data can be taken from it, although preferably, this may be effected by remote deletion. This of course depends on the back-up arrangements, which should be under the organisation's control. For staff who die in office, remote deletion may be the only viable way to go. It is hardly feasible to turn up at house of mourning asking to see the deceased's laptop.

14.3.2.18 At **5.5.6.1** we remarked that on most electronic devices, deletion is a two-stage process. Usually pressing the delete button will simply remove the available pointers to the data but leave the data in situ, where it is freed up to be overwritten, when some other data (or software) is input. Deletion of the pointers alone means that the data is still recoverable when an examination of all the device's locations takes place. Readers should study **5.5.6** for more detail on this.

14.3.3 Privacy considerations

14.3.3.1 The Commissioner's *BYOD* guidance notes that introduction of a BYOD policy usually leads to more staff monitoring:

- in order to ensure that devices (and the organisation's data) can be located, so that a remote wipe of data is possible;
- of internet traffic, in order to check security of transmission and to check that personal (or other confidential) data is not being disclosed in breach of company policy.

14.3.3.2 As we have seen at **14.2**, monitoring of communications intrudes on employees' privacy: the rules explained in **14.2** must always be considered. BYOD can also be particularly intrusive—as the devices are personal, staff will be also be using them for personal purposes, outside work time. If staff are still allowed to let family members use the device, then monitoring may also capture information about family members. *BYOD* recommends that organisations are clear as to whether such monitoring will occur (para.40). Such monitoring is highly intrusive, so is likely to be difficult to justify. If it involves monitoring of communications of family members, or over communications services which the employer does not control, it is also likely to be illegal under the Investigatory Powers Act 2016 s.3 (**14.2.3**).

14.3.3.3 These considerations may also mean that the controller should have conducted a data protection impact assessment (DPIA), since BYOD may engage systematic monitoring and/or data concerning vulnerable data subjects (a staff member's children, for example). These are two of the criteria for considering DPIAs in WP 248 pp.9–11 (**13.5.3**).

14.3.4 Other data protection considerations

14.3.4.1 While the main risks from BYOD are security related and the threat to staff privacy, the Commissioner's *BYOD* guidance also reminds that there are other risks (paras 41–45). In particular:

- if personal data is processed locally, it will be harder to ensure that the data is kept up to date and it will be harder to ensure that it is deleted when it should be. Implementing a BYOD policy where devices connect to a central repository of data which the organisation controls is the better approach;
- it will also be harder for an organisation to ensure that it has located all relevant personal data as necessary to respond to a request from an individual to exercise their rights (for example, of erasure).

14.3.5 Contract considerations

14.3.5.1 The expansion in the number of devices accessing the controller's system may have contractual implications. In ***SAP UK Ltd v Diageo Great Britain Ltd*** [2017] EWHC 189 (TCC), Diageo had a software licensing arrangement with SAP. Diageo interfaced new software to SAP's software so that Diageo's sales representatives could now manage customer calls on the system and some Diageo customers could also access the system. The terms of the licence were based on the number of users and these additional users resulted in a very much higher fee payable to SAP. Any possibility of this will need to be investigated before any decision to implement BYOD.

14.3.6 Implementing Bring Your Own Device

14.3.6.1 Once a controller has examined the risks of BYOD to its organisation, it must decide whether to ban BYOD or go ahead with it. If it wishes to go ahead with BYOD, it needs:

- to decide whether to conduct a DPIA and if so do this at once;
- to ensure that its IT department is able to manage the move to BYOD. To that end the department will need:
  - to have sufficient staff to advise staff members on all aspects of BYOD;
  - to specify the devices and operating systems etc that can be used;
  - to assist the data protection professional in drafting the Policy, including
- specifying security mechanisms (encryption, dumb terminals, etc.); and
- specifying back-up procedures—preferably automatic;
  - to decide what level of support can be provided for the devices;
  - to decide to what extent (if at all) to be able to provide replacement devices for members of staff whose own devices are no longer available to process the personal data;
  - to consider whether there are any implications for software licences in allowing data to be used on or accessed form additional devices; and
  - to have clear guidance as to the extent to which they can or cannot monitor staff's use of BYOD (**14.2**);
- to establish with the data protection professional a clear policy on BYOD and ensure it is understood by all relevant staff;
- to monitor regularly the running of BYOD and if necessary change the policy accordingly.

CHAPTER 15

Law Enforcement and The Intelligence Services

15.1 PROCESSING FOR LAW ENFORCEMENT PURPOSES

15.1.1 Scope of the Law Enforcement Directive and Part 3 of the DPA 2018

15.1.1.1 At the same time as the GDPR was adopted by the EU, a Law Enforcement Directive (2016/680) was also adopted. Like the GDPR, the Law Enforcement Directive (LE Directive) was to come into force after a grace period of two years—in this case by 6 May 2018. As it was a Directive and not a Regulation, it required Member States of the EU to transpose the provisions of the Directive into their own legislation. Part 3 of the DPA 2018 is the UK's implementation of the LE Directive.

15.1.1.2 The purpose of the LE Directive is to provide data protection provisions crafted to fit the particular circumstances of law enforcement—crime prevention, detection, prosecution and sentencing.

15.1.1.3 Article 1(1) of the LE Directive sets the scene:

> "*This Directive lays down the rules relating to the protection of natural persons with regard to the processing of personal data by competent authorities for the purposes of the prevention, investigation, detection or prosecution of criminal offences or the execution of criminal penalties, including threats to pubic security*".

15.1.1.4 Part 3 of the DPA 2018 and the LE Directive[1] apply to the processing of personal data for law enforcement purposes by competent authorities. Each of these terms is considered below. The provisions can also be relevant to processors acting on behalf of competent authorities. The provisions are not, however, relevant if an individual or private sector organisation processes personal data concerning the prevention or detection of crime: the CJEU regards these as activities of the State or State authorities, not of individuals (***Sergejs Buivids v Datu valsts inspekcija*** (C-345/17) (and the other cases mentioned there) [42]). The LE Directive (and the DPA 2018) replace Council Framework Decision 2008/977/JHA of 27 November 2008 on the protection of personal data processed in the framework of police and judicial co-operation in criminal matters which set out rules for sharing of personal data between competent authorities in the EU and which was implemented in the UK by the (now repealed) Pt 4 of the Criminal Justice and Data Protection (Protocol no.36) Regulations 2014. However, the DPA 2018 also applies to *all* personal data processed by competent authorities for law enforcement purposes in the UK, even when there is no sharing of personal data with other Member States.

15.1.1.5 Part 3 of the DPA 2018 comprises ss.29–81 and also Schs 7–8. The Information Commissioner has issued a Guide to *Law Enforcement Processing (Part 3 of the Bill)*, which we have referred to as the *LE Guide*.

Competent authorities

15.1.1.6 These are listed at DPA 2018 Sch.7. Competent authorities can also be "*any other person if and to the extent that the person has statutory functions for any of the law enforcement purposes*" (s.30(1)(b)). However, intelligence

[1] The UK has to opt-in to European Commission measures adopted under Title V of the Treaty on the Functioning of the European Union (the Treaty of Rome or TFEU). Title V relates to judicial co-operation on criminal matters and police co-operation. The UK has chosen to opt-in to some measures which relate to processing of personal data, but not to opt-in to others. This means that, whilst the provisions of Pt 3 of the DPA 2018 will always be relevant, the LE Directive itself may not always be relevant. The House of Lords European Union Committee Report on *The UK's Opt-in Protocol: Implications of the Government's Approach* (Ninth Report of Session 2014–15) is a useful summary of the UK's approach to the Opt-in Protocol.

services are *not* included in the definition (s.30(2)). They are dealt with in Pt 4 of the DPA 2018 (**15.2**).

15.1.1.7 Schedule 7 includes government departments, police, other investigatory authorities (such as HM Revenue and Customs and the Serious Fraud Office), those involved in offender management and probation services and other investigatory authorities, such as the Director of Public Prosecutions. Regulators also appear: The Financial Conduct Authority, for example, and the Information Commissioner herself, and the Scottish Information Commissioner, are also listed. Schedule 7 also lists some private sector organisations—in particular those who have contracted for the running of prisons or young offender institutes, secure training centres or prisoner escort services. There is a mechanism to amend the authorities listed at Sch.7 (ss.30(3)–(6)).

15.1.1.8 As to examples of competent authorities not in Schedule 7, the *LE Guide* suggests local authorities who prosecute trading standards offences or the Environment Agency when prosecuting environmental offences.

Law enforcement purposes

15.1.1.9 These are defined at s.31 as the purposes of

> "*the prevention, investigation, detection or prosecution of criminal offences or the execution of criminal penalties, including the safeguarding against and the prevention of threats to public security*".

As the Explanatory Notes make clear at para.175:

> "*Not all processing of personal data by a competent authority will be for law enforcement purposes. This is because, where a controller determines that the processing will take place for another purpose, for example, for HR purposes, this will be general processing and governed by either the GDPR or the applied GDPR regime*".

Role of processors

15.1.1.10 The law enforcement provisions will mostly be relevant to those authorities (or contracted private sector organisations) with law enforcement functions. However, processors acting on behalf of such organisations should also be aware of the provisions. As with the GDPR, obligations in relation to security are placed directly on processors (**15.1.5.24**) and there are also direct obligations to keep specific records of processing and logs of automated systems (**15.1.5.12**). Processors can be liable to individuals, and subject to penalties, for failure to comply with these provisions (**15.1.7**). Lastly, of course, the nature of the processing and the instructions given to processors may also be affected by the specific obligations which apply to controllers (for example, in relation to categorising fact and opinion and different categories of individuals (**15.1.3.33**)).

15.1.2 Key concepts

15.1.2.1 The key concepts—of personal data, a (structured) filing system, controller and processor are identical to those used in the GDPR, although there is a slight nuance in the definition of processor. A processor is, at s.32(3), "*any person who processes personal data on behalf of the controller (other than a person who is an employee of the controller)*". (In the GDPR, at art.4(8) a processor is "*a natural or legal person, public authority, agency or other body which processes personal data in behalf of the controller*", a definition repeated in art.3(9) of the LE Directive.) Section 33(2) then goes on to include a bespoke definition of an employee noting that the term "*in relation to any person, includes an individual who holds a position (whether paid or unpaid) under the direction and control of that person*". The Explanatory Notes comment that this is included so that "*in this context, police officers and special constables (who are office holders rather than employees) are treated as an extension of their chief officer*".

15.1.2.2 The Explanatory Notes also have a useful example of joint controllers:

> "*For example, the Police National Computer is managed on behalf of all police forces in the UK with individual chief constables jointly determining the purposes and means of the processing of the personal data held on the database. In this situation, the chief constables will be acting as joint controllers*".

15.1.3 Data protection principles

15.1.3.1 Section 34(1) sets out the core data protection principles which apply to law enforcement processing. The principles are:

1) lawful and fair processing;
2) specified, explicit and legitimate processing;
3) personal data to be adequate, relevant and not excessive;
4) personal data to be accurate and kept up to date;
5) personal data to be kept no longer than is necessary;
6) personal data to be processed in a secure manner.

15.1.3.2 To readers familiar with the 1998 Act, the principles will be familiar from principles 1–5 and principle 7 in Sch.1 Pt I to that Act. They are substantially the same as the core principles set out at art.5(1) of the GDPR. The Explanatory Notes, at para.180, suggest that the difference with the GDPR is that:

> "*there is no requirement for data to be processed in a transparent manner. This omission recognises the inherent sensitivities of processing for law enforcement purposes by competent authorities*".

15.1.3.3 To the extent that EU law applies to law enforcement processing, so that the LE Directive is relevant, this statement would seem to be incorrect as rec.26 of this states that

"*any processing of personal data must be lawful, fair and transparent in relation to the natural persons concerned...*".

15.1.3.4 There are also ad hoc references to transparency elsewhere in Pt 3—although it is certainly given less prominence than in the GDPR. The *LE Guide* says in relation to the GDPR's principles:

"*Transparency requirements are not as strict, due to the potential to prejudice an ongoing investigation in certain circumstances*".

Principle 1: lawful and fair processing

15.1.3.5 The DPA 2018 s.35 provides that "*the processing of personal data for any of the law enforcement purposes must be lawful and fair*". The *LE Guide* glosses "lawful and fair" as follows:

"*'Fairness' generally requires you to be, where appropriate, clear and open with individuals about how you use their information, in keeping with their reasonable expectations.*
'Lawful' processing means authorised by either statute, common law or royal prerogative, or by or under any other rule of law. It also meets one of the conditions for processing under Data Protection legislation. For example, Part 5 of the Police and Criminal Evidence Act 1984 confers statutory authority for the taking and retention of DNA and fingerprints (this applies to England and Wales). Also, the Domestic Violence Disclosure Scheme relies on the Police's common law powers to disclose information where it is necessary to do so to prevent crime".

15.1.3.6 The LE Directive, art.8(2), further provides that:

"*Member State law regulating processing within the scope of this Directive shall specify at least the objectives of processing, the personal data to be processed and the purposes of the processing*".

Rules for "normal" personal data

15.1.3.7 The DPA 2018 s.35(2) provides that:

"*The processing of personal data for any of the law enforcement purposes is lawful only if and to the extent that it is based on law and either–*
a) the data subject has given consent to the processing for that purpose, or
b) the processing is necessary for the performance of a task carried out for that purpose by a competent authority".

Rules for sensitive processing

15.1.3.8 The GDPR art.9 contains additional restrictions on processing of "special categories of data". The DPA 2018, s.35(8), refers to "sensitive processing"—which means processing of the special categories of data set out in GDPR art.9 (the categories are listed out in full in s.35(8)). There is then, at s.35(3), a proviso that such processing may only take place as set out:

- in s.35(4)—which allows processing where the individual has given consent (as set out at s.35(2)); or
- in s.35(5)—which permits processing where it is "strictly necessary" for law enforcement purposes and where at least one of the conditions in Sch.8 is met.

15.1.3.9 The *LE Guide* notes that "strictly necessary" means that "*the processing has to relate to a pressing social need, and you cannot reasonably achieve it through less intrusive means*". The conditions in Sch.8 are that the processing is:

- necessary for judicial and statutory purposes;
- necessary for the administration of justice;
- necessary to protect the vital interests of the data subject or another individual (unlike the equivalent GDPR condition, there is no requirement that the data subject be incapable of providing consent);
- necessary to safeguard children or individuals at risk;
- related to personal data which is manifestly made public by the individual;
- necessary for legal claims;
- necessary when a court acts in its judicial capacity;
- necessary for preventing fraud; or
- necessary for archiving purposes in the public interest, or for scientific or historical research purposes or for statistical purposes (unlike the equivalent Sch.1 conditions, the public interest requirement is only stated in relation to archiving).

15.1.3.10 Save as mentioned above, the conditions are identical to the equivalent conditions set out in Schedule 1 of the DPA 2018. The conditions relating to vital interests and data manifestly made public are taken from the LE Directive itself, at art.10(b) and (c).

15.1.3.11 In addition, whenever sensitive processing takes place, the additional safeguards set out in s.42 must be in place. These safeguards require:

- that the controller maintains a document which explains its procedures for complying with the data protection principles in respect of the relevant processing and explains its policies as regards retention and erasure, including giving an indication of how long the personal data is likely to be retained;

- that the above documents (referred to as the "appropriate policy document") must be retained, reviewed and made available to the Commissioner on request at no charge throughout the period of processing and for six months thereafter.

15.1.3.12 Further, any record of processing maintained by the controller, or its processor, must confirm:

- whether the processing is carried out with consent, or, if based on a Sch.8 condition, which condition;
- how the processing satisfies the s.35 (lawfulness) requirement; and
- whether the personal data is retained and erased according to the policies described in the appropriate policy document and, if not, why not.

15.1.3.13 To give a GDPR point of comparison, these are substantially the same as the additional safeguards set out in the DPA 2018, Sch.1, Pt 4 which apply to many of the additional conditions for the processing of special category data.

The role of consent

15.1.3.14 The drafting in s.35 which relates to consent is odd. The DPA 2018 s.35(2) states that personal data can be processed for law enforcement purposes "either" with consent, "or" where the processing is necessary for the performance of a task carried out for law enforcement purposes by a competent authority. Where data is processed with consent in this way, then this also allows "sensitive processing", of more intrusive categories of data, to take place. The provisions, therefore, seem to allow competent authorities to use consent to legitimise the processing of personal data on occasions when the processing is not actually necessary for law enforcement purposes. The effect must be unintentional.

15.1.3.15 By contrast, the LE Directive, at art.8(1) provides that:

"*Member States shall provide for processing to be lawful only if and to the extent that processing is necessary for the performance of a task carried out by a competent authority for the purposes set out in Article 1(1) (law enforcement purposes) and that is based on Union or Member state law*".

Recital 35 re-iterates this, noting that:

"*... The performance of the* [law enforcement] *tasks ... institutionally conferred by law to the competent authorities allows them to require or order natural persons to comply with requests made. In such a case, the consent of the* *data subject, as defined in Regulation (EU) 2016/679* [i.e. the GDPR], *should not provide a legal ground for processing personal data by competent authorities. Where the data subject is required to comply with a legal obligation, the data subject has no genuine and free choice, so that the reaction of the data subject could not be considered to be a freely given indication of his or her wishes. This should not preclude Member States from providing, by law, that the data subject may agree to the processing of his or her personal data for the purposes of this Directive, such as DNA tests in criminal investigations or the monitoring of his or her location with electronic tags for the execution of criminal penalties*".

15.1.3.16 Recital 37 also notes that:

"*. . . The processing of such [sensitive] data should also be allowed by law where the data subject has explicitly agreed to the processing that is particularly intrusive to him or her. However, the consent of the data subject should not provide in itself a legal ground for processing such sensitive personal data by competent authorities*".

15.1.3.17 The Article 29 Working Party adopted an *Opinion on some key issues of the Law Enforcement Directive* on 29 November 2017 (WP 258). This notes that:

"*The consent of the data subject can never in itself constitute a legal ground for the processing of special categories of data in the context of the Directive. This is a major difference in comparison to the GDPR and this difference is stressed explicitly in Recital 35 which considers that Member States may provide by law, that the data subject may agree to the processing of his or her personal data for the purposes of this Directive.*
In the light of this, the WP29 concludes that voluntary agreement should only be considered as an additional safeguard under the law. . .".

Principle 2: specified, explicit and legitimate purposes

15.1.3.18 Section 36 provides that:

"*a) the law enforcement purpose for which personal data is collected on any occasion must be specified, explicit and legitimate, and*
b) personal data so collected must not be processed in a manner that is incompatible with the purpose for which it was collected".

There are specific rules for certain types of additional processing.

15.1.3.19 For processing for other law enforcement purposes (e.g. data processed by the police in an investigation and then used and processed by the Crown Prosecution Service for prosecution), s.36(3) applies. This provides that personal data can be processed for any other law enforcement purpose, "*whether by the controller that collected the data or another controller*" provided that the controller is "*authorised by law to process the data for the other purpose, and the processing is necessary and proportionate to that other purpose*".

15.1.3.20 For processing for non-law enforcement purposes, s.36(4) provides that such processing must be authorised by law. The rules for such processing would then be found outside of Pt 3 of the DPA 2018—either in the GDPR, the applied GDPR, or, for processing by the intelligence services, in DPA 2018 Pt 4.

Processing for archival etc. purposes

15.1.3.21 Part 3 allows personal data processed for law enforcement purposes to be processed for archiving purposes in the public interest, scientific or historical research purposes, or statistical purposes. Where the archiving etc. is also for law enforcement purposes, then art.4(3) of the LE Directive requires that there are appropriate safeguards for individuals. The DPA 2018 sets these out at s.41 (replicating the GDPR related conditions from s.19, but without the special arrangements for approved medical research)—requiring that the processing is not permitted if:

> "*a) it is carried out for the purposes of, or in connection with, measures or decisions with respect to a particular data subject, or*
>
> *b) it is likely to cause substantial damage or substantial distress to a data subject*".

15.1.3.22 Where the archiving etc. is not for law enforcement purposes, then s.36(4) would apply—i.e. the processing would need to be authorised by law. Presumably the special rules dealing with processing for archiving etc. set out in the DPA 2018 could serve this purpose.

Data sharing with competent authorities outside the UK

15.1.3.23 On some occasions, there may be specific conditions or restrictions which apply to the processing of personal data for law enforcement purposes—i.e. in addition to those under the DPA 2018. The LE Directive, art.9(4), provides that competent authorities cannot impose conditions on authorities in other Member States which do not apply equally in the original Member State. However, where there *are* additional restrictions which apply to law enforcement processing, then the competent authority must notify such conditions to any recipient of the data. These rules are transposed at s.80—which also provides that UK competent authorities must comply with any restrictions imposed by competent authorities in Member States.

Principle 3: adequate, relevant and not excessive

15.1.3.24 This is set out at s.37. There is a useful gloss as to how this applies in the Explanatory Notes, which refer to previous guidance by the Information Commissioner which:

"*provided that in practice this term meant that controllers should ensure that:*
- *they hold personal data about an individual that is sufficient for the purpose it is being held for in relation to that individual; and*
- *they do not hold more information than is needed for that purpose*".

Principle 4: accurate and kept up to date

15.1.3.25 More specific details are included here by comparison with the GDPR principle and the earlier principle under the 1998 Act. Section 38(1) provides that:

"*a) personal data processed for any of the law enforcement purposes must be accurate and, where necessary, kept up to date, and*
b) every reasonable step must be taken to ensure that personal data that is inaccurate, having regard to the law enforcement purpose for which it is processed, is erased or rectified without delay".

15.1.3.26 Section 38(4) also provides that all reasonable steps must be taken to ensure that inaccurate, incomplete or no longer up to date data is not transmitted or made available for law enforcement purposes. Importantly, this also means that the quality of the data must be verified before it is transmitted or made available; if it is transmitted, information which allows the recipient to assess accuracy, completeness, reliability and currency is also shared; and, if it later emerges that that the data was incorrect or the transmission was unlawful, then the recipient must be notified without delay (s.38(5)).

15.1.3.27 There are additional provisions relating to data quality—differentiating between fact and opinion and different categories of data subject. Section 38(2) requires that "*personal data based on facts must, so far as possible, be distinguished from personal data based on personal assessments*" (data in witness statements, for example). As regards data subjects, s.38(3) requires that, where relevant and so far as possible, a clear distinction must be made between personal data relating to different categories of data subjects—such as suspects, those convicted of an offence, victims, witnesses and others with information about offences (which in the LE Directive specifically references contacts or associates of offenders and suspects). The *LE Guide* notes that:

"*There may be instances where an individual falls under more than one of these categories. For example an individual may be both a victim and a witness in a certain case, or indeed an offender in one case and victim/witness in another. You will therefore be required, where relevant and as far as possible, to have processes and procedures in place to distinguish between such categories*".

Principle 5: kept no longer than necessary

15.1.3.28 As with principle 4, the DPA 2018 (and the LE Directive) contain more detail on what is required here than under the GDPR. Section 39(2) notes that:

> "*Appropriate time limits must be established for the periodic review of the need for the continued storage of personal data for any of the law enforcement purposes*".

The Explanatory Notes remind us that in some cases there are specific rules addressing this—for example, in England and Wales, the Police and Criminal Evidence Act 1984 deals with retention of fingerprints and DNA profiles, with retention periods differing depending on whether or not an individual has a conviction. There is also a framework provided by the College of Policing (the Management of Police Information). The rules in this area reflect legal challenges to data retention for law enforcement purposes, leading to cases at the European Court of Human Rights and the Supreme Court[2]. These cases have also led to the creation of a Commissioner for the retention and use of biometric material: the Biometrics Commissioner (*https://www.gov.uk/government/organisations/biometrics-commissioner* [Accessed 14 May 2019]). More detail on these cases and relevant rules can be found in Rosemary Jay & Angus Hamilton, *Data Protection Law & Practice*, 4th edn (London: Sweet & Maxwell), paras 6–66 to 6–73.

Principle 6: processed in a secure manner

15.1.3.29 Section 40 requires that:

> "*personal data processed for any of the law enforcement purposes must be so processed in a manner that ensures appropriate security of the personal data, using appropriate technical or organisational measures (and, in this principle, 'appropriate security' includes protection against unauthorised or unlawful processing and against accidental loss, destruction or damage)*".

Section **15.1.5.24** contains more commentary on the provisions of Pt 3 in relation to security.

15.1.4 Data subject rights

General

15.1.4.1 Individual rights are addressed in Ch.3 of the law enforcement provisions of the DPA 2018. As in the GDPR, individuals have rights to be given information, to access data, to rectify, erase and restrict processing and not to be subject to significant and entirely automated decisions. There are no rights to portability (which is irrelevant in a law enforcement context) or to object to processing. As will be seen below, the detail of the rights can vary from the com-

---

[2] These include ***S and Marper v United Kingdom*** [2008] Apps 30562/04 and 30566/04, and ***R. (on the application of GC) v Metropolitan Police Commissioner*** [2011] UKSC 21; and ***Tele2 Sverige AB v Post-och telestyrelsen*** and ***Secretary of State for the Home Department v Tom Watson*** (conjoined cases C-203/15 and C-698/15, respectively).

parator GDPR right. As under the GDPR, in most circumstances, no charge can be made for dealing with individuals rights (s.52(5)).

15.1.4.2 There are also exemptions from the rights (except the right not to be subject to an automated decision), where compliance would itself obstruct or prejudice law enforcement purposes, public security, national security, or the rights and freedoms of others (**15.1.4.30**). In addition, according to ss.43(3)–(4), the rights (again, other than automated decision-making) do not apply to personal data contained in judicial decisions or other documents created by or on behalf of a court or other judicial authority relating to a criminal investigation or proceedings. The Explanatory Notes comment that:

> "*Instead, access to such 'relevant personal data'* [the term used in s.43(4)] *will be governed by the appropriate legislation covering the disclosure of information in criminal proceedings, such as (in England and Wales) the Criminal Procedure and Investigation Act 1996*".

The Information Commissioner's *LE Guide* goes on to note that:

> "*This provision only applies if the judge or other judicial authority is the controller and the relevant personal data is contained in a judicial decision or in other documents which are created during a criminal investigation or proceedings and made by or on behalf of the judge or judicial authority. For example, the 'relevant personal data' may be contained in judge's notes*".

15.1.4.3 There are general rules, at s.52, which apply whenever information is provided to individuals under Ch.2. Section 52(1) requires that information is provided in a "*concise, intelligible and easily accessible form, using clear and plain language*". Recital 39 in the LE Directive adds that it should be "*adapted to the needs of vulnerable persons*". Where an individual makes a request in a particular form (i.e. electronic, paper, oral), then s.52(3) provides that the controller should provide the information "*in the same form as the request where it is practicable to do so*". Subject to this provision, s.52(2) provides that the information can be provided in electronic form. Because individuals could make valid requests orally, the *LE Guide* recommends that "*it is good practice to have a policy for recording details of all the requests you receive, including verbal* [sic] *requests*".

15.1.4.4 Section 52(4) suggests that, where the controller has reasonable doubts about the identity of the person making the request, the controller may request additional information to allow the confirmation of identity. This also delays the date on which the controller must start dealing with the request.

Right to information

15.1.4.5 This is split into two obligations. Section 44(1) contains a list of information which must always be made available to data subjects. However, this obligation can be met by making the information "*generally available to the public*", so via a publicly posted privacy policy. This must include information as to:

- identity and contact details;
- contact details of any data protection officer;
- purposes of processing; and
- the existence of individual's rights (other than the automated decision-making right), including rights to complain to the Information Commissioner and her contact details.

15.1.4.6 Section 44(2) then requires more detailed and case specific information to be given "*in specific cases for the purpose of enabling the exercise of a data subject's rights*". This list includes:

- the legal basis for processing;
- information about retention periods or the criteria used to determine these;
- where applicable, information about categories of recipients (including recipients in third countries or international organisations); and
- such further information as is necessary to enable the exercise of the data subject's rights under Pt 3 of the DPA 2018. Section 44(3) notes that this last obligation may be relevant where "*the personal data being processed was collected without the knowledge of the data subject*".

15.1.4.7 It is worth noting that "recipient" is a defined term and "*does not include a public authority to whom disclosure is or may be made in the framework of a particular inquiry in accordance with the law*" (s.33(5)). So, there is no obligation to tip the individual off that data has been sent to a competent authority for a specific enquiry. Recipients do, however, include "*any person to whom the data is disclosed, whether a third party or not*" with the result that, as with the GDPR, information must be given about the types of departments within the controller which have received the personal data.

15.1.4.8 The *LE Guide* contains an example of the way these provisions work together—and of the way the exemptions (**15.1.4.30**) may apply:

> "*You have a generic privacy notice on your website which covers basic information about the organisation, the purpose you process personal data for, a data subject's rights and their right to complain to the Information Commissioner. You have received intelligence that an individual was present when a crime took place. On first interviewing this individual, you need to provide the generic information, as well as the further supporting information, to enable their rights to be exercised. You can only restrict the fair processing information you are providing if it will adversely affect the investigation you are undertaking*".

Access

15.1.4.9 Section 45 provides that a data subject is entitled to obtain from the controller:

> "*a)* *confirmation as to whether or not personal data concerning him or her is being processed, and*
> *b)* *where that is the case, access to the personal data and the information set out in subsection 2*".

The additional information referred to at subs.2 is:

- the purposes and legal basis of processing;
- the categories of personal data;
- the recipients or categories of recipients, including details of those in third countries or international organisations;
- the retention period or the criteria used to determine this if it is not possible to provide the period;
- the individual's rights of rectification, erasure and restriction; and
- the right to complain to the Commissioner and her contact details.

15.1.4.10 Most of this is all very familiar from the GDPR. In addition, the individual is entitled to "*communication of the personal data undergoing processing and of any available information as to its origin*". This is different from the GDPR, which provides that "a copy" of the data must be provided. This sounds less onerous than the GDPR obligation—an impression which is confirmed by rec.43 of the LE Directive, which notes that:

> "... *Where such communications include information as to the origin of the personal data, the information should not reveal the identity of natural persons, in particular confidential sources. For that right to be complied with, it is sufficient that the data subject be in possession of a full summary of those data in an intelligible form, that is to say a form which allows that data subject to become aware of those data and to verify that they are accurate and processed in accordance with this Directive, so that it is possible for him or her to exercise the rights conferred on him or her by this Directive. Such a summary could be provided in the form of a copy of the personal data undergoing processing*".

15.1.4.11 The *LE Guide* says

> "*You can restrict the amount of personal data you supply when it is necessary and proportionate to 'protect the rights and freedoms of others'. If information contains the personal data of an individual and that of third parties, you have to consider whether it is reasonable to disclose this information and whether this would adversely affect the rights and freedoms of others*".

However, as the *LE Guide* points out:

> "*Unlike the GDPR, where you can contact the individual to clarify the request if it involves a large amount of personal data, there is no similar provision under Part 3 of the Act. In practice, you may need to contact the requester to clarify the request but this will fall within the timescale for responding to the request*".

15.1.4.12 The time period for responding is set out in s.54 and is one month from the later of: when the request is received; when information requested to confirm identity is provided; or, if a fee is charged for an unreasonable or excessive request, when the fee is paid. This period can be extended by secondary legislation (adopted under the negative resolution procedure)—but any such regulations cannot extend this beyond three months. This same time period also applies to requests to erase or restrict data.

Rectification

15.1.4.13 Section 46 provides that a controller must rectify personal data at the request of the data subject if it is inaccurate (s.46(1)) (where the request must be met without undue delay), or if it is incomplete (s.46(2)). In appropriate cases (for example, if original data must be retained for evidential purposes), then the obligation to update data may be met by providing a supplementary statement (s.46(3)).

15.1.4.14 If the controller is required to keep personal data in its uncorrected form for evidential purposes, but the data is inaccurate, then s.46(4) provides that, instead of correcting the data, the controller must "restrict" processing of the data (as to which, see below). Once personal data has been corrected, then a competent authority must also notify any competent authority from which it obtained the original, incorrect, data (s.48(7)). This includes competent authorities in other Member States. In addition, if the data has been disclosed to others, then the controllers must notify the recipients, who must similarly rectify, erase or restrict the processing of the personal data (s.48(9)).

Erasure and restriction

Erasure

15.1.4.15 Section 47(1) provides that:

> "*The controller must erase personal data without undue delay where –*
>
> *a)* *the processing of the personal data would infringe section 35, 36(1) to (3), 37, 38(1), 39(1), 40, 41 or 42, or*
>
> *b)* *the controller has a legal obligation to erase the data*".

The sections listed at a) are the data protection principles. However, the additions to the principles (dealing with distinctions between fact and opinion; categories of data subject; checking retention periods; and passing on information necessary to allow others to assess the quality of personal data) are not included in the list—so a failure to follow these supplemental requirements does not necessitate erasures.

15.1.4.16 Section 47(1) is a free-standing obligation on the controller to erase data—irrespective of whether or not a request has been made by an individual. This is not just a slight of drafting—it is confirmed in s.47(4) which notes that:

"*A data subject may request the controller to erase personal data or to restrict its processing (but the duties of the controller under this section apply whether or not such a request is made)*".

Restriction

15.1.4.17 The obligation to restrict personal data applies:

- where personal data should be rectified—but cannot be because it must be maintained for evidential purposes (s.46(4));
- where personal data should be erased because the data protection principles have been breached or there is a legal obligation to erase—but, again, this cannot be done, because the data must be maintained for evidential purposes, (s.47(2)); or
- where an individual contests the accuracy of the personal data, but it is not possible to confirm whether the data is accurate or not (s.47(3)).

Again, as with erasure, s.47(4) provides that there is an independent obligation on the controller to restrict in these situations, irrespective of whether or not the individual has asked for this to be done.

15.1.4.18 Under the GDPR (art.18(2)), restriction of data means that:

"*personal data shall, with the exception of storage, only be processed with the data subject's consent or for the establishment, exercise or defence of legal claims, or for the protection of the rights of another natural or legal person or for reasons of important public interest of the Union or of a Member State*".

This formulation cannot work for restriction of law enforcement processing given that, in many cases, the data will have to be processed for evidential purposes. Instead, s.33(6) of the DPA 2018 provides that:

"*'restriction of processing' means the marking of stored personal data with the aim of limiting its processing for the future*".

15.1.4.19 Recital 47 of the LE Directive notes that:

"*... Methods to restrict ... could include ... moving the selected data to another processing system, for example for archiving purposes, or making the selected data unavailable. In automated filing systems the restriction should in principle be ensured by technical means*".

The Explanatory Notes go on to say (paras 199 and 200):

> "*Restricted data should be processed only for the purpose which prevented its erasure.*
> *Restrictions on processing of data may be given effect by moving the data to another system, for example for archiving purposes, or making it unavailable by applying strict access controls. The fact that the processing of the personal data is restricted should be indicated on the system, for example, through flagging*".

The *LE Guide* would seem to be incorrect on this point, therefore, when it states that

> "*when processing is restricted, you are permitted to store the personal data, but not further process it*".

15.1.4.20 Where an individual contests the accuracy of personal data, and the processing has been restricted because this cannot be confirmed, then (as under GDPR), the controller must notify the individual before lifting the restriction (s.48(10)). As with erasure, the controller must notify recipients of the personal data that it has restricted processing of it and, if the recipients are still responsible for processing the data, these recipients must in turn also restrict processing (s.48(9)).

Exceptions and enforcement via the Information Commissioner

Exceptions for law enforcement and national security purposes and to protect the rights and freedoms of others

15.1.4.21 There are exceptions from all of the rights (except automated decision-making), which allow the controller to restrict compliance:

> "*wholly or partly, ... to the extent that and for so long as the restriction is, having regard to the fundamental rights and legitimate interests of the data subject, a necessary and proportionate measure to –*
>
> *a) avoid obstructing an official or legal inquiry, investigation or procedure;*
> *b) avoid prejudicing the prevention, detection, investigation or prosecution of criminal offences or the execution of criminal penalties;*
> *c) protect public security;*
> *d) protect national security;*
> *e) protect the rights and freedoms of others*".

These restrictions are set out separately in relation to each right at ss.44(4–7), 45(4–7) and 48(3–6). However, they all operate in the same way and address the same concerns.

15.1.4.22 The first four exemptions all relate to law enforcement or national security purposes. The last is much broader. As the *LE Guide* notes, this would allow data to be withheld from an access request if it relates to other individuals or third parties more generally. The reference to the exemption applying "*to the extent that and for so long as*" restriction is necessary emphasises the case by case nature of the way the exemptions must be applied. This is also emphasised in rec.44 to the LE Directive, which notes that they should be assessed "*. . . by way of a concrete and individual examination of each case*". The *LE Guide* gives an example of the way this works:

> "*An individual you are investigating for tax fraud makes a request for all their personal data that you hold. You can only restrict the amount of personal data you provide in so far as disclosing it will prejudice an active investigation. P45 forms, or records on the individual's income which were self-reported for instance, are information they are aware of and therefore withholding it is unlikely to be unjustified. However, you can clearly restrict access to investigative files and evidence which you have gathered*".

15.1.4.23 Where compliance is restricted, wholly or partly, then the controller must also advise the individual of this, in writing and without undue delay. The controller must advise that compliance with the request has been restricted; the reasons for this; and the individual's right to make a request to the Commissioner under s.51 (to check the lawfulness of the restriction); to lodge a complaint with the Commissioner; to apply to court under s.167 (compliance ordered by the court).

15.1.4.24 Notifying an individual that a restriction has been applied could, itself, tip the individual off and accordingly the provisions dealing with the exemptions all provide for a further exemption where compliance with this information duty would undermine the purpose of the restriction. As noted at para.198 of the Explanatory Notes a "Neither Confirm Nor Deny" response may be appropriate here. However, the controller always has to explain the individual's rights to pursue the matter via the Information Commissioner or the courts.

15.1.4.25 These are powerful exemptions and, taken together, it may be difficult for individuals to challenge them. For this reason, two sets of protective provisions are important. First, where a controller not only applies an exemption, but also does not tell the individual of this, arguing that this would prejudice the relevant purpose, then the controller must always record the reasons for the decision not to notify the individual. This record must be available to the Commissioner on request (ss.44(7), 45(7) and 48(6)). Second, s.51 allows individuals to exercise their rights through the Commissioner. Where a controller has restricted its compliance, as set out above, then the affected data subject may ask the Information Commissioner to check that the controller has done so lawfully. The Information Commissioner has discretion as to how to deal with such a request, but, according to s.51(3), may exercise any of the powers conferred by s.142 (information notice) or s.146 (assessment notice **3.4.2.4**). Once the Commissioner has done this, she must advise the individual if the action was lawful. If she is not satisfied it was lawful, she *may* (s.51(6)) also inform the individual of any further steps she is considering taking by way of enforcement. In both cases, the Commissioner must also advise the individual of her right to apply to court under s.167.

National security certificates

15.1.4.26 Where the reason for non-compliance with data subject rights is that compliance would prejudice national security, then the provisions at s.79, relating to national security certificates, are relevant. These allow for certificates to be issued by a Minister either in respect of a specific restriction (this personal data must not be provided to this data subject, because of the risk to security s.79(2)(a)) or in more general terms (e.g. any personal data held in a particular system, or in connection with a particular investigation, should not be provided in response to an access request s.79(s)(b)). National security certificates are conclusive and the Commissioner's enforcement powers under Pt 6 do not apply in relation to them. There are powers to challenge the issue of a certificate via the Tribunal. The provisions relating to national security certificates in connection with law enforcement processing, the applied GDPR and the provisions of the DPA 2018 dealing with national security itself are all substantially identical. For this reason, we have considered them all together, at **15.2.7**.

Manifestly unfounded or excessive requests

15.1.4.27 Controllers are also excused from compliance in the case of requests of this nature. In this case, as under GDPR, they are given the choice of refusing to act on the request or charging a reasonable fee to deal with the request (s.53(1)). Sections 53(4) and (5) provide that the Secretary of State may specify limits on fees by regulations, subject to the negative resolution procedure.

15.1.4.28 Section 53(2) gives one example of a manifestly unfounded or excessive request, where it "*merely repeats the substance of previous requests*". Many more are given in the Explanatory Notes, which para.208 state:

> "*. . . may include requests that are repetitious, are malicious in intent or where they represent an abuse of the rights to access, for example by providing false or misleading information. Similarly, data subjects might attempt to use the right of subject access as a means to harass law enforcement bodies with no real purpose other than to cause disruption to the organisation. This can be in the form of repeated requests over a relatively short period of time or extending over several years, or where the controller has provided the data subject with their personal data through an alternative disclosure mechanism*".

Section 53(3) provides that if, in proceedings, there is an issue as to whether this provision applies or not, it is for the controller to show that the request is manifestly unfounded or excessive.

Significant automated decision-making

15.1.4.29 Section 49 introduces safeguards for such decision-making. The section applies to decisions "based solely on automated processing" where the decision "*produces an adverse legal effect concerning the data subject, or significantly affects the data subject*". The requirement that the legal effect must be "*adverse*" differs from the similar provision in the GDPR.

15.1.4.30 Section 49(1) provides that any such decisions may only be made if they are required or authorised by law. In addition, under s.50(2), the controller must notify the data subject, as soon as reasonably practicable, that a decision has been made on this basis. The data subject then has one month within which they can require the controller to reconsider the decision or to make a new decision so that it is not based entirely on automated processing. The controller, in turn, has one month to do this and to confirm to the individual of the steps taken to comply and the outcome of this—presumably explaining the outcome of the new decision.

15.1.4.31 There are no exemptions to this right to have decisions remade. However, this is unlikely to be significant because, as the Explanatory Notes mention (para.49),

> "*in practice, currently automated decision-taking that leads to an adverse outcome is rarely used in the law enforcement context and is unlikely to have any operational implications*".

Part 3 has not implemented art.11(3) of the LE Directive—which states that:

> "*Profiling that results in discrimination against natural persons on the basis of special categories of personal data referred to in Article 10 shall be prohibited* ...".

There is, however, a mechanism for additional safeguards to be introduced via secondary legislation (s.50(4)).

15.1.5 Controllers and processors (and accountability and security)

Controller's obligations of accountability

15.1.5.1 As under the GDPR, an accountability principle is introduced. Controllers must

> "*implement appropriate technical and organisational measures to ensure, and to be able to demonstrate that, the processing of personal data complies with the requirements of this Part* [of the DPA 2018]" (s.56(1)).

The concept of technical and organisational measures is defined at s.55 but is essentially the same as that under the GDPR. These measures may include appointment of a data protection officer and policies and s.56 also provides that the measures must be reviewed and updated where necessary.

15.1.5.2 An obligation of data protection by design and by default is placed on controllers at s.57. As with the overall accountability obligation, this is essentially identical to that under the GDPR.

Joint controllers

15.1.5.3 The DPA 2018, s.58(1), states that:

> "*Where two or more competent authorities jointly determine the purposes and means of processing personal data, they are joint controllers for the purposes of this Part*".

Where this is the case, they must "*in a transparent manner, determine their respective responsibilities for compliance . . . by means of an agreement between them*". This is not necessary if it is determined by enactment (s.58(2)). The agreement must designate the controller which is to be the point of contact for data subjects (s.58(3)). However, unlike the GDPR, there is no obligation to make the arrangement between the authorities available to individuals.

15.1.5.4 The main difference between GDPR and law enforcement processing in relation to joint controllers is that, unlike under the GDPR, joint controllers for law enforcement processing are not jointly and severally liable towards individuals for that processing. The LE Directive, at art.21(2) did allow Member States a discretion to allow individuals to pursue rights against any of the joint controllers, however, this has not been implemented in the DPA 2018. Similarly, s.152 of the DPA 2018 provides that the Information Commissioner cannot issue enforcement notices in relation to a joint controller unless that organisation is actually responsible for compliance with the provision in question.

Relations with processors

15.1.5.5 As under the GDPR, the processor may only process personal data on instructions from the controller, or to comply with a legal obligation (s.60). Although the DPA 2018 does not state this, Art.23 of the LE Directive makes clear that this has to be an obligation under European Union or Member State law. A processor which fails to do this and which, as a result, itself determines the purposes and means of processing "*is to be treated for the purposes of this Part as a controller in respect of that processing*" (s.59(8)). This corresponds to GDPR art.28(10).

15.1.5.6 Where a controller appoints a processor, they may only do so where the processor can provide guarantees to implement appropriate technical and organisational measures to comply with the law enforcement related provisions set out in Pt 3 of the DPA 2018, in particular ensuring compliance with individuals' rights (s.59(2)). Any appointment of a processor must be governed by a "*contract in writing between the controller and the processor*" (s.59(5)). The formulation here is slightly different from that in the GDPR and in the LE Directive itself, both of which refer to contracts which are "*binding on the processor with regard to the controller*". In most cases, data processing agreements will clearly be directly between a controller and the processor, so that the difference in wording will not matter. However, this is not always the case—for example, where there are joint controllers wishing to appoint a processor, or where with agreement of the controller a sub-contractor is engaged, or where data processing services are provided by a processor to a government department and non-departmental public bodies for which it is responsible pursuant to one master services agreement. Here, the narrower wording of the DPA 2018 seems to dictate direct agreements between every relevant controller and the processor.

15.1.5.7 Sections 59(5)–(7) set out certain terms which must be included in the contract with the processor. These are very similar to those at art.28(3) of the GDPR, although a small number of the more prescriptive provisions under the GDPR have not been included:

- there is no requirement for the contract to require the processor to take all measures required to implement appropriate security (art.28(3)(c));
- although the processor must make available all information required to demonstrate compliance, there is no express requirement to agree to audit (art.28(3)(h))—although one would imagine that any competent authority would insist on this;
- there is no obligation to assist the controller in relation to data protection impact assessments and breach reporting etc. (art.28(3)(f)); and, lastly
- there is no obligation to notify the controller if the processor believes that an instruction is illegal (art.28(3)(h) indent).

Co-operation

15.1.5.8 There is a general obligation on controllers and processors to co-operate, on request, with the Commissioner in the performance of her tasks (s.63).

Records of processing activities and logging

Records of processing activities

15.1.5.9 Section 61 requires controllers and processors to maintain records of processing activities, which are to be available to the Information Commissioner on request. Again, the obligation is extremely close to that under the GDPR, save that there are additional obligations here for controllers to include details of the legal basis for processing and details of any use of profiling. Profiling is defined at s.33(4) with the same definition as that in the GDPR at art.4(4). For ease of reference this is:

> "*any form of automated processing of personal data consisting of the use of personal data to evaluate certain personal aspects relating to an individual, in particular to analyse or predict aspects concerning that individual's performance at work, economic situation, health, personal preferences, interests, reliability, behaviour, location or movements*".

Logging

15.1.5.10 Retaining system logs in order to be able to prove the confidentiality and integrity of the data is not a new concept—and has been considered by the European Court of Human Rights to be a requirement under the right to private life (***I v Finland***, App. No.20511/03, 17 July 2008). The LE Directive and Pt 3 of the DPA 2018 now introduce this as a specific requirement for controllers and processors—but only in relation to automated processing.

15.1.5.11 Section 62 introduces a requirement to keep logs of at least the following processing operations:

- collection;
- alteration;
- consultation—where the logs must include date, time and justification of consultation and, so far as possible, the identity of the person who consulted the data;
- disclosure (including transfers)—where the logs must again show date, time and justification and, so far as possible, the identity of the person who disclosed the data and of the recipients of the data;
- combination; and
- erasure.

15.1.5.12 Retaining IT logs which include information about persons accessing personal data itself involves processing of personal data—which must be compliant with data protection legislation. With this in mind, s.62(4) notes that such logs may only be used for one or more of the following purposes:

"*a) to verify lawfulness of processing;*
b) to assist with self-monitoring by the controller or (as the case may be) the processor, including the conduct of internal disciplinary proceedings;
c) to ensure the integrity and security of personal data;
d) the purposes of criminal proceedings".

15.1.5.13 The DPA 2018, s.62(5) provides that the records must be made available to the Commissioner on request. The provision does not state for how long the records must be maintained. However, the Information Commissioner makes her Office's Records Retention Schedule available as part of her Office's publication scheme. This includes a retention period of 12 months for their own IT audit logs.

15.1.5.14 The Explanatory Notes, at para.218, make the important point that:

"*Logs of erasure should not reference the data itself – there is no need to retain a record of what was erased as that too would also be a record. Rather, the log should be able to specify that an item of data was erased on a specific date by a specific person*".

15.1.5.15 There are transitional arrangements in relation to the logging requirement. These are at Sch.20, Pt 4, para.14(1). They apply until 6 May 2023 and provide that there is no need to create a log "*if and to the extent that compliance ... would involve disproportionate effort*".

15.1.5.16 Logging only applies to automated processing systems. However, the Explanatory Notes at para.216, and paraphrasing rec.57 of the LE Directive, note that:

> "*The processing of personal data in non-automated processing systems (that is, paper based filing) also needs to be appropriately monitored by controllers and processors, and there should be in place methods of demonstrating lawfulness of processing, and data security and integrity. This may be through logs of other forms of records*".

Data protection impact assessments and prior consultation

15.1.5.17 Section 64 sets out the obligation to conduct data protection impact assessments for high risk processing—that is processing "*likely to result in a high risk to the rights and freedoms of individuals*". Whereas the GDPR gives examples of processing (at art.35(3)) which will amount to a high risk, where a DPIA will be required, the LE Directive and the DPA 2018 do not. This would seem to give competent authorities somewhat more discretion to determine what amounts to a high risk. The *LE Guide*, when discussing DPIAs, the examples from the GDPR in any event. As these examples include "*processing on a large scale of ... personal data relating to criminal convictions and offences ...*" this does little to assist competent authorities in determining when a DPIA may, or may not, be required.

15.1.5.18 The requirements for the DPIA are very similar to those under the GDPR, although (as with the threshold for the DPIA) they are slightly less prescriptive. In particular:

- whereas GDPR requires a systematic description of the processing, here it may be general;
- the suggestion in the GDPR, that "where appropriate" it may be necessary to take into account the views of data subjects (art.35(9)), is not included; and
- the suggestion in the GDPR that in some circumstances it may be necessary to check if processing is being carried out in accordance with the DPIA (art.35(11), is also not included

although the provisions in GDPR here would seem to be sensible good practice in any event and are also in line with the Information Commissioner's now withdrawn Privacy Impact Assessment Code of Practice.

15.1.5.19 Where, following a DPIA, there is a high and unmitigated risk, then the controller must consult with the Information Commissioner, providing copies of the DPIA and any other information requested by the Commissioner for the purpose. The Commissioner must provide advice to the controller or processor as appropriate within six weeks, although this period may be extended for an additional month if complexity of processing requires (ss.65(2)–(5)).

15.1.5.20 As with the GDPR, the LE Directive (art.28(2)), also requires that the Information Commissioner be consulted not just by controllers, but also in the case of legislation which relates to law enforcement purposes and relates to the processing of personal data. Schedule 13 para.(1)(c), which sets out additional details of the Commissioner's functions, makes clear that her functions include provision of advice on new legislation.

Security and personal data breaches

Security

15.1.5.21 As under GDPR, an obligation is placed on controllers and processors to implement appropriate technical and organisational measures to ensure a level of security appropriate to the risks. In the case of automated processing, the LE Directive and the DPA 2018 are somewhat more prescriptive as to what this entails. Section 66(2) provides that there must be a risk evaluation, following which measures must be designed to prevent unauthorised interference with systems and unauthorised processing, to ensure that systems function properly and can be restored in case of interruption and that data cannot be corrupted. This corresponds to the classic security requirements of confidentiality, availability and integrity. In addition, there is a requirement to "*ensure that it is possible to establish the precise details of any processing that takes place*" (so a supplement to the more tightly defined logging obligations). Those with responsibility for undertaking this exercise should note that the description of what is required in section 66(2) is not identical to that in the LE Directive. Article 29(2) breaks out security requirements into the more structured and detailed formulation of equipment access control, data media control, storage control, user control, data access control, communication control, input control, transport control and recovery. The DPA 2018 covers the same ground —but the way the requirements are spelt out in the LE Directive leaves less room for argument as to what is required.

Personal data breach reporting

15.1.5.22 Personal data breach has the same meaning as under the GDPR but is separately defined at s.33(3)). The provisions relating to breach reporting are very close to those under the GDPR, save that there are provisions which allow controllers not to report to data subjects where this would prejudice law enforcement and other public interest purposes. For ease of reference:

- controllers must keep a record of all personal data breaches, which is to be made available to the Commissioner to check compliance (ss.67(6)–(7));

- controllers must report personal data breaches to the Commissioner without undue delay and where feasible within 72 hours of becoming aware of the breach (s.67(1)), but this is not required if the breach is unlikely to result in a risk to individuals (s.67(2));
- the report must contain contact details for the controller, the data protection officer and details of the data affected, the likely consequences of the breach and the remedial measures undertaken (s.67(4)) and the information can be provided in phases if necessary (s.67(5));
- where the personal data has been transmitted to the controllers in other member states, then that other controller must told of the breach (i.e. the information in the record of breaches) (s.67(8)). Curiously, this does *not* apply when the data has been provided to other controllers in the UK;
- the processor must notify the controller without undue delay when it becomes aware of a personal data breach (s.67(9)).

15.1.5.23 Where the breach is likely to result in a high risk to individuals then the controller must inform the data subjects without undue delay (s.68(1)). The notice must comply with the general requirements for clear and easily intelligible communications (**15.1.4.3**) and must include contact details, a description of the breach, the likely consequences and what the controller has done to remediate and mitigate possible adverse effects. There is no obligation to notify if the controller had implemented appropriate technical and organisational measures to protect the data (such as encryption) or, since the breach, has taken measures to ensure that risks are no longer likely to materialise (s.68(3)). As in GDPR, there is also an acknowledgement that on some occasions it would involve disproportionate effort to notify on an individual basis—and here a public communication or similar method must be used (s.68(5)). If the controller does not provide a notice, the Information Commissioner may still require notice to be provided (s.68(6)).

15.1.5.24 As mentioned above, the controller does *not* have to provide notice to data subjects "*to the extent and for so long as*" this is a necessary and proportionate measure to avoid obstructing an official or legal inquiry, investigation, or procedure; to avoid prejudicing law enforcement purposes, public security or national security or to protect the rights and freedoms of others (s.68(7)). In this case, the Commissioner cannot require a notice to be provided.

Data protection officers

15.1.5.25 Whereas, under the GDPR, only certain organisations carrying out more intrusive processing have to appoint a DPO, all controllers subject to the law enforcement processing provisions must do so. In practice this makes little difference as they are all likely to be public authorities. The only exception is for courts and other judicial authorities when acting in a judicial capacity (s.69).

15.1.5.26 The professional qualities, position and tasks of the DPO are the same as those under the GDPR arts 37–39. In particular, the DPO must have expert knowledge of law and practice and be competent to perform then relevant tasks but can be appointed on behalf of multiple controllers. The DPO cannot be instructed as to how to perform his tasks, must be free from conflict of interests and cannot be dismissed for performing his tasks (s.70(3)) and must report to the highest management level (s.70(5)). The controller must also provide appropriate resources to allow the DPO to perform his tasks and to maintain his knowledge (s.70(2)). The DPO's details must be published and communicated to the Commissioner (s.69(4)).

15.1.5.27 The DPO's tasks are listed at s.71 and are: informing and advising the controller (and its processors and employees); advising on DPIAs; co-operating with the Commissioner; acting as the contact point for the Commissioner; monitoring compliance with policies and with Pt 3 of the DPA 2018. Individuals may also contact the DPO to exercise their rights or with regard to any other issue relating to the processing of their personal data.

15.1.6 Data transfers to third countries

15.1.6.1 The rules for data transfers to third countries or international organisations set out at ss.73–78 of the DPA 2018 are described in a particularly complex way, with multiple sets of sub-conditions which must be met for transfers to be permissible. There is also duplication of content and extensive cross-referencing. In order to explain the provisions in a more straightforward way, we have not followed the order of the sections in the DPA 2018, although we have taken account of all of its provisions.

15.1.6.2 There are three principles which underlie the transfer rules and which are cumulative:

1) transfers must always be for law enforcement purposes;
2) the recipient must usually be an authority or international organisation with comparable functions to the controller which is transferring the personal data; and
3) there must be adequate protection for the personal data.

15.1.6.3 We have described each of these principles below. The sections also require onward transfer restrictions to be imposed on the recipient of the data and, where data has come from a controller in a Member State, require that controller to be consulted before data are transferred to a third country.

Transfers must be for law enforcement purposes

15.1.6.4 The DPA 2018 s.73(2) provides that personal data may not be transferred unless it is "*necessary for any of the law enforcement purposes*".

The functions of the recipient

15.1.6.5.1 The data importer must either be an international organisation which carries out functions for law enforcement purposes (ss.73(4) and (7)) or it must be a person which has "*functions comparable to those of a competent authority*" (ss.73(4) and 72(2)). The principle, therefore, is that competent authorities should transfer personal data to agencies in other countries which also have law enforcement roles.

Special cases

15.1.6.6 In some cases, controllers can transfer data to non-law enforcement bodies. The rationale for this is explained in para.232 of the Explanatory Notes (paraphrasing rec.73 of the LE Directive):

> "*In specific individual cases, the regular procedures requiring transfer of personal data to a relevant authority in a third country may be ineffective or inappropriate, ... because the transfer could not be carried out in a timely manner, or because that authority in the third country does not respect the rule of law or international human rights norms and standards ... This may be the case where there is an urgent need to transfer personal data to save the life of a person who is in danger of becoming a victim of a criminal offence or in the interest of preventing an imminent perpetration of a crime, including terrorism*".

Not all controllers can rely on this special case. Those who can are listed at s.73(4)(b) —for example government departments and, indeed, the Information Commissioner, are not included in this list, however police forces, HMRC and the National Crime Agency are included.

15.1.6.7 Section 77 sets out the special cases, which are:

- that the transfer is strictly necessary for a (law enforcement) task of the controller which is making the transfer, as provided for by law;
- there are no fundamental rights and freedoms of the concerned data subject which override the public interest in making the transfer;
- it would be ineffective or inappropriate to transfer the data to a relevant authority or international organisation in that country;
- the actual recipient of the data is told of the specific purposes for which the personal data may be processed;
- the relevant authority or international organisation in that third country is told of the transfer without undue delay, unless this would be ineffective or inappropriate of itself; and
- the controller making the transfer must document the transfer and inform the Information Commissioner about the transfer.

15.1.6.8 These arrangements are not intended to affect any international agreements in force with third countries relating to judicial co-operation in criminal matters and police co-operation (s.77(8)).

Adequate protection for personal data

15.1.6.9 Whenever personal data are transferred (whether to a relevant authority or international organisation or in a special case), the controller must ensure that there is adequate protection for the personal data. The concepts—adequacy decisions; other safeguards; derogations—are familiar from the GDPR. However, the details differ and offer more operational choice to controllers, but in return for a greater role for the Information Commissioner in being able to supervise the arrangements.

Adequacy decision

15.1.6.10 Section 74(a) provides that personal data can be transferred to a third country or international organisation where the European Commission has decided, under art.36 of the LE Directive, that there is an adequate level of protection and where such a decision has not been repealed, suspended or amended so as to demonstrate that the Commission no longer considers the protection to be adequate. The matters which the Commission is required to consider when assessing adequacy under Art.36 are identical to those under art.45 of the GDPR. In the event of a no-deal Brexit, then this provision will be replaced by s.74A, which will give the Secretary of State power to adopt such adequacy regulations. The section will spell out the matters which the Secretary of State must consider when assessing adequacy. Section 74B will provide that such adequacy regulations must be kept under regular review. Schedule 21 (further transitional provisions), Part 3, paragraphs 10 and 11 will provide that transfers to Member States and to Gibraltar are to be deemed to be based on adequacy regulations, as are transfers to third countries, territories or sectors, which are the subject of adequacy decisions made by the European Commission under art.36(3) of the LE Directive. These adequacy provisions are very similar to the post no-deal-Brexit adequacy arrangements which will be included in the UK GDPR (**9.4.4** and **9.4.8**) and the conditions which the Secretary of State must consider when assessing adequacy mirror those set out in art.36 of the LE Directive, which, in turn, are identical to those under art.45 of the GDPR.

15.1.6.11 The Explanatory Notes, at para.228, and the *LE Guide* refer to the existing adequacy decisions which have been adopted by the Commission under the Data Protection Directive and state that transfers can be made in reliance on those. However, this does not seem correct (at least according to the European Commission) which, in a document entitled *Adequacy of the protection of personal data in non-EU countries* (accessible on *http://ec.Europa.eu* [Accessed 14 May 2019]) stated that "*These* [existing] *adequacy decisions do not cover data exchanges in the law enforcement sector*". Recital 68 of the LE Directive also states that any decisions under GDPR should be taken into account—so it seems that they are relevant, but not automatically applicable. In the event of a no-deal Brexit, this will also be true – as a result of amendments to Sch.21 Pt 3 which, as mentioned above, refers specifically to adequacy decisions under the LE Directive.

Safeguards

15.1.6.12 As an alternative, s.75 allows personal data to be transferred on the basis of appropriate safeguards, which must either be:

- a legal instrument containing appropriate safeguards, which binds the recipient of the data; or
- self-assessment by the controller

"*having assessed all the circumstances surrounding transfers of that type of personal data to the third country or international organisation,* [where the controller] *concludes that appropriate safeguards exist*".

15.1.6.13 The Explanatory Notes para.230 and paraphrasing LE Directive rec.71, note that a legal instrument could be a bilateral agreement between the UK and a third country, and that the self-assessment route means that:

"*Controllers are able to take into account cooperation agreements concluded between Europol or Eurojust and third countries . . . the fact that the transfer of personal data will be subject to confidentiality obligations and the principle of specificity, ensuring that personal data will not be processed for other purposes than for the purposes of the transfer. In addition, a controller should take into account that the personal data will not be used to request, hand down, or execute a death penalty or any form of cruel and inhuman treatment*".

Presumably the EU-US agreement on personal data protection (Decision (EU) 2016/920), known as the Umbrella Agreement, and providing for protection of personal information relating to prevention, investigation, detection and prosecution of criminal offences, could be an example of such an agreement, although, without special arrangements, post-Brexit, the UK will no longer benefit from the Agreement.

15.1.6.14 Where a controller relies on this self-assessment route, then it must inform the Commissioner about the categories of data being transferred in this way (s.75(2)) and must document the transfer (date and time; name and relevant information about the recipient; justification and description of personal data transferred) and make this documentation available to the Commissioner on request (ss.75(2) and (3)).

Special circumstances

15.1.6.15 Section 76 allows for transfers of personal data, even where the third country or international organisation does not provide adequate protection for personal data, in special circumstances. These could broadly be described as emergency, or case-specific transfers. They could not be used to justify broader, systematic, data sharing schemes. The special circumstances apply where the transfer is necessary:

- to protect the vital interests of the data subject or another person;
- to safeguard the legitimate interests of the data subject;
- to prevent an immediate and serious threat to the public security of a Member State or a third country;
- in individual cases, for any of the law enforcement purposes, or
- for a legal purpose (defined in s.76(4) as being in connection with legal proceedings (including prospective proceedings) relating to law enforcement purposes, necessary for obtaining legal advice in relation to any of the law enforcement purposes, or otherwise necessary for establishing, exercising or defending legal rights in relation to law enforcement purposes.

15.1.6.16 Recital 72 of the LE Directive emphasises that these "*... derogations should be interpreted restrictively and should not allow frequent, massive and structural transfers of personal data, or large scale transfers of data*". In addition, transfers made in reliance on these provisions must be documented (date and time of transfer, name and details of recipient, justification and description of data transferred) and the documentation must be made available to the Commissioner on request (s.76(3)). It will be seen from the provisions at s.76(3) and s.75, that, unless a controller only transfers personal data outside the UK in reliance on adequacy decisions, it will need to retain detailed records of all transfers, on a per-occasion basis.

Rules for onward transfer

15.1.6.17 The detailed data transfer rules would achieve little if the organisation receiving transferred data was not bound by similar considerations. Accordingly, s.78(1) provides that the controller making the transfer

> "*must make it a condition of the transfer that the data is not to be further transferred to a third country or international organisation without the authorisation of the transferring controller or another competent authority*".

Such an authorisation may only be given (s.78(2)) where the further transfer is also necessary for a law enforcement purpose. The authorising authority must also take into account the seriousness of the circumstances leading to the request; the purpose of the original transfer; and the standards of protection for personal data that will apply to the personal data after the subsequent transfer (s.78(3)).

Consulting the originating authorities in EU Member States

15.1.6.18 Where the controller has received the personal data from a competent authority in a Member State, then the controller is not entitled to transfer the personal data to a third country or international organisation without the approval of the original controller of the personal data (s.73(1)(b)). There is an exception to this rule if the transfer is necessary to prevent "*an immediate and serious threat either to the public security of a member state or a third country or to the essential interests of a member State*" so that authorisation cannot be obtained in time (s.73(5)). In this situation, the authority which should have authorised the transfer must be informed without delay (s.73(6)).

15.1.6.19 Where a controller receives a request from a law enforcement authority or international organisation, in accordance with s.78(1), and the personal data originally came from a competent authority in another member State then ss.78(4)–(6) contains equivalent provisions to those above—the originating authority must be consulted and must give authorisation, save in emergency situations.

What about transfers to processors in third countries?

15.1.6.20 The data transfer restrictions in the GDPR apply to controllers and to processors. The mechanisms for adequacy could also apply to processors which import personal data (for example, processor binding corporate rules or standard contractual clauses for transfers to processors in third countries (**9.5.7.17** and **9.5.6.12**). The data transfer provisions in the LE Directive and the DPA 2018 only apply to controllers. However, there appears to be no mechanism for a competent authority to provide adequate protection for a transfer to a processor (or a sub-processor) in a third country. The data transfer rules apply to any transfers to "recipients", defined at s.33(5) as: "*any person to whom the data is disclosed, whether a third party or not . . .*".

15.1.6.21 Data transfers may, in accordance with s.73(4), only take place where the intended recipient is a "*relevant authority in a third country or an international organisation . . .*" or where the exceptional rules at s.77 apply. There appears to be no authority for personal data to be transferred to a processor or sub-processor in a third country.

15.1.7 Enforcement

Enforcement by the Commissioner

15.1.7.1 The Commissioner's powers of enforcement set out in Pt 6 of the DPA 2018 also apply to controllers and processors in respect of the law enforcement provisions in Pt 3. In particular, penalties of up to €20 million and €10 million can be imposed for breach of Pt 3 (DPA 2018 s.157).

15.1.7.2 Section 120 gives the Commissioner a specific international role in relation to enforcement and jurisdictional conflicts. This is similar to the obligations placed on the Commissioner under art.50 of the GDPR (**1.3.8.13**).

Application to court

15.1.7.3 Individuals are able to apply to court to seek compliance orders (s.167, see **3.3.1.2**) and to claim compensation (s.169, see **3.3.1.4–3.3.1.23**). As mentioned at **15.1.5.4** above, joint controllers are not jointly and severally liable for law enforcement related processing, Accordingly, s.167(5) in relation to compliance orders and s.169(4) in relation to compensation, provide that joint controllers can only be subject to an order or to liability if they are, in fact, responsible for compliance with the provision of data protection legislation that is contravened.

15.1.7.4 Processors should note that, as under the GDPR, they can also be subject to compliance orders or compensation orders for law enforcement related processing. As with the GDPR, the processor will only be liable if (s.169(2)) it is involved in the processing and has not complied with an obligation specifically directed at processors or has acted outside or contrary to the controller's instructions. There is a defence for both the controller and processor, as under GDPR, if they can demonstrate that they are not in any way responsible for the event giving rise to the damage.

Whistleblowing

15.1.7.5 Section 81 requires controllers to implement effective mechanisms to encourage reports of breaches of Pt 3 of the Act, where reports may be made either to the controller itself or to the Information Commissioner. These mechanisms must also raise awareness of the whistle-blowing protections in employment rights legislation, which allow employees to claim unfair dismissal if they are dismissed or victimised as a result of blowing the whistle. Section 81(4) also provides that anyone who reports breaches under the section will not breach any obligation of confidence or any other restriction on disclosure of information. The only exception to this is certain disclosures which are prohibited by certain sections of the Investigatory Powers Act 2016 and, while it is still in force, the Regulation of Investigatory Powers Act 2000.

15.1.8 *El Gizouli*

15.1.8.1 The provisions of Pt 3 of the DPA 2018 have been considered in the case of ***The Queen (on the application of Maha El Gizouli) v the Secretary of State for the Home Department*** [2019] EWHC 60 Admin. The claimant, Ms El Gizouli, is the Mother of a British national, Mr El Sheikh, who fought in, and is detained in, Syria and who, according to the Director of National Security in the Home Office, is believed to be a member of a group of terrorists

> *"associated with some of the most barbaric crimes committed during the conflict in Syria. This includes. . .beheading of 27 individuals, including the murders of . . . British citizens David Haines and Alan Henning. . ."* [6].

The UK concluded that there was insufficient evidence to charge Mr El Sheikh. However, the US, did wish to charge Mr El Sheikh and asked the UK for information which would be useful for its investigations. In such cases, the UK usually seeks an assurance that information which the UK provides will not be used in proceedings where the recipient seeks the death penalty. In this case, the Home Secretary took the decision not to require such a commitment: this conclusion was reached after consideration that such a request would be turned down (and that even to request such a commitment could be counter-productive with current senior US leaders), and could also lead the US to detain Mr El Sheikh in Guantanamo Bay instead of trying him in a civilian court. Ms El Gizouli argued that the disclosure of information to the US was unlawful (on various grounds, including breach of the DPA 2018) and that any future disclosure should be prohibited. Ms El Gizouli failed on all grounds. So far as the DPA 2018 was concerned, the court noted that the government parties had given no consideration to the DPA 2018 before disclosing the information [142], but still considered the disclosure to be lawful. More detailed analysis of the data protection points is set out below.

15.1.8.2 The main argument advanced by Ms El Gizouli was that Pt 3 of the DPA 2018 must be interpreted in accordance with the Charter of Fundamental Rights of the European Union and, as this prohibits the death penalty, any processing which could lead to the death penalty must automatically be unfair and unlawful [147]. The court rejected this. Although the LE Directive refers to the EU Charter, as mentioned at **15.1.1.4**, measures which relate to freedom, security and justice (Title V of TFEU) only apply if the UK opts-in to them—so that the LE Directive is relevant to some, but not all, processing of personal data for law enforcement purposes in the UK. In this case, disclosures of personal data by the UK to the US did not take place pursuant to any EU criminal justice measure and was outside the scope of EU law [174]; the EU Charter therefore has no relevance to such processing [178]. The court went on to note that the EU Charter is limited in its territorial scope: because Mr El Sheikh was in Syria, even if the EU Charter was relevant to interpretation of the DPA 2018, Mr El Sheikh would not be able to rely on the EU Charter [185].

15.1.8.3 The case also considered a number of other provisions in the DPA 2018:

- the obligation in the first data protection principle that processing must be "fair" is primarily concerned with transparency and openness: the fact that the US would use the information in capital proceedings would not make the disclosure "unfair" [187];
- the obligation for processing to be "lawful" meant that the processing had to authorised by statute, common law or royal prerogative: failure to keep records prescribed by the DPA 2018 did not result in "unlawful" processing for purposes of the first data protection principle. Further, where the DPA 2018 required documentation to be kept, documentation kept for

other purposes could meet this requirement, it did not require a "bespoke set of documents" [189];

- information about acts of extreme religious violence would *not* be protected as special category data:

"*these provisions should not be interpreted to give a heightened degree of protection in respect of terrorist offences which advance 'a political, religious, racial or ideological cause' compared with non-ideologically driven crimes*" [192];

- the disclosure by the police to prosecuting authorities overseas was not processing for an "incompatible purpose" [196];
- the transfer of personal data to the US could meet the provisions in the Pt 3 (albeit that notice had not been given to the Commissioner, as it should have been under s.75(1)(3)) either on the basis (1) that, as a matter of fact, there were appropriate safeguards in place [203]; or (2) because there were "special circumstances" as provided for in s.76—namely that the transfer was necessary in an individual case for law enforcement or legal purposes (s.76(1)(d) or (e)) [207]; and
- lastly, the court also concluded that, when considering if there were "appropriate safeguards" in place, what mattered was whether such safeguards were in substance in place—there was no requirement for the party transferring the data to give express consideration to this before the transfer [202].

15.2 NATIONAL SECURITY: PROCESSING BY THE INTELLIGENCE SERVICES

15.2.1 Introduction

15.2.1.1 Matters relating to national security fall outside European Union law with the result that, as confirmed by rec.16 of the GDPR, the GDPR does not apply to them. The DPA 2018, Pt 4, does, however, set out the data protection rules which apply to the intelligence services. The DPA 2018 also includes exemptions from data protection obligations, where this is required for national security purposes. The paragraphs which follow describe the substantive obligations which apply to the intelligence services and the way the national security exemptions operate across all of the DPA 2018. As with processing for law enforcement purposes, the provisions on security apply directly to processors as well as to controllers, so service providers working for intelligence services should also be aware of the provisions.

15.2.1.2 Readers should note that, at the date of writing (February 2019), certain of the provisions relating to the intelligence services had not yet been brought into force. These are: s.93 (right to information), s.102 (general obligations of the controller), s.103 (data protection by design), s.104 (joint controllers), s.105 (processors) and s.108 (communication of a personal data breach), as well as certain provisions in the Schedules to the DPA 2018.

15.2.2 Scope of Part 4

15.2.2.1 Part 4 of the DPA 2018 applies to processing by the intelligence services, defined as being the Security Service (i.e. MI5), the Secret Intelligence Service (i.e. MI6) and the Government Communications Headquarters (GCHQ). Part 4 applies to *any* processing of personal data by these services. Unlike Pt 3, therefore, it would for example apply to processing by the intelligence services for human resources purposes. The provisions apply to processing of personal data, wholly or partly by automated means, or of personal data which is in a filing system. The definitions used for these (and other terms) are consistent with those set out in Pt 3—save that a definition of consent is added.

15.2.2.2 The reason behind the inclusion of special provisions for the intelligence services in the DPA 2018 is set out well at paras 41, 42 and 45 of the Explanatory Notes, as follows:

> "*National security is outside the scope of EU law by virtue of Article 4(2) of the Treaty on the European Union, which states that national security is the sole responsibility of each Member State. Therefore the processing of personal data in connection with national security activities and processing by agencies or units dealing with national security issues is not within scope of the GDPR or the LED. Domestic processing of personal data by the intelligence services, comprising the Security Service, the Secret Intelligence Service and the Government Communications Headquarters, is currently governed by the 1998* [Data Protection] *Act. Part 4 of the new Act builds on the existing regime by seeking to adopt the standards of the modernised Convention 108 (which does apply to national security data processing) to ensure processing of personal data carried out by the intelligence services will be in-line with future international standards. It provides for rules on processing personal data in the national security context whilst ensuring that the UK intelligence community can tackle existing, new and emerging national security threats.*
>
> ...
>
> *The regulatory structure applying to the intelligence services is found in other legislation and already imposes restrictions on their activities, including relating to their data handling practices. This includes the Security Services Act 1989, the Intelligence Services Act 1994, the Regulation of Investigatory Powers Act 2000 and the Investigatory Powers Act 2016...*".

15.2.2.3 Much of Pt 4 has been carried across from the 1998 Act (especially the data protection principles and many of the provisions dealing with individuals' rights), although some provisions have been edited so as to be partially in line with Pt 3 of the DPA 2018. As at the date of writing, there is no guidance from the Information Commissioner on Pt 4. Part 4 of the DPA 2018 comprises ss.82–113 and also Schs.9–11.

15.2.3 Data protection principles

Principle 1: lawful, fair and transparent processing

15.2.3.1 Section 86(1) and (2) provides that:

"*(1) ... processing of personal data must be–*
a) lawful, and
b) fair and transparent.
(2) The processing ... is lawful only if and to the extent that–
a) at least one of the conditions in Schedule 9 is met; and
b) in the case of sensitive processing, at least one of the conditions in Schedule 10 is also met".

In considering whether processing is fair and transparent, one must have regard to the method by which the personal data was obtained (s.86(5)). Personal data will be treated as fairly obtained if the data is obtained from a person who is authorised, or required, to supply it by an enactment, or who is required to supply it by an international obligation of the UK.

15.2.3.2 The conditions for processing at Sch.9 are very similar to those in Sch.2 to the 1998 Act. They are:

- that the data subject has given consent;
- the processing is necessary to perform a contract with the data subject or to take steps at the request of the data subject prior to entering into a contract;
- the processing is necessary to comply with a legal obligation on the controller (other than one imposed by contract);
- the processing is necessary to protect the vital interests of the data subject or another individual;
- the processing is necessary for the administration of justice, the functions of either House of Parliament, the exercise of functions conferred by enactment or rule of law, the exercise of any functions of the Crown, a Minister or a government department, or the exercise of other functions of a public nature exercised in the public interest by a person; and
- the processing is necessary for the purposes of legitimate interests of the controller or a third party (i.e. someone other than the controller or a processor or sub-processor), unless the processing is unwarranted in any particular case because of prejudice to the rights and freedoms or legitimate interests of the data subject.

15.2.3.3 "Sensitive processing" s.86(7) corresponds to processing of sensitive personal data under the 1998 Act—with the addition of processing of: information about genetic data; or biometric data uniquely to identify an individual; and of sexual orientation (in line with the definition in the GDPR). As in the 1998 Act, information about offences is included in the definition of sensitive processing.

15.2.3.4 The conditions for sensitive processing at Sch.10 will, again, be largely familiar from the 1998 Act. They are:

- the data subject has given consent (the 1998 Act requirement for explicit consent has been omitted);
- the processing is necessary for employment law related rights and obligations;
- the processing is necessary to protect the vital interests of any person (where the data subject cannot give consent; where the controller cannot reasonably be expected to obtain consent; or—where processing is to protect the interests of someone else—where consent has been unreasonably withheld);
- the processing is necessary to safeguard children and individuals at risk (this is consistent with the new conditions included in the DPA 2018 in relation to GDPR and law enforcement processing);
- the information contained in the personal data has been made public as a result of steps deliberately taken by the data subject (the original 1998 Act wording is retained in preference to the language in the GDPR and the LE Directive. See **4.5.5.7** for comment on the difference in language);
- the processing is necessary for legal proceedings;
- the processing is necessary for the administration of justice, the exercise of functions conferred on a person by enactment or rule of law, for the exercise of functions of the Crown, a Minister or government department, or for the exercise of functions of either House of Parliament (this last provision has been added to the 1998 Act, consistent with the equivalent provisions in the DPA 2018 dealing with processing to which the GDPR applies);
- the processing is for medical purposes (as defined) and is undertaken by a health care professional or someone who owes an equivalent duty of confidentiality;
- the processing is of sensitive data relating to racial or ethnic origin, is necessary to keep the existence or absence of equality of opportunity under review with a view to promoting or maintaining equality and is carried out with appropriate safeguards.

Principle 2: specified, explicit and legitimate purposes

15.2.3.5 The controller must process personal data for specified, explicit and legitimate purposes (s.87(1)(a)). There is also a prohibition on processing personal data for incompatible purposes (at sub-section (b)). However, this has little effect, as s.87(3) goes on to provide that:

> "*Personal data collected by a controller for one purpose may be processed for any other purpose of the controller that collected the data or any purpose of another controller provided that–*
> *a)* *the controller is authorised by law to process the data for that purpose, and*
> *b)* *the processing is necessary and proportionate for that purpose*".

The Explanatory Notes para.251 comment that

> "... *for example, personal data collected by the Security Service for the purpose of safeguarding national security could be processed further for the purpose of the prevention or detection of serious criminal offences, for instance by alerting the relevant law enforcement agency to intelligence suggesting a subject of interest is in possession of a firearm*".

15.2.3.6 There is also an exemption for processing which is necessary for archiving purposes in the public interest or for scientific or historical research or for processing for statistical purposes (s.87(4)).

Principles 3–6

15.2.3.7 The remaining principles are briefer, so have been addressed together here. Principle 3 (s.88) provides that personal data must be "*adequate, relevant and not excessive in relation to the purpose for which it is processed*". Principle 4 (s.89) is that "*personal data undergoing processing must be accurate and, where necessary, kept up to date*". The Explanatory Notes para.253 comment that

> "*this may not always be a straightforward question of fact in cases where it amounts to an intelligence officer's assessment which is based on underlying information which is partial or incomplete*".

15.2.3.8 Principle 5 is that personal data "*must be kept for no longer than is necessary for the purpose for which it is processed*" (s.90). The Explanatory Notes (paras 254 and 255) remind that whilst set periods are not prescribed by the DPA 2018, some processing of personal data by intelligence services is subject to statutory retention periods (for example retention of a bulk personal data set has to be authorised in accordance with the Investigatory Powers Act 2016).

15.2.3.9 Principle 6 is that personal data "*must be processed in a manner that includes taking appropriate security measures as regards risks that arise from processing personal data*". These risk must "*include (but not be limited to) accidental or unauthorised access to, or destruction, loss, use, modification or disclosure of, personal data*". There is more on security at **15.2.4.7** below.

15.2.4 Data subject rights

Right to information

15.2.4.1 Section 93 provides that a controller has to give a data subject information as to:

- the controller's identity and contact details;
- the purposes for processing and legal basis for processing;
- the categories of personal data being processed;
- information as to the recipients or the categories of recipients;
- the right to lodge a complaint with the Commission and the contact details for the Information Commissioner;
- how to exercise the rights granted to individuals under Pt 4; and
- any other information needed to ensure fair and transparent processing.

15.2.4.2 The controller can comply with this obligation by a general notice (unlike the law enforcement provisions (**15.1.4.5**) there is no obligation to supplement this with a specific notice) and does not have to provide the information if the individual already has it. The exemptions in the 1998 Act, which provided that where data was not collected directly from the individual, that there was no obligation to provide a notice if to do so would be impossible, involve disproportionate effort or if the processing is authorised by enactment, have been included here (s.93(4)).

Right of access

15.2.4.3 This follows the provisions in the 1998 Act at ss.7–8 closely. Under s.94, an individual has a right to confirmation as to whether personal data about them is being processed and, where that is the case, to have the information provided, as well as supplemental explanatory information. A copy of the information should ordinarily be provided, in writing, unless this would involve disproportionate effort, or the individual agrees otherwise (s.95(1)). The supplemental information is very similar to the information which has to be provided as part of the right to information, save that it must also include details of the right to rectification and erasure and information as to the period for which the personal data is to be preserved.

15.2.4.4 The controller is able to charge a fee for dealing with the request (up to a maximum amount set by secondary legislation) and the controller does not have to provide the information until any requested fee is paid (s.94(3)). Where the controller reasonably requires information to ascertain the identity of the individual making the request or to locate the data, then the controller does not have to comply unless and until this information is provided (s.94(5)).

15.2.4.5 As under the 1998 Act, there are exemptions where the personal data to be supplied also relates to another individual, in which case, the information should only be disclosed with the consent of that person or if it is reasonable to do so in all the circumstances (s.94(6)–(8)). Where a controller can comply with the request by anonymising information then this should be done, although one must have regard to the likelihood that the requester could identify the third party (s.95(5)). The sections also contain guidance on assessing what is reasonable. There are exemptions where the individual has already made similar requests in the past and where a reasonable interval between requests has not elapsed (s.95(2)–(3)).

15.2.4.6 A controller has to comply with a request within one month (s.94(14)), although there is scope for this to be extended (up to 3 months in total) by secondary legislation. The information which the controller supplies should be the data at the time the request was received—unless the data would have been amended or deleted in the ordinary course of events in between that date and the date the information is provided (s.95(4)).

Automated decision-making and information about decision-making

15.2.4.7 Section 96 sets out a prohibition on taking significant decisions based solely on automated processing of personal data. Significant decisions are those which have legal effects in relation to the individual. There is an exception to this prohibition for decisions which are:

- required or authorised by law;
- based on the individual's consent; or
- taken to consider whether to enter into a contract with the individual, with a view to enter into such a contract or to perform such a contract.

15.2.4.8 Where the decision is required or authorised by law, then additional safeguards apply (s.97)). These are that the controller must notify the individual, as soon as practicable, that the decision has been made and the individual then has up to one month to request the controller to reconsider or to make a new decision not based solely on automated processing. The controller must, within one further month, consider the request and advise the individual of the outcome of this. Individuals' rights in relation to automated decisions used for law enforcement purposes are absolute (i.e. the controller *must* reconsider). This is not the case in Part 4: accordingly, the controller could decide that an exemption applies and that it is not reconsidering.

15.2.4.9 Section 98 introduces a new provision. Irrespective of entirely automated decision-making, this section provides that where the controller processes personal data relating to the data subject and "*the results produced by the processing are applied to the data subject*", the data subject is "*entitled to obtain from the controller, on request, knowledge of the reasoning underlying the processing*". The controller must comply with such a request without undue delay.

Right to object to processing

15.2.4.10 Section 99 gives individuals the right, by notice at any time, to require the controller not to process personal data about that individual at all, or for a specified purpose or manner. The right can only be exercised where

> "*for specified reasons relating to the situation of the data subject, the processing in question is an unwarranted interference with the interests or rights of the data subject*".

There are similar provisions relating to identifying the individual and locating the data as there are in relation to subject access requests (s.99(2)). The controller must notify the individual within 21 days of the request (or the provision of the supplemental required information to identify or locate the data) whether the controller has or intends to comply or the reasons why the controller does not intend to comply.

Right to rectification, erasure and restriction

15.2.4.11 An individual may exercise rights of erasure or restriction by applying to court (s.100). The right to erasure applies where the processing infringes the data protection principles of rights of data subjects. In each case, the court may order the controller to erase or rectify the data without delay. As with processing for law enforcement purposes (**15.1.4.17**), there are special rules relating to restriction where data has to be retained for evidential purposes, or where (in connection with accuracy) the court concludes that the controller is not able to ascertain whether the data is accurate or not. Restriction has to be ordered by the court (s.100(3) and (4))—unlike the law enforcement provisions there is no independent obligation on the controller to implement restriction.

15.2.5 Controller and processor

15.2.5.1 The provisions in this chapter of Pt 4 are particularly light touch, setting out high level principles, with less prescriptive detail than is contained in the GDPR, or other parts of the DPA 2018. There are no requirements to appoint data protection officers or to have records of processing activity, for example.

Accountability for controllers

15.2.5.2 Section 102 places an obligation on controllers to

> "*to implement appropriate measures to ensure and to be able to demonstrate, in particular to the Commissioner, that the processing of personal data complies with the requirements of this Part*".

The exemptions available for national security processing perhaps explain why the emphasis is on demonstrating compliance to the Commissioner, as it will often be harder for individuals to hold the intelligence services to account. As the extensive exemptions below (**15.2.6**) show, it may also be hard for the Information Commissioner to do this.

15.2.5.3 Data protection by design obligations are included (s.103), but these are lighter touch than those elsewhere, without data minimisation obligations. Instead, there is an obligation on the controller to

> "*consider the impact of the proposed processing on the rights and freedoms of data subjects . . . prior to the processing*".

Technical and organisational measures must be designed to ensure that the principles are implemented and that risks to individuals' rights and freedoms are minimised.

15.2.5.4 There is a general provision that anyone who has access to the personal data under the authority of the controller (or a processor), may not process the personal data save on instructions from the controller or to comply with a legal obligation (s.106).

Joint controllers

15.2.5.5 Section 104 provides that joint controllers must, in a transparent, manner determine their respective responsibilities for compliance, by an arrangement between them. This is not necessary if this is determined under or by virtue of an enactment. The arrangement must designate the controller which is to be the contact point for data subjects. As with processing for law enforcement purposes (**15.1.5.3**), there is no obligation to make this arrangement accessible to individuals.

Processors

15.2.5.6 Section 105 provides that the controller must only use a processor which undertakes to implement appropriate measures that are sufficient to ensure that the processing complies with this Part of the DPA 2018 and to provide such information as is necessary to demonstrate this to the controller. There is no requirement for there to be a written agreement, or for set provisions to be included in that agreement. If a processor oversteps the mark, and determines purposes and means of processing, then as with other Parts of the DPA 2018, the processor will be treated as a controller in respect of the processing (s.105(3)).

Security and personal data breaches

15.2.5.7 Section 107 requires each controller and each processor to implement security measures which are appropriate to the risks. In the case of automated processing, then each controller and processor must evaluate the risks and then implement measures designed to prevent unauthorised processing or interference with systems; to ensure that the precise details of any processing that takes place can be established; to ensure that any systems used function properly and can be restored in case of interruption' and that stored personal data cannot be corrupted if as system which is being used malfunctions.

15.2.5.8 The Explanatory Notes para.278 suggest that these measures may include:

"• *record or log keeping to ensure access to and that processing of the data can be audited;*
• *An ability to verify the integrity of the stored data and restore it if it becomes corrupted;*
• *Specific levels of security clearance for staff processing the data;*
• *Restricting physical access to systems holding personal data;*
• *Network security measures to prevent unauthorised access to electronic systems; or*
• *Restrictions on access to data by staff who do not need to* [sic] *access to that element of the personal held by the controller*".

15.2.5.9 Section 108 sets out an obligation on processors to notify personal data breaches to the controller without undue delay. The controller is, in turn, obliged to notify the Information Commissioner—but only of serious personal data breaches, defined as a breach which "*seriously interferes with the rights and freedoms of a data subject*" (s.108(7)). To avoid double reporting, there is no obligation to notify the Commissioner if the breach is reportable under s.231(9) of the Investigatory Powers Act 2016 (s.108(6)). Where a report has to be made, it should be made without undue delay—and if this takes longer than 72 hours, then the controller should also advise the Commissioner of the reasons for delay. There is no obligation to notify data subjects.

15.2.6 Data transfer to third countries

15.2.6.1 The data transfer rules are set out at s.109: a controller may not transfer personal data to a country or territory outside the UK or to an international organisation, unless the transfer is a necessary and proportionate measure carried out for the purposes of the controller's statutory functions or for other purposes provided for, in relation to the controller, in s.2(2)(a) of the Security Service Act 1989 or section 2(2)(a) or 4(2)(a) of the Intelligence Services Act. The Explanatory Notes para.282 note that this allows transfers where necessary:

- in the case of the security service, for prevention and detection of serious crime or for the purpose of criminal proceedings;

- in the case of the secret intelligence service, in the interests of national security or as above; and

- in the case of GCHQ for the purpose of criminal proceedings.

15.2.7 Enforcement and claims

15.2.7.1 As one would expect, the usual enforcement approaches are modified where national security concerns arise. In relation to claims by individuals, the usual provisions by which individuals can enforce their rights via the courts in Pt 6 of the DPA 2018 are disapplied (ss.110(1)–(2)). Instead, individuals' rights to enforce compliance are exclusively those set out in Pt 4 of the DPA 2018.

15.2.7.2 Claims for compensation can be made, however, under s.169. As with the law enforcement related provisions, where joint controllers are concerned, a joint controller will only be liable for compensation if it is, in fact, responsible for compliance with the relevant provision which has been contravened.

15.2.7.3 There is an ability for the intelligence services to claim an exemption from all of the Commissioner's enforcement powers at ss.110(2)(d) and (e), where national security is concerned. There is also an exemption from all of the offences in the DPA 2018 where national security is raised (s.110(2)(e)(ii).

15.2.8 Exemptions

Exemptions from data protection obligations applicable to intelligence services where required to safeguard national security

15.2.8.1 There are wide exemptions from the Information Commissioner's enforcement powers and the offences under the DPA 2018, where this is required for the purpose of safeguarding national security. There are also exemptions relating to:

- the data protection principles (other than the lawful processing obligation);
- the rights of data subjects; and
- the obligation to communicate serious personal data breaches to the Information Commissioner.

Exemptions from other provisions in the DPA 2018

15.2.8.2 There are exemptions from the provisions in Pt 3 (law enforcement processing) where required for purposes of safeguarding national security. Here the exemptions are set out at s.79(1) and they apply in relation to individuals' rights of information, access, to be told about action taken in relation to rectification and access, and to be told of personal data breaches.

15.2.8.3 In the case of the applied GDPR, there are exemptions (art.26(2)) from all data protection principles (except for the lawful processing obligation); data subject rights; obligations to give notice of personal data breaches to individuals; data transfer restrictions; the tasks and powers of the Information Commissioner; the criminal offences under the Act and the provisions allowing representative bodies to bring proceedings on behalf of individuals. Where the GDPR does not apply, individuals have rights to appoint a representative body to make complaints to and about the Information Commissioner, but not to bring any claim for compensation, so an exemption from this provision is less significant here (s.187(2)).

15.2.8.4 Although there is no exemption from the lawful processing obligation under the applied GDPR, s28(1) provides that art.9(1) of the applied GDPR (prohibition on processing of special category data) does *not* prohibit processing of personal data to the extent this is carried out for purposes of safeguarding national security or for defence purposes and with appropriate safeguards for the rights and freedoms of individuals. Section 28(2) also disapplies the usual security standard set out at art.32 of the applied GDPR, instead introducing a general principle that the controller or processor must implement "*security measures appropriate to the risks arising from the processing of the personal data*"—in other words, the security standards which apply to national security related processing are those set out in Pt 4 (**15.2.4.7**). Lastly, the reader may have noted that there are no exemptions for national security purposes in Schs 2–5 (the schedules dealing with the exemptions from the GDPR). This is, presumably, on the basis that the GDPR would not apply to such processing in any event.

The procedure for claiming a national security exemption

15.2.8.5 The procedure for the exemption to apply is set out at s.27 in the case of the applied GDPR, s.79 in the case of law enforcement processing and s.111 in the case of processing by the intelligence services. The procedure is essentially the same in each case, consisting of the issue of a Ministerial Certificate. In the case of the applied GDPR, the certificate can be issued either where required to safeguard national security *or* for defence purposes. The Explanatory Notes to the DPA 2018 note that this is

> "*intended to ensure the continued protection, security and capability of the armed forces and the civilian staff which support them, not just their combat effectiveness*".

Examples of activities which could be covered are given, ranging from military intelligence, assessment of performance of troops, data about former forces personnel who are in the reserves and use of biometric data to maintain security of sites. Certificates may either relate to a specific restriction or may identify the personal data or restriction by way of a general description. Certificates may also have prospective effect. Certificates may be issued by a Minister who is a member of the Cabinet, the Attorney General or the Advocate General for Scotland; they can be issued by way of a general description and can have prospective effect.

15.2.8.6 Certificates are conclusive evidence that an exemption is required on national security grounds. They can be challenged by an appeal to the Information Tribunal. Challenges can be brought directly by a person directly affected by the certificate. The Tribunal's role is to determine if there were reasonable grounds for issuing the certificate (i.e. the Tribunal does not substitute its own decision for that of the Minister). In addition, if there are proceedings where a controller claims that a certificate of general application applies, then any party to the proceedings may appeal the certificate to the Upper Tribunal which will then decide if the certificate applies or not. There is useful discussion of cases involving national security certificates in Rosemary Jay & Angus Hamilton, *Data Protection Law & Practice*, 4th edn (London: Sweet & Maxwell), paras 15–07 to 15–19.

15.2.8.7 There is a requirement at s.130 for Ministers to send copies of all national security certificates to the Information Commissioner. The Commissioner must then publish a record of the certificate (and keep this open to the public)—containing the name of the issuing Minister, the date issued and the text of the certificate. The text must not be published if the Minister determines and notifies the Commissioner that publication would be against the interests of national security, contrary to the public interest, or would jeopardise the safety of any person. Ministers must advise the Commissioner if a certificate is revoked.

Non-national security exemptions for the intelligence services

15.2.8.8 There are additional exemptions for the intelligence services which are set out at Sch.11. These do *not* relate to processing for national security purposes, so do not benefit from the national security certificate approach described above. These exemptions cover:

- data processed for the prevention and detection of crime;
- information required to be disclosed by law or in connection with legal proceedings;
- parliamentary privilege;
- prejudice to judicial proceedings;
- data processed to confer Crown honours and dignities;
- data where compliance would prejudice the combat effectiveness of the armed forces;
- prejudice to the economic well-being of the UK;
- legal professional privilege or duties of confidentiality owed by a lawyer to a client;
- records of intentions of the controller which would prejudice negotiations;
- confidential references given by the controller;
- exam scripts and marks;
- processing for scientific and historical research purposes, for statistical purposes and for archiving in the public interest (in each case in line with safeguards in Sch.11).

15.2.8.9 The exemptions apply to the data protection principles (except lawful processing); data subject rights and the obligation to report serious personal data breaches to the Information Commissioner.

APPENDIX 1

Privacy, Data Protection and the International Dimension

1. The right to privacy
2. The right to data protection and European data protection legislation
3. The OECD guidelines

1 THE RIGHT TO PRIVACY

1.1 International conventions recognise the right to privacy as a fundamental human right. Article 12 of the Universal Declaration of Human Rights provides that:

> *"No one shall be subjected to arbitrary interference with his privacy, family, home or correspondence, nor to attacks upon his honour and reputation. Everyone has the right to the protection of the law against such interference or attacks."*

1.2 The European Convention for the Protection of Human Rights and Fundamental Freedoms (usually called simply "The European Convention on Human Rights") similarly states, in art.8 that:

> *"(1) Everyone has the right to respect for his private and family life, his home and his correspondence.*
>
> *(2) There shall be no interference by a public authority with the exercise of this right except such as is in accordance with the law and is necessary in a democratic society in the interests of national security, public safety or the economic well-being of the country, for the prevention of disorder or crime, for the protection of health or morals, or for the protection of the rights and freedoms of others."*

1.3 The UK transposed the European Convention on Human Rights directly into law by the Human Rights Act 1998 (HRA 1998), with the articles of the Convention which detail the rights set out in Sch.1 to that Act.

1.4 The HRA 1998 generally only obliges public authorities (which include any organisation that performs public functions, including courts and tribunals, but excluding Parliament itself) to comply with convention rights. However, so far as the right to privacy is concerned, the courts have confirmed that this can be raised in disputes between purely private parties. This was confirmed by Lord Nicholls of Birkenhead in the *Campbell* case (**3.3.1.1.5**):

> "*... the values underlying articles 8 and 10 are not confined to disputes between individuals and public authorities*".

1.5 The right to privacy is particularly relevant to organisations which wish to monitor staff emails, phone calls or other activity (**14.2**).

1.6 There is a significant overlap between data protection and the right to privacy. However, the two may not necessarily be identical. Data protection is concerned with use of information, whereas privacy is not just concerned with information—it covers other invasions of personal space. The case of ***Wainwright v Home Office*** [2003] UKHL 53, for example, considered whether the way in which a prison carried out a strip-search was a breach of the right to privacy.

2 THE RIGHT TO DATA PROTECTION AND EUROPEAN DATA PROTECTION LEGISLATION

2.1 Both the Lisbon Treaty (which entered into force in 2009 and replaces earlier treaties setting out the legal basis for the functioning of the European Union) and the EU Charter of Fundamental Rights now contain an explicit right to protection of personal data, separate from a right to privacy (at arts 16 and 8 respectively).

2.2 The earliest European data protection laws were adopted by the German state of Hesse in 1970 and Sweden, in 1973. France, Germany, The Netherlands and the United Kingdom all adopted data protection laws during the 1970s and 1980s.

2.3 In 1995, the European Union adopted Directive 95/46/EC on the protection of individuals with regard to the processing of personal data and on the free movement of such data (Directive 95/46/EC). The different standards in data protection laws between member states was beginning to restrict flows of data and economic activity, between member states (rec.7) and Directive 95/46 was intended to avoid this by harmonizing member state laws.

2.4 In 2016, Directive 95/46/EC was replaced by the GDPR. The replacement of Directive 95/46/EC was prompted by two key motives (explained in recs 6, 7 and 9):

- recognition that the legislation should take account of technological change; and
- recognition that member states had implemented Directive 95/46/EC in quite different ways and that the level of fragmentation was bad for development of online activity.

2.5 European legislation has, therefore, always been concerned both with protecting privacy and with promoting trade—and other interests. As rec.4 to the GDPR notes:

> "*The processing of personal data should be designed to serve mankind. The right to the protection of personal data is not an absolute right; it must be considered in relation to its function in society and be balanced against other fundamental rights, in accordance with the principle of proportionality. This Regulation respects all fundamental rights... in particular the respect for private and family life, home and communications, the protection of personal data, freedom of thought, conscience and religion, freedom of expression and information, freedom to conduct a business, the right to an effective remedy and to a fair trial, and cultural, religious and linguistic diversity.*"

2.6 There are also other EU laws on data protection:

- Directive 2002/58/EC concerning the processing of personal data and the protection of privacy in the electronic communications sector (the Privacy Directive). It sets out data protection rules for the electronic communications sector. It has particular relevance to direct marketing and is considered further at **7.4**;
- Directive 2016/680 on the protection of natural persons with regard to the processing of personal data by competent authorities for the purposes of the prevention, investigation, detection or prosecution of criminal offences or the execution of criminal penalties, and on the free movement of such data, and repealing Council Framework Decision 2008/977/JHA (the "Law Enforcement Directive" or "LE Directive"). The LE Directive came into force on 6 May 2018 and is implemented by the UK by the DPA 2018. The LE Directive is considered further in **15.1**. **Chapter 2** contains more background on the relationship between the GDPR, the LE Directive, UK rules on personal data processing by the intelligence services and other data protection rules (see **2.4**);
- Regulation 2018/1725 on the protection of natural persons with regard to the processing of personal data by the Union institutions, bodies, offices and agencies and on the free movement of such data, and repealing Regulation 45/2001 and Decision No.1247/2002. The Regulation sets out data protection rules which apply to EU bodies. As it is unlikely to be relevant to readers, we have not considered it further.

2.7 Readers should also be aware of the Council of Europe Convention for the Protection of Individuals with regard to Automatic Processing of Personal Data (commonly referred to as Convention 108). The Council of Europe is a body which is older than and distinct from the European Union and now comprises almost all European states—a much wider group than the EU). It opened

Convention 108 for signature in 1981. Convention 108 has also been acceded to by some non-European countries—for example Uruguay acceded to it in 2013. The UK Government passed the Data Protection Act 1984 in order to fulfil its obligations under Treaty 108.

2.8 The Council of Europe updated Convention 108 in parallel with the negotiations to adopt the GDPR and it is consistent with the GDPR. Convention 108 is generally less detailed, leaving more scope for variation by signatories. For example, Convention 108 makes provision for individual rights, including rights of access, but it does not include a right to data portability. It also requires that personal data may only be processed with the individual's consent or in accordance with law, but it does not prescribe the basis for processing in further detail. The UK signed the modernised Convention 108 on 10 October 2018.

2.9 The European Convention on Human Rights, Convention 108 and the GDPR contain consistent and overlapping provisions. A very useful Handbook on European data protection law (2018 edition) has been prepared jointly by the EU Agency for Fundamental Rights, the Council of Europe (and the Registry of the European Court of Human Rights) and the European Data Protection Supervisor. It summarises requirements and cases across all three (and other associated) sources of law and the start of each chapter contains a table which correlates the relevant law and cases. It is a very useful resource—and can be downloaded free from *https://fra.europa.eu/en/publication/2018/handbook-european-data-protection-law* [Accessed 29 May 2019].

3 THE OECD GUIDELINES

3.1 The OECD guidelines governing the protection of privacy and transborder flows of personal data apply beyond Europe. They were adopted in 1980 by the Council for the Organisation for Economic Co-operation and Development (OECD) and were updated in 2013. Unlike Convention 108, the OECD guidelines are not legally binding, although signatories commit to take them into account in domestic legislation.

3.2 The guidelines set out key principles of data protection:

- collection limitation;
- data quality;
- purpose specification and use limitation;
- security safeguards;
- openness;
- individual participation; and
- accountability.

Appendix 2

When are the Parts and Schedules of the DPA 2018 relevant?

	PARTS OF THE ACT	SCHEDULES
General	Part 1: Preliminary Part 5: The Information Commissioner Part 6: Enforcement Part 7: Supplementary and final provisions	12: The Information Commissioner 15: Powers of entry and inspection 16: Penalties 18: Relevant records 19: Minor and consequential amendments 20: Transitional provision
GDPR	Part 2 Chapter 1: Scope and definitions Part 2 Chapter 2: The GDPR	1: Special categories of personal data and criminal convictions etc 2–4: Exemptions etc from the GDPR 5: Accreditaton of certification providers 17: Review of processing of personal data for the purposes of journalism
Applied GDPR	*As for GDPR, plus* Part 2 Chapter 3: The applied GDPR	*As for GDPR, plus* 6: The applied GDPR and the applied Chapter 2
Law enforcement	Part 3: Law enforcement processing	7: Competent authorities 8: Conditions for sensitive processing under Part 3 13: Other general functions of the Commissioner 14: Co-operation and mutual assistance
Intelligence Services	Part 4: Intelligence services processing	9: Conditions for processing under Part 4 10: Conditions for sensitive processing under Part 4 11: Other exemptions under Part 4 13: Other general functions of the Commissioner 14: Co-operation and mutual assistance

APPENDIX 3

ICO Powers of Investigation

Approach	Scope	Comment	Consequence of non-compliance[1]	Procedure[2]	Notice period
No reliance on formal powers	In most investigations, ICO approaches the organisation by correspondence. It sets out what the investigation is about; what information is requested; and what deadlines for reply. The ICO does not exercise formal enforcement powers—rather it "expects" co-operation.		No specific consequences. However, failure to co-operate, or provision of misleading information, will lead to an escalation in enforcement (see below).	No specific procedure.	As specified in correspondence.
Information notice (ss.142–144)	Requires provision of information, where Commissioner reasonably requires this to investigate a breach of data protection legislation. Notice may specify	Regulatory Action Policy notes i.a. the following factors relevant to issue of an information notice: – Risk of harm to individual	*Criminal offence:* knowing or reckless statement which is false in a material respect. *Criminal offence:* destroy or falsify information so	Notice must include the legal basis for notice and why the Commissioner requires the information.	Ordinary notice—time for compliance cannot be before period allowed for appeal and during period of any appeal.

	what is required; format; timing and place for providing information.	– Utility of requiring a formal response within a defined period – Utility of testing responses (as it is an offence to provide misleading information) – Public interest. For urgency, relevant factors include extent to which this may prevent serious harm or serious intrusion; need to prevent falsification of evidence.	as to prevent the Commissioner from inspecting etc. it. Defence if destruction is in the usual course of events.	Notice must state consequence of non-compliance and right to appeal.	Urgency provisions allow Commissioner to require information on 24 hours' notice.
Information order (s.145)	Court order compelling person to provide information required by information notice.	Application to court, but no further procedural information included in the DPA 2018. Failure to comply with a court order punishable as contempt of court.			

Approach	Scope	Comment	Consequence of non-compliance[1]	Procedure[2]	Notice period
	Order to specify form; timing and place for provision of information.				
Assessment notice (s.147)	Notice from the Commissioner requiring controller or processor to permit the Commissioner to assess compliance with legislation i.a. by entering premises, viewing information, taking away copies, observing processing, explaining materials and making personnel available for interview. Notice will specify timescales for compliance (see also notice periods).	Regulatory Action Policy suggests use where ICO has already conducted other investigations and has concluded it is likely there is a breach of the legislation + likelihood of damage or distress to individuals. Another factor would be failure to comply with an information notice within an appropriate time. Triggers for urgent enforcement include need to prevent	Criminal offence to destroy or falsify information so as to prevent the Commissioner from inspecting etc. it. Defence for destruction in the usual course of events.	Notice must state consequence of non-compliance and right to appeal. Urgent notice must include reasons substantiating claim for urgency. Super-urgent notice must include reasons; and explain nature of offence; and the breach must be a substantive breach of the legislation.	Ordinary notice—time for compliance cannot be before period allowed for appeal and during period of any appeal. Urgency provisions allow Commissioner to require compliance on 7 days' notice. Super-urgency provisions allow Commissioner

	Special exemptions for security bodies and certain education bodies.	serious harm or serious intrusion; risk of falsification of materials.		Must not cover domestic premises.	to require compliance on less than 7 days' notice (this could therefore be immediate).
Entry and inspection with warrant (Sch.15)	Can be issued either: 1) In connection with non-compliance and offences under the DPA 2018; or 2) If an organisation has failed to comply with an assessment notice. Allows Commissioner to enter and search premises; to inspect and operate etc equipment, to inspect and operate etc equipment, to inspect and seize equipment; to require copies to be provided; to require persons to provide explanation.		*Criminal offence:* – intentionally to obstruct exercise of a warrant; – to fail, without reasonable excuse, to give required assistance; – knowingly or recklessly to make a statement which is false in a material respect.	Application by Commissioner to judge. Commissioner must provide evidence on oath to satisfy the judge that the conditions on scope are met. Certified copy warrant must be presented by ICO staff and copy left with organisation. ICO must provide receipts for any information removed.	Application on notice to the affected party after the Commissioner has provided 7 days' notice to the occupier of notice at a reasonable tie and occupier has refused, or has not co-operated *or* Judge satisfied that compliance with above conditions would defeat the object of entry;

Approach	Scope	Comment	Consequence of non-compliance[1]	Procedure[2]	Notice period
	Commissioner can exercise reasonable force in executing the warrant. Warrant must be exercised within 7 days of date of issue. Legal privilege exemption does <u>not</u> apply where information relates to intent to further a criminal purpose.				*or* Commissioner has urgent requirement for entry.
Criminal investigations	The procedures above all apply to civil investigations. Breach of the DPA 2018 can lead to criminal proceedings in certain situations (see below). Where the Commissioner suspects a criminal offence has been committed then she follows different procedures (e.g. interviewing under caution).				

	Offences: obstructing the Commissioner in the exercise of a search warrant; falsifying or destroying documents required for an information or assessment notice; knowingly or recklessly misleading the Commissioner (see above); unlawfully obtaining etc personal data (i.e. pretexting); re-identifying pseudonymised data without consent; altering data to prevent disclosure to the data subject. *Self-incrimination protection:* Where information is obtained as part a civil investigation (i.e. one of the mechanisms listed above), then it cannot be used against the organisation in criminal proceedings. There are exemptions which allow information to be used if it is necessary to show that the organisation has itself produced evidence which is inconsistent with the information obtained during a civil investigation, or if it is needed to prove a perjury-type offence.

General principles:
Material where legal advice or litigation privilege could be claimed, relating to advice on data protection, is generally exempt from these powers.
Where data is processed for the "special purposes" (i.e. journalism, literature and artistic purposes), special rules apply.
Where provision of material would infringe parliamentary privilege it is exempt.

1. Non-compliance with any formal action can lead to a monetary penalty (GDPR art.83(6)). Non-compliance with certain formal investigatory powers can be a criminal offence—see below.

2. All "notices" are to be hand delivered or sent by post, to principal office of a corporate body (s.141).

APPENDIX 4

Conditions for Processing Special Category Data

Ref.	Topic	Detail	Policy document + safeguards	Unsuitable consent scenario[1]	Criminal offence variant?	Application to law enforcement authorities
Art.9(2)(a)	Explicit consent	For specified purposes	—	—	Sch.1 Pt 3 para.1. Does not need to be explicit	Does not need to be explicit DPA 2018 s.35(4)
Art.9(2)(b) DPA 2018 Sch.1 Pt 1, Sch.1 Pt 1 para.1	Required by employment or social security or protection law	Carrying out obligations or exercising specific rights of the controller or data subject, in so far as authorised by one of these areas of law	Yes	—	DPA 2018 Sch.1 Pt 1, Sch.1 Pt 1 para.1 applies identically	—
Art.9(2)(c)	Vital interests of data subject or another natural person	Data subject must be incapable of giving consent	—	—	Sch.1 Pt 3 para.30	DPA 2018 Sch.8 para.3 No requirement for data subject to

						be incapable of giving consent
Art.9(2)(d)	Associations and foundations pursuing political, philosophical, religious or trade union purposes	Processing about members, former members or persons in regular contact Only for purposes of the foundation No disclosure without consent of data subject	—	—	Sch.1 Pt 3 para.31	—
Art.9(2)(e)	Manifestly made public by data subject		—	—	Sch.1 Pt 3 para.32	DPA 2018 Sch.8 para.5
Art.9(2)(f)	Legal claims Courts acting in a judicial capacity	Establishment, exercise or defence of claims Includes out of court settlement	—	—	Sch.1 Pt 3 paras 33–34 Condition is broader than that in art.9(2)(f) and retains language from the DPA 1998—covering processing for proceedings, legal advice and	DPA 2018 Sch.8 paras 6–7 As with criminal offence data, language is broader than that in art.9(2)(f)

Ref.	Topic	Detail	Policy document + safeguards	Unsuitable consent scenario[1]	Criminal offence variant?	Application to law enforcement authorities
					which is otherwise necessary to establish, exercise or defend legal rights	
Art.9(2)(h)(h) DPA 2018 Sch.1 Pt 1 paras 2 and 11	Health and social care	Preventive or occupational medicine; diagnosis; provision of care and treatment; management of healthcare and social care systems Processing by persons subject to a duty of confidentiality	—	—	DPA 2018 Sch.1 Pt 1 paras 2 and 11 applies identically	—
Art.9(2)(h)(i) DPA 2018 Sch.1 Pt 1 para.3	Public health purposes in the public interest	By health professionals or others subject to a duty of confidentiality	—	—	DPA 2018 Sch.1 Pt 1 para.3 applies identically	—
Art.9(2)(j) DPA 2018	Archiving, scientific and	Public interest requirement (in GDPR for	—	—	DPA 2018 Sch.1 Pt 1	DPA 2018 Sch.8 para.9

Sch.1 Pt 1 para.4	historical research and statistical purposes	Public interest requirement (in GDPR for archiving; added for others by 2018 Act) Processing must be in accordance with safeguards set out in art.89 and s.19 of 2018 Act			para.4 applies identically	No requirement for research or statistical processing to be in the public interest
CONDITIONS INTRODUCED UNDER ART.9(2)(g) (SUBSTANTIAL PUBLIC INTEREST + UK LAW)						
DPA 2018 Sch.1 Pt 2 para.7	Justice and parliamentary purposes	Administration of justice or exercise of a function of either House of Parliament	Yes	—	DPA 2018 Sch.1 Pt 2 para.7 applies identically	—
DPA 2018 Sch.1 Pt 2 para.8	Equal opportunities monitoring	Identifying or reviewing equality with a view to promoting or maintaining equal opportunity Racial/ethnic origin Religious/philosophical belief Health Sexual orientation Must not be used to take decisions about a particular data subject or be likely to cause	Yes	—	n/a—not one of the specified categories of personal data	—

Ref.	Topic	Detail	Policy document + safeguards	Unsuitable consent scenario[1]	Criminal offence variant?	Application to law enforcement authorities
		substantial damage or substantial damage or distress to an individual Right to object for individuals				
DPA 2018 Sch.1 Pt 2 para.9	Racial and ethnic diversity at senior levels	Promoting or maintaining diversity of individuals with senior positions Racial/ethnic origin must not be likely to cause substantial damage or distress Senior levels is defined	Yes	d)	n/a—not racial or ethnic origin data	—
DPA 2018 Sch.1 Pt 2 para.10	Preventing/detecting unlawful acts	Must be necessary for reasons of substantial public interest	Yes But exception for disclosures to competent authorities or processing in preparation for such a disclosure	b)	Substantial public interest test disapplied	—

DPA 2018 Sch.1 Pt 2 para.11	Protecting the public against dishonesty	Necessary for exercise of a protective function—which is intended to protect the public against dishonesty, malpractice or other seriously improper conduct; unfitness or incompetence; mismanagement in the administration of a body or association; or failures in services provided by a body or association Necessary for reasons of substantial public interest	Yes	b)	Substantial public interest test disapplied	—
DPA 2018 Sch.1 Pt 2 para.12	Regulatory requirements re: unlawful acts and dishonesty	Covers compliance or assisting others to comply Regulatory requirements relating to unlawful acts; dishonesty, malpractice or other seriously improper conduct Regulatory requirements cover legislation, requirements imposed	Yes	c)	Substantial public interest test disapplied	—

Ref.	Topic	Detail	Policy document + safeguards	Unsuitable consent scenario[1]	Criminal offence variant?	Application to law enforcement authorities
		by a person in charge of a function conferred by legislation, or generally accepted principles of good practice relating to a type of body or activity Necessary for reasons of substantial public interest				
DPA 2018 Sch.1 Pt 2 para.13	Journalism and other special purposes	Disclosure of data for journalistic, academic, artistic, or literary purposes In connection with commission of an unlawful act; dishonesty, malpractice or other seriously improper conduct; unfitness or incompetence; mismanagement; failure in services Processing is with a view to publication of	No	—	Substantial public interest test disapplied	—

		the personal data Controller reasonably believes that publication would be in the public interest Necessary for substantial public interest				
DPA 2018 Sch.1 Pt 2 para.14	Preventing fraud	Disclosure or other processing of personal data by or in accordance with arrangements made by an anti-fraud organisation Anti-fraud organisation has the meaning as in s.68 of the Serious Crime Act 2007 ("*any unincorporated association, body corporate or other person which enables or facilitates any sharing of information to prevent fraud or a particular kind of fraud or which has any of these functions as its purpose or one of its purposes*")	Yes	—	DPA 2018 Sch.1 Pt 2 para.14 applies identically	DPA 2018 Sch.8 para.8

Ref.	Topic	Detail	Policy document + safeguards	Unsuitable consent scenario[1]	Criminal offence variant?	Application to law enforcement authorities
DPA 2018 Sch.1 Pt 2 para.15	Suspicion of terrorist financing or money laundering	Necessary for a good faith disclosure under certain sections of the Terrorism Act or Proceeds of Crime Act	Yes	—	DPA 2018 Sch.1 Pt 2 para.15 applies identically	—
DPA 2018 Sch.1 Pt 2 para.16	Patient support and similar groups	Carried out by a not-for-profit body which provides support to those with a disability or medical condition Relates to members of the organisation who are either suffer from the relevant condition, are at risk of so-doing or are relatives or carers of those individuals Relates to racial/ethnic origin; genetic or biometric data; health data; sex life or sexual orientation Is necessary to raise	Yes	d)	Substantial public interest test disapplied	—

		awareness of the condition or to provide support for the condition Is necessary for reasons of substantial public interest				
DPA 2018 Sch.1 Pt 2 para.17	Counselling services	Provision of confidential counselling, advice or other similar services Processing necessary for reasons of substantial public interest	Yes	a) or c) or e)	Substantial public interest test disapplied	—
DPA 2018 Sch.1 Pt 2 para.18	Safeguarding	Processing data about children or vulnerable adults To protect from neglect or physical, mental or emotional harm or to protect well-being Processing of data about particular individuals and types of individuals Processing necessary for reasons of substantial public interest	Yes	a) or c) or e)	Substantial public interest test disapplied	DPA 2018 Sch.8 para.4

Ref.	Topic	Detail	Policy document + safeguards	Unsuitable consent scenario[1]	Criminal offence variant?	Application to law enforcement authorities
DPA 2018 Sch.1 Pt 2 para.19	Safeguarding economic well-being	Processing health data about adults who are less able to protect their economic well-being due to physical or mental injury, illness or disability Necessary for reasons of substantial public interest	Yes	a) or c) or e)	Substantial public interest test disapplied	—
DPA 2018 Sch.1 Pt 2 para.20	Insurance	Processing data about racial/ethnic origin; religious or philosophical beliefs; trade union membership; genetic data or data concerning health for specified insurance purposes Does not cover data about the policyholder or other individuals who will have rights or obligations in respect of the insured person	Yes	d)	Substantial public interest test and specific data category restriction disapplied	—

		Must not be carried out for purposes of measures or decisions relating to the data subject Necessary for reasons of substantial public interest				
DPA 2018 Sch.1 Pt 2 para.21	Occupational pensions	Health data about family members of scheme members Necessary to determine eligibility for, or benefits payable under an occupational pension scheme Processing not for measures or decisions relating to the data subject	Yes	d)	n/a—not health data	—
DPA 2018 Sch.1 Pt 2 para.22	Political parties	Political opinion data by a registered political party, which is necessary for its political activities Must not be likely to cause substantial damage or substantial distress Ability for an individual to serve notice objecting	Yes	—	n/a—not political opinion data	—

Ref.	Topic	Detail	Policy document + safeguards	Unsuitable consent scenario[1]	Criminal offence variant?	Application to law enforcement authorities
DPA 2018 Sch.1 Pt 2 para.23	Elected representatives dealing with requests	By or on behalf of elected representatives (as defined) in connection with their functions Necessary to respond to a request that the representative take action on behalf of the individual	Yes	a) or c) or e) or f)	DPA 2018 Sch.1 Pt 2 para.23 applies identically	—
DPA 2018 Sch.1 Pt 2 para.24	Disclosures to elected representatives	By controllers in response to a request from or on behalf of an elected representative made as set out at para.23	Yes		DPA 2018 Sch.1 Pt 2 para.24 applies identically	—
DPA 2018 Sch.1 Pt 2 para.25	Informing elected representatives about prisoners	Informing members of the House of Commons, National Assembly for Wales or Scottish Parliament about prisoners (including release dates) where the member may not further disclose the information	Yes	—	DPA 2018 Sch.1 Pt 2 para.25 applies identically	—

DPA 2018 Sch.1 Pt 2 para.26	Legal judgments	Publication of, or processing which is necessary for, purposes of publication of, a judgment or decision of a court or tribunal	Yes	—	DPA 2018 Sch.1 Pt 2 para.26 applies identically	—
DPA 2018 Sch.1 Pt 2 para.27	Anti-doping in sport	Processing for anti-doping purposes by a responsible body or disclosures to such a body	Yes—but exception for disclosures to relevant bodies or processing in preparation for such a disclosure	—	DPA 2018 Sch.1 Pt 2 para.27 applies identically	—
DPA 2018 Sch.1 Pt 2 para.28	Standards of behaviour in sport	Measures designed to protect integrity of sport or sporting events Processing necessary for reasons of substantial public interest	Yes	b)	DPA 2018 Sch.1 Pt 2 para.28 applies identically	—

Ref.	Topic	Detail	Policy document + safeguards	Unsuitable consent scenario[1]	Criminal offence variant?	Application to law enforcement authorities
ADDITIONAL CONDITIONS SPECIFIC TO CRIMINAL OFFENCE DATA						
DPA 2018 Sch.1 Pt 3 para.35	Administration of accounts used in commission of indecency involving children	Processing of payment card data (i.e. to cancel an account), where there has been a listed child pornography offence	Yes	—	Specific to criminal offence data only	—

1. Scenario a = tipping off threat; scenario b = consent would prejudice purpose; scenario c = unreasonable to obtain consent; scenario d = reasonable without consent + no objection (see **4.5.6.1** for explanation of these scenarios); scenario e = consent cannot be given in the circumstances; scenario f = processing necessary in the interests of another individual and data subject has unreasonably withheld consent.

APPENDIX 5

Direct Marketing Requirements

Rules for direct marketing by medium

	Consent	**Sale or negotiation exception**	**Preference service**
Post	–	–	Mailing Preference Service
Individuals[1]			
Corporate[2]	–	–	–
Email and SMS			
Individuals	✓	✓	–
Corporate	–	–	–
Live phone calls			
Individuals[3]	–	–	Telephone Preference Service
Corporate	–	–	Corporate Telephone Preference Service

[1] Individual means a living individual and an unincorporated body of living individuals (e.g. a non-Scots law partnership or an unincorporated association, such as a club).

[2] Corporate subscriber means a company per s.735(1) of the Companies Act 1985 or by royal charter or letters patent, a partnership in Scotland, a corporation sole, or any other body corporate or entity which is a legal person distinct from its members.

[3] Note that there are more restrictive rules for direct marketing calls relating to claims management services and pensions schemes. secondary legislation has been introduced under the Financial Claims and Guidance Act 2018 which amends the Privacy and Electronic Communications (EC Directive) Regulations 2003 and creates an opt in regime for these types of calls. The claims management rules apply to "subscribers" and the pension rules apply to "individuals".

Rules for direct marketing by medium

	Consent	Sale or negotiation exception	Preference service
Automated calls			
Individuals	✓	–	–
Corporate[4]	✓	–	–
Fax			
Individuals	✓	–	Fax preference service (individuals and corporate)
Corporate[5]	–	–	

There is always a right to object to processing of personal data for purposes of direct marketing, in addition to the specific requirements above.

[4] Requirement applies where the subscriber is a corporate body, so applies whether call is made to an individual at the company or to a general number.
[5] See footnote 4.

Appendix 6

Complete List of Exemptions

Exemptions under GDPR

Reference	Art.12 (transparency)	Art.13 (notice – direct)	Art.14 (notice – indirect)	Art.15 (access)	Art.16 (rectification and erasure)	Art.17 (erasure)	Art.18 (restriction)	Art.20 (portability)	Art.21 (right to object)	Art.22 (automated decisions)	Art.34 (notice of data breaches)
Purposes for which controller processes personal data do not require identification of data subject and controller can demonstrate that it is not in a position to identify the data subject (art.11(2))											
Manifestly unfounded/ excessive requests (art.12(5))	Controller may either charge a reasonable fee or refuse to act on the request									–	
Identity of the applicant (art.12(6))	–			May require provision of additional information						–	
Data subject already has the information (arts 13(4) and 14(5))				–							

<table>
<tr><th colspan="12">Exemptions under GDPR</th></tr>
<tr><th>Reference</th><th>Art.12 (trans-parency)</th><th>Art.13 (notice – (direct)</th><th>Art.14 (notice – indirect)</th><th>Art.15 (access)</th><th>Art.16 (rectification and erasure)</th><th>Art.17 (erasure)</th><th>Art.18 (restriction)</th><th>Art.20 (portability)</th><th>Art.21 (right to object)</th><th>Art.22 (auto-mated decisions)</th><th>Art.34 (notice of data breaches)</th></tr>
<tr><td>Disproportionate effort/ impossibility (arts 14(5)(b) and 34(3)(c))</td><td colspan="2">–</td><td></td><td colspan="7">–</td><td></td></tr>
<tr><td>Obtaining/disclo-sure of information required by law (art.14(5)(c))</td><td colspan="2">–</td><td></td><td colspan="8">–</td></tr>
<tr><td>Professional secrecy under EU or Member State law requires con-fidentiality (art.14(5)(d))</td><td colspan="2">–</td><td></td><td colspan="8">–</td></tr>
<tr><td>Rights and freedoms of others (arts 15(4) and 20(4))</td><td colspan="3">–</td><td></td><td colspan="3">–</td><td></td><td colspan="3">–</td></tr>
<tr><td>Freedom of expres-sion/legal obligation/ public interest task/ archiving/research/ statistical purposes/ legal claims (art.17(3))</td><td colspan="3">–</td><td>–</td><td></td><td colspan="2">–</td><td>–</td><td colspan="3">–</td></tr>
<tr><td>Exclusions from scope of GDPR (art.2(2))</td><td colspan="11">Regulation (and the DPA) does not apply to processing by a natural person in the course of a purely personal or household activity. For the equivalent exclusion for the applied GDPR, see s.21(3).
Regulation also does not apply to processing of personal data in the course of an activity outside the scope of Union law (art.2(2)(a)); within Chapter 2 of Title V of TFEU; by competent authorities for purposes of law enforcement etc. However, the DPA 2018 does apply to these activities (See Chapter 10, 10.1.2)</td></tr>
</table>

Exemptions under the DPA

These exemptions only apply where the compliance with the relevant GDPR provision would be likely to prejudice, or to prevent, the particular purposes. In the small number of exemptions where this restriction does not apply we have indicated this below. Where the exemption refers to 'preventing' the purpose, this is indicated with an "*"

Heading	**Detail** With the exception of the research, statistics and archiving exemption (Schedule 1, Part 6), the exemptions below all generally contain an exemption from art.5, so far as the provisions of article 5 correspond to the rights and obligations specifically provided for in the exemption.	**Subject information provisions (Arts 13–15)**	**Other individual rights (Arts 16–21)**	**Lawful, fair and transparent processing; Purpose limitation (Art.5(1)(a) and 5(1)(b)**	**Data breach notice (Art.34(1) and (4))**
Sch.2 Pt 1 para.2(1) *Crime and taxation purposes*	Exemption for personal data processed for the purposes of prevention or detection of crime, apprehension or prosecution of offenders, assessment or collection of tax, duty or similar imposition.	Yes	Yes	Yes	Yes
Sch.2 Pt 1 para.2(2) *Crime and taxation purposes (crime and taxation source)*	Exemption where controller 1 can benefit from the exemption and where controller 2 obtains personal data from controller 1 for purposes of discharging statutory functions and processes data for these functions. Exemption applies to the same extent that it would apply to controller 1.	Yes (if the source could rely on this exemption)	–	–	–
Sch.2 Pt 1 para.3 *Crime and taxation risk assessment system**	Exemption for the classification applied to a data subject as part of a risk assessment system operated by a government department, local authority or other authority administering housing benefit, which is operated to assess or collect tax, duties or similar, or to prevent or detect crime or to apprehend or prosecute offenders, where the offence is linked to unlawful use of, or claims for payment out of, public money.	Yes	–	–	–
Sch.2 Pt 1 para.4(1) *Immigration purposes*	Personal data processed to maintain effective immigration control or investigate or detect activities which would undermine this. The exemption only covers certain additional individual rights (erasure, restriction and objection). However, the apparent gaps are probably academic because: – Art.19 (obligation to notify others of erasure or restriction) is academic if there is no erasure or restriction); and	Yes	Some additional rights—see detail	–	–

Exemptions under the DPA

These exemptions only apply where the compliance with the relevant GDPR provision would be likely to prejudice, or to prevent, the particular purposes. In the small number of exemptions where this restriction does not apply we have indicated this below. Where the exemption refers to 'preventing' the purpose, this is indicated with an '*'

Heading	**Detail** With the exception of the research, statistics and archiving exemption (Schedule 1, Part 6), the exemptions below all generally contain an exemption from art.5, so far as the provisions of article 5 correspond to the rights and obligations specifically provided for in the exemption.	**Subject information provisions (Arts 13–15)**	**Other individual rights (Arts 16–21)**	**Lawful, fair and transparent processing; Purpose limitation (Art.5(1)(a) and 5(1)(b)**	**Data breach notice (Art.34(1) and (4))**
	– Art.20 (portability) would not apply in the first place. There is no exemption from art.16 (right to rectification). This seems entirely appropriate: it would seem wrong for an immigration agency to have a right to disregard (valid) requests to correct data.				
Sch.2 Pt 1 para.4(4) *Shared with a recipient which processes for immigration purposes*	Where a controller (controller 1) discloses information relating to the above purposes to another controller, which can rely on the exemption above, then controller 1 can also rely on this—but only to the extent that the recipient could rely on the exemption. This could presumably cover disclosures by an employer to immigration authorities.	Yes (if source could rely on this exemption)	–	–	–
Sch.2 Pt 1 para.5 *Disclosure required by law or in connection with legal proceedings**	Covers personal data which the controller is required, by enactment, to make available to the public; and Disclosures which are required by enactment, rule of law, order of court or tribunal; and Disclosures which are necessary for or in connection with legal proceedings (including prospective proceedings); obtaining legal advice; or are otherwise necessary for purposes of establishing, exercising or defending legal rights.	Yes	Yes	Yes	–
Sch.2 Pt 2 para.7 *Functions designed to protect the public*	Processing by controllers discharging certain functions: – Designed to protect members of the public against dishonesty, malpractice or other seriously improper conduct by organisations involved in financial services,	Yes	Yes	–	–

	or to protect the public against financial loss due to dealing with individuals who have been made bankrupt; – Designed to protect members of the public against other dishonesty, malpractice, seriously improper conduct or other unfitness or incompetence; – Designed to protect against mismanagement etc. of charities; – Designed to secure health and safety and welfare of persons at work, or to protect the health and safety of others as a result of the actions of persons at work; – Designed to protect members of the public against maladministration by or failures in public services provided by public bodies, by the Parliamentary Commissioner for Administration or other listed bodies; or – The Competition and Markets Authority when protecting the public, including by regulating anti-competitive agreements or conduct which is an abuse of a dominant position. The first four categories cover functions conferred by enactment; a function of the Crown, a Minister of the Crown or a government department, or which is of a public nature and is exercised in the public interest.				
Sch.2 Pt 2 para.8 *Audit purposes*	Discharging functions of the Comptroller and Auditor General, the Auditor General for Scotland, the Auditor General for Wales and the Comptroller and Auditor General for Northern Ireland.	Yes	Yes	–	–
Sch.2 Pt 2 para.9 *Bank of England*	Processing by the Bank of England to discharge its functions as a monetary authority, as the Prudential Regulatory Authority or a public function within the meaning of s.349 of the Financial Services and Markets Act 2000.	Yes	Yes	–	–
Sch.2 Pt 2 para.10 *Regulatory functions relating to legal services, the health service and children's services*	Functions of the Legal Services Board, complaints handling functions under the Legal Services Act, the NHS Redress Act 2006, the Health and Social Care (Community and Health Standards) Act 2003, the Children Act 1989 or the Public Services Ombudsman (Wales) Act 2005 or the Social Services and Well-being (Wales) Act 2014.	Yes	Yes	–	–
Sch.2 Pt 2 para.11 *Other regulatory functions*	Functions conferred on other regulators by specified legislation. The regulators include the Information Commissioner and Scottish Information Commissioner and a range of other Ombudsmen, monitoring officers, regulators and authorities.	Yes	Yes	–	–

Exemptions under the DPA

These exemptions only apply where the compliance with the relevant GDPR provision would be likely to prejudice, or to prevent, the particular purposes. In the small number of exemptions where this restriction does not apply we have indicated this below. Where the exemption refers to 'preventing' the purpose, this is indicated with an '*'

Heading	**Detail** With the exception of the research, statistics and archiving exemption (Schedule 1, Part 6), the exemptions below all generally contain an exemption from art.5, so far as the provisions of article 5 correspond to the rights and obligations specifically provided for in the exemption.	**Subject information provisions (Arts 13–15)**	**Other individual rights (Arts 16–21)**	**Lawful, fair and transparent processing; Purpose limitation (Art.5(1)(a) and 5(1)(b)**	**Data breach notice (Art.34(1) and (4))**
Sch.2 Pt 2 para.13 *Parliamentary privilege*	Relevant provisions disapplied where this is required to avoid infringing parliamentary privilege No prejudice test.	Yes	Yes	–	Yes
Sch.2 Pt 2 para.14 *Judicial appointments, independence and proceedings*	Personal data processed to assess suitability for appointment as a QC or personal data processed by individuals, or courts or tribunals acting in a judicial capacity: no requirement to demonstrate that compliance would prejudice the relevant purpose. Provisions also disapplied to the extent that complying would be likely to prejudice judicial independence or judicial proceedings.	Yes	Yes	–	–
Sch.2 Pt 2 para.15 *Crown honours etc.*	Personal data processed to confer crown honours or to assess suitability for certain specified offices (ranging from Church of England appointments, lord lieutenants and the Provost of Eton through to the Astronomer Royal and Poet Laureate). The list of relevant positions can be updated by secondary legislation. No requirement to demonstrate that compliance would be likely to prejudice this purpose.	Yes	Yes	–	–
Sch.2 Pt 3 para.16 *Subject access—rights of others*	Specific exemption from subject access rights where responding to an access request would involve disclosure of information relating to another individual, unless that other individual has consented or it is reasonable in the circumstances to disclose the information without consent. See discussion of this provision in **Ch.6** on individual rights.		–	–	–

Sch.2 Pt 3 para.17 *Subject access—special provisions for health, social and education workers*	Modification of the exemption from subject access where required to protect the interests of another individual where that other person is a health, social or educational worker, where the access request relates to a health, educational or social work record and where the individual has contributed to that record in an official capacity. Where this provision applies, then it is reasonable for the controller to disclose information which relates to the professional without their consent.		–	–	–
Sch.2 Pt 4 para.19 *Legal professional privilege*	Information in respect of which a claim to privilege could be maintained in legal proceedings or, in Scotland, a claim to confidentiality of communications Information in respect of which a duty of confidentiality would be owed by a professional legal adviser to a client of the adviser. No prejudice test (as this would always be the case).	Yes	–	–	–
Sch.2 Pt 4 para.20 *Self incrimination*	No need to comply if this would reveal evidence of the commission of an offence and expose the person to proceedings for that offence. Offences under specified legislation (including the DPA 2018 and laws relating to perjury) do not benefit from this provision. No prejudice test.	Yes	–	–	–
Sch.2 Pt 4 para.21 *Corporate finance*	Processing carried out for corporate finance services (as defined), where compliance would be likely to affect the price of an instrument, or where the relevant person (as defined) reasonably believes that compliance would affect decisions of a person to deal in or subscribe for issue an relevant financial instrument, or to have an effect on business activity or would have a prejudicial effect on the orderly functioning of the financial markets or the efficient allocation of capital in the economy.	Yes	–	–	–
Sch.2 Pt 4 para.22 *Management forecasts*	Processing for purposes of management forecasting or planning in relation to a business or other activity.	Yes	–	–	–
Sch.2 Pt 4 para.23 *Negotiations*	Processing consisting of records of intentions of the controller in relation to negotiations with the individual.	Yes	–	–	–
Sch.2 Pt 4 para.24 *Confidential references*	References given, or to be given, in confidence for the purposes of (or prospective purpose of):	Yes	–	–	–

Exemptions under the DPA

These exemptions only apply where the compliance with the relevant GDPR provision would be likely to prejudice, or to prevent, the particular purposes. In the small number of exemptions where this restriction does not apply we have indicated this below. Where the exemption refers to 'preventing' the purpose, this is indicated with an '*'

Heading	**Detail** With the exception of the research, statistics and archiving exemption (Schedule 1, Part 6), the exemptions below all generally contain an exemption from art.5, so far as the provisions of article 5 correspond to the rights and obligations specifically provided for in the exemption.	**Subject information provisions (Arts 13–15)**	**Other individual rights (Arts 16–21)**	**Lawful, fair and transparent processing; Purpose limitation (Art.5(1)(a) and 5(1)(b)**	**Data breach notice (Art.34(1) and (4))**
	– Education, training or employment – Placing the data subject as a volunteer – Appointment to any office – Provision by the data subject of any service No prejudice test.				
Sch.2 Pt 4 para.25 *Exam scripts and marks*	Information recorded by candidates during an exam – no prejudice test. Marks or other personal data processed to determine results of in consequence of determining results – time period for provision of information is altered where this would otherwise mean that results would have to be provided earlier than the planned announcement. The date for disclosure becomes 40 days beginning on the announcement of results or when the question arises.	Yes	–	–	–
Sch.2 Pt 5 para.26 *Journalistic, academic, artistic and literary purposes*	Broad exemption from all data subject rights (other than automated data processing); all data protection principles; lawful bases for processing; notice of data breaches to the individual; data transfer restrictions; consultation with the Information Commissioner on high risk processing; co-operation and consistency mechanism. Applies where processing is with a view to publication for the special purposes; where controller reasonably believes publication would be in the public interest; and where controller reasonably believes compliance would be incompatible the special purposes.				
Sch.2 Pt 6 paras 27–28 *Research and statistics*	Data processed for archiving in the public interest; scientific or historical research and statistical purposes, in accordance with safeguards at Art.89(1) and s.19 of the DPA 2018 are exempt from most individual rights. For research and statistics, results must not be published in identifiable form.	Yes (only includes subject access rights)	Yes (but only in respect of arts 16, 18	See notes	–

	No derogation from purpose limitation, but GDPR disapplies this so a derogation is not needed. Special condition for processing personal data for these purposes available at Sch.1 Pt 1 para.4.		and 21 for research and statistics) and arts 16, 18, 19, 20 and 21 for archiving in the public interest		
Sch.3 Pt 2 para.3 *Health data processed by a court*	Data concerning health, supplied in a report or other evidence to a court and processed by a court in the course of certain specified proceedings (broadly, related to family, adoption, or children's and young person's hearings), where the rules for those proceedings provide that the data may be withheld. No prejudice test.	Yes	Yes	-	–
Sch.3 Pt 2 para.4 *Requests by persons on behalf of data subjects*	Requests for data concerning health, by someone with parental responsibility for or appointed by the court to manage the affairs of the data subject, but where the health data was provided by the data subject or obtained in the course of examination or investigation of the data subject and the data subject either had expectation that the data would not be disclosed or where the data subject has expressly indicated it should not be disclosed. The bar on disclosure is lifted if the data subject says there is no longer an expectation against disclosure. No prejudice test.	Yes	Yes	–	–
Sch.3 Pt 2 paras 5–6 *Health data and serious harm*	Exemption from subject access in respect of health data where releasing would be likely to cause serious harm to the physical or mental health of the data subject or another individual. Only a health professional may rely on the exemption. A controller which is not a health professional may not disclose health data as part of an access request unless the controller has first obtained an opinion from the appropriate health professional that the serious harm test is not met. No prejudice test.		–	–	-

Exemptions under the DPA

These exemptions only apply where the compliance with the relevant GDPR provision would be likely to prejudice, or to prevent, the particular purposes. In the small number of exemptions where this restriction does not apply we have indicated this below. Where the exemption refers to 'preventing' the purpose, this is indicated with an '*'

Heading	**Detail** With the exception of the research, statistics and archiving exemption (Schedule 1, Part 6), the exemptions below all generally contain an exemption from art.5, so far as the provisions of article 5 correspond to the rights and obligations specifically provided for in the exemption.	**Subject information provisions (Arts 13–15)**	**Other individual rights (Arts 16–21)**	**Lawful, fair and transparent processing; Purpose limitation (Art.5(1)(a) and 5(1)(b)**	**Data breach notice (Art.34(1) and (4))**
Sch.3 Pt 3 para.9 *Social work data processed by a court*	Social work data (as defined), supplied in a report or other evidence to a court and processed by a court in the course of certain specified proceedings (broadly, related to family, adoption, or children's and young person's hearings), where the rules for those proceedings provide that the data may be withheld. No prejudice test.	Yes	Yes	–	–
Sch.3 Pt 3 para.10 *Requests by persons on behalf of data subjects*	Requests for social work data, by someone with parental responsibility for or appointed by the court to manage the affairs of the data subject, but where the health data was provided by the data subject or obtained in the course of examination or investigation of the data subject and the data subject either had expectation that the data would not be disclosed or where the data subject has expressly indicated it should not be disclosed. The bar on disclosure is lifted if the data subject says there is no longer an expectation against disclosure. No prejudice test.	Yes	Yes	–	–
Sch.3 Pt 3 para.11 *Social work data and serious harm*	Exemption from subject access in respect of social work data where releasing would be likely to cause serious harm to the physical or mental health of the data subject or another individual. No prejudice test.		–	–	–
Sch.3 Pt 3 para.12 and Pt 4 para.20 *Data from the Principal Reporter in Scotland*	Applies where a social work or education authority in Scotland holds personal which originated from or was supplied by the Principal Reporter pursuant to its statutory duties, and where the data subject would not be entitled to receive that data from the Principal Reporter. Controller must inform the Principal Reporter that the request has been received and may not		–	–	–

	release the data unless the Principal Reporter confirms that doing so will not be likely to cause serious harm to the data subject or another individual.				
Sch.3 Pt 4 para.18 *Education data processed by a court*	Education data (as defined), supplied in a report or other evidence to a court and processed by a court in the course of certain specified proceedings (broadly, related to family, adoption, or children's and young person's hearings), where the rules for those proceedings provide that the data may be withheld. No prejudice test.	Yes	Yes (not art.19)	–	–
Sch.3 Pt 4 para.19 *Education data and serious harm*	Exemption from subject access in respect of education data where releasing would be likely to cause serious harm to the physical or mental health of the data subject or another individual. No prejudice test.		–	–	–
Sch.3 Pt 5 para.21 *Child abuse data*	No obligation to provide information as to whether the data subject has been the subject of, or may be at risk of, child abuse where the request relates to a child or vulnerable adult and is made by someone with parental authority or who has been appointed by the court to look after the affairs of that person. Does not apply in Scotland. No prejudice test.		–	–	–
Sch.4	Restriction of subject access rights, where provision of the data would be prohibited by other listed legislation. The legislation relates to human fertilisation and embryology, adoption records and reports, statements of special educational needs, parental order records and reports and information provided by the Principal Reporter for children's hearings.		–	–	–
s.26 *National security and defence*	Data processed for the purpose of safeguarding national security or defence purposes; provision for Ministerial certificate. Exemption relevant for the applied GDPR. Extensive exemptions from: – principles – lawful processing and rules for special category data – data subject rights – notification of data breaches to the Information Commissioner – data transfer rules – most provisions relating to enforcement by the Commissioner – offences		See notes		

PRECEDENT 1

Template Employee Privacy Notice[1]

See **6.4.1.1**

1

[*Organisation*] processes personal data about you and is a data controller for this personal data. The categories of personal data we process are:

- [information to identify you—such as your name, picture, home address and contact details and identification numbers;
- information relating to right to work checks;
- information about you or about other family members to provide benefits;
- time and attendance information;
- information about any grievance and complaints;
- information about your role and office location;
- information about compensation, benefits and expenses to allow us to pay you;
- information about experience and education;
- your contract and other legal information;
- records of communications, where permissible;
- information concerning performance, career plans, conduct and, where permissible about violation of laws or breach of company policies;
- medical leave and related information; and
- information about trade union affiliation].

[1] The privacy notice which a controller provides must be accurate and must be specific to the processing which the controller undertakes. Accordingly, it is difficult to provide a 'standard' or template notice. It is often easier to draft a notice when an example is available to show how others have approached the task and the template is provided for this purpose.

We will keep this information, together with data retained from the application and selection process, for the course of the employment relationship and, to the extent permitted, after termination of employment. Our retention policy has more information about this and is available at [ ].

We process this personal data for the following purposes:

- Where the processing is necessary for us to administer our contract with you: This includes recruiting and hiring; administration of payroll and benefits, absence, insurance, occupational health; management of expenses; and handling disciplinary matters and grievances.
- Where the processing is for a legitimate interest of ours, as further listed here: As required to manage our business, including undertaking performance and talent management, managing appraisals and assessments; providing access to our offices; management of our IT systems and infrastructure; to provide company directories and communication services such as e-mail, telephone and internet access. This also includes protecting the security of our premises, assets, systems, and intellectual property and enforcing company policies, including monitoring communications as permitted by law.
- Where the processing is necessary for us to comply with legal obligations or to protect our interests and legal rights, including in connection with legal claims, regulatory and investigative purposes (including disclosure of such information in connection with litigation); and
- With your consent: we collect your picture for use with your contact details in our directory.

We may provide you with more specific notices for some of the processing described above and, if we require your consent, will ask for this at the time we collect your personal data.

Personal data will primarily be processed by employees in Human Resources, IT and finance, and facilities departments. Personal data will be transferred to [*organisation*] Incorporated in the US. The US does not benefit from any European Commission adequacy decisions. We use European Commission approved Standard Contract Clauses to safeguard your personal data. You can find out more information about these Clauses, and obtain a copy of them, by contacting us as set out below.

Personal data may be shared with government authorities and/or law enforcement officials if required for the purposes above and if required for the protection of our legitimate interests. Personal data will also be shared with third party service providers, who will process it on our behalf. These third parties include payroll providers, IT service providers, medical insurance providers, auditors etc.

You have the right to access, correct, erase or restrict our processing of personal data that relates to you or to ask us to pass some data to another organisation in a structured and machine-readable format. You may also have rights to object to the processing of personal data and to request an explanation about the processing or withdraw any consent you have provided. These rights can be exercised by contacting [ ]. There are exceptions to these rights and they may be limited in some situations. For example, access may be denied if making the information available would unfairly reveal personal data about another person or if we are legally prevented from disclosing the information. We are not required to delete or restrict personal data if we need it to administer our contract with you.

Where we collect personal data to administer our contract with you or to comply with our legal obligations, this is mandatory and we will not be able to manage the employment relationship without this information. In all other cases, provision of the requested personal data is optional, but not providing it may affect your ability to participate in certain programmes or systems, where the information is needed for those purposes. For example, you may not be able to participate in a team activity if you choose not to provide the relevant information.

If you have any questions, you can contact your data protection officer by [details]. If you have unresolved concerns you also have the right to complain to data protection authorities in the country where you live, work or where you consider that a breach has occurred.

PRECEDENT 2

Procedures for Dealing with Individual Rights Requests

See **6.1.4.6, 6.5.1.2, 6.5.3.2**

2.1 INTRODUCTION

This Individual Rights Policy ("Policy") sets out the procedures which [*organisation*] must follow to ensure that we meet individuals rights under data protection legislation.

When responding to requests from individuals who exercise their rights, we must:

- respond in a way which does not prejudice the rights of others, where the legislation allows us to take this into account;
- provide personal information to individuals in a secure way; and
- keep appropriate records of the way we have responded to individuals who exercise their rights, so that we can explain our approach if required by the Information Commissioner or at court.

The [Privacy Office/Legal team/etc.] will respond to requests made by individuals concerning the rights set out below in section 3, whether internal (i.e. from a [*organisation*] employee/volunteer] or external (from a [customer/client/etc.]. [*Drafting Note: as an alternative, a company may want the HR team to handle employee individual rights requests*].

2.2 SCOPE

This Policy applies to [all members of the [*organisation*] group/all [*organisation*] entities that process personal information from individuals residing in the European Union].

2.3 INDIVIDUAL RIGHTS

- Data protection legislation grants individuals the following rights when we process their personal information: to be told if personal information about them is being processed and to be given a copy of such personal information;

- to correct inaccurate personal information;
- to be given a copy, in a portable format, of personal information which they have provided or to have such information transferred direct to another organisation, where the personal information is processed:
    - o with their consent; or
    - o to perform a contract with the individual;
- to object to processing:
    - o for purposes of direct marketing, including profiling for purposes of direct marketing;
    - o where the lawful basis for the processing is that it is necessary for [our or a third party's legitimate interests]/[a task which we perform in the public interest or when we exercise official authority]; or
    - o for scientific of historical research purposes or statistical purposes;
- to require their personal information to be erased or to restrict our processing of their personal information; and
- to contest any automated decision which has legal or similarly significant effects, to explain his or her specific situation in respect of such decisions and to ask us to reconsider ensuring that there is human involvement in the decision.

2.4 USING THIS POLICY

This Policy comprises:

- a chart which shows the steps required in all individual rights requests and how they apply to each request;
- template documentation:
    - o for subject access requests;
    - o for checking the identity of the individual and obtaining information to assist in locating personal information[1];
    - o instructing others to assist in providing relevant personal information;
- guidance on reviewing the personal information, including checking with

[1] Controllers will also need to check the identity of individuals who exercise other rights and will need to locate personal data which is processed about them. It is more difficult to provide template documentation for other individual rights, as what is required will vary more significantly by organisation. For example, as portability only applies to automated processing of data which has been provided by the individual and which is processed based on consent or to fulfil a contract, it is probably more likely to be held in central systems and a controller may automate the process of retrieving and porting data, meaning that the documentation to locate and review information may not be necessary at all. We have, however, provided sample responses for all individual rights. Even though the actual responses may vary significantly, it can still be useful to see a sample of such a response.

other individuals if the information also relates to them and checking with health care professionals if the information consists of health information;

- template letters:
  - o providing the information to the individual;
  - o responding to a request to correct personal information;
  - o responding to a request to port personal information;
  - o responding to a request to stop processing personal information;
  - o responding to a request to erase or restrict processing of personal information; and
  - o responding to a request to reconsider a significant decision which has been taken using entirely automated individual decision-making techniques.

2.5 EXCEPTIONS

Exceptions to this Policy may be made only where permitted by law and where a compelling business interest exists. Exceptions must be approved in advance by one of the following [in consultation with the Data Protection Officer]:

- [Head of Privacy/CPO/etc.] (for any exception)
- General Counsel (for any exception)

2.6 ADMINISTRATION

The Policy forms part of the [*organisation*]'s data protection policy, which can be found at [insert intranet link].

The Data Protection Officer owns this policy and must approve any changes to it.

Version History

1.0	[Date]	[Author]	[Description of change]

2.7 Process for Individual Rights Requests

	Access	Rectification	Portability	Objection	Erasure	Restriction	Automated decision making
1. Record-keeping: Identity of individual; date received; due date for response	✓	✓	✓	✓	✓	✓	✓
2. Check identity	✓	✓	✓	✓	✓	✓	✓
3. Locate personal information May include contacting departments with local copies of the data and data processors Keep records of approach to searching	✓	✓	✓	✓	✓	✓	N/A
4. Review personal information and consider exemptions Keep records of approach to applying exemptions	✓	✓	Also consider if right applies in the first place				

5. Prepare copy of personal information to provide to individual Keep records confirming information provided and copy of correspondence	✓	N/A	Or to another controller if requested to do this	N/A	N/A	N/A	N/A
6. Reply to individual If you do not fulfil request, you must provide reasons and explain there is a right to complain to the Information Commissioner and to the courts	Response must contain additional information	✓	✓	✓	✓	✓	Provide meaningful information about logic involved, rather than a copy of the data
7. Notify recipients of the personal information	N/A	✓	N/A	N/A	✓	✓	N/A

ANNEX 1: PRO-FORMA SUBJECT ACCESS REQUEST FORM

[Organisation] **LIMITED**

REQUEST TO ACCESS INFORMATION PURSUANT TO DATA PROTECTION LEGISLATION

Please complete this form if you would like [*organisation*] to confirm if we process personal information relating to you and to provide you with a copy of the information that we hold about you, together with certain supplemental explanatory information. The information that we request in this form will enable us to find the personal information, which you request. Please complete as many sections of this form as are relevant to you.

Your details:

Name: ....

Address: ....

Date: ....

1. Information about services that [*organisation*] has provided to you.

If you are a client of [*organisation's*] and would like to see information that we hold about you, please complete this section.

1.1 Please provide a brief description of the services provided (including dates):

....

....

1.2 Which offices and personnel were involved?

....

1.3 Please provide any [*organisation*] reference numbers (these are likely to be in the following form: [*insert sample number*])

. . . .

2. Marketing information

If you receive direct marketing from [*organisation*] and if you would like to receive a copy of any personal information we process about you in relation to this, please tick here [ ].

If you no longer wish to receive direct marketing from us, please tick here [ ].

3. Billing and account queries

If we hold information about you for billing purposes and you would like to receive a copy of this please complete this section.

3.1 For which period would you like to see information?

. . . .

3.2 Please provide details of any invoice numbers.

. . . .

3.3 Please provide details of [*organisation*] offices and personnel with whom you have been in contact on billing matters.

. . . .

4. Emails

Please complete this section if we hold information about you in emails and you would like to see this.

4.1 During what period would the emails have been sent?

. . . .

4.2 Please provide details of the senders and the recipients of the emails.

. . . .

4.3 Please describe the likely subject lines/content of the emails.

....

5. Miscellaneous

General Information

5.1 If you have used other names and would like to receive information which relates to these names please provide details of these names. We may need you to provide additional Information to confirm how these names are linked to you.

....

5.2 If you would like to receive other information, which we have not listed above, please provide details of the type of information you would like here. Please note that we may need to ask you further questions about this information to allow us to locate it.

....

5.3 For what period would you like to receive this information?

....

Please send the completed form to the Data Protection Officer, [*organisation*]. In addition, for security reasons, we need to ensure that we send information only to the person to whom it relates. Accordingly, please include a copy of [a recent utility bill, your driving licence or passport[2]] with the form so as to allow us to check your identity. Once we have confirmed your identity, we will delete this information securely.

2 The information requested to check identity should be proportionate. For example, if the information is not of a sensitive or financial nature, it may be appropriate just to ask for password used to identity the individual. For a financial services company, the authorisation process used before instructions are accepted could be used.

ANNEX 2: LOCATING ALL INFORMATION RELEVANT TO A SUBJECT ACCESS REQUEST

Individuals are entitled to know whether or not [*organisation*] is processing personal information about them and to be provided with a copy of this information in most circumstances.

[*Organisation*] could either be processing personal information itself, anywhere in the organisation, or could have arranged for a third party to process personal information on its behalf. [*organisation*]'s record of processing activities contains a list of all recipients of personal information – this will include all data processors and departments in the organisation which process personal information for a particular purpose (as well as other external organisations to whom personal information is provided). The record of processing should be consulted to know which departments and processors to ask to assist. Template letters to departmental data protection co-ordinators and data processors are below.

[The record of processing also contains a list of central systems which should be consulted]/[A list of central systems which should be consulted is maintained by . . .].[3] Information from these central systems can be obtained by contacting [*insert department/title of person responsible*].

[3] The record of processing activities does not need to list systems. However, it can be helpful to include this – both to assist in managing access requests and in being able to address other queries about information in the record.

ANNEX 2A: PRO-FORMA ACCESS REQUEST MEMO TO DATA PROTECTION CO-ORDINATORS

To: [*Insert name of data protection co-ordinator*]

From:

Date:

Re: [*Individual details*]—Data Protection Subject Access Request

We have received a request to provide a copy of all personal information which we hold to this individual. Please would you help me by collating and reviewing any information that your department holds in relation to the individual. There are very tight timescales that the legislation lays down within which we have to provide this information. Accordingly, **please would you provide this information to me by [*date*].**

Relevant information

Please would you obtain all information that your business area holds in relation to the individual—whether on computer, paper files, CCTV or any other medium—other than information held on [*list central systems*], which I already have. In particular, please could you check whether you hold any of the following information: [*insert relevant details of computer/paper databases*]. If you hold information about the individual in other systems, please would you let me have details of these systems so that I may update my records.

Before forwarding the documentation to me, please review it and highlight any of the following:

1. Third party information—these are documents or comments which relate to someone other than the named individual, but whom the individual would be able to identify.
2. Health information—any information which relates to the physical or mental health or condition either of the named individual or any other individual should be flagged. We are obliged to obtain medical approval before releasing this information.
3. Commercially inappropriate material—if you believe there is other information which should not be released to the individual (for example because it shows that there are suspicions of fraud, or because it relates to negotiation/disputes with the individual) then please mark this accordingly. The [*Legal department*] will review this information to see if there

is a lawful basis for withholding it under the legislation. **Please do not delete any information: it is a criminal offence to delete or alter information which should be provided pursuant to a subject access request.** If you do not wish it to be released please highlight it (having first made a separate unedited copy of the information which should be sent separately) so that this is drawn to our attention.

If your business area uses third parties (such as archive companies) to hold information about the policyholder please let me have details.

It is important that the information is sent to me in a secure manner. Please do this by [*insert method—e.g. encrypted email/secure document upload facility*].

If you have any queries relating to this request, please call me.

Thank you for your assistance.

ANNEX 2B: PRO-FORMA ACCESS REQUEST LETTER TO DATA PROCESSORS

[*Address of data processor*]

Dear [*insert name of contact*]

Re: [*insert customer reference*]

We have received a request from this individual for a copy of all information that we hold, or which is processed on our behalf. As you may know the individual is entitled to this data protection legislation.

Accordingly, please would you provide me with a copy of all information that you process for us, either on computer, paper, CCTV or any other medium.

Data protection legislation only allows us a very limited period in which to respond to an individual's request. Accordingly, please would you provide the information by [*date*].

Should you have any queries in relation to this, please do not hesitate to contact me.

Thank you for your assistance.

Yours sincerely

ANNEX 3: THIRD-PARTY INFORMATION PROCEDURES

1. The information disclosed by the subject access request may reveal the identity of another individual—either directly, because that person is named, or because the individual making the request will know independently that the information could only relate to a certain person. The Information Commissioner calls this "third party" information. In this situation there could be a conflict between the data subject's right to information and the third party's right to privacy or other rights. If we decide not to comply with the request (in whole or in part) there may be a breach of the subject access rights under data protection legislation. On the other hand, disclosure of third party information as part of a subject access request may expose us to complaint or action by the third party.

2. Data protection legislation provides that the data controller need not provide information in response to the subject access request unless:

   - the individual has given his/her consent; or
   - it is reasonable to release the information without consent.

   It is worth noting that the Information Commissioner regards "disclosure" as meaning revealing information which is not already known to the data subject.

3. The Data Protection Act 2018 sets out guidance on this balancing test at Schedule 2 Part 3 paragraph 17. This states that, in assessing whether it is reasonable to release information without consent, one must have regard, in particular, to:

   - the type of information that would be disclosed;
   - any duty of confidentiality owed to the third party;
   - the steps which the data controller has taken in order to seek consent;
   - whether the third party is capable of giving consent; and
   - any express refusal of consent by the third party.

4. The steps that should be taken to carry out this balancing exercise are:

   - try and anonymise the information but bear in mind that you may still need to seek consent to release the withheld data;
   - usually try and seek consent, unless this is impractical (for example because the third party cannot be located or because the very act of seeking consent would reveal information about the data subject to the third party—in which case you should ask the data subject if they would want this request to be made);
   - if consent is not given, decide if it is reasonable in all the circumstances

to give access. In deciding this take into account the following points, in addition to those listed above:

- o whether the individual is already likely to be aware of the information;
- o whether the third party is the source of the information and the individual needs to know who s/he is so as to challenge the accuracy of the information;
- o the impact the information has had or is likely to have on actions or decisions affecting the individual; and
- o whether the information relates to a professional, in relation to whom special rules apply (e.g. health professionals).

[*The Legal department can provide more guidance on applying these tests, if needed*].

Procedures

5. The following procedures should be adopted to ensure compliance with the third party information provisions in the Data Protection Act 2018:

   - Ask those collating personal information to flag any third party information—either information which names a third party, or from which the individual would be able to infer the identity of the third party.
   - If the information is already known to the individual or is in the public domain then release it. (This would mean that all information supplied by the individual may be released).
   - Does the information relate to a third party in a business capacity? In this case, unless the information is of a particularly sensitive nature, so that its release would be likely to harm the third party, then the information should be released.
   - In all other situations, the individual should be informed that information cannot be released without the consent of the third party. The individual should be asked to confirm that it is in order to contact the third party to ask for consent. This will mean giving details of the individual to the third party.
   - If the individual gives consent, the third party should be approached for consent.
   - If the third party gives consent, the information must be released.
   - If the third party does not give consent, the information should usually be withheld unless this would have a substantial adverse impact on the individual and it would be reasonable in all the circumstances to release without consent.

ANNEX 3A: PRO-FORMA PARAGRAPH TO BE INCLUDED IN LETTER TO INDIVIDUAL

Some of the information that we hold in relation to you also relates to another individual. The Data Protection Act 2018 requires us not to release the information to you without considering the interests of that other individual—in particular, whether or not they have given consent. In order to ask for consent, I would need to advise the third party of your identity and that you have asked for this information. Please let me know if you would like me to proceed with this.

ANNEX 3B: PRO-FORMA LETTER TO THIRD PARTY

[*Name and address*]

Dear [*insert name*]

Re: [*Individual's name*]

I am writing to you in connection with [*insert description of link to individual*].

[*Individual*] has asked [*organisation*] for a copy of the information that we hold in relation to them. Some of this information relates to you as [*insert reason*]. The Data Protection Act 2018 provides that [*organisation*] cannot provide this information to [*individual*] unless it is reasonable in all the circumstances to do so—in particular, taking into account whether you have given consent or not. [I am enclosing a copy of the information for your reference]/[The information consists of [*Insert details*]].

Please would you confirm if you consent to [*organisation*] releasing information that is also about you to [*individual*].

Yours sincerely

ANNEX 4: HEALTH INFORMATION PROCEDURES

The Data Protection Act contains special provisions relating to health, educational and social records. In broad terms, these provide that information must not be released in response to an access request, where doing this would be likely to cause serious harm to the physical or mental health either of the data subject or another person. In addition, the statutory instruments provide that the third party information provisions (which allow information to be withheld which identifies another living individual) do not apply where the individual concerned was a professional responsible for the care of the individual.

Where the individual already knows the medical information, then [*organisation*] may release the information to the individual. However, in all other situations, [*organisation*] must consult with the appropriate medical professional as to whether or not it should release or withhold the information. The appropriate medical professional is the professional responsible for the care to which the records relate. In most cases this is likely to be the individual's GP.

Where an individual requests sight of medical information held on his file but which relates to a third party then the third party information provisions set out Appendix 3 are also relevant. The information may well be confidential to the third party, which is likely to mean that their consent is required before the information may be released.

ANNEX 4A: PRO-FORMA PARAGRAPH TO INCLUDE IN LETTER TO INDIVIDUAL

The information that we hold on file about you includes [*detail of medical information*]. Under data protection legislation, we are required to obtain medical approval before we provide you with a copy of this information. In order to do this, we will need to contact [*your GP*], provide him or her with a copy of the information and ask them to confirm if it is in order for us to forward the material to you.

Please let me know if you would like me to proceed with this [and, if so, advise the name and address of your GP].

ANNEX 4B: PRO-FORMA LETTER TO MEDICAL PRACTITIONER

[*Name and address*]

Dear [*name of medical practitioner*]

Re: [*Name of Individual*]

[*Name of individual*] has advised that you are his general practitioner.

We have recently received a request from [*individual*] for a copy of all information that we hold on file in relation to him or her. As you may be aware, under data protection legislation, where we hold medical information about an individual we are not able to release this information without first checking with the appropriate medical professional. We enclose a copy of the medical information that we hold on file and would be grateful if you would confirm if it is in order for us to release the information, or whether releasing the information would be likely to cause serious harm to the physical or mental health either of the policyholder or any other person.

Thank you for your assistance.

ANNEX 5: EXEMPT INFORMATION PROCEDURES

1. There are a number of exemptions from the need to make information available in response to a subject access request. These cover:

Detail	DPA 2018 reference
Crime and taxation; immigration; disclosures required by law or in connection with legal proceedings	Schedule 2 Part 1
Functions protecting the public or regulatory functions; audit; Bank of England; parliamentary privilege; judicial appointments and legal proceedings; crown honours	Schedule 2 Part 2
Legal privilege; self-incrimination; corporate finance; **management planning; negotiations; confidential references;** exam scripts and marks	Schedule 2 Part 4
Data relating to other individuals (third parties)	Schedule 2 Part 3
Special rules relating to withholding health, social work and education data either from the data subject or from someone making a request on behalf of the data subject Withholding child abuse data from someone making the request on behalf of the child	Schedule 3
Freedom of expression and information	Schedule 2 Part 5
Research, statistics and archiving	Schedule 2 Part 6
National security and defence (likely not in scope for data subject access request: ask for advice)	sections 26, 27 and 28
Requests are manifestly unfounded or excessive (grounds for refusing a request)	GDPR Article 12
Not adversely affect the rights and freedoms of others	GDPR Article 15

2. The exemptions that are likely to be of most practical use are highlighted in **bold.**[4]

3. As they limit individuals' fundamental rights, the exemptions are interpreted narrowly. If [*organisation*] relies on exemptions, it will have to explain to the individual why it has not complied with his or her request. [*organisation*] may also have to explain this to the Information

[4] The organisation may want to provide more detailed guidance on these – this will depend on the level of experience of the person carrying out the review of material.

Commissioner, or to the courts, if the individual makes a complaint or seeks to enforce his or her rights. This means it is important that [*organisation*] documents its approach to application of the exemptions:

- where the request is not met in full because the effort involved in searching would be disproportionate, we must keep a record of:
  - the way the search was carried out – including search terms used;
  - the volume of data returned from the searches undertaken and calculations for the amount of time which would be required to review this information;
  - attempts to alter the search terms so as to enable us to meet the individual's request – including correspondence with the individual asking how the request could be narrowed or the information or processing better identified;
  - sampling of records, to demonstrate that we have checked that search terms are appropriate;
- where the request is not met because it is manifestly unfounded or excessive, then details of all earlier requests and correspondence with the individual should be kept;
- when another exemption is relied on, then we should keep a list of all exemptions relied on and notes to explain the factors considered. If there is a very large volume of material, the notes do not need to relate to each occasion on which an exemption has been applied, but could relate to illustrative examples.
- it is only possible to rely on exemptions if the material has actually been inspected: it is not possible to say that all information a department holds is for purposes of prevention and detection and crime (for example) and therefore must be withheld.
- we must keep a copy of the unedited information returned in the searches and a copy of the information provided to the individual. This should be retained for [insert period] so that we have records to be able to respond to queries or complaints, but which are not retained for longer than is necessary. If a complaint is made, then the records should be kept for so long as the complaint is ongoing and for [insert period] after that.

ANNEX 6A: PRO-FORMA LETTER TO INDIVIDUAL ENCLOSING SUBJECT ACCESS PAPERS

[*Name and address*]

Dear [*individual*]

Re: Data protection—Access Request

Further to your recent subject access request, we confirm that we process personal information relating to you.

[We are enclosing a copy of the information that we hold[5]]/[You may access and download a copy of your data, by going to our secure file transfer site and following these instructions [*insert*]. We want to ensure the security of your data, which is why we use this site to make your data available to you].[6]

In some cases, we have not provided all of the information that we process about you. We have withheld information where: [*insert information about relevant exemptions – for example, it is legally privileged; it also relates to other individuals who have not given consent to us to provide the information to you and where it would not otherwise be reasonable to release the information to you*].

We process your personal information to [*insert purposes*].

The information processed consists of [*insert categories of data – e.g. identification information; financial information; customer service records*].

Your personal information is processed by our [*list departments – e.g. customer service teams*]. We also disclose personal information to third parties who process personal information on our behalf, such as [*insert details – for example, companies providing us with IT support*] and we disclose personal information to [*list other recipients – for example, courier companies to deliver your goods to you/ law enforcement agencies if we are required to do so or if we think this is necessary to protect the rights of others*].

Some of these organisations may be located outside the European Economic Area. Where this is the case [*insert details of adequacy methods under Article 46 of the GDPR – for example, we host personal information on IT systems provided by our parent company, xx, in the United States. xx participates in the EU-US Privacy Shield; when we share personal information with organisations who*

---

5 If the request was made electronically, the information must be provided in commonly used electronic form.

6 Amend depending on how information is provided. Note it must be sent securely.

process the information on our behalf, we put in place standard contract clauses adopted by the European Commission to protect the data].

[The information includes data which we have obtained from [*insert information about data sources – e.g. the electoral register, Companies House, credit reference agencies*[7]].

We keep the personal information for the following periods: [*insert*].

Data protection legislation contains restrictions on organisations which use personal information to take entirely automated decisions, which could significantly affect individuals or have legal effects. We do not carry out this type of processing.[8]

If you consider that any of the personal information should be corrected, or if you object to our processing of the data, or want us to erase or restrict the way we process the personal information, then you may [*contact us at* . . .]. In some circumstances, these rights can be limited – for example if we are required by law to process personal information then it cannot be erased.

If you have a complaint about the way we have processed your personal information, you may contact us at [*insert*]. You may also complain to [court[9] and to] the Information Commissioner (*ico.org.uk*), who is the data protection authority in the United Kingdom.

Yours sincerely,

[7] Credit reference agencies and data vendors may stipulate information that has to be included in correspondence with the individual and in privacy notices. Contracts with them should be checked for this.

[8] If this processing is carried out, then this must be confirmed and meaningful information about the logic involved, the significance and the envisaged consequences of the processing must be provided.

[9] If the organisation has not met the individuals request, then it has to provide information about the right to a judicial remedy (Art.12(4)).

ANNEX 6B: PRO-FORMA LETTER TO INDIVIDUAL ADVISING THAT ADDITIONAL TIME IS NEEDED

[*Name and address*]

Dear [*Individual*]

Re: Data protection—Access Request

We write further to your recent subject access request.

[*organisation*] endeavours to respond to subject access requests within one month. Where necessary, data protection legislation allows organisations additional time to respond to an access request. In this case [*insert reasons linked to complexity or number of requests – e.g. because you have been employed with us for over 15 years, we hold data in numerous systems, many of which are archived. This means that the request is more complex to deal with, because it takes us longer to locate and retrieve your information*]. We will be able to respond fully to your request by [*insert date – which must be no more than 3 months from the date the request was made*].

Yours sincerely,

ANNEX 7: PRO-FORMA LETTER TO INDIVIDUAL MAKING A CORRECTION REQUEST

[*Name and address*]

Dear [*Individual*]

Re: Data protection—request to correct personal information

Further to your recent request, we confirm that we have corrected the personal information we process in relation to you as requested. [*To be included where personal information has been disclosed*] As we explain in our privacy notice, we disclose personal information to other recipients, in particular to third parties who provide services to us, such as [*payroll processing company*] and to [*companies who provide employee benefits and pensions*]. We have also advised these organisations that we have done this. We can provide more information about these recipients: if you would like this, please [contact xxx].

Yours sincerely,

ANNEX 8: PRO-FORMA LETTER TO INDIVIDUAL MAKING A PORTABILITY REQUEST

[*Name and address*]

Dear [*Individual*]

Re: Data protection—request for personal information portability

Further to your recent request, we [attach]/[are making available] a copy of your personal information in a portable format – that is, in a commonly used, structured and machine readable format. [You may access and download a copy of your personal information, by going to our secure file transfer site and following these instructions [*insert*]. We want to ensure the security of your personal information, which is why we use this site to make your information available to you].[10]

To include if not all information processed is in scope for portability; reasons given are illustrative only: You have asked that we make available all the personal information that we process about you in this way. Some of the information that we process about you is [held in paper format/created by [*organisation*]/ [processed to meet our legal obligations]. Data protection legislation provides that this type of information does not have to be provided in portable format. However, if you are interested in a copy of this information in a different format, we can provide this to you. This would still be in electronic format, but would not be structured and machine readable [and we would not provide it direct to another data controller]. If you would like information in this format, please [complete our subject access request form here]/[other contact details].

To include if information has been withheld because an exemption applies: You have also asked us to provide [include relevant description]. [*organisation*] protects [*information*] as a trade secret. Data protection legislation provides that controllers do not have to provide information in a portable format where this would prejudice the rights of others, including the rights of the controller, such as rights to protect trade secrets.

If you have any questions about this, please contact [insert details]. You also have a right to make a complaint to the Information Commissioner, who is the data protection authority in the UK, or to seek a remedy at court.

Yours sincerely,

---

[10] See footnote 5

ANNEX 9A: RESPONSE TO INDIVIDUAL OBJECTING TO DIRECT MARKETING OR PROFILING FOR DIRECT MARKETING PURPOSES

We have received your request to stop processing your personal information for direct marketing purposes/[profiling purposes relating to direct marketing]. We have begun to take the measures necessary for this. These measures may take a short period to implement, so we ask for your patience if by any chance you receive any direct marketing from us before then. *Include if letter addressed unclearly to a group of companies:* Your letter of [*date*] was addressed to [*name*]. There are several companies within our group with similar names: [*details*]. As we are not sure whether you wanted your request for ceasing direct marketing to apply to all of these, we are ceasing all direct marketing to yourself from all such companies. If this does not correctly interpret your request, please advise us as soon as possible.

ANNEX 9B: RESPONSE TO INDIVIDUAL OBJECTING TO OTHER FORMS OF PROCESSING

Form for use where request is accepted: We have received your request to stop processing your personal information for [*relevant purposes*]. We have set in hand the measures necessary for this. These measures may take a short period to implement.

Form for use where request is not accepted. This is context specific – both in relation to the reasons the individual has given for making a request and for the reasons why the request may not be upheld, so the replies are often highly individual: We have received your request to stop processing your personal information. Data protection legislation says that organisations have to stop processing personal information for direct marketing purposes where an individual objects to this. We do not process any personal information relating to you for this purpose. Individuals can also object to processing which is carried out for an organisation's legitimate interests, where the individual has particular grounds to object to this. We process your personal information for the following legitimate business interests: [*list*]. If you can provide information about the particular grounds for your objection, we will consider your request. Please note that this right to object can be overridden in some situations – in particular if we have compelling legitimate grounds for processing which overrides other interests.

If you have any questions about this, please contact [*details*]. You also have a right to make a complaint to the Information Commissioner (*ico.org.uk*), who is the data protection authority in the UK, or to seek a remedy at court.

ANNEX 10: RESPONSE TO INDIVIDUAL ERASURE/RESTRICTION REQUEST

Form for use where request is accepted: We have received your request to [*erase*]/[*restrict*] your personal information for [relevant purposes]. We have done this. As we explain in our privacy policy, we disclose personal information to other recipients – in particular to third parties who provide services to us, such as [companies which send out our email marketing]. We have also advised these organisations that we have [*erased*]/[*restricted*] your data. We can provide more information about these recipients: if you would like this, please [*contact xxx*].

Form for use where erasure request is not accepted. This is context specific – both in relation to the reasons the individual has given for making a request and for the reasons why the request may not be upheld, so the replies are often highly individual. The text here is illustrative to show what a reply may look like: We have received your request to erase your personal information. Data protection legislation gives individuals a right to ask for personal information to be erased in certain circumstances – for example, where the personal information are only processed because the individual has given consent to this and where this consent is withdrawn. In [*organisation*]'s case, we process personal information because [we need this to fulfil our contract with you for banking services and to meet legal obligations on [*organisation*], including to prevent money laundering]. In these circumstances, there is no right to have the information erased. [If you had meant your request to be interpreted as a request to close your account, then you can do this by [*details*]].

Form for use where restriction request is not accepted. This is context specific – both in relation to the reasons the individual has given for making a request and for the reasons why the request may not be upheld, so the replies are often highly individual. The text here is illustrative to show what a reply may look like: We have received your request to restrict use of your personal information. Data protection legislation gives individuals a right to ask for personal information to be restricted in certain circumstances. However, data protection legislation allows organisations to use personal information where this is required to establish, exercise or defend legal claims. You have indicated that you intend to take proceedings against [*organisation*]. We will need to continue to process your personal information for this purpose, as permitted by data protection legislation.

If you have any questions about this, please contact [*details*]. You also have a right to make a complaint to the Information Commissioner (*ico.org.uk*), who is the data protection authority in the UK, or to seek a remedy at court.

ANNEX 11: RESPONSE TO REQUEST FOR REVIEW OF AN AUTOMATED DECISION

This will be specific to the particular processing and circumstances of the individual. The text here is illustrative of what may be needed.

You have asked us to review our decision not to shortlist you for the role of Scientific Process Inspector. The original shortlist had been prepared automatically, however, at your request we have arranged for a member of our human resources department to review you're application, without using the automated CV review system which was originally used. Unfortunately, we have still decided that you do not meet the criteria required for the shortlist. This is because you have no qualifications in a science subject.

If you have any questions about this, please contact [*details*]. You also have a right to make a complaint to the Information Commissioner (*ico.org.uk*), who is the data protection authority in the UK, or to seek a remedy at court.

Precedent 3

Article 28 Data Processing Agreement

See **13.7.4**

3.1 This precedent is a supplemental data processing agreement, which can be used alongside a main agreement for the data processing services. We have assumed that the main agreement would cover (important) matters such as governing law and jurisdiction; limits of liability and indemnities (if required), definition of Client "Group" and rights of third parties to enforce claims arising under an agreement (such as Client group companies).

Data Processing Agreement

This data processing agreement is entered into on [*insert date*] between:

Parties:

[Client]	[*insert [Client] entity and its incorporation details (country of incorporation, registration number and registered address)*] ("**[Client]**"); and
[Supplier]	[*insert Supplier entity and its incorporation details (country of incorporation, registration number and registered address)*] ("**Supplier**")

Recitals:

1. The Client and the Supplier are parties to [*insert Agreement details, e.g. "the services agreement between [Client] and the Supplier dated"*] (the "**Agreement**").
2. The services to be provided by the Supplier include processing of personal data on behalf of the Client. Accordingly and as required by article 28(3) of the General Data Protection Regulation, the Client and the Supplier have agreed to enter into this Data Processing Agreement.

OPERATIVE TERMS:

1. Definitions and interpretation

1.1 In this Data Processing Agreement:

"**Agreement**" has the meaning set out in Recital 1;

"**Data Protection Legislation**" means European Directive 2002/58/EC and the General Data Protection Regulation (EU) 2016/679, and any legislation and/or regulation implementing or made pursuant to, or which amends, replaces, re-enacts or consolidates them and all other applicable laws relating to processing of personal data and privacy that may exist in any relevant jurisdiction, including, where applicable, the guidance and codes of practice issued by supervisory authorities [*Drafting Note: a supplier may wish to narrow the definition—1) so as to specify the particular country laws which apply and 2) so as to avoid including guidance from supervisory authorities in the definition*];

"**data controller**", "**data processor**", "**data subject**", "**personal data**", "**processing**" and "**appropriate technical and organisational measures**" shall be interpreted in accordance with applicable Data Protection Legislation in the relevant jurisdiction;

"**Security Breach**" means any accidental, unauthorised or unlawful destruction, loss, alteration, or disclosure of, or access to the personal data that the Supplier processes in the course of providing the Services; and

"**Services**" means the services to be provided by the Supplier to [Client] pursuant to and as further set out in the Agreement.

1.2 In the event of any conflict or inconsistency between the provisions of the Agreement and this Data Processing Agreement, the provisions of this Data Processing Agreement shall prevail. Save as specifically modified and amended in this Data Processing Agreement, all of the terms, provisions and requirements contained in the Agreement shall remain in full force and effect and govern this Data Processing Agreement.

2. Relationship of the parties

2.1 The Supplier agrees that [Client] is [members of its Group are] the data controller and the Supplier is the data processor in relation to the personal data that the Supplier processes in the course of providing the Services.

2.2 When the Supplier processes personal data in the course of providing the Services the Supplier will:

(a) process the personal data only in accordance with written instructions from [Client], [(which may be specific instructions or instructions of a general nature as set out in this Agreement or as otherwise notified by [Client] to the Supplier from time to time)] [*Drafting Note: Square bracketed language is optional but may be useful to give flexibility as to how instructions are provided*]. If the Supplier is required to process the personal data for any other purpose by [UK,] European Union or Member State laws to which the Supplier is subject, the Supplier will inform [Client] of this requirement first, unless such law(s) prohibit this on important grounds of public interest; and

(b) at all times comply with applicable Data Protection Legislation and notify [Client] immediately if, in the Supplier's opinion, an instruction for the processing of personal data given by [Client] infringes applicable Data Protection Legislation;

3. Details of the personal data processing

3.1 The processing activities, including the subject matter of the processing, the nature and purpose of the processing and the categories of data subjects are as set out below:

(a) The subject matter, nature and purpose of the processing involves [*provide a description of the processing operations* that *the Supplier will undertake. For example: hosting of data or processing personal data in invoices and bank account details to administer an accounts payable service on the Client's behalf*];

(b) The categories of data subjects are [*provide a description. Example: business contacts of the Client and the Client's employees and contract staff*];

(c) The types of personal data to be processed are [*provide a description. Example, name and bank account information; amount payable and narrative for payment*]; and

(d) The processing [does not involve the processing of any special categories of personal data]/[involves the processing of the following categories of personal data: *list*].

3.2 The duration of the processing will be [*insert period*] or for such longer or shorter period as the Supplier provides data processing services under the Agreement.

4. Assistance

4.1 The Supplier shall assist [Client] [and members of its Group], always taking into account the nature of the processing:

(a) by appropriate technical and organisational measures and in so far as is possible, in fulfilling [Client]/[its Group]'s obligations to respond to requests from data subjects exercising their rights;

(b) in ensuring compliance with the obligations pursuant to Articles 32 to 36 of the General Data Protection Regulation, taking into account the information available to the Supplier; and

(c) by making available to [Client] all information which [Client] reasonably requests to allow [Client] to demonstrate that the obligations set out in Article 28 of the General Data Protection Regulation relating to the appointment of processors have been met.

4.2 [To the extent that such assistance is not included within the Services, the Supplier may charge a reasonable fee for any such assistance, save where assistance was required directly as a result of the Supplier's own acts or omissions, in which case such assistance will be at the Supplier's expense;] [*Drafting Note: the GDPR does not address possible charges by the Supplier. Suppliers will want to ensure there is a right to charge for assistance; customers may wish to restrict this.*]

5. Security measures and personal data breaches

5.1 The Supplier shall implement and maintain appropriate technical and organisational measures to protect the personal data against unauthorised or unlawful processing and against accidental loss, destruction, damage, theft, alteration or disclosure. These measures shall be appropriate to the harm which might result from any unauthorised or unlawful processing, accidental loss, destruction, damage or theft of the personal data and having regard to the nature of the personal data which is to be protected. [As a minimum, these should include the requirements set out in [*security measures document*] [*Drafting Note: it is advisable to include specific security measures. Supplier's standard security policies may provide a useful point of cross reference to determine whether the imposition of additional charges is appropriate, assuming that the customer is content with the level of commitment given in such policy/ policies*].

5.2 In the event of a suspected Security Breach, the Supplier will:

(a) take action immediately[, at the Supplier's own expense,] to investigate the suspected Security Breach and to identify, prevent and mitigate the effects of the suspected Security Breach and to remedy the Security Breach;

(b) notify [Client] [immediately]/[without undue delay] [and provide [Client] with a detailed description of the Security Breach including:

(c) the likely impact of the Security Breach;

(d) the categories and approximate number of data subjects affected and their country of residence and the categories and approximate number of records affected;

(e) and the risk posed by the Security Breach to individuals; and

(f) the measures taken or proposed to be taken by the Supplier to address the Security Breach and to mitigate its adverse effects

(g) and provide timely updates to this information and any other information [Client] may reasonably request relating to the Security Breach; and

(h) not release or publish any filing, communication, notice, press release, or report concerning the Security Breach without [Client]'s prior written approval (except where required to do so by law).] [*Drafting Note: language in square brackets is not mandated by GDPR but customers will usually want assurances about the information which the Supplier will provide in the event of a security breach, so that the customer has comfort that it will be given sufficient information as to allow it to meet its obligations.*]

6. Involvement of other persons

6.1 The Supplier shall not give access to or transfer any personal data to any third party (including any affiliates, group companies or sub-contractors) without the prior written consent of [Client]. Where [Client] does consent to the Supplier engaging a sub-contractor to carry out any part of the Services, the Supplier must include in any contract with the third party provisions in favour of [Client] which are equivalent to those in these terms and as are required by applicable Data Protection Legislation. For the avoidance of doubt, where a third party fails to fulfil its obligations under any sub-processing agreement or any applicable Data Protection Legislation, the Supplier will remain fully liable to [Client] for the fulfilment of the Supplier's obligations under these terms.

6.2 The Supplier shall ensure that personnel required to access the personal data are subject to a binding duty of confidentiality in respect of such personal data [and take reasonable steps to ensure the reliability and competence of the Supplier's personnel who have access to the personal data] [*Drafting Note: not required under GDPR but may be useful for customer to include.*]

6.3 The Supplier shall ensure that none of the Supplier's personnel publish, disclose or divulge any of the personal data to any third party unless directed in writing to do so by [Client].

7. Audit

7.1 The Supplier shall allow [Client] and its respective auditors or authorised agents to conduct audits or inspections during the term of the Agreement [and for [12] months thereafter, which will include providing access to the premises, resources and personnel of the Supplier and sub-contractors used in connection with the provision of the Services,] and provide all reasonable assistance in order to assist [Client] in exercising its audit rights under this paragraph. The purposes of an audit pursuant to this paragraph include verifying that the Supplier is processing personal data in accordance with the Supplier's obligations under these terms. [*Drafting Note: provisions in square brackets are not mandatory under the GDPR but may be useful for customers*].

8. Termination

8.1 At the end of the Services, upon [Client]'s request, the Supplier shall securely destroy or return such personal data to [Client] [and/or members of its Group], and delete existing copies unless European Union or Member State laws requires storage of such personal data.

9. Data transfers

9.1 The Supplier will not process personal data outside the [UK or] European Economic Area, or a country in respect of a valid adequacy decision has been issued by the European Commission, except with the prior written consent of [Client].

[*Drafting Note: the paragraphs which follow are only relevant if the Client does wish to authorise data transfers outside the EEA. The Client should select the appropriate provisions*].

9.2 In the event that the [Client] gives its consent to the Supplier transferring personal data outside the European Economic Area and a relevant European Commission decision on which the [Client] has relied in authorising the data transfer is held to be invalid, or that any supervisory authority requires transfers of personal data made pursuant to such decision to be suspended, then [Client] may, at its discretion, require the Supplier to cease processing personal data to which this paragraph applies, or co-operate with it to facilitate use of an alternative transfer mechanism.

[*Drafting Note: Select the next paragraph if the Supplier will commit to standard contract clauses—see* **Precedent 4**.]

9.3 The Supplier agrees to comply with the obligations of a data importer as set out in the Standard Contractual Clauses for the transfer of personal data to data processors established in third countries adopted by the

European Commission decision of 5 February 2010, published under document number C(2010) 593 2010/87/EU (the "**Standard Contractual Clauses**"). The Supplier acknowledges that [Client] [and members of its Group identified by Client] will be a data exporter. In particular, and without limiting the above obligation:

(a) the Supplier agrees to grant third party beneficiary rights to data subjects, as set out in clause 3 of the Standard Contractual Clauses, provided that the Supplier's liability shall be limited to the Supplier's own processing operations; and

(b) the Supplier agrees that the Supplier's obligations under the Standard Contractual Clauses shall be governed by the law(s) of the Member State(s) in which the [Client] entity that is the data exporter is established; and

(c) the details of the appendices applicable to the Standard Contractual Clauses are as set out in the recitals to this Data Processing Agreement and at paragraph 2 above and the security measures required are set out at [*insert description of where security measures are specified*].

[*Drafting Note: Select the next paragraph if the Supplier participates in Privacy Shield (see* **Precedent 4**).]

The Supplier confirms that all processing personal data is covered by the Supplier's Privacy Shield certification. The Supplier agrees to maintain its Privacy Shield certification throughout the term of the Agreement and the Supplier will promptly notify [Client] in writing if the Supplier ceases to maintain, or anticipates the revocation or withdrawal, or is otherwise challenged by any regulatory authority as to the status of, or makes a determination itself that the Supplier can no longer meet the Supplier's obligations under, the Privacy Shield.

[*Drafting Note: Select the next paragraph if the Supplier relies on processor binding corporate rules.*]

The Supplier confirms that all processing of personal data is covered by the Supplier's Processor Binding Corporate Rules, the terms of which are incorporated into these terms. The Supplier agrees that [Client], as data controller, has the right to enforce these Processor Binding Corporate Rules against the Supplier, including a right to compensation in the event that the Rules are breached. [*Drafting Note: if Supplier has processor BCRs, then it will have client contract language which has been approved by data protection authorities which will look something like this paragraph. Supplier's approved language should replace this paragraph.*]

SIGNED ON BEHALF OF THE PARTIES:

On behalf of the [Client]:

Signature:

Name:

Position:

Date:

On behalf of the [Supplier]:

Signature:

Name:

Position:

Date:

PRECEDENT 4

Useful Clauses for use with Data Transfers

See **9.4.2.3, 9.5.4.14, 9.5.4.19**

4.1 As explained in **Ch.9**, when an organisation transfers personal data to a recipient which participates in Privacy Shield, or which has processor binding corporate rules, certain terms should be included in the contract between the exporter and the importer (**9.5.4**). These are set out below.

4.2 In addition, because of uncertainty over the status of data transfers caused by ongoing litigation and the requirement for the Commission to keep adequacy decisions under review, it is generally advisable for anyone exporting personal data to an arm's-length third party to include further assurance provisions, requiring the importer to assist in the event that the transfer mechanism relied on is invalidated (**9.5.4.19**). In intra-group arrangements, the exporter could likely rely more on shared interest in compliance so that such provisions should not be necessary.

4.3 If the exporter is relying on standard contractual clauses to transfer personal data to a data processor (**9.5.4.12**), then these terms include most of the provisions required in a data processing agreement by art.28. However, a few additional provisions should be agreed and the template below addresses this. Of course, if an organisation exports personal data to a processor relying on Privacy Shield or processor binding corporate rules or an adequacy decision, then art.28 terms must also be included. The precedent at **P3** may assist here.

General further assurance provision to be used to address the risk of an adequacy decision being invalidated

In the event that the European Commission decision, or UK regulations, authorising the data transfer mechanism referred to [*insert cross reference*] is held to be invalid, or that any supervisory authority requires transfers of personal data made pursuant to such decision to be suspended, then [Client] may, at its discretion, require the Supplier to cease processing personal data to which this paragraph applies, or co-operate with it to facilitate use of an alternative transfer mechanism.

Supplier participates in Privacy Shield:

4.4 The Supplier confirms that all processing of personal data is covered by the Supplier's Privacy Shield certification. The Supplier agrees to maintain its Privacy

Shield certification throughout the term of the Agreement and the Supplier will promptly notify [Client] in writing if the Supplier ceases to maintain, or anticipates the revocation or withdrawal, or is otherwise challenged by any regulatory authority as to the status of, or makes a determination itself that the Supplier can no longer meet the Supplier's obligations under, the Privacy Shield.

Supplier relies on processor binding corporate rules:

4.5 The Supplier confirms that all processing of personal data is covered by the Supplier's Processor Binding Corporate Rules, the terms of which are incorporated into these terms. The Supplier agrees that [Client], as data controller, has the right to enforce these Processor Binding Corporate Rules against the Supplier, including a right to compensation in the event that the Rules are breached.

[Note: if the Supplier has processor BCRs, it will have client contract language which has been approved by the supervisory authorities which will look something like this paragraph. The Supplier's approved language should replace this paragraph.]

Terms to be incorporated into a wider commercial agreement, which supplement the C2P standard contractual clauses so as to meet the requirements of the GDPR Art.28

1. The parties have entered into the standard contractual clauses (processors) adopted by Commission Decision C(2010)593 (the "standard contractual clauses"). The definitions set out in the standard contractual clauses shall apply to this [amendment]/[appendix].

2. The parties agree:

   a. that the duration of the processing of personal data will be [*for so long as the importer provides services to the* exporter]; and

   b. to amend the standard contractual clauses as set out below.

   c. Clause5(a) shall be amended as follows:

"*The data importer agrees and warrants:*

(a) to process the personal data only on behalf of the data exporter and in compliance with its written instructions and the Clauses; if it cannot provide such compliance for whatever reasons, it agrees to inform promptly the data exporter of its inability to comply, in which case the data exporter is entitled to suspend the transfer of data and/or terminate the contract;".

   d. The data subject's rights to enforce Clauses 3(1), 3(2) and 3(3) in accordance with Clause 3 of the standard contractual clauses shall extend to the provisions in paragraph 3 below.

3. The data importer agrees and warrants:

a) in addition to Clause 5(a) of the standard contractual clauses, to comply with the data exporter's instructions with regard to transfers of personal data to a third country or an international organisation;

b) notwithstanding Clause 5(a), if the data importer is required to process the personal data for any other purpose by European or Member State [or United Kingdom domestic] law to which it is subject, the processor shall inform the data exporter of that legal requirement before processing, unless that law prohibits such information on important grounds of public interest;

c) to ensure that persons authorised to process the personal data have committed themselves to confidentiality or are under an appropriate statutory obligation of confidentiality;

d) at the data exporter's request, to assist the data exporter by appropriate technical and organisational measures, insofar as this is possible, for the fulfilment of its obligations (or, where relevant, a Client's obligations) to respond to requests for exercising data subject rights laid down in the applicable data protection law;

e) in addition to Clause 5(d)(ii) of Schedule 3, to notify the data exporter, without undue delay, if it becomes aware of any breach of security leading to the accidental or unlawful destruction, loss, alteration, unauthorised disclosure of, or access to personal data transmitted, stored or otherwise processed ("**Security Incident**") and take such steps as the data exporter may require, within the timescales required by the data exporter, to remedy the Security Incident, assist with notifying such Security Incident to supervisory authorities or data subjects (by the data exporter or, where relevant, a Client) and provide such further information as the data exporter may request;

f) in addition to Clause 5(c), to implement technical and organisational security measures in accordance with Article 32 of the GDPR;

g) at the data exporter's request, to assist the data exporter with its compliance with its obligations pursuant to Articles 32 to 36 of the GDPR (including the obligations relating to privacy impact assessments and consultations with supervisory authorities in relation to the processing of personal data) taking into account the nature of processing and the information available to the data importer;

h) in addition to Clause 5(e), to make available to the data exporter all information necessary to demonstrate compliance with the obligations laid down in Schedule 3, this Schedule 4 and Data Protection Law;

i) notwithstanding Clause 12(1), only retain personal data where European Union or EEA member state law [or United Kingdom domestic law] requires storage of the personal data; and

j) notify the data exporter immediately if, in the data importer's opinion, an instruction for the processing of personal data given by the data exporter infringes the applicable data protection law.

PRECEDENT 5

[Organisation] Data Protection Policy

See **13.8.2.2**

5.1 INTRODUCTION AND SCOPE

a. This Data Protection Policy sets out [Organisation]'s obligations when it processes personal data. It also sets out what [Organisation's] employees and contractors must do when they handle [Organisation] personal data.

b. [This Policy applies to [Organisation]'s European operations and to others at [Organisation] who receive data from [Organisation]'s European operations – for example, European employee data. It also applies to [Organisation]'s operations outside Europe if they monitor individuals in Europe (for example for online advertising) or they intend to provide goods or services to individuals in the EU].

[*Drafting Note: 1) If the Organisation only operates in the EEA or, post Brexit, the UK, then this paragraph will not be necessary. However, if an international group wishes to use this policy, then it will need to explain when the policy applies. We have suggested that the policy applies in line with the territorial scope of the GDPR and to data which has been transferred from Europe. The latter is not strictly necessary—here the organisation receiving the data will need to comply with the relevant data transfer mechanism it uses, which may not be identical to the GDPR. However, for ease of implementation it may be easier to apply this policy. 2) For ease of use, we have referred to European operations. However, the reader may wish to be more precise and to talk about EU, or EEA, depending on where it has establishments.*]

5.2 WHAT IS PERSONAL DATA AND WHAT IS A DATA SUBJECT?

a. Personal data is any information about an identifiable living individual. You may see documents which talk about "data subjects": this is what data protection law calls individuals. An individual is identifiable where:

i. [Organisation] holds clear direct identifiers – such as, name or full postal address; and/or

ii. It is reasonably likely that [Organisation] can identify the individual by other reasonable means. For example, an employee ID number where HR can link this to employee name, or customer reference number, where customer support can link this to name or address.

b. Online identifiers – such as cookie IDs and device IDs – are also covered by the law, as are, decisions made about individuals and subjective opinions held about people.

c. Sensitive personal data is any information about health, religion, sex life or orientation, racial or ethnic origin, political opinions, trade union membership, genetic data or biometric data used to uniquely identify a person (such as fingerprints or facial recognition). Information about criminal convictions, or alleged criminal activity is governed by very similar rules, so where this Policy refers to sensitive personal data this also includes criminal offence data.

d. You may collect personal data in a variety of ways, such as: from recruitment agents, correspondence with employees or with customers.

5.3 What is processing?

Processing is *any* use that [Organisation] makes of personal data. This includes obtaining or creating personal data, amending it, storing it, sharing it, or even accessing, anonymising or deleting it.

5.4 What obligations does [Organisation] have?

[Organisation] must comply with the General Data Protection Regulation ("**GDPR**") and laws such as the Data Protection Act 2018 and Privacy and Electronic Communications (EC Directive) Regulations 2003 in the UK. [Organisation]'s obligations under these laws are set out in this Policy.

5.5 What are my obligations?

All employees and, where applicable, contractors of [Organisation] must comply with this Data Protection Policy and any additional policies which [Organisation] introduces. Failure to comply with this Policy may result in disciplinary action. The Annexes to this Policy contain supplemental notes for those working in HR [etc. . .]. [*Drafting Note: it is often useful to have department specific annexes which contain more focused guidance for that department.*]

5.6 CORE DATA PROTECTION PRINCIPLES

[Organisation] follows these data protection principles when processing personal data:

a. Lawfulness, Fairness and Transparency

Always process personal data fairly – in line with individual's reasonable expectations – and lawfully.

Tell individuals how [Organisation] will use their personal data

i. Individuals must understand how their personal data will be collected and used. When developing a new product or activity that will involve personal data, consider how individuals will be informed.

ii. When [Organisation] collects personal data **directly** from individuals, it should provide notice **at the time of such collection.**

iii. When [Organisation] collects personal data from **another** source, it should provide notice within a reasonable period, but **no later than a month**, after the data was obtained by [Organisation]. If [Organisation] intends to communicate with the individual, or disclose the data to a third party, then the information must be provided no later than that communication or disclosure.

iv. The privacy notice must contain the information listed in Annex 1.

v. [Organisation] must ensure that privacy notices are: concise, intelligible, use clear and plain language, which is suitable for the audience; easily accessible; and provided in writing (which can include electronic means), unless the individual asks for the information to be provided orally.

vi. If the purposes for processing personal data change, [Organisation] must provide a further privacy notice before the new processing takes place – speak to [Legal] [*Drafting Note: change as appropriate*] if you think that a purpose for which you process personal data is not already covered by the applicable privacy notice.

Justify all processing

i. Only process personal data where [Organisation] can meet one of the grounds for processing in the legislation. These include

   a. The individual has given consent to the processing;

   b. The processing is necessary to perform a contract with the individual, or to take steps at the request of the individual before entering into a contract;

c. The processing is necessary for compliance with a legal obligation to which [Organisation] is subject; or

d. The processing is necessary for [Organisation]'s legitimate interests or those of a third party, unless the interests of the individual override those interests.

ii. The Annexes have guidance on the relevant grounds for each [Organisation] business area.

iii. [Organisation] must only process sensitive personal data if it can satisfy one of the additional sensitive data grounds. Suitable grounds for each [Organisation] business area are listed in the Annexes.

b. Purpose Limitation

Say what you do and do what you say...

i. [Organisation] must only process personal data for purposes which are legitimate and which [Organisation] has told the individual about, as part of the Transparency principle (see 6a above) and in the Record of Processing (see 6f below).

ii. [Organisation] must not process personal data for any incompatible purpose – if you want to do this, speak to [Legal] [*Drafting Note: change as appropriate.*]

c. Data Minimisation and Accuracy

Use limited, quality data

i. [Organisation] must make sure that personal data is adequate and relevant for the purposes for which it is processed and limited to what is necessary for the purpose of processing. Do not collect more personal data than needed just because it *may* turn out to be useful later.

ii. It must also make sure that personal data is accurate and, where necessary, kept up to date; and take all reasonable steps to correct or delete inaccurate personal data.

d. Storage Limitation

Don't be a data hoarder!

i. [Organisation] must determine for how long it needs to process personal data for a particular purpose and only keep personal data for this period. At the end of this period, [Organisation] must erase the personal data, or ensure that the data doesn't allow individuals to be identified.

ii. Specific details about the retention periods that [Organisation] has adopted for its different purposes and processing activities are set out in [Organisation]'s [Data Retention Policy] which can be found [insert the name of the relevant portal]. [*Drafting Note: change policy titles as appropriate.*]

e. Integrity and Confidentiality

Stay safe

i. [Organisation] must keep all the personal data it processes secure, and protected against 'unauthorised or unlawful processing and accidental loss, destruction or damage'. It does this by implementing various security measures which are listed in [the Information Security Policy] on [name of the portal]; and also implementing the measures which it imposes on its data processors (as described in section 8 below).

ii. [Organisation] must also implement a data breach response programme so that it can log, remediate and report any data breaches as required by law. The process which [Organisation] has implemented is described in [its Data Breach Policy] which can be found on [name of the portal]. [*Drafting Note: change policy titles as appropriate.*]

f. Accountability

Look good, and be good

i. **Privacy by Design and Default:** [Organisation] must be able to demonstrate its compliance with this Policy and with applicable data protection law. [Organisation] must ensure that privacy issues have been considered from an early stage in implementing services and procedures (*privacy by design*), and that, by default, only the minimum amount of personal data necessary is being processed (*privacy by default*). [Organisation] has drafted a New Project Checklist and guidance to ensure that these requirements are considered at the outset of any new project or initiative – this can be found on [name of the portal].

[*Drafting Note: change as appropriate. We have suggested that a new project checklist could be used, but there could be other ways of ensuring that this obligation is met.*]

ii. **Data Protection Impact Assessment:** In certain cases – high risk processing – [Organisation] may be required to carry out a data protection impact assessment (DPIA). A DPIA is a check conducted on a specific area of an organisation's operations to identify and minimise non-compliance risks. The New Project Checklist and guidance also considers DPIAs.

iii. **Record of Processing:** [Organisation] is required to keep a formal record of its processing activities.

[*Drafting Note: insert action depending on whether you will rely on teams to take ownership of their* respective *sections within the RPA or this will be centralised.*]

5.7 INDIVIDUAL RIGHTS—RESPECT THEM!

[Organisation] must deal promptly with requests from individuals to exercise their data protection rights. If you receive a request from an individual please forward it to [ ].

Individuals have the following rights:

a. **Access:** to obtain (i) confirmation whether [Organisation] processes their personal data; (ii) a copy of the personal data (in a commonly-used electronic form, if the request is made electronically); and (iii) provision of supporting explanatory information.

b. **Portability:** to request that their personal data is "ported" (i.e. transferred) to a specified third party, or to the individual him or herself, in a machine-readable and structured format (e.g. CSV files). There are exemptions – for example, this only applies to personal data which has been provided by the individual or collected automatically from the individual, which is held in digital format, and which [Organisation] processes with the individual's consent or to fulfil a contract with that individual.

c. **Rectification:** to request correction of inaccurate personal data.

d. **Objection:** to object to: (i) processing for direct marketing purposes; (ii) profiling based on direct marketing; and/or (iii) processing based on [Organisation]'s legitimate interests.

e. **Erasure** (a.k.a. the "right to be forgotten"): to request that personal data is erased in certain situations, for example, where: (i) the processing is based on consent and the consent is later withdrawn; or (ii) the individual has validly exercised a right to object and wishes the data to be erased.

f. **Restriction:** to request that personal data is "restricted" (i.e. block/pause) whilst complaints (for example, about accuracy) are resolved, or if the processing is unlawful but the individual objects to erasure.

Individuals also have rights not to be subject to decisions taken solely on the basis of automated processing of personal data of an individual (i.e. no human involvement in the decision) which produce legal effects, or have similarly significant effects, unless taking such decisions is permitted by law. There are limited exceptions to this. [[Organisation] does not use automated individual decision-making technology]. [*Drafting Note: if the Organisation does use automated decision taking, then more detail would need to be included here. This would be context specific.*]

5.8 SHARING PERSONAL DATA WITH THIRD PARTIES AND INTERNATIONAL TRANSFERS

a. **Data processors** are other organisations which process personal data on behalf of a controller. [Organisation] may appoint processors to help it process personal data (e.g. a payroll provider).

b. When appointing any data processor to collect, store or use personal data on [Organisation]'s behalf, [Organisation] must:

  a. **Before Engagement:** Ensure that the data processor provides **satisfactory assurances** about their data protection practices – [Organisation] has drafted a Processor Contract Review Checklist which must be checked for every data processor contracts, and which can be obtained from [Legal] [*Drafting Note: change as appropriate*]; and

  b. **On Engagement:** Sign the data processor up to specified **data processing terms** – [Organisation] has drafted template terms which must be entered into with all data processors, and which can be obtained from [Legal] [*Drafting Note: change as appropriate*]; and

  c. **Post Engagement:** Confirm on an appropriate periodic basis (as determined by [IT]) that the assurances provided before engagement about their data protection practices remain valid – the Supplier Due Diligence Checklist must be sent to all data processors on an [TBC] basis. [*Drafting Note: change as appropriate.*]

c. Where [Organisation] transfers personal data to data processors or data controllers which are based outside the EEA (which includes data processors accessing the personal data from outside the EEA e.g. in order to provide IT support services), a data transfer mechanism must be put in place unless that country has been deemed adequate by the European Commission. Speak to [Legal] [*Drafting Note:* **change** *as appropriate*] if you suspect that personal data is being transferred outside the EEA, for example, as part of your team's activities, a project you are involved in or a system that you use.

5.9 TRAINING

[Organisation] must, and does, provide training on this Policy and [Organisation]'s other data protection-related policies, procedures and obligations to all employees and contractors when they join [Organisation], and then on an [annual] basis. [*Drafting Note: change as appropriate.*]

5.10 AUDITS AND MONITORING

[Organisation] audits compliance with this Policy and other data protection-related policies; and will implement appropriate corrective actions to rectify any non-compliance. If you think that this Policy is not being complied with in any way at [Organisation], please bring this to the attention of [Legal]. *Drafting Note: change as appropriate*]

5.11 UPDATES OF THE POLICY

[Legal] [*Drafting Note: change as appropriate*] is responsible for communicating changes to this Policy, and will also provide a brief explanation of the reasons for any notified changes to this Policy.

5.12 PUBLICATION AND FINAL PROVISIONS

[Organisation] will publish this Policy and any other amendments to it [name of the portal]. [*Drafting Note: change as appropriate.*]

5.13 EFFECTIVE DATE: [INSERT]

Contact: You can raise any questions or concerns in relation to this Policy by contacting: [Legal]. You should also contact Legal if you think you need an exception to a rule in this Policy. [*Drafting Note: change as appropriate.*]

ANNEX 1

1. **Information which must be provided to individuals when collecting their personal data directly from them:**

   a) The identity and the contact details of [Organisation] [and of [Organisation]'s DPO];

   b) The purposes and the legal basis for the processing;

   c) The legitimate interests of [Organisation], where applicable;

   d) The recipients or categories of recipients of the personal data;

   e) Any international data transfers, including the location of any recipients and the methods used to ensure the adequate protection of those transfers (and how to obtain details of those methods);

   f) Data retention periods;

   g) Their rights under data protection rules;

   h) The process available to individuals to withdraw any consent;

   i) Whether the individual is obliged to provide the personal data and the possible consequences of failure to provide such data; and

   j) The existence of automated decision-making, including profiling, and the logic involved.

2. **Information which must be provided to individuals when collecting their personal data another source:**

   a) All of the information stated in paragraph 1 of this Annex 1 above;

   b) The categories of personal data obtained from the third party; and

   c) The sources of the personal data – information must be as precise as possible (e.g. identify whether this source is a private or public source; and the type of organisation/industry/sector).

HR ANNEX

1. Grounds for processing personal data

[Organisation] HR can collect and process personal data where it is necessary for the following purposes:

Type of data	Ground for processing	Example
Normal data: e.g. names, contact information, job title, bank details etc.	Necessary to perform a contract	Processing payroll data, administering benefits and pensions, managing employee mobility, facilities management disciplinary procedures etc.
	Necessary to comply with a legal obligation and for exercising rights in the field of employment, social security and social protection law	Collecting information required for statutory sick pay purposes
	Consent	Use photos of employees for internal/external communication purposes
Sensitive data: e.g. medical information, sexual orientation, disabilities, information revealing ethnic origin or political opinions, trade union membership, biometric data etc.	Necessary to comply with a legal obligation and for exercising rights in the field of employment, social security and social protection law	Sickness or disability information for administration purposes, background checks, Administering benefits etc.
	Data Protection Act 2018, Schedule 1, Part 2, para.8 (additional obligations apply here – consult [legal])	Information regarding general equal opportunities monitoring

When using **consent** as a ground for processing you should keep in mind that it must be presented clearly and separately from any other terms (e.g. not incorporated into the employment contract). Consent must also be freely given, specific and give separate options for different types of processing. In addition, it should be as easy to withdraw as to give consent.

In an employment context it can be hard to prove that consent has genuinely been "freely given". Therefore, where possible, you should avoid relying on consent for processing employee data. In addition, if you rely on consent and employees decide to withdraw it you won't be able to process their data anymore.

2. Transparency

[Organisation] has prepared privacy notices for applicants and employees. These are available on the [name of the portal where these documents are accessible]. [*Drafting Note: change as appropriate.*]

3. Data quality

[Organisation] employees] can correct their personal data using [self-serve tools]. HR should take reasonable additional steps to check data – for example by prompting individuals to check that their personal data is accurate on a periodical basis. [*Drafting Note: change as appropriate.*]

PRECEDENT 6

Allocating Responsibilities between Joint Controllers (article 26)

See **13.7.5.5**

6.1

Ref.	**Summary**	**Controller A**	**Controller B**
arts 15–21	Handling individual rights requests from data subjects: • to access data • retrieve it in portable form or provide to another company • to rectify data • to ask for it to be erased • to restrict the data (= storage but no live use pending resolution of dispute) • to object to processing (other than "do not market" requests *Describe how these will be handled in practice between the organisations. For example, these could be handled in full by either Controller A or Controller B, or they may be shared, perhaps with A dealing with initial customer requests but then handing the request on to B for advice on validity and for technical implementation of the request, or vice versa*		

art.21(2)	"Do not market" requests *This could be combined with the above, but often there is a separate process for this*		
arts 13–14, art.7	Obligation to provide a privacy notice and responsibility for obtaining consent (where required) and proving this (i.e. the UI) *The Privacy Notice must tell data subjects about the other Controller Typically the controller who first deals with the data subjects will handle the Privacy Notice*		
art.26(1)	Point of contact for data subjects *Any designated privacy point of contact for data subjects—e.g. the DPO or DP Professional*		
art.22	Restriction on automated decision making		
art.5	Ensuring data quality: Accurate, relevant, up to date, not kept for longer than necessary		
art.5(1)(f) and arts 32–34	Security: Ensuring appropriate technical and organisational measures—including a breach reporting process		
arts 5(2), 6, 9 and 24	Accountability – being able to demonstrate compliance, including: – Maintaining a record of processing (art.30) – Understanding what the lawful basis for all processing is (arts 6 and 9) – Ensuring that new processing has a lawful basis and is compatible with any original purpose—and that a data protection impact assessment is performed as necessary (arts 5(1)(b) and 36) – Developing and rolling out policies (art.24)		

	– Ensuring systems are designed with privacy in mind (art.25) – Ensuring contracts with processors are put in place and monitored etc. (art.28) – Considering if a DPO is needed (art.37)		
art.44 on	Data transfers Ensuring transfers of data outside the EEA (or UK post-Brexit) are made with appropriate protection *Describe Standard Contractual Clauses, Binding Corporate Rules or other safeguard*		

Index

LEGAL TAXONOMY

FROM SWEET & MAXWELL

This index has been prepared using Sweet and Maxwell's Legal Taxonomy. Main index entries conform to keywords provided by the Legal Taxonomy except where references to specific documents or non-standard terms (denoted by quotation marks) have been included. These keywords provide a means of identifying similar concepts in other Sweet & Maxwell publications and online services to which keywords from the Legal Taxonomy have been applied. Readers may find some minor differences between terms used in the text and those which appear in the index.

Suggestions to: sweetandmaxwell.taxonomy@thomson.com

(all references are to paragraph number)